Consumer
Behaviour

Second Edition

Martin Evans

Ahmad Jamal

Gordon Foxall

WILEY

A John Wiley and Sons, Ltd., Publication

Copyright © 2009   John Wiley & Sons Ltd, The Atrium, Southern Gate, Chichester,
West Sussex PO19 8SQ, England

Telephone: (+44) 1243 779777

Email (for orders and customer service enquiries): cs-books@wiley.co.uk
Visit our Home Page on www.wiley.com

Reprinted in June 2012

Other Wiley Editorial Offices

John Wiley & Sons Inc., 111 River Street, Hoboken, NJ 07030, USA

Jossey-Bass, 989 Market Street, San Francisco, CA 94103-1741, USA

Wiley-VCH Verlag GmbH, Boschstr. 12, D-69469 Weinheim, Germany

John Wiley & Sons Australia Ltd, 42 McDougall Street, Milton, Queensland 4064, Australia

John Wiley & Sons (Asia) Pte Ltd, 2 Clementi Loop #02-01, Jin Xing Distripark, Singapore 129809

John Wiley & Sons Canada Ltd, 6045 Freemont Blvd, Mississauga, ONT, L5R 4J3, Canada

Wiley also publishes its books in a variety of electronic formats. Some content that appears
in print may not be available in electronic books.

Library of Congress Cataloging-in-Publication Data

Evans, Martin (Martin J.)
  Consumer behaviour / Martin Evans, Ahmad Jamal, and Gordon Foxall. – 2nd ed.
    p. cm.
  Includes bibliographical references and index.
  ISBN 978-0-470-99465-8 (pbk. : alk. paper)   1. Consumer behavior. I. Jamal, Ahmad, 1965-
II. Foxall, G. R. III. Title. IV. Title: Consumer behavior.
  HF5415.32.E933 2009
  658.8′342 – dc22

                                      2008053856

British Library Cataloguing in Publication Data

A catalogue record for this book is available from the British Library

ISBN 978-0-470-99465-8

Typeset in 10/12pt Plantin by Laserwords Private Limited, Chennai, India
Printed and bound by Grafos S.A., Barcelona, Spain

CONTENTS

About the Authors   xi

Preface to the Second Edition   xiii

Acknowledgements   xvi

PART 1 INDIVIDUAL ASPECTS OF CONSUMER BEHAVIOUR   1

CHAPTER 1   Consumer Motives and Values   3

CHAPTER 2   Consumer Response to Marketing Actions: 1 Exposure, Attention, Perception   45

CHAPTER 3   Consumer Response to Marketing Actions: 2 Learning and Attitudes   89

CHAPTER 4   Consumer Response to Marketing Actions: 3 Action, Post-Purchase
                 Dissonance, Consumer Involvement   125

CHAPTER 5   Consumer Demographics   154

CHAPTER 6   Consumer Psychographics   190

ARTICLE   D Smeesters and N Mandel (2006) Positive and Negative Media Image Effects
                 on the Self. *Journal of Consumer Research*, Vol 32, pp 576–582   228

PART 2 SOCIAL AND GROUP ASPECTS OF CONSUMER BEHAVIOUR   239

CHAPTER 7   Social Group, Tribal and Household Buying Influences   241

CHAPTER 8   Culture and Subculture   284

ARTICLE   S McKechnie and C Tynan (2006) Social Meanings in Christmas Consump-
                 tion: An Exploratory Study of UK Celebrants' Consumption Rituals. *Journal
                 of Consumer Behaviour*, Vol 5, pp 130–144   320

PART 3 INTEGRATED APPROACHES TO CONSUMER BEHAVIOUR   337

CHAPTER 9   New Product Buying   339

CHAPTER 10   Repeat, Loyal and Relational Buying   369

CHAPTER 11   Data-Based Consumer Behaviour   404

CHAPTER 12   Consumer Misbehaviour   435

CHAPTER 13   Organizational Buying Behaviour   458

ARTICLE   P A Norberg and D R Horne (2007) Privacy Attitudes and Privacy-Related
Behavior. *Psychology & Marketing*, Vol 24(10): 829–847   481

Glossary   495

References   513

Index   547

DETAILED CONTENTS

PART 1 INDIVIDUAL ASPECTS OF CONSUMER BEHAVIOUR | 1

CHAPTER 1   Consumer Motives and Values | 3

Introduction	3
Motivation	6
Maslow's Hierarchy of Needs	11
Freudian Theory of Motivation	15
Jungian Motivation	22
Memetics	23
Cognitive Dissonance as Motivator	23
Motivation and Shopping	24
Values	28
Motivation Research	31
Means–End Chain Analysis and Laddering	33
TNS Case Study – Understanding Consumer Needs – Racing Past the Barriers: The Success of the Apache Motorcycle in India	35
Summary	43
Questions	43
Further Reading	44

CHAPTER 2   Consumer Response to Marketing Actions: 1 Exposure, Attention, Perception | 45

Introduction	45
Exposure	47
Attention	51
Perception and Interpretation	64
Symbolism in Perceptual Interpretation	86
Summary	87
Questions	87
Further Reading	88

CHAPTER 3   Consumer Response to Marketing Actions: 2 Learning and Attitudes   **89**

Introduction   89
Learning   90
Knowledge and Expertise   104
Attitudes   105
Summary   123
Questions   123
Further Reading   124

CHAPTER 4   Consumer Response to Marketing Actions: 3 Action, Post-Purchase Dissonance, Consumer Involvement   **125**

Introduction   125
Action   125
Post-Purchase   129
Involvement   141
TNS Case Study – Information Processing and Memory Limitations – So What Does the Scottish Executive Do Anyway? – Brand Development in Government Communications   150
Summary   151
Questions   152
Further Reading   153

CHAPTER 5   Consumer Demographics   **154**

Introduction   154
Age and Generational Cohorts   156
Gender   170
Sexuality   180
Social Grade   183
Income   188
Summary   188
Questions   189
Further Reading   189

CHAPTER 6   Consumer Psychographics   **190**

Introduction   190
Lifestyle   191
Lifestyle, Values and Demand Mapping   196
Summary   224
Questions   224
Further Reading   227

ARTICLE   D Smeesters and N Mandel (2006) Positive and Negative Media Image Effects on the Self. *Journal of Consumer Research*, Vol 32, pp 576–582   228

PART 2 SOCIAL AND GROUP ASPECTS OF CONSUMER BEHAVIOUR   239

CHAPTER 7   Social Group, Tribal and Household Buying Influences   **241**

Introduction	241
Social Groups	242
Tribal, Virtual Groups and Postmodern Consumer Behaviour	253
Virtual Groups	260
Family Influences on Consumer Behaviour	266
Summary	281
Questions	282
Further Reading	282

CHAPTER 8   Culture and Subculture   **284**

Introduction	284
Culture	285
Values	290
Cultural Differences and Similarities	291
Use of Humour	298
Spanning Cultures	298
Subcultures	300
TNS Case Study – The Apache Motorcycle Advertising Campaign in India	315
Summary	317
Questions	318
Further Reading	319

ARTICLE   S McKechnie and C Tynan (2006) Social Meanings in Christmas Consumption: An Exploratory Study of UK Celebrants' Consumption Rituals. *Journal of Consumer Behaviour*, Vol 5, pp 130–144   320

PART 3 INTEGRATED APPROACHES TO CONSUMER BEHAVIOUR   337

CHAPTER 9   New Product Buying   **339**

Introduction	339
Foundation Theory	340
Adapters vs Innovators	349
Two- and Multi-Step Flows of Communications	352
Summary	366
Questions	367
Further Reading	367

CHAPTER 10   Repeat, Loyal and Relational Buying   **369**

Introduction	369
Repeat Purchasing Behaviour	370

Beyond Repeat Purchasing: Loyalty   374
Loyalty   381
TNS Case Study – A Marketing Research Model by TNS to Measure Loyalty   384
Beyond Loyalty: Relational Consumption   392
Summary   402
Questions   403
Further Reading   403

CHAPTER 11   Data-Based Consumer Behaviour   404

Introduction   404
Understanding Consumer Behaviour from Personalized Behavioural Data   405
Understanding Consumer Behaviour via Personalized Profile Data   416
Biographics and Individualism   428
Consumer Reaction to Individualized Consumer–Organization Interaction   429
Summary   432
Questions   433
Further Reading   433

CHAPTER 12   Consumer Misbehaviour   435

Introduction   435
Consumer Misbehaviour Typologies   437
Idealistic Rationale for Misbehaviour   440
Consumer Misbehaviour with Respect to Marketing Activities   445
Behaviour Balances   454
Summary   456
Questions   456
Further Reading   457

CHAPTER 13   Organizational Buying Behaviour   458

Introduction   458
Characteristics of Organizational Markets and Organizational Buying   460
The Decision-Making Process   463
Buying Classes and Phases   467
The Buying Centre: Roles and Complexity   470
Major Influences on Organizational Buying Behaviour   471
Summary   478
Questions   479
Further Reading   480

ARTICLE   P A Norberg and D R Horne (2007) Privacy Attitudes and Privacy-Related
           Behavior. *Psychology & Marketing*, Vol. 24(10): 829–847   481

ABOUT THE AUTHORS

Martin Evans is a Senior Fellow at Cardiff Business School, having been Head of Marketing and Strategy there. He previously held professorial posts at the Universities of Portsmouth, Glamorgan and West of England. His industrial experience was with Hawker Siddeley and then as a consultant to a variety of organizations over 30 years. Martin's specialist areas include direct marketing, consumer behaviour, and marketing research and information and he has over 180 publications including nine books, mostly in these areas. He is an academic prizewinner at the International Marketing communications Conference, the Academy of Marketing, the Learning and Teaching Support Network (ITSN) and Institute of Direct Marketing. He is a Fellow of both the Chartered Institute of Marketing and Institute of Direct Marketing. He has Editorial Board experience for eight academic journals and was founding and managing Editor of the Journal of Consumer Behaviour. Martin has discussed his research on both radio and TV.

Ahmad Jamal is a Senior Lecturer in Marketing and Strategy and the Coordinator for the Ethnic Marketing Research Group and Programme Director for the MSC in Strategic Marketing at Cardiff Business School. He holds a PhD in Consumer Behaviour from the University of Bradford. Ahmad is a former Deputy Secretary of the Academy of Marketing UK, a member of Association of Consumer Research, European Academy of Marketing and a Senior Examiner for the Chartered Institute of Marketing. He also acts as the Vice President for Western Europe, the Academy for Global Business Advancement (AGBA) and is the Managing Editor for Journal of Global Business Advancement. His research interests include cross-cultural consumer behaviour, self-concept, service quality, brand evaluations and customer satisfaction, and he has published widely in leading academic journals. His major areas of teaching include consumer behaviour, advertising and other forms of marketing communications.

Gordon Foxall is a Distinguished Research Professor at Cardiff University. His chief research interests lie in psychological theories of consumer choice and consumer innovativeness and their relationships to marketing management and strategy. He has published some 16 books and over 250 articles and papers on these and related themes and has previously held professorial appointments at the Universities of Strathclyde, Birmingham and Keele. He is a Fellow of both the British Psychological Society (FBPsS) and the British Academy of Management (FBAM) and was recently elected an Academician by the Academy of Learned Societies for the Social Sciences (AcSS).

PREFACE TO THE SECOND EDITION

Consumer behaviour is dynamic: the environment within which we, as consumers, behave is constantly changing – social attitudes change, marketers change the way they understand and target us, markets fragment, and so on. The academic literature on consumer behaviour is also constantly changing so this new edition provides updated coverage of contributions from psychology, sociology and social psychology. We also provide integrated coverage of newer perspectives such as how marketers are increasingly basing their understanding, segmentation and targeting of consumers on personalised data about consumers. Another area that integrates approaches and theory in a more eclectic manner is what might be seen as the *mis*behaviour of consumers. Consumers can buy too much, or buy and use illegally and we explore these issues in contemporary society. For completeness we have added a new chapter on organizational buying behaviour (OBB). This, we believe, is important because much marketing is in the B2B arena. Even if academics do not always include OBB in their direct teaching, students will have access to this material in the text.

We believe it is important to go well beyond a basic text in today's learning climate, because there are significant challenges to learning and teaching strategies for consumer behaviour. Where these might not be unique to consumer behaviour, they are particularly relevant to the area. Students do not always engage as fully with theory and academic literature as academics often hope and expect. Our text takes this on board and provides thorough and rigorous coverage of theories on Consumer Behaviour. Consumer Behaviour can be seen by some students as abstracted theory and, as such, they sometimes (albeit quite adeptly) report theory, but don't engage with it sufficiently to be able to analyse, evaluate or apply it to practical consumer behaviour contexts. There is not much point in merely reporting - even if it is accurate. Marketers need theory to inform their practice, so we are keen to develop students' abilities to apply theory.

Our approach contextualises consumer behaviour within marketing practice and the marketing curriculum and is very much concerned with how marketers can use, and apply, consumer behaviour theory. We therefore provide examples throughout the text of how each theory can be applied. We understand contemporary students and how to write to engage them. Our approach draws from the style of distance learning (having written for the Open University) and so we have made the text more participative than is sometimes the case. The style is deliberately student-friendly and concise, so it doesn't overwhelm the reader. It is accessible and indeed manageable for a *one or two semester* module.

Cases and Examples

Since publication of the first edition we have successfully negotiated with Marketing Week, the Direct Marketing Association, TNS Sofres, the Future Foundation and several brands and advertising agencies for the inclusion of cutting edge case studies, examples and research. The result is that we are able to offer, in the text and on the accompanying web site, a selection of clippings from Marketing Week, many print and TV advertisements, Future Foundation report summaries, as well as many more case studies, again on both the web and in the text itself.

Journal Articles

To encourage students to engage with academic literature we again incorporate articles from double-blind reviewed consumer behaviour journals. We know that the inclusion of the articles in the first edition helped students and lectures make a leap from 'book learning' to a wider engagement with the literature. We have updated these with new relevant recent articles, and provide notes on the companion website. We feel that once students experience some research findings in the form of the original source, not just someone else's summaries, they will develop a hunger to explore more of what the academic journals can offer.

Think Boxes

We continue the use of Think Boxes throughout the text to encourage students to, well, think! These little stop-off points encourage engagement with the issues dealt with at that point, so the reader can bring their own experiences and thoughts on the matter into play – so going beyond a more passive way of learning. The Think Boxes, together with the end of chapter questions, provide plenty of scope for insightful and fun engagement with the material and provide material for seminar exercises.

Book Companion Website

We have also been able to update and significantly expand the student and lecturer support through our extensive web site at **www.wileyeurope.com/college/evans**.

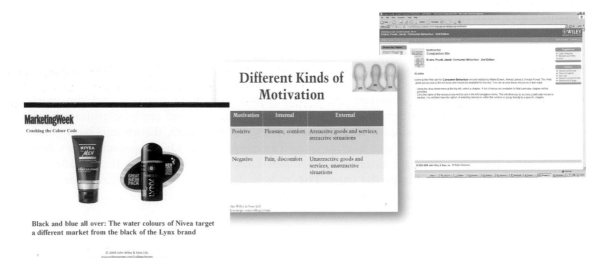

The lecturer companion site provides a full **Instructor's Manual,** with ideas as to how to answer the questions in text but also provides further questions, projects and case teaching notes. There is a **Test Bank,** which is also Blackboard and Web CT compatible, and expanded, visually rich **PowerPoint slides.** New to the website are **Video Clips of TV adverts** for use in the classroom with teaching notes. There is also extra **Case Material** from Marketing Week, TNS and DMA awards. There are also fuller Future Foundation Research Reports.

For students, the website provides self-test **multiple choice quizzes,** all the full length **journal articles, research summaries, extra cases, weblinks** and an **online glossary.**

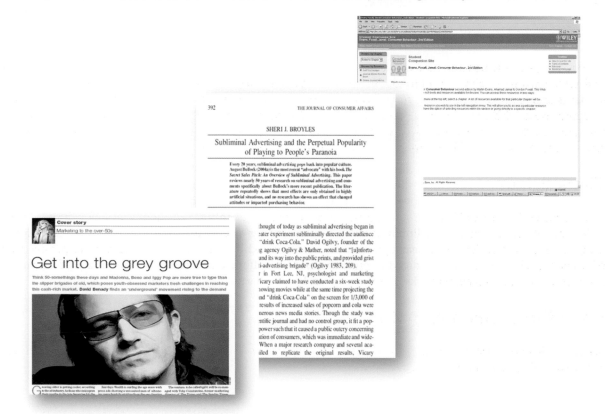

Our web material is 'living': we regularly update the articles from Marketing Week, for example, which therefore maintains a contemporary commentary on how marketers understand consumer behaviour. We feel that this provides a powerful synergy with the academic content and appreciate your feedback via the website.

ACKNOWLEDGEMENTS

We are very grateful for the help, support and encouragement of all at John Wiley & Sons: especially, Sarah Booth, Nicole Burnett, Deb Egleton, Claire Jardine and Anneli Mockett. We thank students on the courses we have taught, over several decades. They have given us encouragement and inspiration to produce a student friendly book and they have shown us how to achieve this.

We have also had extremely thorough reviews of the 1st edition and other material by five reviewers and we have been able to improve the book as a result of their very constructive feedback. Thank you kindly.

The many case studies, clippings from the marketing press, research reports and examples of advertising campaigns that appear throughout the book and on the accompanying web site, have been provided by individuals, companies and organizations. We offer our gratitude to the following for granting permission to include these works:

Rachel Boldy
Direct Marketing Association (DMA)
The Future Foundation
Sam Gould
Vicky James
Marketing Week
Professor Clive Nancarrow
TNS

Last but certainly not least, we offer our thanks and love to our families for encouraging us, but also our apologies for neglecting them during the writing process. Your support, as always, keeps us going.

Martin Evans, Ahmad Jamal and Gordon Foxall
Cardiff Business School

PART 1

INDIVIDUAL ASPECTS OF
CONSUMER BEHAVIOUR

CHAPTER 1   Consumer Motives and Values

CHAPTER 2   Consumer Response to Marketing Actions 1: Exposure, Attention and Perception

CHAPTER 3   Consumer Response to Marketing Actions 2: Learning and Attitudes

CHAPTER 4   Consumer Response to Marketing Actions 3: Action, Post-Purchase Dissonance, Consumer Involvement

CHAPTER 5   Consumer Demographics

CHAPTER 6   Consumer Psychographics

ARTICLE: D Smeesters and N Mandel (2006) Positive and Negative Media Image Effects on the Self. *Journal of Consumer Research*, Vol 32, pp 576–582.

We open the book with an exploration of consumers as individuals. That is, we use many theories and concepts from psychology to explain how consumers behave.

We start (Chapter 1) with an exploration of what motivates consumers and in doing so we explain the difference between needs and wants. For this we draw from theories of motivation based on the work of, for example, Maslow, Freud and Jung. We also extend our critical examination of concerns over marketing's role in exploiting the human condition, which tends to aspire for more and more. We are privileged to be able to include a major and current case study on motivation provided by TNS Sofres.

The next three chapters (Chapters 2, 3 and 4) also draw mainly from psychology as we take you through a sequential model of how consumers can respond to marketing activities. We have extended our coverage of how marketers tackle consumers' selective exposure patterns. There are new examples of gaining attention and we expand our coverage of consumers' perceptual and learning processes, how they develop attitudes toward products and services and indeed how marketers can use a knowledge of all this in their promotional campaigns. For example, there is more on sensory discrimination, memory, knowledge, attitude change and impulse buying. What happens after purchase is also of great relevance. We examine how post purchase doubt can occur and also how markets can reassure consumers that they have indeed bought the right thing. We extend the satisfaction-dissatisfaction issue with attribution and equity theories. Much depends on the level of involvement consumers have with the product or service concerned, so we have expanded aspects of low and high involvement from both a consumer and marketer perspective.

We then turn (in Chapter 5) to demographic characteristics of individuals and how these can influence their buying behaviour. There are many implications for marketers as well, of age/generational cohorts, gender, sexuality and social grade. We provide evidence of how consumers of different ages are interested in different things and how their mindsets need to be taken on board by marketers targeting them. Gender is an interesting factor in consumer behaviour: men and women behave differently as consumers – and marketers often use gender stereotypes but not always in ways that are appreciated by their targets. We also introduce sexuality here because many marketers are keen to appeal to what they see as relatively lucrative gay market segments. Social Grade (based on occupational groups) has long been used by marketers but we are critical of this classification on a number of grounds, despite its continued use. The 2nd edition extends and updates this coverage, especially in terms of age and gender.

Part 1 also covers what we call consumer psychographics (Chapter 6). This includes personality, lifestyle and self-concept theory. There was initial and probably fairly obvious excitement about the prospect of matching brand personalities with consumer personalities. The logic being that consumers buy things that reflect their personality and we have extended our coverage of personality as a dimension in consumer behaviour and link this with consumer decision-making styles. However, we show that many consumers want to hide aspects of their real personality and portray different traits. As a result, self-concept theory has some mileage in explaining consumer behaviour because it shows how some consumers buy brands that are congruent with how they see themselves or how they want others to see them. We have expanded our coverage of self-concept theory and extended it into the contemporary arena of the virtual and online self and also into individualism.

Some specific traits, however, such as innovativeness and inner-directedness do hold useful clues for marketing activity. We explore consumer lifestyles as researched via anonymized market research that attempts to uncover consumer activities, interests and opinions. The coverage is extended into a blend of lifestyle, values and demand mapping.

We conclude Part 1 with the inclusion of a full research article on the effects of female stereotyping on the self.

Throughout Part 1, there are practical examples and references to material, including other actual research articles, which can be accessed via the accompanying web site. We are grateful for permission to include clippings from *Marketing Week*, cases from the DMA and TNS and reports from the Future Foundation.

CHAPTER 1
CONSUMER MOTIVES AND VALUES

CHAPTER OBJECTIVES

After engaging with the material presented in this chapter and its associated exercises and reading, you should be able to:

- Distinguish between needs and wants.
- Apply theories of motivation to how consumers behave.
- Explain consumer values and how they relate to motives.
- Define motives for 'going shopping'.
- Demonstrate an awareness of motivation research techniques, their nature and application.

INTRODUCTION

The understanding of customer **needs and wants** is one of the major underpinning constructs of the **marketing concept**. The nature of being **market-orientated** rather than **product-orientated** requires organizations to consider who their (best) customers might be, where they are, how to target them and with what. An important starting point is to understand what it is they really 'want'. This is not as easy as it might sound. A company might be making 8 mm drills and at first sight it might seem logical for the company to focus on 'selling' 8 mm drills. However, customers don't buy 'drills' so much as 'holes': that is, what the product (or service) can do for them, rather than what it is in its tangible form. Indeed the DIY store Homebase has used the slogan: 'Make a house a home.'

Source: Homebase

EXAMPLE 1.1

The concept of market orientation can be illustrated in many ways. Charles Revson, the founder of Revlon cosmetics stated, 'In the factory we make cosmetics; in the drugstore we sell hope.' Or, as in the 'Roadmaster' advertisement, marketers imply they can fulfill dreams.

Reproduced by permission of Pacific Cycle Inc.

In other words it isn't the physical composition or features that are being purchased, but rather the benefits consumers might derive from their purchase. An advertisement for Canon microcomputers depicted a variety of situations in the life of a man. Each box in the press advertisement showed, variously, the man at the office working on business plans, with employees in a negotiating situation, with clients in a selling situation, on the squash court and at home with his family. This multifaceted way of life fits very well in this postmodern era of persons fulfilling many roles. Each of these boxes had captions: forward planning, employee relations, clinching the deal, playing hard, and being a dad. The implication of course was that a prospective Canon computer buyer would not be buying RAMs, ROMs and hard disks, but would be buying something that takes over the tedious and time-consuming chores, thus allowing the buyer more time for the important things in life, and therefore being more successful at them, including being a better squash player and parent!

A Sainsbury's television commercial featured a mother and young son at the checkout. When the items were rung up on the till, the display did not show prices but, for example: 'mum's night off' for a pizza, 'breakfast in bed' for a packet of croissants.

Throughout all this the son looked glum: they had perhaps had a row. When the gingerbread man was rung up, the display was 'peace offering'!

In an episode of *Star Trek: The Next Generation*, Captain Picard reports to the crew his time-travel visit to 20th century Earth. He said he 'actually saw automobiles'.

The crew didn't know what this meant but Data the android accessed his databanks to reveal that automobiles were 'an ancient earth device used primarily for transportation, also seen as a source of status and virility often a prime ingredient in teenage mating rituals'!

The classic way for marketing to focus on the 'benefits approach' is to identify needs of the target and to match one or more product or service features that are in some way relevant with each need. Then each feature can be converted, using a 'which means' approach, into a benefit that can satisfy that need (Table 1.1).

Needs	Features	Benefits
Identify needs	**Select relevant features**	**Convert features into benefits that satisfy needs**
Newly married couple who have just moved into a newly built house	This drill-bit set includes a set of masonry and wood/metal bits	This drill-bit set can help you turn your house into a home by allowing you to personalize it by hanging shelves, pictures, etc.
Shy and retiring 18-year-old who has just started university and wants to make some new friends	Designer-label jacket	This jacket will help you fit in and become part of the in-crowd.
A young woman who wants to experience life to the fullest and wishes to make a statement about her individuality	A navel-piercing service	Piercing your navel makes a statement. It says something about who you are and you've never before experienced anything like the feeling it gives you.

Table 1.1: Needs, features, benefits

This approach is not new. The advertisement here for Biro pens demonstrates the conversion of features into benefits (yes, there is a brand called Biro, even though we often tend to think of the 'ball point pen' product category as this brand: the brand becomes the commodity).

Customer needs and requirements should not, however, be totally satisfied: business is not altruistic because it needs to make a profit in order to stay in business and grow. What is needed is a crucial compromise of satisfying organizational goals and satisfying customer needs, which can lead to competitive advantage in increasingly crowded marketplaces. This chapter explores how marketing can interpret and use motivation theories in these respects and provides practical examples of their application. We start with a discussion of motivation and motivation theories, then extend this into coverage of values. The chapter closes with a brief exploration of research approaches to investigating consumer motives and values.

THINKBOX

FUTURE FOUNDATION RESEARCH:
Social and Cultural Capital

Related to the increasing importance of networks and the skills required to navigate them is what we refer to as 'social capital' and the growth in what has been called 'cultural capital'. In today's service economy, it is access to services, networks and the consumption of culture that plays a critical role in defining one's individual status – the critical currency of the modern world is in many ways cultural capital. By this we mean the knowledge and experience of arts, culture and hobbies that help to define who we are and, critically, differentiate us from others. Sociologists such as Rifkin and Bourdieu argue that we are moving from an era of industrial to cultural capitalism, where 'cultural production is increasingly becoming the dominant form of economic activity' and securing access to the many cultural resources and experiences that nurture one's psychological existence becomes just as important as holding property. Whether that culture is 'high' (opera) or 'low' (celebrity watching), you can differentiate yourself, gain kudos and access to opportunities by having cultural knowledge or experience ('been to the match', 'seen the play'); by having cultural capital. This phenomenon is particularly important because surely the management of this 'cultural' capital is more complex than that of physical goods and the components of cultural capital need to be maintained and nurtured regularly – another pressure in modern life we believe is key to understanding the complications people face.

Looking ahead, it's likely we will see an ever-wider range of experiences as we work on building our cultural capital. And as we all realize that networking in both social and work environments is important, we will want not only to hone our skills in communication but also acquire and use the modern communication technologies that can help us. The connections you have and the capabilities and influence of your friends and families – your 'social capital' becomes critical. We will also probably notice the reduced influence of traditional institutions and the growing importance of 'personal' authorities one has. Clearly there is potential here for the public and private sectors to provide the tools that improve networking and building social capital.

As you will know from Chapter 8, this does not refer to cultural differences across societies, but rather our consumption of the more artistic/experiential/cultural aspects of life. What are your views here?

Reproduced by permission of Future Foundation http://www.futurefoundation.net/

MOTIVATION

Motivation is a basic concept in human behaviour and thus, also in consumer behaviour. Motivation can be described as the driving force within individuals that moves them to take a particular action. This

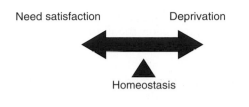

Need satisfaction   Deprivation

Homeostasis

- We strive for a state of equilibrium (*Homeostasis*)
- Physiological needs (e.g. hunger) move us away from this
- But so do *social* and *psychological* needs

Figure 1.1: The homeostasis see-saw

driving force is produced by a state of tension, which exists as a result of an unfulfilled need that moves us away from psychological equilibrium or **homeostasis** (Figure 1.1).

Indeed, motivated behaviour is activity that is directed towards the attainment of a goal or objective. As we have indicated, not all **motives** derive from physical drives. Having satisfied their hunger and other physical needs, people may be found buying such items as fashionable clothes or cosmetics. Evidently, the motives behind this behaviour originate quite separately from those that involve the satisfaction of the physiological drives (also called **biogenic drives**) of, for example, keeping warm and 'needing' to eat and drink in order to live. A whole range of **psychogenic** drives (e.g. the desire to be appreciated or to have status or feel 'at one with one's self') stem from our social environment, **culture** and social group interactions. Many such as Belk *et al.* (2003) even argue that **want** (or desire), which is fundamentally social in nature, is the major driving force or motivation behind much of our contemporary consumption.

Every individual has the same need structure, but different specific needs will be to the fore in different individuals at various points in time and according to different cultural and social contexts. In critical mode, Mishan (1971) argued that marketing adds to dissatisfaction, rather than satisfaction:

> Advertising, taken as a whole, conspires first to make men feel that the things that matter to them are the material things of life: the goods, services and opportunities provided by the economy. Second, it conspires to make men dissatisfied with what they have – so goading them into efforts to increase their 'real' earnings so as to acquire more of the stuff produced by modern industry. (p 244)

He also maintained that the plethora of versions of products and services, with relatively little differentiation (apart from the 'emotional') again added to consumer anxiety and dissatisfaction. He preferred less choice but greater real differentiation.

So, marketers are often accused of creating a need for a product or a service that would not exist except due to some aggressive and repetitive marketing activities that educate, inform and even persuade consumers to buy those products and services. For example, most advertisements strive to portray products in such an emotional and persuasive manner that consumers start to think that they ought to buy those products even if that specific brand is not a necessity for sustaining life. However, our proposition is that marketing does not create needs, rather it encourages us to want or desire brand X by associating its acquisition with the satisfaction of a latent need.

Indeed Marx (1867/1967) wrote:

> A commodity is, in the first place, an object outside us, a thing that by its properties satisfies human wants of some sort or another. The nature of such wants, whether for instance they spring from the stomach or from fancy, makes no difference.

However, he was not convinced about them satisfying our needs because he also said that the danger of continual aspirations to *have* things was that it creates the illusion that *having* is a way to happiness. We just want more and more and are constantly distant from happiness.

EXAMPLE 1.2

MarketingWeek

Many Western societies have high levels of personal debt. The ongoing worldwide financial crisis of 2008 reflected a degree of over-stretching of credit levels. Can we accuse marketers of encouraging the acquisition of materialistic lifestyles that are not sustainable? Not sustainable at an individual level but also at 'planet' level.

1. Individual level

ASA Condemns Littlewoods Ads

The Advertising Standards Authority (ASA) has condemned retailer Littlewoods for sending out a mailer encouraging young women to go into debt.

The mailer, which portrayed a young woman living a glamorous lifestyle on credit, was sent out by Littlewoods-owned Shop Direct Financial Services to more than 75 000 Additions Direct customers.

The ASA decided that Additions Direct's Direct Plus mailer was irresponsible because it was designed to appeal particularly to young women and was likely to be seen as encouraging carefree impulsive spending on credit.

The mailing features phrases such as "Hot dates won't last until payday" and "No cash required".

It also featured a series of cartoon scenes of a young woman with accompanying captions. One scene showed the woman and a man at home watching TV with the caption "Back at the flat... 40" LCD TV nice one! How does she do it? "

Shop Direct Financial Services, which owns Additions Direct, says the animated story format was intended to target customers in a "fun" and "informative" way, and points out that it did include details of the interest rate.

Marketing Week, 'ASA Condemns Littlewoods Ads' 10 November 2008, p.6. Reproduced by permission of Centaur Media Plc.

2. Planet level

The same *Marketing Week* article (2008) reported another ASA ruling against a TV commercial. This Ad was for Malaysian palm oil and it claimed it was produced in a sustainable way. Indeed so many of our food products contain palm oil. A mailer from the WWF in December 2007 stated: "in the last 20 years Borneo lost an area of orang-utan habitat 8 times the size of Wales, 100 years ago there were an estimated 230,000 orang-utans, 10 years ago 115,000, but now less than 32,000 remain in the wild. . .less we act now there could be no orang-utans left within 30 years''.

THINKBOX

Check out how widespread the use of palm oil is in foodstuffs. Do we really need to use this oil as much? Is it human greed that is destroying the planet's resources and inhabitants?

Is this sustainable? Does it matter? Are marketers just responding to human motivation?
Does the continual acquisition of 'things' make us happier?
What do you think?

Tangible and practical uses of products are often subordinated to more symbolic values. In a useful chapter on how consumers use the *things* we buy to communicate more symbolic meaning with others, Gabriel and Lang (1995, Chapter 3) draw from Theodor Adorno's philosophical thinking of post-war Germany. Adorno and others, from what became known as the **Frankfurt School**, saw social symbolism of products often outweighing their more practical use values. The work of Vance Packard (1957) extended this to assert that as the *practical* is subordinated in favour of the more frivolous, we are unduly influenced by the persuasive powers of marketing.

Various forms of marketing communications (e.g. advertising, personal selling, branding, sales promotions, direct marketing, packaging) contribute by conveying **symbolic meanings** about who we are and the way we can relate to ourselves and to others in the society. On this basis, products and services can be strategically positioned in competitive marketplaces and marketing communications (in particular) can, at an operational level, benefit from an understanding of the key aspects of motivation theory because specific message appeals can be based on such analysis.

www. **For more on symbolic consumption, read the article by Piacentini and Mailer (2004), Symbolic Consumption in Teenagers' Clothing Choices, on the accompanying web site at** www.wileyeurope.com/college/evans.

Furthermore, marketers can restructure and shape how human needs are manifested by introducing and producing products that did not exist before (Firat *et al.*, 1995). For instance, the need for transportation and mobility was restructured and reshaped by the production and consumption of cars and televisions. Due to the modern organization of life and the relationships of work and home, we have witnessed a reorganization of the transportation and entertainment systems at both the society and individual levels leading to changes in our consumption and expenditure patterns (Firat *et al.*, 1995).

Might consumers' buying behaviour not only reflect their desire to buy benefits, but with the aggregation of their purchases even define them? Are we what we buy (Belk, 1988)?

McAlexander *et al.* (2002) propose that, from a marketers' perspective, it is worth exploiting consumers' desire not only to buy benefits but also an experience. They suggest that this can gain competitive advantage by focusing: 'not merely on the product and its positioning but also on the *experience* of ownership and consumption'. The concept of experiential consumption is explored in Chapter 10.

THINKBOX

Our central proposition, then, is that marketing does not create needs but shapes the manifestation of these via wants for specific brands and types of products.

Do you think that marketing creates needs? Explain your position.

How do you feel about the proposition that many of the things we buy lack real use value and are merely bought for their symbolism to ourselves and to others?

Positive and Negative Motivation

Positive and negative motivation may be distinguished as **approach** and **avoidance**, respectively. As positive motivation, people are looking for positive situations, positive mood, pleasure, sensory gratification, intellectual stimulation, social approval and comfort: things that may enrich their lives and are worthwhile to strive for and goals that they want to reach (Figure 1.2). Holidays and entertainment are examples of products and services appealing to a positive motivation.

With negative motivation, people are motivated to escape from negative situations, negative mood, pain, illness and discomfort such as a headache: they want to avoid and remove problems. For example, people do not like to be stranded on a motorway when their cars break down suddenly and hence the motivation to purchase the breakdown cover. Similarly, a consumer while buying a washing machine may opt to buy an extended warranty for up to five years to avoid inconvenience and pain associated with calling and paying for expensive repairs if the machine breaks down.

We discuss **cognitive dissonance** later in this chapter (and in Chapter 4) and this is another example of how we are motivated to avoid states of disequilibrium.

Internal and External Motivation

Motivation is either internal ('from within a person') or external ('from the environment'). Internal motivation is concerned with instinct, need, drive or emotion. It often has a physiological base, for example hunger, thirst, sexual needs and need for stimulation. We explore aspects of deep-seated inner

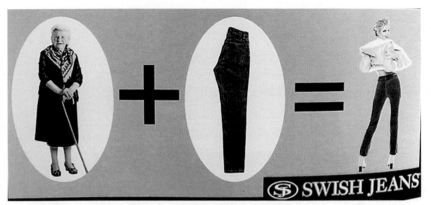

Figure 1.2: Positive motivation
It's not how you really are, but how the advertisement suggests you might become. But does marketing
sometimes promise the undeliverable, leading to consumer discontent?
Source: Swish Jeans

drives in the later section on **Freudian motivation. External motivation** is based on an attractiveness
of environmental stimuli such as products and services and often becomes **internal motivation** in the
form of preference for products, services and situations.

Operant conditioning and vicarious learning (explored in more detail in Chapter 3) are based
on the attractiveness of goods and services and the reinforcements these goods provide for consumers
through their benefits. Operant conditioning is concerned with the strengthening of behaviour through
reinforcement. If consumers select a brand or product type they may be positively reinforced by the
benefits of the product. But if these benefits are absent, there can be a 'negative' reinforcement of not
repeating the same buying experience. Vicarious learning (Chapters 3, 7 and 9) relates to the imitation
drive of people. Many will try to imitate celebrities and fashion models. They imitate the clothing,
movements and typical characteristics of these role models and in this way external motivational drives
are often triggered. Combining positive and negative motivation with internal and external motivation
gives the four types of motivation of Table 1.2.

At this point we turn to specific theories of motivation and how the work of the marketer and consumer
researcher can be informed by these.

Motivation	Internal	External
Positive	pleasure, comfort	attractive goods and services, attractive situations
Negative	pain, discomfort	unattractive goods and services unattractive situations

Table 1.2: Different kinds of motivation

MASLOW'S HIERARCHY OF NEEDS

Perhaps the most widely cited theory of motivation is that of Maslow which is represented as a hierarchy of
needs (Figure 1.3). Maslow's proposition is that needs at one level must be at least partially satisfied before

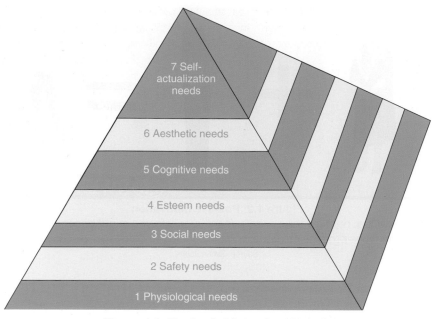

Figure 1.3: **Maslow's hierarchy of needs**

those at the next level become important in determining our actions. The satisfaction of a lower-order need triggers the next level of needs into operation, demanding new patterns of behaviour on the part of the individual. Naturally the basic needs must be met first (adequately, if not completely). But once the physiological (biogenic) needs have been satisfied, the individual turns their attention to the fulfillment of more advanced psychogenic requirements such as social acceptance and self-esteem. People may also have needs for 'cognition', that is to know and to understand things, and Maslow's level 5 reflects this. Many will have a need for learning for its own sake, for example. There can also be a need for creativity and for outlets for artistic, creative and aesthetic drives (level 6). The final stage in the motivational hierarchy is the need for what Maslow calls **self-actualization**. While he does not define this term with any real degree of precision, it appears to represent the attainment of what other psychologists call *self-realization*, the process in which the individual has the opportunity to invest all their talents and abilities in activities that they find meaningful: activities that help develop **personality**, for example through leisure activities and creative pastimes.

The significance of the hierarchy to marketing is great. It clearly demonstrates that a need refers to more than mere physiological essentials. Other forces driving our behaviour can come from a concern for our safety, social integration, personal recognition, learning, appreciation of our surroundings or from the perceived importance of spiritual satisfaction.

www. Take a look at this web site for more on Maslow's theory:
http://www.businessballs.com/maslow.htm

The hierarchy can be criticized; for example, Maslow suggested that as societies develop they move further up the hierarchy in terms of their most relevant needs to tackle. It could be argued here that not everyone will move up the ladder in quite the same way, perhaps missing some levels and perhaps moving back down to lower level needs. An illustration of this would be where, in Western industrialized countries, at the same time as attempting to satisfy social and higher levels of the hierarchy, many will be heavily orientated to, for example, safety and security as a result of fears about criminality, the violent society and terrorism. An advertisement by the Discovery Television channel for documentary programmes about terrorism pictured an airplane flying close to two tower blocks of flats. The copy headline was: 'Terrorism has changed the way we view the world.' Marketing clearly recognizes how even the most developed societies have strong and rekindled safety needs. This is evidenced by the plethora of advertisements for personal alarms, life assurance policies and home and car security devices. Chubb locks, for example, use the copy: 'Pick your own lock before a burglar does . . . and lock out unwelcome visitors.'

Some expensive products will target lower-level needs. Prior to the slightly more trendy Volvo advertising of today, the company promoted 'safety' as a key benefit of its cars for many decades (Figure 1.4). But even in 2006 Volvo targeted mothers with children between 3 and 5 years old via a direct mail campaign that focused on the car's safety features for children (Precision Marketing 2006). Volkswagen's Polo model has also been subject to 'safety' messages:

So, in the context of the discussion of consumer motivation, such criticisms are relatively pedantic. We present Maslow to reinforce the point that consumers can be motivated by more than the 'essentials' of physiology and that there can be changes, over time, to what motivates individuals. Maslow's theory makes a distinction between what may be termed physical/inherited needs and learned needs. The latter are not innate but acquired by the individual through social interaction.

© DDB London. Photography by Henrik Knudsen. Reproduced with permission

Identifying which needs are especially salient within different market segments is a task for marketers and market researchers. To demonstrate this, a useful illustration is the toothpaste market. Many of us might think, 'Toothpaste is toothpaste' and that we all use it in similar quantities for similar reasons. Table 1.3 adapts a classic piece of research into an apparently non-differentiated market. It shows that consumers may be assigned to different segments for a variety of reasons and can, on this basis, be targeted with different marketing mixes.

Figure 1.4: Example of how marketers have targeted Maslow's 'safety' needs
Reproduced by permission of Volvo Car UK Ltd and Abbott Mead Vickers BBDO

	Sensory segment	Sociable segment	Worrier segment	Independent segment
Main benefit	flavour	bright teeth	decay prevention	price
Demographic factors	children, young people	teens	large families	men
Lifestyle factors	hedonistic	active	conservative	concerned with value

Adapted from Haley (1968)

Table 1.3: Toothpaste consumer benefit segments

So, whereas brands of fluoride toothpaste may be tangibly and chemically very similar, they will often be targeted at different market segments. Even the brand *names* used can suggest this, on the basis of varying benefits being sought: Close Up, Aquafresh, Ultrabrite and Macleans. The imagery surrounding the advertising of these brands similarly suggests the difference between 'features' and 'benefits'. Some might show two mothers with their children in a dentist's waiting room. One child has to have several fillings and the other does not. Explicitly there might be references to the brand used by the child who has no cavities, suggesting that this is the brand for 'you', if you want to prevent tooth decay and hence satisfy a need or value to safeguard yourself (needs at level 2). Implied, however, is an even stronger benefit that if you don't use this brand as a parent, in some way you are not such a good parent (needs at levels 2, 3 and perhaps 4).

Recently, Colgate, in Figure 1.5, heavily promoted the benefit of fresh breath.

Figure 1.5: Toothpaste 'benefits'
Example of a marketer recognizing that different market segments will be motivated by different needs and therefore providing a basis for 'benefit segmentation'.
© Colgate-Palmolive Company 2005. Designed by Jim Richards, addicted2tv.com

EXAMPLE 1.3

Direct mailings for pensions aimed at the 18–35s have shown that in order to secure an assured future, a second pension is increasingly desirable (level 2). BUPA has used the advertising strapline: 'You're amazing, we want to keep you that way.' This and campaigns for life assurance, especially covering family members, can be linked with level 2 but also, because of the implied concerns for loved ones, we can see level 3 being activated (i.e. social needs) and additionally, more personal esteem needs from level 4 (our self-esteem can be enhanced by feeling we are looking after those for whom we have some responsibility). Social needs are also portrayed by BT's 'Friends and Family' and 'It's Good to Talk' campaigns. Perhaps, rather incredulously, we can see a possible use of self-actualization and its 'utopian' nature in Bounty Bar (a chocolate bar) advertisements claiming 'a taste of paradise'?

There is evidence of a trend toward self-actualization as reflected in **individualism**. We explore this further in Chapters 6 and 11 but it is worth a brief mention here. During the 1970s in the UK and the USA this trend was identified and led, among other things, to the Regan and Thatcher election campaigns from the late 1970s and into the 1980s, based on 'self-reliance' (BBC, 2002a; McNulty and McNulty, 1987). 'Standing on one's own feet' and 'freeing the individual from the state' were the sorts of mantras of those elections and were manifestations of research at the time that was put forward as evidence of the self-actualizing consumer, by the creator of the VALS lifestyle research in USA and confirmed more recently (McNulty, 2002). Indeed in UK, research reported by Publicis (1992) suggests that from 1973 to 1989 there had been a shift in motivators from 'level 1 and 2' functional and rational factors (40% to 27% of the population) and 'level 3' other-directedness (static at 35%) to more **inner-directedness** levels 4 to 7 (25% to 38% of the population). So although we started by suggesting a criticism of Maslow that not all societies will continue to progress up the hierarchy, there is evidence to suggest this can happen within some.

Alderfer (1972) proposed a similar, if more simple, model. This is still based on the principle of progression through categories of motivation; in this case, existence, relatedness and growth. His ERG model. In empirical research, more support is found for the ERG model than for the Maslow hierarchy, although the Maslow hierarchy remains popular with many (Wahba and Bridwell, 1976).

Other theories explain individual differences in motivation. For instance, consumers are likely to be different in their need for achievement, power and affiliation (McClelland, 1961) and their need for cognition (Cohen *et al.*, 1955). Similarly, McGuire classified motives into two broad categories: cognitive and affective. **Cognitive motives**, as per McGuire (1974, 1976), reflected motives that emphasized an individual's need for being adaptively orientated towards the environment and for achieving a sense of meaning. **Affective motives** emphasized an individual's need to achieve satisfying feeling states and to attain emotional goals.

FREUDIAN THEORY OF MOTIVATION

Consider the following: owners of sports cars verbalize reasons for purchase as being able to accelerate safely during overtaking manoeuvres. This, however, might just be a *good* reason, and the underlying *real* reason might be that the sports car helps attract the opposite sex or is even a substitute mistress. This is not as far-fetched as it might sound and was actually the theme of a classical advertising for the MGB GT car in the early 1980s. The copy headline for that advertisement read: 'Psychologists say a saloon car is a wife and a sports car is a mistress.' The MGB advertisement played on the proposition that not only are consumers buying benefits rather than features, but also that the benefits can sometimes satisfy more deeply seated needs by using the slogan 'Psychologists say a saloon car is a wife and a sports car is a mistress.' In this case, the sports car would be considered to be a subconscious symbol.

Sigmund Freud's psychoanalytic theory underpins this thinking and distinguishes three basic structures of the mind: **Id, Ego** and **Superego** (Table 1.4).

Structure	Level
Superego	Conscious
Ego	Subconscious
Id	Unconscious

Table 1.4: Id, ego and superego

Id

The **id** is the unconscious, instinctive source of our impulses: a source of psychic energy. It is a beast looking for immediate hedonistic gratification (pleasure), self-interest and a short-term perspective. The Id tries to satisfy whatever delivers pleasure without regard for wider implications for others, so in this way we can say that it works on the **pleasure principle**. Freud argued that the libido, sexuality, is the driving force of the id but the more general interpretation is that the id is the reservoir of 'base' instincts and these could be sexually or violence-related or even be traumatic experiences from the past which linger in the unconscious and exert influence on conscious and subconscious processes. There is a large degree of 'internal' motivation here, based on deeply seated instinctive drives.

Many people believe that consumers may be influenced at the unconscious level with 'subliminal' advertising. Subliminal advertising is supposed to exert influence on behaviour while consumers are not aware of the influence attempt of this type of advertising. Examples of subliminal advertising are short flashes, such as 'Eat popcorn' or 'Drink Coca-Cola' inserted in a film in New Jersey. These flashes were too short to be consciously observed (Packard, 1957).

As we know, although films appear convincingly as movement, they are composed of a series of still frames. The speed through the projector gives the impression of movement. The point is that our senses are not quick enough to distinguish each single frame. The idea behind the experiments was to apply this knowledge and it was thought that the single-frame insert would not be consciously noticed but, because it did physically appear on the screen for a fraction of a second, there would be a chance that the receivers' subconscious might accept the message. Indeed, for the test products, Coca-Cola and popcorn, more was sold during the commercial break (after the 'subliminal' message in the form of this additional single frame was shown) than was the case in 'control' audiences where the insets were not projected.

The approach was pounced on by the media and, as a result of general public concern, subliminal advertising was made illegal in many countries. However, other experiments attempting to replicate the results were not entirely conclusive about its effectiveness.

Subliminal images may also be inserted in pictures, in a scrambled or hidden way, e.g. the word 'sex' to be read in the ice cubes in a glass of whisky (Key, 1973). The suggestion is that these hidden flashes or pictures are being unconsciously observed and processed and, without any cognitive defence or screening by the superego, transmitted to the mind of consumers. These subliminal messages exert a strong effect on behaviour without people knowing that they are influenced. It is reassuring for consumers, perhaps, that in a review article (which we reproduce on the accompanying web site) Broyles (2006) submits that subliminal advertising is ineffective.

Even the popular notion that we are unconsciously influenced by pheromones, a sort of surreptitious aroma that we all secrete, is not yet proven. The obvious application is in the formulation of perfumes that might encourage greater sexual attraction of one to another (Small 1999).

But if subliminal advertising should work, it would bring many ethical questions to the fore as to whether this type of advertising would be allowed or not. Nevertheless there is sufficient concern for the legislation to remain.

Superego

However, the **superego** represents the internalized representation of the morals and values of those important to us in society and operates at the conscious level. In this way the superego is more of an 'external' motivator. It consciously controls our behaviour by seeking to make it fit with these internalized norms. It is our social conscience and can conflict with the id.

Ego

The **ego**, on the other hand, responds to the real world and acts in a mediating role between the id and reality (so the **reality principle** operates here). It does not operate at the conscious level but neither is it submerged into the unconscious; instead it is a subconscious mediator between the other two elements. Thus it controls our instinctive drives and tries to find a realistic means by which we can satisfy our impulses, or socially acceptable (to satisfy the superego) outlets that will adequately address the id drives (Figure 1.6).

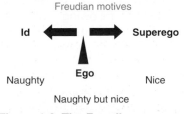

Figure 1.6: The Freudian see-saw

THINKBOX

In Figure 1.7, the id suggests what we 'really' want to wear or see, but which might not be entirely socially acceptable in public. Our superego reflects our social conscience and is what we see as being socially acceptable, but which probably doesn't satisfy the id enough. The ego comes up with styles which satisfy the id acceptably but which are also socially acceptable in public.

Id   Superego   Ego

Figure 1.7: Naughty, nice, naughty but nice

Source: Ann Summer's, www.annsummers.com (Id); Freemans plc, www.freemans.com (Superego and Ego).

EXAMPLE 1.4

If a main tenet of the theory is the conflict and ultimate compromise between the id, the superego and the ego, consider the effects of alcohol. In a classic television anti-drink advertising campaign, the same scene was played twice, through the perceptions of the two main characters. First, a man was drinking more and more and (through his eyes) becoming more sophisticated, suave and attractive to the women around him. Then the same episode was played as if through her eyes: a drunk was getting more and more obnoxious. What this nicely demonstrates is the effect that alcohol can have on reducing the constraints of the superego.

Indeed, in a series of advertisements for Pernod, the copy, in a variety of different settings, read 'Pernod: free the spirit'. Apart from the obvious play on words, it could also be equated with the notion of freeing the id. When on holiday in a foreign country we often don't know of the local norms and some will deliberately ignore them so that there is little perception of social constraints at all. Again the id can be free and this might explain the **misbehaviour** (see Chapter 12) of binge drinkers in Spanish resorts and elsewhere.

Even ice cream has been promoted with a similar 'free the id' appeal (Figure 1.8).

Tapping the id, but in a way that can ultimately be manifested in a socially acceptable way, is the key to this approach. Consider the following: 'Why do people take so much pleasure in immersing themselves in warm water? One theory is that it awakens distant memories of floating in the comfort of the womb.' This was actually part of the copy for a British Gas advertisement!

Figure 1.8: Freeing the id?
Free the spirit: free the id via alcohol – and even with ice cream you can 'lose control'.
Source: General Mills UK. Image courtesy of the Advertising Archives

THINKBOX

Next time you attend, or just see pictures of a carnival or Mardi Gras (or indeed go clubbing) check out the 'outfits' that some of the revelers are wearing – very few would probably be worn anywhere else. Are they satisfying id drives in a more direct manner than might be accepted by their superego at the next lecture?

Reproduced by permission of Bianco Footwear AS.

Source: Jean Paul Gaultier, Image courtesy of the Advertising Archives

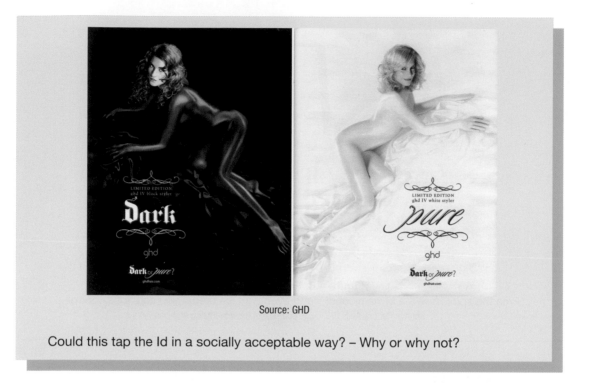

Source: GHD

Could this tap the Id in a socially acceptable way? – Why or why not?

Lasswell's (1948) **theory of the triple appeal** is useful for practical implementation of Freud-based marketing messages. This states that to be successful the message must appeal to all three elements of the mind. If not and it appeals only to the id, for instance, its effects will be immediately negated by the superego. If the appeal is purely to the superego, the social conscience is in danger of being too 'goody-goody' and won't address what really motivates us, and if the appeal is pure 'ego' it can be too logical and therefore lacks 'appeal'. So, Lasswell would opt for an appeal that was a touch 'naughty' but also 'nice'.

EXAMPLE 1.5

It might be suggested that appeals to the id can be made in other subconscious ways. Pack designs could trigger subconscious sets of associations; for example, when there is phallic and

Photo: Martin Evans

other symbolism in the designs, shapes, textures and materials. Also, consider the scope for 'voice under' messages as part of in-store music tracks declaring you must not steal, but which (at the conscious level) are inaudible.

Marketers might attempt to tap the id in such a way as to encourage what some might regard as rather dubious purposes. The purchase of a camcorder, for example, might be explained via a number of 'good' reasons but the 'real' reason might not be one that all purchasers would verbalize (Figure 1.9)!

Figure 1.9: 'Good' and (dubious) 'real' motives
Good and real reasons for buying a camcorder . . .
© Sanyo Europe Ltd. Reproduced by permission

Other messages might attempt to tap the subconscious id drives with what superficially would appear to be rather obscure references. Take, for instance, an advertisement in which a woman is about to eat a toffee apple. She wears a bracelet on her wrist in the form of a snake and the copy reads: 'Adam just cured my fear of snakes.' The advertisement is actually for gold jewellery, but there is plenty of Freudian symbolism here (Adam and Eve, 'forbidden fruit' and the phallic symbolism of snakes). This might go completely over the heads of the target market, at least at the conscious level, but if it reaches the id then it might well be doing what was intended.

The problem with the unconscious, of course, is that it is very difficult to identify and research – even its very existence. Different psychoanalysts might well interpret research findings in different ways and so the whole approach attracts critical attention.

It was not Freud himself, of course, who introduced the marketing world to this theory, but rather his nephew, Edward Bernays in 1920s America. He introduced the concept of linking subconscious desires with the acquisition of products and brands (BBC 2002b). He used celebrity endorsement (which we discuss in Chapter 9) and he was even instrumental in introducing the approach into political marketing in order to repress what many saw as a latent human savagery than can lead to horrors such as Nazism.

THINKBOX

Another of the major contributors to the adoption of psychoanalytical approaches in some areas of marketing was Ernest Dichter. Durgee (1991) provided an interpretation of Dichter's motives for consumption. These included eroticism, power and reward but also Maslow type motives such as social acceptance and security.

There is a very interesting reading on the accompanying web site that explores his contribution. The paper by Fullerton (2008) is critical of what he sees as Dichter's overly subjective interpretations of his motivation research studies and the lack criticality of the methodology used within them.

Read the article and critically analyze the points made.

However, new developments in **direct marketing** might increase the use of id appeals. For example, Club 18–30 targeting of what they see as the 'real' reason for young people to go on their holidays (i.e. sex on holiday) is barely disguised ('Beaver Espania', 'One swallow doesn't make a summer', 'the summer of 69'). We suggest that this sort of 'id' appeal would generally not be acceptable in mass media communications that reach the mass of the population with little targeting. But the direct approach perhaps allows for this, providing these risqué messages are targeted at the 'like-minded' in a discreet and confidential way; for example, through direct mail. In one mailing, Club 18–30 portrayed a couple of dolls having sex with the headline, 'coming soon'. In this way, the more 'private' message, which direct communications provide, could give added momentum for Freudian messages which are almost *all* id.

JUNGIAN MOTIVATION

Jung also proposed an unconscious, but that it is divided into:

1. Experiences that were once conscious but now sufficiently repressed, suppressed, ignored or forgotten, that they are now unconscious. Jung argued that if they resurface they can explain intuition. This is Jung's 'personal unconscious'.
2. Experiences that are equally unconscious but which derive from our previous ancestral existence(s). Such motives hidden in the unconscious reflect a more spiritual collectivism from the past. This is Jung's 'collective unconscious'.

He proposed a series of what he called 'archetypes'. These are image-types that we all possess, albeit at the unconscious level. One such archetype is the 'shadow'. This reflects our dark, often anti-social side and we can manifest it by seeing enemies around us or the dark unknown or what we know (if the superego rises) is forbidden. We can also ascribe our own less acceptable shadow traits onto others and this is a way of explaining what might be illogical blame or creating scapegoats. Sometimes we might repress our more positive characteristics into the shadow if family or social circumstances present any taboo. Dreams can also be the expression of shadow archetypes and some advertising might even attempt to stir such manifestations of the unconscious. For more on Jung and his archetypes, see Knox (2002).

MEMETICS

We wonder if a new consumer motivator is in the process of being identified and exploited. **Memetics** has recently attracted significant attention (Dawkins, 1989; Blackmore, 1999; Marsden, 1998, 1999; Williams, 2002). Whereas a gene passes forms of behaviour down (vertically) through the generations, a meme acts as a sort 'horizontal' communicator of how to behave. The difference, however, is that memes work more like a viral contagion. A good example of the principle is how it is often difficult not to start yawning if others are yawning (Marsden, 1998). Could memes go some way to explaining the spread of what at times appears to be an epidemic of suicides? It might be an unconscious communication, thus having some relationship with the Freudian paradigm discussed above and be one which might be most enduring if instilled at an early age. Or is it akin to vicarious learning, which we explore in Chapter 3?

Will it become possible to 'create' a meme that marketers can use to communicate through societies, with consumers becoming infected with a mind virus that is not recognized consciously, but which results in them suddenly joining the next fad or fashion? Some say this is nearly possible, and research is being conducted to 'design and engineer highly infectious memes that could be used in marketing campaigns' (Marsden, 1998).

www. | **Take a look at this web site for more on memes and memetics:**
www.geocities.com/persistentmemes/articles.html

THINKBOX

In 1957, with respect to what we might see today as straightforward mass media advertising such as TV advertising, Vance Packard raised concerns about its 'hidden persuasion' potential. He wrote: 'Eventually – say by AD 2000 – perhaps all this depth manipulation of the psychological variety will seem amusingly old-fashioned. By then perhaps the biophysicists will take over "biocontrol", which is depth persuasion carried to its ultimate' (Packard, 1957:195).

What do you think?

COGNITIVE DISSONANCE AS MOTIVATOR

The final motivation theory we have space to explore here is the need to avoid or reduce cognitive dissonance (Festinger, 1957). This is discussed in more detail in Chapter 4 but, briefly, it is a condition reflecting a tendency towards mental unease (the homeostasis see-saw again) which occurs when an individual holds two attitudes, ideas, beliefs or other cognitions that are not in harmony with each other. In this situation the person tries to reduce dissonance – perhaps by dropping a cognition, perhaps by strengthening one. Dissonance is therefore a factor in motivation because it leads the individual to change their opinion, attitudes or behaviour in order to reach a state of 'consonance' or homeostasis.

For example, there is dissonance in a smoker who knows that smoking is dangerous to health. The smoker is motivated to reduce the dissonance, perhaps by stopping or reducing the smoking behaviour or by not reading (or screening out) the messages conveying the dangers of smoking. Another well-known example of cognitive dissonance theory concerns the post-decisional doubt expressed by purchasers of new cars. The existence of dissonance among such customers was deduced from their tendency to seek further information about the model just bought despite having previously considered several alternatives. There is a degree of reassurance that many buyers seek, to confirm their choice. Marketing responds with 'welcome packs' for new customers (especially for new customers of mobile phone companies), 'congratulations' messages on joining the 'family' of owners, after-sales service and the use of comparative advertising in which competitors' offerings are not seen in such good light as their own. Chapter 4 explores dissonance as a **post-purchase** phenomenon in more detail, but in this chapter we submit that dissonance reduction and/or avoidance is a clear motivator for many consumers.

MOTIVATION AND SHOPPING

In a shopping context, we can think of motivation as the driving force within consumers that makes them shop. Table 1.5 presents some of the shopping motives identified by previous research. The well-known work of Tauber (1972) concerns the identification of a number of shopping motivations with the premise that consumers are motivated by a number of personal and social needs. The personal motives include the needs for role-playing, diversion, self-gratification, learning about new trends, physical activity and sensory stimulation. The social motives identified by Tauber (1972) include the needs for social experiences, communication with others, peer group attractions, status and authority, and pleasure in bargaining. Similarly, Westbrook and Black (1985) and Arnold and Reynolds (2003) identify a number of interesting shopping motivations. It is worth noting that, for some consumers, a shopping experience can be potentially entertaining, playful and fun, emotionally involving and a mechanism of escaping from the daily routines. In this way it reinforces the earlier view that we buy less for tangible functionality than for social and psychological symbolism that satisfy higher-level needs. Even the *process* of buying can be more important than the resulting product acquisition itself. We explore negative dimensions of this (for example, compulsive buying) in our chapter on **consumer misbehaviour** (Chapter 12).

For other consumers, however, *shopping* can obviously be task-orientated (e.g. I have to buy this as part of my day-to-day routine) and is a very rational activity to satisfy more physiological needs.

By knowing and exploring consumers' motivations for shopping, researchers have been able to profile shoppers into different segments and have examined similarities and differences among these segments. Table 1.6 presents characteristic features of different shopper segments based on Sproles and Kendall's (1986) work on mental orientations that characterize consumers' approaches to making shopping choices. Marketers can improve their targeting efforts by developing marketing communications that emphasize key features of the shopping experience (e.g. depict the shopping experience as a delightful adventure or emphasize value for money). They can also improve store designs and store layouts (e.g. tailor store atmospherics to the needs of a particular segment).

Tauber (1972)

- **Diversion** highlights shopping's ability to present opportunities to the shopper to escape from the routines of daily life and therefore represents a type of recreation and escapism.
- **Self-gratification** underlines shopping's potential to alleviate depression as shoppers can spend money and buy something nice when they are in a down mood.
- **Physical activity** focuses on consumers' need for engaging in physical exercise by walking in spacious and appealing retail centres, particularly when they are living in urban and congested environments.
- **Sensory stimulation** emphasizes the ability of the retail institutions to provide many sensory benefits to consumers as they can enjoy the physical sensation of handling merchandise, the pleasant background music and the scents.
- **Social and communication** motives feature shopping's potential to provide opportunities to socialize, meet and communicate with others with similar interests.
- **Peer group attraction** stresses consumers' desires to be with their reference group.
- **Status and authority** reflect shopping's ability to provide opportunities for consumers to command attention and respect from others.
- **Pleasure of bargaining** reflects consumers' desires and abilities to make wiser decisions by engaging in comparison shopping and special sales.

Westbrook and Black (1985)

- **Anticipated utility** – the benefits provided by the product acquired via shopping.
- **Role enactment** – identifying and assuming culturally prescribed roles.
- **Negotiation** – seeking economic advantage via bargaining.
- **Choice optimization** – searching for and securing precisely the right products to fit one's demands.
- **Affiliation** – with others directly or indirectly.
- **Power and authority** – attainment of elevated social position.
- **Stimulation** – seeking novel and interesting stimuli.

Arnold and Reynolds (2003)

- **Adventure shopping** – to seek stimulation, adventure, and feelings of being in a different world.
- **Social shopping** – for enjoyment of shopping with friends and family, socializing while shopping and bonding with others.
- **Gratification shopping** – for stress relief, to alleviate a negative mood and as a special treat to one's self.
- **Idea shopping** – for keeping up with trends and new fashions and to seek new products and innovations.
- **Role shopping** – for getting enjoyment as a consequence of shopping for others.
- **Value shopping** – reflecting shopping for sales, looking for discounts, and hunting for bargains.

Table 1.5: Shopping motives

Shopper category	Characteristics
Quality-consciousness shoppers	They look for highest possible quality while shopping; like to shop carefully, systematically and may not feel satisfied with just-good-enough brands.
Brand-conscious shoppers	They seek out more expensive and famous brands; like to perceive price–quality link, have positive attitudes towards departmental and speciality stores selling expensive and popular brands and may prefer best-selling, heavily advertised brands.
Novelty-fashion-conscious shoppers	They seek to buy novel and fashionable items; like to seek pleasure and excitement out of discovering new things, want to keep up to date with new styles and trends.
Recreational shoppers	They look for pleasure, fun, recreation and entertainment out of shopping.
Value-conscious shoppers	They seek bargains and look for deals; are concerned about getting best value for money; engage in comparison-shopping.
Impulsive shoppers	They tend to buy on impulse; do not like to plan their shopping; remain unconcerned about how much they spend.
Confused shoppers	They tend to get confused by over-choice of brands and information; likely to experience information overload.
Brand-loyal shoppers	They to tend to like and buy same brands again and again; likely to have developed particular behaviours and habits.

Table 1.6: Classification of shoppers based on Sproles and Kendall's (1986) consumer decision-making styles

www. Addis and Holbrook (2001) on the conceptual link between mass customization and experiential consumption: An explosion of subjectivity, Journal of Consumer Behaviour, Vol 1 No 1 pp 50–66 can be found on the accompanying web site and it explores a variety of issues relevant to the current chapter: hedonistic versus utilitarian consumption, experiential consumption as well as aspects of relational consumption, relevant to Chapter 10.
www.wileyeurope.com/college/evans

THINKBOX

Jonathan Porritt has been reported by Smith (2007) as stating 'Fascism, Communism, Democracy, Religion, but only one has achieved total supremacy. Its compulsive attractions rob its followers of reason and good sense. It has created unsustainable inequalities and threatened to tear apart the very fabric of our society. More powerful than any cause or even religion, it has reached into every corner of the globe. It is Consumerism'

Smith (2007) Stop Shopping ... or the Planet will go Pop, Observer, 8 April 8–9

Critically analyse and evaluate this statement:

'When I'm watchin' my TV and a man comes on and tells me
How white my shirts can be
But, he can't be a man 'cause he doesn't smoke
The same cigarettes as me
I can't get no' ... (you know what)

Jagger & Richards (1965)

Does this imply that marketers try but fail to satisfy our needs?

THINKBOX

FUTURE FOUNDATION RESEARCH:

Experience Economy

Just in the way that, in the modern economy, manufacturing is declining and service industries are rising even more, for the modern consumer functional satisfaction is giving way to the search for psychic benefits. For millions, it is relatively easy to procure household durables and leisure products. Few really take eating-out to be that special a treat any more. Leisure is ubiquitous, and in 'leisurizing' our experiences we are creating an experience economy – one where consumers are demanding instant stimulation, innovation and originality. Modern marketing realizes that there are fewer and fewer mere products these days and more and more agents of enhanced personal experience. Novel executions in the field of customer service, invitations to accomplishment, elegance in presentation and setting all appeal to consumers' appetites to convert humdrum consumption into psychic treasure. This raises difficult issues for marketers trying to position their brand within their consumers' multiple experiences. Does a bookstore-chain sell a quiet space for reverie and friendly encounter or just books at competitive prices? Does a bottle of whisky give you a nice drink or the permission to be quietly and successfully alone at the end of the working day, just before bed? Is an airline a supplier of movement or a stress alleviator? When so many products can simply no longer deliver unassailable innovations at the level of functions and features, how can competitive advantage for a brand really be sustained? Consumer culture is driving people to seek the promise of unexpected and delightful experiences. An entire encyclopedia of communications challenges arises from this idea.

The summary, here, of the Future Foundation Report of the same name extends our discussion of 'features versus benefits'. What are your reactions to this?

Reproduced by permission of Future Foundation http://www.futurefoundation.net/

VALUES

Higher-level needs approach the status of **values**, which are critical determinants of behaviour (Baier, 1969). Rokeach (1968) regarded a value as 'an enduring belief that a specific mode of conduct or end-state of existence is personally or socially preferable to an opposite or converse mode of conduct or end-state of existence'. For Schwartz and Bilsky (1987) values transcend specific situations and one of the most widely accepted value inventory is the Rokeach Value Survey (RVS). The RVS measures 18 **instrumental values** and the same number of **terminal values** (Table 1.7). Instrumental values are related to preferred modes of conduct such as honesty and friendliness which people know can lead to being accepted by others and to having good relations with others. Instrumental values are thus means to reach a goal. Terminal values are more related to end-state goals such as wisdom, happiness and freedom. Products and services may also be related to terminal values; for example, Coca-Cola and its connotation of US values.

Vinson and Lamont (1977) devised a model of consumer value systems by arranging values at three different levels and giving a hierarchical arrangement to them (Figure 1.10).

Instrumental Values	Terminal Values
Ambitious	A Comfortable Life
Broad-minded	An Exciting Life
Capable	A Sense of Accomplishment
Cheerful	A World at Peace
Clean	A World of Beauty
Courageous	Equality
Forgiving	Family Security
Helpful	Freedom
Honest	Happiness
Imaginative	Inner Harmony
Independent	Mature Love
Intellectual	National Security
Logical	Pleasure
Loving	Salvation
Obedient	Self-respect
Polite	Social Recognition
Responsible	True Friendship
Self-controlled	Wisdom

Source: Adapted from Rokeach (1973)

Table 1.7: The Rokeach Value Survey

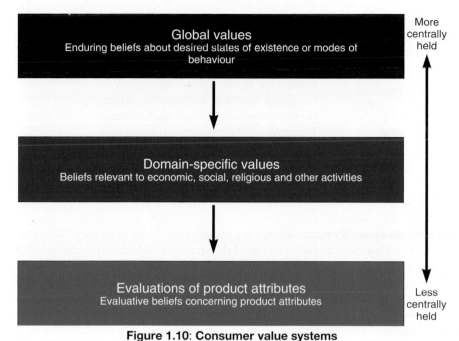

Figure 1.10: Consumer value systems
Source: D. Vinson, J. Scott and L. Lamont, 'The Role of Personal Values in Marketing and Consumer Research', *Journal of Marketing* 41 (April 1977), pp. 45–50. Reproduced by permission of American Marketing Association

In different cultures, different values have been found and we discuss this in more detail in Chapter 8. However, it is worth introducing Hofstede's (1980) study on work-related cultural values in 40 countries. This identified four major dimensions: power distance, uncertainty avoidance, femininity/masculinity and individualism/collectivism. The power-distance emphasis refers to the extent to which a particular society or its members tolerate an unequal distribution of power in the society. In cultures with large power distance, people tend to have their rightful places in the society. They also tend to respect old age, and status is valued to show off power. People in low power-distance cultures try to look younger than they are and the powerful people try to look less powerful. The uncertainty-avoidance emphasis refers to the extent to which people tend to feel threatened by uncertain, risky and ambiguous situations. People in cultures with large uncertainty-avoidance tend to appreciate the need for rules and formality to structure their lives. They also tend to value competence, which leads them to value experts. In masculine cultures, people tend to value achievement and success and there is a significant role differentiation between males and females. In feminine cultures, people tend to value caring for others and quality of life and there is less role differentiation. People in individualist cultures tend to look after themselves and their immediate family only whereas, in collectivist cultures, people tend to value belonging to groups that look after them in exchange for loyalty.

Similarly, Western values are characterized by 'separatedness' in the sense of people being relatively independent and individualistic (as the Publicis [1992] research above suggested). The Harley Davidson strapline, 'We don't care how everyone does it ... we prefer to go our own way'

Country	Values
UK	Singularity, difficult to express feelings, not tactile
France	Search for quality of life/well being
Italy	Religious idealism, community, curiosity
Spain	Human interaction, sharing, harmony
Germany	Tangible reality, concrete pleasure

Source: Adapted by the authors from Harris Research (1998) European Values Research Report, London

Table 1.8: European values

encapsulates this, whereas non-Western cultures are more 'connected' in terms of being more interdependent and collective. The Fuji Bank in Japan has used the strapline, 'Meeting clients' needs is half the story, meeting society's needs is the other half.' Furthermore, Harris Research (1998) has found differing values within Europe as summarized in Table 1.8. Similarly, Caillat and Mueller (1996) compared the cultural variables manifest in US and UK commercial messages for beer advertising, including dominant cultural values. The study found that the US commercials perpetuated predominantly US cultural values (e.g. achievement, individualism/independence, and modernity/newness) whereas UK commercials presented predominantly UK cultural values (e.g. tradition/history and eccentricity). Their findings led them to conclude a standardized message strategy among the US and UK beer markets might not be very effective, because of differences in cultural values.

People are not born with their values. Rather, values are passed from one generation to another; they are learned. Engel *et al.* (1986) point out that some values are relatively constant while others are subject to change. They propose that the triad of families, religious institutions and school plus early lifetime experiences leads to a model of **intergenerational value transmission** (Figure 1.11).

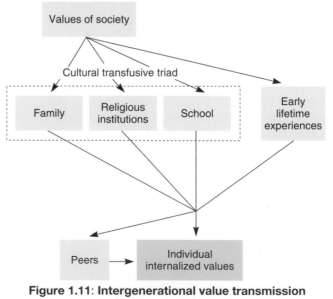

Figure 1.11: **Intergenerational value transmission**
Source: Adapted from Engel *et al.* (1986)

This analysis is developed in the next section discussing motivation research methods because it provides a framework for research; namely, to explore a hierarchical sequence of how consumers perceive product **attributes**, their **consequences** and what these then reveal about their values (**means–end chains**).

MOTIVATION RESEARCH

It is apparent from the foregoing that the identification of consumers' motives is a complex business. The difficulties involved in discovering directly the precise motivating factors that shape buying behaviour led some marketers and consumer researchers to devise techniques for exposing hidden motives. Such techniques sometimes need to reveal suppressed and repressed motives and some are briefly discussed below. Most marketing research textbooks will provide more detailed expositions and a discussion paper by Tadajewski (2006) traces the ups and downs of motivation research techniques over the best part of a century and extends this to the development of more experiential interpretive research methodologies.

Projective Techniques

If persons are relieved of direct responsibility for their expressions, they will tend to answer more freely and truthfully. **Projective tests** are designed to achieve this end. These are called 'projective tests' because respondents are required to project themselves into someone else's place or into some ambiguous situation. Consider the following examples of projective tests:

Third-Person Tests

In **third-person tests**, the respondent is encouraged to reply through some third party. The rationale is that there are both 'good' and 'real' reasons for behaviour. 'Good' reasons are socially acceptable (e.g. to buy environmentally friendly products). 'Real' reasons are sometimes not socially accepted. While 'good' reasons will probably be given in response to a direct questioning approach, such as 'Why did you buy this?', these answers may only be partially true. There may be a 'real' reason for behaviour that either the respondent is unwilling to admit or unable to recognize. An indirect question – for example, 'What sort of people buy this?' or 'Why do people buy these?' – might be sufficient to reveal 'real' reasons for behaviour.

EXAMPLE 1.6

A classic piece of market research years ago investigated the reasons for poor sales of the newly introduced instant coffee. The widely quoted study of instant coffee usage illustrates that there can be 'good' and 'real' reasons for behaviour (Haire, 1950). The indirect questioning approach employed in this project was to ask women what sort of housewife would have compiled the shopping lists shown in Table 1.9. One half of the sample had list 1, which differed from list 2 only by having instant coffee included. The instant-coffee shopping list was seen to have been drawn up by a lazier, less well-organized woman who was described as not being a good housewife. Direct questioning, on the other hand, revealed good reasons for preferring real coffee, which revolved around the product not tasting as good as drip-grind coffee. Respondents were considered to be unwilling or unable to reveal their true (real) reasons for not buying instant coffee.

Shopping list 1	Shopping list 2
11/2 lb hamburger	11/2 lb hamburger
2 loaves Wonderbread	2 loaves Wonderbread
Bunch of carrots	Bunch of carrots
1 can Rumfords baking powder	1 can Rumfords baking powder
1 lb Nescafé instant coffee	1 lb Maxwell House drip-grind coffee
2 cans Del Monte peaches	2 cans Del Monte peaches
5 lb potatoes	5 lb potatoes

Reprinted with permission from the Journal of Marketing, published by the American Marketing Association, Haire (1950) Projective Techniques in Marketing Research, Vol 14, pp 649–656

Table 1.9: Haire's shopping list

Source: Betty Crocker
Image courtesy of the Advertising Archives

Another example was Mary Baker cake mix. This was also not selling well and motivation research led to the conclusion that more had to be done by the consumer than just adding water to the cake mix, in order to overcome what again was thought to be an overly convenient way of baking a cake. The omission of the dried egg component was seen as the solution and apparently was enough to allow the consumer to feel that they had contributed at least a little more, creatively. Indeed, this particular research became somewhat notorious because it was felt that baking a cake was so much a creative process for women that it was symbolic of childbirth! Perhaps, following extreme interpretations such as this, there was a degree of a backlash against psychoanalytic methods in marketing.

Word Association Test

This type of test, also known as 'free association', involves firing a series of words at respondents who must state immediately which other words come into their minds. Word association tests can be used to determine consumer attitudes towards products, stores, advertising themes, product features and brand names. A frequent association with 'Volvo', for many years, was 'safety'.

Psychodrama

Here, the respondent is asked to play a role and, to do so, they are given a complete description of the circumstances. For instance, the role-playing of respondents to depict two alternative painkillers with other respondents playing the role of the pain. How the 'painkiller' tackles the 'pain' might lead to the copy strategy in direct response and other advertising campaigns (Cooper and Tower, 1992).

Cartoon Test

Informants are presented with a rough sketch showing two people talking. One of them has just said something represented by words written into a 'speech balloon' as in a comic strip. The other person's balloon is empty and the respondent is asked how this other person might reply (Figure 1.12). The idea is that the respondent's *own* feelings are *projected* through that reply.

Figure 1.12: Cartoon test

MEANS–END CHAIN ANALYSIS AND LADDERING

As mentioned in the 'Values' section, a useful technique is repeatedly to ask the respondent (words to the effect of) 'What does that mean to you?'. For example, it is typical to start with product or service attributes such as those shown in Figure 1.13 and to encourage the respondent to work through

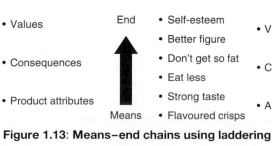

Figure 1.13: Means–end chains using laddering

a series of 'consequences' towards their own motives and values. Product features or attributes are thus 'creating' benefits, and these benefits are contributing to the realization of consumer needs and values. The sequence of 'attributes → benefits → values' is called a 'ladder' or a means–end chain (Gutman, 1982; Reynolds and Gutman, 1988).

Take a look at the article by Woodside (2004), Advancing Means-End Chains by Incorporating Heider's Balance Theory and Fournier's Consumer Brand Relationship Typology, which is accessible from the accompanying web site: www.wiley.com/go/evans. We refer to this again in Chapters 3 and 11 because it integrates concepts from those chapters with the means–end chain approach.

We again refer you to the article on the accompanying web site by Ronald A Fullerton (2008): Mr MASS Motivations Himself: Explaining Dr Ernest Dichter, Journal of Consumer Behaviour, Vol 6, No 6, pp 369–382.

THINKBOX

An earlier era – forget social, psychological or subconscious-based motivation appeals – this one just told the market what the product does:

Do you think marketing would be more honest using these more basic appeals?

THINKBOX

FUTURE FOUNDATION RESEARCH
Complicated Lives

Consumers in recent years have witnessed a 'choice explosion' in which the range of choice in various markets has grown exponentially. Our ability to handle information has grown, but has not kept pace with the choice explosion. Despite unprecedented affluence, consumers seem little happier. Their expectations are continually increasing, bringing with them complexity and complications. The growth of individualism is undoubtedly manifesting itself in a more internally-focused definition of identity, with multiple identities simultaneously negotiated, often resulting in genuine, or perceived, 'anxiety'. Changing age and household structures are undermining traditional stereotypes and giving rise to more complex family structures, including the more fluid and self-definitional nature of 21st-century family.

How can companies respond to the growing individualization of consumption? Are some consumers feeling the pace? Are some tending towards greater 'burn-out' and downshifting? Brands will need to think carefully about how to position themselves to be seen as removing the complication from consumption.

This summary of the Future Foundation report of the same name raises further questions about consumer motivation but also introduces some of the ideas we explore in more detail in Chapter 6, notably *self-concept theory* and the notion of multiple roles. It also provides some foundation for our coverage of postmodernism in Chapter 7. What do you think about the main findings summarized here?

Reproduced by permission of Future Foundation http://www.futurefoundation.net/

CASE STUDY **1.1**

TNS CASE STUDY: Understanding Consumer Needs

Racing Past the Barriers: The Success of the Apache Motorcycle in India

Poonam V. Kumar
TNS – Asia Pacific & Middle East

Prasad Narasimhan
TVS Motor Company India

Introduction

The motorcycle market in India has, in the past, been a sellers' market with enormous waiting lists of buyers. The focus had been on producing technically better machines with functional benefits such as fuel efficiency being the major point of differentiation. Segmentation was based on price tiers and branding limited to corporate values to reassure about quality and after sales service. However, things have changed. The market has become more competitive.

Changing Lanes

Never strangers to trying avenues other than the conventional, safe and the familiar, TVS took the bold decision to look beyond improving functional performance for a solution. Rather than taking a scattergun, trial and error approach, TVS decided to attempt to understand what the market needed. They had access to the best technical and design consultants in the world, and were confident that once the market gaps were identified and understood, the task of creating a suitable product would not be very difficult. There was also a hesitant realization that consumer decisions were not wholly rational and that there were elements that went beyond functional parameters. How else could they explain the less than successful launch of models that surpassed others on fuel efficiency?

The decision to explore building the brand as a platform for a deeper consumer connection was taken. A research proposal to segment the market on needs was asked for, the initial reaction to which was a mix of both scepticism and enthusiasm.

The Tool Box

The research consisted of several stages. The first was a qualitative exploratory phase to uncover the need structure of the market. This was followed by quantitative need based segmentation to validate the need structure and measure the sizes of the need segments. Mapping and measuring of existing brands on the needs landscape helped to identify where the opportunity lay. Concepts were developed and tested and THEN finally the technical design team given the direction to develop/identify a suitable product that expressed the desired brand positioning. This represented a complete paradigm shift in the method of client working and thinking, where most of the earlier launches (the successful ones as well as not so successful) had emerged from the engineering and draftsman drawing boards.

NeedScope, TNS's proprietary system was identified as the most suitable solution.

The NeedScope System

Two concepts form the theoretical basis of Need-Scope – a marketing model and an archetypal framework.

The marketing model describes how brands and needs are two sides of an equation and should fit together. Needs are layered into three levels:

The outer, most easily accessible, layer of consumer needs is the rational layer and is satisfied by the functional benefits the product delivers. The Indian two-wheeler market was largely competing at this need level – there was increased fragmentation on prices, varying combination of features,

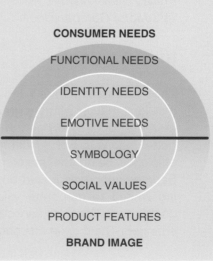

CONSUMER NEEDS

FUNCTIONAL NEEDS

IDENTITY NEEDS

EMOTIVE NEEDS

SYMBOLOGY

SOCIAL VALUES

PRODUCT FEATURES

BRAND IMAGE

performance and mileage. The only route to competitive advantage seemed to be engineering innovation, leading to long new product development (NPD) cycles, high-risk launches without any means to secure long-term advantage as all the big three had equal access to international state of art technology.

The second layer has to do with sociology – the need to identify with particular groups in society. These needs are met by the social values or character of the brand – a brand for young people, for women, upscale, etc. Interestingly, the market was not very well differentiated at this layer either, except through a default pricing route.

And finally, at the heart of the model are the emotive needs. These are the core drivers of brand choice, the engine that powers the consumer's relationship with the brand.

The marketing model, therefore, is not just an emotive model. It recognizes that consumers have needs at all levels, and that the rational or functional level serves as a screener, the first stop, which if not satisfied will keep the brand out of the consumer's consideration set. However, this is not the layer at which loyalty can be built and it is necessary to go below the surface. Starting with the rational, the model systematically uncovers the inner need layers. There is also no hierarchy – no layer is considered more important than the others. The needs are interlinked and only when cohesively met across all three layers, will a powerful connection be struck with the consumer.

The second concept is the NeedScope archetypal framework:

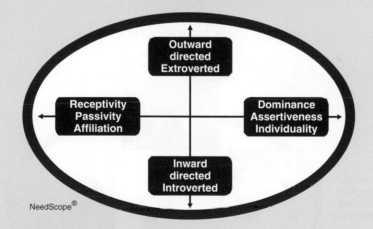

NeedScope®

Two axes are the fundamental anchors of the framework. The horizontal is the 'I vs. We' axis. The right side represents the drive for individualism and self-assertion. This is the need to stand out, to feel superior, to be admired and to stay ahead of others. The left is about the fundamental sense of belonging – the need for acceptance, togetherness, friendship and warmth.

The vertical dimension divides the model into the extroverted and introverted poles. The top is about energy directed outwards – release, stimulation, freedom. The bottom is about energy that is inwards – more contained and controlled and therefore less visible. While these are polar opposites, there are no hierarchies or negatives. The space represents alternative strategies that consumers use to resolve their needs. It must also be pointed out that this is a needs rather than a consumer framework. Consumers are multi-faceted and have multiple needs, depending on the context of the category and occasion.

The space can be dissected in many ways, but in its most basic way we can identify six archetypes. Archetypes are the unchanging constant in human beings that hold over time, across different geographies and cultures. For example, everyone recognizes and connects with the nurturing care of the Mother, the appealing purity of the Innocent, the determined courage of the Winning Hero beating odds,or the irresistible sensuality of the Seductress. These archetypes are found in culture after culture, they anchor our worlds and our belief systems. Carl Jung calls this the collective unconscious.

Taking the Emotional Leap Forward

For the TVS story, the market was largely operating at the functional layer. The only brand that had broken out of this mould was Pulsar, from a competitor house, with enviable success. Clearly the Indian consumer was not just ready for a more meaningful dialogue, but was actually seeking more than functional promises.

We started with qualitative research with recent buyers of motorbikes and those intending to buy a motorbike in the next few months. Using projective techniques and the NeedScope framework, needs were uncovered at all layers:

The Needs Landscape

Breaking free, Pleasures & thrills

Feeling accepted, confident, comfortable

Asserting Individuality, Power & Superiority

Feeling safe and in control.

Some of the key insights that came through are given below.

- Modernity is at the heart of the category. The market had moved away from the family orientation scooter days. Consumers were looking for contemporary expression in keeping with the optimism and hope of the new generation. This had to be reflected in both the design and the emotive proposition.

- Stability, reliability and trust, which were critical strengths of the TVS corporate brand were now taken for granted, important to have, but no longer enough with which to build a differentiated proposition.
- The new brand would therefore have to stand-alone; in fact perhaps lead the shift of TVS image towards modernity.
- And to succeed In this direction, there was a need to alter the thinking and functioning of existing stalwarts within the company, with their strong technical orientation.

The next stage was the quantitative segmentation based on needs. There were six need states identified:

Six Need Segments

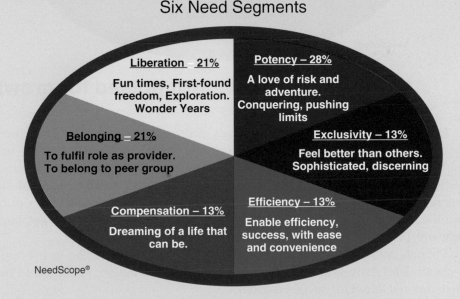

NeedScope®

The archetypes are clearly evident. Exclusivity is about asserting one's status, looking and feeling better than others. The brand has to reflect sophistication, knowledge and authority. The social values of Exclusivity are premium, international and exclusive. Functionally, the bike needs stronger safety assurances that only a discerning buyer understands and visible enhancement features to match. In contrast, Affiliation is a need to belong, to own the tried and trusted, to be appreciated by the family and to feel good about one's self. The social values are that of a newly married person, ready to settle down. Functional needs are pillion comfort, low maintenance value and an assured resale price.

The size of the need states indicates the dynamic shift of the market towards more modernity and individualism. Of the market, 62% is weighted towards self-expression and status needs:

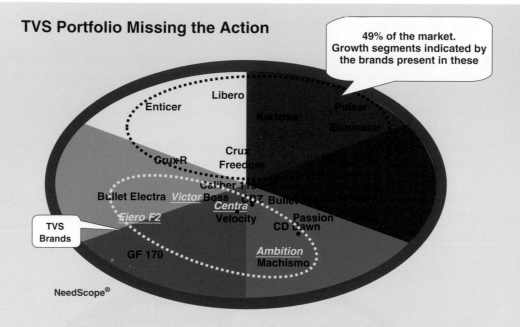

Brands were then mapped on the needs landscape based on how consumers perceived them. Pulsar, the big success in the market, was unsurprisingly in Potency. The TVS brands were **all** clustered in the lower part of the affiliative section of the map. Clearly, all of them were drawing imagery and symbology from the affiliated, reliable image of the corporate brand. The position of the TVS brands indicated sub-optimal utilization of the portfolio and the absence from the more dynamic and growing part of the market was a cause of concern. TVS clearly had to get back into the action.

Potency and Liberation, being large and growing were identified as the opportunity. An in-depth need state-brand fit analysis showed that Liberation, rather than Potency was a more optimal target for several reasons:

- Potency, while larger and exciting, already had a formidable competitor in Pulsar. There was a high risk of becoming a me-too launch unless something dramatically different was created.
- While the need to create a new brand rather than a new TVS model was recognized, it was also clear that the auto being a high ticket buy, the signature of an established company is needed for market acceptance and consequently there would be some influence of the company brand. The Potency need state with its macho, rugged individualism was just too distant to be targeted credibly with TVS's affiliative imagery.
- Liberation had a younger skew, which opened up the opportunity to target a new social group – the first-time bike buyer. With the market size growing, the profile of the buyer was getting younger and this segment was expected to grow even further as the shift of the older middle-class consumers towards four-wheelers had begun.

The first step was to understand Liberation at all layers of needs.

- Emotively, Liberation represents the wonder years in a man's life. The first taste of freedom, the first coming into adulthood. A time of freedom, fun, exploration of the world and experiences before responsibility and the realities of life take over. The bike in this need state symbolizes a rite of passage – the boy becomes a man – and is the ideal partner to explore spaces, both physically and emotively. In the physical sense it is about mobility. Emotionally it is about reaching places you've never been.
- Liberation evokes the heady kick and excitement of youth, the exciting discovery of adulthood and the bike is integral as a source of pleasure.
- There was a definite younger skew demographically, but the need also extended to the Young at Heart. For the young man, the motorbike is a symbol to flaunt his adult status (personified as a girlfriend for fun, romance). With older men it is about recapturing moments gone by, the wish for evergreen enduring youthfulness.
- The social values of the need state are therefore younger men in the golden period between boys and adult men. The need has a strong peer context, typical to that life stage. The need for affiliation, togetherness is also reflected in the relationship with the bike – a buddy with whom to share the fun.
- With every brand boasting of an international collaboration, it was decided that this was not a differentiating or for that matter much of a motivating proposition any more. International technology is of course desirable, but there is also an emerging pride and comfort especially among the youth about Indianness and being Indian.
- Functional delivery needs to live up to the vibrant need for a trendy, cool experience – a combination of speed, power, pick up and trendy looks. Advanced technology to reflect the fast paced lifestyles of the emerging Indian youth.

Two concepts were developed and tested on the same frame of reference.

And so the Apache was born!

Symbolism – living life in the moment. Targeting that part of every man that brings back the wonder years – of Freedom, of Irresponsibility, of LIVING! A sense of release, exploration and the anticipation that the world is waiting for you! For the newly initiated, the promise of discovering a new world, for the young at heart, the recapturing of a time gone by, a retreat to Ladland! About living life to the fullest and making most of the moment.

- Social values – unattached, young, popular men with lots of friends and popular among girls.
- Functional promise – stylish looks, really cool accessories, power and pick up, lightness to reflect the mood, easy maintenance.
- Reason to believe – driven by those who young people identify with and look like (not celebrities). The brand had to be the rage of the moment; something that everyone is talking about. This was brought about by innovative co-sponsorship and partnership of events and promotions – on Channel V and MotoGP.

- Advertising – the tonality is irreverent, but inoffensively so. Fun, easygoing, defying conventions and conservatism without becoming rebellious or edgy.

The television commercial is set to a rap tune, but the words are in an Indian language – in tune with the current youth's desire for a blend of the international with the Indian – a distinct flavour of modern India.

The strongly evocative emotional proposition was also translated into trendy style and irresistible features. Notably, the much used propositions of reliability and mileage promises were absent.

The seeming purposelessness about the functional promises reinforced the indulgent wonderful irresponsibility of the carefree, fun emotive positioning.

All activities and touch points were aligned with the symbolic positioning – partnership promotion with a trendy retail outlet, sponsorship on MotoGP sports.

In all, Apache is a brand where all layers of needs and all marketing touch points were in perfect harmony and therefore the rewards, recognition and success inevitably had to follow.

Questions

1. What were the former characteristics of the market in India?
2. How was the market changing?
3. What roles did qualitative research and quantitative research fulfil?
4. What insights are drawn from existing theory?

This case study is based on a paper given at ESOMAR Annual Congress, Berlin, September 2007 by Poonam Kumar, Motivational Research, APAC Region, TNS Asia, India & Prasad Narsimhan TVS Motor Company, India (ESOMAR Copyright).

There is a full version of the case on the accompanying web site:

www.wileyeurope.com/college/evans

SUMMARY

■ It might be tempting to assume that a 'need' would be for the necessities of life whereas a 'want' would be for something that is merely desired in, perhaps, a 'luxury' sense. This is *not* the marketing view. Marketing sees 'needs' as being any motivator that encourages some sort of behavioural response. In this way, a need can certainly be for the necessities like food and drink, but can equally be for more social and psychological reasons. Needs are motivational forces providing direction and intensity of behaviour: both approach and avoidance behaviours. Approach behaviour results from a positive motivation (sensory gratification, intellectual stimulation and social approval). Avoidance behaviour results from a negative motivation (problem avoidance and problem removal).

■ Motivated behaviour occurs when an individual perceives an external goal (incentive) and experiences internally a need or drive which stimulates them to reach that goal. Motives can be classed as biogenic (psychological and safety needs) or sociogenic (affective, esteem and actualization needs). Both of these types of motive are useful in marketing planning. Cognitive dissonance may also motivate.

■ Maslow provides a view of human motivation which is hierarchical, moving from physiological to social, psychological and spiritual needs. Freud on the other hand suggests we are motivated by deep-seated drives, which we do not always recognize at a conscious level.

■ Satisfaction of needs and wants is a major emphasis of the marketing concept and they are often activated through social interaction, observation, vicarious learning (imitation), advertising and just due to the presence of products. Marketing may make latent needs manifest (through specific wants and desires) but it does not create needs in people. People are not always aware of the 'real' needs determining their behaviour, so advertising may sometimes appeal to these subconscious and unconscious needs.

■ Marketers can improve the effectiveness of their targeting activities by investigating the reasons consumers go shopping. Consumers can be motivated to shop by personal and social motives, hedonistic and utilitarian motives and cognitive and affective motives.

■ Values are more enduring and can be gleaned from means–end chain research. Other forms of research are important for exploring what motivates consumers, such as projective techniques.

QUESTIONS

1. **Find some examples of Freudian symbolism in advertising and packaging.**

2. **Using your course as a product/service, create a needs–features–benefits framework and discuss its use in marketing the course.**

3. **Discuss the reasons why consumers go shopping.**

4. **Find *three* press advertisements and for each of these:**
   a. **Decide what are the likely target market and promotional objectives, based on media and message used and your knowledge of competition within such markets.**

b.   What do Maslow and Freud contribute to explaining the message used and motivational factors in the target market?

5. Choose a product or service, and then design projective techniques to explore why consumers do or do not buy it.

6. 'Marketing creates needs'. Discuss.

7. What are values? Provide examples of consumer values in different cultures.

FURTHER READING

Elliott R (1999) Symbolic Meaning and Postmodern Consumer Culture, in **Brownlie D** *et al.* (eds) (1999) *Rethinking Marketing*, Sage, London. This chapter concisely summarizes the key issues in symbolic consumption and contextualizes them within postmodern society.

Packard V (1957) *The Hidden Persuaders*, McKay, New York. No marketing student should miss this one. It might be old and some of the content will seem dated, but the critical analysis of the use of consumer psychology for marketing purposes will still provide food for thought.

Woodruffe-Burton *et al.* **(eds)** (2005) Toward a Theory of Shopping, *Journal of Consumer Behaviour*, Vol 4, No 4. This Special Issue of *JCB* is an excellent amalgam of research for a number of countries. These papers contribute much to our understanding of consumer shopping behaviour.

CHAPTER 2
CONSUMER RESPONSE TO MARKETING ACTIONS: 1
EXPOSURE, ATTENTION, PERCEPTION

CHAPTER OBJECTIVES

After engaging with the material presented in this chapter and its associated exercises and reading, you should be able to:

■ Integrate the application of concepts from psychology within the first stages of a model of how consumers respond to marketing activity.
■ Explain why consumer exposure to marketing activity is selective and suggest ways for marketers to overcome this.
■ Examine ways of creating conditions for a greater likelihood that consumers will attend to the marketing message/offering.
■ Apply some of the principles of the psychology of perception to increase the likelihood that consumers will interpret the message/offering in the intended manner.

INTRODUCTION

In this chapter we introduce a model of how consumers respond to marketing activities with a view to providing some theoretical and practical implications. The model is called the **hierarchy (or sequence) of communication effects**: exposure, attention, perception, learning, attitude, action, and post-purchase (Figure 2.1). This is not necessarily a sequence that consumers follow in all situations, but it provides a logical framework for integrating concepts from psychology to explain how consumers can respond to marketing activity. We will be discussing these *staged* responses in the current chapter and the next two chapters. You need to bear in mind that there are several other sequential models such as: 'AIDA' (attention–interest–desire–action) (Tosdal, 1925; St Elmo Lewis, circa 1900); the slightly more expanded model proposed by Lavidge and Steiner (1961) and labelled by Palda (1968) the 'hierarchy of effects'. This includes the following stages: awareness, knowledge, liking, preference, conviction and

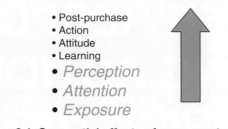

- Post-purchase
- Action
- Attitude
- Learning
- *Perception*
- *Attention*
- *Exposure*

Figure 2.1: Sequential effects of response to marketing

purchase. There are also the stages leading from awareness to adoption (Robertson, 1971), which are discussed in Chapter 9 on new product buying.

In order to understand consumer response to marketing activity, we need to start from what is known as exposure. Consumers do not watch every TV advertisement or read every marketing message in store or in the print media. Indeed many consumers will 'channel hop' while watching TV in order to avoid advertisements (**zapping**) or fast-forward through the advertisements in programmes they have recorded (**zipping**). As a result, consumers' exposure to marketing activity is selective. However, when an advertising message comes into contact with a consumer's **senses** (see 'Sensory Systems', under 'Perception and Interpretation' later in this chapter), we say that the consumer is being exposed to the message. In other words, now the message has a *chance* of being noticed by the consumer. There are many forms of marketing activities – such as branding, packaging, point of sale materials, in-store displays, web sites and sales promotional offers etc. – all of which must be placed within the range of a consumer's senses in order to get a chance of being noticed. Obviously, without being exposed, there is no chance that a consumer will respond to any sort of marketing activity. The trouble is that not all consumers expose themselves to all marketing activities, advertising, media and distribution channels, so there are significant implications here for media and distribution channel selection. But even if the marketing message or offering is in the right place, there is no guarantee that the target group will see it. The marketer's main concern is then to attract the attention of consumers. Attention is the stage when the consumer simply notices or sees the message. There are particular techniques that can be employed here, as the section on attention explores.

After being exposed to the message and after paying attention to it, the consumer makes sense of the message. At this perception stage, the consumer recognizes, selects, organizes and interprets the message (Harrell, 1986). They may not do so in the way marketers would like them to, but this fact reinforces the value of exploring the psychology of perception here, because it is from this that shared ways of interpretation can be encouraged.

Learning is the stage whereby the consumer remembers the message by storing it in **memory**. This stage is characterized by applications from the psychology of learning. Although the intended meaning of the message might be understood and remembered, this is not the same as the development of a favourable predisposition. At the attitude stage, the consumer responds *affectively*, taking a more or less favourable position on the message and thereby establishes a positive or a negative attitude towards it. Thus the attitude stage is, as the name suggests, concerned with attitude theory and how consumer attitudes develop and can be changed. We explore learning and attitudes in the next chapter.

These stages in the hierarchy determine whether an action will take place and what kind of action (trial, purchase, usage, asking for more information).

However, once a purchase has been made, this is not the end of the process. At the post-purchase stage, the consumer responds by expressing satisfaction or dissatisfaction towards the advertised brand or engages in positive or negative **word-of-mouth** communication with others. One solitary transaction is not the purpose of marketing, which is concerned with regular and mutually satisfying transactions. The study of cognitive dissonance can be of benefit in this regard. Action and cognitive dissonance are explored in Chapter 4. Satisfaction with the purchase is a good starting point for repeat purchasing, which could be cultivated to develop **loyalty, advocacy** and even relational interaction between the organization/brand and consumer. Later chapters explore **repeat purchasing** (Chapter 9), loyalty and relational marketing (Chapter 10).

For the current chapter, we start by exploring the initial sequence of exposure–attention–perception. These are sometimes described as being subsets of the perceptual process.

EXPOSURE

In order to be effective, marketers have to make sure that consumers are exposed to their marketing activities. From the marketing point of view, **exposure** is ensuring that the marketing offering or message is in the right place, for the target market to (at least potentially) have access to it. Exposure is a basic requirement if marketers want to change consumer perceptions, attitudes or behaviour.

For instance, in order to make media selection decisions, marketers conduct research to profile the target customers they need to reach. For some of your projects or assignments in Marketing you may well have used some of the many market reports to profile buyers in a product-market. MINTEL, Keynote, Market Assessment and the **Target Group Index (TGI)** all provide the characteristics of those who buy in different product categories (and sometimes specific brands). Such profiling can include demographics (see Chapter 5), psychographics (see Chapter 6) or geodemographics (see Chapter 11) and once the marketer has a clear picture of the target market it is necessary to use profiles of the sorts of people who read/see (ie 'expose' themselves to) different media. Unfortunately, not all potential customers read all newspapers, listen to all radio or read all posters: we all exhibit selective exposure in this respect. A 'matching' exercise then takes place, so that those publications or TV programmes that are more likely to be read/seen by the intended by the target market are selected.

There is a well-developed industry that provides such readership and viewing data. The National Readership Survey, for example, researches the profile of print-media readership, in such demographic terms as age, gender, social grade, family circumstances (see Chapters 5 and 7), lifestyle (see Chapter 6), ethnicity (see Chapter 8) and geodemographics (see Chapter 11).

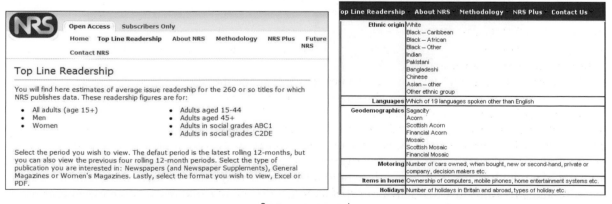

Source: www.nrs.co.uk

The Target Group Index (TGI) is one of the largest market research surveys in the UK with an annual sample size of about 25 000 respondents. As well as profiling the characteristics of people who buy in different product categories and specific brands, the TGI also profiles those who read different publications, again according to a variety of characteristics.

	elements	total	British Airways: AIR TRAVEL: Airlines Flown Holidays	Easyjet: AIR TRAVEL: Airlines Flown Holidays	Britannia: AIR TRAVEL: Airlines Flown Holidays	Air 2000: AIR TRAVEL: Airlines Flown Holidays
total	Sample	23,479	1,946	1,216	1,094	1,103
	(000)	44,862	4,357	2,784	2,071	2,216
	vert%	100%	100%	100%	100%	100%
	horz%	100%	9.71%	6.21%	4.62%	4.94%
	Index	100	100	100	100	100
Daily Mail	Sample	3,180	363	196	198	188
	(000)	5,625	751	403	358	365
	vert%	12.5%	17.2%	14.5%	17.3%	16.5%
	horz%	100%	13.4%	7.17%	6.37%	6.49%
	Index	100	138	116	138	131
The Sun	Sample	4,894	261	165	259	242
	(000)	8,295	534	389	467	440
	vert%	18.5%	12.3%	14.0%	22.6%	19.8%
	horz%	100%	6.44%	4.68%	5.63%	5.30%
	Index	100	66	75	122	107
The Guardian	Sample	679	121	84	20	28
	(000)	1,242	254	194	36.3	55.8
	vert%	2.77%	5.82%	6.98%	1.75%	2.52%
	horz%	100%	20.4%	15.7%	2.92%	4.49%
	Index	100	210	252	63	91

The **Guardian**	Index
I CONSIDER MYSELF INTERESTED IN THE ARTS	350
I BUY FAIR TRADE PRODUCTS WHERE AVAILABLE	347
I PREFER TO TAKE HOLIDAYS OFF THE BEATEN TRACK	335
I AM INTERESTED IN OTHER CULTURES	320
A SINGLE EUROPEAN CURRENCY WOULD BE A GOOD THING FOR BRITAIN	314
I LOOK ON THE WORK I DO AS A CAREER NOT JUST A JOB	243
I AM PREPARED TO PAY MORE FOR GOOD QUALITY WINE	242

Sun	Index
I WEAR DESIGNER CLOTHES	176
I CANNOT RESIST BUYING MAGAZINES	175
I READ DAILY NEWSPAPERS MORE FOR ENTERTAINMENT THAN NEWS	172
ADVERTISING HELPS ME CHOOSE WHAT TO BUY	170
A REAL MAN CAN DOWN SEVERAL PINTS AT A SITTING	167
MONEY IS THE BEST MEASURE OF SUCCESS	160
I AM A TV ADDICT	158
I REALLY ENJOY A NIGHT OUT AT THE PUB	157

SOURCE: GB TGI 2004 Spring (Jan 2003 - Dec 2003)

Other industry bodies provide data on exposure to other media. For example, RAJAR profiles radio audiences and POSTAR provides data on outdoor poster audiences. Broadcasters' Audience Research Board (BARB) is the body that provides data on television audiences.

Monthly Viewing Summary				
Total Viewing Summary				
Jul-07 ▼ OK				
HOURS OF VIEWING AND SHARE OF AUDIENCE Including Timeshift - 4 weeks ending 29th Jul				
	Average Weekly Viewing per person		Share of Total Viewing	
	July(Hrs:Mins)	June (Hrs:Mins)	July(%)	June(%)
ALL/ANY TV	23:56	23:56	100.0	100.0
BBC 1 (incl. Brkfast News)	5:27	5:27	22.7	22.7
BBC 2	1:57	1:57	8.2	8.2
TOTAL BBC1/BBC2	7:24	7:24	30.9	30.9
ITV (incl. GMTV)	4:30	4:30	18.8	18.8
CHANNEL 4/S4C	2:15	2:15	9.4	9.4
five	1:16	1:16	5.3	5.3
TOTAL/ANY COMM. TERR. TV	8:01	8:01	33.5	33.5
Other Viewing	8:31	8:31	35.6	35.6

Representative samples of households around the country agree to report on their TV viewing. A typical approach, used by STATSCAN in South Wales was to provide households with an automatic recording device, the set meter. This records which channel the TV is tuned to and a people meter is for each household member to 'press their button' whenever they enter or leave the room, in order to measure audiences not just the activity of the TV set. One of your authors was a panelist and has to declare that it is likely that not everyone will use the people meter for very long, hence is there a question of 'garbage in, garbage out'?

In addition, panelists are asked to scan the bar codes of what they buy so that markets can assess the effect, in the 'shopping basket', of their advertising activity, in this case, not only to assess 'exposure' but also effectiveness through subsequent stages of the model we discuss in Chapters 2–4.

Photos: Martin Evans

So, while keeping in mind the profile of their target audience and budgetary constraints, marketers want to make sure that an appropriate proportion of their target market is exposed to their message. Their decisions are based on what is known as reach. Reach is the percentage of target audience that would be exposed at least once to your advertised message if you advertised in a medium (such as a newspaper or a magazine). The reach of a newspaper or magazine is different from the number of copies sold. Since more than one reader may read a newspaper copy, the reach of a newspaper is usually larger than the number of copies sold. Similarly, reach of a medium is different from the reach of a part of the medium. Not all readers see all pages of a newspaper and thus miss several advertisements. TV viewers do not see all programmes and commercials. Advertising reach is thus generally lower than medium reach.

However, 'reach' is not sufficient for media selection: costs are also important and British Rate and Data (BRAD) provides information on advertising costs and indeed on circulation statistics.

THINKBOX

If a marketer has identified from research along the above lines that publications A and B could equally reach their market, which should they select?

Suppose NRS might suggest these two could reach targets equally well in terms of segment profile

BRAD	PUBLICATION A	PUBLICATION B
Full Page Mono	£16 300	£40 500
Circulation	391 000	1,040 000

You might go for the cheaper, or you might go for the one with the greater circulation, but can you think of a way of combining these two measures?

Exposing consumers to a message just once may not be enough for understanding or acceptance of the message. Therefore, a message is often repeatedly delivered during a particular time period. **Frequency** is the number of times a message is placed or shown during a particular period of time. For example, a high-profile TV advertisement may be shown 60 times or more during just one month. In many media plans, the reach and a minimum or average number of exposures is the objective.

When it comes to television audiences and their exposure to commercials, it is commonplace to calculate television ratings (TVRs). This is a measure of how far a communications channel 'reaches' into the target market. For example, specific TV commercial time slots might reach 100% of the target audience. It might also be thought that to make an 'impact', three exposures would be needed. This is known as 'opportunities to see' (OTS). In this case, the calculation to determine TVRs would be $100 \times 3 = 300$ TVRs. But is it realistic to expect 100% of target market to be reached? Would they all be watching these specific commercials? Probably not, so different calculations can be made based on experience or further research.

Perhaps 50% of the target audience might more realistically be reached and it might be thought that there should be more exposures of the commercial to make an impact (often six have been found appropriate). So now the TVR calculation would be $50 \times 6 = 300$ TVRs.

Clearly this adds cost because each exposure is costing air time (often £50,000 per 30-second commercial). So this has to be balanced against the realistic 'reach' of time slots and the estimated number of needed OTSs. This raises the issue of how many exposures is optimal before what is known as **wearout,** or over-exposure, occurs. It is difficult to generalize because of the nature of the message, the media and indeed audience mood changes. But some campaigns use slightly different executions of the same central theme or message in order to keep a campaign fresh.

EXAMPLE 2.1

An interesting example of advertising reach concerns the audiotape producers Maxell. Rather than selecting media according to the traditional television ratings approach, they asked tape **users** directly what their favourite programmes were. The result was a six-week TV campaign leading up to Christmas with many slots at slightly unconventional times such as 2 a.m. The campaign cost £330 000, which was very inexpensive for a six-week television campaign of the intensity employed.

A number of years ago Lea and Perrins sauce ran a campaign which incorporated door drops of free samples, a small bottle of sauce banded onto magazine covers and sales of the bottle through Tesco for a loss leading price of 19p (Lovell, 1997). In all cases targets were invited to send for a recipe book in exchange for providing data about themselves (nine questions' worth). The exercise was designed to gather data for targeting purposes. By matching the data collected with lifestyle profiles (see Chapter 11) it was found that Lea and Perrins customers were absolutely 'average', nothing peculiar to them seemed to emerge. However, one of the specific questions enquired about television viewing habits; 43% of the Lea and Perrins users said they watched morning programmes on ITV. Had the company relied solely on their demographic and lifestyle profiling, they would not have selected this particular scheduling (i.e. off-peak television advertising) and thus they saved valuable resources and satisfied exposure criteria very effectively.

The society in which we live is characterized by **fragmentation** of media, which poses some serious concerns about the ability of marketers to reach large number of consumers using a mass medium such as TV (Rust and Oliver, 1994). Therefore, achieving the right level of exposure may not be as simple as it sounds. Rather than relying on a single mass medium, marketers can still reach their target audiences by using multiple media (Magrath, 1992).

THINKBOX

In order to appreciate the difficulties marketers have in putting their messages in front of you, consider the number of ways in which *you* avoid them. For example, think of the number of TV advertisements you deliberately zip or zap, the number of print messages you won't even look at and the range of publications you do not read but which would be logical ones in which to advertise to reach people like you.

Do you have Personal Video Recorder (PVR) which allows you to fast forward exactly 30 seconds (i.e. through a typical TV commercial)? If so, you are exhibiting **advertisement avoidance** by deliberately trying to dodge marketing messages.

A different example of exposure avoidance is in a controversial device known as the Mosquito. This 'emits a modulated 17 khz sound that proves to be of great annoyance to teenagers but leaves most over 20 years of age unaffected' (Willmainson, 2005). The point of this is for marketers running shops, or shopping malls, to deter youngsters from gathering in the vicinity and possibly causing trouble and hence affecting business.

Try the sound for yourself at: http://www.compoundsecurity.co.uk/

Is this something that you would not want to expose yourself to? If you ran a neighbourhood row of shops on a run-down housing estate, would you want to deter gangs from gathering?

On the other hand, do you exhibit **voluntary exposure**, by, for example, 'opting in' to receive mail shots, emails or phone messages about products or brands in which you have an interest? You might, in this case, provide marketers with what they call 'permission marketing' approaches.

Another issue for you to consider concerns internet advertising. Bearing in mind that a report by Softscan (2008) found that over 97% of emails sent in December 2007 were unsolicited, 'spam', do you feel that you are exposed to more pop-ups, emails or other marketing messages than you really want? Or have you invested in additional software to screen them out?

Product placement, by which marketers manage (often by paying the programme or film makers) to expose their brands within a TV programme or movie. If James Bond refers to a certain brand of champagne or drives a particular brand of car, it is difficult for you not to be exposed to this. Similarly, your favourite TV 'soap' might expose brand X of sauce in the kitchen table. What is your view of product placement?

ATTENTION

Even if the marketing offering is in the right place, there is no guarantee that the market will see it or pay **attention** to it. Therefore, while exposure is important, it is not enough to ensure that consumers will respond to a marketing activity such as an advertising message. Consumers often scan the media to see whether there is something interesting on TV or in the newspaper. As such, they focus on what is relevant to them. They continue to focus their attention on relevant messages, be they editorial or news (**initial**

attention). If the message is not really important for them they continue scanning the medium for what might be (**persistent attention**).

Attention reflects the amount of mental energy or effort that we allocate to stimuli. We normally pay selective attention to marketing stimuli and are often unaware of most of such stimuli in our environment. Marketers, though, want us to pay **focal attention** to their advertised messages to utilize more of our cognitive processes while responding to their marketing efforts. The probability that we will pay focal attention to marketing activities goes up if they have some relevance and are of interest to us.

For example, consider the case of a print advertisement for a washing machine. Most of the advertisement may go unnoticed by us (that is, we will ignore reading the detailed part of the message) if we do not need to buy a washing machine. However, we are likely to pay focal attention to the details of the message (e.g. washing speed, washing load, energy ratings, etc.) if we are already considering buying a new washing machine. Similarly a mobile phone enthusiast will consciously and voluntarily make use of mental ability to process the information and pay focal attention to most mobile phone advertisements.

Although not an entirely reliable estimate, there are several suggestions that every UK consumer is exposed to at least 2000 promotional messages a day but that they probably notice less than 5%. Americans are exposed to 18 million unsolicited telephone calls daily and receive 3 000 coupons each per year (Hallberg, 1995). Davidson (1997) suggests that the average consumer in Spain and Italy is exposed to over 20 000 commercials per year. He also submits that £1 m worth of advertising probably only buys 0.1% share of consumer exposure. Goddin (1999) suggests that in the USA there are over 3 000 marketing messages per day and that, on average, each US citizen had $1 000 spent on them via direct targeting in 1998.

All of this suggests that there is an increase in what is known as advertising **clutter** (too many messages bombarded at consumers). A cumulative effect of clutter is that consumers can become sceptical and can employ advertising avoiding strategies (such as zipping and zapping) to maintain control over their psychic space (Speck and Elliott, 1997). This poses an additional challenge for marketers because they have to make sure that their message is noticed by consumers. A further complication relates back to the number of exposures and wearout: if too many exposures, **habituation** means that we attend less to the over-familiar. However, habituation is likely to be less and attention spans greater if the consumer is more involved with the product or brand (see Chapter 4).

Four aspects of attention may be distinguished:

1. Gaining attention: This is important but a difficult task given the clutter of commercial messages.
2. Holding attention: Once gained, attention needs to be held in order for the actual message to be conveyed.
3. Leading attention: Attention must be guided toward the message and not to peripheral elements in the communication.
4. Distracting attention: This is usually ineffective, unless the arguments of the message are weak, in which case distraction might prevent consumers from discovering the weakness of the arguments.

Techniques to Gain and Hold Attention

At the attention stage, marketers are concerned with attracting and maintaining attention and there are particular techniques that can be employed to accomplish this. Among these is the use of colour, movement, position of the message, size, conditioned response, novelty, humour and participation.

Use of Colour

On a general level, colour tends to arrest the attention more than monochrome and indeed different colours have different attention values. The warm colours (orange and red) advance toward us, having the effect of making whatever it is appear larger, whereas the cooler colours (blue) recede, making the message appear smaller. On this basis red is often cited as having the highest attention value. Having said this, there can be problems associated with the use of red. At the time of writing, the Royal Mail's automated sorting machines could not read addresses printed in black on a red background and this presents enormous difficulties every Valentine's Day when the use of red envelopes is commonplace.

Using colour in packaging to gain attention is particularly useful for fast-moving consumer goods where a consumer often has to make an instant choice at the point of purchase. A clever use of colour in packaging can draw attention to the brand and can break through the competitive clutter. It can symbolize brand values and can send a powerful emotional signal to consumers.

Different colours have been found to affect search times in store. Jansson *et al.* (2004) investigated a variety of colours and hues and found that basic colours can reduce consumer search times more than non-basics and that there could be real benefits in employing these issues when designing point of sale materials.

It has been found that primary colours particularly attract children, and yellow especially attracts young children (Littlewood, 1999). Furthermore, in studies it is proposed that women are more likely to be attracted to colourful direct mail envelopes than are men (see later coverage of Neurolinguistic Programming under Perception, Chapter 5 and our discussion of 'gender').

EXAMPLE 2.2

In a classic case in the USA, a whisky company supplied display racks to a department store. Whenever a customer physically got close to the rack, a mechanism in the rack released a bottle so it fell, only a short way, to be held again by the rack. This was wonderfully successful at gaining attention; nearly all the customers lunged forward to try to catch the falling bottle. However, although this achieved the aims of the attention stage, it had negative effects on subsequent stages, being thought of as a rather 'sneaky' trick. There is an important message here. Whatever happens in one stage can affect other stages. In this case the attitudes formed were somewhat negative, even though the attention was supremely achieved.

Movement

Movement is another technique used to gain attention. Thus advertising on television or in the cinema is often considered more effective at generating attention than static press or direct mail messages. Many outdoor posters 'move' or at least the message rotates, as can be seen at many sporting events.

EXAMPLE 2.3

Movement and Outdoors Posters

The following posters demonstrate the potential attention value of movement:

© Russell Signs Ltd. Used with permission

© Russell Signs Ltd. Used with permission

This sign literally set the world alight when it appeared outside the News International building on the Highway in Wapping, East London. Fuelled by Calor gas via a complex system of pipes and valves, it was 'alight' for two hours in the morning and evening rush hour periods for eight days and although the emergency services had been informed and given their permission, apparently many public spirited drivers felt moved to contact the fire brigade on their mobile phones to report the fire!

This full-size helicopter was made from fiberglass, with fully working rotors and internal smoke machine and was erected on London's busy Cromwell Road.

However, it is possible to simulate movement in a still picture and this is often done effectively with blurred backgrounds suggesting a moving foreground (Figure 2.2). Video cassettes within direct mailings

Figure 2.2: Speeding sports car
BMW: The simulation of movement in print advertising to attract attention.
Source: BMW. Image courtesy of the Advertising Archives

allowing the use of movement are becoming more popular for communicating messages. Similarly there are interactive communications via the Internet and multimedia messaging services (MMS) via mobile phones which can incorporate graphics, music and video clips.

A variation on *movement* is the use of holography.

EXAMPLE 2.4

Attention: Movement and Holographic

Moving, holographically-projected images might similarly attract attention, partly because of their relative novelty but also because of the sequential message 'uncovered' (see Figure 2.3)

Figure 2.3a: Holographic window display attract attention

Source: www.mediazest.com

Figure 2.3b: Holographic 'Puma' prowling the sports shop

Source: www.mediazest.com

Sound

Even if a consumer is watching TV, they might not always attend to the commercials. This could be an opprtunity to check the programme listings for what's on next. Their visual attention diverted, a commercial employing the sound of classic pop music tracks could redirect their attention. Millward Brown (2007, cited in Hemsley 2007) studied brands' use of sound and suggested that marketers could benefit from using sound more, in order to cut through the clutter of advertising messages.

THINKBOX

Have you ever turned the sound down on the TV when the commercials come on?

Some marketers believe that by broadcasting commercials at a higher volume than the programmes the consumers will notice them more. Perhaps they notice but do not necessarily attend to them – the sound might even be muted.

www. There is more on the use of sound in the following case on the book companion web site:
Hemsley (2007) Let the Music Play, Marketing Week, 19 April, pp 33–34

Position

The position of the message is also important in gaining attention. The outside back cover of a magazine, for example, means that the advertising message can be noticed even without opening the magazine at all. Some marketers might include the main component of the message on the envelope of a mailing to increase the chances of it being noticed. Others, however, believe that by doing this, recipients might be more likely to discard the piece before opening because it would be clear it was a piece of direct mail. Variations on this theme include letting an enticing part of the message (e.g. the incentive) show through the window of the envelope. Some believe that the right-hand page attracts more attention than the left because as we browse through the pages from the beginning, it is the right page that is uncovered first. Those, however, who start with the sports page on the rear of a newspaper may well disagree and argue that the left-hand page is the one that is usually noticed first. If a double-page spread is employed then there are no competing messages and so attention could be more likely because of this. A compromise is to cover a double-page spread with a message but using just half of each page.

The 'golden section' technique or 'law of thirds', known by architects and artists, can also be employed. This suggests that if a rectangle is divided into thirds, both vertically and horizontally, then the eye goes to the points of intersection (Figure 2.4). Placing important parts of the copy or graphics at these points might therefore make them more prominent. Additionally, in the context of direct mail, if some of the message is moved to the postscript or 'PS', it is often the case that this will be the part of the letter that is especially noticed and remembered.

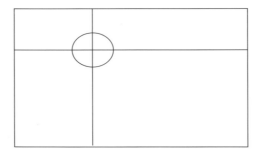

Figure 2.4: The golden section

The 'eye camera' is useful for tracing the path that the eye takes over a 'space' such as a mailing, advertisement, poster, or even store shelf displays (Figure 2.5). In this way different colour combinations or different positions of copy headline can be tried out to find the most effective version for attracting attention to the key parts of the message.

The eye camera traces the path the eye takes. This can help determine the best positioning for a poster or even the main message within an advertisement, in order for it to be noticed. This can also help in 'leading attention' to what the marketer hopes will be noticed.

Retail marketers have long recognized the importance of position of point of sale material, product category and brand positioning in store. Manufacturers might provide inducements for retailers to position

Figure 2.5: **Eye camera**
Source: Eye-tracks From "Wave 4" Visibility Study 10th October 2007 POSTAR

'their' brands in prime locations, such as eye level (which can be at a low level if the brand is targeted at children (see Chapters 5 and 7)).

As the 'hemispheral lateralization' case study on the accompanying web site discusses, different sides of the brain deal with different functions and are related to which part of our vision is activated. Those elements of the message that are in the middle of our vision (**focal vision**) are processed by both sides of the brain. Our peripheral vision is subject to a sort of crossover in the brain, with left peripheral messages being dealt with in the right brain and right peripheral message elements dealt with in the left hemisphere (Janiszewski, 1989).

This is potentially of great significance, since the left side of the brain deals with more logical analysis and deals with words, for example. So maybe elements such as the description, in words, of the characteristics of a brand should be positioned to the right (in order to be processed by the left brain).

The right side of the brain is more concerned with holistic and subjective issues, so perhaps the more emotional images and appeals of a message need to be positioned on the left of the advertisement in order to be processed by the right brain.

Size

The size of the message has also been the focus of marketing discussion. This is not, however, a straightforward matter. Doubling the size of a message is unlikely to double attention. A suggestion is that attention increases as the square root of the message size increases (Rudolph, 1947).

'Over-sized' outdoor posters have become more popular among some marketers as can be seen in Figure 2.6.

Figure 2.6: Oversized outdoor poster
© Russell Signs Ltd. Used with permission

Conditioned Response

Yet another approach to gaining attention uses known conditioned responses. We attend, almost automatically, to the sound of a telephone ringing and this approach is used to good effect in direct response radio advertising. Other examples include the introduction to a radio advertisement with a statement such as 'Here is a news flash'. A major direct marketer, Avon Cosmetics, uses a ringing door bell and the 'Avon calling' slogan in its promotional approach. See Chapter 3 for a discussion of the theory behind conditioning. The work of Pavlov underpins much of this.

It might be reassuring that few drivers attend to posters on the rear of buses when overtaking. Although it might equally be disturbing that nearly 6% do!

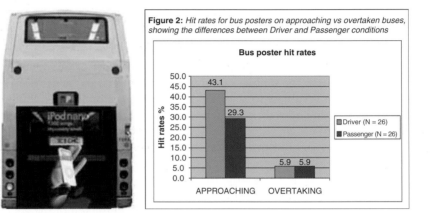

Figure 2: *Hit rates for bus posters on approaching vs overtaken buses, showing the differences between Driver and Passenger conditions*

EXAMPLE 2.5

MarketingWeek

Tracking Tool is an Eye-Opener

So what is eye tracking? Eye tracking lends itself very well to traditional advertising and marketing research, in print and online. Companies such as Bunnyfoot have pioneered its use in these arenas, even extending to in-game advertising.

CAD interactive often has a wider remit for our user research than just marketing and we are generally tasked with understanding cognitive reaction to brand, message and content and how customers physically interact with booking forms, self-help, navigation and rich media.

During a recent research project we used eye tracking and the PEEP methodology (don't talk, just look), followed by a traditional use-and-talk lab interview. We then combine these findings with quantitative click-map stats (overlay of where users are clicking on the website). The end results are both fascinating and worrying. On their own, the eye tracking and click-map stats contradict how people interact with a page.

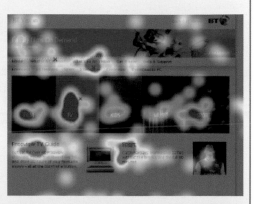

Users are looking at and clicking on the main navigation in a consistent fashion, but are interacting very differently with page contents.

An example of this is where there is a linked title with copy below and a related image. The majority of users read the title but click on the image. If you relied on eye tracking alone, then you would find that the image is ignored and the title is the most important element, relying solely on clickmap analysis shows the reverse.

The reason the eye tracking does not correlate with the location users are clicking on is because eye tracking does not pick up peripheral vision, it only registers what people are looking directly at.

On certain pages of the site there is an interesting trend emerging. Users tend to spend more time gazing at the animations and on-site graphics more than the written content. However, despite their focus, it does not mean that images are always used as a point of navigation. The chart below shows the vast majority of Web users (68%) clicked on headings and titles compared to 18% whose gaze fell on them. Yet, 39% of users' gaze was captured by animation, but only 9% clicked on them. Graphics tell a similar story, with 30% of Web users' gaze being captured by them, yet only 15% clicked on a graphic. Text links do not have the same disparity – they attract 13% of Web users' gaze and 8% click on them to help them navigate the site.

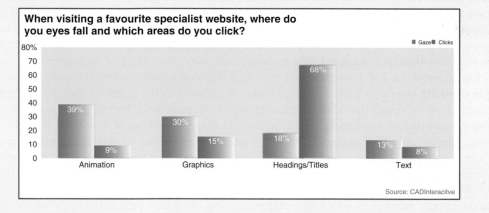

The research also shows that users are looking at key information on screen, yet have no recollection or recall of it. This is particularly true of pages that have a number of different prices displayed around the page or pages that have a large amount of similar information.

Once we put the results through our customer insight intelligence tool – which reviews key website information to produce a top-level executive summary that pinpoints usability and accessibility problems – and combine wider sources of user interaction data we can build an incredibly detailed and sometimes conflicting user story.

This research shows that eye tracking offers an immensely powerful insight into user behaviour, cognitive recognition and through PEEP, realistic user interaction.

However, eye tracking is only a tool and one that fits well with other usability research services, like remote Web tracking, statistical analysis, holistic reviews and traditional lab research.

Eye tracking can show how people use sites and services in a more realistic way as they don't need prompting, but they are still in a lab, undertaking a task on-demand. Yet, for the first time, we can watch, in detail, exactly how a person interacts, without the need for software downloads, prompts or labs.

Relying on eye tracking alone, especially in untrained hands will lead to unnecessary interface changes being implemented and the real problems going undetected. Combining eye tracking with other usability tools will provide marketers, designers and site owners with a complete understanding of their users.

Anyone can buy or rent an eye tracker, so before engaging their services check that they have a robust methodology in place and are not just using eye tracking for hype or for the sake of using technology.

Marketing Week, 25 October 2007, pp 32–33. Reproduced by permission of Centaur Media Plc.

Novelty

If a message is in some way different it may stand out and thus attract more attention. For instance, a monochrome TV advertisement is likely to gain attention because people are not as accustomed to them as they are to colour advertisements. An unusual and distinct message can elicit feelings of surprise due to what is known as **schema discrepancy**. When the contents of a marketing communication message are different from generally expected beliefs, attitudes and/or behaviours, then they are likely to be perceived as incongruent, followed by feelings of surprise. For example, Alden *et al.* (2000) report that as the familiarity with the situation depicted in a message increases, the effect of incongruity on surprise also increases. For example, a TV advertisement may first depict a generally familiar situation to consumers (e.g. people drinking beer in a pub) and then show an unusual event (such as the slamming of the door by a stranger). This increases the effect of incongruity on surprise and thereby gains consumer attention.

The use of surprise in marketing communications can not only gain attention but also encourage consumers to spend more. For instance, while investigating the effect of in-store surprise or unexpected coupons (e.g. electronic shelf coupons, peel-off coupons on product packaging) on consumer behaviour, Heilman *et al.* (2002) reported that the use of the surprise coupon increased the size of the shopping basket and the number of unplanned purchases made on that shopping trip.

In practice many marketers place the distinctiveness of their communications at the top of their priorities. The direct mail industry has a strong track record of employing unusual and attention grabbing mailings. All sorts of items have been sent in mailings and this makes the medium extremely capable of delivering innovative creative ideas (Figure 2.7).

Certainly, communications do need to stand out from the crowd but because many consumers may be risk averse, communications must also create a sense of familiarity. Thus, the marketer needs to be careful when using novel messages. For example, in an outrageous mailing in USA, Barnes (2001) describes:

a pigeon in a cage was first trialled . . . the idea was that recipients would attach their response to the leg of the pigeon which would return 'home'. Surprised at the low response rate, post-campaign research revealed that instead of the birds being released, they were killed and eaten [by some recipients].

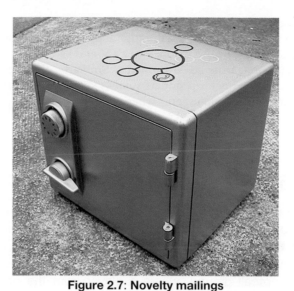

Figure 2.7: Novelty mailings
Telewest mailed a locked safe and a web site address to 2000 IT managers. The web site gave the safe combination access number and the safe included shredded money to reflect a fraction of the sum that the advertiser's secure data transfer system could save.
Photograph: Martin Evans

Another problem of course is that novelty lasts only a short time so the employment of this approach must be especially dynamic to maintain its distinctiveness. It is clear, though, that marketers are very proactive in this area and they do try different approaches (Figure 2.8).

Humour

The use of humour in marketing communications is often very effective in getting attention and improving brand recognition (Sternthal and Craig, 1973; Weinberger *et al.*, 1995). Weinberger and Gulas (1992)

Figure 2.8: Novelty
The two cars glued to a poster were advertising Araldite glue, not Ford.
Source: Huntsman LLC. Image courtesy of the Advertising Archives

quote prior research to suggest that 94% of advertising practitioners hold the view that humour is an effective attention-getter. In a study involving TV, radio and print advertising, Weinberger *et al.* (1995) found that the use of humour varied by the media type. TV and radio advertisements used humour two to three times more often than magazine advertisements. Similarly, the use of humour also varied with product type. Humour was used mostly for products such as snack chips, beer, chewing gum, candy, soft drinks, toilet bowl cleaners and laundry detergents whereas it was used least often for high-risk items such as sports cars, motorcycles, jewellery and insurance.

EXAMPLE 2.6

Andruss (2001) quotes a TV ad by FedEx Express that featured a football team's young equipment manager who felt distressed over the whereabouts of five missing boxes of uniforms he had shipped to Madrid for a big match. He was told by an older man that he did not need to worry as long as the boxes were shipped with FedEx (but they were not). The ad then showed a football ground, where a player from the opposing team was about to attempt a penalty kick. As the camera pulled out, viewers saw that the equipment manager's team was defending its goal without uniforms or a stitch of any other kind of clothing. The tagline of the ad stated: 'Let FedEx take the load off your shoulders.' The campaign resulted in an immediate jump in unaided brand awareness levels among the target audience, which in this case consisted of small and medium-size business owners across Latin America.

Although not especially novel, the use of ambient media can attract attention:

Photo: Martin Evans

Participation

Not only is it important to attract the attention of consumers, but also the marketer must hold the attention and convey the message. Attention-getting devices are numerous, but if attention is attracted by methods inconsistent with the message or the situation, this attention is readily lost. Attention may be held by encouraging the audience to participate, such as exemplified by the following outdoor posters.

EXAMPLE 2.7

Interactive Posters

Interactive Bus Stop Posters:

A bus stop poster for Pretty Polly showed a young woman wearing Pretty Polly's Baroque lingerie range. A strategically placed button placed just beneath her cleavage encouraged the viewer to "Press for lift." and this resulted in an audio message being played from the poster giving information about the new range of Pretty Polly lingerie.

Another illustration of interaction with posters concerns the link that can be made via mobile phones and smart codes on posters:

This 12m × 6m 3D display was manufactured to imitate a "Las Vegas" style sign using the latest computer chip technology.

© Miles Calcraft Briginshaw Duffy & Pretty Polly. Reproduced with permission.

© Russell Signs. Reproduced with permission.

Messages which work in this way might be ambiguous or incomplete and for this reason the audience (sometimes through a double take) is encouraged to attend to the message more than would otherwise be the case, in order to complete the message and to make sense of it (the Zeigarnik effect, named after B. Zeigarnik in 1927).

This is known as the **law of closure** (see 'Gestalt Approaches to Perception Organization', below), which suggests that consumers often enjoy 'filling in the gaps' for themselves.

Personalization

As Chapter 11 explores, marketers are increasingly personalizing their interaction with customers and potential customers. Mailings addressed to the correct householder are more likely to be attended to than those merely addressed to 'the occupier'. Digital printing now affords personalization of letters, catalogues and magazines.

Photo: Martin Evans

PERCEPTION AND INTERPRETATION

Once noticed, the message/offering should be perceived and interpreted or understood in the intended way. For this stage we draw information from the psychology of **perception**. Engel *et al.* (1986) understand perception to mean 'the process whereby stimuli are received and interpreted by the individual and translated into a response'.

Sensory Systems

Consumers become aware of their environment through the five senses, as we mentioned at the beginning of the chapter, but we explore sensation here because as well as being the 'receptors' they can also determine how we interpret messages. Table 2.1 summarizes the sort of perceptions that can follow from each 'sense'.

The retail environment provides marketers with many opportunities to play on consumers' senses in order to develop and maintain their relationships with brands (Fulberg, 2003; Jackson and Fulberg, 2003). Often, marketers use the term **store atmospherics** to refer to approaches that tap consumers' senses.

Perceiving through	Illustration
Vision	Use of colour, pack/product/logo designs are important.
Sound	Music sound tracks to TV advertisements can affect how the advertising message itself is interpreted; use of fast music in-store to speed up the momentum of shopping; pleasant music likely to arouse positive emotions. Fulberg (2003) suggest that our right, more emotional, brain processes music and this fits with our earlier discussion of the use of well-known pop classics, because of the support this can give brands. The article on the accompanying web site explores more on the perception and use in marketing of sound (Hemsley 2007).
Touch	Not well researched, but North Europeans are not as tactile as South Europeans (important for face-to-face sales); consumers like to touch fabrics (fabric swatches in fashion catalogues) and this can create problems for on-line marketers. Do women touch fabrics more than men when shopping for clothes? A variation of touch is that some fabrics might be uncomfortable or irritating to the skin for some consumers.
Taste	Blind tests show importance of brand image (see examples in text).
Smell	Aroma (synthetic or real) of bread baking in store to suggest the bread is really fresh; palm trees in travel agents to conjure up nostalgic memories of holidays in warm climates. Audi produced a leather outline of one of their cars as a stick-on to a press advertisement. The leather swatch allowed consumers to experience the smell of Audi leather seats.

Table 2.1: Perception and the use of senses

EXAMPLE 2.8

An example of how the law of closure can attract attention in order to 'solve the puzzle' is the use of mobile phone 'text' language. For example, G8 yor M8s. This is being used in advertising to both show a degree of street credibility of brands but also to hold attention for a few more seconds because of its superficial ambiguity.

Posters for Disneyland Paris by Ogilvy Mather Direct are based on capturing images from 8 mm cinefilm before production and end up as 3-D holograms, which are expensive but attention grabbing (Stokes, 1997).

Sometimes the type of participation is not the intended response. One poster advertisement for Levi's jeans actually had a pair of 501s glued to the poster itself. The result was that many people clearly noticed the message because many of them tried to get the jeans, but of course they were positioned too high on the poster for this to be an easy matter (Figure 2.9). This sort of physical participation on the part of the consumer was not intended but demonstrates the attention-grabbing value of the ad as well as the jeans-grabbing aim (of consumers).

Figure 2.9: Attention and participation

Some marketers are experimenting with **multisensory brands**. For example, Nike found that 845 of respondents in a test preferred the trainers in a room infused with a floral scent compared with the same trainers in a non-scented room (Lindstrom, 2005). This is because 'A strong brand appeals to all five senses'. Sounds of products in use are being incorporated in advertising, such as the sound of cereals 'snapping, crackling and popping'. The 'scratch and sniff' technique has of course been used for a long time in magazine adverts for perfumes. As Flynn (2005) states: 'Using multiple senses to create a brand experience can make the experience more powerful and differentiate the brand.'

EXAMPLE 2.9

Spies and Hesse (1997), in a study of two furniture stores in Germany with different store atmospheres, found that consumers' moods improved with pleasant, but deteriorated with less pleasant, store atmospheres. Similarly other sensory elements such as sound, often examined as music, can influence consumers' responses to advertising (e.g. attitudes towards the advertisement) and to the retail environments (e.g. spend more money or stay longer in the shop).

One supermarket study found a 38% increase in sales when the supermarket played slow music compared with fast music (Milliman, 1982). In comparison with visual and taste cues, it is often difficult for consumers to recognize and/or label smell cues (Ellen and Bone, 1998). Their ability to recognize odour may be influenced by other cues. For instance, our ability to recognize a lemon scent is much higher if the scent is contained in a yellow rather than, say, a red container (Ellen and Bone, 1998).

Similarly North et al. (1999) investigated the extent to which stereotypically French and German music influenced selections of French and German wines by supermarket customers. During a two-week testing period, they placed French and German wines of the same price and sweetness on the shelves with appropriate national flags and played French and German music on alternate days. Findings revealed the sale of French wine increased when French music was played whereas the sale of German wines increased when German music was played.

Figure 2.10 shows a marketer attempting to engage the senses.

It has also been discovered that beers can be perceived as having different taste sensations according to the type of music being played in the background. Apparently the (same) beers tasted stronger when the music harmonized and weak or watery when the music was harsher (Holt-Hansen, 1978). A similar result was obtained in an experiment in which the preference for a ball-point pen was greater when shown with attractive music than with unattractive music (Gorn, 1982). Beverland et al. (2006) provides further research on the use of music in-store.

Figure 2.10: Five senses ice cream
Reproduced by permission of Unilever UK.

The development of the Internet as a shopping medium reduces the scope for sensory experiences. However, it has been found that consumers do desire sensory stimuli, yet many on-line retailers do not provide appropriate surrogates (Parsons, 2004).

 Take a look at Parsons (2004), Sensory Stimuli and E-Tailers, Journal of Consumer Behaviour, Vol 5 No 1, which can be accessed via the accompanying book web site at www.wileyeurope.com/college/evans

How consumers interact with store atmospherics is also relevant and there are three aspects of this: **proxemics, kinesics** and **paralanguage**. Proxemics refer to how people use physical space as a means of conveying information. For example, if the buyer stands far away from the seller, the implication is dislike, thus reducing the likelihood of a transaction. Kinesic behaviour involves the use of body positioning and movement as well as eye contact to indicate one's feelings. Here, greater eye contact between buyer and seller is generally associated with a more positive feeling between the two parties. Realizing this, we would expect the seller to use eye contact as a selling device. One might use various gestures (head nods, hand movements, etc.) to determine effect.

Finally, paralanguage refers to the particular choice of words used to transmit information. Yawns, loudness and tempo of voices are also elements of paralanguages. If the consumer felt positively about the sale, they might use words such as 'here' and 'this' as opposed to 'there' and 'that'. When asked about the product at hand, the seller might indulge in an over-inclusion strategy, where responsibility is diffused by attributing it to more than one source.

A case study on the accompanying web site explores proxemics, kinesics and paralanguage further.

THINKBOX

Next time you spend time in a shopping mall, make a note of the number of times your various senses are touched by marketing activity.

Are there any differences between men and women in terms of how tactile they are when browsing in shops and malls?

Sensory Marketing Research

It is interesting to note that market researchers are aware of not only what respondents say but also how they say it. Habershon (2004), for example, is keen to use facial expressions of respondents to supplement their actual words, thus combining both sight and sound within market research. For example, 'The sixty anger expressions share certain core configurational properties which distinguish them from the family of fear expressions, disgust expressions and so forth' (Ekman and Freisen, 2003). In addition, consumer researchers are using brain scans to reveal the nature of brain activity when processing marketing information (Leighton, 2004).

Following from the above-mentioned 'multisensory brands', Lindstrom (2005) describes the need for a measure of consumer reactions that spans the senses – a 'Sensogram'.

Neurolinguistic Programming (NLP)

A relatively recent development in marketing has been the transfer of findings from neurology to understanding how the human brain processes marketing information, such as advertisements. This is explored further in Chapter 5 but useful writings on the topic include: White (2005), Du Plessis (2005) and Addison (2005).

Perception Organization

In this section we build up a typology of conventions for perceptual organization, how we make sense of sensory inputs. First, try interpreting the pictures in Figure 2.11.

Figure 2.11: KAZON
If each were a brand, in which product category would they be?
Source: D Bernstein, *Creative Advertising* (Harlow: Longman, 1975), p. 128

These pictures were used to demonstrate the importance of *how* messages are presented (Bernstein, 1975). These versions of a hypothetical brand were presented to respondents, who were asked to what sort of product category they might belong. Version 1 produced no uniform reply and nothing very spontaneous was forthcoming. It was seen by different people as being a range of very different categories. Version 2, however, started to produce more rapid replies and ones which were a bit more focused: on a brand stamped on a car tyre or tea chest, presumably because of the stencilled style. Version 3 was stronger again. Most people readily thought of a comic or a powerful cleaner. Version 4 also produced fairly spontaneous and similar responses: a travel company of some kind, such as a ferry operator, airline and so on. The point of Bernstein's experiment was to convey the important message for marketers that the way in which something is presented can affect consumers' perception of it. Even the pronunciation of KAZON might influence how consumers perceive it.

Convention 1
Perception is not isolated to the substantive element of a message. Clearly there are important implications here for logo and pack design.

The interpretation of KAZON also shows that if we already hold an image of a brand's logo, a similar logo might be thought to be for a brand in the same product category.

Convention 2

The law of similarity means we are likely to interpret a new message in a similar way to something already in our existing experience. Sometimes the most recent and similarly presented stimulus determines how the newly presented stimulus is perceived: the **primacy effect**.

Figure 2.12 depicts two images in one picture. The experiment here was based on a split sample. One half of the sample was informed that they were going to be shown a picture of an old woman and the other half of the sample a picture of a young woman. Although it did not work with all respondents, most of those expecting to see the old woman saw this image first in the picture (with many going on to see the other image as well) and most of those expecting to see the young woman saw this image first, again with many going on to see the other image as well. To go from one image to the other one has to turn a kind of 'mental switch'.

Figure 2.12: **The old and the young woman**
Which do you see first: an old woman or a young woman? This is a good illustration
of an important principle of the psychology of perception. We see what we expect to see.

Convention 3

Our interpretation of a message is often based on 'expectations'. Consider one of the marketing mix elements, 'physical evidence': one of your authors witnessed a vehicle careering down a motorway with 'car valeting' engraved on its side. It was in a decrepit state: not exactly encouraging anyone to call for further details.

Similarly, food is expected to be presented in certain ways. The version of the right might taste exactly the same but because of the colouration, might even induce sickness.

Gestalt approaches to perceptual organization

Gestalt psychology stresses the fact that perception of a stimulus does not occur in isolation from a host of other variables. The German word *Gestalt* means 'whole' or 'entirety'. This section explores aspects of how we organize our interpretation of messages and sensory inputs. However, rather than producing a list, we invite you to engage with several issues as a way of building up to a series of conventions on perception.

Have a look at Figure 2.13 and you probably won't have any difficulty in seeing two messages: either a glass or two faces in profile looking at each other, depending whether you use white or black as the 'figure' or the 'background'.

Figure 2.13: Figure–ground relationships

Convention 4

'Figure–ground' relationships can influence how something is interpreted. You can't see both images at the same time.

This was used to great effect in some of the 1930s advertising campaigns by Shell. The classic images were interpreted differently depending on which was taken as the figure or ground.

Earlier we mentioned the law of closure as a way of gaining attention. In that respect, messages which are incomplete and ambiguous can encourage us to take notice just because of their strangeness.

Convention 5

The law of closure can be effective if it encourages consumers to solve the puzzle themselves because they are spending more time interpreting the message.

In Figure 2.14, the two lines are the same length but we are likely to perceive the bottom one to be longer because its 'wings' extend our perception outwards whereas the top line's more inwardly directed wings take our interpretation to a more contracted shorter length. This is an example of the law of continuity.

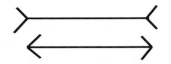

Figure 2.14: Visual Illusions

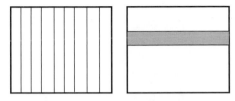

Figure 2.15: Extending Lines

In Figure 2.15 there is another variation on this process of our minds 'extending' lines. The boxes are the same size and shape but the left hand one might appear taller and thinner if our minds continue the thin vertical lines upwards. This is used in fashion design where, for example, pinstripe suits are supposed to make the wearer appear taller and thinner. Actually the approach does not necessarily produce a 'slimming' effect because where there are extra curves/bulges, the thin lines sometimes are seen to waver, thus accentuating the problems! Larger swirling patterns might be better at disguising such shapes. Conversely, the other 'pack' might appear to be wider and squatter because we continue the wide horizontal band sideways. Perhaps this explains why broad hoop designs on rugby jerseys can make the wearer appear broader than he really is.

EXAMPLE 2.10

The Newcastle Brown poster (Figure 2.16) depicts an irate cat and a bottle of Newcastle Brown. The image here was from a poster in Cardiff and the authors have asked students at Cardiff University if they understand this message. Very few did and complained it was just too ambiguous. Clearly there is another piece of information needed to make sense of this one. As many from Tyneside (more than 300 miles from Cardiff) will know, Newcastle Brown is known as 'the dog'. Armed with this piece of information, the consumer might indeed look twice at the ambiguity but soon fit the pieces together. The ambiguity and its solution can greatly enhance the attention value of marketing messages. But there is no point in assuming the majority of the target audience will have the missing pieces of the advertising jigsaw. This demonstrates that there are different **frames of reference** within a country as well as between countries.

When targeting is more accurate, advertisers and consumers can have fun with messages. For example, another in the Newcastle Brown series pictured a can of the beer with the ring pull having just been opened and the spray forming a speech balloon in which the word 'woof' appeared.

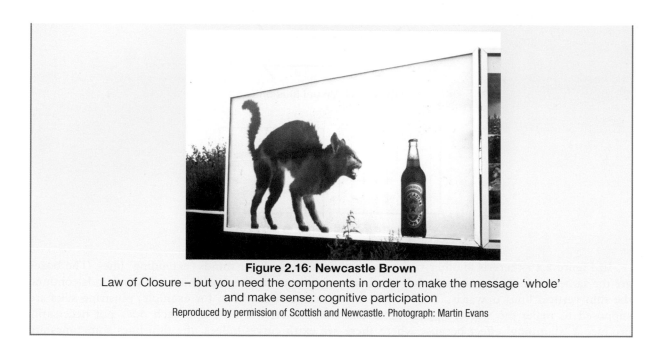

Figure 2.16: Newcastle Brown
Law of Closure – but you need the components in order to make the message 'whole'
and make sense: cognitive participation
Reproduced by permission of Scottish and Newcastle. Photograph: Martin Evans

Convention 6

The law of continuity encourages the consumer to continue an element of a stimulus in a particular direction. A core marketing module might well have taken you through the various Ps of marketing; however, when you, as a consumer, perceive a brand, it is likely that you do not think atomistically in terms of each 'mix' element in isolation from the rest. Instead you probably think of the whole brand experience. Gestalt perceptual processes are ultimately based on the whole being greater than the sum of the parts.

THINKBOX

© Getty Images. Photographer: John Gichigi. Reproduced with permission

Could the Canadians (red and black) have conveyed a more intimidating size and shape if the design of their shirts emphasized their shoulders more?

Convention 7

The whole is greater than the sum of the parts.

www. **Have a look at this web site, which discusses aspects of gestalt perception:**
http://www.cultsock.ndirect.co.uk/MUHome/cshtml/perception/
percep4.html

THINKBOX

BMW used the tagline, 'A car is more than the sum of its parts', to encourage a $2 + 2 = 5$ sort of interpretation of the car.

How can a brand be more than the sum of its parts?

Colour

Under 'Attention' we discussed the use of colour in attracting attention. In this perception stage, we return briefly to the use of colour. Different colours can transmit different meanings and emotions. Most colours have both positive and negative meanings and of course different colours are more or less fashionable at different points in time.

For example, Cadbury's use of purple in its packaging is very effective in communicating 'luxury' and 'quality' images to consumers (Figure 2.17). For many years, Virgin has cleverly used the red colour in its logo as well as in most of its packaging materials to send a clear signal to consumers that it is an active, stimulating and energetic brand. The phone company Orange not only uses the colour orange extensively in its branding; it even uses it as its name.

Use of particular colours in communication is like making a fashion statement. Just as fashion and trends change, so does the use of different colours by marketers. That is why most manufacturers of cars change 30% of their colour offerings every year and rely on the expert advice of colour consultants well before a particular colour is introduced (Triplett, 1995).

The meanings associated with colours are culture-specific and hence people in different cultures can associate different meanings to the same colour. For instance, in a cross-cultural study of colour meanings and preferences involving eight different countries, Madden *et al.* (2000) found that red was perceived as active, hot and vibrant across all countries. However, while black and brown were perceived as 'sad' and 'stale' across all cultures, yet the same colours had additional meanings of being 'formal' in Brazil, Colombia, China and Taiwan and of being 'masculine' in Austria, Hong Kong and the United States. The meanings associated with colours can change across cultures but within cultures as well. For instance, in the USA, while black clothing generally conjures up funereal images, in urban markets across America, black clothing is perceived as 'trendy' (Gimba, 1998). Table 2.2 summarizes colour perceptions in the USA as per Kanner (1989).

Figure 2.17: Use of purple by Cadbury
© Cadbury Schweppes plc. Reproduced by permission

Colour	Perceived meanings
Red	Exciting, hot, passionate, strong
Green	Secure, calm, natural
Blue	Authority, commands respect
Black	Sophisticated, mystery, power
Yellow	Warmth, novelty, caution

Summarized by the authors from Kanner (1989).

Table 2.2: Colour perceptions in the USA

Source: www.virgin.co.uk
Even Virgin's in-house guide starts with the statement 'Red is the lifeblood of our look'

Marketers also need to take into account the needs of those consumers who have colour-deficient vision and who cannot perceive some of the colours that people with normal colour vision can (Kaufman-Scarborough, 2001). A student was reprimanded while on placement with a company a few years ago. His role was a 'rep' for a cosmetics company and although he knew he was mildly colour-blind, he managed to totally confuse the colour-coded shampoo packs and stocked his retail customers with the wrong product versions.

EXAMPLE 2.11

MarketingWeek

Cracking the Colour Code

In today's visual-obsessed society, where consumers have more choice and less time than ever before, it has never been more important for marketers to invest in the design and look of their product or logo. Take the perfume industry, where as much as 50% of the cost of a bottle of perfume can be accounted for by packaging and advertising – often more than is spent on the scent itself.

Research supports the importance of a brand's visual appearance to consumers. One study by the Institute for Colour Research revealed that people make a subconscious judgement about an item within 90 seconds of initial viewing, and that up to 90% of that assessment is based on colour. Another study by the University of Loyola reveals that colour increases brand recognition by up to 80%.

Yet how much time and budget do marketers and manufacturers devote to thinking about the colours they choose for their products and marketing materials? Many successful brands have arrived at a winning colour combination, but it is often the result of years of trial and error, rather than a more focused and scientific approach.

By applying the principles of colour psychology, marketers can arrive at the right colour combination more quickly and reliably. The following analysis considers the use of colour by five different brands and is taken from a report commissioned by in-store marketing company Catalina Marketing.

The 11 basic colours have fundamental psychological properties that are universal, regardless of the shade, tone or tint. Each of them has potentially positive or negative psychological effects depending on the colour combinations chosen.

For example, the positive attributes of red can include physical strength, warmth, energy and excitement. But in a negative light it can signify defiance, aggression and strain.

The tone of each colour also has an impact. Each of the millions of colours that the human eye can see falls into one of four colour groups.

Generally speaking, colours from the same group harmonize with each other and reinforce each other's good points. Conversely, combining colours from different groups has an undermining effect and can emphasize the less attractive aspects of a colour.

The difference that colour can make becomes clear when comparing two brands from the same product category. For example, in the male toiletries market Lynx and Nivea both target appearance-conscious men, but the difference in their packaging reflects the different groups they aim to reach.

Black and blue all over: The water colours of Nivea target a different market from the black of the Lynx brand.

As an upbeat product range for young men, Lynx has taken the hi-tech route, using colours we might normally associate with motorbikes, or mobile phones. Black does not reflect cleanliness or freshness (which could be seen as important attributes in the toiletries market), but it has come to stand for sexiness, especially for males. Targeted at a market that has traditionally shied away from personal hygiene products, there is nothing girlie about this range.

The Nivea approach is much more subtle and the products communicate male cleanliness rather than manliness. Reassuring and water-related colours are used throughout the range – for example white for calming products, aqua for cleansing and stronger blue for invigorating. Nivea is selling on practical product benefits and a trustworthy reputation.

It is even possible for two brands in the same category to use the same colour, yet create a different response from consumers. For example, both Sainsbury's and Iceland use orange in their branding – a colour that stimulates appetite and is therefore highly appropriate for a supermarket.

Sainsbury's has focused on tastebuds with its Jamie Oliver advertising and Taste the Difference range. Its current choice of orange is more earthy and textured than the previous logo, and works well with cream to give a sense of rich, natural flavour. This orange communicates naturalness, some quirkiness ('try something new today'), and good sound principles.

By contrast, Iceland's orange is higher energy, more upbeat and combined with white, suggests low prices. Iceland supports this with red, a dynamic, energizing colour. This is not a shop to browse in – more a place to get what you need and move on.

But you don't always have to follow conventions. Sometimes using an unexpected colour can be a good way to make a statement about your brand. For example, Apple's initial use of white was a bold move considering electronic goods had been black or silver for many years. However, this only paid off thanks to the high quality and perfect finish of the products – anything less substantial would feel cheap in white.

The psychological properties of the 11 basic colours:

Colour	Positive	Negative
RED	Physical courage, strength, warmth, energy, basic survival, 'fight or flight', stimulation, masculinity, excitement	Defiance, aggression, visual impact, strain
BLUE	Intelligence, communication, trust, efficiency, serenity, duty, logic, coolness, reflection, calm	Coldness, aloofness, lack of emotion, unfriendliness
YELLOW	Optimism, confidence, self-esteem, extroversion, emotional strength, friendliness, creativity	Irrationality, fear, emotional fragility, depression, anxiety, suicide
GREEN	Harmony, balance, refreshment, universal love, rest, restoration, reassurance, environmental awareness, equilibrium, peace	Boredom, stagnation, blandness, enervation
VIOLET	Spiritual awareness, containment, vision, luxury, authenticity, truth, quality	Introversion, decadence, suppression, inferiority
ORANGE	Physical comfort, food, warmth, security, sensuality, passion, abundance, fun	Deprivation, frustration, frivolity, immaturity
PINK	Physical tranquillity, nurture, warmth, femininity, love, sexuality, survival of the species	Emotional claustrophobia, emasculation, inhibition, physical weakness
GREY	Psychological neutrality	Lack of confidence, dampness, depression, hibernation, lack of energy
BLACK	Sophistication, glamour, security, emotional safety, efficiency, substance	Oppression, coldness, menace, heaviness
WHITE	Hygiene, sterility, clarity, purity, cleanness, simplicity, sophistication, efficiency	Sterility, coldness, barriers, unfriendliness, elitism
BROWN	Seriousness, warmth, nature, earthiness, reliability, support	Lack of humour, heaviness, lack of sophistication

Source: www.colour-affects.co.uk

Colour clearly plays a crucial part in catching the modern-day consumer's eye. According to the Henley Centre, 73% of purchase decisions are now made in store. Consequently, catching the shopper's eye and conveying information efficiently are critical to successful sales. In today's world of myriad choices no brand can afford to ignore the impact of colour. More importantly, why would anyone want to give that potential advantage away to the competition?

Catherine Shovlin, founder of Customer Interpreter, contributed to this week's Trends Insight.

Marketing Week, 11 October 2007, pp 28–29. Reproduced by permission of Centaur Media Plc.

Convention 8
Colour can influence perception.

Have a look at these web sites, which explore the use of colour in general and in marketing:
http://www.infoplease.com/spot/colors1.html
www.colour-affects.co.uk

Sensory Thresholds

A further consideration is that our perceptual senses have limits. These are called **absolute sensory thresholds**. The point here is that, although a message might exist, our senses are not capable of picking up all sensory inputs. We have already introduced the 'Mosquito' which can be heard by people under about 20 years but not by older people.

Our hearing or sight is not as acute as that in some members of the animal kingdom. One implication of this has already been discussed in a different context – subliminal messages (in Chapter 1). If a message is below our sensory threshold it is just possible that although the message is not perceived consciously it might be subconsciously.

EXAMPLE 2.12

'Veteran' readers may remember that between 'A Day in the Life' and the 'run-out' (first pressing only) track of the Beatles' *Sergeant Pepper* album a 15 kilocycle pitched dog whistle sounds. If played with a dog in the room, this can produce strange behaviour from the animal because, unperceived by the human listener, the dog whistle on this track would be clearly heard by the dog!

A marketing application of the sensory threshold concept is the use of an audio message as part of supermarket muzak that says something to the effect of 'I must not steal'. The message might be below the sensory threshold to be consciously heard but perhaps it reaches the mind unconsciously (see Chapter 1). If so, by definition, the receiver is not consciously aware of the message so does not put up emotional barriers to the message and may therefore react as intended.

As discussed in Chapter 1 and as evidenced by Broyles (2006) there is little for consumers to really worry about in terms of being manipulated unconsciously – probably.

Have a look at the following web sites, which explore subliminal perception in greater detail:
http://www.arts.uwaterloo.ca/~pmerikle/papers/
SubliminalPerception.html
http://www.csicop.org/si/9204/subliminal-perception.html

Sensory Discrimination

A variation on this sensory threshold point concerns sensory discrimination. That is, can we always detect differences between similar sensory inputs? The marketing application here is reflected in the many taste tests that are regularly conducted. A recent group of students, for example, conducted a taste test as part of their marketing research module. Before the test most claimed to like chocolate, and that they preferred one particular brand. Indeed many claimed that they would be able to identify that brand in a blind test (in which all brand identification is removed). Respondents stated which sample of chocolate they preferred and which brand they generally preferred. Most also thought that the sample they liked in the test was also their generally preferred brand, but of course it was not. This sort of experiment demonstrates the importance of branding, advertising imagery, packaging and so on, in affecting consumers' perception of a marketing offering. It again shows the importance of the 'whole' over the components of the marketing mix.

Often, retailer brands try to emulate national brands in terms of packaging. For example, Figure 2.18 shows national and retailer packs of men's cosmetics. This is an attempt to reduce discrimination between brands in the hope that consumers might go for the cheaper own label because it looks the same as the highly advertised national brand. This is another example of the law of similarity.

Figure 2.18: Attempt to narrow sensory discrimination
The black packs are of the retailer and manufacturer versions respectively.
Would you mind which you bought?
Photograph: Martin Evans

THINKBOX

We bet that you will probably say that you prefer particular brands of beer, chocolate, fast food, colas etc. but can you *really* identify them in blind tests? Try this with some friends. If you do not always identify your claimed preferred brands, what does this say about:

1. Your perceptual process, and
2. The power of branding, packaging and advertising?

THINKBOX

Do YOU have any qualms about buying the cheaper imitator brand? Why?
How do you think the imitated brands feel about this and why?

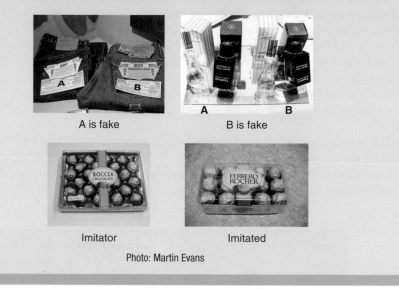

A is fake   B is fake

Imitator

Imitated

Photo: Martin Evans

EXAMPLE 2.13

Some years ago, Pretty Polly tights had a heavy Ad spend using women's legs.

Aristoc Tights had a much smaller Ad spend but used similar approach. Research found that consumers thought the Aristoc Ads were actually Pretty Polly Ads so consumers saw the brands as the same and Aristoc were really advertising Pretty Polly.

Source: Pretty Polly

Source: Aristoc

Images courtesy of the Advertising Archives

Just Noticeable Difference

Another dimension of sensory discrimination, concerning the degree to which consumers might or might not notice a change in some marketing message, product design or package, is what is known as the 'just noticeable difference' (JND). Consider the incremental changes in pack design in Figure 2.19.

Figure 2.19: Pack design changes
Each change might not always be noticed, even though the cumulative effect
over time is significant.
Reproduced by permission of Robert Opie

Many marketers will use their knowledge of this to make changes over time in such a way as not to make it obvious that they are making changes. But minor changes to pack design can keep the brand appearing fresh and up to date even if the changes are not particularly noticed.

The same logic can apply to changes to price levels. Rather than a major change in one move, the product might be moved up or down the price ladder in stages, such that each sequential change is barely noticed by the majority of consumers. Those who are especially involved (see Chapter 4) with the product or service concerned are, however, more likely to spot these incremental changes. Conversely, if a marketer actually wants consumers to notice a price difference – for example, when marking-down stock for a 'sale' – they would try to ensure that the change was above the JND. Miller (1962) has suggested such a price change (for 'sales' to be noticed) should be around 25% of the previous price and anything less would not be effective.

The JND is the degree of change needed for a consumer to notice a difference between two stimuli 50% of the time. Experimentation on JND has a long history and it was Weber in 1834 who found one of the most robust relationships in any psychological concept. Weber found that if a stimulus is initially 'intense' or strong, a greater change is needed for individuals to notice it. He used the senses of sight and sound for his research and came up with a formula for the relationship between the strength of the initial stimulus and the degree of change needed to be noticed:

$$\frac{\Delta I}{I} = K$$

where ΔI = the JND,
I = the strength or intensity of the stimulus, and
K = a constant, which is different for each sense.

Weber's work was applied to marketing by Miller (1962).

For example, consider a change in the weight of a tin of tuna fish. In research it might be found that, from the initial 300 g size, 50% of respondents only noticed a difference in the amount of tuna for their toasted sandwiches when it reached 280 g.

Therefore, substituting in Weber's formula:

$$\frac{21\,g}{300\,g} = 0.07 (\text{a 7\% change in tin weight is needed before a change is noticed})$$

In other words, the marketer might 'get away' with reducing the tin to 280 g and consumers would not notice the difference.

The 'constant' means that for other sizes of similar products – e.g. a large 600 g tin of salmon might be reduced to 558 g (600 g – 7% = 558 g) – consumers would not notice the difference in the amount of fish. It has been found that because of different 'constant' values for taste and smell, marketers of ready meals, for example, might need to manipulate the aroma of a 'new improved' dish more than its taste, in order to ensure a difference is noticed.

THINKBOX

Manufacturers of light bulbs could have taken advantage of the JND by selling 95-watt bulbs. As with cars advertised as having a 2-litre engine (when it is really 1975cc) the light bulb manufacturer might say you are getting the light of a 100-watt bulb for less usage of electricity, assuming the consumer might not be able to tell the difference in brightness between 95- and 100-watt bulbs.

Is this a rip-off?

Selective Attention and Perception

We have already said that consumers are bombarded daily with many thousands of messages. One way of coping with this constant bombardment of information and persuasion with which the individual has to contend is through selection of what is perceived.

The precise manner in which the person allows some messages to penetrate or 'get through' while rejecting others depends on their values, motives and attitudes as well as their social situation, current interests and preoccupations. Messages which are in tune with what the individual already believes stand a much better chance of gaining attention and being perceived than those which are at odds with their preoccupations or tangential to their interests and needs. **Perceptual vigilance** is where consumers are open to what they are interested in and even seek it. **Perceptual defence** is where consumers avoid messages that are not congruent with their view of the world. We discuss this further in Chapter 4.

The fact that different individuals might perceive the same message differently, or selectively, might lead to the conclusion that the above discussion is totally irrelevant, that there is nothing we can do to affect perception. This is very far from the truth because the more we understand about the perceptual process, both generally and of the target market concerned, the more we can ensure that intended receivers of the message will interpret the message in the intended way. The A and B regions in Figure 2.20 are the fields of experience of the sender and the receiver. Region C is the common frame of reference for the message between sender and receiver. If the sender of the message understands the frame of reference of the receiver and puts the message in terms that mean the same to both sender and receiver, there is a greater chance of effective communication. The receiver will then perceive and understand the message in the intended way.

For example, consider a crooked sign in long-hand writing advertising fresh eggs, found along a country lane and outside a rustic country cottage. This would probably be congruent with the receiver's frame of reference for 'happy hens' and free range eggs. The same sign in a city centre probably wouldn't be. Conversely, if the sign read 'flying lessons' then the receiver might be less tempted to ask for further details in the rustic cottage than in a more urban setting!

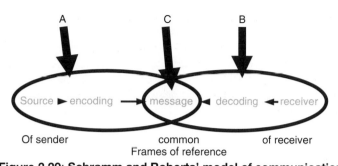

Figure 2.20: Schramm and Roberts' model of communication

Source: W Schramm and D Roberts (eds), *The Process and Effects of Mass Communication.* (Urbana IL: University of Illinois Press, 1971).

As we mentioned earlier, there are so many distractions for the consumer these days, such as advertising clutter, all of which constitute **noise** in the communications process and can hinder the message either getting through at all or being interpreted in ways other than the intended.

EXAMPLE 2.14

The recent outsourcing of call centre provision to other countries – for example, India – has seen unusual training of the operatives, in order for them to work within a similar frame of reference to those who call them. They are trained to know about current UK weather and storylines in TV soaps so they can converse more casually.

This shows that the interpretation of meaning is also dependent upon the context of the consumer's own cultural knowledge and understanding. That is why perceptions of reality differ from consumer to consumer as each person interprets social and physical stimuli so that these fit their overall culturally determined world view.

Product Perception

It should be clear by now that it is important to look at things from the consumer's perspective. That is, rather than thinking in terms of what we are *making* and *selling*, marketers should empathize more and think in terms of *what benefits* consumers buy and how they perceive products and brands.

How consumers perceive a range of brands can be researched to build **perceptual maps**. How consumers perceive the product in terms of image relative to competing offerings (Ries and Trout, 1986) is extremely important and marketers should use an understanding of this to position their own brands. In this way, brand positioning is not actually something that is done *to* a product – rather it is something that marketers do to the minds of consumers.

EXAMPLE 2.15

Figure 2.21 shows an example of perceptual mapping. Respondents are asked to position different brands along various continua and then to position their ideal brand relative to existing brands.

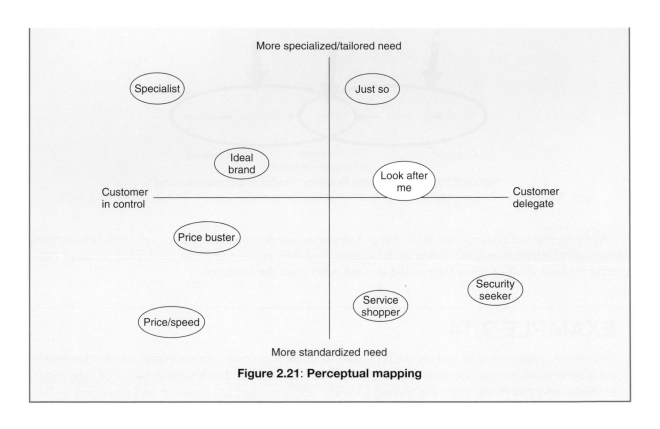

Figure 2.21: Perceptual mapping

Perception and Evoked Sets

If consumers mapped a range of brands, it is likely that they would not be aware of some of the brands in a product or service category. This is known as their **unawareness set**. They may be aware of some brands and be able to bring to mind some of them which they consider purchasing – this is called the **evoked set**. They may also know some brands but remain indifferent to them. This is called the **inert set**. They can also know and reject brands based on experience or information. This is called the **inept set**. Through the use of marketing communications, marketers aim to make sure that a right kind of brand association (see Chapter 3) is created in consumers' minds (e.g. cool, innovative, trendy). However, becoming part of consumers' evoked set is often a hard task because only few brands get their place here.

Perception and Intangibility of Services

Intangibility means that services cannot be touched or grasped. Intangibility also means that services are incorporeal – that is, they do not have physical bodies and they do not exist in physical space and therefore they cannot be sensed by our physical senses (Mittal, 2002). The intangibility of services poses some additional challenges when it comes to perceiving and comprehending services and developing communication programmes for them (Legg and Baker, 1996; Grove *et al*. 2002). Table 2.3 presents an overview of creative approaches as suggested by the service advertising literature to address the problem of intangibility and other services problems (Legg and Baker, 1996; Mittal, 2002).

Creative message treatment	Examples
Show the physical components of a service delivery process	The AA van rescuing a stranded customer
Focus on the tangibles	Show physical facilities, equipment, appearance of personnel
Use vivid information	Any information that creates very strong mental image of service
Use specific and concrete language	'Strong research capability', 'Sound analysis', 'Experts in delivery'
Use relevant tangible objects to improve comprehension	'Under the traveller's umbrella'; 'The Nationwide blanket of protection'
Use interactive imagery	Direct Line's use of moving telephone, Lombard Direct's use of talking telephone
Present objectively document data on past performance	The punctuality record of a train company
Show a typical service delivery event	An employee going out of the way to help a customer
Show testimonials from customers about some aspect of service	A letter from a satisfied customer
Show a typical customer experiencing the service	A customer getting a good deal for his home insurance; 'Quote me happy' campaign by Norwich Union Direct
Encourage people to speak positively about the service and use personal endorsement	BT's use of 'It's good to talk' campaign
Educate customers for service process	easyJet's web site providing information to customers about what they need to do during the service delivery
Communicate backstage operations, rules and policies to improve confidence	A service company showing their backstage operations in a TV ad
Use dramaturgy	AA's dramatic use of service delivery process

Table 2.3: Creative approaches to improve consumers' perceptions of services

Because of the intangible nature of services, it is difficult for a service organization to understand how its customers perceive and evaluate the quality of its services (Parasuraman *et al.*, 1985; Zeithaml, 1981). However, customers make inferences about service quality on the basis of tangibles (the buildings, the physical layout, etc.) that surround the service environment. Support for this argument comes from empirical evidence suggesting that the tangible, physical surroundings of the service environment can have a significant impact on customers' affective responses and their behavioural intentions (Wakefield and Blodgett, 1999). Dabholkar *et al.* (1996) reported similar findings, that the tangible aspects of department stores do influence customers' perceptions of service quality.

Legg and Baker (1996) argue that even when consumers comprehend services and realize that the service is useful in satisfying their needs, they may still experience difficulties in developing a list of potential service providers in their minds. Advertising helps to create brand identities by associating a brand's name with some sensory images (e.g. a symbol, logo, graphics or other visual form). Mittal (2002) argues that creation of brand identity is easier for a physical product because it has a tangible form which acts alongside the associated visual forms to lead to clear brand identity. However, in the case of services, symbols alone have to do the job of creating brand identity by capturing the core meaning or essence of the service. For example, many service providers use relevant phrases or logos to create a clear brand identity in consumers' minds (e.g. Direct Line, loans4you.com, insure.com).

Mortimer (2001) conducted qualitative interviews of creative directors in the UK and reported that the respondents perceived intangibility to be the most prominent characteristic of services. The respondents suggested a greater emphasis should be placed on personal recommendations and on not promising something that could not be delivered. They also believed services relied upon trust and relationship and therefore clear and consistent branding campaigns to build familiarity and trust were important for service advertisers. The issues of loyalty and relationships are discussed in Chapter 11.

SYMBOLISM IN PERCEPTUAL INTERPRETATION

Marketers are sometimes turning to the study of symbols and signs (semiotics). Here, marketing messages will have three elements: the 'object' (e.g. the product/brand itself), the 'sign' (e.g. the imagery used in the message) and the 'meaning' (which is how the recipient interprets the message) as shown in Figure 2.22.

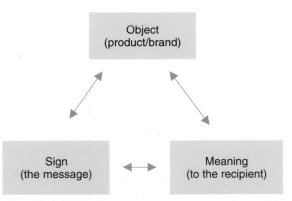

Figure 2.22: Semiotics triad

The marketer can:

1. Relate signs in the message directly to the product or brand; for example, using an *icon* that is almost as good as a picture of the product, such as a telephone on wheels to promote a telephone-based motor insurance company.
2. Relate signs in the message that share common properties; for example, using an *index*, such as depicting scented flowers in the advertising of an air freshener.
3. Relate signs in the message that have agreed associations; for example, using a *symbol* such as the US cowboy to create the 'rugged' persona for Marlboro cigarettes (that is, before the model died of lung cancer).

SUMMARY

■ The model of pre- and post-purchase buying stages introduced in this chapter is an example of a 'hierarchy of effects' sequential model. Such models allow the discussion of what otherwise might appear to be discrete topics within a more integrated framework. In this chapter we have explored the concepts of exposure, attention and perception.

■ There are important implications for the placing and timing of marketing messages in order to match the intended target market's likely exposure to media. Similarly, there are techniques which marketers can employ to increase the likelihood of their messages being noticed. In order to gain attention, marketers can use movement, or simulated movement, novelty, participation and colour.

■ From the marketer's perspective, it is clearly important for consumers to notice marketing activity and then to respond in the way the marketer intends. Perception, which refers to the reception and interpretation of external stimuli by an individual, begins with the process of sensation and is a selective operation. Without attention being given to a stimulus, perception will not take place; and people give their attention largely to those things in which they have an interest, or which are novel, or from which they derive pleasure and satisfaction. Consumers react to advertisements, products, packages and so on according to their motives, attitudes and social situation, and each individual's perception of these marketing mix elements is unique to him or her.

QUESTIONS

1. **Identify and discuss some of the widely used techniques to gain and hold consumer attention. Conduct an experiment to test your ideas.**

2. **What is perception? What is the role of our five senses in perception? Use some common examples to illustrate.**

3. **Services are characterized by many features, such as their intangibility. Use your own examples to discuss the impact of intangibility on services advertising. How can marketers resolve those problems?**

4. **Select some press advertisements or packages that are good illustrations of the use of any of the following:**
   a. **Perception of colour**
   b. **Use of visual illusions**
   c. **Ambiguity and participation.**
   How might theory be applied in each case? What is the likely effectiveness?

5. **Provide examples of the JND principle from price, pack and product changes. Conduct an experiment to measure the JND for a change in the price of a brand of beer.**

6. Consumers' exposure to marketing messages is selective. How can marketers take account of this in their media selection?

7. Provide examples of the application of Gestalt psychology in consumers' perpetual processes.

FURTHER READING

Foxall G, Goldsmith R and Brown S (1998) *Consumer Psychology for Marketing*, 2nd edn, International Thomson Business Press, London. This is a good summary of a number of aspects of psychology within the marketer–consumer context. It examines cognitive processes such as perception, learning and attitudes. There is also coverage of motivation, lifestyles, consumer choice, postmodern consumers and consumer behaviour within social and consumption environments.

Jackson M and Fulberg P (2003) *Sonic Branding*, Palgrave, Basingstoke. 'Silence is golden', as the Tremeloes asserted in their 1967 song. However, it isn't, according to this book. There is much to be gained from the use of sound in branding and this is the book from which to learn. It also provides wider coverage of what brands are and how they communicate with consumers.

CHAPTER 3
CONSUMER RESPONSE TO MARKETING ACTIONS: 2
LEARNING AND ATTITUDES

CHAPTER OBJECTIVES

After engaging with the material presented in this chapter and its associated exercises and reading, you should be able to:

■ Integrate the application of concepts from psychology within a model of how consumers can respond to marketing activity.
■ Apply aspects of behavioural learning to increase the likelihood of consumers remembering and learning about the marketing message/offering.
■ Apply aspects of cognitive learning to increase the likelihood of consumers remembering and learning about the marketing message/offering.
■ Analyse and evaluate different approaches to explaining the link between attitudes and behaviour.
■ Explain different approaches to attitude formation and change.

INTRODUCTION

The last chapter focused on exposure, attention and perception stages of our **hierarchy of effects** model. This chapter moves the discussion forward by focusing on the learning and attitude stages of the model (Figure 3.1). If the consumer noticed and interpreted the marketing message in the intended way, we now need to explore ways of encouraging the consumer to learn effectively about the marketing activity, to remember the message and then to develop favourable emotions and intentions toward it. In this chapter we explore aspects of both learning and attitude and provide examples of how these concepts apply to consumer behaviour. We also show how marketers can benefit from understanding these concepts.

- Post-purchase
- Action
- Attitude
- Learning
- Perception
- Attention
- Exposure

Figure 3.1: Sequential model of response to marketing

LEARNING

Assuming that the marketing offering is interpreted appropriately, **learning** is concerned with ensuring it is remembered in the intended way. Marketing communication may be considered to be concerned with teaching consumers about various marketing offerings. If this is the case, marketing itself can benefit from knowing about how consumers learn about things.

Learning vs Memory

As consumers we continuously learn new information which may or may not be stored in our memory. Hence, it is worth noting here that learning and memory are interrelated yet different concepts. Learning deals with how we acquire new information whereas memory is the internal recording of information or experiences and is related to our ability to store, retain, and subsequently recall information. Figure 3.2 illustrates three important processes or stages related to the memory including encoding (i.e. the information is sensed, received and processed), storage (i.e. the information is permanently recorded) and retrieval (i.e. information is recalled when needed). Understanding the three processes helps us understand various memory types explained in the following section.

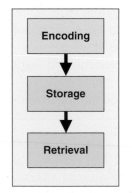

Figure 3.2: Memory processes

Memory Types

Sensory Memory
Not all of the information is stored in our memory on a long-term basis and hence there are different memory types and memory stores each having different functions, capacity and duration. For

P	Q	R	S
C	K	L	T
X	V	Z	A
Q	O	D	S

Figure 3.3: Sensory memory illustration

instance, sometimes we sense information temporarily, only for few seconds, but do not analyse it and hence the information is lost very quickly. This characterizes sensory memory which allows a very short representation of information while being processed via our senses. The sensory memory forms automatically without any attention or interpretation. To illustrate, imagine you visit your local optician who examines your eyesight. Imagine that during the examination, the optician accidentally presses an electric switch and, as a consequence, you see and read an illuminated screen on the wall in front of you with four rows of alphabet letters each row having four alphabets (Figure 3.3). The optician quickly realizes his mistake and turns the switch off. Now the question is how many letters can you recall in each row in the exact order and for how long can you do this? You may be able to recall all or some of the letters momentarily but not for long because your memory of the letters is likely to fade as soon as you start having a conversation with the optician. The situation can obviously be very different if you deliberately wanted to memorize the alphabets and hence allocated more attention and mental ability in recognizing and memorizing the letters. The example illustrates that sensory memory is short lived (just long enough to process information for its basic physical characteristics) and needs our attention before becoming part of what is known as short-term memory.

Short-term Memory

Assume you are talking to a sales person over the phone and the person mentions a free phone number to call and asks you to note it down. However, you don't have a pen handy and hence try to remember the number on its own but, as soon as the phone call is over, you forget the phone number. The situation reflects short-term but conscious and active processing of incoming information known as short-term memory (or working memory). Short-term memory is limited in capacity (you may consciously encode between five and nine pieces of information) and is also short-lived meaning you can only store information for as little as 30 seconds. That is why consumers often find it convenient to carry around a shopping list while shopping or 'things to do' list while at work as our capacity to store information in short-term memory is limited. Moreover, consumers find it convenient to repeat the information either in their minds or verbally to improve their chances of retaining the information in short-term memory longer than the usual 30 seconds. Similarly, chunking or grouping the information into little but meaningful groups can also help in retaining the information. That explains why consumers find it convenient to split the telephone numbers into little subgroups. For instance, it may be difficult for a consumer to remember a number such as 0870345675 in one go but easier if the number is presented as 0870 345 675 (notice the little spacing in between groups of numbers).

Long-term Memory

The information from short-term memory can be encoded into long-term memory, which can store information for longer periods of time. The memory process of encoding (Figure 3.2) controls the movement of information form short- to long-term memory whereas the retrieval process controls the flow of information from long- to short-term memory as and when the information is needed to be recalled. The long-term memory organizes and stores the new piece of information and ties it up with other bits of information that already exist. Long-term memory can be categorized into semantic memory, which refers to the organizing and storing of factual information (independent of context) and episodic memory, which refers to the organizing and storing of information specific to a particular context (e.g. as to where and when an event happened). Forgetting is our inability to retrieve previously stored information. This could be caused by many factors including the probability that the information was never encoded into long-term memory in the first place (encoding failure) or that, for some reason, we are unable to retrieve the information from long-term memory (retrieval failure). Whatever the case, it is worth noting that some of the information is explicitly stored and retrieved, while other information is based on implicit learning and is not based on conscious recall of information (Anderson, 1976).

In summary, learning and memory are closely interrelated, but different, concepts and it is worth noting here that learning is also closely associated with perception: learning influences perception and, in turn, depends on it. Also, both processes are intimately connected with, and shaped by, the individual's motives (Chapter 1), attitudes (this chapter) and personality (Chapter 6). Learning can be explored by using either a behavioural or cognitive approach.

Behavioural Learning

The behavioural approach to learning is based on what is known as the stimulus–response model which argues to study the learning processes most objectively by focusing on stimuli and responses. The approach assumes that learning involves a behaviour change, is largely the result of environmental events and hence internal cognitive processes are not studied.

Within the behavioural school of thought, there are two popular approaches to learning: **associationist learning** (or **classical conditioning**) and **instrumental learning** (or **operant conditioning**). We discuss both of these in the following sections.

Associationist Learning: Classical Conditioning

THINKBOX

Are there some smells that always remind you of something from your past? For example, there might be certain seaside aromas of sea and trees. You might have had a good holiday and in your memory this is linked with days of taking in these smells. Might you, therefore, associate the artificial aroma of palm trees in a travel agency with buying a good holiday?

When you hear a music track from, say, the summer of when you were 16, do you associate that tune with what you were doing that summer?

Associationist learning is based on the early work of the Russian physiologist Ivan Pavlov (1928) and on the work of Skinner (1938). Pavlov considered learning to be essentially concerned with stimulus–response relationships. His experiments included observation of dogs' responses to different stimuli. He observed

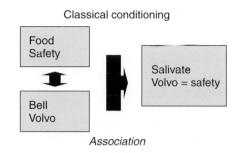

Figure 3.4: Associationist learning: classical conditioning

that the dogs in his experiments salivated when they were presented with food. However, there was nothing exceptional about this. It is a natural and even automatic response to a stimulus like presentation of food. What was really fascinating was that he also observed that the dogs salivated not only when they were given the food but also whenever they heard the footsteps of the assistants who brought the food to them. Pavlov went on to present various other stimuli at the same time as presenting the food. Again the dogs salivated. This process (repeated 'paired stimuli') was also tried with other stimuli (the sound of a tuning fork, light bulb being flashed, etc.). After repeatedly presenting food with these other stimuli, Pavlov again presented 'the other' stimulus by itself and the dogs salivated to just the tuning fork, light bulb and so on, even though no food was present. What he argued was that an unnatural response to the light or sound had been conditioned into the animals. This type of learning became known as classical conditioning and is summarized in Figure 3.4 with its application to the car market.

Marketing might not operate precisely at the level of Pavlov's experiments but the principles are used every day. If marketing understands the target market's frame of reference (see Chapter 2) – for example, status appeals/benefits or sex appeals/benefits – it can present that relevant appeal repeatedly and the market is likely to respond favourably to the appeal itself. But then if the brand is presented at the same time, with plenty of repetition of this paired stimuli approach, the market may well learn to associate the brand with that particular appeal/benefit.

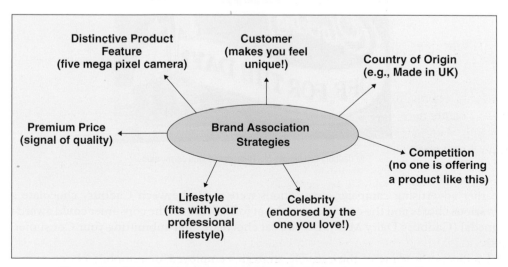

Figure 3.5: Potential brand association strategies for a mobile phone

THINKBOX

We are sure that you remember our example earlier in this chapter concerning memorizing telephone numbers. Consider this example but in the current context of 'association'. What is the intended association here?

Source: Hastings Direct

In Chapter 1, we argued that marketing does not create needs, but rather encourages a want for a specific product because of the association between the acquisition of the product/service and the satisfaction of a need. This is the basis of the associationist learning approach. The approach explains why consumers learn to associate certain beliefs and feelings with certain brands and many of our preferences are learned this way. Advertising plays a key role in creating and reinforcing existing brand associations in consumer minds. For example, Cadbury has used an appeal that associates the end of the working day with their chocolate.

© Cadbury Schweppes plc. Reproduced with permission

In an earlier advertising campaign associations were made between Cadbury chocolate and having completed various chores and the copy suggested that following this, the consumer could award themselves the CDM medal (Cadbury Dairy Milk). Do you eat chocolate after submitting your Consumer Behaviour assignment?

Figure 3.5 illustrates some of the possible strategies employed by a mobile phone manufacturer to create distinct brand associations in consumers' minds.

THINKBOX

Brand association can be negative, however. Why so in this case?

Here's a clue...

Photo: Martin Evans

EXAMPLE 3.1

In Figure 3.6, an advertisement for rail travel creates an association between road travel and discomfort. This also reflects the approach of increasing negative emotions toward competing products/services and is explored in more detail in Chapter 4, in our coverage of cognitive dissonance. Similarly, the advertisements for IKEA presented in Figure 3.7 create an association between sleeping and discomfort.

Figure 3.6: Associating a competing product with discomfort
Reproduced by permission of Scotrail and DDB London

Figure 3.7: Associating sleeping with discomfort
Source: Ikea

Further examples of association concern the use of celebrities in advertising. In Figure 3.8, for example, Madonna's characteristics and what she stands for may well transfer to the brand (Versace) she is endorsing in the advertisement (see Chapter 9). Similarly, through the constant pairing of specific music to a brand in a TV ad, marketers aim to condition the response of consumers.

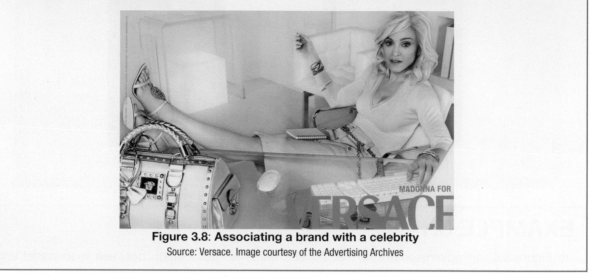

Figure 3.8: Associating a brand with a celebrity
Source: Versace. Image courtesy of the Advertising Archives

Despite research that indicates that conditioning using celebrities can produce strong and enduring attitudes to brands (Till *et al.*, 2008), many marketers, however, are becoming increasingly wary of associating their brand with celebrities, as we discuss further in Chapter 9. This is because of what might be the unpredictable 'misbehaviour' of the celebrities in their private or public lives or indeed their negative comments about the brand they are supposedly endorsing (Benady, 2008).

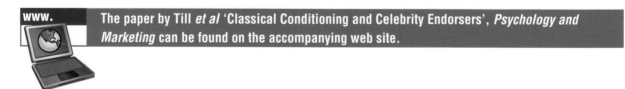

www. The paper by Till *et al* 'Classical Conditioning and Celebrity Endorsers', *Psychology and Marketing* can be found on the accompanying web site.

Although not a specific marketing application, but especially writing from Cardiff we cannot resist a couple of rugby examples. Some years ago the then Coach of the England rugby team, Geoff Cooke, decided that the support that the Wales team received from home supporters in the Cardiff stadium was so significant that it needed to be counteracted. Specifically, he wanted to reduce the power of the Welsh anthem, before kick-off. He played especially passionate versions of this to the England players but as a soundtrack alongside a film of great England tries against Wales in Cardiff (yes, there have been some!). The idea was to encourage the England players to associate the Welsh anthem with good English play.

In the 2007 Rugby World Cup, one of the biggest upsets was France beating New Zealand in the quarter final. The French coach encouraged his team to refer to their opponents as 'New Zealand' rather than as the 'All Blacks', because of the powerful and scary associations so many teams have had for many decades with the name 'All Blacks'.

Our accompanying DVD includes a Dulux paint commercial in which different colours are associated with appropriate sounds. For example, 'Siesta' is overlaid with the sound of a clock ticking peacefully. Colour association can be important and Chapter 1 explored some of the components of this and the chapter-end article by Sholvin (2007) is useful in our current context.

THINKBOX

The associations attached to a large number of well-advertised brands can be explained by this process (Table 3.1)

- Volvo = safety
- Golf GTI = sporty
- BMW = quality
- Levi's = youth
- Wrangler = cowboys
- Benetton = colourful

Table 3.1: Some famous brand associations

Try this for yourself. Get a friend to list some well-known brands and then to ask you to spontaneously come up with what they mean to you. You might be surprised at how your associations match marketers' intentions as reflected in the advertisements for these brands.

Instrumental Learning: Operant Conditioning

This is another behavioural approach to explaining learning and it relates to the consequences that similar responding has produced in the past. Skinner's work resulted in operant conditioning. Here, the frequency of occurrence of a specific behaviour is modified by the consequences of the outcome of that behaviour. This learning approach recognizes that learning can be encouraged and even reinforced through the use of positive and negative reinforcers. Generally speaking, marketers want to increase the rate at which learning takes place and to reduce the rate at which consumers' memory decays. For example, several researchers have drawn on studies of the psychology of reinforcement. Reinforcement is closely allied to one of the oldest and simplest of laws that psychology has produced – the **law of effect** – which states that actions that are enjoyed or satisfying are repeated (Figure 3.9).

For instance, by offering a price reduction (e.g. 10% off on everything bought) at the time of purchase, marketers can increase the probability that the consumer will repeat their behaviour (e.g. will shop at the store again). Similarly, a customer is likely to walk past a store where their complaints were met with abusive outbursts. Walking past and shopping elsewhere avoid such aversive consequences and are said to be negatively reinforced; i.e. their rate of repetition is increased by avoidance/escape rather than by approach.

Now, it is obvious that a consumer who purchases a particular brand is likely to repeat this buying pattern only if they derive an acceptable minimum level of satisfaction from the purchased item.

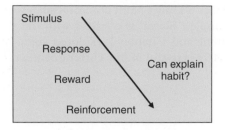

Figure 3.9: **Operant (or instrumental) conditioning**

Consumers who are disappointed in their choices are likely to switch to alternative brands. For this reason, advertising and other promotional efforts must make claims which can be borne out by the consumer's post-purchase experience of the product (see our coverage of cognitive dissonance in the next chapter); the strength and amount of reinforcement are directly related to the number of behavioural repetitions the customer makes.

When the outcome of buying the same product/service is similarly rewarding over repeated purchases, the consumer can develop a habit of buying that brand. In this way, operant conditioning can go some way to explaining **habitual buying**.

Continued positive reinforcement from habitual buying may be difficult to break, but at the same time a single disappointing reaction to a particular brand may not be enough to overcome all the reinforcement that has previously taken place.

THINKBOX

Consider your own buying behaviour. To what extent can your buying be explained by operant conditioning? What other factors might be involved?

Repetition is clearly an important dimension of behavioural learning and marketers need to consider the number of 'exposures' of the message that should be used. We have already covered 'reach and frequency' in Chapter 2, but there are issues that are especially pertinent to the learning process, which we examine here.

Repetition Effects

As we have seen, repetition of 'paired stimuli' can help create associations via classical conditioning but, in a wider context, how many exposures are needed for optimal learning of the message? The concept is also sometimes known as **advertising wearout** and we discussed this in Chapter 2 in terms of the diminishing marginal effects of repetition. There is a clear link here with the reinforcement stage of operant conditioning because without repetition it is difficult for solus marketing activity per se to aid retention. It is not valid to state precisely how many exposures are needed because of individual learning characteristics, the nature of the message itself, its timing and influence of competing messages and influences from the environment.

However, a somewhat glib rule of thumb is that four categories of exposures might be needed. The first, to achieve awareness, the second exposure to relate the message to the target consumers' frame of reference (to show relevance), and the third to remind of the benefits of the product or service concerned. As we discuss in the next chapter, it is also the case sometimes that consumers seek reassurance, after they have purchased something, that they have done the right thing. So a fourth category of exposure can be helpful at that stage. We also suggest that there is likely to be a degree of repetition of exposures for each of these four stages, but the precise number depends on the product, the message, the consumer and a host of situational and competitive factors, making a definitive and universally applicable number of exposures difficult to state. The general point is surely pertinent, though, that repetition effectiveness increases over a certain number of exposures, then stabilizes and eventually declines.

www. Visit the following web site for a summary of classical and operant conditioning:
`http://www.wilderdom.com/personality/L9-1ClassicalConditioning.html`

Cognitive Learning

From a cognitive perspective, learning involves mental processes that are not necessarily reflected in overt behavioural changes. In other words, learning occurs whether or not there is an observable behavioural change in the learner and hence the need to look beyond the stimulus–response processes. The cognitive approach is sometimes equated with the mind being a black box with a stimulus being the input and a response being the output. With cognitive learning the focus is very much on what happens within the black box (mind) and the nature of the cognitive processes involved in learning.

The cognitive learning approach puts emphasis on studying cognitive processes (e.g. logical reasoning, abstract thinking, imagination, insights and appreciation), which influence learning mechanisms. Here, learning is viewed as a process of relating new information to previously learned information in the mind. For instance, consumers often engage in **reasoning** when they encounter some information in their lives (e.g. brand information) and deduce their own conclusions regarding the information's suitability, relevance and importance to them. This may involve integration of new information with existing knowledge already stored in memory or the evaluation of a brand's attributes against some criteria to determine brand suitability. Consumers devote more effort, time and cognitive energy than with behavioural stimulus–response-based learning.

The level of involvement which a consumer has with the situation is important, too. We discuss involvement in the next chapter but it is worth mentioning the **passive learning** theory of Krugman (1965). He stated that when consumers are exposed to mass media, either they lack personal involvement or they exhibit a high degree of involvement. In the low-involvement mode, consumers process very little of the information received, but repeated exposures to the information leaves a basic perceptual structure in the mind leading to low-involvement learning. But even with low-involvement situations, learning is more than a mere stimulus–response sequence.

We can also learn by observing others, thinking about what they are doing and how it might apply to ourselves. The imitation of the behaviours of others is known as vicarious learning. Not only can a consumer observe the actions of others – and, when the perceived consequences of their actions are seen to be positive and attractive, the consumer may well imitate that behaviour – but also they can avoid those actions seen to be unattractive.

© Getty Images. Photographer: Dave Hogan/Stroger. Reproduced with permission

A range of consumer behaviours (such as shopping, interaction with sales assistants, brand selection and consumption) can be modelled for consumers who pattern their future actions on the basis of examples observed.

Gestalt Contributions to Learning

In the previous chapter we discussed gestalt approaches to perceptual organization. The gestalt school of psychology is also relevant here, in terms of explaining learning processes. A major figure within the gestalt school was Kohler, who proposed that learning took place in more of a cognitive way than the behavioural stimulus–response approach could achieve. He demonstrated this with a number of experiments with apes, and one ape in particular displayed **insight** by being able to put the components of a problem together to form a (greater) whole, or a solution. These experiments were conducted around the same time as Pavlov's but Kohler thought there was more to human learning than mere stimulus–response relationships. Kohler presented apes with a variety of puzzles.

One such puzzle involved an ape in an almost bare cage, with a bunch of bananas hanging from the roof. The architecture of the cage made the bananas difficult to reach. Kohler left a table in the corner of the cage. What the apes wanted was to learn how to get the bananas, but they were left to solve the problem on their own. Nothing much happened for some time until one ape, Sultan, eventually moved the table to be underneath the bananas, stood on the table and managed to reach the fruit. Kohler described the extra element of mental processing in the learning process needed to solve problems as 'insight'.

Photo: Martin Evans

The law of closure, the law of similarity and the law of continuity have already been discussed in Chapter 2 as contributing to how consumers can be encouraged to attend to and then interpret messages. We return to the gestalt approach here because, where consumers need to devote relatively significant amounts of mental processing to learning about a marketing message/offering, that learning can itself be especially effective and enduring. This is because the consumer has to participate in the marketing activity and, as the old adage has it, *learning by doing* is often more effective.

So the marketing implication is that because the 'problem' is not solved at the immediate superficial level, by encouraging participation, marketers are tapping into this process of insight.

EXAMPLE 3.2

The British Army wanted to tempt sceptics to consider joining the service, by enticing them through TV and web channels. The law of continuity could be reflected in recent TV commercials for the Army. The TV provides a film clip of an incident but stops abruptly and directs the viewer to the web site for a further installment and additional information. The campaign, created by Publicis Dialog, told the personal stories of soldiers. They started on TV, radio and print and continued on armyjobs.mod.uk.

The campaign achieved 207 987 unique visits in the first month and, to date, there have been 290 000 Army pathfinder conversions.

EXAMPLE 3.3

To celebrate the '30 years in the making' proposition for the launch of its new Golf MK5. Volkswagen took over all advertising in an issue of *Auto Express*, backing this up with a special insert designed to cultivate prospects for future marketing activity, as well as for its prospect conversion programme, which feeds people's details to dealers when they are most likely to be responsive to offers.

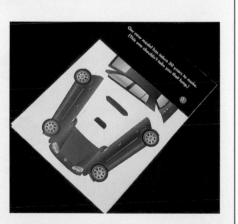

Not only did the insert encourage interactivity by giving readers the opportunity to make a paper model of their own Golf, but it incentivized response with the chance of winning a Bang & Olufsen TV – an aspirational product for this audience. The ad allowed prospects to respond via three channels: a coupon; by phone; and online.

Not only did Volkswagen get a 4.05 response rate, but it also received calls asking for more copies of the insert. This gathered 5 271 prospects at a cost per response of just £5.68.

Another example of encouraging more effective learning through 'doing' was reflected in an Oxfam mailing. This included a tape measure which could be used to measure whether one's child's arm was small enough that they could be classified as suffering from malnutrition, as given in enclosed tables of wrist diameters of malnourished children. The process of comparing a well-fed Western child with a starving one in a poor country adds more to learning about the general issue than a mere copy headline requesting donations to Oxfam.

A somewhat more dubious example comes from France and concerns a poster campaign. The first poster showed a bikini-clad woman and copy to the effect that in two days' time she would remove her top half. Two days later another poster appeared with the woman topless and copy promising the bottom half would be removed in another two days. Sure enough on the appointed day another version appeared with the woman, now naked with her back to the camera! The copy this time merely stated that the company keeps its promises. The objective here was to show potential advertisers (the poster was run by the poster owners themselves) that the poster *medium* could produce more responses than many clients had thought.

In this way, the campaign used the gestalt law of continuity because the images told a story which needed all three, in sequence, to make sense. The approach required the recipient to engage with the story, which tapped insightful learning. Although this would probably have been ambiguous to the consumer, it would make more sense to advertisers who were sceptical about the poster medium being able to be responsive within days rather than the common belief (at the time) that a poster could only be held for a month.

Figure 3.10: Learn by participative 'doing'
Reproduced by permission of Proximity London and Volkswagen Group UK Ltd.

THINKBOX

Discuss gestalt psychology and its role in developing 'participative' marketing messages. Does 'tapping insight' work for you, when you are encouraged to 'learn by doing' when marketing activity uses gestalt laws?

It is also suggested that younger segments are more interested in participative marketing messages than are older segments – do you see this among the young people you know? Why, or why not?

Can the 'advertising crossword puzzle' sometimes detract from the message to be learnt: we play the game and spot as many films from the mosaic of images, but don't learn the basic message of entering a competition by drinking more Stella Artois?

Stimulus Generalization and Discrimination

Once learned, a consumer can often extend their response to other similar stimuli. For instance, in the case of a popular brand, consumers are likely to be already familiar with the brand and are likely to hold some favourable, strong and unique brand-related images and associations in memory. On the basis of this, and using the principle of stimulus generalization, the brand name can be extended to new product categories, hoping that consumers will react positively to the new products. This practice is known as 'family branding strategy' and is very popular among marketers. Other marketers encourage stimulus generalization (that is, usually, making their brand look and sound like a competitor), hoping that the consumers' feelings for the competitor's brand will be generalized to their own brand. Also, as discussed on Chapter 1, by using similar packaging to national brands, own label brands can be perceived in a similar light and this can reduce the need for spending as much on promotional activity as is spent on national brands. This is also why some national brands defend their packaging or logos with vigorous litigation against those who copy them (Jack, 2007).

'Stimulus discrimination' refers to consumers learning to make different responses to similar stimuli. Some consumers have strong brand preferences and learn to discriminate among essentially identical products. Marketers of well-known brands often aim to make their brand distinctive in consumers' minds so that the consumer will discriminate and associate positive feelings only with their brands and not with their look-alikes. But, as we discussed in Chapter 2, consumers do not always discriminate: remember the case of Pretty Polly and Aristoc tights?

Measurement of Learning

Most measurements of learning involve some verbal response to interviewer questions. The answers indicate the degree of awareness, recognition and/or recall aroused in the respondents by the (e.g.) advertising. What is measured is the proportion of each sample who, on being shown an advertisement, claim to have noted it (the **recognition method**), or who, on being shown a brand advertised in a magazine they have read, can 'play back' enough of the advertisement to indicate that they have in fact seen it (the **aided recall method**).

The limitation common to these studies is that the respondent's claim of having been exposed to advertising cannot be taken at face value. Recognition scores do not necessarily decrease with the increase in time since reading, through memory loss, as might have been expected. This suggests that the respondent was 'recognizing', not the advertisement they had actually seen, but the likelihood that this was the kind of advertisement they would have noted, given the opportunity. Recognition could also result from previous purchases rather than be the cause of later ones.

Respondents also sometimes claim to recognize 'control' advertisements they could not have seen. The extent of misclaiming can be related to the respondent's interest in the product advertised, and other personal characteristics. Such studies also appear to be ineffective as predictors of future behaviour. What is retained by respondents may have nothing to do with their subsequent purchases. **Selective retention** operates here as well. Indeed the selective processes affect all stages so far – **selective exposure, selective attention, selective perception** and selective retention. The techniques and theory on which to base marketing approaches, however, provide potential means for ensuring a reasonable degree of uniformity of response even though there is equally the potential for individualistic responses.

KNOWLEDGE AND EXPERTISE

Knowledge is what we know and what we have stored in our memory as a function of learning. Knowledge can be of two types: objective knowledge is the actual information about a stimulus stored in the memory and subjective knowledge reflects our own perceptions of what or how much we know about the stimulus (Park *et al.*, 1994). What consumers think they know and what they actually know can be different and the level of correspondence between the two is called calibration. Marketers are often interested in creating, reinforcing and measuring consumer brand knowledge, which can be defined in terms of the personal meaning about a brand including brand features, brand attributes, benefits provided by the brand, brand imagery, thoughts and feelings associated with the brand and attitudes and experiences relevant to the brand (Keller, 2003). More specifically, advertisers are interested in finding out the extent to which consumers have stored brand-related information in their short-term or long-term memories. Earlier, it was stated that the long-term memory organizes and stores new information by linking it up with the existing information. Hence, long-term memory is a network of nodes, which represents stored information or concepts, and connecting links, which represent the strength of association between nodes (Anderson, 1983). As per Keller (1987), exposure to advertising can produce different types of nodes in our memories such as brand specific information (e.g. its benefits, features, attributes), advertisement specific information (e.g. the message, style, tone), the identity of advertised brand, the way product works and affective responses (e.g. positive emotions). The information stored in the memory can be influenced and modified as a consequence of our experiences with the brand and other means such as word of mouth information.

Moreover, it was stated earlier that the retrieval as a memory process (Figure 3.2) controls the flow of information from long- to short-term memory as and when the information is needed to be recalled. There could be many clues or prompts that could help stimulate recall and retrieval of a stored piece of information from long-term memory. When a specific cue (known as a recognition cue) such as a familiar name is matched exactly against the contents of our long-term memory, we recognize that name. However, there are occasions when we use a general cue to search memory and hence the cue is known as a recall cue.

In a marketing context, many studies have demonstrated that consumers use two types of cues during decision making: intrinsic information cues and extrinsic information cues. Intrinsic cues are those that are specific to a particular product and include the physical attributes such as shape, design, style and ingredients of a product (Lee and Lou, 1996; Ulgado and Lee, 1993). On the other hand, extrinsic cues are considered to be not part of the physical product itself although they are product related (e.g. price, brand name, country of origin). Both intrinsic and extrinsic cues can remind customers what they already know and hence help them in their product evaluations (Jamal and Goode, 2001). It is possible that over a period of time, consumers may become more aware of the extrinsic information cues and thus may rely more heavily on them during the product evaluations than the intrinsic cues. Richardson *et al.* (1994), for instance, examined the relative importance of extrinsic versus intrinsic cues in determining perceptions of store brand quality for five products (i.e. regular potato chips, French onion chip dip, chocolate chip cookies, cheese slices, and grape jelly). Findings suggested that evaluations of store brand grocery items were mainly driven by extrinsic cues rather than intrinsic cues.

THINKBOX

To what extent do you really know about different brands? Compare and contrast your brand knowledge for different brands within each of the following product categories:

a) Cereals
b) Window double glazing
c) Life insurance
d) Computer games

In practical terms, some consumers may be more knowledgeable than others depending on their interactions and familiarity with the brand (e.g. past experiences) and their levels of expertise, which refers to an ability to perform product or brand related tasks successfully as well as an understanding of and knowledge about various attributes in a product/service category (Alba and Hutchinson, 1987). Consumer research has suggested a number of ways in which expert consumers are very different from novice customers and Table 3.2 compares and contrasts some of these differences. Interestingly, sometimes consumers can overestimate their expertise, which may cause them to believe that getting additional information may not provide them with any new facts and hence they may not process the information properly.

ATTITUDES

If the hierarchy of effects 'sequence' has 'worked' so far, then the message has:

- been communicated via appropriate vehicles to reach the target market
- gained attention
- been interpreted the intended way
- been remembered in the intended way.

We are now concerned with developing favourable **attitudes** toward the marketing offering/message.

In simple terms, an attitude is a complex mental state involving what we know, our feelings, our values and dispositions to act in certain ways. As per Loudon and Della Bitta (1993), an attitude is 'an

Experts in comparison with novices are more likely to:	Novices in comparison with experts are more likely to:
– Search for new information – Have highly developed conceptual structures, and as such, are better equipped to understand the meaning of new information – Have enhanced skills in distinguishing between important and unimportant and relevant and irrelevant information – Restrict acquisition to relevant and important information – Process information more deeply to identify what is relevant and what is not	– Process information selectively – Select information on the basis of expediency rather than relevance or importance – Are less able to comprehend and evaluate product related facts – Select peripheral cues in the message – Use heuristic processing and utilize information cues such as brand image, price, and country of origin – Weight those attributes that are easily understood

Table 3.2: Experts vs novices: a comparison of some of the differences

enduring organization of motivational, emotional, perceptual and cognitive process with respect to some aspects of the individual's world'. This is useful, especially at this stage in the book, because it serves to reinforce the integration of some of the concepts explored so far (e.g. motivation, perception and learning).

A person's attitude is a major outcome of the learning processes that we discussed earlier in the chapter. That is, on the basis of whatever is learned about the stimulus or object, an individual develops either a liking or a disliking towards it. More specifically, an attitude refers to a predisposition to respond in a consistent or predictable manner to a stimulus. This explains why attitudes are always towards some stimulus (or 'object'). The stimulus can be anything, such as a physical or a social object (e.g. a brand, a retail store or even a person), an action (e.g. going to watch a football match or make a purchase), an idea (e.g. capitalism) or even advertising. From advertisers' point of view, consumers can have attitudes towards the advertisement itself or towards the advertised brand, both of which are important for them to understand.

The Structural Approach to Attitudes and Attitude Change

One of the most enduring approaches to attitudes is the proposition that an attitude has three components: cognitive (beliefs), affective (emotions) and conative (intentions) (Figure 3.11):

• A *cognitive* component – this consists of a person's beliefs or knowledge about an issue or an object, such as the reliability of a car or its fuel consumption. These beliefs might not be accurate in terms of product specifications or objective assessments of reliability, but are in many ways more important because they reflect how the individual perceives the case to be, even if there is a mismatch between their beliefs and reality.
• An *affective* component – this consists of a person's feelings or emotions about the issue of the object; these feelings can be 'positive' or 'negative'. These are based on the beliefs about the object that the individual holds.

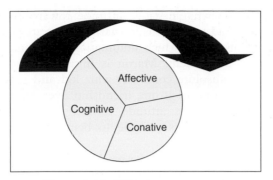

Figure 3.11: **Attitude components**

• A *behavioural* (conative) component – this consists of how the individual is likely to respond to the object based on what they know about it and how they feel about it; that is, that individual's 'readiness to respond behaviourally' to the object.

This approach has been especially useful in researching attitudes (see later section) because it provides a framework for devising questions that cover each component in order to be able to measure attitudes holistically.

The structural approach also helps in the definition of communications objectives, message creation and campaign evaluation. Objectives can be defined by discovering the nature of beliefs with regard to the marketing 'object', whether 'affect' is favourable or unfavourable, and whether the target audience exhibits any intention to buy. Messages can be tailored depending on what is discovered during this analysis. Campaigns may also evaluated by measuring these same dimensions over the course of the campaign (and before–after it) in order to identify if it changes attitudes.

Balance Theory

Related to the concept of cognitive and affective components is Heider's (1958) balance theory, which argues that consumers try to maintain a degree of balance between cognitive and affective components and in this respect the approach is congruent with cognitive consistency. If we experience inconsistency between the components, we will change our attitude in order to create harmony. The theory provides a 'triad' framework of the consumer, the attitude 'object' and some other person (Figure 3.12).

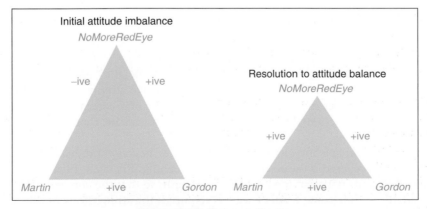

Figure 3.12: Balance theory

For example, Martin has a somewhat negative attitude toward Microsoft because he perceives it as having a world-dominating and monopolistic marketing strategy. Microsoft introduces a new software product called 'NoMoreRedEye' which automatically eliminates red eye from digital photographs as Windows Explorer opens them. Martin is initially negative toward 'NoMoreRedEye'. However, his friend Gordon is an absolute computer whiz kid and recommends the product highly. Martin's attitude toward Gordon is one of strong friendship over many years. The imbalance needs resolving. Martin could either change his attitude toward Gordon or toward 'NoMoreRedEye'. In this case he changes (but only just) his attitude to being more positive toward 'NoMoreRed-Eye'.

The balance theory has important implications for marketers and is yet another explanation of the use of celebrities in marketing messages. A brand toward which a consumer has a slightly negative attitude can be seen in a different light if a celebrity who is especially liked by the consumer is used to endorse it and thereby transfers the positive attitude to the brand.

www. In Chapter 1 we discussed the means–end chain approach to uncovering motives and values, and recommended an article on this to you. That same article also incorporates Heider's balance theory within the means–end chain method, and is accessed via the accompanying book web site at www.wileyeurope.com/college/evans:

Woodside A G (2004) Advancing Means-End Chains by Incorporating Heider's Balance Theory and Fournier's Consumer-Brand Relationship Typology, Psychology and Marketing, Vol 21 No 4 pp 279–294

THINKBOX

Have you ever changed any attitudes in the way implied by Heider's balance theory? Why or why not?

How else could the theory be used by marketers and consumers?

Attitude Measures

Marketers are often keen to discover consumers' attitudes towards their product offerings or the offering of their competitors. They can measure attitudes using different rating scales. However, measuring attitudes requires special consideration because it is far too easy and superficial to ask a respondent a question like this: 'What is your attitude towards Bloggo Brand?' only to receive a reply along the lines of 'I like it', or 'It's all right'. While such feelings may be important, it would be of greater use to uncover the reasons for such feelings and the type of actions in which they are likely to result; that is, using the tri-component structural approach to attitudes.

If intentions are based on specific elements of knowledge (beliefs) and evaluations, these beliefs and evaluations need to be discovered if the results are to be meaningfully used. Furthermore, such attributes are perceived by respondents with varying degrees of strength, so that the concept of degree in measuring attitudes is unavoidable. While some form of scale is required, the straightforward like/dislike continuum would be of only limited value. A more useful approach is to compile a series of scales, each measuring a

For the direct mail you receive, in general do you think it is:

	1	2	3	4	5	
Interesting	1	2	3	4	5	Uninteresting
Informative	1	2	3	4	5	Uninformative
Intrusive	1	2	3	4	5	Not intrusive
Entertaining	1	2	3	4	5	Not entertaining
Damaging to the environment	1	2	3	4	5	Not damaging to the environment
Relevant to you	1	2	3	4	5	Not relevant to you

Figure 3.13: **Semantic differential**

different attribute of the same attitude. If a department store wishes to identify any scope for improvement on the one hand and perceived strengths to accentuate on the other hand, there are a variety of attitude scaling methods that can be employed and these are outlined below.

Semantic Differential Scales

The **semantic differential** incorporates a set of five- or seven-point bipolar scales (Figure 3.13). The scales are characterized by opposites such as good/bad, active/passive, hot/cold, rough/smooth and strong/weak. For example, consumers can be asked to express their attitudes towards the direct mail that they receive by ticking or circling a number on the scale. One advantage of the semantic differential is that it provides a convenient way of comparing attitudes to different elements (e.g. the same scales could be used to elicit responses to mobile phone marketing, interactive television, email marketing, as well as direct mail) on the same scales, and a useful pictorial representation can be produced to compare attitudes to all of these objects.

Likert Scales

Respondents may be presented with a series of statements about the topic concerned, and asked to indicate their degree of agreement with each, according to a five-point scale ranging from 'strongly agree' to 'strongly disagree'. It is important, though difficult in practice, for the range of statements offered to cover the range of cognitive, affective and conative aspects that any given topic involves. Figure 3.14 shows a version of the Likert scaling technique, where a mixture of positive and negative statements allows respondents' consistency to be checked.

Both the semantic differential and Likert scales can be used quantitatively by assigning values to each scaling position, and average scores for all respondents' replies can be calculated, either for each scale or in an overall summation.

We have to be very careful with attitude measurement, however. As is often the case with the use of opinion polls to predict voting behaviour, respondents might not always reveal their true attitudes toward political parties or to their voting intentions. Indeed these intentions may change right up to the moment of slipping their voting card into the ballot box.

Across a range of attitude measurement studies, respondents frequently answer according to how they think the interviewer might like them to respond, or to how they think 'most' people would feel about the issue. The latter is called the **bandwagon effect** (Nancarrow *et al.*, 2004). Also, what people say they

Please indicate your level of agreement or disagreement with the following statements:

	Strongly agree				Strongly disagree
I like having product or service information communicated to me by organizations	1	2	3	4	5
I like to decide for myself when and where to look for product or service information	1	2	3	4	5
The more that organizations know about me, the better they can meet my needs	1	2	3	4	5
I really don't mind about marketers having my personal details	1	2	3	4	5
There is a need for strong laws to control the sharing of personal information	1	2	3	4	5
For the direct mail I receive, marketers have generally got my details correct	1	2	3	4	5
I like to deal with organizations over the phone	1	2	3	4	5
I like to deal with organizations through the post	1	2	3	4	5

Figure 3.14: Likert scaling

intend to do and what they actually do are usually quite different and frequently have no relevance to their attitudes. According to Kauffman *et al.* (1997), 'People lie consistently and people's behaviours are going to lag behind what they say.' Engel *et al.* (1995:394) agree with Kauffman *et al.* (1997) and state that:

> People do distort or hide their true feelings, particularly when the topic is heavily value laden such as alcohol and tobacco consumption, environmentalism and nutrition, yet accurate prediction of specific behaviour requires the use of specific measures that correspond to behaviour.

THINKBOX

Try to analyse the components of your attitudes towards the course you are studying. How might these be converted into a questionnaire to investigate students' attitudes toward the course?

Fishbein's Multi-Attribute Model (Attitude Toward Object Model)

According to Fishbein (1973), our attitude towards an 'object' (e.g. a product or a brand) is predicated upon what we consider to be an appropriate range of beliefs about that object and how we evaluate these. Respondents might be able to score brands or products along each semantic differential scale (belief) but they might not regard all bipolars as of equal importance or favourableness. So the idea is to elicit not only a rating along each belief scale, but also a favourableness rating of each scale. Multiplying the two for each scale and aggregating the scores provides a more meaningful analysis. The attitude is thus the summation of the weighted belief scores.

Please place an X on each of the following scales to indicate your beliefs about how these universities rate on these features:

	Strongly Agree	Agree	No View	Disagree	Strongly Disagree
I believe the University of Cardiff has excellent research ranking	X	4	3	2	1
I believe the University of Poppleton has excellent research ranking	5	4	3	X	1
I believe the quality of teaching at the University of Cardiff is good	5	X	3	2	1
I believe the quality of teaching at the University of Poppleton is good	5	4	X	2	1
I believe the social environment at the University of Cardiff is reasonably good	5	X	3	2	1
I believe the social environment at the University of Poppleton is reasonably good	X	4	3	2	1
I believe the University of Cardiff has excellent library facilities	5	4	X	2	1
I believe the University of Poppleton has excellent library facilities	5	4	3	X	1
I believe the University of Cardiff has very good computing facilities	5	4	X	2	1
I believe the University of Poppleton has very good computing facilities	5	4	3	X	1

Figure 3.15a John's beliefs about two universities

Please place an X on each of the following scales to indicate the extent to which each of the following is important to you:

	Strongly Agree	Agree	No View	Disagree	Strongly Disagree
It is important for me to study at a university with excellent research ranking	5	4	3	X	1
It is important for me to study at a university with good teaching quality	X	4	3	2	1
It is important for me to study at a university with a reasonably good social environment	X	4	3	2	1
It is important for me to study at a university with excellent library facilities	5	4	X	2	1
It is important for me to study at a university with very good computing facilities	5	4	X	2	1

Figure 3.15b Attribute importance by John

Attribute	Attribute importance	Attribute score for Poppleton	Attribute score for Cardiff
Quality of research	2	2	5
Quality of teaching	5	3	4
Library facilities	3	2	3
Social environment	5	5	4
Computing facilities	3	2	3
		56	68

Figure 3.15c John's overall attitude towards each of the universities

Figure 3.15: Illustration of Fishbein's multi-attribute model (expectancy value)
Worst score for a single attribute would be (importance) 5 x (rating) 1 = 5 and best score would be (importance) 5 x (rating) 5 = 25

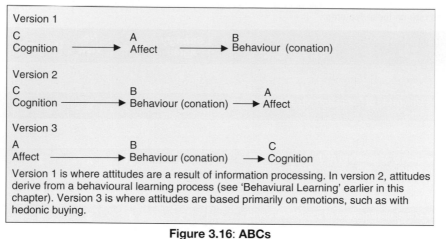

Figure 3.16: ABCs

Source: Adapted by the authors from Solomon *et al.*, 2003

For instance, imagine John is an A-level student and that he is going to university next year. He is asked to indicate his beliefs about two universities on a scale of 1 to 5 for each of the attributes such as research quality, teaching quality, library facilities, social environment and computing facilities (Figure 3.15a). John is then asked to indicate the importance *to him* of each of the attributes using a scale of 1 to 5 (Figure 3.15b). The ranking scores for each attribute are reported in the second and third columns of Figure 3.15c. The results for attribute importance are reported in the first column of Figure 3.16c. The researcher then multiplies scores for each of the attributes with its corresponding importance score and adds them together. The summed weighted belief scores of 56 and 68 represent John's attitudes towards each university.

Alternative Attitude Models

As we have seen, there are clear uses of the tri-component approach within the structural approach to attitudes but at the same there are criticisms of it and there are different views as to the sequence between cognition, affect and conation.

For example, the conative component is sometimes not seen as a determinant of consumer attitudes, rather attitudes are viewed as *determining* the conative component. That is, a person's behavioural intentions will depend on their attitudes. It is not difficult to find reports that cast doubt on the relationship between consumer attitudes and behaviour in the marketplace (Festinger, 1964; Wicker, 1969; Calder and Ross, 1973).

So, different sequences are available for how cognition, affect and conation operate. Solomon *et al.* (2003) provide a summary of these. They apply the hierarchy of effects specifically to attitudes. They call conation 'behaviour' (but remember this is actually *intention* to behave, not actual behaviour) and, as a result, use the 'ABC' acronym (Figure 3.16).

Thus there is a continuing debate about how attitudes predict behaviour, regardless of their structure and formation. Having said this, it can be assumed that some knowledge of an individual's attitude will increase the likelihood of understanding the individual's intended and actual behaviour. The most significant development in the use of attitudes as a predictor of behaviour has probably been the recognition of additional predicting variables, used to overcome some of the problems. For example, it is also likely that attitudes depend to some extent on the level of the involvement in the topic or purchase issue, by each individual. We recognize this and explore the nature and implications of 'involvement' in the next chapter.

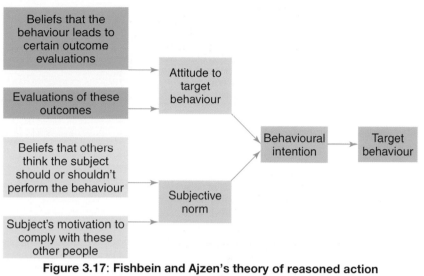

Figure 3.17: Fishbein and Ajzen's theory of reasoned action
M Fishbein and I Ajzen, Belief, Attitude, Intention and Behavior, Reading, MA: Addison-Wesley, 1975.

Other such variables might be unpredicted and uncontrollable, such as social or peer pressure. We explore these issues as specific concepts in consumer behaviour in Chapter 7 but they also contribute to another set of attitude models discussed in this chapter. The potential influence of both attitudes and social influences is explicitly recognized in Fishbein and Ajzen's (1975) theories of reasoned action and planned behaviour.

The Theory of Reasoned Action

The theory of reasoned action extends the original tri-component model by the inclusion of what other (relevant) people might be perceived to think about the topic (object). This is the key addition and is called the 'subjective norm'. Figure 3.17 graphically summarizes this theory.

The Theory of Planned Behaviour

The theory of planned behaviour states that the influence of your partner or parents will play an important part in your decision, and the amount of knowledge that you have, be it instrumental (i.e. knowledge-based) or experiential (i.e. feelings-based), will also affect your decision. Other factors could affect attitude here, such as a lack of need, a lack of finance, change in circumstances and a lack of motivation. The theory of planned behaviour is an extension of reasoned action theory (Ajzen, 1988; Ajzen and Madden, 1986). Attitude toward the behaviour and subjective norm are further extended to include perceived control. This factor refers to ease or difficulty in performing the behaviour and it is assumed to reflect past experience as well as anticipated obstacles (Figure 3.18).

This model predicts behaviour by the intention to perform that behaviour. Behavioural intention is then split into three elements: attitude towards the behaviour, subjective norm, and perceived behavioural control. Attitude towards behaviour is predicted by salient beliefs about a behaviour, weighted by the subject's estimation of the likelihood that performing the behaviour will result in a given outcome. Subjective norm is predictive by normative beliefs about what relevant other people (salient others) would advise, modified by the subject's motivation to comply with the advice of those people. Perceived behavioural control is measured through control beliefs that may help or hinder the individual in carrying out that behaviour (Fishbein and Ajzen, 1975).

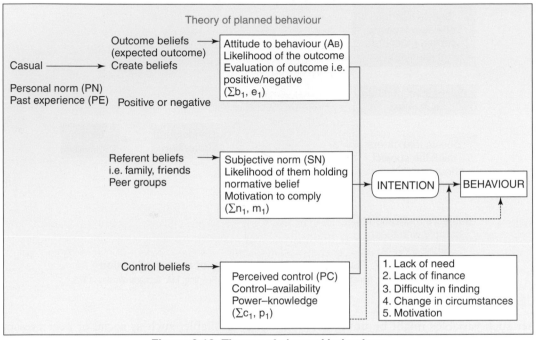

Figure 3.18: Theory of planned behaviour
The correlation is stronger if you have the relevant strength.
Normative salient beliefs determine the thoughts easily brought to mind.
Global measures to cover AB, SN and PC
Product sum Σb_1, e_1, Σn_1 and $\Sigma\, c_1\, p_1$
Source: M Fishbein and I Ajzen, Belief, Attitude, Intention and Behavior, Reading, MA, Addison-Wesley, 1975, p 48

The Functional Approach to Attitudes

Attitudes can serve many functions for consumers as proposed by Katz (1960) and therefore it is important for marketers to study and understand these functions. He attributes four functions to attitudes:

1. The instrumental function, in which the individual assesses the utility of objects for the attainment of their goals;
2. The ego-defensive function, in which the individual uses attitudes to protect their **self-image** by emphasizing their place in their social world;
3. The value-expressive function, by which the individual expresses their central values and self to others; and
4. The knowledge function, by which the individual constructs the meaning of their world, or gives explanation to both physical and metaphysical phenomena.

Instrumental Function

This is an extension of operant or instrumental learning as discussed earlier in this chapter. If a purchasing experience is satisfying (rewarding), not only are we more likely to repeat it but also we are likely to develop favourable attitudes toward it.

Ego-Defensive Function

There might be an initial desire for a product but a consumer might not be able to afford, for example, a sports car. They might develop unfavourable attitudes toward it by 'defending' their psyche by deciding such a car is, actually, too flashy and ostentatious for someone in middle age. They might also decide that it would be totally unpractical for collecting those shelving units from the local DIY store and indeed someone who has developed a bit of middle-aged spread might find difficulty getting in to the car and even greater difficulty getting out.

Value-Expressive Function

Whereas ego-defensive attitudes actually cover up true feelings (e.g. toward that sports car), value-expressive attitudes deliberately communicate these true feelings, values and self-image (see Chapter 6 for coverage of self-image).

The brands we buy and display or talk about can reflect inner values and our self-image. For example, the purchase of a Harley Davidson motorbike often goes beyond its functions as a mode of transport and allows the values and self-image of the owner to be observable. The consumer who tries to be an ethical consumer might seek a savings account from a financial services company which makes a point about only investing ethically (e.g. not in arms companies or companies which exploit child labour in poor countries, etc.). In such cases, the consumer will display positive attitudes toward Harley Davidson, or the Cooperative Bank, even if their friends don't want to consume the same products/services.

Knowledge Function

As we saw in the previous chapter, we do not 'expose' ourselves to all marketing media/messages and certainly don't 'attend' to the increasing bombardment of marketing activity which is coming through a plethora of media. Indeed attitudes help in the filtering process and extend the 'selective' concepts discussed in the previous chapter. For example, consumers who are especially interested in cars will have favourable attitudes toward almost any new marketing activity concerned with cars.

THINKBOX

How do your attitudes affect your purchasing of durable products?

Changing Attitudes and Behaviour

A great deal of marketing effort is aimed at persuasion, which may be defined for our purposes as 'attempted attitude and behaviour change'. Social psychology has been helpful in this regard in that certain principles of attitude change have been presented in the literature of that discipline. Attitude change remains, none the less, an inexact science.

Attitudes are essentially stable structures and are not easily modified. Thus the first fact on which social psychologists and marketers agree firmly is that attitude change is a difficult and expensive enterprise.

Marketers can think of the attitude components and attempt to focus on one of them in their efforts to change attitudes. For example, in the 2005 UK general elections, the Labour Party produced a leaflet aimed at British Muslims to change their cognitions or beliefs by claiming that Labour's long-standing ties with British Muslims helped Labour deliver a range of benefits for the British Muslim community. The idea here was to change British Muslims' attitudes towards Labour by drawing attention to a number of benefits (which would otherwise go unnoticed) in the context of Labour's controversial involvement in the Iraq war.

Credibility and Discrepancy

Whatever the marketing goals are, the marketing manager endeavours to produce the maximum of attitude change in the market, given budgetary and time constraints. The extent to which this succeeds depends on the credibility attributed to the source of marketing messages by the audience.

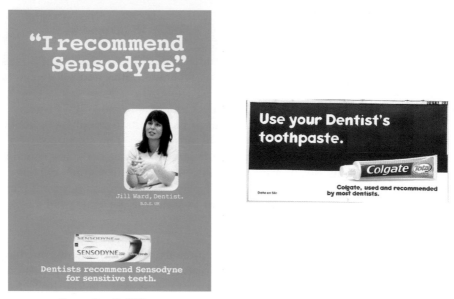

Source: GlaxoSmithKline

Credibility includes both expertise and trustworthiness (Zimbardo and Ebbesen, 1970). In a seminal study into credibility effects, Hovland and Weiss (1951) showed that Americans were more likely to change their attitudes to believe in the possibility of building atomic-powered submarines when a message arguing that this could be done was attributed to a highly credible source, namely J. Robert Oppenheimer, the famous physicist. Persons who were led to believe that the source of the message was the official Russian newspaper *Pravda* were very unlikely to believe that atomic submarines were a feasible proposition! At the time the Americans perceived *Pravda* to be little more than a propaganda tool of (iron curtain) Russia.

Advertisements which feature popular singers, actors, footballers and so on (e.g. Figure 3.8, the use of Madonna in a Versace advertisement) attempt to persuade members of the audience to ascribe the message they receive to a highly credible source. If 'experts' endorse a product, their opinion appears more trustworthy and, especially in view of the fact that many consumers tend to discount much of what persuasive advertising claims, the use of a credible source may be crucial in gaining the audience's attention and in ensuring that selective perception does not cause the message to be screened before it is even considered. (See, also, our coverage of different types of 'power' that social groups can wield, in Chapter 7.)

The exploitation of such methods of opinion change is limited, however. Hovland *et al.* (1953) report that after a few weeks the positive influence of highly credible message sources and the negative effects of low-credibility sources are extinguished. This has important budgetary implications for advertising. Often expensive celebrities are used in advertising as highly credible sources, but their continued use may not only be costly but also may produce diminishing returns relatively quickly in terms of the impact of their credibility.

THINKBOX

It is worth considering a recent development in the role of trust in changing attitudes. One of the hormones found naturally in the body is oxytocin. When subjects inhaled extra oxytocin in an experiment, it was found to have the effect of increasing trust on the part of the person inhaling.

Could it be that the dissemination of oxytocin via, for example, air-conditioning systems in car showrooms might have the effect of enhancing the trust invested in car salespeople? Although it is unlikely that we currently have the technology for achieving this, it raises issues for the future.

Do some research to investigate the current state of this issue, and think about your own position on the value – and ethics – of the approach.

(Kosfeld *et al.*, 2005)

Content and Organization

The content and organization of marketing communications also have implications for the modification of consumers' attitudes. One of the recurrent themes in attitude research is the role that fear plays in persuading people to alter their opinions and behaviour. A considerable body of research findings that relate fear to persuasion has been accumulated, as is shown by a classic review by Sternthal and Craig (1974). First, persuasion through fear is closely related to the credibility of the message's source. The higher the credibility of the originator, the greater the amount of attitude (and, generally, behavioural) change that occurs directly as a result of the fear appeal. This seems to be the case because greater cognitive dissonance (see Chapter 4) can be created when the audience believes that the message source is authoritative than when it is able to deprecate the fear appeal's origin, and cognitive dissonance is resolved through a change in attitude or behaviour or both. Where a low-credibility source is used, message recipients are likely to avoid the fear-inducing message by means of selective attention and perception.

Second, Sternthal and Craig show that characteristics of the message's audience may moderate fear appeals as happens for those whose coping ability is less developed; persons high in self-esteem are vulnerable to fear appeals as are those whose 'perceived vulnerability' is low – e.g. non-smokers or light smokers perceive themselves as having low vulnerability to lung cancer and are more easily persuaded by fear appeals related to cancer than are heavy smokers.

Third, fear appeals are usually effective only when a means of escape from the threatened consequences is clearly depicted in the message. Failure to indicate how the message recipient can avoid the threatened effects of non-compliance with what the message advocates may simply result in the recipient's avoiding the message itself by means of perceptual defence mechanisms. This is important because it has been shown that threats of a social nature (giving offence to others or being ostracized) is more effective than threats of physical consequences. People appear to assume that horrifying things simply will not happen to them and are not easily persuaded to, say, give up smoking, by being shown the physical consequences.

It is probably easier in the case of threats of social disapproval to indicate to the audience how the more unpleasant consequences of their behaviour can be avoided.

For example, anti-drink-driving campaigns may be more effective when they portray the effects on family and loved ones of a tragic death of a child due to drink-driving than if the message focuses on the drink-driver. The same can be said about advertising that promotes social causes such as reduction of violence against women. For instant, the advertisements by Women's Aid shown in Figure 3.19 uses shocking images to change our attitudes towards domestic violence.

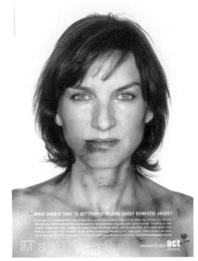

Figure 3.19: **Image used in a Women's Aid campaign**
Source: Women's Aid

EXAMPLE 3.4

Figure 3.20: Generating empathy
©MS Society UK/Saatchi & Saatchi. Reproduced by permission

Saatchi & Saatchi devised a campaign for the Multiple Sclerosis Society to coincide with the London Marathon. The ads appeared in the national press and on cross-track posters in the London Underground. The aim was to contrast the debilitating effects of the disease with the able-bodied runners, using a switch device to show the unpredictable way in which MS can switch off parts of the body (Figure 3.20). Part of the problem for the agency was the recognition that people donate to charities for which they feel empathy, yet relatively few have direct experience of MS. Hitting the right tone was essential to generate that empathy.

Figure 3.21: Fear of Aging: Nivea

This case study demonstrates the sensitive yet powerful use of a fear appeal to change attitudes toward multiple sclerosis (DMA Awards 2003). Fears such as the fear of aging is demonstrated in Figure 3.21.

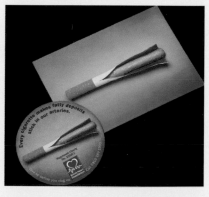

One of the best remembered ads of 2004, the British Heart Foundation's fatty cigarettes campaign, hit the message home for many smokers of just what smoking was doing to their bodies.

Judges said that this entry showed an 'insert into how to cut through what can be very bland messages' in this type of campaign. Showing a fatty substance dripping out of cigarettes, the ad explained how cigarettes cause a fatty build-up in the arteries. Unlike many anti-smoking campaigns, it focused on the cigarette rather than the smoker, an approach research has shown is more likely to draw in the campaign's core target market of serial quitters.

The campaign launched on January 1 – a time 23 per cent of smokers make a new year's resolution to give up the habit. Supported with poster, press and ambient activity, the campaign also generated £900 000 of free publicity in the form of press articles and coverage on all TV networks' new programmes.

Smokers responded in droves. The British Heart Foundation recorded 83 635 visits to the campaign microsite during January and February alone, and of the 54 219 smokers who made contact, 90 per cent were from the core audience of repeat quitters. Seven weeks after the end of the campaign, 34 per cent of callers still hadn't touched a cigarette.

Figure 3.22: **Two-sided appeal**
This accepts that attitudes toward Marmite are quite polarized and even plays on this to good effect.
©Unilever. Reproduced by permission

A consideration which also concerns the content and structuring of advertising messages is that of the one-sided/**two-sided appeal** (Figure 3.22). Should persuasive messages include elements which are unfavourable to the product or service which is being marketed? On the face of it there might appear to be no case for presenting potentially damaging information to any audience, no matter how sophisticated and educated it may be, for any amount of damage to the company's image or its brand images must surely result in lost sales and reduced profit. Despite such natural misgivings, there is fairly conclusive evidence that, within a specified context, two-sided appeals (those which incorporate arguments for and against the product or brand) may be more effective than one-sided appeals.

The constraints on this technique are threefold:

1. The market or segment receiving this message must be currently unconvinced of the message's attractiveness (i.e. consumers who are at present not buying the brand and those whose current attitudes make them unlikely to do so in the near future are ideal targets for two-sided appeals).
2. Those most persuaded by the two-sided appeal tend to be highly educated (the academic practice of presenting both sides of an argument seems to appeal to those who have received large amounts of formal education).
3. The technique is advisable where there is a likelihood that the audience will find out about the less attractive (or even unattractive) side of the product anyway (Figure 3.23).

Repetition

As discussed above, with respect to learning, repeating persuasive messages is important and this also helps develop and change attitudes. Indeed learning theory is useful in assessing the extent to which repetition contributes to attitude change. In most cases, repetition certainly appears to be positively related to consumers' expressed intentions to buy, and these are often a good guide to purchasing behaviour. There is always the possibility, however, that constant repetition may lead to boredom and psychological fatigue and that it may then reduce the consumer's intention to buy. The consumer's rate of learning (change in behaviour) is, as we have seen, related to reinforcement through experience of the advertiser's claims and so it is likely that repetition to people who do not buy the product or who have had unfavourable experiences with it may serve only to instill existing negative attitudes.

THINKBOX

Nudge Nudge...know what I mean?

On an assumption that people seem to act irrationally or at least don't always make 'good' decisions, Thaler and Sunstein (2008) suggest that situations can be contrived in which people can feel that they make decisions in their own best interests. This 'choice architecture' can 'nudge' people into decision making that the persuader desires.

The reader is encouraged to explore 'Nudge', not least in the political context that, in 2008, it became a hot topic (the consequences of which post-date our writing!).

In Wisconsin, USA, rural drinking and driving by young men was a problem. There was status and driving powerful cars and drinking was seen as masculine within the peer group. The innovative solution to changing attitude and behaviour was to provide stretched limos at cost price. The logo of the scheme, Road Crew, emulated the Harvey Davidson approach. The combination was seen as a fun and convenient alternative which avoided drink-driving and by-passed the macho taboos.

Source: http://www.dot.wisconsin.gov/library/publications/topic/safety/roadcrew-twopage.pdf

Attitude Reinforcement

An alternative to changing attitudes is to reinforce those attitudes which already exist among consumers who are favourably disposed to the firm's product brand. There may be scope for increasing sales frequency or for developing new uses for the product. Associated with this is the creative use of word-of-mouth advertising, which will be dealt with in Chapter 9. Denigration of the opposition has also been suggested as an alternative to attitude change (Chapter 4).

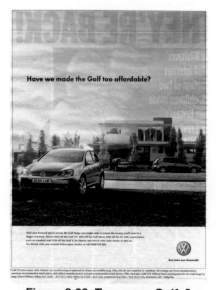

Figure 3.23: Too many Golfs?
This VW advertisement is mildly self-critical in that it questions the company's pricing policy.
Reproduced by permission of Volkswagen UK

Figure 3.24: Advertising to change public attitudes towards drink and driving by the Drinkaware Trust
(www.drinkawaretrust.org.uk)

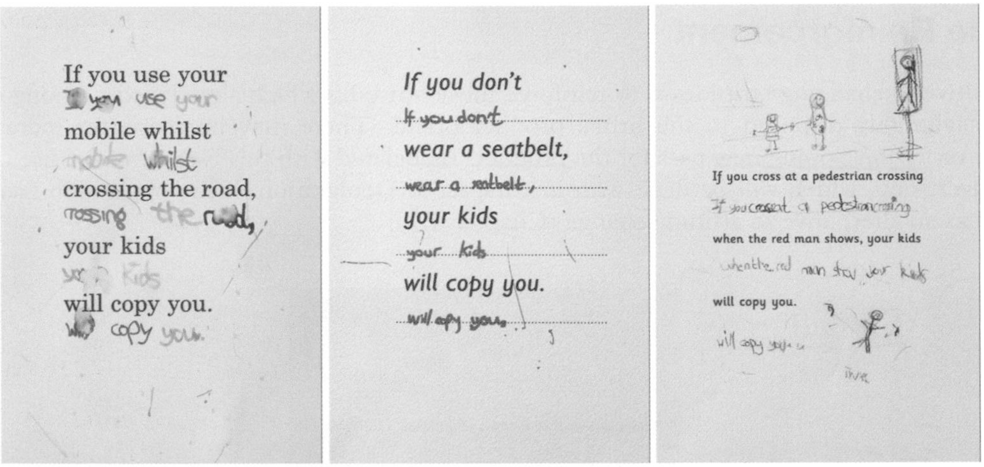

Figure 3.25: Advertising to change public attitudes towards wearing seat belts
http://www.thinkroadsafety.gov.uk/campaigns/parents

THINKBOX

Figures 3.24 and 3.25 illustrate some efforts made by social marketers with a view to change public attitudes towards drinking and driving and the wearing of seat belts while driving.

What factors make you change your attitude toward a company or brand?

Give examples of effective and ineffective attitude changing messages from your own experience.

SUMMARY

- We have seen that consumer behaviour is a process of learning; it is modified according to the customer's past experience and the objectives they have set.
- There are a variety of ways of analysing the learning process. We have explored the application within a consumer–marketer context, looking at the behavioural 'classical' and 'operant conditioning' approaches and the more cognitive (e.g. gestalt) approach.
- Then we examined 'attitudes', which refers to a predisposition to behave in a particular way when presented with a given stimulus, and attitudes towards people, places, products and things are classified as favourable (positive) or unfavourable (negative). Attitudes are composed of three elements or dimensions: cognitive, conative and affective. Behaviour and attitudes are related and each may influence the other, but attitudes and behaviour are not always entirely consistent, and it has even been claimed that attitudes may stem from behaviour rather than vice versa. For marketing, it is usually only important that attitudes and behaviour vary together in some consistent way. There are several ways of testing or measuring attitudes and some examples have been given.
- Attempts to change attitudes have included methods relating to the credibility of message sources and the amount of discrepancy involved in the communication. Discrepancy may be greater when the source's credibility is high. Fear appeals also work well when source credibility is high. Presenting both sides of an argument may induce more attitude change in an educated audience which is sceptical of the advertiser's claims.
- The next chapter takes us into the final stages of this model, namely the 'action' stage which serves to convert positive affective and conative attitudinal constructs into a behavioural outcome and then into post-purchase re-evaluation of this action.

QUESTIONS

1. Explain classical conditioning and operant conditioning. Using some print advertisements, discuss how these theories have been applied to achieve a desirable impact.

2. Find some press advertisements or packages that are good illustrations of the use of associationist learning. How effective are they likely to be? Why?

3. Analyse and evaluate the proposition that consumers learn effectively when messages encourage participation (e.g. the 'learning by doing' examples in this chapter).

4. In the text we state that memory and learning are related but different concepts. What is meant by this? Give examples of different types of memory. Explore the further relationship between learning, memory and knowledge and in what sense expert consumers are different from novice consumers.

5. How would the theory of reasoned action be applied to a study into consumer attitudes toward the use of mobile telephony by marketers? Design a questionnaire for a marketer.

Wanting to explore 18- to 24-year-old students' attitude towards receiving marketing messages via their mobile phones.

6. How would Katz's functions of attitudes apply to your own purchasing behaviour?

7. How good at changing attitudes are:
   a.   Fear appeals
   b.   Two-sided appeals
   Find ads that use these approaches. How could you use research findings to judge their effects?

FURTHER READING

Atkinson R L *et al.* **(eds)** (1999) *Introduction to Psychology*, 12th edn, Wadsworth. This classic psychology text provides more details of the underpinning psychological concepts we explore in Chapters 1–4. We especially recommend Atkinson *et al.*'s coverage of perception and learning.

East R (1997) *Consumer Behaviour: Advances and Applications in Marketing*, Prentice Hall. This consumer behaviour text has particularly useful chapters covering attitudes (for this chapter) and loyalty (for Chapter 10).

Shovlin C (2007) Cracking the Colour Code Marketing Week 11 October 28-29.

Till B D, Stanley S M and Priluck R (2008) Classical Conditioning and Celebrity Endorsers, Psychology and Marketing.

CHAPTER 4
CONSUMER RESPONSE TO MARKETING ACTIONS: 3
ACTION, POST-PURCHASE DISSONANCE, CONSUMER INVOLVEMENT

CHAPTER OBJECTIVES

After engaging with the material presented in this chapter and its associated exercises and reading, you should be able to:

- Explain techniques that encourage consumers to act upon marketing activities.
- Explain impulse buying and customer satisfaction as important concepts.
- Apply cognitive dissonance theory to help explain how consumers can respond after purchase.
- Explain involvement and discuss implications of levels of involvement for consumer behaviour and for the relevance of sequential models of response to marketing activity.

INTRODUCTION

The two previous chapters have taken us through most of the pre-purchase stages of our sequential model. We now complete these with the 'action' stage followed by what happens post-purchase (Figure 4.1). Marketers are not merely concerned with a one-off purchase but to encourage repeat purchase (as we discuss in Chapter 9, and loyal and even relational buying as we explore in Chapter 10). In this chapter, we provide a discussion and application of a variety of concepts which can help explain not only post-purchase behaviour (such as cognitive dissonance) but also **involvement** which can help marketers determine the extent and nature of the relevance of sequential (hierarchy of effects) models.

ACTION

The whole rationale behind this model is that there is no simple checklist of marketing activities that results in instant **action** by consumers. The previous stages of response move potential customers through pre-purchase events so that there is a better chance of the conversion of 'intend to buy' into 'buy'.

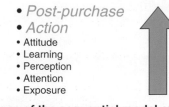

- *Post-purchase*
- *Action*
- Attitude
- Learning
- Perception
- Attention
- Exposure

Figure 4.1: **Final stages of the sequential model of response to marketing**

Impulse Buying

Even the gimmicks aimed at **impulse buying** (sometimes referred to as unplanned purchasing) are to some extent dependent on some level of prior understanding and involvement (see later in this chapter) in the product or service. For example, point of sale promotions will themselves be building upon the above sequence of events. Consumers engage in impulse buying when they experience a sudden but powerful and persistent urge to buy a product offering immediately, with diminished regard to the consequences of buying the offering (Rook, 1987). It is often an unplanned decision, which may happen in less than a second and is a common and prevalent feature of the marketplace. We may wrongly assume that impulse buying is associated only with low-value, low-involvement purchases (e.g. soft drinks, chocolates and potato crisps) but as per Rook (1987), it could also be associated with high-value and high-involvement products (e.g. VCRs, microwave ovens, and even a vacation cruise). According to Rook (1987), impulse buying is relatively extraordinary and exciting, emotional rather than rational and is likely to be perceived as bad rather than good. There appears to have been an increase in unplanned purchasing in UK; 44% of consumers in 2007 agreed that they easily give in to temptation when shopping compared with 31% in 1983 (Future Foundation, 2007). The same research suggested that younger consumers are especially susceptible: 69% of 15–24 s compared with just 255 of the over 65 s. This even extends to age differences concerning the rows that couples have over unplanned purchases which had not been previously agreed!

Greater affluence can fuel impulse buying: it can be seen to be not only more affordable but the risk can be tolerated more. The other side of the 'cash rich' scenario, is 'time poor' and as consumers become more time hungry they might bother less with planning shopping lists and hence buy more on a whim whilst in the store.

THINKBOX

Do you normally buy on impulse? Do you think it is a rational or an emotional decision?
Have you had rows with a partner over unplanned purchases?
Share your ideas with a friend who has also bought on impulse.

It might also be assumed that no 'pre-purchase' stages would be relevant with this, but Bayley and Nancarrow (1998) found that there are four styles of impulse buying and we can assume that pre-purchase stages are relevant for some of these: accelerator impulse, compensatory impulse, breakthrough impulse and blind impulse. Accelerator impulse buying is driven by a desire to stock up for a future need. For example, a housewife may buy on impulse to confirm that she is a good carer for her family. *Compensatory impulse* buying occurs when the buyer either feels 'down' and low in self-esteem and uses sudden purchases as a prop or if purchaser rewards themselves for achieving something or after completing a tedious or difficult chore and use a surprise purchase as a reward. In an old chocolate advertisement, for example, Cadbury depicted people achieving something and then rewarding themselves a medal; a CDM (Cadbury's Dairy Milk).

The *breakthrough impulse* buying is intriguing. It can include some high-value products such as cars and even houses! It appears that the purchaser suddenly decides that whatever underlying emotional conflict with which they have been wrestling can be resolved by a step change in their lives. 'A few years ago Winnie went out to buy a spare set of car keys and signed up for a new car' was how one respondent described an impulse purchase in this category. Another one revealed: 'After a row with his wife he jumped into the car to drive around and cool down. He drove past a house for sale and something made him stop. He put an offer on it there and then and went back to tell his wife the good news'. Finally, *blind impulse* buying is probably what we tend to think of as impulse buying: buying with no underlying purpose and no regard for the fulfilment of any needs of either a functional, social or psychological nature.

An earlier approach to impulse buying, by Stern (1962), identified four forms of impulse buying:

1. Pure impulse buying, where the consumer breaks a normal purchasing pattern by buying on sudden grounds of novelty or escapism.
2. Reminder impulse buying, where the item is suddenly 'remembered' as being wanted because the consumer recalls that stocks are low or that they intended at some point to buy it.
3. Suggestion impulse buying, where the consumer goes through a very rapid evaluation on the spur of the moment without any prior knowledge of the product.
4. Planned impulse buying, where the consumer intends to buy, but 'what' is not decided prior to the shopping trip. That is, they know they will buy something, perhaps on the basis of special offers. The 'specials' in stores such as Lidl provide an example of how some consumers know in advance that something from that range will be bought.

However, within the context of postmodern society, impulse buying can work as an act of freedom allowing consumers to fulfill their desires and feel in full control of their lives (Thompson *et al.*, 1990). It can also allow consumers to reinforce their self-identities. That would probably explain why consumers often end up buying clothes on impulse. One would also imagine that impulse buying is linked to hedonistic shopping experiences whereby sense of adventure and thrill, feelings of excitement and escapism can all lead to a reduction of self-control. Buying on impulse can also be a personality trait (called 'impulsiveness trait'), which refers to a person's tendency to buy spontaneously, unreflectively, immediately and kinetically (Rook and Fisher, 1995). That is a consumer with a high impulsiveness trait is likely to be more receptive and open towards buying spontaneously.

Certain retail environments such as airports, funfairs, casinos and even car boot sales appear to be particularly suitable for impulse buying. For instance, while waiting at the airport, consumers can engage in impulse buying for a variety of reasons (Table 4.1). Crawford and Melawar (2003) argued that marketers could take a number of steps to increase the possibility that consumers will buy on impulse in environments such as airports. They suggested reducing stress levels and anxiety (e.g. locate flight screens in visible locations), inducing browsing (e.g. provide open and attractive retail environment) and reducing normative traits (e.g. stress the rationality of impulse buying via promotional materials).

THINKBOX

Think of a retail setting other than airports. What steps can marketers take to encourage impulse buying given the range of effects identified by Crawford and Melawar (2003)?

	Illustration
The holiday effect	Consumer is going on a holiday with high levels of excitement and more disposable income is at hand than normal
The family effect	Consumers think of buying gifts for family and friends
The guilt effect	Business travellers buying for spouse and children to compensate for the loss of family time due to business travel
The reward effect	Consumers' self-indulgence
The occasion effect	Easter, Christmas, Mother's Day, Valentine's Day, birthday
The exclusivity effect	You can only buy certain products in specific travel related environment such as airport
The effect of forgetting	I forgot to bring my umbrella
The effect of confusion	Information overload causing impulse buying
The effect of disposing	I need to get rid of some leftover foreign currency

Based on G Crawford and T C Melewar, The Importance of Impulse Purchasing Behaviour in the International Airport Environment, *Journal of Consumer Behaviour*, Vol. 3 No 1 (2003), p. 85© John Wiley & Sons, Ltd. Reproduced with permission.

Table 4.1: Impulse buying at the airport

In Chapter 6 we discuss self-concept theory and it has been suggested that impulse buying can be perceived by some consumers to help them get closer to their ideal self-concept (Dittmar, 2000; 2007). But it is also pertinent to point out that this might be self defeating, because striving toward an ideal, if some distance from how the person actually sees themselves, can lead to increased disillusionment (Richins, 1991). Richins also proposes that this can be partly explained by the proposition that the larger this gap, the lower the person's overall self-esteem. He is concerned that marketing activity can over glamourize such that the benefits implied can simply be unachievable.

Related to this, there can also be associations with a consumer's personality (Belk, 1985; Dittmar, 2000). Those whose personality traits include higher levels of materialism or sensation seeking have been found to be more likely to buy unplanned products (Bellenger and Korgaonkar, 1980).

Marketing can and does, of course, encourage impulse buying. Supermarket checkouts might be the obvious example (have you added a bar of chocolate or chewing gum to the conveyor belt whilst waiting?) as is the use of eye-level positioning (different for adult and children's products).

Point of purchase (PoP) display material provided by suppliers can entice, as can price offers, multipacks and 'buy one get one free' sale promotion offers (BOGOFs). In-store atmospherics can also encourage unplanned purchases: the use of colour, lighting, aromas and music can all enhance a 'buying mood'.

THINKBOX

There have been social concerns over targeting children with checkout, point of sale and eye-level 'goodies'. What is your position on this and on the wider issue of the use of atmospherics in stores to encourage purchasing beyond that which was planned?

Marketing technology provides greater scope. There is now a plethora of television channels devoted to selling items and some consumers might watch, almost as if watching a conventional programme, only to suddenly think 'oh that would be nice to have' and hence more impulse buying. The internet, with its surfing facility, allows consumers to browse and once some coveted item is found, the ease and speed of placing the order bypasses the more time-consuming shopping trip: pre-empting second thoughts?

Telemats in stores can lure shoppers to special offers and even guide them to the appropriate aisle. Is it likely that we will also see mobile phones being the vehicle for marketers to target members of loyalty schemes whilst in-store. Their location being tracked in real time via GPS and previous transactional data accessed. Relevant offers (according to the marketer) might be sent by text message or video message encouraging shoppers to add other items to their basket. It is certainly already the case that 'personalised vouchers can be redeemed in store simply by scanning the phone at point of sale' (Benjamin, 2007).

Further encouragement for us to buy something unplanned can come from the novelty of interactive posters. Using short code technology, a virtual discount voucher can be sent from the poster to a mobile phone and all the consumer needs to do is to show their handset at the checkout. Have you bought anything because of the novelty of the method?

POST-PURCHASE

Response or purchase at the action stage does not represent the end of consumer response to marketing efforts. Marketing is concerned with satisfied customers, good relationships with customers, repeat purchasing and/or the spreading of goodwill, as can be the case with loyal advocates. **Post-purchase** advertising and other product information on packages and labels are important for consumers to structure their product experience. For example, a consumer who buys a bottle of wine would like to learn about the **country of origin** of the wine, the type of grapes and other related information. The wine may even taste better knowing this information. Some wine distributors provide this sort of 'added value' and it can help develop relationships with their customers. There is further coverage of this in Chapter 10, but here we first focus on two important post-purchase phenomena called 'satisfaction' and 'cognitive dissonance'.

Customer Satisfaction

Customer satisfaction is the attitude-like feeling of a customer towards a product or service after it has been used. It is generally described as the full meeting of one's expectations (Oliver, 1980). The concept of satisfaction is important for marketers because it is the essence of success in today's highly competitive world of business. Marketers often try to become market-oriented and customer-focused and in doing so improving customer satisfaction becomes an important corporate goal for them. In fact, satisfaction is a major aim of all of our marketing activities and is a key influence in the formation of future purchase intentions. For instance, a satisfied customer is very likely to share their experiences with others, thereby engaging in what is known as positive **word-of-mouth advertising**. Similarly, a dissatisfied customer is very likely to switch brands and/or complain, thereby engaging in negative word-of-mouth advertising.

Related to the concept of satisfaction is anticipated satisfaction (Shiv and Huber, 2000). Consider, for example, a consumer who is deciding between two brands of mobile phone. One has the latest digital camera and is really light to carry; the other has a low price and is relatively heavy to carry. When this consumer approaches this decision with a view to developing anticipated satisfaction, they are likely to pay more attention to those attributes that are vivid in nature (attributes which are easy to visualize and construct imagined experiences – in this case, the digital camera and the weight of the phone) than to less vivid attributes (in this case, the price).

Therefore, the consumer is more likely to choose the mobile phone with the camera. Thus, anticipated satisfaction is not related to the actual performance or use of the product but rather to consumers' imagined ideas about how the product is going to function.

Antecedents of Customer Satisfaction

Disconfirmation Paradigm

In order to understand what causes satisfaction, researchers have widely relied on the **disconfirmation paradigm**, which views satisfaction with products and brands as a result of two cognitive variables: pre-purchase expectations and disconfirmation. According to Peters and Olson (2005), 'pre-purchase expectations are beliefs about anticipated performance of the product; post-purchase perceptions are the consumer's thoughts about how well the product performed. Disconfirmation refers to the differences between the two' (p 403). In other words, post-purchase perceptions are compared with pre-purchase expectations and this comparison process determines disconfirmation (Figure 4.2). For example, when the perceived performance exceeds a customer's expectations (this is a positive disconfirmation), then the customer feels satisfied. On the other hand, if the perceived performance falls short of customer's expectations (this is a negative disconfirmation), then the customer feels dissatisfied. Empirical research has generally supported this view. For instance, Churchill and Surprenant (1982) reported that when customers perceived the product performing better than expected, they became more satisfied. When actual product performance far exceeds expectations – that is, when there is a big difference between them – then consumers feel delighted (Oliver, 1997). This obviously depends upon initial expectation levels, and if consumers already have higher expectations, then delighting customers can be a very difficult task. Also, when consumers are not familiar with a product category or the brand (if they have never used

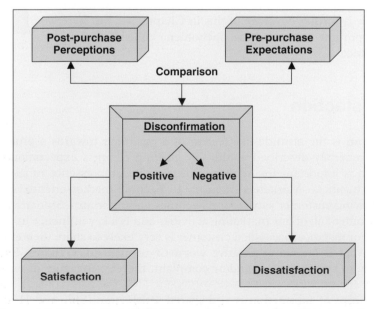

Figure 4.2: Customer satisfaction and the disconfirmation paradigm

it before or never heard of it), then they are very likely to have some poorly formed expectations about the product or the brand. So it might be that once consumers' knowledge and familiarity goes up, their expectations go up as well (Jamal and Naser, 2001).

Attribution Theory

Moreover, attribution theory (Mizerski *et al.*, 1979; Weiner, 2000) also helps to explain why consumers can feel satisfied or dissatisfied. As per attribution theory, consumers seek explanations for the causes of outcomes. For instance, you may have purchased a microwave but it has stopped working after a few days and hence you may seek an explanation for this negative outcome. Your attributions would have three dimensions, all of which may influence your satisfaction/dissatisfaction judgements: focus (i.e. is the outcome due to your own fault as you did not use it as per manufacturer's instructions or is it due to the manufacturer who supplied a low quality product?); controllability (i.e. do you have any control over the outcome or is it under the control of an external source?); and stability (i.e. is the cause of the outcome temporary or permanent?). Consumers are thought to be more satisfied when they attribute favourable outcomes to themselves and negative to others (Oliver, 1993). For instance, when consumers attribute an unfavourable service outcome (e.g. unable to buy a train ticket using a self-serving machine) to an external source (e.g. service provider), they are likely to feel dissatisfied (Meuter *et al.*, 2000). Interesting, in the case of internet bank customers, Jamal (2004) reported that customers continued to prefer the same service provider despite encountering dissatisfying incidents (e.g. unable to log in quickly) as they appeared to attribute the negative service outcome to the technology and not to the service provider. You may also note that some products or services lend themselves to stable attributions while others are more readily associated with unstable attributions (Weiner, 2000). For instance, imagine you bought and disliked the taste of a mass produced food item, such as a pasta sauce, then you may not buy it in the future because you would expect the next jar of pasta sauce to taste exactly the same. However, in the case of internet banking, one episode of dissatisfying incident may not deter you from using the service again because you are probably uncertain about your future liking or disliking of the service.

Equity Theory and Other Factors

Equity, defined as a 'fairness, rightness or deservingness judgement that consumers make in reference to what others receive' (Oliver, 1997:194) is also considered as an important determinant of satisfaction. In other words, equity is your evaluation of what you consider as fair or right based on a comparison of outcomes (e.g. value, utility and pleasure gained out of the transaction) relative to inputs (e.g. cost and effort involved) in a market exchange situation. For instance, you may spend a lot of time and energy in browsing the internet, finding the relevant information, seeking price comparisons and finally buying a computer from a well-known retailer where you interacted with a sales person who also ended up spending their time and effort in explaining the product features and different pricing options to you. From your point of view, you are likely to feel satisfied if you perceive that you got a fair (i.e. equitable) treatment in the exchange process in terms of your inputs (time, effort and money) and output (a good quality computer at an affordable price) relative to sales person's inputs (e.g. selling time and effort) and outputs (e.g. commission, profit margin for the retailer). This is because, as our inputs-to-outcomes ratio decreases, we are more likely to view our interactions with companies and their staff in a positive manner. The equity theory also helps us understand why customers, who receive an organization-initiated recovery (the firm realizes the mistake and takes a corrective action on its own), feel much happier and delighted than the ones who end up complaining and then receive a positive response from the firm, because they made no effort in complaining and hence their input was less while the outcome was similar (Voorhees *et al.*, 2006). Notice, however, that our perceptions of fairness are likely to be biased towards ourselves in the sense that we seek to gain more out of the exchange process (e.g. seeking a large price discount and yet believe it is a fair deal!).

We stated earlier that satisfaction is an attitude like post-consumption evaluative judgement. However, the evaluative aspect of the judgement varies along a pleasant-unpleasant continuum and both product evoked evaluations and emotions (e.g. affective responses) coexist and make independent contributions to satisfaction judgements (Mano and Oliver, 1993).

Consequences of Customer Satisfaction

Just as some researchers have looked at the causes of satisfaction, others have looked into consequences of satisfaction and dissatisfaction, which include exit, complaining behaviour, word-of-mouth advertising and repurchase intentions and loyalty. We will discuss repurchase intentions and loyalty in a later chapter.

Complaining Behaviour

If you are not satisfied, then you have the option of complaining, which is a very good way of getting rid of your anger and frustration. Obviously, it is in the interest of marketers to listen to customer complaints

and provide solutions with a view to improve satisfaction levels, but the trouble is not everyone complains. This could be, in part, due to politeness (Lerman, 2006), perceived responsiveness of firm or service provider and lack of time and effort (Voorhees *et al.*, 2006), or the fact that some people are willing to suffer in silence hoping that things will get better in the future (Hirschman, 1970).

Voice, Third Party Actions and Private Actions

There are three types of complaining behaviour: voice, third-party actions and private actions (Singh, 1988). Voice refers to complaining behaviour directed towards the offending party such as the manufacturer or the service provider and can take the form of making a complaint in person, making a telephonic call, writing an email or a letter or online feedback form. In third-party actions, complaining behaviour is channelled through a third party, which, though not directly involved with the offending organization or service provider, still carries some authority or influence over it. For instance, you may write to a newspaper, to a public sector organization (e.g. Office of Fair Trade or Consumers Direct) or an industry association (e.g. Advertising Standards Authority) to express your views and make a complaint. The internet has provided additional opportunities for consumers to express their anger via dedicated web sites that encourage consumers to share their grievances and concerns with those in similar situations. In private actions, the complaining behaviour is channelled to consumers' own social circle (e.g. family and friends). This can take the form of word-of-mouth recommendations, which will be covered in detail in the later section, but first we will look at important determinants of voice.

THINKBOX

Have you ever used a dedicated website to voice your complaints? If yes, which one? Did you get any feedback from the website or from other consumers in similar situations? Do you believe the complaint websites are effective in exerting pressure on companies to listen to consumers? In what sense are these websites a better alternative to voicing your concerns directly to the manufacturer, or to the service providers?

Your tendency to complain may be a function of your personality traits (Bodey and Grace, 2007). For instance, a person can be risk seeker (i.e. engages in activities even when the possible outcome is likely to be negative) or risk aversive (e.g. only engages in an activity when there is a strong probability of a positive outcome). Risk seekers, in comparison with risk aversive persons, are more likely to complain because there is often a high level of uncertainty attached to achieving a positive outcome through the complaint process. Similarly, some consumers experience higher levels of propensity to complain or their likelihood of seeking redress or expressing dissatisfaction is higher than others and hence they are quite likely to engage in complaining behaviour. The propensity to complain can, however, depend on the severity of the situation including the extent of the damage, corporate reputation of the firm and the ease with which you can make a complaint using the marketing channels. Also, when there are greater chances of some kind of redress (e.g. the store will listen to my complaint), then consumers are more likely to complain. Moreover, a person may have a very strong perception of their ability to achieve a successful outcome via the complaining process and hence their level of perceived ability and motivation (e.g. time, monetary cost, perceived benefit) to complain are also important determinants of complaining behaviour. In addition, and as per the equity theory, you are very likely to complain when you attribute blame to someone else rather than yourself.

Word of Mouth

As an outcome of satisfying (or dissatisfying) experiences, consumers may engage in positive (or negative) word-of-mouth (WOM) communications. When the WOM is positive, it is defined as an 'informal, person-to-person communication between a perceived non-commercial communicator and a receiver regarding a brand, a product, an organization, or a service' (Harrison-Walker, 2001:63). Not everyone who is satisfied with a product or service engages in positive WOM but those who could be classified as market mavens (Feick and Price, 1987) and/or opinion leaders/innovators are very likely to engage in positive WOM recommendations. Hence, to encourage WOM activity, an increasing number of companies offer monetary (e.g. a £20 gift voucher) or non-monetary incentives (e.g. a free CD) to existing customers for making a positive referral.

EXAMPLE 4.1

First-time customers usually try Laphroaig single malt whisky, distilled on the Isle of Islay, on the recommendation of a friend.

Publicis Dialog emailed 25 000 members of the Friends of Laphroaig inviting them to recommend friends who would appreciate a taste of 10-year-old Laphroaig, and offering them the chance to win a trip to Islay.

The friends were then mailed a personalized pack with a sample of Laphroaig and information about the product and its loyalty scheme.

The campaign exceeded targets, with 63 per cent of recommended friends applying for miniatures.

However, consumers can and do share their dissatisfying experiences with others and, thus, engage in negative WOM advertising (Richins, 1983). The extent to which a person engages in negative WOM can

Goal for engaging in negative WOM	Explanation	Goal likely when consumers experience the following
Comfort search	Seeking comfort, moral support or understanding	Disappointment, uncertainty
Advice search	Engaging in negative WOM in order to gain cognitive clarity	Disappointment, uncertainty
Bonding	Decreasing interpersonal distance and strengthening social bonds	Regret
Entertaining	Keeping a conversation going and amusing the conversational partner	Regret
Self-representation	Managing another's impression, or image of oneself	Regret
Warning	Helping the receiver make a satisfying purchase decision	Regret and disappointment
Venting anger	Blowing off steam by expressing the emotion	Anger, frustration and irritation
Revenge	Behaviour performed to harm someone else (e.g., the brand or firm), in response to feeling of being harmed	Anger, frustration and irritation

Source: Based on Wetzer *et al.* (2007)

Table 4.2: Link between emotions and goals for engaging in negative WOM

depend on perceived justice (based on equity theory) and severity of the problem. Engaging in negative WOM allows consumers to release their anger, irritation, disappointment and frustration while regaining control over a bad situation and gaining sympathy from others. Table 4.2 presents a range of goals for engaging in negative WOM activity based on a recent work conducted by Wetzer *et al.* (2007) in which they investigated the link between consumption related emotions (e.g. anger, frustration) and goals for engaging in negative WOM. As indicated in Table 4.2, consumers who experience anger, frustration, or irritation appear to have some destructive goals (e.g. taking revenge) for engaging in negative WOM. On the other hand, those who experience disappointment, uncertainty and regret appear to have some constructive goals (e.g. seeking comfort, advice and bonding) for engaging in negative WOM. A challenge for marketers is how best to manage the negative WOM as recent developments in internet technology have facilitated the spreading of negative WOM via online communities, chat rooms and emails. When consumers complain or engage in negative WOM, they are actually relieving their cognitive dissonance, which we discuss in detail in the following section.

THINKBOX

Have you ever complained to a manufacturer, retailer or service provider? What was the response? Do you think it was a good idea to complain? As a marketer, what would be your response to consumers' complaints?

Cognitive Dissonance

Cognitive dissonance is a kind of psychological tension resulting from perceived inconsistencies in cognitions (Festinger, 1957). For example, imagine you have just purchased a new car after a fairly extensive pre-purchase search and evaluation of alternatives. Your final choice is probably a bit of a compromise because no car is completely tailored to the requirements of each individual customer. Having said this, you are likely to view your choice as highly satisfactory. However, there may have been other cars available that you believed had some superior design features. These slightly contradictory cognitions can produce dissonance and you may ask yourself if you have made the correct choice. The level of dissonance is a function of the importance of the cognitions to the individual. So, if the point about other design features is very minor, the level of dissonance might be negligible. If, however, you drive your new car home and your next-door neighbour, who you see as being especially knowledgeable about cars, says, 'Why on earth did you buy that? That model has a terrible repair record!', your level of dissonance could be very substantial indeed. Cognitive dissonance is a motivator in that the individual tries to reduce it. In the above example, a high level of dissonance over the car might lead the buyer to seek supporting evidence for his decision, to reassure himself that he has done the right thing. Indeed, much advertising is aimed at people who have already made a purchase, in order to help them overcome dissonance, reassure them of their purchase decision and to ease the way for a repeat purchase or at least to spread positive messages to others. It is also worth emphasizing that dissonance is not the same as dissatisfaction. Dissatisfaction produces dissonance, yes, but a generally satisfying purchase may also produce cognitive dissonance if some of the cognitions over it are slightly inconsistent with each other.

EXAMPLE 4.2

Take the example reported by Jones (1996), which we also discuss in Chapter 10, concerning the missing ashtray from his BMW. The BMW dealer had forgotten to replace the ashtray after a service but a chance call to a Lexus dealer resulted in them collecting the ashtray from BMW and delivering it to Jones! Even though he had been a loyal BMW owner for 12 years, this seemingly minor incident over the ashtray raised dissonance in his mind. The Lexus dealer's actions suggested to him that there would be less dissonance if he were a Lexus customer, so that's what he became.

Although we are discussing dissonance in the post-purchase phase (because it applies particularly well here), it can occur in the pre-purchase phase as well. We can usually perceive positive and negative cognitions whenever we are faced with alternatives, so the mental processing of these pros and cons can obviously lead to levels of confusion and doubt over the best choice. Therefore, the onus is on the interactive relational marketer to provide the target with information, which will help the individual overcome such dissonance. It might appear obvious to suggest that we emphasize consonant cognitions (positive aspects of the product). However, there are occasions when a slightly negative set of points can be made as well. The use of two-sided arguments has been suggested as being effective for more educated audiences. Charity marketers often draw attention to the 'downside' of, for example, parting with one's hard earned money but (the upside is) for a very good 'cause'. The marketer might also emphasize how many satisfied customers there are. For example, a satellite broadcaster used the copy headline, 'Half a million people can't be wrong.' Marketers can also extend this by targeting specific individuals as endorsers or **opinion leaders**. The targeting of **opinion formers** (e.g. journalists) is also a highly sophisticated business, as we discuss in Chapter 9, with the aim of securing positive and relevant 'editorial' coverage by those who are likely to be perceived as being independent, credible experts. This can 'reassure' customers that they have bought the right product.

Strategy	Action
1. Change one's behaviour	Stop smoking
	Change to smoking cigar or pipe
2. Distort the dissonant information	Refuse to accept cancer connection
3. Minimize the importance of the issue	Say there is more chance of death in a car crash
4. Ignore dissonant information and seek consonant information	Seek social support

Table 4.3: Dissonance reducing strategies in smoking

Another example of dissonance comes from the cigarette-smoking market and this provides us with something of a framework for overcoming dissonance or avoiding it in the first instance. Smoking cigarettes is initially a positive and rewarding activity. There is initially no dissonance. However, receiving messages about health risks and negative societal reactions to smoking poses a problem and leads to the psychological tension of dissonance. Table 4.3 shows four generalized ways of overcoming dissonance.

The first method looks simpler than it really is. Changing our behaviour by stopping altogether (apart from being easier to say than to achieve) might reduce the dissonance resulting from the health and social warnings. All the positives for the individual (the nicotine, etc.) have gone, and dissonance can arise over not smoking! The individual might turn to eating more, especially mints, and this might lead to dissonance over gaining weight or tooth problems! Less dramatic changes in behaviour, such as to smoking cigars or a pipe, might enable the individual to reassure herself that the health risk might be less and that, although dissonance still exists, it is not at the same level and therefore it might be manageable. Once the cigar smoker, however, realizes that the result from smoking cigars in the same way that he smoked cigarettes (inhaling) can be even more damaging, then dissonance will clearly rocket again!

The second method is to refuse to accept that there is a strong or proven link between cigarette smoking and health problems. It has been found that some smokers rationalize their behaviour in this way. They say there might be a correlation but not necessarily a causal link. The point here is that if dissonance is based on the balance between positive and negative cognitions, by reducing the perceived level of the negative ones, dissonance can thus be reduced to a tolerable level.

The third strategy reduces the importance of all of the cognitions. By convincing ourselves that the issue is relatively insignificant in our lives we might still experience dissonance over it, but at a much reduced and acceptable level. We might, of course, increase dissonance over driving, especially if we drive and smoke at the same time!

The fourth approach is a variation on the second. Rather than distorting that which is dissonant, we might seek more of that which is consonant. The argument that our friends are fit and healthy and that they smoke serves to accentuate the positive cognitions to an extent that they outweigh the dissonant cognitions. Early cigarette advertising actually used this approach and depicted young, fit and energetic smokers with the implication that 'You too can be like this if you smoke this brand'! Even sporting heroes were used in such smoking advertisements.

Figure 4.3 shows how marketing messages of that bygone era depicted, somewhat unethically, healthy people to reassure that smoking cigarettes will not do harm. Indeed the copy of one reads 'For your throat's sake, smoke Craven A' and the other implies the endorsement of women (see Chapter 9 for more on endorsement) with a probable aim of encouraging women to take up smoking at a time when it was predominantly a male preserve.

Based on the above discussion we can transfer the general strategies into workable approaches in marketing. It might appear obvious to suggest that we emphasize the consistent cognitions (positive aspects

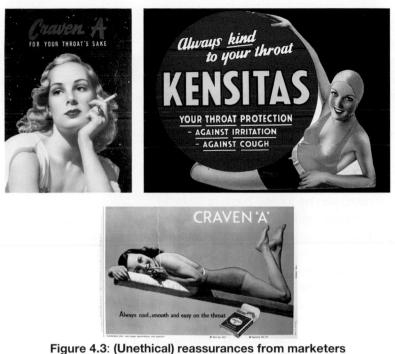

Figure 4.3: (Unethical) reassurances from marketers
Overcoming dissonance: healthy women smoke (seeking social support) and it's good for you (!) (using positive cognitions).
Reproduced by permission of Robert Opie

of the product) and indeed this is based on the balancing act between the consonant and the dissonant aspects. However, there are occasions when a slightly negative set of points can be made as well. The use of two-sided arguments has been suggested as being effective for more educated audiences (see Chapter 3). Another example is the old Volkswagen advertisement which showed the Golf being advertised as slower than a competitor, with the tagline 'Once again, our GTi is about to be left standing'. The small print, however, went on to point out the extra safety and other features that the Golf possessed. This also takes us to the implication that there are dissonant elements of competing products. This is again based on the balance between the consonant and dissonant. We perhaps try to increase dissonance over competing products. Comparative advertising, although banned in some countries, is used extensively in others. In the UK, for instance, it is not uncommon for advertisements for model X car to show the market leader as well and to emphasize, selectively, only a few features such as the smaller boot that the competitor has. The other car might be the market leader but 'ours' is so much less expensive and still comes with many similar features. Asda has led some of its advertisements with reports from independent price comparison checks that Tesco or Sainsbury's had so many lower prices, but then reports that Asda has more.

EXAMPLE 4.3

This case provides a good example of several of the theories expounded in this book.

Visit Wales wanted to see whether a creative approach would help challenge the perceptions of high-values non-responders towards an autumn break in Wales – by turning the concept of rain into a positive. The mail pack went to members of the Visit Wales website and generated an

additional £5 757 in revenue for Wales. In the current context it shows how the Wales tourist board engaged in an
attitude change campaign by incorporating a two-sided
message (Wales can be wet but that can be fun in itself)
and you can kit yourself out appropriately – even using
the rain poncho sent in the mailshot. It also illustrates
dissonance reduction by minimizing the importance of
the dissonant (wet) cognition. The case reflects Heider's
balance theory (Chapter 3): the initial triad is inconsistent, but the negative to Welsh holidays (because of the
negative to wet holidays) can be turned positive by tackling the wet holidays barrier head on. Finally, the Wales

case reminds us of negative and positive motivations (Chapter 1). In that sense it is an example of
an attempt to turn a negative motivation (wet holidays) into its positive counterpart (walking in the
rain – in suitable attire – can be invigorating!).

Another good illustration of a two-sided appeal was an advertisement for new homes. The
two-column message listed the advantages of buying a new home in one column, such as a
10-year guarantee, the latest fittings, new electrical systems and energy-saving heating. In the
other column were the negatives associated with buying a 20-year-old house, e.g. the need to
spend money on a new kitchen, electrical rewiring and the replacement of windows.

Figure 4.4 shows a poster for Bird's Eye curries, prompting consumers to investigate what is
lurking in their curries, especially artificial ingredients which cannot be identified by simply looking
at the product. The effect might be to increase dissonance over these competing brands, hence
tipping the balance in favour of Bird's Eye.

One of the most seminal examples of building dissonance over a competitor occurred during
the 1979 UK general election, when the Conservative Party took a swipe at the then incumbent
Labour Government (Figure 4.5). The basis was high levels of unemployment but it is interesting
to note that after the Conservative win in 1979 unemployment rose.

Figure 4.4: Increasing dissonance over competing brands
Reproduced by permission of Bird's Eye, a division of Unilever plc. Illustrated by Anthony Burrill

Figure 4.5: Comparative/negative advertising
© Conservative Party. Reproduced with permission.

Perhaps unfortunately, modern political campaigning seems mostly to 'knock' opposition parties.

THINKBOX

The building dissonance approach is also to be seen in the music industry.

Record companies strive to get their CDs into the 'charts', not only because this means they sell more at that stage and get more airplay but also because once a recording can be promoted as 'a hit' it appears to give additional credibility and to reduce potential dissonance. The buyer can think that if they are silly to buy, then millions of others are as well, and that is unlikely!

The same applies to the book market. Faced with rows of novels, the one with 'million seller' on the cover can attract the buyer in the same way.

Music programmes even describe new releases as 'future hits'. Are consumers more likely to buy if the CD is described as a 'hit' or 'future hit' than if there were no 'charts' at all?

What does this say about our buying behaviour?

Related to this is offering reassurance through after-sales service and warranties. This is again very prominent in the car market and reflects the pragmatic view that cars are complicated pieces of machinery and that no car is tailor-made for each individual customer, so there are bound to be both consonant and dissonant cognitions. However, if the marketer emphasizes that, if anything goes wrong, there is nothing for the consumer to worry about, there need be no dissonance after purchase because the company will look after the purchaser. Network Q in 2005 used the copy headline: 'With 114 checks on every Network Q car, peace of mind comes as standard' (Figure 4.6).

Another approach is based on the strategy of reducing the importance of the issue. How many of us have bought a garment in a 'sale' and it doesn't fit too well or in daylight the colour is pretty

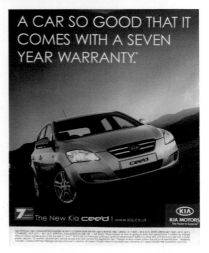

A CAR SO GOOD THAT IT COMES WITH A SEVEN YEAR WARRANTY.

The New Kia cee'd | www.kia.co.uk

Figure 4.6: Reassurance

Consumers know very well that a car is a complicated product and things can go wrong. They seek reassurance that if there are problems, these can be resolved easily.

© Vauxhall Network Q. Reproduced by permission

awful? We are sometimes able to reduce this dissonance to a tolerable level and even go back and buy something else from the 'sales', because we rationalize it as 'a bargain' and therefore it doesn't matter so much!

Even where there might appear to be a degree of social disapproval for a purchase because the product is not a major brand and therefore lacks the conspicuousness of image that another might convey, marketers can help reduce dissonance by reminding consumers that product functionality is more important than the froth of branding:

EXAMPLE 4.4

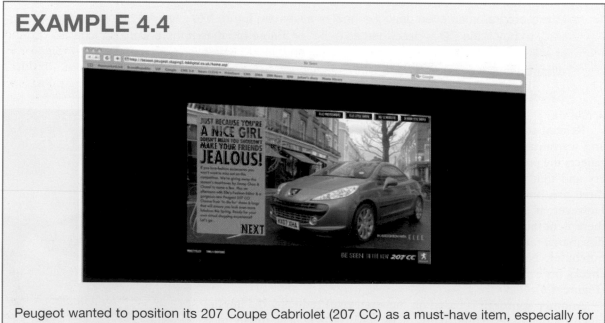

Peugeot wanted to position its 207 Coupe Cabriolet (207 CC) as a must-have item, especially for women.

Euro RSCG ₄D Digital created a shopping-themed website in the style of women's lifestyle and fashion magazines. Visitors were encouraged to enter a virtual shopping competition by creating a customized film of a woman driving round London's fashion hotspots.

They could create a video for their friends and email them the link. There was also a chance to win clothes, an exclusive shopping trip and a 207 CC. Inserts in women's magazines such as *Elle*, *Glamour* and *Grazia*, along with banner advertising on their websites, drove visitors to the site.

The site attracted 21 500 unique visitors and there were 15 500 entrants to the competition. Visitors emailed 3 000 referrals to friends, with 42 per cent of these generating a response. The campaign raised awareness of the car, with over a third of consumers not familiar with the 207 CC previously; 77 per cent of visitors said the car appeared more attractive after using the site. Despite being designed to raise brand awareness, the execution also created 191 test-drive requests.

Judges said the campaign 'drew you into the product in a unique way. Rather than being about the car it sold you a version of what having the car was like. It was exciting, visual and fun'.

Disposal Behaviour

An important post-purchase phenomenon is the disposal behaviour, which concerns the disposal of used-up products including those products that we no longer need. Consumers engage in a variety of disposal behaviour including throwing away, recycling, selling/swapping, giving away or keeping it for an extended period of time. Consumers tend to throw away products due to the convenience factor or to make room for new products. Technological advancements have led to shortened product life cycles for some products (e.g. mobile phone, computers, printers), which along with a desire to buy the latest model puts extra pressures on consumers to dispose of their old products. Some consumers are chronic keepers as they tend to keep products for a fairly long period of time even when they no longer use or need the products. That would probably explain why some people tend to have a large pile of products (e.g. old monitor, cables) in their attics or cellars. While some of the items may be kept for their nostalgic value or due to an emotional attachment (e.g. remind them of a loved one), most of the other items are kept in the hope of using them some time in the future.

INVOLVEMENT

Before we leave the sequential model it is worth saying that levels of involvement that customers have with the product category or the specific purchase issue can go some way to determining the value of such models. As we have seen through the last two chapters, consumers' response to marketing activity and indeed their decision-making can be depicted as a sequential cognitive process. However, we must take account of the level of involvement that consumers show in the decisions they make, their personal interest and engagement in the process.

Involvement is commonly defined as the consumer's personal interest in buying or using an item from a given product field, an approach which nicely summarizes the personal, product and situational components of the relationship.

A person's level of involvement depends on personal relevance and the inherent interests, needs and values of the individual, which motivate them towards the object of involvement. Personal components include self-image, which we introduced above as having a similar effect on impulse buying. If we perceive our self-image as being likely to be enhanced by purchase, then involvement can increase (Venkatraman, 1988) and when a particular product is seen in this way, involvement can 'last' – that is, it is enduring involvement.

Enduring involvement, then, continues out of sustained interest in the product category. When a consumer perceives something to be of personal relevance and of interest, it means that it is self-related and in some way instrumental in achieving certain life goals and values (Celsi and Olson, 1988). There can be some intrinsic sources of personal relevance (e.g. knowledge associations based on experiences with a product and which are stored in the memory); these do not change across situations and remain relatively stable. Therefore, enduring involvement is relatively stable and longer-lasting.

The product's physical characteristics can also influence a person's level of involvement (Zaichkowsky, 1985). Product related components include the concept of perceived risk. Here, if a consumer perceives a product purchase to be risky (e.g. uncertainty as to whether it will do the job, or even do them some physical harm, or doubt over self-image enhancement) then involvement can again be higher. Some products, such as high-performance cars, seem inherently involving because of their complexity, risk and cost, while others, such as toothpaste, seem uninvolving by comparison because of their familiarity, low risk and low cost (Laaksonen, 1994). In fact, while this is true in a general way, involvement is actually a relationship rather than a property of this or that product or service. It reflects not only the degree of uncertainty experienced by a consumer when they are faced with consideration of a product but also the personal characteristics of the consumer (some people find everything more involving than others) and on the situation in which purchase and consumption take place.

Situation components, then, include the consumption context: whether consumed socially or more privately, or indeed consumed by another in the family or as a gift to another. This component explains why involvement with the same product can change from time to time. The purchase of wine for an 'ordinary' family meal might be lower than when a similar meal is served at a dinner party (Zaichkowsky, 1985). It is perhaps also the case that involvement in, for example, fashion changes over time as we age: there could be higher involvement at age 18 than 80?

Marketing activities are one example of situational influence because they help activate self-relevant consequences, goals and values. Since most situational sources of personal relevance are changeable, the **situational involvement** can also change when the situation changes (Celsi and Olson, 1988). Situational involvement, then, is short-lived because the interest is related to an event (e.g. buying a dress for a wedding). However, consumers can be involved with a product category (e.g. mobile phones) but also with a brand (e.g. Nokia), an advertisement (e.g. a print ad for Nokia), or a medium (e.g. the Internet or shopping method).

Indeed the previous chapter introduced Krugman's passive learning theory (1965). He related learning to consumers' levels of involvement and he was one of the first to explore the nature and implications of low involvement for TV as an advertising medium. His hypothesis was that TV can act as a sort of wall-paper: the medium itself is animate but the consumer inanimate, and as result consumers do 'take in' some TV advertising but in a fairly random manner based mostly on repetition effects (passive learning; see the previous chapter) but it does not have much effect on changing attitudes because consumers are not heavily involved with the medium.

Several researchers (Krugman, 1965; Grass and Wallace, 1974; Childers and Houston, 1984) suggest that when involvement is low, the passive learning effect of TV advertising is effective, but for higher involvement contexts, print media can be more effective. This is because in the latter it is the consumer who has to be animate when the medium in inanimate.

THINKBOX

It is perhaps possible to refute some of this today. Much TV advertising is more engaging and participative than in the 1960s because we have the 'red button' to interact with the advertiser in real time. Also, most TV advertisements now include a direct response mechanism such as a telephone number or web site address, facilitating further interaction.

In this sense is the consumer sometimes less passive or inanimate than in a previous era – and TV as an advertising medium even more animate than ever?

Consumers can also be involved with a purchase decision itself (e.g. deciding between alternatives when buying a mobile phone). There can also be response involvement, which refers to the cognitive and behavioural consequences that arise from the associated levels of enduring and situational involvement. For example, a person's enduring involvement with a product category, say mobile phones, and situational involvement with a given situation (e.g. buying one as a birthday present for a daughter) should have significant cognitive and behavioural consequences pertaining to the buying of a mobile phone in this particular context.

It has been suggested that a highly involved consumer might not accept many other opinions on the issue (they have a narrow 'latitude of acceptance') and instead might reject many others (a wider latitude of rejection). This is based on Sherif's **social judgement theory** (Sherif and Hovland, 1964) and explains why a consumer might selectively perceive messages about an issue to be more favourable than perhaps they really are, if that message is within their latitude of acceptance. This is referred to as the **assimilation effect**. Whereas a message which is within a consumer's latitude of rejection (and as suggested, these could be many for an involved consumer) can be interpreted as even more unfavourable than perhaps it really is (this is the **contrast effect**). It has further been suggested that more involved consumers might have a narrower repertoire of brands from which they choose (because of their narrow latitude of acceptance) but at the same time might consider more factors for evaluating this narrower range of alternatives (Rothschild and Houston, 1977) because their degree of search and information processing can be high.

Social judgement theory also proposes that someone who is less involved with the issue might accept a wider range of opinions from others on it (that is they have a wider latitude of acceptance) or have a wider latitude of non-commitment toward the issue. This can afford marketers some scope for interesting consumers in a wider range of brands options because they are more open to alternative views. At the same time, however, being so uninvolved means that they don't seek information and view advertising in a similar way as in Krugman's passive learning approach. Familiar brands might be purchased on the basis of familiarity and lack on perceived need or inclination to explore alternatives. Rothschild and Houston (1977) found the reverse, for uninvolved consumers, compared with their finding for the involved: that is, more brands considered but on fewer factors and this was supported by Gensch and Javagli (1987) in their study of farmers' selection of suppliers.

To (object to be judged) is:			
1	Important	_:_:_:_:_:_	Unimportant*
2	Boring	_:_:_:_:_:_	Interesting
3	Relevant	_:_:_:_:_:_	Irrelevant*
4	Exciting	_:_:_:_:_:_	Unexciting*
5	Means nothing	_:_:_:_:_:_	Means a lot to me
6	Appealing	_:_:_:_:_:_	Unappealing*
7	Fascinating	_:_:_:_:_:_	Mundane*
8	Worthless	_:_:_:_:_:_	Valuable
9	Involving	_:_:_:_:_:_	Uninvolving*
10	Not needed	_:_:_:_:_:_	Needed

Totaling items gives a low of 10 to a high of 70
* Indicates item is reverse scored. For example, a score of 7 for item no. 1 (important/unimportant)
would actually be scored as a 1.
Adapted from Zaichowsky (1985)

Table 4.4: Zaichowsky's semantic differential measures involvement

Measurement of Involvement

As we have seen, there are a number of types of involvement, contexts for it and a number of components that different researchers have proposed. To combine all in an accepted measurement instrument has not been easy or perhaps, as yet, achieved. However, Zaichowsky (1985) and McQuire and Munson (1992) have developed useful measures (see Tables 4.4 and 4.5).

Michaelidou and Dibb's (2006) paper is commended to you as one that also provides a concise summary of involvement with clothing and the useful empirical research approach leads to the findings that enduring involvement with clothing is based in part on the enjoyment of the shopping process per se and partly on the importance of clothing symbolically expressing self and reflecting lifestyle.

Their paper is on the accompanying website and is also useful as it shows a method of measuring enduring involvement (Figure 4.6). As will be seen this includes 'self expressive', 'hedonic', 'importance' and 'interest' dimensions of involvement.

- I would be interested in reading about this product
- I would read a *Consumer Reports* article about this product
- I have compared product characteristics among brands
- I usually pay attention to advertisements for this product
- I usually talk about this product with other people
- I usually seek advice from other people prior to purchasing this product
- I usually take many factors into account before purchasing this product
- I usually spend a lot of time choosing what kind to buy

Table 4.5: McGuire and Munson's Likert scale measures enduring involvement using a personal involvement inventory

Involvement and Hierarchy of Effects

So, higher involvement with purchase decisions leads to consumers spending more time and effort and indulging in extensive information search. Zaichkowsky (1985) also suggests that involvement affects

Item	Dimension of Involvement
1. It gives me pleasure to shop for clothes	Hedonism
2. I can think of instances where a personal experience was affected by the way I dressed	Importance
3. Because of my personal values, I feel that clothing ought to be important to me	Importance
4. I enjoy buying clothes for myself	Hedonism
5. I rate my dress sense as being of high importance to me	Importance
6. Clothes help me express who I am	Self expression
7. I attach great importance to the way people are dressed	Importance
8. It is true that clothing interests me a lot	Interest
9. The kind of clothes I buy do not reflect the kind of person I am	Sign value
10. I buy clothes for pleasure they give me, not others	Hedonism
11. Clothing is a topic about which I am indifferent	Interest
12. Clothing is not part of my self-image	Self expression
13. Relative to other products, clothing is most important to me	Importance
14. Buying clothes feels like giving myself a gift	Hedonism
15. I am not at all interested in clothes	Interest

Source: Michaelidou and Dibb, 2006

Table 4.6: Measures for enduring involvement in the clothing market

consumers' cognitive (e.g. information searching, processing, attention, satisfaction) and behavioural (e.g. early adoption of a product) responses.

Blending our coverage of a hierarchy of effects model in the last two chapters with the current examination of involvement, Celsi and Olson (1988) investigated the role of involvement (defined as self-relevant knowledge that is activated in a given situation) in consumers' attention and comprehension processes. Their findings indicated that as consumers' involvement increased, subjects allocated more attention to the advertisements, exerted greater mental effort during comprehension of those ads, increasingly focused on product-related information contained in the ads and engaged in extra elaboration of the product information during comprehension.

In fact, consumers' motivation to process information is often conceptualized in terms of consumers' involvement with the information stimuli. Figure 4.7 illustrates low and high involvement with decision making and also with different types of learning.

Consumers go through the sequential model under high-involvement conditions whereas there is less evidence of applicability of sequential models under low-involvement conditions.

	High involvement	Low involvement
Decision-making	Sequential models	Less evidence for sequential models
	Cognitive learning	Passive learning
Habit	Loyalty	Inertia
	Instrumental conditioning	Classical conditioning

Figure 4.7: Involvement and hierarchy of effects (sequential) models

THINKBOX

Think of a low-involvement decision and a high-involvement decision that you made recently. To what extent do you think your decision-making differed in the two situations?

In order to move consumers' involvement from low to high, marketers could:

1. Link the brand with an involving issue. For example, high cholesterol is an important issue for some and therefore the clear linking of brands, such as Benecol, which lower cholesterol, can help to increase consumers' involvement with what otherwise might be a rather boring product (margarine). Marks and Spencer try to increase involvement in its brand of food by suggesting that it is 'not just food, it is M&S food'.
2. Link the brand with an involving personal situation, such as advertising a satellite car-navigation brand on radio when harried commuters might be struggling through the rush-hour traffic.
3. Link the brand with a more hedonic motivation, such as in Figure 4.8, which shows a Häagen-Dazs advertisement that links ice cream with even more 'involving situations' using a sensory appeal.
4. Link the brand with a message style which is itself involving, such as the cinema quality 'blockbuster' advertisements that Guinness often produce. Interactive outdoor advertising is increasingly encouraging participation with consumers as the examples below (and on p 376) suggest:

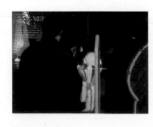

Source: http://www.mediazest.com/index-products.html

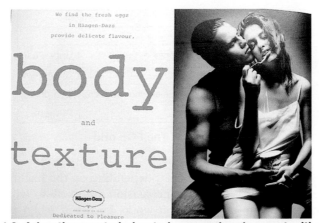

Figure 4.8: Advertisement aiming to increase involvement with a brand
Source: General Mills UK

5. Associating a brand with a celebrity. We introduced this in the previous chapter where we discussed this under associationist learning and we return to the issue in Chapter 9, where we explore the influence of opinion formers and opinion leaders.
6. Building relationships with consumers. We explore this in more detail in Chapter 12, but suffice to provide an example here: the buying of groceries might not be the most involving for many consumers but the personalization dimension of loyalty schemes can involve consumers. Sainsbury's send birthday cards to its members.

Information processing and attitude change are determined by involvement and consumers' motivation to process information. High involvement leads to a **central route to persuasion**, which 'views attitude change, resulting from a person's diligent consideration of information that she or he feels is central to the true merits of a particular attitudinal position' (Petty *et al.*, 1983:135). Consumers pay strong attention to the product-related features and other relevant factual information and consciously elaborate potential outcomes. Attitude change here is relatively enduring, predictive of behaviour and is resistant to counter-persuasion. Under high-involvement conditions, an advertising message is likely to affect cognition, then attitudes and then behaviours (Krugman, 1965).

On the other hand, low involvement leads to a **peripheral route to persuasion** whereby consumers pay limited attention to non-product features and feelings. Here the information processing is largely unconscious with no or very limited elaborative activities. Using some simple cues (e.g. opinion of an expert) consumers make simple inferences about the merits of the advocated position (Petty *et al.*, 1983).

Under low-involvement conditions, an advertising message is likely to affect cognition, then behaviours and then attitudes (Krugman, 1965).

The central route deals with the message *content* and the peripheral route with the *execution* of the message (use of humour, celebrities, music and so on). Central route processing depends on much of what we have discussed in the preceding two chapters: attention, perception, learning and then attitude formation. Peripheral route processing, however, can be more spontaneous depending on how the style of the message appeals to the consumer. As the well-known lyrics go: 'It ain't what you do, it's the way that you do it.' These arguments are based on what is known as the **elaboration likelihood model**

Involvement	Motives	
	Think	Feel
High	Pension scheme	Sports car
	Economy car	Cosmetics
Low	Washing and cleaning products	Soft drinks
		Burgers

Figure 4.9: The FCB grid

(Petty and Cacioppo, 1983). The model argues that, depending on the likelihood of a message-relevant thought occurring, different methods of inducing persuasion are likely to work best. That is, when the elaboration is high, the central route to persuasion works best, but when the elaboration is low, the peripheral route will work best. The model has significant implications for message strategy and message content. For example, when there is high involvement, attitude change can best be achieved by presenting high-quality arguments and presenting a lot of rational and detailed information. On other hand, under low-involvement conditions, attitude change can best be achieved by using some peripheral cues (e.g. attractive models, delightful music, expert persons).

Another related approach is summarized in Figure 4.9, which presents a simple grid model used by Foote, Cone and Belding, a major advertising agency, to analyse consumer–product relationships. The grid also shows the typical locations of several different products. The **FCB Grid** (Berger, 1986) is based on two concepts: consumers' involvement and their salient knowledge, meanings and beliefs about the product.

Some products are considered primarily in terms of rational factors, such as the functional benefits of using the product. These are termed **think products** in the grid model. Included in this category are such products as investments and car batteries, all products purchased primarily for their functional consequences.

In contrast, **feel products** are considered by consumers primarily in terms of non-verbal (visual or other types) images and emotional factors, such as psychosocial benefits and values. For instance, products purchased primarily for their sensory qualities, such as ice cream and cosmetics, as well as products for which emotional consequences are dominant, such as flowers or jewellery, are feel products in the FCB Grid. An example of the practical application of this concept can be seen on the use of scent strips for perfume products, which allow consumers to experience 'feel' products. Marketing research shows that consumers are more likely to buy products that they have sampled. Scent strips on press advertisements can be a very effective marketing communication device.

THINKBOX

Think about a recent purchase of a product. Was it a 'feel' product or a 'think' product? How do you know? Is the feel/think dichotomy relevant to all products? What about services?

The appropriate message strategy depends on the product's position in the grid. Sometimes, a product can be 'moved' within the grid, from a 'think' to a 'feel' product.

There are, however, some limitations of this model as reported by Rossiter, Percy and Donovan (1991). For example, they criticize the method of conceptualizing involvement for the FCB grid and

	Type of motivation	
	Informational (negative motivations)	Transformational (positive motivations)
Low-involvement decision-making	Examples: aspirin, light beer, detergent,	Examples: candy, regular beer, fiction novels
High-involvement decision-making	Examples: microwave oven, insurance, home renovations	Examples: vacations, fashion clothing, cars

Figure 4.10: Involvement and motivation
Based on J R Rossiter, L Percy and R J Donovan, A Better Advertising Planning Grid, Journal of Advertising Research, October/November 1991, pp. 11–21. Reproduced by permission of Cambridge University Press

Motives	Typical Emotional States
Information Motives	
Problem removal	Anger-relief
Problem avoidance	Fear-relaxation
Incomplete satisfaction	Disappointment-optimism
Mixed approach-avoidance	Guilt-peace-of-mind
Normal deception	Mild annoyance-convenience
Transformation Motives	
Sensory gratification	Full-elated
Intellectual stimulation	Bored-excited
Social approval	Apprehensive-flattered

Table 4.7: Information motives and transformation motives

argue that it does not distinguish brand choices from wider product category choice and this affects the think–feel issue. So both involvement and think–feel constructs are seen to be limited. As a result we have the *Rossiter–Percy Grid* (Figure 4.10), which is claimed to be more robust and provide richer insights. It operates in two ways: first, it recognizes a difference between brand recall and brand recognition, and second, it incorporates positive and negative motivations with high and low involvement. Positive motives are referred to as transformational motives and negative motives as informational, with their accompanying emotional states (see Table 4.7).

A significant implication here is that although it might be obvious that negative motives produce negative emotions, they can also lead, in time, to more positive feelings, for example, because the dissonance can be the motivator to overcome the negative (as we discussed earlier in this chapter) and hence return to something approaching equilibrium.

By understanding how consumers might react to specific brands, the implications of the four quadrants of the Rossiter–Percy Grid are:

1. *Low-involvement/negative motivations* To attack negative motivations a simple-solution approach is suggested and marketers should not worry too much if consumers don't like the style of message. In order to attack the low-involvement dimension, marketers should keep the benefits relatively clear but not in proliferation. They should be easy to learn from a few exposures.

2. *Low-involvement/positive motivations* In order to attack the low-involvement dimension here, marketers should use repetition of exposures in order to 'build up' reinforcement. For positive motivations, the approach should find an emotional appeal, which is relevant to the consumer in order to encourage liking of the message.

3. *High-involvement/negative motivations* To attack negative motivations here, marketers need to ensure positive reaction to the main point of the message rather than the peripheral issues. In order to exploit the high-involvement dimension, marketers should employ convincing appeals, which do not over-claim benefits. Comparative messages might be useful when consumers perceive relatively similar brand alternatives.

4. *High-involvement/positive motivations* To exploit positive motivations, marketers relate emotional benefits of the product very clearly to the target segment's lifestyle and motivations and should not be overly concerned whether the style of message is liked. In order to exploit high involvement, marketers should provide useful information for those who are highly involved, and should make relatively strong claims for their product or service

www. Have a look at this article, which is accessible from the accompanying web site at www.wileyeurope.com/college/evans:
Hansen, T. (2005). Perspectives on Consumer Decision Making: An Integrated Approach. *Journal of Consumer Behaviour*, Vol 4, No 6. It explores relationships between attitudes, involvement and emotional buying and the role that price and quality play in consumer decision-making.

CASE STUDY 4.1

TNS CASE STUDY: Information processing and memory limitations

So what does the Scottish Executive do anyway? – Brand development in Government communications

Chris Eynon, TNS UK

Where an organization markets many different brands and services (or products) there is a limit to how much a consumer can take in and be expected to piece together to form an overview of that organization. This is in part due to information processing and memory limitations but also reflects the understandable lack of motivation to do the marketers' jobs for them. The full case study on the web site demonstrates how the Scottish Executive tackled this issue.

When the Scottish Executive set out to bring greater structure to its communications by clustering its 28 campaigns under a smaller number of umbrella themes, it seemed both logical and expedient to adopt existing campaign identities for this purpose. Little was it imagined, when TNS was appointed to check out the acceptability of this approach, that this research would lead to the development of a completely new brand framework which would be whole-heartedly adopted across all Scottish Executive communications.

The research quickly identified the weaknesses of the proposed approach, in the disparate nature of the current campaign routes and in their lack of perceived wider relevance. From our recommendations, the brand family of Safer Scotland, Healthier Scotland, Natural Scotland, Smarter Scotland and One Scotland was developed – not only a consistent and integrated structure, but also extending beyond the level of *identity* to real *brand values* to which the target audience could aspire. These were rounded off through the research-assisted adoption of a series of impactful and emotive graphic images, appealing to national sentiment through the use of the Scottish saltire.

The contribution of research to the development of Scottish Executive communications branding was therefore both highly significant and extremely effective.

1. In terms of a consumer's capacity for 'information processing' what can we learn from this case?
2. What would you judge to be the value of the emotional component of the approach and describe how it is employed?

A full version of this case study appears on the accompanying web site for this book: www.wileyeurope.com/college/evans

Reproduced by permission of TNS.

SUMMARY

■ In this chapter, we have reviewed ways of encouraging consumers to 'act' and to respond positively after purchase. We have also introduced moderators of the sequential approach, in the form of involvement.

■ Impulse buying is a pervasive and characteristic feature of the purchasing behaviour of most of us. Consumers can buy all sorts of products on impulse – low and high value, and low and high risk. Impulse buying allows consumers to reflect their self-view and their identities. Certain retail environments, such as airports and casinos, are particularly suitable for impulse buying, and marketers can take a number of steps to improve the probability of impulse purchasing happening.

■ Customer satisfaction is a post-purchase attitude like feeling and is an important theoretical as well as practical concept. Some of the widely known antecedents of customer satisfaction include expectations, disconfirmation of expectations, performance, affect, equity and attributions, whereas complaining behaviour, negative word-of-mouth advertising and repurchase intention are outcomes of dissatisfaction.

■ Cognitive dissonance can occur before purchase as well as after purchase. When alternatives are presented there will usually be both consistent and inconsistent cognitions about each. Marketing can help avoid cognitive dissonance and help reduce it if it is experienced. If a purchase is not satisfying, dissonance arises, because of inconsistent cognitions, dissonance can still occur. The objective is to keep dissonance to a minimum and to encourage repeat purchase or at least the spreading of goodwill. Involvement can help explain the degree to which the pre-/post-purchase sequential model applies to different consumers. Consumers can become involved with product categories, brands, advertisements, communication media and even purchase decisions. Involvement reflects the product's relevance to a consumer and can be enduring, situational and response-driven. Personal relevance can be driven either by some intrinsic personal sources such as knowledge associations based on experiences or by some extrinsic, external sources such as marketing communication activities. Higher levels of involvement often lead to a central route to persuasion whereas lower levels lead to a peripheral route to persuasion. In either case, marketers can aim to employ different strategies to consumers' attitudes. There are other integrating models that build on involvement including the elaboration of likelihood model, the FCB Grid and the Rossiter–Percy Grid. Marketers in general and advertisers in particular can use them to decide brand positioning and spot advertising opportunities.

QUESTIONS

1. **What is impulse buying? Use your own examples to suggest how marketers can encourage impulse buying.**

2. **What is customer satisfaction? How can marketers prepare to offer it? What are its antecedents and consequences?**

3. **What is word of mouth? Why do consumers engage in word of mouth?**

4. **What is post-purchase dissonance? Give your own examples. Did you go on to buy the same products/services/brands again? What did you tell others about them?**

5. **Choose brands for which you have:**
   a. **low involvement, and**
   b. **high involvement.**

   How does theory explain your behaviour with respect to these brands? How can marketers increase consumer involvement?

6. a. **How can involvement be measured?**

b. How do Sherif's social judgement theory and Krugman's passive learning theory help explain consumer involvement?

7. Compare and contrast the FCB, elaboration likelihood and Rossiter–Percy models. How do they explain your buying behaviour for some selected brands? How do they suggest marketers should target you?

FURTHER READING

Festinger L (1957) *Cognitive Dissonance*, Stanford University Press, California. This is the original and seminal work from which marketers have borrowed and adapted the term 'cognitive dissonance' within the context of consumer behaviour, especially but not exclusively post-purchase. Future Foundation (2007)

Rossiter J R, Percy L and Donovan R J (1991) A Better Advertising Planning Grid, *Journal of Advertising Research*, October/November, pp 11–21. This paper is also a seminal contribution. It extends the FCB Grid and the concept of involvement to their own Rossiter-Percy Grid. The paper is well worth reading

CHAPTER 5
CONSUMER DEMOGRAPHICS

CHAPTER OBJECTIVES

After engaging with the material presented in this chapter and its associated exercises and reading, you should be able to:

- Comprehend how demographics contribute to an understanding of consumer behaviour.
- Analyse and evaluate the role played by age in explaining consumer behaviour.
- Analyse and evaluate the role played by gender in explaining consumer behaviour.
- Analyse and evaluate the role played by social grade in explaining consumer behaviour.

INTRODUCTION

Consumer demographics are important for marketers because consumers can be targeted using variables such as age, gender and occupation. But 'why', when this is sometimes seen to be an outmoded approach: 'segmenting consumers according to social-demographics used to be regarded as highly sophisticated . . . it can still shed light onto customer preferences and propensities . . . this is no longer enough' (Cubitt, 2008:23). We tend to subscribe to this view. Indeed, although we discuss age, gender, social grade and family circumstances in various other parts of the book, we devote just this one dedicated chapter to demographics. Cubitt's proposition is mainly predicated on the wealth of personalized data to which marketers now have access and this is explored in more detail in Chapter 11. The value of demographics, however, is not to be dismissed and does add substantively to the stock of knowledge of consumer behaviour.

Consumer behaviour differs with demographic variables. For example, many of our purchases vary by age category, also, men and women can behave differently as consumers. For instance, because of

	Used chicken/burger restaurant in the past three months %	Used any chicken restaurant in the past three months %	Used any burger restaurant in the past three months %	Do not use chicken/burger restaurants %
All	55	45	32	14
Men	58	47	35	14
Women	52	44	28	14
16–19	83	78	54	6
20–24	78	65	53	2
25–34	77	66	50	5
35–44	68	59	39	7
45–54	55	43	26	15
55–64	38	27	18	20
65+	19	14	8	30
AB	50	42	27	18
C1	57	45	32	13
C2	59	48	35	12
D	62	54	37	15
E	45	38	26	13
Age of own children in household				
0–4	77	69	46	4
5–9	79	73	43	5
10–15	71	65	38	6
Any 0–15	73	66	41	6
No children	48	38	28	17

Table 5.1: Market report profiling – visiting habits of chicken/burger restaurants – detailed demographics, based on 2 083 adults, aged 16+

differences in male and female roles in different cultures, men and women end up performing different tasks and behaviours. Marketing has not, traditionally, explored **social class** but uses a surrogate (**social grade**) based on occupational grouping, and this is a demographic variable that has certainly been questioned in recent years, as we shall see later. Incidentally, family circumstances such as stage in the family life cycle, family size and composition can be regarded as demographic factors, but we leave these to Chapter 7, where we explore group, including family, influences on consumer behaviour. Similarly ethnicity, sometimes considered a demographic factor, is examined in Chapter 8.

If any of your course projects have involved conducting an analysis of specific markets, it is quite likely that you will have referred to some of the commercial 'market reports' in your library, such as MINTEL, Keynote, the Target Group Index (TGI) or Market Assessment. These profile customers who buy various products according to the demographic characteristics of age, gender and social grade (occupation) (Table 5.1).

THINKBOX

Go through Table 5.1 and try to infer reasons for the figures given.

Clearly, demographic factors can differentiate buying behaviour but to what extent do they actually explain differences? That is, it might be relatively easy to infer reasons but is inference a dangerous practice?

Not only are demographic characteristics still found in the commercial market reports from MINTEL, Keynote, Market Assessment and so on but also they are included as important profile questions in many consumer research studies. They are relatively easy to collect and, as a result, they can provide consumer researchers and marketers with very useful data.

In the following sections we explore the traditional demographic characteristics of age, gender and social grade and whether they still provide any value to the process of understanding consumer behaviour. We also discuss consumer sexuality, which is becoming an important base for marketers to segment their markets.

AGE AND GENERATIONAL COHORTS

Marketing Week, 1 May 2008. Reproduced by permission of Centaur Media Ltd.

Rather than looking at the issue of age from only a chronological perspective, we can combine **chronological age** with other age perceptions (Table 5.2). This means biologically we have a physical age; psychologically we grow, learn and mature through what we learn and our experiences (also, the 'spirit might be willing but the flesh is weaker'); and socially we develop as a result of our interaction with others, from family to **peer** and **reference group** (Treguer, 2002). Also, certain people (e.g. the

Chronological age	Number of years that you have lived since birth
Biological age	An estimate of your present position with respect to your potential lifespan
Social age	Age in terms of social roles and habits; this is concerned with different roles you take during the life cycle indicating your standing in society
Cognitive age	This is your self-perceived age (the age you perceive yourself to be, related to your self-concept); this can include subjective age and personal age
Subjective age	Your self-perception with reference to other age groups (e.g. middle-aged, elderly, old)
Personal age	This is also based on your self-perceptions and comprises four age dimensions: feel age (how old you feel), look age (how you look), do age (how involved you are in doing things favoured by someone important in your life); and interest age (how similar your interests are to those of a particular age group)
Other perceived age	This is a subjective evaluation of your age status as assessed by others

Source: Based on B Barak and LG Schiffman, Cognitive Age: A Non Chronological Age Variable, *Advances in Consumer Research*, Vol 8 (1981), pp 602–606. Reproduced by permission of the Association for Consumer Research

Table 5.2: Age categories

elderly) cope very well with age transitions and have a higher tendency to perceive themselves to be younger than their actual age. This influences a range of their behaviours including their satisfaction levels with brands and with others around them. Cognitively young consumers lead active lives, enjoy many of the same goods and services as younger and middle-aged consumers and are a good target for products such as travel services, automobile and recreational services (Stephens, 1991). **Cognitive age** has some very useful implications for advertising because feeling younger than your actual age is important (Stephens, 1991). For instance, while targeting the 55 + age group, marketers can use relatively young actors and spokespersons to improve the effectiveness of their advertising message. Similarly, they can portray the elderly in healthy and activity pursuits and depict more family-related interactions. However, keep in mind that the idea of cognitive age applies not only to the elderly but also to different age groups (e.g. young and middle-aged) who all have a certain cognitive age.

Barak (1987) provided a framework for explaining cognitive age, which includes: felt age (how old we feel, which is a component of self concept: see Chapter 6), look age (how we look, which is also a component of self-concept), group referral (identification with groups/tribes: see Chapter 7), do age (activities engaged in to 'escape') and interest age (engaging with experiences).

One approach, then, is to consider how those from specific 'generations' behave as consumers. Each cohort will have gone through the same era and will have had similar experiences during their formative years as adults. A major implication of the **generational cohort** approach is that marketers are given clues as to what to say to each cohort segment and how to say it, on the basis of the formative events experienced within each cohort. Indeed Belk (1988) has asserted that 'Possessions are a convenient means of storing the memories and feelings that attach our sense of past' and in this way the consumption patterns of generational cohorts can be predicated on important symbolism.

We start by exploring several specific age segments: the burgeoning 'grey' market, including baby boomers and first, young consumers. However, we will hold back a discussion of children and their buying behaviour and influence to Chapter 7 because this again needs to be integrated with wider aspects of **family buying behaviour**.

THINKBOX

The Who sang about 'My Generation' and each era has its own music which captures the ethos of the times. This means that the late teen and early twenties phase is significant in our development.

Recently the Gangsta rap genre appears to use stronger and stronger images and extreme lyrics. In the 1990s, the Spice Girls attempted to sing about post-feminist self-confidence in 'Wannabe' (but they really really wanted was 'zagazig ah' – perhaps not fully following through a post-feminist political call to revolution?). In the 1980s, Frankie Goes to Hollywood recommended 'Relax', the Undertones advocated 'Teenage Kicks' in 1978 and in 1968 the Beatles considered a 'Revolution'. Our personal development as we move from child to adult is full of contradictions and the tensions due to our physical and emotional development. We want to find our own identity, yet value the security of the family. At the same time, because of the former, we are prone to rebelling against the latter, producing difficult-to-deal-with tensions.

How does your generational cohort interact with the world? What music reflects your formative years? Why?

What do you think your cognitive age is? What should marketers do to satisfy your age requirements? Contrast your views with those of a friend.

It has been suggested that whereas 'adults' define themselves by their occupations, youths are 'defined by their consumption patterns. Brands and products are therefore of critical importance to teenagers' (Gillespie, 2003) and this is clearly congruent with the multiple roles of self-expressive behaviour discussed in the next chapter and the phenomenon of tribal behaviour (in Chapter 7) which facilitates a degree of individualism and even narcissism but within the safety of a group.

A major generational cohort, and in some sense the first to be especially recognized as such, was the generation born in the years following the Second World War; that is, between 1945 and 1965. This explains the subsequent divisions of generations based on a 20-year generational span (i.e. allowing individual development to about age 20) and the mid-decade periods. However, we 'work backwards' here, from the most recent adult/young adult generation, those born between 1977 and 1994.

Generation Y (or 'N') (16–33 year olds in 2010)

Those born between 1977 and 1994 have been termed **Generation Y** or the Millennial Generation (Adam Smith Institute, 1998). Sometimes this cohort is labelled the 'N-Gen' after 'the net' and the 'information revolution' which has been such a major impact on their development (Schewe and Meredith, 2004). Many in this category have been found to be materialists, brand-orientated, risk-takers, keen on business, hedonism and illegal drugs and having disrespect for politics. But they are not as cynical as their predecessor, **Generation X** (see below). The Future Foundation (2000) extended this research and found Generation Y to be more accepting of multi-nationals and less interested in protesting. Further analysis of Generation Y has been conducted by Shepherdson (2000) and Gofton (2001). If this group were targeted, this profile could provide useful clues as to the sort of message and media to use and reach them.

Davidson (2003) discusses them as being introspectively and self-expressively motivated:

They are only interested in their personal lives, the parties they go to, the clothes they wear ... the absence of community ... the cult of celebrity provides an exciting surrogate community ... celebrity (provides) a real identity in a sea of mock individuality.

THINKBOX

a) As Goode (2008) declares, 'reaching the 18–34 year old age demographic is a real challenge for advertisers, as this group is spending less time consuming print and broadcast media'. But perhaps the mobile phone is the vehicle?
The internet-enabled mobile using engaging experiences and links with social networking sites will be the route to Gen Y. What do you think and why?

b) About 40% of 18–24 year olds voted in the 2005 General Election in UK, compared with over 60% of the equivalent age group in 1992 (Baines, 2006).
Influences over voting intention are varied but TV debates between party leaders – so often rejected by the incumbent party – were cited by 29% of the 18–24s: much higher than any other age group:

	All	18–24	45–54
Internet	2	9	1
Newspapers	14	15	15
Opinion Polls	3	6	2
Party Election Broadcasts	12	22	10
TV Debates Between Party Leaders	18	29	17
Views of Local Candidates	23	9	19

Table 5.3: IpsosMORI (2005) reported in Baines (2006)

What do you take from this research and how would you advise politicians?

THINKBOX

FUTURE FOUNDATION RESEARCH
Youth Trend

It seems that today's generation of young people is somewhat at odds with our perception of youth as rebellious, anti-establishment and idealistic: today's youth are on average quite inclined towards global capitalism, show little interest in politics, seem willing to participate fully in society and to embrace the entrepreneurial ideal. Brought up in an era of ever increasing affluence, they have come to expect a life of fulfilment and excitement, which they seek through various forms of escapism.

Source: Times Higher, cover, 26 June 2008

Do you recognize your generation from any of this? If not, why not?

Reproduced by permission of The Future Foundation http://www.futurefoundation.net/

Generation X (or Baby Busters) (34–44 year olds in 2010)

This group was born approximately from 1966 to 1976 and the name 'Generation X' was coined by Coupland (1991). Indeed he probably started the sequence of 'alphabetical' generations because Gen X was the first so labelled back in the early 1990s. They have become important spenders – demanding their own products and searching for their own identity. A complicating factor is that this group has been found to be especially individualistic and sceptical of marketing activity. O'Donohoe and Tynan (1998), for example, found that young adults are indeed advertising-literate. This doesn't make them difficult to reach, but it is proving harder to influence them. Coupland (1991), Bashford (2000) and Ritchie (1995) have analysed their behaviour and attitudes. Ritchie, for example, declares that 'Xers' have known much more advertising all their lives, compared with older generations but that they do not

> dislike advertising ... they dislike hype ... overstatement, self importance, hypocrisy and the assumption that anyone would want to be disturbed at home by a salesman on the telephone [but] they do not reject the concept of conspicuous consumption. (Ritchie, 1995:159)

Research International (1996) also found these young adults (by then in their 20s) to be dismissive of advertising that insults intelligence, knocks competitors or tries too hard to be 'hip'. Coupland provides a series of values of Xers, some of which are reproduced in Table 5.4.

Xers might also be more interested in engaging with marketing rather than being passive receivers of it. If so, marketing can provide some of what Generation X might be looking for – that is, greater interactivity and participation in marketing communications.

Value	Definition
Divorce assumption	A form of *safety net-ism*, the belief that if a marriage doesn't work out, then there is no problem because partners can simply seek a divorce.
Anti-sabbatical	A job taken with the sole intention of staying only for a limited period of time (often one year). The intention is usually to raise enough funds to partake in another, more personally meaningful activity such as water-colour sketching in Crete or designing computer-knit sweaters in Hong Kong. Employers are rarely informed of intentions.
Legislated nostalgia	To force a body of people to have memories they do not actually possess: 'How can I be a part of the 1960s generation when I don't even remember any of it?'
Spectacularism	A fascination with extreme situations.
Cult of aloneness	The need for autonomy at all costs, usually at the expense of long-term relationships. Often brought about by overly high expectations of others.
Voter's block	The attempt, however futile, to register dissent with the current political system by simply not voting.
Yuppie Wannabes	An X Generation sub-group that believes the myth of a yuppie lifestyle being both satisfying and viable. Tend to be highly in debt, involved in some form of substance abuse and show a willingness to talk about Armageddon after three drinks.
Me-ism	A search by an individual, in the absence of training in traditional religious tenets, to formulate a personally tailored religion alone. Most frequently a mishmash of reincarnation, personal dialogue with a nebulously defined god figure, naturalism and a karmic eye-for-eye attitude.
Strangelove reproduction	Having children to make up for the fact that one no longer believes in the future.
2 + 2 = 5-ism	Caving in to a target marketing strategy aimed at oneself after holding out for a long period of time. 'Oh, all right, I'll buy your stupid cola. Now leave me alone.'
Down-nesting	The tendency of parents to move to smaller, guest-room-free houses after the children have moved away so as to avoid children aged 20 to 30 who have boomeranged home.

Source: Adapted by the authors from D Coupland *Generation X: Tales for an Accelerated Culture*, London, Abacus, 1991. Reproduced by permission of Time Warner Book Group UK

Table 5.4: Xers

THINKBOX

Consider the difference between a (passive) advertising message for Marlboro cigarettes and a more participative approach which involved a 'treasure hunt'. Here, an advertisement announced a competition and gave a telephone number that entrants should call. The telephone contact involved asking the caller various questions and it gathered some personal data for a company database. If the quiz questions were correctly answered, a mail pack was sent; this included a letter, a map and a video. Each contained 'clues' as to where the 'hidden treasure' could be found and the recipient played the role of a treasure hunter.

Are younger market segments more likely to engage with this sort of participative marketing message than older segments?

Indeed, in their interpretation of their research in 35 countries, Research International (1996) suggested that practical implications of the young adult perspective would lead to 'interactive, challenging relationships' between advertiser and consumer. This is congruent with the postmodern (see Chapter 7) construct of **hyperreality** (Firat and Schultz, 1997).

THINKBOX

You are quite likely to be within Generation Y. How do the above descriptions 'fit' your outlook and consumption behaviour, and those of your contemporaries?

Between X and Boomer

From a major research programme, Taylor Nelson Sofres (2004) found the 35 to 50 age group to 'dip in and out' of things. They switch their pursuits and relationships and want relatively immediate results from their activities. 'They enjoy watching do-it-yourself and cookery programmes on TV (rather than doing it themselves).' This reinforces research about the *cellular household*: 'Family viewing is extremely rare with family members spread around the house, watching different TV sets' (Collins, 2004). Marketers will be heartened by the findings that 35- to 50-year-old men are very interested in clothes, appearance and brands and enjoy shopping (Taylor Nelson Sofres, 2004).

Baby Boomers (45–65 year olds in 2010)

We turn now to consider the first of the generational cohorts identified as such, those born between 1945 and 1965. The **baby boomers** – those born in the years following the Second World War – have very distinctive attributes and have became a very important target for marketers. They were involved in a massive social revolution which changed music, fashions, political thought and social attitudes forever (Fifield, 2002). They were the generation to grow up in the 1960s when the term 'teenager' hadn't been used previously. They were not 'small adults' who, in previous generations, had worn similar clothes to their parents. The new generation, however, wanted their own culture, their own fashions and music, and their own social attitudes, which rejected the values of their parents. Coupled with this desire for ownership of their thoughts and lives, the baby boomer generation was the most affluent (generally) of any 'youth market' until their era, so they were able to engage in the consumer market, and marketers responded with a fashion and music explosion which we had previously not experienced.

They had their formative years in the 1960s and 1970s and saw and engaged with significant developments such as rock and pop music, youth fashion, the women's 'liberation' movement, the freedom that 'the pill' gave to sexual behaviour and world events such as 'Vietnam' and the 'Cold War'. They engaged in a tremendously optimistic youth culture. Famously, Jack Weinberg of University of California was quoted in 1965 as saying 'we don't trust anybody over 30'. The so called summer of love of 1967 was more of a movement to shed conservatism, advance peace and social revolution and wasn't really restricted to that particular summer. Indeed the Beatles' 'Revolution' track was published in 1968. Dylan wrote 'Johnny's in the basement mixing up the medicine, I'm on the pavement thinking about the Government' (Dylan, 1965). It did not take long, however, for optimism to turn sour. The reaction of the 'establishment' to such social movements as that against the Vietnam war led some to question whether change could be achieved. In 1972 David Bowie wrote 'and my brother's back at home with his Beatles and his Stones, we never got it off with that revolution stuff – what a drag, too many snags'. Then social causes seemed to give way to greater individualism. In 1976 the Sex Pistols 'sang' about 'Anarchy in the UK'. Perhaps the Punk movement heralded a new generation: Generation X (which indeed was the name of a punk band).

The Baby Boomer cohort, however, is now turning 50. There are over 20 million people aged over 50 in the UK, and this figure will approach 25 million by 2021 (Ahmad, 2002). Such a consumerism-literate market should be extremely attractive. Indeed, in USA a baby boomer turned 50 every 6.8 seconds in 2001. The large segment coupled with its purchasing power – it was the first to become empowered as consumers – means it is a favourite target for marketers.

Overall, they are relatively wealthy, in terms of inheritance from their parents. That previous generation was 'blessed' with low house prices when they bought and a lifestyle which was much less materialistic. As a result their estates have often (but clearly not always) been cascading down to the new over-50 market. Many have a 'cognitive age' less than their 'chronological' age' and therefore act much more youthfully than their age might suggest (Szmigin and Carrigan, 2000, 2001). In other words they have a youthful **self-concept** (Moschis, 2003), and we explore self-concept theory in the next chapter.

The Over-50s

The over-50s in the UK hold 80% of the country's wealth and 40% of spending (£145 billion pa) and is not only the only segment that is growing but also the one that has more disposable income than all the others combined (Cummins, 1994; Bond, 1997) (see Figures 5.1 and 5.2).

Worldwide there are 600 million people over 60 years of age, and by 2050 there could be 2 billion. Their growth as a proportion of the population has been cited as a worrying factor in many countries (Moschis, 2003): more pensioners than the smaller workforce will be able to support but, from a consumption perspective, it is obvious that they are very important to marketers. But it is foolish to lump these together in just one segment (Gunter, 1998; Treguer, 2002). There are those in their sixties and seventies and indeed the over-70s who are from other generations with lifestyles and attitudes of their own (Table 5.5).

Research amongst the over-50s has revealed several characteristics. The over-50s don't like to be portrayed as 'old' but at the same time would see through attempts to portray them as 'young', so caution is needed. They often prefer to keep their youthful self concept: 'the notion that a person of a certain age is like a person of any age, can be rather effective' (Moschis, 2003), as suggested in Figure 5.3.

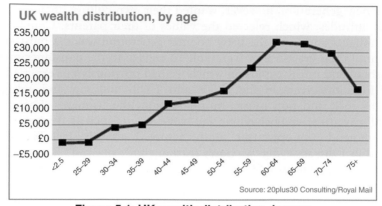

Figure 5.1: UK wealth distribution, by age

Source: 20plus30 consulting/Royal Mail (2007), reported in Marketing Week (2007) Generation LX 24 May 40–41

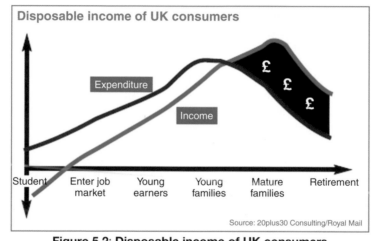

Figure 5.2: Disposable income of UK consumers

Source: 20plus30 consulting/Royal Mail (2007), reported in Marketing Week (2007) Generation LX 24 May 40–41

There has certainly been an explosion of magazine titles aimed at various over-50 groups, demonstrating that the market is not homogeneous and that the various groups can be reached. The profiling in this sector is not merely on the basis of age, however; social grade and geodemographics are also being used and there is a trend toward overlaying this with attitudinal research. An example of this comes from the analysis of the TGI in 1993 (Cummins, 1994) which found, based on shopping attitudes and behaviour, that there are 'astute cosmopolitans', constituting about 19% of the 50 to 75s and who are discerning consumers. There are also the 'temperate xenophobes' (20% of 50 to 75s) who are less likely to go abroad or eat 'foreign food'. The 'thrifty traditionalists' make up 20% and a further 19% are 'outgoing funlovers'. The largest group is the 'apathetic spenders' (21%) who use credit cards to extend their purchasing power beyond what they can really afford (Cummins, 1994). The over-50s can be more loyal: 'The problem with young consumers is that they are "flippy". As soon as someone else targets them they jump ship. The mature consumer tends to be more loyal and they tend to do more business' (Cooper, 2003).

There is another issue for marketers and consumer researchers, here: 'As soon as you target the mature sector, people are worried that it's going to upset their youth market, but not if you use niche channels like direct mail and the internet' (Cooper, 2003). Saga is a major direct marketer, for instance, that is focused on the over 50s.

55–64s

Take more holidays than the average and more than half are planning two or more holidays in the next 12 months.

Certain charities such as blind causes, cancer and the elderly appeal to the over-55s more than the norm.

65–74s

Favourite activities are gardening, crosswords, reading. A significant proportion enjoy classical music, support the National Trust, do voluntary work and play bridge. They have an above-average number of long-term savings plans.

75–84s

Less likely to have travelled abroad in their lives, buy a significant amount of plants and vitamins through the mail but are unenthusiastic about other mail order purchases.

85+

Have fewer interests but continue to favour gardening, classical music and current affairs. They are significant charity supporters despite lower incomes.

Source: Adapted by the authors from the Telegraph Group reported in E. Carling, Grappling with the Grey Market, *Marketing Direct* (1999)

Table 5.5: Over-50s

Figure 5.3: Pragmatism regarding their future but still remembering the good times of the 1960s is a theme of some marketers' appeals, as is the case with Liverpool Victoria's use of Cilla Black and a '60s retro appeal

This takes us back to cognitive age and behaving as old as one feels can lead to some potentially embarrassing behaviours. As Featherstone (1991) proposes 'youth styles and lifestyles are migrating up the age scale and as the 1960s generation ages they are taking some of the youth-oriented dispositions with them'. The old cliché of being embarrassed by one's father dancing conjures images probably not to be dwelt on, but does signal wider implications for consumer behaviour and marketing. Goulding and Shankar (2002) for example found that 30–40 year olds join the dance/rave culture for the cognitive age reasons including reflecting self-expression (see Chapter 6) and new social groups and communities (see Chapter 7). They sometimes appear to be motivated by products that will enhance youthful appearances; they can cope with a fragmented lifestyle (see Chapter 7 for postmodernism). They also seem to be driven by materialism and 'brands' and by sensation ('escapism and adrenaline driven activities'). Goulding and Shankar (2002) suggest that marketers will be interested in this group, not only because of their clear engagement with the consumer society but also because they are often earlier adopters of new products (see Chapter 9) and because they often have higher disposal incomes, partly because they have deferred having children to later in life and sometimes not at all.

Figure 5.4: But there are times when age catches up

Figure 5.5: Baby boomers are as young as they feel and as old as they are
A slight spoof on a classic Wonderbra advertising campaign and is actually an advertisement by Age Concern.
See Evans and Rowland (1996) for a discussion of the semiotics of campaigns.
© Age Concern England. Reproduced by permission. Image courtesy of the Advertising Archives

THINKBOX

Marketers are sometimes criticized for not targeting older segments appropriately. Simcock and Sudbury (2006) for example report that their content analysis of TV advertising in UK revealed 'an apparent reluctance by marketers ... to portray older

models'. As we have already seen, advertising creatives are overwhelmingly young, so could part of the problem be that they find empathizing uncool?
Consider this view from within the motor industry:

The car dealers often despair of the marketing initiatives they see. The focus is on the young or the young family, even for the point of sale in showrooms . . . older people often have 2 or 3 cars per family, yet manufacturers get hung up on items like cup holders. (Pulham, 2003)

A major issue, then, surrounding this is that marketers tend to target younger age segments yet the 50–60 segment buy two-thirds of all cars, more long-haul holidays than younger segments and even 25% of all toys (Sclater, 2003). Datamonitor (2003) speculates that one reason for the relative neglect is that half the staff in advertising agencies are themselves under 30 and it has been suggested that it is not always seen to be 'cool' for these to design advertising 'creative' for older segments (Cooper, 2003). It probably isn't a case, however, of allocating older staff to older accounts, as Cooper suggests; whatever age group media planners are shouldn't affect what they're planning. They should be experienced enough to target the demographics of their clients irrespective of their own interests.

Could you design an advertising campaign for package holidays aimed at, say, the 55–64s?

Changes in birth and death rates over time determine cohort size and it is well known that many Western countries are experiencing a shift toward older profiles of their populations. Indeed Europe has been described as 'undergoing a demographic winter and now Europe is an elderly continent' (Institute for Family Policy, 2008). The European Union has six million more over 65s than under 14s, compared with the situation in 1980 when there were 36 more children than pensioners (Institute for Family Policy, 2008).

Population:[1] **by sex and age, 1971, 2006 and 2031**

United Kingdom

Millions

I Mid-year estimates for 1971 to 2006: 2005-based projections for 2031. See Appendix, Part 1: Population estimates and projections

Source: Office for National Statistics Government Actuary's Department:Governement Registar Office for Scotland: Northern Ireland Statistics and Research Agency

THINKBOX

Are you the first born in your family?

If so, are you eager to discuss any high involvement purchases that you are about to, or have made?

Research suggests this to be the case, more so than if you are a 'later-born' (Nancarrow *et al.,* 1999).

Psychology has long found birth order to be a determinant of behaviour and personality. Not least because parents often devote much time to the first born child and later borns sometimes get less attention. This can have the effect that first borns expect to receive more attention and even have more parental pressure on them to succeed.

First borns are perhaps more likely to turn to others when under stress (social stroking as the psychologists have it). It is on this that proposition that first borns might turn to others for support when buying high involvement or high risk products, is predicated. Nancarrow *et al.*'s research supports this and suggests that marketers can target first borns because it can be simple to identify birth order via a simple and relatively non-controversial market research survey question.

From your experience of birth order in your family or families that you know, what could be the implications of this, for consumer behaviour and marketing action?

Gremlins: the New Batch

Chapter 7 explores the role of children in family buying but we turn here to a brief review of the consumer behaviour of children and how marketers use this knowledge. According to Childwise (2006) the 9–13s spend £3 bn themselves and influence £30 bn (see Chapter 7). In a rather disturbing study of 9–13 year olds, 70% of children have a TV in their rooms, most with a video or DVD, 40% also watch horror as well as children's programmes (Nairn *et al.*, 2007). Approximately 57% would be happier if they had more money to buy things themselves. Should these findings raise concerns for society?

Cairns (2006) states that 'child culture is complex and its relationship with the adult world even more so'. Children engage with old fashioned toys and games but also with explicit and violent video games, with similar passion. Ten year olds have internalized about 400 different brands; Nairn (2006) reported that a young child in a qualitative study, on entering a branch of Boots, asked her mum if they were going to buy a car that day:

Source: Ford Motor Company Ltd.   Source: Boots UK Ltd.

Marketers are not only interested in children for their current engagement with their products but in terms of how they will be as adult consumers in years to come (MacDougall and Chantrey 2004). A key aspect of this is, of course that the 9–13 year olds of today have grown up in a 24/7, internet, mobile phone world. TV will not be the major advertising vehicle for them. Advergames and viral marketing could be the interactive media to succeed in their lives. MacDougall and Chantrey drew from child psychology, which suggests that even at 6 months a child is beginning to form mental images of brand logos, and in USA, 20% of three year olds (before they can read and write) signal requests for specific brand products.

There are concerns that children are growing up too soon and marketing is one culprit: fuelling their maturity into adult consumerhood. Kilby (2006) for example asks whether brands and marketers are hijacking childhood. Consider a web site (missbimbo.com) which allows such young girls to create bimbos. *Marie Claire* magazine (2008) was furious about the site's facilities to allow girls to give their bimbos boob jobs and sexy lingerie. The magazine reports Hibberd, of Parentkind as warning that 'after playing the game some will aspire to have breast operations and take diet pills . . . a nine year old fails to appreciate the irony and sees the bimbo as a cool role model'.

Does the Barbie web site encourage girls to engage with a fun fantasy childhood or bypass it?

Source: www.barbiegirls.com

The many children's games playable from the 'mousebreaker' web site are supported by a plethora of adult advertisements:

Source: www.mousebreaker.com

Horgan (2006) shows a strange and disturbing paradox: 11 and 12 year olds can be worried about bullying, the dark and about their parents splitting up. There has also been media attention given to a generation in which parents are worried about letting their children walk to local shops, to school or to go anywhere by themselves. Yet Horgan also describes the 11–12s ('inbetweenies') as 'a media savvy age group and the children's descriptions of 'good' advertising read like a classic advertising brief'.

THINKBOX

FUTURE FOUNDATION RESEARCH
Longevity

One of the most significant demographic shifts occurring within society is the ageing of the population. Before 2025, the number of people aged between 45 and 64 will have increased by 3.5 m, while average life expectancy will be 82, the fruit of medical advances and healthier living. There is already a lively public debate about how enhanced longevity will be financed as concepts such as retirement and pensions are forced to adjust to dramatically new conditions and expectations. Discussion about longevity has in many senses deepened the narrative of life-stage planning; it has brought home to individuals just how much preparation the forward organization of their lives might require. At a general level this gives a basis for company-to-consumer dialogue in a number of markets. At the same time, more and more spending power is going to be pushed into the higher age brackets as we work longer, enjoy the benefit of non-state pensions and exult in steadily accumulating home property values. It is also likely that the next generation of older consumers will not think of themselves in a twilight phase at all, but rather carry forward all the expectations of good service, more fun and richer experiences that have matured inside them across this age of affluence. It is old hat, however, to predict a cult of old age. Every service that can hold back a wrinkle, control the menopause, extend the active sex-life, restore hair in the right places and rejuvenate a tired appearance will find a continuously excitable market. Grey hair will mean wisdom to some, and a little more cellulite to many.

What are your views here?

Reproduced by permission of The Future Foundation http://www.futurefoundation.net/

Consumer researchers often joke about their analysis of demographic data being 'broken down by age and sex'. We now turn from age to sex, or at least *gender*.

GENDER

Women account for about 80% of household buying decisions (Gardner, 2008) and marketers target women even if they are not the user of the product. Even where there is a 'joint' use, as in the case of condoms, women are important purchasers. In that market, 95% of purchases traditionally were by men but now, women buy one-third of all condoms (Cubitt, 2004). This phenomenon is replicated in many consumer markets and is one of the themes of this section. Another theme is the changing social roles of men and women and how these are reflected by marketers' actions.

Often, such reflection is via gender stereotyping but, although this has been used extensively over many decades, it hasn't always escaped criticism (Nokes, 1994; Rees, 1995; Murray, 1995). Reliance on

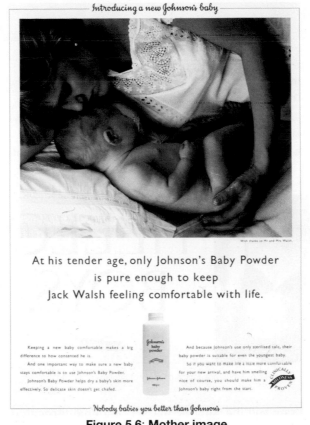

Figure 5.6: Mother image
This image powerfully reflects the strength of maternal instincts.
© Johnson & Johnson Ltd. Reproduced by permission. Image courtesy of the Advertising Archives

'mother' (Figure 5.2) or 'mistress' or 'career woman' images of women in advertising sometimes attracts complaints on sexist or offensive grounds, as have some more recent demeaning images of men.

In 1970s there appeared to be only two main female stereotypes, the mother image and the mistress image and indeed if one goes back to the advertising of that decade, it is littered with what we might regard as sexist female stereotyping. The 1980s, however, saw greater female independence in society. Gender roles changed and more women joined the work force. Marketing was not always adept at replaying these changing roles. An advertisement for Crest hotels being a case in point – the tagline being 'I've finally found a hotel that treats me like a man': were women really wanting to be treated like men?

The pressure, and to some extent reality, of 1980s society was, however, depicted in a classic VW Golf advertisement, in which there is clearly a partnership breakdown and the woman leaves home throwing away her fur coat (good!) but she keeps her Golf keys.

The 1990s and beyond have seen further changes in gender roles whereby what was termed 'girl power' came to the fore. We have already commented on the Spice Girls' attempt at taking the feminist movement forward with rather limp and meaningless lyrics, but Annie Lennox and Aretha Franklin were somewhat more powerful with their version of 'The Sisters are Doing it For Themselves'. Women were more assertive as reflected in the Wonderbra campaign which attracted much attention as portraying independent assertiveness rather then sexism.

	20–24	45–54	65+
My partner does some housework, less than me and that's OK	33	37	35
Does some but not enough	8	4	4

Source: Woman 2000 Report: Household chores.

Table 5.6: Sex roles not changing fast enough? Percentages

Source: Winderbra. Image courtesy of the Advertising Archives

Increases in the divorce rate and the 'singles' market (imposed through divorce or by decision) have added to the more general changes in sex roles, with women becoming more individualistic through their own careers rather than being housewives per se. The previously cited study of family life across the EU, conducted by the Institute for Family Policy (2008), found that a marriage broke down every 30 seconds across Europe. Two-thirds of marriages in Belgium, Luxemburg and Spain ended in divorce. Related to this, the report found that there are more Europeans living alone: 54 million. Marketing to women, however, may still be in need of updating.

As female roles change, so do those of men, but perhaps not as fast as women would like (Table 5.6).

EXAMPLE 5.1

Could Figure 5.7, for example, be seen as sexist by men?

The revolutionary Levi's advertisement of the 1980s saw a 'stripping' Nick Kaman in a launderette. Innocent enough even then, but it introduced new ways of depicting men in advertising. Since then we have witnessed an increase in the portrayal of naked or near-naked men in advertising. The use of naked women has often been criticized as sexist, but what about naked men? In 2008 Francoise Xavier appeared in Diet Coke TV commercials. The storyline seemed to be that three young female office workers deliberately get trapped in a lift to be rescued by the engineer. The implication is that more took place between the four of them.

Lee Jeans attracted attention in 1997 with its 'girl power' advertisement. The ASA received many complaints on the grounds of sexism (against men) but rejected them:

Figure 5.7: Sexist male advertising?
© Sanyo Europe Ltd. Reproduced by permission

Source: Lee Jeans

Are these ads sexist toward men? Why or why not?

We have seen a variety of male stereotypes such as those we might term: 'caring sharing new man', the 'family' man, the 'yob lad', 'modelling' man, 'househusband' man, as well as gay images. Female stereotyping has been criticized for decades but could it be that male images might come in for the same treatment? In a study by Elliott and Elliott (2005), young men did not respond particularly positively to the portrayal of naked/sexual male imagery in advertising, homophobia being one major theme to emerge; as was another, which 'identified body consciousness and vanity as female traits'.

In a broader context, in a study conducted by the market research agency Capibus on behalf of the Chartered Institute of Marketing (CIM) (2000), 48% of a sample of 1013 adults in UK thought women are inaccurately stereotyped in advertising but only 39% thought men were inaccurately so stereotyped.

What the advertising does	Illustrations	Why is it bad?
Projects sex stereotypes of a weaker role of women in life.	Show women as submissive; in constant need of alteration or improvement; feeling ashamed of themselves; dissatisfied in life; confused, childish, contradictory, or generally in need of help.	This leads to beliefs among women that they are or they ought to be weak, mindless and in need of help. Ignores the true role of women in society such as that of successful professional women.
Redefines attractiveness from something natural to an unattainable ideal; leads to erosion of self-esteem with no room for inner beauty.	Show impossible youth, impossible perfection, which is inhuman and (in most cases) can only be accomplished with professional make-up and hairstyles.	Encourages women to desire to attain impossible perfection and body figure; it becomes difficult for many women to gain jobs in certain areas (e.g. flight attendants); leads to higher levels of frustration among women as the standard seems unattainable; causes problems among teenagers who wish to look too thin (many eat too little)
Portrays women as 'things' or 'mere sex objects'.	Use stunningly disordered models, fragmented body parts; women displayed as dolls or animals; a woman's face as a mask, and her body as an object.	Leads to destruction of women's true self; may cause violence against women.

Source: Based on J A Cohan, Towards a New Paradigm in the Ethics of Women's Advertising, *Journal of Business Ethics*, Vol 33 No 4 (2001), pp. 323–337. Reproduced with kind permission of Springer Science and Business Media.

Table 5.7: Ethical issues in women in advertising

Sex appeals produced interesting results: 59% of 15 to 24s said they enjoy the use of sex to promote a product but this fell to just 23% of the over-65s; and 60% of women disliked the approach compared with just 37% of men.

Marketing cannot afford to assume all women to be homogeneous (and similarly for men). Indeed as we act out multiple roles 'in the post millennial society individuals will be able to pick and choose different gender schemes or choose not to care about gender at all' (Kacen, 2000).

In fact, Cohan (2001) identifies three major ethical issues related to advertising messages targeted at women (Table 5.7) and makes a compelling argument urging the advertising industry to project images and values which women hold as important, and to discontinue the use of stereotypical images. Cohan's argument is not to give up sex appeal altogether but to become more inclusive by showing images of not only young but also older women with less than perfect figures with a more natural look.

However, not all advertising is bad or leads to such consequences. For example, the cosmetics industry has successfully used sensual images of females to convey benefits to consumers.

EXAMPLE 5.2

Figure 5.8: Things appear to have changed
Packaging suggesting 'the weaker sex' and a 1900 advertisement for what appears to be little more than a face mask. This was aimed at men to control their wives smoking in public – and even their 'excessive talking'!
© Alcoa Inc. Reproduced by permission. Image courtesy of the Advertising Archives

Figure 5.9: But have they . . . sexy or sexist?
Is this demeaning to women because she is in a state of undress? Is it demeaning to men because she is dominating him with a whip? Or is it merely reflecting mutual sexuality humorously?
© Skechers Footwear USA/Phil Mucci Photography LLC. Reproduced by permission

Many also think that if the message is targeted at a suitable audience using an appropriate medium (e.g. a specialist magazine), then there is less chance that the contents of the message will be perceived as offensive by someone. Jaffe and Berger (1994) argued that, due to a rise in number of working women, advertisers were already using modern images of women. An example that was quoted included the projection of a superwoman image, where they manage the demands of their jobs and their homes with little help from others. For example, advertisers often project an egalitarian women image in the advertisements where woman and husband (both working) share the household chores together. Jaffe and Berger (1994) investigated the effect of these modern female role portrayals in print ads for food products, and found that the egalitarian portrayal was the most effective role portrayal among many segments of the female market.

It will be interesting to monitor campaigns such as the one run for Dove soap, in which female models who are not of 'catwalk' appearance are used. These models reflect and celebrate 'real' women of many different sizes and shapes. Will this break the mould or will women be drawn to what appears to be the aspirational supermodel stereotypes?

Source: Dove, Image courtesy of the Advertising Archives

This *Marketing Week* clipping describes advertising that still does not adhere to European sexual guidelines for advertising alcohol.

EXAMPLE 5.3

MarketingWeek

Girl's Clothes Disappear, But Then So Does the Beer

Where is this mythical lager that improves sexual success? The Diary has certainly yet to discover it.

According to the European Forum for Responsible Drinking (EFRD), 57 of the 109 alcohol ads that were non-compliant with industry guidelines failed to meet the sexual and/or social success guidelines (*MW* last week).

The latest beer to fall foul of this is Rubbel Sexy Lager from Belgium. Not only did Bucking-hamshire Trading Standards complain about the lager's name promoting sexual success, but the fact the bottles' labels feature an image of a woman in a swimsuit that can be scratched off to reveal her naked body didn't really help either. Consequently the Portman Group has banned Sexy Lager from being sold.

But as far as the Diary's concerned the main issue has been missed here – what are the implications if the rumours that delabelling a bottle denotes sexual frustration are true?

Marketing Week, 19 April 2007. Reproduced with permission of Centaur Media Plc.

THINKBOX

Naked female models were found to be less interesting and more insulting to women than to men (Dishman 1993). But less so if relevant to the product (Tinkham & Reid 1988). Even for men, sexual images are not good at communicating a brand's message, they are more effective at gaining attention (Reichert *et al* 2001). Society has become desensitised to explicit sexual content and images (Zimmermann and Dahlberg 2008). Reichert and Lambiase (2003) suggested a typology. Dress/nudity from tight fitting to nudity), Sexual Behaviour (hugging, kissing, voyeurism and more intimate), Sexual Referents (double entendre, innuendo, setting, camera angles), Sexual Embeds (objects symbolising sexual body parts). Stern (1991) has suggested a trend to 'commercial pornography'. What are your views?

EXAMPLE 5.4

Diago wanted to increase Baileys consumption outside the Christmas season and build brand loyalty. Chemistry Communications Group created a campaign centred on The Bailey Lounge. This promoted the idea of drinking Baileys in new ways during a social occasion. About 200 000 members of the Baileys relationship marketing programme were targeted.

Initial communications were designed to woo the customer, with attention made to their preferred mode of contact, such as mail, email or SMS. Longer-serving members are encouraged to engage more with the brand through, for example, digital activity. Sites such as Baileys' Egg Directory used amusing Easter-themed content to give new serving suggestions.

Diago also invited members to divulge what their simple pleasures were by postcard. There were 5 000 respondents and the material collected was collated into a coffee-table book that was sent to new members and sold through Baileys.

The campaign achieved remarkable results, with recipients drinking 300% more in 2005–06 and 224% in 2006–07, compared with the control group. Judges said it was 'faultless in how it communicated Baileys' story. It was perfectly pitched at its target audience'.

© Direct Marketing Association. Reproduced with permission.

Understanding Consumer Behaviour via Information Processing Styles

This is concerned with the idea that the male and female brains might 'work' differently. Information processing style has been generally reviewed by Kitchen and Spickett-Jones (2003) but the point in the current section concerns possible gender differences as identified by Moir and Moir (1998). Males tend to be selective processors of information and use heuristics cues, whereas females tend to be comprehensive processors of information paying attention to all of the information (Darley and Smith, 1995; Meyers-Levy and Maheswaran, 1991).

Neurolinguistic programming – NLP, as it is termed – is already being used in practice to target consumers; for example, Tunney (1999) explains the use by Marketing Focus of NLP to identify 14 different types of information processing styles. Ford is also using brain scans to detect which car designs prompt different responses, and the Open University with London Business School evaluate TV commercials via brain scans. As Steven Rose, director of brain and behaviour research at the Open University states,

> What would be worrying if marketers, governments or police felt they could control people's thoughts by manipulating brain processes in this way ... I am not sure marketing are going to be looking at this ... but I would be surprised if they don't. (Leighton, 2004)

Previous research also suggests that females are more likely to communicate their internal emotional states than males, who are normally reluctant to disclose their intimate feelings such as those that imply any weakness or dependence on others or vulnerability (Kring and Gordon, 1998). The gift-giving literature in consumer behaviour suggests that women are the primary gift-givers because of their greater concern to show care and love to others (Cheal, 1988). Similarly, Fischer and Arnold's (1990) study of Christmas gift-giving among men and women found that women, in comparison with men, were more involved in this sort of activity.

EXAMPLE 5.5

Evans *et al.* (1999, 2000) drew from findings in neurology based on MRI scans of male and female brains as they processed information (by reading). Female brains generated more activity from more areas of the brain than did male brains. The researchers propose that women were using more elements of messages (colour, imagery, words, etc.) to form meaning and as a result left and right, front and back areas of their brains 'lit up' when reading material. As for men, their brains showed less activity, and the supposition was that they were focusing more on fewer specific elements of the messages, mostly the words, to make sense of it (Figure 5.10). Consumer behaviour based on neurolinguistics therefore suggests that women respond well to bright colours, photographs and images, and men respond well to bold headlines, bullet points and graphs.

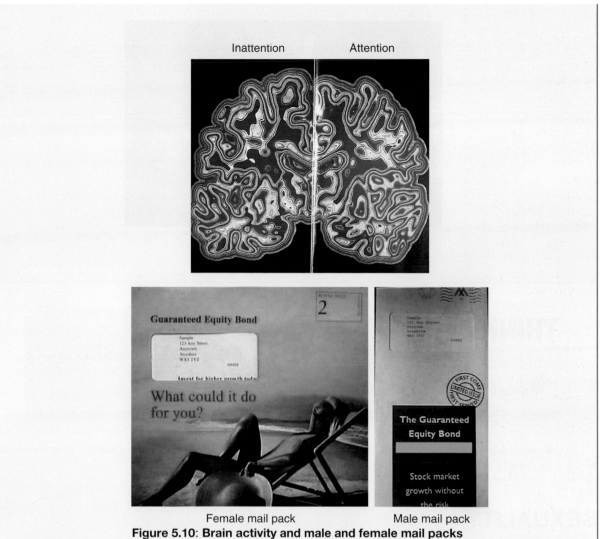

Inattention   Attention

Female mail pack   Male mail pack

Figure 5.10: Brain activity and male and female mail packs
Brain activity: P Laybourne and D Lewis, Neuromarketing: The Future of Consumer Research?, *Admap* (May 28–30 2005), pp 28–30. Reproduced with permission of Admap, the world's primary source of strategies for effective advertising, marketing and research. For more information visit www.admapmagazine.com.
© World Advertising Research Center. Mail packs: © Target Direct. Reproduced by permission.

The exception within this study concerned cars. Women appeared more interested in the facts such as running costs, safety features and fuel consumption, and men more concerned with image and appearance (Figure 5.11) and, perhaps in a Freudian sense (see Chapter 1), whether the car has a long red bonnet!

Figure 5.11: Boys and their toys
© Target Direct. Reproduced by permission

THINKBOX

Does marketing accurately reflect male and female buying behaviour? Why, or why not?

Do male and female brains 'work' differently?

So, as with age, gender, although being an apparently straightforward demographic characteristic, hides a multitude of implications for the marketer.

SEXUALITY

An extension of gender is **sexual identity**. Most of us are male or female (there are some who are transgender/transsexual) but the concepts of masculinity and femininity are aligned along a continuum based to a large extent on:

- the socialization of our culture (men kiss each other in some cultures but not others) (Solomon, 2004)
- our own self-image (see the next chapter)
- how we use our bodies to reflect this and indeed how we clothe, enhance and even physically modify our bodies to achieve the image we wish to project to others.

Androgyny and bisexuality are mixes of the two poles of the continuum. Marketers can appeal to our opposite pole in appropriate circumstances (Figure 5.12).

Marketing is also increasingly interested in the gay market segments. Gay men, for example, spend twice as much on clothing and four times as much on grooming as straight men do. Dodd *et al.* (2005) have explored the extent to which young gay men are 'dependent' on clothing purchases and whether marketing exploits this too far. They are often relatively more affluent, in higher socio-economic groups (see next

Figure 5.12: Masculine self
Masculinity–feminity is not just a biological issue but is also a cognitive continuum.
© Jim Beam Brands Co. Reproduced by permission

section) and have few dependants (MINTEL, 2001). The segment is easier to reach nowadays because there are more gay magazines and TV programmes as well as access via the Internet (MINTEL, 2001) and sponsorship of gay events (e.g. by Smirnoff, Levi's and Virgin). Even as far back as 1994, Time-Warner considered introducing a magazine for gay men (Ritchie, 1995:158).

However, despite such targeting, Shoffman (2006) states that 'New UK laws will require companies to understand how to meet the needs of Britain's 3 million gay and lesbian customers who now account for more than £70 billion in earnings'. A comprehensive review of the gay market can be found in MINTEL (2001)

Gay men have also been found to be more responsive to new products and might be a good target in the early stages in the life of new products and services, in terms of the early adopter and opinion leadership constructs discussed in Chapter 9.

£1.4 billion spent on leisure each year
£730 million spent on the home each year
90% eat out regularly
79% take more than two holidays per year
Lesbians earn £3000 more than the average UK woman
27% have higher education
42% spend more than £500 pa on clothes
50% gay men wear Levi's
More than 30% spend between £50 and £100 on CDs pa
35% visit a gay club or pub each week
65% claim they will boycott gay-unfriendly places

Bass's portfolio of gay clubs/pubs turned over £8.7 million
  in 1995–1996: up 18% year on year.

Source: Adapted by the authors from Rainbow TV (1997)

Table 5.8: Gay consumer behaviour

The significance of the gay market cannot be underestimated – Middleton (1997) said it was worth around £12 million. Gay women earn around £3000 pa more than is average for women and '40% of gay men are estimated (in 1997) to have an annual income in excess of £25,000' (Middleton, 1997). In research conducted by Rainbow TV, it was found that 46% of the gay population had taken a foreign holiday in the previous year compared with 29% of the entire population (Rainbow TV, 1997) and 80% take two or more holidays each year (Table 5.8)

As is discussed in Chapter 11, with reference to geodemographics, the gay market can potentially be identified and profiled from census data. But in the meantime we turn to one of the consumer researchers' most used profile characteristics, social grade.

EXAMPLE 5.6

In a recent Levi's ad, one woman is 'kissing' another and has her hand in the pocket of yet another. The woman on the left tries to pull her away. According to Levi's America: 'The image is actually of the same girl and is intended to depict a "virtual reality" of her expressing different aspects of her personality. The Australian marketing team said that the campaign was designed to position women as confident, sassy and self-empowered. The ad also fits with our long tradition of respecting and celebrating diversity and freedom of expression.' The advert below is a more direct gay image used by the Diesel brand.

Figure 5.13: This Diesel clothing advertisement used an overtly gay image
© Diesel. Reproduced by permission. Image courtesy of the Advertising Archives

Take a look at Oakenfull and Greenlee (2005), Queer Eye for a Gay Guy: Using Market Specific Symbols in Advertising to Attract Gay Consumers without Alienating the Mainstream, Psychology and Marketing, Vol 22 No 5 pp 421–440, accessed via the accompanying book web site at www.wileyeurope.com/college/evans.

SOCIAL GRADE

Especially in the past, marketers have acknowledged that there is a degree of social stratification, but they have long avoided researching possible segments on the basis of social class in any true sociological sense. This would involve rather complicated assessment of income, wealth, power and skill.

In the UK, instead of this, social grade is determined via the occupation of the 'chief income earner in the household'. A sixfold **classification** results: A, B, C1, C2, D, E (Table 5.9). This was devised by the National Readership Survey in 1956. The main 'dividing line' is between C1 and C2, above which there are non-manual occupations and below which there are manual ones (Market Research Society, 2004). Many commercial market research programmes have found significant differences in buying behaviour between respondents in the various social grades: have a look at the MINTEL or other such reports in your library (remember Table 5.1). The traditional justification for the continued use of social grade is basically twofold (Market Research Society, 1981). First, it is simple to research. All that is required is for data to be analysed according to the occupation of the 'chief income earner in the household'. Second, social grade appears to have been a reasonably good discriminator of buying behaviour as you will find in many (but not all) product-markets profiled in MINTEL-type reports. There is debate over the extent to which social grade reflects lifestyle patterns but despite all of this it is used widely by advertisers for profiling and targeting consumers.

Grade	Description	1991	2004
A	Top of profession	3	3.5
B	Middle management	10	21.5
C1	Teachers/students	24	29.1
C2	Skilled manual	30	20.9
D	Semi-skilled manual	25	6.2
E	L/R unemployed, state pensioners	8	9.1

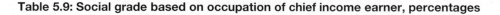

Table 5.9: Social grade based on occupation of chief income earner, percentages

During the 1980s in particular, a number of significant criticisms of social grade were made. There are inevitable anomalies in its use. For example, significant proportions of those earning above the national average are C2DE, so the traditionally strong correlations between social grade and income have been destroyed. Some in C2, such as highly skilled manual workers, will be earning more than some middle managers in group B and some full-time students in C1 will be earning less than some manual workers in D.

It has also been shown that of 400 respondents to earlier surveys who were re-interviewed to confirm their social grade, 41% had been allocated to the wrong group, and this is an indication of instability of the system (O'Brien and Ford, 1988).

Another problem concerning social grade is that although there might be some correlations between social grade and purchase, how can this be used? Certainly it is relevant for selecting appropriate advertising media based on the matching of segment social grade with the social grade profiles for different media. But there could be dangers in inferring values and attitudes of those in each social grade in order to create marketing communications messages. These more *affective* dimensions might not be caused by occupation. Furthermore, in the context of the urban industrialized environments where social networks can be complex and fluid in nature, it is often difficult to think of a group of consumers as a community of individuals who are bound together by a common social grade or social status (Henry, 2005).

EXAMPLE 5.7

MarketingWeek

Is it Still as Simple as ABC?

For over half a century, UK advertisers have categorised the population according to the jobs people do.

The ABC$_1$ social grading system has become the first port of call for brand owners looking for information about their consumers and is the primary trading currency for newspaper, television and radio sales.

But the value of the system – launched by the National Readership Survey in 1956 – is being called into question. In an age of one-to-one internet marketing and as a mass of lifestyle and postcode data about households becomes available, many market researchers believe social grading has had its day.

As society becomes increasingly diverse and people's aspirations change, the six monolithic divisions – A, B, C$_1$, C$_2$, D and E – which are worked out according to the respondents' professional positions and how many staff report to them, appear, to some, increasingly clumsy. That said, when adding in information about the regions where people live and their age, the data gets richer and more complex.

But an array of alternative profiling methods have been launched, with products from Experian, Acxiom and CACI dividing the population into ever smaller and more tightly focused groups. These are based on past consumption habits, location and lifestyle data. Meanwhile, other research methods have focused on people's attitudes rather than their behaviour or economic and demographic information.

Proponents of social grading accept that simply measuring audiences by jobs, age and region is very general, but insist that it still has many uses and will continue to help advertisers target their products at the right people for a long time to come. One critic of the social grade system is Nick Murray, planning director at KLP. He says that those media using the ABC_1 measures are generally in decline, from ITV1 to national, daily and weekly newspapers. By contrast, media that are more segmented are growing. "We are now a cellular society, made up of attitudinal rather than economic or demographic groups," he says.

Groups and Subgroups

While social grade may inform the beginning of any research process, Murray favours the social values measures developed by Dr Liz Nelson (founder of Taylor Nelson, now owned by Sofres) in the early 1970s. These are based on Maslow's hierarchy of needs and categorise people into three broad groups. There are the "sustenance driven" settlers, who crave safety and belonging. Then there are "outerdirected" types who search for esteem from others through the products they buy and experiences they enjoy. Then there is the "inner-directed" group who are autonomous and decisive, nonmaterialistic and enthusiastic in challenging orthodoxies. These are the so-called "self-actualisers". Each of these groups is further split into between seven and 12 sub-groups.

Murray says: "Society is moving progressively from a situation in the early 1960s where the biggest group was the sustenance-driven, to the situation today where the outerdirecteds are the biggest groups and inner-directeds are growing most quickly."

This research method was sold by Taylor Nelson when it was acquired by Sofres in 1997 and is now owned by research company Consumer Insight. People are allocated to the psychographic categories according to answers to 400 questions about attitudes and products asked in an omnibus survey conducted every two or three years. Among banal enquires such as "how often do you wash your hair?" penetrating questions about attitudes to credit risk and fear of crime are dropped in. As David Anthony at Consumer Insight says: "The key to it is that when you understand people's values, you can understand the things they do as opposed to segmentation on behaviour. Two different people could own a BMW for completely different reasons, one for esteem, the other might be for the performance and thrill of driving it."

Segments – Chicken or Egg?

A further attack on the social grade system – and a criticism of much market research – is that marketers have got segmentation the wrong way round. They should create segments on the basis of data they receive rather than making people fit into pre-established criteria.

Arguing against fitting people into broad categories, David Arrowsmith, strategy manager for customer intelligence at research company SAS UK, gives the example of two men with similar profiles. Both were born in 1948, grew up in the UK and have been divorced and remarried. They both have grown-up children, are wealthy and both take skiing holidays in the Alps. A quick look at these characteristics might lead to the opinion that they belong in the same consumer segment. But one is Prince Charles. The other is Ozzy Osbourne.

Prince of Darkness, Prince of Wales: On paper Ozzy and Charles could belong to the same consumer segment. That's where the similarities end.

As Arrowsmith says: "ABC$_1$ type categorisations emerged when the marketing industry didn't have the ability or mechanism to collect and store information at an individual level. As industry trends and consumers have evolved, we now realise just how non-individual and unrepresentative ABC$_1$ categorisations have become."

He believes marketers are getting frustrated with the ABC$_1$ system as it doesn't allow them to do the sort of targeting they know they can achieve. "It is all about efficiency and return on investment," he says. "Ten years ago it wasn't cost-effective to target in the way it is today."

But Guy Consterdine, a market research consultant, says that the success of the new profiling techniques do not undermine the utility of the social grade system. "It is wrong to dismiss social grade as an outdated, anti-diluvian method of measuring people. In cases where you have not got your own research defining the market in the most appropriate way, there is still power left if you use it with other data such as age." In one exercise for the NRS, he says: "Social grade emerged as one of the most important variables in predicting the readership of newspapers and magazines." He adds that social grade is still a key measure when it comes to recruiting respondents for market research surveys.

Other supporters of the social grade classification point out that it is in fact based on more complex data than at first appears. NRS, which owns the social grade data, uses Ipsos MORI to carry out some 35,000 surveys of households each year. Included in these half-hour interviews are seven questions relating to occupation and responsibility. Factors such as the number of staff that report to the respondent and whether they have professional qualifications are taken into account. Ipsos MORI has a team working on the data and constantly updates the definitions of jobs included. There are some 3,500 jobs on the database.

This information is made available to subscribers to the non-profit making NRS, including members of the Institute of Practitioners in Advertising, the Newspaper Publishers Association and the Periodical Publishers Association. The data can then be used by media agencies to plan campaigns according to social grade, age and region.

Ipsos MORI confirms that about 4% of the population are in the A category, 22% are Bs, 29% are C1 while 21% are C2. The D category accounts for about 16% of the population and E for 8%.

One criticism is that retired people receiving a state pension are automatically put into the E category whatever their previous job. But it should be pointed out that if they live on a non-state pension, they are categorised according to the job they held which gave them that pension.

Another supposed inconsistency concerns the relationship between income and social grade. A plumber or builder could earn more money than a company director depending on the circumstances of each.

Inescapable Discrepancies

Geoff Wicken, TGI development director at BMRB and a supporter of the system, says there will always be discrepancies, adding: "My view is that at a broad-brush level, social grade is still fairly good, it still discriminates. We do ask income questions on TGI and if you cross-tabulate income versus social grade, there is a strong correlation between people in higher social groups being more likely to have higher incomes."

Another social grade sceptic is Iain Dawson, communications planning director at EquiMedia. He says alternatives such as Mosaic, Acorn and Cameo provide a far deeper insight into audiences, though none has so far been able to dominate the market. "For example, there are 11 Mosaic groups at the top level – and it is simply a lot more difficult to remember 11 than six. Equally, we are not conversant with descriptors such as Symbols of Success or Welfare Borderlines and few people are able to tell the difference between Happy Families and Suburban Comfort. With 40 to 50 types at the next level, this is just the tip of the descriptors iceberg."

One of the main arguments against the social grade system is that society has changed fundamentally since the system was introduced in the 1950s. The new generations of baby-boomers are much more individualistic than their parents, who tended to adhere to stricter class-based behaviour. These days the prince and the working class chap from Birmingham might holiday in the same place. However, against this view, there is evidence that the UK has one of the lowest levels of social mobility in Europe. The upsurge in mobility between the 1960s and 1980s appears to have been a temporary phenomenon according to some research and the social grades are now as valid as they ever were.

Much of this debate is another front in the battle between above the line advertising with its broadbrush appeal to large groups and more targeted marketing. Opponents of this direct approach claim that marketing budgets are more effectively spent through segmenting audiences into ever smaller groups.

It seems doubtful that the controversy will rage for another half century. As mass media decline, alternatives to the social grading system will eventually make the ABC1 approach look quaintly outdated.

Marketing Week, 2nd August 2007, p.31–32. Reproduced by permission of Centaur Media Plc.

Recent attempts to improve social classification do not bode well, either. The census of 2001 has produced eight (rather than the previous six) categories but excludes the over-75s (Zelin, 2003). Indeed the new system has been found to be as good a discriminator of purchase activity as the 'ABC 1' system, but Rose (1999) could not recommend it as a replacement for social grade. However, the previous system was based on households (occupation of chief income earner in the household) whereas the new system is at individual level, so the marketer might be tempted to at least experiment with this because of the stronger potential of data at individual level. However, in comparative research, the Market Research Society (2004) concluded that the old social grade model was a better discriminator than the new socio-economic classification (SEC) and indeed the latter 'would have none of the advantages we would look for in a new system' (Market Research Society, 2004). It is, therefore, perhaps not surprising that the 2001 census output included both the new SEC and the standard (ABC1) social gradings (Market Research Society, 2004); but maybe it is surprising that it attracts such criticism itself.

INCOME

It is worth a very brief mention of 'income'. Although this is not a component of defining social grade it is perhaps inherent in the extremes of social grade categorization. Lawson (2007) reports that the highest earners have grown faster than those at the national income mean. The percentage growth of earning over £100 000 pa has been 10% per year over the previous five years (compared with just 5% growth in those earning between 20 and £30k pa). Lawson (2007) also reports the Ledbury Research/HM Customs and Revenue research which found that 1% of the top earners in UK account for 21% of total hotel spending, they are prone to be early adopters and indeed opinion leaders (see Chapter 9).

Although family circumstances and ethnicity are sometimes discussed under the 'demographics' heading, we explore these in other chapters ('family' within Chapter 7 along with children's involvement with consumption issues; and ethnicity in Chapter 8).

SUMMARY

- In this chapter, we explored some of the relevant and meaningful demographic variables and their implications for marketers. In particular, we looked into the roles of age, gender, sexuality and social grade in explaining consumer behaviour.
- An age is something we all possess but equally it is inevitable that we all 'age'. The notion of generational cohorts is important in marketing because it identifies the key outlooks possessed by people within different age groups, and this knowledge can inform marketing communications messages greatly.
- Gender leads to male and female stereotypes in marketing activity but there are more involved issues. Masculinity and femininity are not absolute but are positioned differently along a continuum for each individual. Information processing styles can vary according to this, and the whole area is further complicated by sexuality and self-image (which can change in different social circumstances).
- Marketing's widespread use of social grade has come under critical scrutiny in recent years and, although it can apparently reveal differences in buying behaviour, we need to be wary of the accuracy of the data and also need to ask ourselves why such differences are there. That is, does social grade explain behaviour? Or is there merely a coincidental link? Nevertheless, social grade is an important indicator of consumer lifestyle and is widely used in marketing communications for profiling consumers.
- Income, as a discrete variable, can clearly and logically determine some consumption behaviour, but it is the seriously rich who disproportionately fuel the consumption economy and many marketers are keen to take a share of their wallet.

QUESTIONS

1. How will Generations Y and X differ in consumer behaviour and favourite marketing style?

2. Baby boomers are significant in terms of their numbers and affluence. How good is the marketing aimed at them?

3. What do you think of the way marketers use gender stereotyping in advertising?

4. Should marketers use sexuality as a targeting base? Why (and how)? Or why not?

5. From which social grade do you come? How far does this explain your buying behaviour?

6. Explore the buying behaviour of your own age cohort and compare with that of your parents' age cohort.

7. Analyse and evaluate the proposition that the male and female brains process information differently.

FURTHER READING

Gunter B (1998) *Understanding the Older Consumer*, Routledge and Treguer J P (2002) 50 + Marketing, Palgrave. The 'average' student (if there is such a creature), is not usually over 50. However, the 'older' consumer is becoming very important to marketers, yet relatively few marketers who devise campaigns for the over-50s are themselves over 50. These two books provide important and interesting perspectives on these older consumers.

Market Research Society (2004) *Occupation Groupings: A Job Dictionary*, Market Research Society, London ISBN 0906117275. Our coverage of social grade in UK in this chapter showed that the occupation of the chief income earner in a household determines the social grade to which they belong. This short work by the MRS lists pretty well every occupation and the corresponding social grade.

Moir A and Moir B (1998) *Men Don't Iron: The Real Science of Gender Studies*, HarperCollins, London. This book distils a great deal of research from around the world about the differences between men and women. What about feminism or equality, you say. Well, read on and you will discover that gender differences are more than the result of social or cultural pressure. The science of the brain is examined and applied in this book and adds much to the ongoing debate.

CHAPTER 6
CONSUMER PSYCHOGRAPHICS

CHAPTER OBJECTIVES

After engaging with the material presented in this chapter and its associated exercises and reading, you should be able to:

- Demonstrate an understanding of psychographic profiling of consumers.
- Analyse and evaluate the contribution of consumer personality to understanding consumer behaviour.
- Analyse and evaluate the contribution of 'traditional' lifestyle research to understanding consumer behaviour.
- Analyse and evaluate the contribution of self-concept theory to understanding consumer behaviour.
- Recognize the relative contributions of demographics and psychographics to understanding consumer behaviour and for targeting.

INTRODUCTION

Our coverage of **psychographics** includes **lifestyle**, personality and **self-image**. As the 'psycho' component suggests, the approach is more concerned with trying to get beneath the skin of consumers and to be able to explain their behaviour in greater depth than the 'profiling' approach of demographics can. This chapter examines each of these psychographics dimensions in turn but also reflects on the relative and synergistic contributions of psychographics and demographics to understanding consumer behaviour and for the targeting of marketing activity.

LIFESTYLE

Lifestyle is a mode of living as reflected in consumers' unique patterns of attitudes, interests and opinions. Lifestyle is important because one can develop deeper insights into consumer behaviour by looking at how consumers spend their time and what they think of various elements of their environment. One can also get a closer idea of consumers' motives, feelings and beliefs because lifestyles are reflections of self-concept.

There are two approaches to lifestyle: what we term **traditional lifestyle** and **contemporary lifestyle**. It is the former that we concentrate on in this chapter because the latter, which is discussed in Chapter 11, is less to do with 'psycho' dimensions of consumer behaviour and more with what consumers claim they actually do. Indeed the latter is mainly used to create lists of named consumers who claim to buy specific brands. But our focus in this chapter, on traditional lifestyle marketing, is to explore consumer activities, interests and opinions (**AIO analysis**) using market research techniques which do not reveal individual consumer identities.

Traditional lifestyle research has been based typically on the presentation to respondents of a series of statements (**Likert scales**).

One of the most significant sources of consumer data is the Target Group Index, based on survey research conducted by the British Market Research Bureau (BMRB). The survey was launched in 1969 in the UK but is now run in more than 60 countries. In the UK the fieldwork is conducted throughout the year, from an annual sample size of about 24 000 adults and data released quarterly. The data presents profiles of consumers in many product markets and includes the type of demographic data we saw in the previous chapter. However, what is pertinent here is that the TGI now houses up to 290 lifestyle (Likert Scale) statements. These are designed for the measurement of respondents' activities, interests, opinions and values across many different sectors (e.g. health, travel, media, food and so on).

Table 6.1 reproduces a short selection of the lifestyle statements used in the TGI. Respondents are presented with these statements and asked to give their degree of agreement with each. From this there are two main alternative ways of analysing the data.

First, because the Target Group Index also provides an extremely comprehensive profiling of the sorts of consumers who buy a range of products and brands, it is possible to cross-tabulate the sort of consumer who buys 'Bloggo' brand not only with age, gender and social grade but also with any or all of the attitudes, interests and opinions (AIOs) reflected in the lifestyle questions (see Figure 6.1).

For example, the buying of a particular brand of lager might be associated with young males from C1 and C2 social grades. By cross-tabulating with the lifestyle questions, it might be revealed that these

- I buy clothes for comfort, not for style
- Once I find a brand I like, I tend to stick to it
- I always buy British whenever I can
- I dress to please myself
- My family rarely sits down to a meal together at home
- I enjoy eating foreign food
- I like to do a lot when I am on holiday

Source: British Market Research Bureau (1987), Target Group Index.

Table 6.1: Some TGI statements

Definitely Agree Statements

Private Eye Target: THE GUARDIAN

Pop: 46,791 Resp: 24,023

Pop: 1,272 (000) Resp: 692

	Index	(000)	Resps	Vert%	Horz%
I CONSIDER MYSELF INTERESTED IN THE ARTS	350	512	262	40.3	9.51
I BUY FAIR TRADE PRODUCTS WHERE AVAILABLE	347	324	158	25.5	9.44
I PREFER TO TAKE HOLIDAYS OFF THE BEATEN TRACK	335	240	111	18.8	9.11
I AM INTERESTED IN OTHER CULTURES	320	500	274	39.3	8.7
A SINGLE EUROPEAN CURRENCY WOULD BE A GOOD THING FOR BRITAIN	314	347	199	27.3	8.53
I AM A REGULAR CINEMA GOER	276	117	68	9.23	7.51
I LOOK ON THE WORK I DO AS A CAREER NOT JUST A JOB	243	340	150	26.7	6.61
I AM PREPARED TO PAY MORE FOR GOOD QUALITY WINE	242	255	129	20.1	6.58

BMRB INTERNATIONAL   SOURCE: GB TGI 2004 Spring (Jan 2003 -Dec 2003)

Definitely Agree Statements

Private Eye Target: THE SUN

Pop: 46,791 Resp: 24,023

Pop: 8,824 (000) Resp: 5,039

	Index	(000's)	Resp	Vert%	Horz%
I WEAR DESIGNER CLOTHES	176	488	199	5.53	33.1
I CANNOT RESIST BUYING MAGAZINES	175	314	175	3.56	33.1
I READ DAILY NEWSPAPERS MORE FOR ENTERTAINMENT THAN NEWS	172	698	432	7.91	32.5
ADVERTISING HELPS ME CHOOSE WHAT TO BUY	170	279	170	3.61	32.1
A REAL MAN CAN DOWN SEVERAL PINTS AT A SITTING	167	455	276	5.61	31.4
MONEY IS THE BEST MEASURE OF SUCCESS	160	677	423	7.67	30.1
I AM A TV ADDICT	158	516	326	5.85	29.8
I REALLY ENJOY A NIGHT OUT AT THE PUB	157	1709	840	19.4	29.6

BMRB INTERNATIONAL SOURCE: GB TGI 2004 Spring (Jan 2003 - Dec 2003)

Figure 6.1: Definitely agree statements

buyers tend *not* to like healthy eating, but do enjoy the hedonism of sun, sea and sex package holidays. Media usage can similarly be profiled against lifestyle questions:

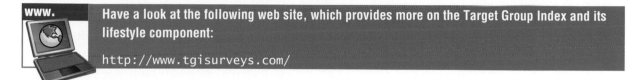

www. Have a look at the following web site, which provides more on the Target Group Index and its lifestyle component:

`http://www.tgisurveys.com/`

The second main way of using the data, whether it be TGI or other traditional lifestyle data, is to explore the full range of lifestyle answers in order to group consumers into segments within which there is a strong degree of homogeneity in terms of their activities, interests and opinions.

EXAMPLE 6.1

In the 1980s, Levi Strauss in USA went through a new product development programme concerning a range of upmarket men's suits. The market research programme that was involved, revolved around an attempt to discover 'lifestyles'. This included eliciting degrees of agreement with statements such as:

- 'Dressing right is a complete mystery to me'
- 'I dress to please my friends'
- 'I think of myself as very fashionable in the clothes I wear'
- 'I dress to conform to what others seem to expect'
- 'Others often ask my advice when it comes to clothes buying'

Each emerging 'cluster' would then be allocated a somewhat glib title. In the Levi lifestyle research programme, for example, the main clothing segments were labeled as: the 'classic independent', the 'mainstream traditionalist', the 'price shopper', the 'trendy casual' and so on. This sort of profile would not only help determine appropriate product/service features but also help to arrive at an advertising message which is congruent with the segment's lifestyle.

In the UK a lifestyle typology was compiled by Taylor Nelson's Applied Futures (McNulty and McNulty, 1987) and identified the following segments: the belonger, the survivor, the experimentalist, the conspicuous consumer, the social resistor, the self-explorer and the aimless (Table 6.2). The self-explorer group was the fastest growing, which further reinforces one of the propositions of this chapter – namely that some markets have become more orientated to **self-expression** and individualism. This traditional form of lifestyle (AIO) segmentation provides useful insight into what makes people 'tick'. It is based on traditional market research – administering Likert scaled statements concerned with activities, interests and opinions to a sample of consumers. The data is anonymized and the resulting profiles are very useful for determining the style and mood of promotional messages.

The Applied Futures typology in the UK was derived from the 'values and lifestyle' research programme in USA (VALS) and the latest version of this is summarized in Figure 6.2 with the sorts of research questions shown via the link on the accompanying web site. At the time of writing you could even answer these questions online and be profiled accordingly.

Lifestyle category	Characterized by	Percentage of population
Belonger	Place great store by home, family, country, the establishment, etc.	19
Survivor	Disposed towards identification with groups and accepting of authority. Self-expression and creativity are irrelevant.	16
Experimentalist	Attracted to all that is new and different, always looking for new ideas, items and experiences	12
Conspicuous consumer	Energy is directed toward the consumer dream via material possessions, take their cues from reference groups, non-critical of advertisers, followers of fashion	18
Social resister	Seeks to maintain the status quo, controlling self, family, society, suppressing self in favour of duty and moral obligation	15
Self-explorer	Self-aware and self-concerned people, self-expression important	14
Aimless	Uninvolved and alienated, aggressive towards the system, resentful of its failure to provide employment	6

Table 6.2: Taylor Nelson's lifestyle typology

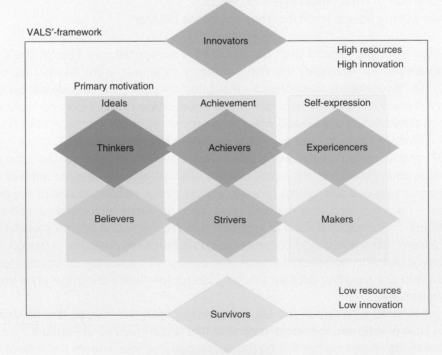

Figure 6.2: VALS
Source: http://www.sric-bi.com/VALS/presurvey.shtml

Figure 6.3 summarizes a current profiling of the UK according to this form of lifestyle research.

 SELF-ACTUALIZERS Seeking the highest levels of personal development, they are people- and relationship-oriented and consequently are tolerant and empathetic. Innovative and experimental by nature, they are open, sociable, far-sighted and non-materialistic. They have the self-confidence to back their own judgement and the vitality to sweep others along with them. ***18% of UK population***

INNOVATORS Self-confident risk-takers, they seek out the new and the different and set their own targets to achieve. ***8% of UK population***

ESTEEM-SEEKERS Acquisitive and materialistic they aspire to what they see as the symbols of success, both in terms of 'possessions' and 'experiences'. ***23% of UK population***

 STRIVERS Looking towards outer-directedness, image and status are important but only to provide acceptance from their peer group so hold on to traditional values. ***10% of UK population***

CONTENTED CONFORMERS Want to be 'normal' so go along with the herd. Accepting of their lot, they are comfortable and contented in the secure world they have created. ***24% of UK population***

 TRADITIONALISTS Risk-averse, they look to traditional values and behaviours for guidance. Quiet and reserved, they hang back and try to blend in with the crowd. ***11% of UK population***

DISCONNECTED Stand apart and are embittered, and therefore apathetic. Tend to live in the ever-present now, not thinking of tomorrow's consequences. ***7% of UK population***

Figure 6.3: Consumer Insight's 'Social Value Groups' 2005

Reproduced by permission of Consumer Insights: http://www.insightmc.com/insightmc groups3.htm

www. Have a look at this web site, which provides more on the VALS Lifestyle and Values Group and allows you to respond to a version of the survey itself:

http://www.sric-bi.com/VALS/presurvey.shtml

The following web site provides more on the Consumer Insights UK Social Value Groups:

http://www.insightmc.com/insightmc groups3.htm

EXAMPLE 6.2

Figure 6.4: Five types of Japanese lifestyle

May R (2005), Reproduced by permission of Consumer Insights: http://www.jmrlsi.co.jp/english/sizing/insights/2004/cons2.gif

LIFESTYLE, VALUES AND DEMAND MAPPING

Referring back to Chapter 1, we discussed means–end chains to uncover underpinning values. With lifestyle research, there is a progression the other way; that is, interests, activities and opinions can help explain behaviour and buying activities, which in turn can inform target marketing approaches

(Orth *et al.*, 2004). Brunso *et al.* (2004) also explore these links and show that values can be the 'top' level and product perceptions the 'bottom' level, with lifestyle usefully providing an intervening system. The means-end chain can be used to work both ways – from product attributes to reveal values via lifestyle or from values via lifestyle to reveal product or brand perceptions, in a 'goal directed' manner.

EXAMPLE 6.3

MarketingWeek

Demand Mapping and the Art of Customer Attitude Profiling

Broadcaster ITV has its problems, but how well they are addressed may depend on work currently being done by director of marketing and commercial strategy Clare Salmon.

Salmon has been 'demand mapping' TV audiences – delineating various groups of viewers by factors such as whether they are addicted to or anti TV, keen on new technologies such as the internet and set top boxes, their viewing habits ('flick and dip' or 'disciplined') and so on.

Her research has revealed six distinctive segments. They include the likes of pro-technology but anti-TV 'plugged in achievers' (who account for 14% of the population), anti-technology, anti-TV 'cultural connoisseurs' (12%), TV loving trend followers (20%), home-loving, anti-technology 'TV addicts' (13%) and the list goes on. By overlaying her own proprietary research with BARB and other data she has developed not only a picture of their TV preferences, but their lifestyles, incomes and so on.

The result underlines the challenge now facing ITV (hardly any programmes appeal to all segments across the board), while also opening up new opportunities. ITV now knows much better what sorts of programmes to broadcast and what sort of marketing initiatives it needs to attract viewers to these programmes, to get the mix of audience its advertisers are looking for. Even if absolute audience figures don't grow dramatically, the value of these audiences could.

Segmenting target markets by attitude as well as by demographics is hardly new, of course. But what's exciting is our growing ability to fuse attitudinal understanding with hard data to get the best of both worlds.

Strategy consultants Roland Berger have developed a similar approach. They started their research from an unusual place. Instead of asking consumers about things that brand managers fret about (like product usage and brand associations), they focused on what really matters to individuals in their daily lives, regardless of their brand preferences. In an enormous exercise, they analysed open-ended conversations with thousands of different individuals to identify common themes which they turned into a bank of attitudinal statements. Having tested it in 70 000 surveys across 16 countries for ambiguities, omissions and overlaps, they claim they can generate a good picture of an individual's outlook on life: the core values they hold dear. The statements themselves are pretty simple and straightforward, such as 'the best experiences are those you have with friends or family'; 'I often do things on the spur of the moment' or 'I am most annoyed by busy and hectic environments'. People tend to embrace or reject them in similar clusters, leading the consultants to suggest that there are 19 core values commonly held across Europe.

The values cover a vast territory. They include 'New & Cool' (adrenalin-seeking, rule-flouting, rebellious pushing of the limits), 'Clanning' (searching for warmth, friendship, belonging and team spirit), 'Personal Efficiency' (making best use of one's time, performance focused), 'Proven' (favouring authority, experience, reliability, tradition), 'Purism' (seeking simplicity, understatement, reducing things to their essentials), and so on.

Because every individual embraces or rejects each of these values to a different degree, and because the research is made up of a bank of many 'yes or no' answers, it is possible to use statistical pyrotechnics (multi-dimensional scaling analysis) to create a 'values profile' of each individual – and to depict this profile visually.

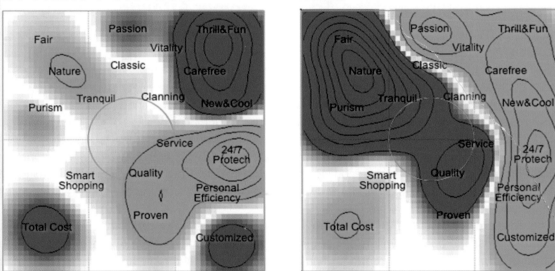

Figure 6.5: The attitudes of individuals, Dr Hans Petersen and 'Mike'

Figure 6.5 shows an example of two very different individuals, Dr Hans Petersen and 'Mike'. The blue areas show values that the individual positively embraces, compared to the other individuals in the sample. The more contour lines it shows, the more strongly committed the individual is, with each contour line representing a degree of statistical significance. The red areas highlight values that the individual positively rejects. A white area shows that when it comes to these values the individual is perfectly representative of the sample – they do not stand out as caring more or less than the people with whom they are being compared.

Both Hans and Mike are positively attracted to the value '24/7 Pro-Tech' – which means they are keen on the latest technology and scientific innovation, want quick and efficient access to information, and favour cold transactions. But the similarities end there. For Hans, things like 'Quality and Service' are important, as is concern for the environment. He's turned off by 'Thrill & Fun' and values such as 'Carefree', 'Vitality' and 'Passion'. Mike, on the other hand, lives for these values while keeping a sharp eye out for best value. He's positively irritated by altruistic concerns for fairness and the environment, and for boring, traditional priorities such as quality and service.

Along with the core values research, Roland Berger also conducts usual-suspect lifestyle, demographic and brand preference data. The individual profiles can then be aggregated to create profiles of brand buyers versus non-buyers, category users versus non-category users, different social groups, and so on – once the initial research is done, the data can be sliced and diced at will.

Figure 6.6 shows the values profiles of BMW buyers and Aldi shoppers in Germany. They could hardly be more different.

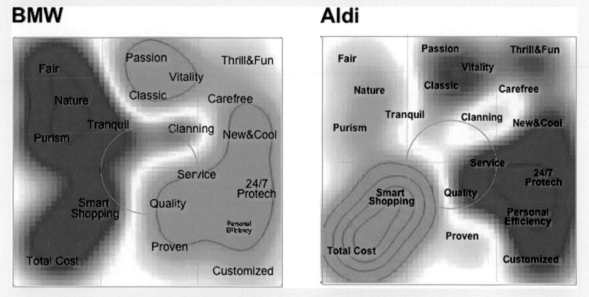

Figure 6.6: Profiles for the values of BMW and Aldi customers

A new book (that I must admit to have an interest in) describes the many ways this value profiling can be used to align a brand's emotional and functional propositions to target markets (in a similar way to the ITV example), to sort out messy brand architectures, identify innovation opportunities, manage agency creative, and so on.

It's also intriguing to see how the value profiles of brand users differ across countries. Whether in Europe or China, for example, Nike buyers embrace common core values such as 'New & Cool' and '24/7 Pro-Tech'. They also reject other values representing purism and tranquillity. However, there are subtle differences. While European Nike buyers embrace the values of 'Carefree' (light-hearted optimism, spontaneity, playfulness), Chinese Nike buyers positively reject them: carefree communications could work well in Europe but bomb in China.

Marketers have always stressed the need to offer both functional and emotional value. Both are expressions of underlying values. Wouldn't it be nice if, at last, we found some robust ways of uniting these two poles in a seamless data-driven, practical manner?

Alan Mitchell, www.alanmitchell.biz

Marketing Week, 9th November 2006, pp 24–25. Reproduced by permission of Centaur Media Plc.

Before we leave traditional lifestyle research it is worth linking this with our coverage of demographics in the previous chapter. The nearby Thinkbox provides a short case study, which demonstrates the combined use of these methods of understanding consumers in order for marketers to devise marketing mixes.

THINKBOX

Dragon Foods Ltd (DFL) is about to introduce a new, instant breakfast food. The product requires no preparation, and can be used as a meal substitute or as a snack, and as a dietary or nutritional food. According to a recent study of lifestyles and food consumption needs conducted by DFL, the following **lifestyle segments** could be considered potential buyers of the product:

1. Harried commuters – busy career people who need a source of energy and nutrition but who don't have time to prepare and eat a complete breakfast meal.
2. Career women – women whose work prevents them from making sure that their children eat a full and balanced breakfast.
3. Snack-servers – housewives who ensure that their children do eat a full and balanced breakfast, but who also want to provide them with good-tasting snacks as an added source of energy.
4. Calorie-counters – dieters looking for tasty, filling and nutritious meal substitutes.

Additional demographic data reveals the following:

1. Harried commuters – young career people, single or married with no children mostly college-educated, employed in ABC1 occupations.
2. Career women – married women, aged 25–45 with two or three children of school age, employed in mostly B and C1 occupations.
3. Snack-servers – married women, aged 23–40 with one or two children of school age or younger, husbands employed in C1C2 occupations.
4. Calorie-counters – men and women, aged 18–49, from all walks of life, with no other distinguishing characteristics other than the common perceived need to diet.

Suppose DFL decided to select the harried commuters as its target market:

1. Recommend a suitable marketing mix, showing how the demographic and lifestyle profiles respectively could contribute to determining each element of the mix.
2. How far can Dragon Foods combine all segments with a marketing mix?

www. Take a look at the following web site, which provides more on the Target Group Index and its fusion with customer data:

http://www.firstt.co.uk

Personality Variables

The word 'personality' is frequently used to refer to the capacity of a person for popularity, friendliness or charisma. However, these might be specific personality dimensions that an individual might possess. Someone who is unpopular, aloof and unfriendly still has a personality. We all have a personality and it is this that provides the essential differences between one individual and another. Personality, according to this interpretation, consists of the mannerisms, habits and actions that make a person an individual and thereby serve to make them distinct from everyone else. Eysenck *et al.* (1975) define personality as 'the relatively stable organization of a person's motivational dispositions arising from the interaction between biological drives and the social and physical environment'. Personality is thus a function of innate drives, learned motives and experience. The various themes in definitions of personality are brought together by Kempner (1976) where the term is explained as 'that integrated organization which determines each individual's pattern of behavioural responses to the environment', so that 'the study of personality is essentially the study of differences between people'. Like lifestyle, marketers can use some **personality traits** as the basis of segmenting their target market.

Psychoanalytic Theory

One of the first major ideas to inform personality research was provided by Sigmund Freud, who proposed that our personality is the result of the polarizing forces of the id and superego and the intervening and balancing mechanism of the ego. We discussed the implications of this for understanding consumer behaviour and for marketing activity in Chapter 1.

Trait Theory

Traits are an individual's characteristic ways of responding to the social and physical environment. Examples are aggression, honesty, anxiety, **independence** and sociability. You might think that for marketers it is an attractive segmenting approach to match brands with consumers' personalities, the logic being that we buy products and services that in some way reflect or extend our personality traits.

Quite widely known are the **personality big five** factors, which are extraversion, openness, agreeableness, conscientiousness and emotional stability and each factor consists of a continuum of more specific interrelated traits (John and Srivastava, 1999; see Table 6.3). This implies that consumers may be high or low or in between along the continuum of traits with most consumers scoring in the middle.

This is sometimes referred to as the multi-trait approach because several dimensions measure a more holistic personality. Single trait approaches on the other hand focus on one dimension. This is something we return to shortly. It is interesting to remind ourselves of the coverage of birth order in the previous chapter. Nancarrow *et al.* (2001) explore this and report that Sulloway (1995) found significant relationships between birth order and this 'big five'.

THINKBOX

Think of a person you know very well and describe them using the Big Five Personality Factors and their associated personality traits. How and in what sense does the person differ from yourself? You may note that the personality traits of consumers are often high or low on a continuum of traits, hence you would only be talking about the degree to which someone is extrovert or not and so on.

Emotional Stability	
Calm	Anxious
Secure	Insecure
Self-satisfied	Self-pitying

Extraversion	
Sociable	Retiring
Fun Loving	Sober
Affectionate	Reserved

Openness to Experience	
Imaginative	Practical
Independent	Conforming
Variety Seeker	OK with routine

Agreeableness	
Soft hearted	Ruthless
Trusting	Suspicious
Helpful	Uncooperative

Conscientiousness	
Organized	Disorganized
Careful	Careless
Disciplined	Impulsive

Table 6.3: The big five personality factors

EXAMPLE 6.4

Two classic studies, which attempt to link traits with product use, concern the ownership of cars. Both were carried out in the United States and, among other things, involved car owners' preferences towards buying either a Ford or a Chevrolet. Evans (1959) cites as the stimulus for his research the fact that, while mechanically and in designer terms these types of car were almost identical, advertisers had tried to create very different brand images for them based on what they assumed to be profiles of car buyers. Likely Ford owners were popularly portrayed as independent, impulsive, masculine and self-confident, while probable Chevrolet buyers were presented as conservative, thrifty, prestige-conscious, less masculine and moderate. A standard personality test (the Edwards Personal Preference Schedule) was used to measure these personality traits and others which might be relevant. The test was administered to owners of one or other make of car.

In a first trial based solely on the personality test scores of subjects, Evans was able to predict successfully whether an individual owned a Ford or Chevrolet in 63% of cases, 13% more than would have been the case in a purely chance situation. In a second experiment, using only socio-economic measures of the individual, these predicted correctly in 70% of tries. In a third experiment where a combination of both sets of consumer characteristics were used, Evans failed to improve his accuracy beyond that of his first try. Clearly, none of these results is sufficiently reliable to be of much value to the car manufacturer who wants to segment his market on the basis of consumer personality. A replication of part of this work by Westfall (1962), which used the Thurstone Temperament Schedule in place of the Edwards scale, also failed to distinguish satisfactorily between Ford and Chevrolet owners by personality traits, though it succeeded in distinguishing convertible owners from non-convertible owners; persons who scored low on the measures of activity, vigour, impulsiveness and sociability had a lower-than-average chance of owning a convertible.

Although cars have figured in a number of surveys, a wide range of products and brands have now been covered by tests, as is shown in the accompanying tables. Table 6.4 shows that research has involved a variety of traits. The results can be briefly summed up as follows: there is a mass of evidence that personality traits are linked with product and brand choice but the associations are, in the main, very weak. Correlation coefficients of the order of 0.3 or below are very common in these studies, showing that the proportion of variability in consumer purchase patterns that can be explained in terms of personality traits is quite small. However, a single trait such as innovativeness has been deployed in marketing for many years and we explore this in Chapter 9.

	Product/Brand	Traits	Results
(a)	**Fords/Chevrolets**	Achievement, deference, exhibition, autonomy, affiliation, intraception, dominance, abasement, change, heterosexuality, aggression	Allowed correct prediction of 13% more buyer's choices than chance alone would give
(b)	**Car types**	Activeness, vigour, impulsiveness, dominance, stability, sociability, reflectiveness	'No personality differences between Ford and Chevrolet owners.' Low activity related to low convertible ownership.
(c)	**Magazines**	Sex, dominance, achievement, assistance	Less than 13% of purchase behaviour variance explicable in terms of personality for
	Cigarettes	Dominance, aggression, change, autonomy	magazines or cigarettes.
(d)	**Toilet tissue**	45 traits	Personality of no value in prediction of brand loyalty, number of units purchased or colour of tissue.
(e)	**Private brands**	Enthusiasm, sensitivity, submissiveness	Less than 5% of purchase variance explained by these three traits; other traits of no value.

Source: Derived from (a) Evans (1959); (b) Westfall (1962); (c) Koponen (1960); (d) Advertising Research Foundation (1964); (e) Myers (1967).

Table 6.4: Personality and product choice: some examples

Consumer Decision Making Styles

Related to the notion of personality trait is the concept of consumer decision-making styles, which is defined as a mental orientation characterizing a consumer's approach to making shopping choices (Lysonski *et al.*, 1996; Sproles and Kendall, 1986; Walsh *et al.*, 2001). The underlying idea is that consumers engage in shopping with certain fundamental decision-making styles. Table 6.5 illustrates the decision-making styles and their implications for understanding the shopping behaviour of consumers. Empirical studies have largely validated their applicability in different countries such as New Zealand (Durvasula *et al.*, 1993), Korea (Hafstrom *et al.*, 1992), Germany (Walsh *et al.*, 2001), US, Greece, New Zealand and India (Lysonski *et al.*, 1996) and Qatar (Jamal *et al.*, 2006).

Investigating consumer decision-making styles can be very useful for marketers as they can segment their market accordingly and develop relevant marketing programmes. For instance, Jamal *et al.* (2006)

Mental orientation	Explanation	Implications
Quality consciousness	The tendency to seek perfection or highest possible quality in products while shopping	Tend to shop more carefully, more systematically; good enough brands cannot guarantee satisfaction
Brand consciousness	The tendency to seek the more expensive, well-known famous brands	Likely to perceive price-quality link, have positive attitudes towards departmental and speciality stores selling expensive and popular brands; may prefer best selling, heavily advertised brands
Novelty-fashion consciousness	The tendency to buy novel and fashionable items to seek	Likely to keep up to date with style with variety seeking as part of their orientation; experience pleasure and excitement for seeking and discovering new things
Recreational shopping	The tendency to seek pleasure, fun, recreation and entertainment out of shopping	Likely to feel increased excitement and have feelings of perceived freedom; engage in fantasizing and feelings of escape from routine tasks
Value consciousness	The tendency to seek bargains and look for deals	Likely to be concerned about getting best value for money and may engage in comparison shopping
Impulsiveness	The tendency to buy on impulse	Likely not to plan their shopping and remain unconcerned about how much they spend
Confusion	The tendency to get confused by over-choice of brands and information	Likely to experience information overload
Brand loyal orientation	The tendency to like and buy same brands again and again	Likely to have favourite brands and stores and to have formed habits in choosing them

Table 6.5: Consumer decision-making styles and shopping

recommended using experience-based advertising message strategy focusing on what it feels to use a brand or service to target recreational shoppers. This is because such consumers are likely to focus on messages that are perceived to be self-relevant, self-fulfilling and idealistic. Also, they are likely to experience increased arousal, heightened involvement, perceived freedom, fantasy fulfilment and escapism (Babin *et al.*, 1994). Moreover, in the case of value conscious shoppers, Jamal *et al.* (2006) recommended using marketing communication messages with typical sales promotional offers and price reductions. These types of messages are likely to provide savings and convenience benefits to consumers improving their overall shopping experience (Chandon, Wansink, and Laurent, 2000; Davis, Inman and McAlister, 1992).

Type Theory

Another approach to personality analysis involves the classification of various types of personality. The classification of people as introverts and extroverts is a well-known example, which stems from Carl Jung's psychoanalytical theories.

The possibility that trait theorists have been looking in the wrong place for applicable information on the links between consumers' personalities and their consumption habits has led some researchers to substitute **personality type** variables in their marketing investigations: but the results have only been a little more encouraging than those for trait research discussed above.

For instance, we might consider the work of Cohen (1967). He used the research paradigm advanced by Horney (1950) (classifying consumers into compliant, aggressive or detached types). Compliant individuals are anxious to be with others, to receive love, recognition, help and guidance. Such needs may make them over-generous and over-sensitive so that they shy away from criticism and allow others to dominate them. They are essentially conformists. Aggressive people tend to be achievement-orientated, desire status and see life as a competitive game. They seek the admiration of others through being outgoing in their behaviour and may exhibit what are often called 'leadership qualities'. Finally, detached individuals try to separate themselves from others both emotionally and behaviourally; they do not seek responsibility or obligations and do not try to impress other people. Each of these personality types contains sufficient unique traits to be conceptually distinct from the others, though in practice it is probable that many individuals possess elements of more than one.

In consumer tests, Cohen was able to match these personality types with product/brand preferences and usage rates. For instance, highly compliant people were more likely than less compliant types to use mouthwash, prefer 'Dial' soap, and drink wine at least several times per month. Those respondents scoring high on aggression bought more men's deodorant than low-aggression types. The compliant and detached persons drank tea at least several times a week while the others drank it much less frequently.

Fruitful as these results appear to be, it is important to note that Cohen presents only selected data and that no statistically significant relationships were found for a wide range of products including cigarettes, dress shirts, men's hairdressing, toothpaste, beer, diet products and headache remedies. Nevertheless, this particular study tends to give encouragement to the use of personality type as a meaningful concept for consumer behaviour research. Preferences for media offerings were also discovered, taking the personality/consumer choice relationship beyond brand selection and usage rates. Aggressive individuals, for example, preferred exciting television programmes, and magazines like *Playboy*. Compliant persons more readily chose more homely programmes and typically read *Readers Digest*. The detached subjects had more mixed and ambivalent preferences.

Brand Personality

As we saw in Chapter 1, consumers buy benefits and even a degree of emotional engagement with brands. Just as humans have personality traits, brands are also sometimes invested with personality dimensions. For instance, Aaker (1997) identified five brand personality dimensions – sincerity, excitement, competence, sophistication and ruggedness – using 631 respondents who rated 37 brands on 114 personality traits.

However, while there may be apparent similarities between human personality traits and those associated with a brand, there are some differences in the way in which they are formed (Aaker, 1997). For instance, we infer human traits on the basis of our observation of a person's behaviour, physical attributes, attitudes, beliefs and other demographics. In contrast, our perceptions of brand personality traits are formed due to our interactions (both direct and indirect) with the brand. For example, consumers normally have stereotypical perceptions of brand users, those who are associated with the brand (e.g. employees working for a brand) and brand endorsers (e.g. expert spokespersons or celebrities). McCracken (1988) argued that the images associated with these persons identified with a brand are transferred directly to the brands, leading to some distinct perceptions of brand personalities in our minds. Similarly, marketing efforts including advertising styles, product features and attributes, brand names and logos also contribute indirectly towards the formation of distinct perceptions of brand personalities in our minds.

A related approach views human personality as being the meanings constructed by an individual to describe the inner features and characteristics of another individual, based on observations of that individual's behaviour (Allen and Olson, 1995; Aaker and Fournier, 1995). Transferring this to brands, consumers can make attributions about the brand's personality (its inner characteristics) on the basis of behaviours and actions performed by the brand. This means that to create a meaningful and effective brand personality in consumer minds, marketers need to make sure that their brand is perceived to be doing things actively (e.g. use of animations or use of brands as characters in a story). There is also a relationship approach to brand personality research (Fournier, 1995; Aaker and Fournier, 1995). It is postulated that consumers develop trait inferences on the basis of their observation of behaviours undertaken by a brand in its capacity as an active, meaningful and a contributing dyadic partner. The trait inferences which are generated in this manner collectively summarize our perceptions of brand personality (Fournier, 1995). Moreover, leadership personification can also influence brand personality. Example 6.5 illustrates this very well.

EXAMPLE 6.5

Virgin is one of the world's most recognized and respected brands covering businesses in a range of sectors such as mobile phones, transportation, travel, financial services, leisure, music, holidays, publishing and retailing. Virgin brand stands for money, quality, innovation, fun and a sense of competitive challenge. The charismatic personality of its founder, Sir Richard Branson, has played a key role in developing the overall attractiveness, distinctiveness, and self-expressive value of Virgin's brand personality. Consequently, the brand is now one of the most admired brands in the UK with significant levels of brand engagement and brand attachment shown by consumers.

Source: www.virgin.com

www.

Woodside (2004) was commended in Chapter 1 in discussing the means–end chain approach to uncovering motives and values, and in Chapter 3 because it also incorporates Heider's balance theory within the means–end chain method. It incorporates Fournier's brand relational constructs as well.

AG Woodside, Advancing Means-End Chains by Incorporating Heider's Balance Theory and Fournier's Consumer-Brand Relationship Typology, can be accessed via the accompanying book web site at `www.wileyeurope.com/college/evans`.

Social Character Research

Inner-/Other-Directedness

A related approach to personality and consumer choice research derives from the behavioural categories put forward by Riesman in *The Lonely Crowd* (1950). Riesman uses social character to sum up the individual's personality type. His system has three categories: tradition-direction, other-direction and inner-direction, each of which has implications for attitudes and behaviour. Tradition-directed are those whose values and behaviour stem from the past. Inner-directeds have a strong personal sense of what sort of behaviour is correct and other-directeds' values, attitudes and behaviour are largely acquired from others. Table 6.6 summarizes a possible approach to target inner- and other-directed people. Examples of how marketers might target inner-directedness are shown in Figure 6.7 and an example of how they might target other-directedness is shown in Figure 6.8.

If you consider the 'inner-directed' category, you may well remember our earlier discussion of lifestyles and the emerging prevalence of the self-explorer and other 'inner-directeds'. This is also of relevance later in this chapter where we discuss further implications of consumers whose inner-directedness is manifested in being self-expressive through their consumption.

www.

Take a look at the following web site, which offers a link to an article summarizing Riesman's Lonely Crowd work.

`http://www.robertfulford.com/LonelyCrowd.html`

Self-Monitoring

Self-monitoring is the degree to which persons adapt themselves to their social environment. Persons high in self-monitoring behave chameleon-like and are always trying to make good impressions on others. It is important for them to be accepted by others.

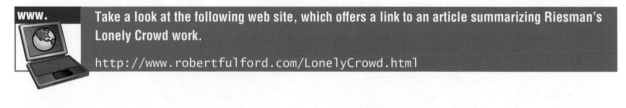

Product	Inner-directed approach	Other-directed approach
Painkiller	Don't spoil your leisure time Showing individual involved with DIY	Don't spoil your leisure time Showing a group in a pub

Table 6.6: Inner- and other-directed appeals

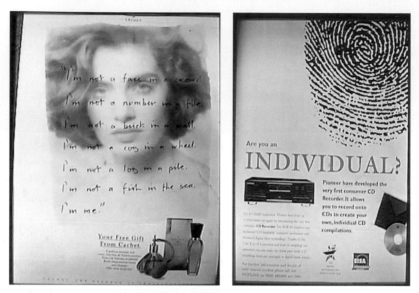

Figure 6.7: Inner Directed Appeals

Figure 6.8: Other Directed Appeals
Source: Diesel

They tend to buy products and brands that contribute to making favourable impressions on their reference group. Persons low in self-monitoring behave more according to their own beliefs and attitudes, and are less influenced by the perceived or actual approval of their social environment. Inner- and other-directedness looks similar to self-monitoring, but is somewhat different. Inner-directed people are concerned with their own thoughts and problems.

Other-directed people are more social and looking for contacts with other people. To distil much of the research into the use of personality in understanding consumer behaviour for marketing targeting purposes, there are some personality traits that offer much scope and these are: **innovativeness**, and **inner-** versus **outer-directedness** and the **self-concept**. As mentioned earlier, innovativeness is discussed in more detail in Chapter 9 on new product buying.

Perhaps one of the problems with personality in explaining consumer behaviour is that an objective personality test might reveal our true personality but we might not know that this is how we are or we may not agree with it. Second, we might want to disguise our true personality and therefore buy brands that in some way extend those traits we want to portray, and perhaps different traits at different times in different social circumstances. This leads us to a consideration of how we might want to be and how we think we are, rather than how we actually are, according to some externally determined personality tests and criteria. This is self-concept theory.

Self-Concept

This variation on the personality theme in consumer psychographics is based not on what sort of personality consumers possess, as identified through administering standardized personality inventory tests, but on how consumers perceive themselves.

Self-concept refers to all of the subjective thoughts and feelings that a person has about themselves as an object (Rosenberg, 1979). It is formed in an interaction process between a person and others in which the person strives for self-enhancement (Grubb and Grathwohl, 1967). It can encompass different things such as 'role identities, personal attributes, relationships, fantasies, possessions, and other symbols that individuals use for the purpose of self-creation and self-understanding' (Schouten, 1991:413). You can view self-concept from different perspectives (Sirgy, 1982). For instance, taking a psychoanalytical approach, you can consider it to be a self-system inflicted with conflict (recall the discussion about tensions between the id and the superego). Take a cognitive perspective and you can describe self-concept in terms of information processing about the self. Take a more symbolic route and you can treat self-concept as a function of interpersonal interactions. Whatever the case, the self-concept develops over time, is not innate (you have to learn it), has the purpose of protecting and enhancing your ego, is unique (it propels individualism in your mind and we explore this later in this chapter) and it includes self-related knowledge and beliefs that are stored in your memory (Graeff, 1996b; Onkvisit and Shaw, 1987). Indeed, it has been found that over time greater congruence between preferred brands and self-image can develop (DeLozier and Tillman, 1972).

There have been many empirical tests of self-concept's explanatory ability regarding consumer behaviour, since Grubb and Gratwohl's (1967) theoretical approach over 40 years ago. For example, Dornoff and Tatham (1972) found that self versus store image can explain store choice. Grubb and Hupp (1968), Grubb and Stern (1971) and Kressmann et al. (2006) found it to be relevant in car markets, perhaps helping consumer research to change gear and accelerate out of the cul-de-sac of 10 years previously when personality assessment somewhat stalled in the car market.

Dimensions of Self

Self-concept is a multidimensional concept and can include actual self, ideal self, social self and ideal social self (Figure 6.9). The variants of 'self' are based on the actual self and the more aspirational ideal self (sometimes referred to as the **looking-glass self**).

	Actual self	Ideal self
Private context	How I see myself now	How I would like to see myself
Social context (looking-glass self)	How I think others see me	How I would like others to see me

Figure 6.9: **Actual and ideal self in a private and social context**

In research by Dorlich (1969) and Ross (1971) the relevance of self-concept for 'privately' versus 'socially' consumed products was explored. Neither found significant support for their hypotheses that socially consumed brands would match the aspirational ideal self more than actual self, or the corollary that privately consumed brands would be more congruent with actual self images. However, Graeff (1996b) found support for the former, if not the latter. He proposed that much research on public/private contexts focuses on products that seem inherently to be one or the other and that it could be more realistic to explore the role of conspicuousness in actual consumption situations. By doing this he found that conspicuousness did not moderate for actual versus ideal self congruence with brand image (Graeff 1997).

EXAMPLE 6.6

MarketingWeek

The Priory Highlights Mental Health Care

The Priory Group, the independent mental health services provider, is highlighting the services available at its 16 UK hospitals.

The integrated campaign is the second of four the group intends to run. It will last 12 months and will focus on four areas – addictions, eating disorders, adolescent mental health and day therapy services.

In the first of two ads, a girl is upset by what she sees in a mirror, despite being incredibly thin with bones sticking out. The ad suggests she has an eating disorder. The second ad shows the order in which people with eating disorders often give up the five main food groups. The last picture shows a gravestone.

The ads will run in regional and national press and have been created by Blackburn-based agency Touch Marketing and Design.

Marketing Week, 28 Jun, 2007, p.6. Reproduced by permission of Centaur Media Plc.

There is clearly lack of clarity is this area, but Solomon (2006) and Hawkins *et al.* (2007) conclude that it is probably reasonable to expect brand images of socially expressive products to match more with ideal self- than with actual self-image and less socially charged products to match more with actual than ideal self-image. They both, however, reinforce the situational context for product use, which also comes from Aaker (1999) along with Graeff's (1997) research.

THINKBOX

In Chapter 5 we discussed gender and sexuality and provided examples of how some consumers will identify with sexual identities which might not obviously reflect their physiological gender. It is pertinent to reflect again on these issues in the context of self-concept theory. Our culture and more local group and family influences (see Chapters 7 and 8) exert gender role pressures on us, in terms of how we act and dress.

But to what extent do you think that our sexual identity is also shaped by our actual and aspirational ideal-self images?

Also, to what extent do you think that our actual and ideal **body images** are accurate and relevant in developing, reflecting or determining sexual identity?

Multiple Selves

There is a discussion about whether self-concept is stable and consistent over time or whether it changes in different situations (Markus and Kunda, 1986). Since we are influenced by others and want to influence others in return, plus the fact that we are with different 'others' on different types of occasions, the general view is that we can all have 'multiple selves' or **multiple identities**. In other words, self-relevant thoughts and feelings can change once you change the social context or situation. For example, when

© Roberto Delpiano. Reproduced with permission.

you are talking to your boyfriend or girlfriend in private, you have a different set of feelings and thoughts about yourself than when you appear in a job interview

These multiple selves coexist in our memory and we tend to activate a particular self, making it more salient depending on a particular situation or context. For example, Jamal and Chapman (2000) reported that respondents in their study experienced multiple selves and identities, revealing their differences and similarities with other groups.

This means a consumer is likely to subscribe to several self-images within their life sphere depending upon the situational context. The implication is that marketers need to facilitate the co-presence and aggregation of individuals having a multiple sense of being by emphasizing the experiential qualities of their products and by reinforcing feelings of consumers in different contexts (Jamal, 2003). A related concept is the notion of **possible selves**, which is a kind of self-relevant knowledge pertaining to how individuals think about their potential and about their future. These are the sorts of selves that you could become or you are afraid of becoming (Markus and Nurius, 1986).

Extended Self

Extended self is based on the idea that we can value certain possessions to the extent that they become part of ourselves (Belk, 1988). The possessions could include external objects, such as brands and collections, but also animals: do we sometimes become like our pets (see Figure 6.10) because we use them as a sort of surrogate for self?

Belk also suggested that other people can extend ourselves, such as partners and even children. That is, do some adults 'live through' their children? Citing the work of McClelland (1961), Belk (1988) argued that possessions become part of ourselves when we are able to exercise some degree of control and power over them. Just as valuing possessions leads to them becoming part of ourselves, losing them also leads to a loss or lessening of ourselves.

Figure 6.10: Using animals as a surrogate for self?
Source: Mars

Our purchases become an extension of ourselves and the ultimate of this process is where we buy 'modifications' to our body such as tattoos, plastic surgery or body piercings (Figure 6.11). There are serious social responsibilities arising from this that marketers are not always keen to address (see Chapter 12). The 'ideal' body image as marketers stereotype it in their advertising or on fashion catwalks (yes, that's just as much 'marketing' as a advertisement) is often difficult for all to achieve. It can lead to eating disorders and body mutilation. It is further complicated by the fact that what is culturally seen to be a desirable body shape varies across cultures, so this reinforces the power of others (see Chapter 7).

The approach is based on an interaction between our self-image and symbols in our environment and is referred to as symbolic interactionism. This is based on the idea that we and our behaviour are influenced by our interactions with the society at large and with our reference groups. We will discuss the influence of reference groups in a later chapter, but it is important to note here that symbolic interactionism leads to an interesting form of research. Rather than investigating single products and consumers' self-concepts, it might be more meaningful to explore groupings of products which symbolize similar things (even if the products themselves are totally unrelated). For example, consider a selection of designer labels across product categories and whether this portfolio might reflect self-concept synergistically. Marketers often depict upmarket cars in advertisements for upmarket jewellery and vice versa.

Figure 6.11: Extending our self-image by modifying our body

THINKBOX

Along with all the variations of the self-concept discussed so far, consider also that we all act out multiple roles. Think about how different you are in today's 2 p.m. lecture from how you were in the club at 2 a.m. on Saturday – or how you are with your family and various other people. Indeed we might be with the same people but in different circumstances and will act out different selves each time.

What are the implications for marketing of your multiple selves?

Virtual Self-Image

The dramatic rise of online communities and in particular social networking, has brought about another dimension of multiple roles and multiple selves: what might be termed the virtual self.

A virtual persona can be posted, and this can meet and interact with virtual friends and exchange virtual information about activities, interests, opinions, purchasing behaviour and so on.

Second Life (www.secondlife.com) affords a new self to be created – an incarnation (or avatar) of one's self in a virtual but 3D environment. Name, age, body image, sexual identity can all be created in this virtual persona. The appearance, however, is a bit like the images in computer games.

Source: www.secondlife.com

Social network sites such as Facebook connect people with friends and others who work, study and live around them. People use Facebook to keep up with friends, upload an unlimited number of photos, share links and videos, and learn more about the people they meet' (Facebook, 2008). We return to the implications of such social networking sites in Chapter 7 where virtual group behaviour is explored.

facebook

Email:

Password:

☐ Remember me

Login

Forgot Password?

Already a Membe

facebook

Facebook is a **social utility** that **connects you** with the people around you.

Everyone can use Facebook — Sign

Source: www.facebook.com

THINKBOX

facebook

Back to "Facebook"   Remove label "Facebook"   Report

Please delete my details from your system

show details Nov 2

Alan Burlison   I have deactivated my Facebook account, it seems o

Peter from Facebook to me

Hi Alan,

If you deactivate, your account is removed from the site. However, we save all your profile content (friends, photos, interests, etc.), so if you want to reactivate sometime, your account will look just the way it did when you deactivated. If you do want your information completely wiped from our servers, we can do this for you. However, you need to remove all profile content before we can do this. Once you have cleared your account, let us know and we'll take care of the rest.

...acting Facebook,

But could the Eagles' *Hotel California* apply to your virtual self: 'you can check out anytime you like but you can never leave'!? (Felder, *et al.,* 1976)

Also, could a virtual self-image be a manifestation of the sort of id drive that we discussed in Chapter 1?

Self-Image Congruence

The importance of self-concept lies in the fact that consumers tend to buy products (or at least some) that are perceived to be similar to their own self-concept. In other words, we have our own self-image and we can psychologically compare that with those of a typical user of a brand (Sirgy, 1982). Consider, for example, the case of a university student who views herself as a modern, trendy, flexible and cool person. She may be influenced by a particular brand of a computer that she views as being used by individuals who are also modern, trendy, flexible and cool. During such a psychological comparison, the product-user image interacts with the consumer's self-concept, generating a subjective experience referred to as **self-image congruence** (Sirgy *et al.*, 1997). When the comparison is between a consumer's actual self and brand/product-user image, it is known as **actual self-image congruence**.

Similarly, consumers can have **ideal self-image congruence and social self-image congruence and ideal social self-image congruence** depending on the type of self-concept (ideal self, social self, ideal social self respectively) used in the comparison process (Figure 6.12). Moreover, the self-congruency influences consumer behaviour through certain motives such as the needs for self-consistency (i.e. the tendency to behave consistently with one's own view of self), self-esteem (i.e. the tendency to seek experiences that enhance one's self-concept), social consistency and social approval motives, and is regarded as an important predictor of consumer behaviour (Sirgy, 1982).

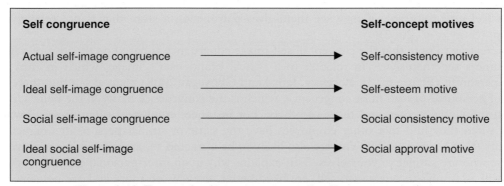

Figure 6.12: Types of self-congruence and self-concept motives
Source: Adopted from Sirgy *et al.*, (2000)

Self-image congruence is important because research has shown that it affects a number of consumer behaviours (e.g. brand preferences and evaluations, purchase intentions, attitudes toward brands, satisfaction). For instance, Jamal and Goode (2001) investigated the effects of self-image congruence on brand preference and satisfaction using a questionnaire, which was sent to 500 consumers of precious jewellery in five major cities of the UK. A total of 118 completed questionnaires were received back and their analysis led to the conclusion that self-image congruence was a very strong predictor of consumers' brand preferences and a good predictor of consumer satisfaction. It was also found that individuals with higher levels of self-image congruence were more likely to prefer the brand and enjoy higher levels of satisfaction with the brand as compared to those with lower levels of self-image congruence. Similar findings have been reported by more recent studies investigating the effects of self-image congruence in the retail banking sector (Jamal, 2004) and automobiles (Jamal and Al-Mari 2007).

Self-image congruence is of high relevance to advertisers also because they can tailor the contents of their messages depending on the degree of self-image congruence experienced by their target consumers. For instance, Graeff (1996b) conducted an experiment among 100 consumers to test whether advertising messages could be used to activate a person's self-concept and whether this activation had any effect on product evaluations and attitudes towards brands. Their general hypothesis was that the effect of self-image congruence would be greater for those who viewed advertisements that encouraged them to think about their self-concept than for those who viewed advertisements that encouraged them to think about functional attributes of the product (e.g. physical product quality). Their findings revealed that activating self-concept through advertisements had a significant effect and led to the generation of more favourable attitudes towards the brand and the ad. Similarly, advertisements that encouraged customers to focus on functional product quality reduced the effect of self-image congruence on brand and ad attitude.

Consumers can vary in their degree of self-image congruence experienced; some can experience higher levels while others can experience lower levels. Factors such as price, income, product life cycle, consumer involvement, product utility, value and a person's level of expertise can moderate the effects of self-image congruence (Onkvisit and Shaw, 1987; Jamal and Al-Mari, 2007). Similarly, as we have seen, the effects of self-image congruence are likely to be stronger for products that are conspicuous in nature and are publicly consumed (e.g. cars and jeans) than those that are less conspicuous in nature and are privately consumed (e.g. soap and underwear). Marketers can, however, remedy this situation by bringing the privately consumed products out and making them more conspicuous through advertising (Onkvisit and Shaw, 1987).

In the context of retail stores, it has been argued that the greater the degree of congruence between a shopper's self concept and the retail patron image, the greater the likelihood that the shopper would patronize the retail store (Sirgy *et al.*, 2000). This helps to explain why, in a retail context, consumers sometimes feel uncomfortable if they see themselves patronizing a store that is not reflective of their self-concept (Sirgy *et al.*, 2000).

It is interesting to note that the concept of self-image congruence is based on the idea of a fit between how consumers see themselves in relation to a typical brand user's image, which in turn reflects a person-to-person fit (Figure 6.13). Recently, Jamal and Gboyega (2008) pointed out that there are many examples of person-to-person fit or congruence, which is the congruence between the beliefs, norms and goals of an individual person and those of others. For instance, employees often remain loyal to their employers when they find that other employees have the same or similar personality characteristics as that of theirs (Van Vianen, 2000). You are also likely to be attracted to, and have more positive attitudes about those who are similar to yourselves. This explains why in an inter-personal context, partners, who are perceived as similar to one's own self, are liked better, are trusted more and are perceived as more attractive compared to dissimilar partners (Bendapudi and Berry, 1997).

Utilizing the notion of person-to-person fit, Jamal and Gboyega (2008) investigated the effects of self-employee congruence (i.e., the fit between service employee image and that of a customer during the service delivery process) on a number of relational factors such as satisfaction towards service employees, loyalty towards the employees and the overall satisfaction towards the service provider. Findings suggested that self-employee congruence was a strong predictor of personal interaction, relationship satisfaction and loyalty towards the service employee.

Furthermore, as per Jamal and Gboyega (2008), the notion of self-image congruence also parallels the concept of person-organization fit or congruence, which is defined as the congruence or fit between the beliefs and norms of individual persons and those of an organization (Netemeyer *et al.*, 1997; O'Reilly *et al.*, 1991). Empirical evidence suggests that job satisfaction and commitment towards the organization can be higher when there is a person–organization fit (Lauver and Kristof-Brown, 2001). In a consumer behaviour context, you can think of a fit between you as a consumer and a particular organization as a brand (Figure 6.13) and when this occurs we say a self-brand congruence is established. This may well explain why many of us admire leading brands such as Virgin, which has some very strong and favourable brand associations. The notion of self-brand congruence is very similar to that of self-brand

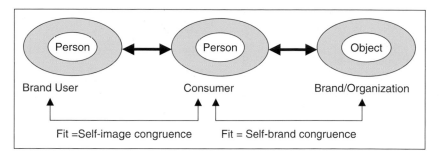

Figure 6.13: **Self-image congruence and self-brand congruence**

connection (Escalas and Bettman, 2003), which can be explained as the extent to which consumers incorporate a brand into their self-concept. Consumers normally achieve self-brand connection when they use some specific brand associations to either form their self-images or to communicate their self-images to others (Escalas and Bettman, 2005). This has implications for the way we relate to others such as reference groups and hence a further discussion of this will appear in a later chapter.

THINKBOX

Compare and contrast the typical brand users' imagery for each of the following brands and then list the features down against each brand. In other words, what sort of person uses each of the following brands?

Brand Name	Typical Brand User Image
Volvo	
Starbucks	
Microsoft	
Apple iPod	
Calvin Klein	
Nike	
Rolex	

Self-Concept Research Mechanics

The self-concept approach can be based on semantic differential scales showing series of bipolar adjectives, on which respondents may be asked to position how they see various brands, and/or themselves and/or their ideal self-concept. The brand preferred would then be the one closest to (having the greatest degree of congruence with) the segment's self-image or ideal self-image. With distance scores this degree of congruence is calculated and this helps to identify appropriate brand images to create and project (Figure 6.14).

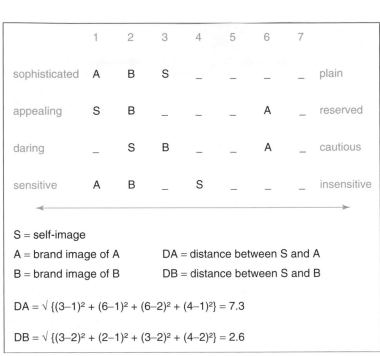

Figure 6.14: **Self-concept distance scores (seven-point scale)**

The smaller the distance score, the greater the degree of congruence between brand and self-images. Brand preferences can be predicted on the basis of such congruence.

An Alternative Approach for Measuring Self-Image Congruence

Sirgy *et al.* (1997) proposed an alternative method of measuring self-image congruence. Rather than using product-user images and self-images, they suggested measuring self-image congruence experience directly using Likert-type scales (Table 6.7). The method induces subjects to conjure up the product-user image right at the moment of response rather than through the use of some predetermined images. Sirgy *et al.* (1997) then compared the predictive validity of the two methods (old and new) in six studies involving different customer groups, products, consumption settings and dependent variables. Their findings provided support for the high predictiveness of the new method over and beyond the old one.

Inner-Directedness, Self-Concept and Self-Expression

An integration of Inner-Directness and Self Concept Theory leads to the concept of self expression and Aaker (1999) has shown, for example, that consumers use brands as a means of non-verbal self expression.

For teenagers, especially, the search for individuality is manifested in a 'search for identity and belonging' thus supporting the importance of tribes: 'the majority tend to be more transient and consumer led. Kids can buy a look, an identity and an attitude: 'you can even purchase a potato peeler that reflects your 'crazy' personality' (Davidson, 2003).

The Clarks Shoe advertisement reflects this: 'Be Your Own Label'.

This, for some market segments, affords further insight because there is evidence suggesting that some people are becoming more orientated to self-expression in the form of individualism as opposed

- First, ask your respondents to think about a particular product (e.g. athletic shoes or women's apparel and clothing style).
- Then ask them to think about the kind of person who typically uses that product. Ask them to imagine that person in their minds and describe the person using some personal adjectives (e.g., stylish, classy, modern, sexy etc.,).
- Once they have done this, ask the respondents to indicate their agreement or disagreement to the following statements*:

  - This product (brand X) is consistent with how I see myself (in situation X).
  - Using this product (in situation X) reflects who I am.
  - People similar to me use this product (brand X in situation X).
  - This product (brand X) is a mirror image of me (in situation X).
  - The kind of person who typically uses this product (in situation X) is very much like me.

- Ask your respondents to mark their responses on a Likert-type scale ranging from 1 to 5 or 1 to 7.

*Statements included here are for illustration only. See Sirgy *et al*. (1997) for their use of different statements in different contexts.
Source: Based on JM Sirgy *et al*., Assessing the Predictive Validity of Two Methods of Measuring Self-Image Congruence, *Journal of the Academy of MarketingScience*, Vol 25 No 3 (1997), pp. 229–241.© 1997.

Table 6.7: Alternative method for measuring self-image congruence

to following mass social movements. In Chapter 5 we proposed an historical progression from the social optimism of the 1960s pop culture to the more anarchic (individualistic) mood of 1970s Punk. Indeed The Henley Centre (1978) predicted this trend as far back as the 1970s when they discussed household behaviour as being 'cellular' rather than 'nuclear' - households were beginning to do things together less and less and beginning to behave more independently: families were not eating together as often and having TV and sound systems in their 'own' rooms.

The greater resulting pluralism in the market today has been confirmed by The Henley Centre for Forecasting (1992) and The Future Foundation (2008). The extract, below, from one of the latter's Reports provides interesting and significant implications for consumer behaviour, society and marketing.

Source: Clarks

THINKBOX

FUTURE FOUNDATION RESEARCH
Fluid Identities

Our concept of self is an increasingly fluid and malleable one. We are free to be actors in so many different roles: at home, as parents, at work, as managers, at play, as aspirants, at the point of purchase, as customers. Modern communications technology allows individuals - a most revolutionary concept - to control the revelation of their identities. Online, you can buy and sell and leave comment and opinion without anyone knowing your real name. You can take on virtual identities as you enter unfamiliar environments and connect with other 'individuals' across the world. As a number of unfortunate scandals and controversies have affirmed, this extra layer of consumer empowerment has its dark, criminal side. Yet it is interesting to note how substantially the technology has been democratised. One can be different people online - a power that an individual but not a company can enjoy.

Many analysts have noticed just how quickly ad hoc alliances can form online to create protest movements rooted in quickly shared information and advice. Such energised networks give a possibility of prompt initiative that the pre-Net years could not sustain. Marketers already realise that in appealing to consumers they must reach out to multiple personalities, to a fluidity that can be influenced by cultural and social mores day by day. The challenge is how to sustain loyalty and consistency of product offering whilst still appealing to different aspects of consumers' personality.

We delve more into the extension of self via virtual selves online, in chapter 7, but what do you think of the findings as summarized here?

Reproduced by permission of The Future Foundation http://www.futurefoundation.net/

The concept of postmodernism also includes a greater individualism, **pluralism** and even fragmentation (Van Raaij and Schoonderbeek, 1993).

THINKBOX

Consider the fragmentation in some markets: does this choice reflect individualism, or does it fuel it or does it just confuse us all?

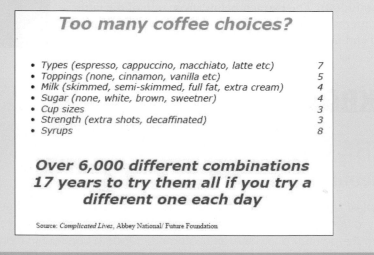

Too many coffee choices?

- Types (espresso, cappuccino, macchiato, latte etc)   7
- Toppings (none, cinnamon, vanilla etc)   5
- Milk (skimmed, semi-skimmed, full fat, extra cream)   4
- Sugar (none, white, brown, sweetner)   4
- Cup sizes   3
- Strength (extra shots, decaffinated)   3
- Syrups   8

Over 6,000 different combinations 17 years to try them all if you try a different one each day

Source: *Complicated Lives*, Abbey National/ Future Foundation

Further evidence of the trend toward individualism was uncovered during the 1970s and led, amongst other things, to the Regan and Thatcher election campaigns from the late 1970s and into the 1980s based on 'self reliance' (BBC, 2002b). 'Standing on one's own feet' and 'freeing the individual from the state' were the sorts of mantras of those elections and were manifestations of research at the time that revealed individualism (McNulty, 2002).

The eras of mass customization and more personalized direct and interactive marketing provide the means to achieve some of this and Chapter 11 explores the matter further.

Research reported by Publicis (Block, 1992) suggests that from 1973 to 1989 there had been a shift in 'motivators' from functional and rational factors (from 40% to 27% of the population) and 'outer-directedness' (static at 35%) to more 'inner-directedness' (from 25% to 38% of the population), again reinforcing evidence of this significant shift in orientation.

EXAMPLE 6.7

Some group discussions conducted for Levi Strauss in the mid-1980s revealed general praise for Levi's advertising in which rock music soundtracks were used. Many in the groups, however, expressed their own personal music tastes to be orientated towards different specific music styles of the time. The result was a poster campaign that showed 12 head shots of different young people who clearly had different fashion tastes, many of them music-based (Figure 6.15). The copy subheading reads: 'Blue jeans cut twelve ways'.

Figure 6.15: Levi Individualism Haircuts

Figure 6.16 gives a further example of marketers' use of self-expression and individualism in their understanding of and subsequent targeting of consumers.

Figure 6.16: Self-expression

Individualized car number plates appeal to many who want to personalize their cars and allow others to see the link between themselves and the car they drive

© DVLA. Reproduced by permission

Even business can reflect individualism as a marketing vehicle:

Photos: Martin Evans

In Europe, well over 50 million people now live solitary domestic lives (Institute for Family Policy, 2008). Living alone facilitates greater scope for individualism, or dare it be said, selfishness? As Willmott and Nelson (2003) discuss, individualism does mean that it is individualism versus society. Their work with the Future Foundation found that a function of wanting products that are more congruent with their personal needs, the notion of 'collective individualism' is now evident (Future

Foundation, 2008). There is, perhaps, danger in being too much of an individual, so the compromise is to engage with the new tribalism (Patterson, 1998, Nancarrow and Nancarrow 2007) of the postmodern world. Chapter 7 explores this a little more but essentially consumers can play out their multiple and individualistic roles in such fragmented tribes as brand communities or 'loyalty clubs', music genres and online communities such as Second Life or Facebook, as introduced above. Consumers can switch between many of these anytime we want.

The Undesired Self

In the same way that within 'motivation' there are 'avoidance' motives, because of negative consequences, Hogg and Bannister (2001) describe the **undesired self**. Here the 'image congruence' approach is modified to allow exploration of undesired end states and undesired self-images. Hogg and Bannister (2001) report qualitative research that reinforces the importance of significant others in determining what is 'undesirable'. An implication is to link negative consequences of, say, drink-driving with negative consumer stereotypes in order to discourage that behaviour (see Chapter 12). A UK TV advertisement showed how social embarrassment can be an undesired end state when an individual enters a fancy dress party as an elf only to find all the others are all dressed as Elvis (claiming that he thought his invite had stated elves!).

www. Have a look at Todd (2001) Self-Concept: A Tourism Application, Journal of Consumer Behaviour, Vol 1 No 2 pp 184–196, accessed via the accompanying book web site at www.wileyeurope.com/college/evans

THINKBOX

FUTURE FOUNDATION RESEARCH

Body of the Body

Appearance manipulation is now socially endemic. The concept attracts every age, background and income group. In our defect intolerant society, taboos are being shed forever on fixing our crooked teeth, small breasts or bulbous tummies. As a result, cosmetic surgery is becoming more common (there has been a 30% rise in procedures during 2008), faster (90 minute facelifts are now available), and more trivial (*Zoo* magazine has given away cosmetic procedures as prizes). We refer to this phenomenon as the cult of perfection in appearance. Whether our defect intolerance is morbid or simply a normal element of an affluent consumer society, is a topic hotly debated. However, irrespective of judgement, this phenomenon is certainly here to stay.

Do you think we have an intolerance of what society seems to perceive as defects? Is it a function of the affluent society?

Reproduced by permission of The Future Foundation http://www.futurefoundation.net/

SUMMARY

■ Lifestyle can be researched in different ways. This chapter has explored traditional lifestyle, which is researched via traditional market research techniques using anonymized samples of consumers giving their degree of agreement with a series of Likert statements covering activities, interests and opinions. The approach can be especially helpful in getting beneath the consumer's skin in order to devise relevant promotional messages, which fit with their outlook in life.

■ Personality refers either to an extensive range of separate behavioural traits (honesty, perseverance and hostility, for instance) or to overall types of character and response (extrovert and introvert). In spite of some high hopes and prima facie evidence that aspects of consumers' purchase behaviour might be closely related to their personality traits, empirical verification of this association is still lacking. Some traits are of value to marketers, however, such as innovativeness and inner-directedness/self-expression.

■ Self-concept theory overcomes some of the problems with personality in that this is concerned more with how individuals think of themselves (or want others to see them) than with how they actually are. This is important because much consumption is to do with covering up personality aspects we don't want others to see and with extending those traits we do want others to think we possess.

QUESTIONS

1. **Consider the following situation:**

   A self-concept study was conducted for a cosmetics company with a view to creating a marketing mix for a new perfume based on matching brand images with self-images.

   The cosmetics company had recently taken over another company and, among other products, had acquired a perfume. This was to be relaunched on the basis of their self-concept study findings.

   Respondents were shown three 'advertisements' for perfume. The advertised 'brands' were given three different themes. One used a prestigious, sophisticated theme (the possible brand name here was 'La Vogue'); the second a sensual, slightly naughty theme ('Vamp'); and the third a romantic theme ('Romano'). Each 'advertisement' included appropriate narrative, picture sequences and models. The results are shown in Tables 6.8, 6.9, 6.10 and 6.11. Respondents were asked to position their reactions on each of the scales. In Table 6.8 we see how respondents perceived the three 'brands'. There was, of course, no difference between the perfumes in a chemical sense – the three advertisements were merely three different ways of marketing the same product.

	Left	1	2	3	4	5	6	7	Right
1	luxurious	L			VR				plain
2	lustful	V				L		R	innocent
3	classical			LR			V		fashionable
4	sophisticated	L			R		V		unsophisticated
5	unadventurous		L				VR		adventurous
6	discriminating		L		R			V	undiscriminating
7	shy		LR				V		unreserved
8	prestigious	L				R	V		not prestigious
9	sensitive		R		L		V		insensitive
10	inhibited		L	R				V	uninhibited
11	romantic	R		L			V		unromantic
12	sexy	V				R	L		unsexy

L = La Vogue, V = Vamp, R = Romano.

Table 6.8: Brand Images

	Left	1	2	3	4	5	6	7	Right
1	luxurious					✓			plain
2	lustful			✓					innocent
3	classical				✓				fashionable
4	sophisticated					✓			unsophisticated
5	unadventurous			✓					adventurous
6	discriminating						✓		undiscriminating
7	shy			✓					unreserved
8	prestigious						✓		not prestigious
9	sensitive		✓						insensitive
10	inhibited			✓					uninhibited
11	romantic			✓					unromantic
12	sexy				✓				unsexy

Table 6.9: Self-Images

a. Calculate the distance scores for each brand against each of the two variants of self-concept. On this basis, decide which brand image you will select and with which version of 'self' it will be matched.

b. Decide which of the image dimensions you will select for the 'brand-self' matching determined in question 1a. Also, use the demographics in Table 6.9 to determine the demographic segment you intend to target. (Table 6.9 shows the profile of those respondents who actually preferred the brand you selected in question 1a.)

c. Have a go at compiling a marketing mix for this brand. Explain the relative contributions of the self-concept and demographic information in devising each mix element. Be specific over these contributions, to produce a detailed 'mix' including: product range, package design, size, colours, on-pack information, brand name, price levels, selection of retail outlet type and location, promotional media and details of any TV or print promotional messages (not just 'copy headlines').

1	luxurious	|__|__|__|_✓_|__|__|__|	plain
2	lustful	|__|__|__|__|__|__|_✓_|	innocent
3	classical	|__|_✓_|__|__|__|__|__|	fashionable
4	sophisticated	|__|__|__|_✓_|__|__|__|	unsophisticated
5	unadventurous	|__|__|__|__|__|_✓_|__|	adventurous
6	discriminating	|__|__|_✓_|__|__|__|__|	undiscriminating
7	shy	|__|_✓_|__|__|__|__|__|	unreserved
8	prestigious	|__|__|_✓_|__|__|__|__|	not prestigious
9	sensitive	|✓_|__|__|__|__|__|__|	insensitive
10	inhibited	|__|__|__|__|_✓_|__|__|	uninhibited
11	romantic	|_✓_|__|__|__|__|__|__|	unromantic
12	sexy	|__|__|_✓_|__|__|__|__|	unsexy

Table 6.10: Self-Ideal Images

socio-econ	age			
	18–25	26–35	36–49	50+
A	14	8	8	5
B	22	11	7	3
C1	21	10	9	2
C2	19	8	5	—
D	9	2	—	—
E	7	1	—	—
Totals	92	40	29	10

Table 6.11: Demographic profile of respondents

2. Draw up a lifestyle questionnaire to measure your fellow students' activities, interests and opinions. Conduct some interviews and see if an analysis of the data produces well-defined homogenous clusters.

3. Do we 'buy things that extend our real personality'?

4. Conduct-personal interviews with three fellow students with a viewing to identifying decision-making styles for each one of them using Table 6.5. Compare and contrast your own decision-making style with those identified via interviews.

5. Discuss the concepts of multiple selves. Do you exhibit different personas in different contexts? Are the concepts of the extended self and virtual self used by people you know? How and why?

6. Define self-image congruence. Why are marketers interested in identifying self-image congruence of their target customers?

7. Explore individualism, its manifestations and implications for marketers.

FURTHER READING

Baudrillard J (1999) *The Consumer Society: Myths and Structures,* Sage. This is a work that emanates more from sociology than marketing. It provides a very insightful – and critical – examination of consumption within contemporary society. It extends our coverage of self and individualism, of lifestyles and consumption as affected by the media (in our terms, marketing).

Willmott M and Nelson W (2003) *Complicated Lives: Sophisticated Consumers, Intricate Lifestyles, Simple Solutions,* John Wiley & Sons, Chichester. The Future Foundation is a major research organization and think tank which explores changes in society as they affect companies and markets. This book brings together much of their recent work and is recommended highly. It extends our coverage of individualism, demographics and emerging lifestyles.

Here, at the end of Part 1, we present an academic article from the *Journal of Consumer Research*. The article, by Smeesters and Mandel (2006) addresses the issue of female stereotyping in advertising (see Chapter 5) but also explores methodological approaches to measuring 'self perception' (see Chapter 6).

Q1 Explore the issues raised here for how consumers react to thin (or heavy) body images in advertising.

Q2 What are the implications of this research for measuring aspects of 'self'?

PART 1   JOURNAL ARTICLE

POSITIVE AND NEGATIVE MEDIA IMAGE EFFECTS ON THE SELF

Dirk Smeesters and Naomi Mandel*
Reproduced from Journal of Consumer Research, Inc. Vol. 32 (2006) 576–582.

We examine several factors that determine whether exposure to thin (or heavy) media images positively or negatively affects consumers' appearance self-esteem. We find that the effects of exposure to models in advertisements depend on two moderating factors: (1) the extremity of the model's thinness or heaviness, and (2) the method by which self-esteem is measured (free responses vs. rating scales). We also establish the underlying role of self-knowledge activation by examining response latencies in a lexical decision task.

A model-thin body is now considered an ideal that every woman should admire and achieve (Wertheim *et al.* 1997). This article examines how exposure to thin (or heavy) media images affects women's appearance self-esteem. Richins (1991) demonstrated that women were less satisfied with their own physical appearance after they viewed advertisements featuring thin, attractive models. A number of other researchers have confirmed that exposure to thin media images can negatively affect body-image perception (Meyers and Biocca 1992) and assessment of one's own attractiveness (Martin and Gentry 1997). However, there is also evidence that exposure to thin models in magazines can lead to self-enhancement (Henderson-King and Henderson-King 1997) and thinner self-ratings (Mills *et al.* 2002) than exposure to larger body images. Thus, it remains unclear under which conditions such exposure results in assimilative or contrastive shifts in self-evaluation. In this article, we integrate some of these previously divergent findings and extend Richins's (1991) work by documenting circumstances under which exposure to idealized pictures of women in ads exerts positive or negative effects.

*Dirk Smeesters is assistant professor of marketing at Tilburg University, P.O. Box 90153, 5000 LE Tilburg, The Netherlands (d.smeesters@uvt.nl). Naomi Mandel is assistant professor of marketing in the W. P. Carey School of Business, Arizona State University, Tempe, AZ 85287-4106 (naomi.mandel@asu.edu). This research was supported by a Marie Curie Intra-European Fellowship grant from the European Commission to the first author.

We examine the roles of two potential moderators: extremity of the model's build (i.e., whether the model is extremely or moderately thin/heavy) and response mode (i.e., the way in which participants' self-judgments are measured). According to Mussweiler (2003), assimilation or contrast in self-evaluation depends on which type of accessible self-knowledge becomes accessible as a result of social comparison. Comparison with a moderate standard (e.g., a moderately thin model) should render standard-consistent self-knowledge accessible and result in assimilation, while comparison with an extreme standard (e.g., an extremely thin model) should render standard-inconsistent self-knowledge accessible and result in contrast. The response mode, used to assess the self-evaluative consequences of social comparison, may also play an important role. A free-response measure is more likely to reflect an individual's accessible knowledge than the more often used rating-scale measure (e.g., Richins 1991), which may instead show contrast because of reference-point use (Mussweiler and Strack 2000).

Our research contributes to the existing literature in several ways. As already described, previous studies provided mixed results of exposure to body images in the media. In addition, most prior research has examined moderators of assimilation or contrast in the context of explicit social comparison designs, but almost never in the case of implicit comparison designs (Stapel and Suls 2004). We revisit Richins's (1991) suggestion (which was not directly tested) that individuals implicitly compare themselves to the model in an ad without explicit instructions to do so. We also examine the mechanism underlying our effects

via a lexical decision task, which measures which type of self-knowledge becomes accessible after exposure to various types of advertising models.

Conceptual Background

People have a natural drive to evaluate their own attributes and abilities, which they do by comparing themselves with others (Festinger 1954). A comparison to a thin (or heavy) model is considered to be upward (or downward) social comparison, since thin people are perceived more positively than heavy people (Wertheim *et al.* 1997). Prior research has uncovered assimilation as well as contrast effects in self-evaluation as a result of social comparison. Upward comparisons can result in decreased self-satisfaction, and downward comparisons can result in increased self-satisfaction (e.g., Richins 1991). On the other hand, an upward comparison target might also serve as an inspiration or role model, while exposure to a downward comparison standard can result in feelings of discouragement (see Stapel and Koomen 2001).

Mussweiler (2003) proposed the "selective accessibility model" to explain whether assimilation or contrast occurs. The first stage in this cognitive model is standard selection, which can be manipulated by providing comparison targets, such as thin or heavy models. The second stage is comparison, which is influenced by selective accessibility. The comparison is made by a quick holistic assessment of the similarity between the self and the standard. The individual making the comparison will search her memory for evidence of similarities or dissimilarities between the self and the target. Perceived similarities indicate that the standard resembles the self, which results in the activation of standard-consistent information about the self. Perceived dissimilarities indicate that the standard does not resemble the self, which results in the activation of standard-inconsistent information about the self. The final stage, evaluation of one's own abilities, is highly dependent on the information selectively retrieved during the second stage. Subsequent selfevaluation should assimilate to the standard when it is based on accessible standard-consistent information about the self. However, self-evaluation should contrast away from the standard when standard-inconsistent information about the self is accessible.

Differences in perceived similarity between the self and a comparison standard can determine the occurrence of contrast or assimilation in self-evaluation (Lockwood and Kunda 1997). For example, Häfner (2004) manipulated participants' perceived similarity to models in ads by altering the headlines to read "same body – same feeling" or "feel the difference," and found assimilation effects among participants primed on similarity and contrast effects among those primed on dissimilarity. Moderately thin or moderately heavy models are more likely to be viewed by magazine readers as "possible selves" (Markus and Nurius 1986), either currently or in the future, than extremely thin or extremely heavy models. Therefore, we expect to find assimilative self-evaluations after participants view pictures of moderately thin/heavy models and contrastive self-evaluations after participants view pictures of extremely thin/heavy models. When comparing oneself to a moderately thin model, knowledge that one is thin should become accessible, and when comparing oneself to a moderately heavy model, knowledge that one is heavy should become accessible (Mussweiler 2003). Comparing oneself to an extremely thin or extremely heavy model, on the other hand, should increase the accessibility of knowledge that one differs from the model. As a result, an individual should express higher self-esteem when having access to knowledge that one is thin than knowledge that one is heavy.

Although related, our studies diverge from those of Mussweiler, Rüter, and Epstude (2004) and Mussweiler and Strack (2000) in that we do not explicitly ask participants to make a comparative judgment between themselves and the advertising models before providing self-judgments. If Richins's (1991) assertions are correct, the initial comparison should spontaneously occur when participants view an ad featuring a thin or heavy model. While much of the existing social comparison research uses explicit comparison instructions (Stapel and Suls 2004), in real life, individuals usually compare themselves with others in an implicit and spontaneous manner (Wheeler and Miyake 1992). Under such circumstances, both assimilation and contrast may occur, depending on "a host of factors, such as, for example, the distinctness and extremity of the primed person information" (Stapel and Blanton 2004, 479).

Another factor that is expected to influence our participants' self-judgments is the way in which these judgments are measured, known as the response mode (Payne, Bettman, and Johnson 1992). According to Mussweiler and Strack (2000), a rating-scale measure is dependent on reference-point use when a comparison standard is provided. When answering a rating scale (such as a Likert scale), the standard serves as a reference point to anchor the scale (Lynch, Chakravarti, and Mitra 1991), which leads to contrast when comparing oneself to the standard (Mussweiler and Strack 2000). A free-response measure is not affected by reference-point use but rather reflects the effects of knowledge accessibility. For example, Mussweiler and Strack (2000) demonstrated that comparing oneself to a moderate exemplar of drug use (e.g., Frank Zappa) increases the accessibility of standard-consistent knowledge about one's own drug use, producing assimilation on a free-response measure. However, when answering a rating scale, Zappa serves as a reference point, producing contrast away from the standard. Therefore, when a rating scale is used, we expect lower self-ratings when consumers are exposed to thin models than to heavy models, regardless of the extremity of the model's build (replicating Richins's [1991] contrast results).

In summary, we expect both the extremity of the model's size and the response mode to influence participants' self-esteem responses, as described in the following hypotheses:

H1a: When completing a free-response measure, participants will demonstrate higher self-esteem after exposure to moderately thin models than after exposure to moderately heavy models (i.e., an assimilation effect) and lower self-esteem after exposure to extremely thin models than after exposure to extremely heavy models (i.e., a contrast effect).

H1b: When completing a rating-scale measure, participants will demonstrate lower self-esteem after exposure to thin models than after exposure to

heavy models, regardless of the extremity of the model's size (i.e., a contrast effect).

Experiment 1

A pretest was used to select advertisements containing female models for the following four conditions: moderately thin, extremely thin, moderately heavy, and extremely heavy. Participants were 62 female university students who completed a paper-and-pencil test in exchange for course credit. Each participant viewed an advertisement booklet containing 23 ads with female models. Participants rated each model in terms of size (-5 = extremely overweight, 5 = extremely thin) and attractiveness (-5 = extremely unattractive, 5 = extremely attractive). Based on these scores, we selected four advertising models in each condition. Tukey post hoc comparisons ($\alpha = .05$) revealed that all four conditions differed significantly from each other in terms of size but not in terms of attractiveness. Extremely thin models ($M = 3.56$) were judged as thinner than moderately thin models ($M = 2.48$), who were rated as thinner than moderately heavy models ($M = -1.39$), who were rated as thinner than extremely heavy models ($M = -2.44$). A second pretest, using 123 female university students, confirmed that participants perceived the moderate (thin and heavy) models from the first pretest as more similar to themselves than the extreme (thin and heavy) models ($F(1, 122) = 4.29, p < .05$).

Method

In the first experiment, 62 female university students participated for course credit. Each participant was randomly assigned to one of the four conditions of the 2 (model size: thin vs. heavy) $\times$

2 (extremity of model size: moderate vs. extreme) between-subjects design. The first task was labeled "Advertisement Questionnaire." Participants received a booklet containing eight full-page color ads: four ads with models, pertaining to their condition, and four filler ads with no models. The order of the eight ads was randomized. Participants indicated on five-point scales whether the ads were original, convincing, and/or informative. Following a short filler task, participants received an "Attitude Questionnaire." The first part of this questionnaire consisted of the Twenty Statements Task (TST; Kuhn and McPartland 1954), where participants complete 20 self-descriptive statements ("I am __"). This free-response task can validly assess individuals' momentary self-conceptions, such as appearance (Gardner, Gabriel, and Lee 1999). Next, participants completed the Appearance Self-Esteem Scale on a five-point scale (Heatherton and Polivy 1991), which represented the rating-scale measure. Finally, participants completed a short questionnaire, which indicated that no participants correctly guessed the true nature of the study.

Results and Discussion

Two independent judges, blind to the conditions and the hypotheses, scored participants' TST answers. For each participant, the judges selected self-descriptive statements, either positive or negative, that referred to the participant's own physical appearance (e.g., "I am pretty," "I am slim," "I am heavy," "I am unsatisfied with my appearance"). The judges showed a high level of agreement ($r = .81$). Based on the selected statements per participant, two other independent judges, also blind to the conditions

and the hypotheses, rated each participant's perception of her own physical appearance using a five-point scale that ranged from 1 (very negative about her own physical appearance) to 5 (very positive about her own physical appearance). Ratings of the two judges were highly correlated ($r = .91$, $p < .001$) and were combined into a single score. Our analysis for the free-response measure was based on these judged ratings. We also conducted an analysis on the difference between the number of positive and negative self-descriptions about one's own appearance. This analysis was highly similar to the analysis on the judged ratings.

We conducted a 2 (model size: thin vs. heavy) $\times$ 2 (extremity of model size: moderate vs. extreme) $\times$ 2 (response mode: free response vs. rating scale) ANOVA with model size and extremity of model size as between-subjects factors and response mode as a within-subjects factor. This analysis revealed a three-way interaction between model size, extremity of model size, and response mode ($F(1, 58) = 11.62$, $p < .01$), which is illustrated in Figure 1.

Analysis of the free-response measure revealed a model size $\times$ extremity interaction ($F(1, 58) = 15.29$, $p < .001$). Participants exposed to moderately thin models had higher appearance self-esteem ($M = 3.60$) than participants exposed to moderately heavy models ($M = 2.38$), resulting in an assimilation effect that supports hypothesis 1a. Participants exposed to extremely thin models had lower appearance self-esteem ($M = 2.63$) than participants exposed to extremely heavy models ($M = 3.53$), resulting in a contrast effect that also supports hypothesis 1a. Analysis of the rating-scale measure revealed only a main effect of model size ($F(1, 58) = 14.50$, $p < .001$), providing evidence

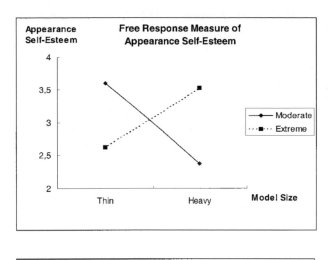

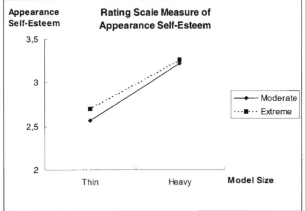

Figure 1: Experiment 1 results: Appearance self-esteem as a function of model size, extremity of model size, and response mode

to support hypothesis 1b. Participants exposed to thin models ($M = 2.63$) had lower appearance self-esteem than participants exposed to heavy models ($M = 3.29$).

These results suggest that the extremity of the standard and the response mode determine to what extent comparison with a standard leads to assimilative or contrastive self-evaluations. When judging themselves via free responses, participants displayed self-esteem that varied as a function of the extremity of the standard. However, when participants judged themselves on a rating scale, we only obtained a contrast effect. These findings imply that in addition to selective accessibility, self-evaluative comparisons also suggest a reference-point mechanism that may be used for subsequent judgments. Thus, the contrast effects found for extremely thin and heavy models on both the free-response and the rating-scale measures appear to result from a different underlying process: knowledge accessibility in the case of the free-response measure and reference-point use in the case of the rating-scale measure. Experiment 2 was designed to provide further evidence for the role of knowledge accessibility in self-evaluation when comparing oneself to models in ads.

Experiment 2

In experiment 2, we tested the underlying process by which self-knowledge becomes accessible after exposure to thin versus heavy models by using a lexical decision task. This task measured the accessibility of words designating thinness, words designating heaviness, and neutral words. These words were preceded by subliminally presented self primes (words related to the self, e.g., *I* or *me*), or control primes (words unrelated to the self). Subliminal exposure to self primes has been demonstrated to activate the selfconcept (Dijksterhuis *et al.* 1998). Lexical decision trials preceded by self primes increase the specific accessibility of knowledge related to the self, whereas trials preceded by control primes do not (Dijksterhuis *et al.* 1998).

If selective accessibility plays a role in the comparison with advertising models, standard-consistent self-knowledge should become more accessible when participants compare themselves to moderately thin models (i.e., knowledge that one is thin should become accessible) or moderately heavy models (i.e., knowledge that one is heavy should become accessible). On the other hand, standard-inconsistent self-knowledge should become more accessible when participants compare themselves to extremely thin models (i.e., knowledge that one is heavy should become accessible) or extremely heavy models (i.e., knowledge that one is thin should become accessible). Hence, participants should respond more quickly in identifying words that are related to the self-knowledge that has become accessible.

H2: In the presence of a self prime, participants exposed to moderately thin models or extremely heavy models will respond faster to words associated with thinness than to words associated with heaviness or neutral words, whereas participants exposed to moderately heavy models or extremely thin models will respond faster to words associated with heaviness than to words associated with thinness or neutral words.

Participants tend to compare themselves automatically with advertising models (Richins 1991), but the self-evaluative effects of such a comparison should only occur when participants are asked to judge themselves (as in experiment 1) or are nonconsciously primed to think about themselves (as with self primes; Dijksterhuis *et al.* 1998). On the other hand, lexical decision trials preceded by control primes should reflect only the knowledge associated with the standard (Dijksterhuis *et al.* 1998) because the self is not activated. In particular, we predict here an interaction between model size and the target words. Exposure to moderately or extremely thin models should lead to the activation of thinness knowledge, whereas exposure to moderately or extremely heavy models should lead to the activation of heaviness knowledge, as specified in hypothesis 3:

H3: In the presence of a control prime, participants exposed to thin models will respond faster to words associated with thinness than to words associated with heaviness or neutral words, whereas participants exposed to heavy models will respond faster to words associated with heaviness than to words associated with thinness or neutral words, regardless of the extremity of the model's size.

Method

Participants were 84 female university students who participated for course credit. They were randomly assigned to one of the following four conditions: moderately thin, moderately heavy, extremely thin, or extremely heavy. This resulted in a 2 (thin vs. heavy models; between-subjects) × 2 (moderate vs. extreme; between-subjects) × 2 (self primes vs. control primes; within-subjects) × 3 (thin vs. neutral vs. heavy target words; within-subjects) experimental design.

Upon arrival in the laboratory, participants were told they would participate in two unrelated studies. First, participants completed the same "Advertisement Questionnaire" as in experiment 1, containing (a) the four ads with models, pertaining to their condition, and four filler ads with no models, and (b) several five-point scales on which participants indicated whether the ads were original, convincing, and/or informative. After this task, participants sat in front of a computer monitor and performed a word-recognition task. The instructions on the screen informed them that they should focus on the screen every time a string of X's appeared. They were told that this string would be followed by a word or a nonword and that they should identify, as fast as possible, whether the word existed or not. Participants responded by either pushing the "1" (word) or the "3" (nonword) on the keyboard. To reduce variance in response latencies, participants were asked to keep their hands near the buttons throughout the task.

The lexical decision task consisted of 42 trials, with six practice trials and 36 critical trials. The critical trials consisted of 18 trials in which the target word was an existing word and 18 trials in which the target word was a random letter string (e.g., *golrr*). Of the 18 existing target words, six words were associated with thinness (e.g., *thin, slender*), six words were associated with heaviness (e.g., *heavy, fat*), and six words were unrelated to thinness or heaviness (e.g., *calm*). Half of the target words were preceded by a self prime (*I, my, me*), and the other half were preceded by a control prime (*on, the, a*). We created two lists for this task, so that three specific words that were preceded by a self prime in one list were preceded by control primes in the other list and vice versa. The 36 trials were randomly presented. At the beginning of each trial, a row of X's appeared on the center of the screen for 1,000 ms. The prime then appeared in the same location for 15 ms and was immediately masked by the string of X's again for 500 ms. Then the target word appeared, overwriting the mask, and remained on the screen until participants made a lexical decision, which was timed by the computer. After each decision, the screen remained blank for 2,000 ms. Following the lexical decision task, participants answered a final questionnaire, which tested for any suspicion about the aim of the experiment or awareness of the subliminal primes. None of the participants guessed the aim of the experiment or connected the first task of the experiment (ad ratings) with the second task (lexical decision task). After being informed that they had been exposed to subliminal primes, none of the participants could recall the words that were primed. They were not even aware that any primes had been presented.

Results and Discussion

Only the results for the target words were included in the analysis. To reduce the distorting effect of outliers, data points that were 3 standard deviations above or below the mean for each word (1.2%) were considered outliers and dropped from the analysis. The remaining latencies were subjected to a 2 (model size: thin vs. heavy) × 2 (extremity of model size: moderate vs. extreme) × 2 (primes: self primes vs. control primes) × 3 (target words: thin vs. neutral vs. heavy) ANOVA, with the last two factors being within-subjects.

The ANOVA revealed a four-way interaction between model size, extremity of model size, primes, and target words ($F(2, 160) = 7.62$, $p < .01$), as illustrated in Figure 2. To test our specific hypotheses regarding self primes and control primes, we conducted two separate 2 (model size: thin vs. heavy) × 2 (extremity of model size: moderate vs. extreme) × 3 (target words: thin vs. neutral vs. heavy) ANOVAs, with the last factor being within-subjects, on the response latencies for each type of prime. The ANOVA for the self primes revealed a three-way interaction between model size, extremity of model size, and target words ($F(2, 160) = 11.83$, $p < .001$). Participants exposed to moderately thin models responded faster to thinness words ($M = 476$ ms) than to neutral words ($M = 516$ ms; $F(1, 80) = 4.91$, $p < .05$) or heaviness words ($M = 520$ ms; $F(1, 80) = 6.57$, $p < .05$). Participants exposed to moderately heavy models responded faster to heaviness words ($M = 484$ ms) than to neutral words ($M = 521$ ms; $F(1, 80) = 4.06$, $p < .05$) or thinness words ($M = 527$ ms; $F(1, 80) = 5.95$, $p < .05$). Further, participants exposed to extremely thin models

reacted faster to heaviness words ($M = 477$ ms) than to neutral words ($M = 518$ ms; $F(1, 80) = 5.17$, $p < .05$) or thinness words ($M = 515$ ms; $F(1, 80) = 4.80$, $p < .05$). Participants exposed to extremely heavy models reacted faster to thinness words ($M = 473$ ms) than to neutral words ($M = 519$ ms; $F(1, 80) = 6.39$, $p < .05$) or heaviness words ($M = 522$ ms; $F(1, 80) = 7.97$, $p < .01$). These results support our predictions in hypothesis 2.

The ANOVA for the control primes revealed a two-way interaction between model size and target words ($F(2, 160) = 6.81$, $p < .01$), supporting hypothesis 3. Participants exposed to thin models reacted faster to thinness words ($M = 485$ ms) than to neutral words ($M = 517$ ms; $F(1, 80) = 7.63$, $p < .01$) or heaviness words ($M = 516$ ms; $F(1, 80) = 8.99$, $p < .01$). Participants exposed to heavy models reacted faster to heaviness words ($M = 489$ ms) than to neutral words ($M = 516$ ms; $F(1, 80) = 4.00$, $p < .05$) or thinness words ($M = 520$ ms; $F(1, 80) = 8.76$, $p < .01$).

The results confirmed that moderate and extreme comparison standards lead to a selective increase in the accessibility of different subsets of self-knowledge, as indicated by response latencies to words preceded by a self prime. It appears that self-knowledge consistent with the standard became accessible after exposure to moderate comparison standards, and standard-inconsistent self-knowledge became accessible after exposure to extreme comparison standards. These results foster strong support for a selective accessibility explanation of the assimilation and contrast effects obtained with the free-response measure in experiment 1.

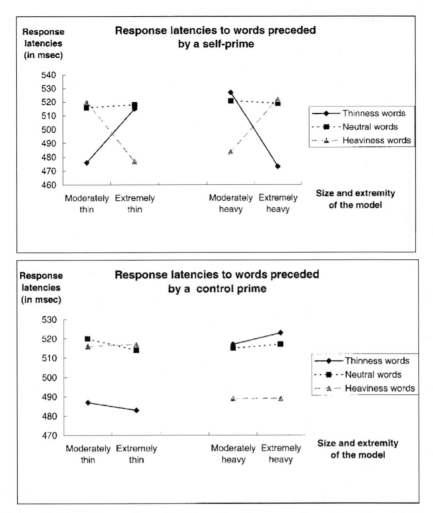

Figure 2: Experiment 2 results: Reaction times as a function of model size, extremity of model size, prime, and target word

General Discussion

Richins (1991) demonstrated that exposure to idealized advertising models can negatively alter self-perceptions by lowering individuals' satisfaction with their own bodies. Some prior studies supported these findings, whereas other studies obtained self-enhancing effects. In our research, we provide two factors that should be taken into account when studying self-evaluative effects following implicit social comparison with advertising models. First, the extremity of the comparison standard seems to be a crucial factor in determining assimilation and contrast effects. Second, whether assimilation or contrast occurs also depends on whether the self-evaluation question is framed as a free-response measure or as a rating scale. Furthermore, the findings of experiment 2 confirmed, via a lexical decision task, that the assimilation and contrast effects obtained with a free-response measure were due to selective accessibility of different subsets of self-knowledge. Comparison with a moderate standard increases the accessibility of standard-consistent self-knowledge, such as knowledge that one is thin (or heavy) when comparing oneself to a moderately thin (or moderately heavy) model. Comparison with an extreme standard increases the accessibility of standard-inconsistent self-knowledge, such as knowledge that one is heavy (or thin) when comparing oneself to an extremely thin (or extremely heavy) model. Our results also stress the importance of using a free-response measure to assess the consequences of social comparison for the self. A free-response measure reflects what becomes cognitively accessible in a consumer's mind during exposure to thin media images. Therefore, the free-response measure seems to be a more realistic measure of appearance self-esteem than the rating-scale measure, which is affected by reference-point use. These findings might have important implications for researchers who draw conclusions from consumers' self-ratings by using rating scales.

Our two studies also confirmed Richins's (1991) suggestion that women compare themselves spontaneously and automatically with the models in advertisements. However, in contrast to Richins's findings, we demonstrated that exposure to thin models does not necessarily have a negative impact on one's self-esteem. On the contrary, exposure to moderately thin (but not extremely thin) models has a positive impact on one's self-esteem. Our findings might explain why *Mode* magazine, which featured only plus-sized models, folded after just 4 yr because of low circulation rates (Morris 2002). Fashion and beauty magazine readers may aspire to achieve the thin ideal pictured on the cover, and without promises of attaining such an ideal, there might be no reason to buy the magazine.

Future research should examine whether our results are universal or could be moderated by other factors. One obvious moderating factor is body mass index (BMI). In our experiments, we measured BMI, but this factor did not affect our results. However, most of our participants resided within normal ranges of BMI (between 19 and 25). Therefore, future research should examine to what extent our results differ for consumers outside that BMI range. All of the participants were young, female university students, and thus we also cannot say whether these findings extend to men or individuals in other stages of life. Future research might also examine the effects of exposure to thin (or heavy) models on more consumer-oriented variables, such as purchase intention, product preference, or consumer spending. Further research might also examine the duration of the effects of exposure to such ads. Perhaps exposure to idealized images has only a temporary effect. However, given the pervasiveness of the idealized images one encounters daily, effects might be more enduring.

[*Dawn Iacobucci served as editor for this article.*]

References

For full references to this text please see the website.

SOCIAL AND GROUP ASPECTS OF
CONSUMER BEHAVIOUR

CHAPTER 7   Social Group, Tribal and Household Buying Influences

CHAPTER 8   Culture and Subculture

ARTICLE: S McKechnie and Caroline Tynan (2006) Social Meanings in
Christmas Consumption: An Exploratory Study of UK
Celebrants' Consumption Rituals, *Journal of Consumer
Behaviour*, Vol 5, pp 130–144

Having explored a number of individual aspects of consumers and how these can explain their buying behaviour, we turn, in Part 2, to social influences on consumers.

Here, there are powerful forces exerted by various social groups on consumers to conform to various group norms. We therefore analyse (in Chapter 7) the role of reference groups in this process and the types of social power they exert. We extend the coverage here and make links with self-concept theory. A recent phenomenon is postmodernism and we expand the implications of this for consumer buying behaviour. This is sometimes reflected in the emergence of tribes and tribal buying behaviour. Another recent development is the virtual group. People are increasingly interacting via the superhighway rather than face-to-face. This includes interaction as consumers, either with other consumers (to exchange buying experiences) or with organizations. We have expanded and updated coverage of these issues, including, for example, Flashmobbing.

We then turn to the family (also in Chapter 7). This is obviously the first 'group' that individuals experience and it exerts important influences over buying behaviour. We examine the changing nature of many Western families as manifested in, for example, an increase in the singles market. Families change over time and the family life cycle concepts is very useful for explaining and even predicting consumer behaviour over time. Within families, there can be significant division of labour in terms of the buying process and we explore not only the role of men and women but also that of children. The latter are increasingly influential and marketers are well aware of this. It is, however, not only the children themselves who can 'pester' but also parents can sometimes be targeted to buy expensive 'image brands' for their children. This is not necessarily because their children want them but because the parents want their children to portray certain images. There are further updates here, in terms of the family life cycle, the family DMU and the influence of children in buying behaviour.

Chapter 8 is then concerned with other aspects of social influence: culture and subculture. Here, we explore aspects of cultures, cultural meaning rituals. It is clear that many marketers are keen to globalize their marketing, but sometimes this can lead to problems because different cultures view the world in different ways. Marketers need to recognize such differences in how they target international markets if they are not to offend cultural traditions and values. It is all too easy to offend when communications media cross international boundaries so readily, such as the Internet. The meaning transfer model is further extended in this edition and we have expanded and updated our discussion of cultural and subcultural influences on buyer behaviour.

We also expand aspects of ethnicity here and show how these subcultures are a growing and important component of many societies. We extend our coverage of acculturation in this edition. Marketers are increasingly targeting ethnic segments and we extend our examination of some of the implications of this.

Our 'reading' for Part 2 is an article that explores how cultural rituals provide social meanings, as contextualized in Christmas in Britain.

Throughout Part 2, there are practical examples and references to material, including other actual research articles, which can be accessed via the accompanying web site. We are again grateful for permission to include clippings from *Marketing Week*, cases from the DMA and TMS and reports from the Future Foundation.

CHAPTER 7
SOCIAL GROUP, TRIBAL AND HOUSEHOLD BUYING INFLUENCES

CHAPTER OBJECTIVES

After engaging with the material presented in this chapter and its associated exercises and reading, you should be able to:

■ Understand the nature of social group influence in consumer behaviour.
■ Apply different types of group influence to consumer behavior and marketing.
■ Appreciate the dynamic nature of society and its effects on groups such as tribalism, postmodernism and virtual groups.
■ Analyse and evaluate how families buy through different stages of development and change.
■ Assess relative contributions of family members to the buying process.
■ Explore the nature of pester and parent power and discuss some of the ethical issues in targeting to children.

INTRODUCTION

Homo sapiens is a social species. As a result we interact with others constantly. Each of us is a member of a family and may belong to great variety of social groups such as university, work, leisure related and friendship groups. We don't all need to be extrovert or 'soul of the party' types: others in a group often influence us and we can also be the influencers within these groups. There are also groups to which we aspire to belong or at least identify with even if they are not membership groups.

Through societal developments including what is referred to as postmodernism, there are significant changes in the nature of groups. We now have a plethora of constantly changing groups (sometimes referred to as **tribes**) and some groups operate virtually, via the Internet, yet they all hold powerful implications for consumer behaviour and marketing.

Many of the decisions made by consumers are taken within the environment of the family and are thus affected by the desires and attitudes of other family members. Many products are purchased on behalf of other members of the buyer's household, perhaps as gifts, and these purchases inevitably reflect some degree of joint decision-making. Even the most personal of purchases can be influenced in some details by the behaviour of the buyer's family and this social group demands special attention from consumer researchers. The family has also been affected by modern and postmodern factors, resulting in a number of different 'models' of the family, such as the single-parent household and indeed the single household.

This chapter explores these aspects of groups within a consumer behaviour context and with implications for marketing.

SOCIAL GROUPS

In many cases, group influence is instrumental in determining an individual's buying behaviour. Sprott back in 1958 wrote that a group is 'a plurality of persons who interact with one another in a given

context more than they interact with anyone else'. In essence, a human group involves several persons who share common goals or purposes and who interact in pursuance of these objectives; each member of the group is perceived by others as a group member and all members are bound together by patterns and networks of interaction over time. The interdependence of group members is made enduring by the evolution of a group ideology which cements the beliefs, values, attributes and norms of the group (Kassarjian and Robertson, 1973).

Behavioural scientists also refer to primary groups and secondary groups. Primary groups are characterized by their size and by the close relationships that take place within them. Examples of primary groups are the family (discussed later in this chapter), a seminar/tutorial group of students, and the 'mile high hang-gliding society' at your university. Secondary groups are made up of more than one primary group and examples include your students' union, and the wider social system within a company or university.

Consumer research is also concerned with informal groups, which occur 'spontaneously' on the basis of common interests and the geographical closeness of members rather than formal groups, which are usually officially organized groups with a more rigid structure. Informal organization occurs, however, within formal organizations and is inevitably influenced by the 'official' structure of its environment.

Reference Groups

Any individual or a group of individuals that can significantly influence your behaviour could be called your 'reference group' (Bearden and Etzel, 1982). Reference groups are significant to the extent that consumers aspire to be like them, emulate them, listen to them, identify with them and buy what they buy. The question is why these groups are important to us as consumers. In response, you may quote Maslow's Hierarchy of Needs and argue that we have a need for belonging, for affection and for love, etc., and hence we tend to associate ourselves with the reference groups. However, the fact is that consumers use reference groups as sources of attitudes, beliefs, values or behaviours (even a single person, for example a celebrity, who carries out this function is also known as a reference *group*). These

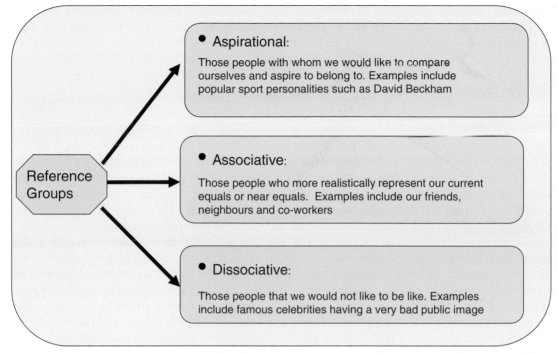

Figure 7.1: **Types of reference groups**

groups perform certain important functions for consumers. For instance, the reference group can provide settings and can enforce standards of behaviour. It can also act as a point of comparison against which consumers evaluate themselves. This is particularly useful because by social comparison we are able to judge the consequences of our behaviour. As the significance, importance and value of a reference group to us increases, so does the likelihood that our buying behaviour will be influenced by the reference group.

Three distinct uses of the term 'reference group' can be traced in the sociological literature and all of them are useful in consumer research. They are:

1. Groups with which the individual compares themselves, their attitudes, their behaviour, their performance; this could be a formal contractual group (e.g. the person is a member of the group, approves the group values and has a regular interaction with the group) or an informal group or person.
2. Groups to which the individual aspires to belong.
3. Groups whose social perspectives are assumed by the individual as a framework of reference for their own actions (Shibutani, 1955).

Figure 7.1 presents three types of reference groups to which a consumer can turn as a standard for behaviours. Aspirational groups can be either anticipatory aspirational: anticipation of membership at some future date, and symbolic aspirational: there is little chance of membership, but nevertheless a strong affiliation with the group's norms and behaviour, such that there can be vicarious (see Chapter 3) bond with the group. The use of Beckham, in Figure 7.1, would be an example of the latter version. However, of particular interest is the dissociative reference group type; these are groups or individuals whose behaviour, beliefs and values the individual deliberately avoids adopting as their own. Reference groups can also be categorized into normative referents and comparative referents. Normative referents include those who provide us with norms, attitudes and values through direct interaction. Examples include parents, teachers and peers. On the other hand, comparative referents provide us with standards of achievement to which we aspire and examples include sports heroes and entertainment figures. A further classification is socially proximate and socially distant referents.

Types of Reference Group Influence

According to Park and Lessig (1977), reference group influence can be manifested in three main ways. First, an information influence when, for example, a consumer is considering buying a product and seeks information about brands in that product category, from family, friends, perceived experts (including those who belong to an association and those who work with the product as a profession). In doing so, the individual can also make inferences by watching the behaviour of others (e.g. endorsement or a seal of approval from an expert, or by observing the type of products used by others). This type of influence works because we aim to seek information in order to be able to make informed decisions.

Second, there is a utilitarian influence (or normative influence) which concerns a degree of conformity (see below) with the behaviour or norms of a group with which the consumer wants to identify. For example, an individual may purchase a brand because they want to comply with the expectations of others (e.g. family members or workmates or those with whom they interact regularly). This influence works well if the individual perceives that their behaviour is visible or known to others and that the significant others in the group can mediate some rewards or punishment and indeed when the use of the product is conspicuous. Third, there is a value expressive influence (or identification influence), which is where the consumer buys, for example, a brand, which they think will enhance their image among others in the group, because the brand is expressive of values, norms, behaviour and/or lifestyles of the group. This influence works particularly well when the individual likes those in the reference group.

As consumers, we wish to be psychologically associated with others in order to enhance our self concept. Many organizations offer 'affinity' credit cards which some consumers will see as a way of visibly projecting their own affinity with that organization and its values. Many charities, for example, offer such a credit card.

THINKBOX

Provide examples from your own experience or that of people you know, of each of the following: information, utilitarian and value expressive influence.

You need to note that reference group influence depends upon whether the product category/brand is a publicly consumed luxury, a privately consumed luxury, a publicly consumed necessity or a privately consumed necessity (Bearden and Etzel, 1982). We say a product/brand is public if other people know that you have got the product/brand and they can identify it with little or no difficulty.

A product/brand is said to be private when you use it at home in such a way that others (except your immediate family) are not aware of it. There are some similarities here with our discussion of self-concept theory in Chapter 6, where we explored private and social contexts for consumption. Figure 7.2 summarizes the effects of different contexts on reference group influences.

Publicly consumed luxury Examples: golf clubs, snow skis, sailboats **Strong reference group influence** on both whether or not the product is owned and the specific brand which is purchased (because both the product and the brand are visible to others)	**Privately consumed luxury** Examples: TV games, bread maker, paper security shredder **Strong reference group influence** on product (everyone has it, so you have to have it) but a **weaker influence** on specific brand (because the brand consumption is hidden from public gaze)
Publicly consumed necessity Examples: wrist watches, clothing, cars There is a **weak reference group influence** on whether or not the product is owned (because you have to have it as everyone has it) but **a strong reference group influence** on the specific brand which is purchased (because everyone will see it)	**Privately consumed necessity** Examples: mattresses, duvets, freezers There is a **weak reference group influence** on **both** whether or not the product is owned and on the specific brand which is purchased (neither product nor brand is visible to others)

Figure 7.2: **The context of consumption and reference group influence.**
Based on WO Beardon and MJ Etzel, Reference Group Influence on Product and Brand Purchase Decisions, Journal of Consumer Research, Vol 9 (1982), pp. 183–194.

THINKBOX

Together with the above analysis, consider the following framework for assessing reference group influence:

Reference Group Influence	
Weak	**Strong**
Behaviour is not conspicuous	Conspicuous behaviour or consumption
Behaviour is unimportant to group norms	Behaviour is important to group norms
Individual is confident about their own position on the behaviour and perceives the group to hold a certain position	Individual is not confident of their own position and perceives the group to hold a less clear position

Why is it important for marketers to know which type of influence is dominant for different consumers or for different products? You are already aware that the marketplace is characterized by similarity of choice and abundance of similar products and hence an understanding of reference group influences can be leveraged to separate a product from the rest.

Susceptibility to Interpersonal Influences

Consumers have different personality traits and one such trait is consumers' susceptibility to interpersonal influences (CSIN), which is defined as "the need to identify or enhance one's image with significant others through the acquisition and use of products and brands, the willingness to conform to the expectations of others regarding purchase decisions, and/or the tendency to learn about products and services by observing others and/or seeking information from others" (Bearden, Netemeyer, and Teel, 1989, p.474). Consumers vary in their susceptibility to interpersonal influences and some consumers can be more susceptible to social or interpersonal influences than others and vice versa. This susceptibility is likely to be enhanced when a consumer is highly worried about the inferences other people make or may make about his/her behaviour (Netemeyer *et al*, 1992). In an empirical work, (Netemeyer *et al*, 1992) found that those with high levels of susceptibility to interpersonal influences are more likely to purchase products that they perceive will lead others to make some favourable evaluations of them and avoid purchasing products that will lead others to evaluate them negatively. The susceptibility also varies across cultures with varying degrees of individualism/collectivism (Mourali *et al.*, 2005). For instance, French Canadians (less individualistic) were found to be more susceptible to normative influence than their English Canadian counterparts.

Reference Groups and Self-concept Theory

In Chapter 6, we explained self-brand connection as the extent to which we incorporate a brand into our self-concept. Reference groups can be an important source of brand meanings and associations and hence the need to link self-concept theory with reference group theory. In an experimental study, Escalas and Bettman (2005) argued that consumers can use brands for the creation and representation of their self-images and for the presentation of these images to others with a view to achieve some identity goals. This process results in a linkage that bridges the brand and the self. It was further argued by Escalas and Bettman (2005) that the extent to which the self-brand connection occurs can depend on the degree to which the consumer associates with their associative reference group. For instance, if you consider yourself to be an innovative person and members of your associative group (e.g. your friends) tend to use a brand (e.g. Hewlett Packard) which stands for innovation, then you may also choose to use that particular brand as a symbol of how innovative you are and hence make a connection between the brand and your self-concept. As per Escalas and Bettman (2005), you are very likely to have a more positive self-brand connection when you perceive that your associative group uses the brand and that you have a positive fit with your associative group. The same is likely to happen when you aspire to belong to an aspirational reference group. Moreover, a consumer is likely to be strongly influenced by their associative group when they are seeking self-verification goals such as seeking out and interpreting situations and adopting behavioural strategies that are consistent with their existing self-conceptions. Similarly, a consumer is likely to be strongly influenced by their aspirational group when they are seeking a self-enhancement goal such as trying to make a good impression on others around them.

Later, Escalas and Bettman (2005) extended their work on self-brand connection making a distinction between the use of brand associations deriving from one's own group (an in-group such as associative reference group) versus groups to which one does not belong or does not wish to belong (an out-group such as dissociative reference group). Their findings indicated that when a brand is perceived to be consistent with an in-group, self-brand connections go up, whereas brands perceived to be consistent with the out-group have a less positive effect on self-brand connection. Moreover, the negative effect of out-group brand association on self-brand connection was found to be higher for those with independent selves than for those with interdependent selves. In other words, consumers with individualistic orientation do care more about who is using the brand than those who have a collectivistic orientation. For example if you are not a member of a group and do not desire to be a member of that group (e.g. fans of a celebrity that has a very bad public image), then you are very likely not to use the brand that is being used by members of that external group in an attempt to distance yourself from the symbolism attached with the brand and, this is very likely to happen, if you have more individualistic tendencies than collectivistic ones.

Conformity and Independence

Group membership involves the individual in the acceptance of a degree of conformity and that the group itself evolves norms of behaviour which specify the ideal actions to which members should conform. Social groups also tend to have a system of rewards and sanctions through which adherence to group norms is reinforced positively and thereby encouraged, and deviance is punished and thus discouraged. Ultimately groups may exclude members who flout the norms which other group members accept and to which they conform. Figure 7.3 reflects marketers' understanding that pressure to conform can be a useful advertising appeal.

Figure 7.3: A conformity appeal
Buy this and you'll have great hair like me.
Reproduced by permission of Wella ShockWaves.

While conformity is an inevitable feature of social groups, absolute compliance is never found. Independence is also a valued trait for many people. Even in buying situations where people choose the same brands of a product as their friends, they often select an alternative colour or display their independence in some way. The motive, which is responsible for this desire to maintain freedom, has been called reactance and there is experimental evidence to suggest that, where compliance is forced, individuals will do their best to achieve some degree of autonomy and independence (Venkatesan, 1966).

EXAMPLE 7.1

Several interesting experiments have shown that, under laboratory conditions at least, individuals tend to shape their judgements so that they fit in with the opinions and behaviour of others. Asch (1955) reports a series of tests which relate expressed opinions to social pressure and which confirm that there is a strong desire in most people to conform to group judgements. Groups of about eight people were asked to match a single line on one white card with a line of similar length on another card which contained several lines. Each member of the group selected the corresponding line individually in a prearranged order. All of the group members except the last to report his answer were working for the experimenter, however, and gave patently false answers. The point of the experiments was to ascertain the reaction of the final group member to report – he alone was the subject of the tests. He could either trust his senses and refuse to conform with the majority or he could go along with the rest of the group despite the evidence of his visual sense.

In almost 37% of the cases, subjects chose to conform to group pressures even though the chosen line was clearly unequal to the reference line. This occurred despite the fact that in control tests – where no groups contained stooges and where no one was under any pressure to do anything other than what his senses suggested – less than 1% of cases resulted in mistakes being made.

Individual subjects varied considerably; some were willing to conform all the time to group pressures while others consistently refused to do so, and few subjects changed their minds after showing initial conformity or independence. Further trials were conducted to find out whether the size of the majority was more important than its unanimity. Groups ranging from two persons to 15 were used in these tests but, beyond a group size of three, increases in size had little further effect on conformity. Whatever the group's size though, the presence of a disturbing element – another person in league with the experimenter who chose to disagree with the majority, sometimes agreeing with the subject, sometimes not – reduced the majority of a great deal of its power and made it easier for the subject to disagree with the group.

Venkatesan conducted an experimental study of consumer behaviour which was intended to throw light on the questions of conformity to social pressure and the possibilities of reactance occurring in consumer decision-making situations. One hundred and forty-four college students were asked to select and evaluate one of three men's suits which were identical in style, colour and size and which were denoted simply by letters of the alphabet: A, B and C. Information provided for the subjects included the suggestions that the suits were from different manufacturers, that there were differentials in quality from one suit to another, that previous studies carried out at a prestigious research centre had established that the best suit could be identified by experts, and that the study in which the subjects were taking part was to determine whether buyers were capable of selecting the best suit.

For purposes of comparison, three experimental conditions were created:

Condition 1

This involved a control group in which subjects evaluated the suits independently, reported separately on them, and received no group pressures to conform or comply.

Condition 2

This involved groups of four subjects, three of whom were in league with the experimenter. The seating arrangements were manipulated so that the confederates reported first, orally, that the best suit was B, thus establishing a group norm for the naive subject to conform or reject.

Condition 3

This was similar to Condition 2 but there was an attempt by the experimenter at engineering reactance, and the responses of the three confederates in each group were accordingly specified thus:

Confederate 1: I am not sure if there is a difference – it is not great; but if I have to choose then B is the *best* suit.

Confederate 2: (Looking at Confederate 1) You say B . . .Well, I cannot see any difference either – I will 'go along with you' – B is the *best* suit for me.

Confederate 3: Well you guys chose B. Although I am not sure, I am *just going along* to be a good guy. I choose B too.

When it came to the real subject's turn, the situation had already been structured so as to reduce his choice.

The results, which are displayed in Table 7.1, are consistent with the hypothesis that consumers generally conform to group norms when making brand choices but reject attempts at inducing them to make particular brand decisions.

In Condition 1, where no social influence attempt was made, the distribution of responses did not differ from what chance would have predicted by a significant amount. In Condition 2, where conformity was promoted, the proportion of choices cast in favour of suit B was greater by a significant amount than chance would suggest (i.e. than one third), which indicates that conformity to a group norm is to be expected. However, in Condition 3, where compliance was induced, the proportion of choices of suit B was not significantly different from one third, indicating that consumers who realize they are being forced to conform to the group's standards may react by deliberately asserting their independence.

It is worth a reminder about 'individualism' here. In Chapter 6 we explored the trend toward greater degrees of self-expression and pluralism in society and this can lead to increased independence but, even with this, the individual will usually want the security and accepted behaviour norms which groups can provide.

Suit	Condition 1	Condition 2	Condition 3
A	17	11	14
B	10	22	14
C	20	9	19

Table 7.1: Conformity and independence in consumer choice

THINKBOX

Consider the clothing market. To what extent do people wear garments to reflect their individualism and/or desire to conform?

Conformity is not the only dimension of group dynamics that has interested social researchers. Group cohesiveness has also attracted attention. Cohesiveness has been described as 'the overall level of attraction towards the group' which 'can be equated with "loyalty"' (Argyle, 1969). It is this factor of cohesiveness which makes a group something more than a mere collection of individuals; it involves feelings of belongingness and integrity, and develops as the group fulfils the interpersonal needs of its members. The more importance a member attaches to the group, the more likely they are to adopt its norms, including its consumption patterns. However, cohesiveness can not guarantee similar buying behaviour.

Cohesiveness is also closely connected with the affective nature of the group and this suggests methods of measuring cohesiveness. For example each member can be asked how much they want to stay with the group and the scores averaged across its members. Another approach is based on the likings and dislikings of one member for the rest of the group.

Moreno (1953) introduced the method of sociometry to measure cohesiveness in groups; this method essentially involves asking group members which other person(s) they would prefer to share some activity with or to select those who would surely be unsuitable for that activity.

The results of a sociometric approach produce a sociogram, such as in Figure 7.4. This indicates the respondent pictured at the centre is a popular individual with whom everyone wishes to interact, and the bottom right is an 'isolate' individual with whom no one wishes to interact in the context specified. The triangle formed by (1), (2) and (3) represents a clique.

Leadership

The third and final facet of group dynamics that is useful for understanding consumer behaviour is the evolution of positions of leadership within groups and the formation of hierarchies. Leaders are usually

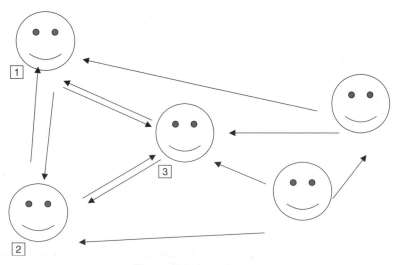

Figure 7.4: A sociogram

defined as those who most frequently initiate action within the group, though this activity must, of course, be clearly relevant to the goals of the group whether formal or informal. Argyle (1969) comments that the emergence of hierarchies in groups is a universal human phenomenon and that, whatever the size of the group, some people communicate more than others. Other group members, perhaps less sure of their opinions, tend to look to the leader for ideas and inspiration. The person with most ideas, and who puts them forward persuasively, inevitably assumes a position in the hierarchy which reflects this while others delegate the propagation of ideas to them. Leadership may also be based on popularity and there is a tendency for the 'best-liked group member' to have some degree of leadership. In this case, they are then instrumental in releasing tensions, and questioning the role of the group and its members.

We explore two specific aspects of group hierarchies in Chapter 9: opinion leadership and opinion forming.

EXAMPLE 7.2

Stafford (1966) carried out an experiment involving ten already existing groups of housewives each with approximately four members. The groups were ranked on the basis of cohesiveness tests from one to ten, the first group being the most cohesive, the tenth, the least. The housewives were asked to select one of four brands of bread over a period of time and to obtain all of their bread from the source indicated by the experimenter. The four 'brands' of bread were, in reality, identical save that their wrappers were identified by a single letter of the alphabet: H, L, M or P. Analysis of the housewives' choices at the end of the experimental period indicated that the group's favourite brand was identical with the leader's best-liked brand for the five most cohesive groups. After that, the relationship broke down but the study demonstrates the influence of the group and its leader and suggests that this is strongest where loyalty and belongingness are highest. Although this was an experimental test, the housewives were unaware of the nature of the test, and the conclusion that primary groups affect brand choice appears to be a valid one.

Social Power

Group influence is determined by the power the group wields. There are different types of social power as proposed by French and Raven (1959):

- Referent power operates when a consumer identifies with or admires the group or person. Examples of this are (as we discuss in Chapter 9) when celebrity endorsers are used effectively in advertising.
- Information power operates when a consumer perceives someone as possessing knowledge about the issue. This also relates to examples in Chapter 9 where we discuss opinion-forming journalists. For example, motoring journalists writing in motoring magazines might seem to be knowledgeable about cars. The knowledge may or may not be real – just perceived to be there.
- Legitimate power is where a consumer thinks that the position of the referent confers authority in the context concerned; for example, police officers in the law enforcement context. Sometimes it is possible to simulate legitimate power in advertising, by portraying someone who might not in reality be a policemen or doctor, but the uniform/white coat they wear gives them assumed authority. In a cross-cultural context, members of a collectivist culture normally associate legitimate power with groups like the family elders.
- Expert power is where there really is a good degree of expert knowledge on the part of the referent. Here, well-known experts can be especially influential, such as a world famous astronomer advertising a telescope.

- Reward power is similar to what Park and Lessig describe as 'utilitarian influence', because it operates when responding favourably to the referent results in positive reinforcement (Chapter 3) by the group. For example, the purchase of the trendiest trainers might be rewarded by the approbation of the individual by their group, if trendy trainers are part of their credo.
- Coercive power can be the opposite of reward power. It encourages conformity by explicitly or implicitly threatening some form of intimidation. Fear appeals in advertising can be based on this, as can the more personal intimidation of the less desirable forms of 'foot in the door' personal selling.

Negative Reference Groups

The discussion so far has referred mainly to groups with which the consumer positively identifies and in many cases will aspire to have some sort of link with. Such groups are therefore termed aspirational groups. The notion of negative reference groups or avoidance or disassociative groups is also relevant here. These are groups or individuals whose behaviour, beliefs and values the individual deliberately avoids adopting as their own. It is probable that consumers select reference groups which are compatible with their self-images and ideal self-images, and that the use of inconsistent distant others in advertisements will elicit a positive response only in consumers who have already adopted the appropriate groups as personal reference points. Any distant reference group is bound to affect some segment of the market in this way and care must be taken to measure the possible extent of this before marketing plans are operationalized.

Membership and Non-Membership Reference Groups

We might belong, as members, to some groups by token of being in an 'age group' or 'occupational group'. We might, of course be in a membership group to which we have to be rather more proactive, such as joining the university Mile High Club or Business Society. There are several factors that can help determine whether someone is more or less likely to join a membership group. These include the physical closeness to the group. This is called proquinquity and you might have joined groups of friends in your immediate neighbourhood or school, when younger. Sometimes the frequency of coming across people can increase the likelihood of joining as a social group; this is the exposure effect.

Non-membership groups on the other hand are groups to which, at least at present, we do not belong but either anticipate joining or use in the more aspirational reference way as discussed earlier and below.

A framework for studying the reference effects of non-membership groups has been put forward by Bourne (1956) who identified conspicuousness as the most pervasive product attribute involved in reference group influence. Conspicuousness, however, can mean two things: not only must the product be capable of being seen and perceived by others; it must also stand out and command attention.

In a seminal exposition of consumption, Veblen (1899) posited that consumers used others higher in the social hierarchy and emulated some of their consumption patterns. In this way he developed the notion of conspicuous consumption with which we are familiar today. Veblen's ideas link so well with several of the theories in this book. For example, he suggested that consumers are constantly seeking the status of some higher order, as reflected through their consumption. This parallels our argument that Maslow's hierarchy (Chapter 1) is constantly leading us to aspire onwards and upwards such that we are never fully satisfied. As affluence grows, the consumption patterns of those whom we use (as in the above analysis) as reference groups also change over time and hence we have a dynamic consumer culture. Veblen's rather elitist framework (consumers look to those in a higher social strata) does not entirely fit with society today. It is more likely that the aspirational use of reference groups can be 'trickle up', 'trickle across', as well as 'trickle down' (Evans, 1989).

Product valency	Brand valency	Examples
Strong (+)	Strong (+)	Cars, cigarettes, beer, drugs
Strong (+)	Weak (−)	Air conditioners, instant coffee, black and white TV
Weak (−)	Strong (+)	Clothing, furniture, magazines, refrigerator (type), toilet soap
Weak (−)	Weak (−)	Soap, canned peaches, laundry soap, refrigerator (brand), radios

Source: Adapted by the authors from FS Bourne, *Group Influence in Marketing and Public Relations*, Foundation for Research on Human Behaviour, 1956, p. 8

Table 7.2: Reference group influence

Bourne recognized that the influence of reference groups varies from product to product and set out to isolate those product areas where reference group influence was particularly strong. He claimed that the strongest influence occurred in relation to those products and brands about which people had evolved strong norms specifying ideal behaviour on usage patterns, brand preferences, and so on.

Further empirical work allowed Bourne to attach 'valencies' to the brands of certain products and to product groups themselves, denoting high or low reference group influence. Four possibilities exist: strong product valency with either strong or weak brand valency, and weak product valency with either strong or weak brand valency. Table 7.2 shows the products which Bourne allocated to each of these four categories.

THINKBOX

We covered the Theory of Reasoned Action (TORA) in Chapter 3. How do the social group influences discussed in the current chapter relate to TORA? Recall that TORA takes into account the effects of Normative Beliefs (what a significant other person in a consumer's life thinks about what the consumer is intending to do (e.g. purchase a computer)) and the extent to which a consumer is willing to comply to others. Therefore, social group influences play an important role in predicting intentions.

TRIBAL, VIRTUAL GROUPS AND POSTMODERN CONSUMER BEHAVIOUR

In Chapter 5 we plotted some dimensions of the progression of individualism. In the current chapter we explore influences of a more social nature. The two are not mutually exclusive. Indeed the rather contradictory blend of individualism and conformity can be examined in the context of the equally contradictory realm of postmodernism. Consumers can express individuality but within the safety of groups; this is one aspect of the postmodern consumer. It can be reflected in the re-emergence of tribal behaviour manifested in a number of ways. For example, individualism, as discussed in the previous chapter, can be seen in the extended self image. Here, as we saw, some consumers literally extend themselves via cosmetic surgery or the addition of tattoos and piercings: thus joining what can be ephemeral and vaguely linked tribes.

Goths   *Indie*

Numetal   *Pop princess*   *Rude Boy*

Soulstress   *Teenclubber*

Figure 7.5: Teenage and football tribes
© BBC Radio & Music Interactive. Reproduced by permission.
© Getty Images. Photographers: Thomas Lohne & Torsten Silz. Reproduced with permission.

The examples in Figure 7.5 imply that consumers might want to identify with style or behaviour groups and this leads us into the area of tribal behaviour. Indeed this is the logical blending of an extension of individualism and group conformity as also explored by Patterson's (1998) tribes or the style groups of Evans and Blythe (1994).

For teenagers, especially, the search for individuality is manifested in a 'search for identity and belonging' (Davidson, 2003) thus supporting the importance of tribes: 'The majority tend to be more transient and consumer led. Kids can buy a look, an identity and an attitude,'(Davidson, 2003). Perhaps the first teenage tribe was the 'Teddy boy' group. In the 1950s, for the first time, teenagers had more disposable income than teenagers of earlier generations and they wanted to display their independence from parents in the way they dressed, the music they liked and the behaviour they displayed. No longer did teenagers look like younger versions of their parents; they had their own and different dress codes.

EXAMPLE 7.3

Figure 7.6 shows an example of marketers attempting to exploit consumers' desires to conform to the norms of tribal groups. Sometimes apparent individualism is actually tribal social group behaviour: different enough, but within the safety of a group.

Figure 7.6: Tribal group influence
Source: Versace

Unlike a market segment, the tribe consists of heterogeneous consumers with different demographic features who are capable of collective action and act as advocates for their causes (Cova and Cova, 2002). This has some important implications because marketers may not be able to treat consumers as a homogeneous market segment. However, the problem can be resolved by paying attention 'to the tacit and the visceral, especially the feelings of the consumers' (Firat and Shultz, 1997:198) which unite consumers in the tribes. Rather than focusing on building relationships between consumers and the firm directly, marketers can position their brand as a supporter of tribal links among consumers aiming to develop more *affective* consumer loyalty (Cova and Cova, 2001, 2002).

Maffesoli (1996), Bauman (1992) and Cova and Cova (2001, 2002) argue for a reverse movement in which consumers are joining together by developing strong emotional bonds (e.g. sharing of same tastes, habits, intellectual pursuits or participating in events like animal rights protests or anti-capitalism campaigns). This ephemeral and unstable grouping of consumers who are joined together by sharing emotions, feelings and passions on a relatively small scale is termed as a tribe. However, unlike the archaic tribes, a consumer can belong to many tribes at a time because the boundaries of such a grouping are conceptual rather than physical (Cova and Cova, 2002). Also, membership of such a group transcends traditional cultural, national and race barriers – anyone sharing the same space and a common sentiment can join the tribe, which has a less articulated but differentiated form (Cova, 1997).

Further work on consumer tribes appears in Cova et al. (2007).

THINKBOX

When you were a teenager, to which tribes did you belong? What were the norms and buying behaviour involved?

It is also worth pausing to consider the multiple and fluid groups to which we all now belong and postmodernism can, to some extent, explore this. Consider the music market. 'Modernism' resided in the relatively few 'boxes' of the modern era, for example, rock, progressive, R&B, etc. But in the postmodern era there is tremendous pluralism, for many confusing pluralism. There are now multiple music pastiches as reflected in the sampling by current bands of earlier clips and the result is gangsta rap, jungle, hiphop, house, hardcore, acid jazz, boogie woogie, trance, world fusion...

You try to complete the list and relate each to your own tribal subculture!

The 'modern' epoch of the post world war era now sees postmodernism taking over. Brown analyses the dimensions of postmodernism and identifies the 'aesthetic': ' the modern era of the Beatles, Stones, Beach Boys, Dylan...has sundered into a multiplicity of modalities...house, jungle, techno, rap, roots, drum 'n' bass, sped garage...which are parasitic upon (sampling) pastiches of...Beatles/Oasis (Brown, 2003). Compare the 1960's Arndale shopping centres with the current lifestyle themed shopping malls of today. He also notes a socio-technology dimension: 'the world of the www, 24 hour banking, satellite TV, soundbitten and spindoctored politics, mobile phoneophilia, 3 minute culture, pick 'n' mix lifestyles and serial monogamy...ephemerality, instability, proliferation, fragmentation...and above all, chaos...upheaval' (Brown, 2003).

Postmodernism chaos is also reflected in a shift from relative certainty, for example, we used to 'know' which foods were good for us, now the plethora of conflicting reports make things less certain. The optimistic social environment of the 1960s, which we introduced in Chapter 6 has given way to consumer cynicism and irreverence. The Future Foundation has shown how consumer cynicism has grown (Figure 7.7).

This clearly has implications for markets: to perhaps be more open and honest with their campaigns, because many postmodern consumers are savvy about 'marketing ploys', have more choice, so can switch almost at will and can easily reject the unwanted. The plethora of alternatives (see the coffee example in Chapter 6), individualism and few rules is certainly and especially reflected in our behaviour as consumers.

THINKBOX

You are at the heart of this and can identify with all of this; probably more so than the old codgers who teach you. You see the chaos of the postmodern world: being cynical, streetwise, interested in style, less interested in voting, see families break up and possibly live more for the present.

Do you agree? Why or why not?

Table 7.3 summarizes some of the conditions operating within postmodernism. Hyperreality reflects a postmodern desire for experiencing man-made theme parks rather than nature-made natural environments.

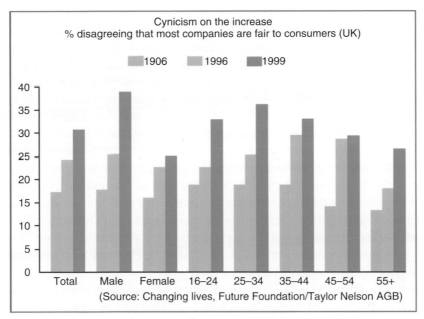

Figure 7.7: Consumer cynicism
Changing Lives, Future Foundation/Taylor Nelson AGB. Reproduced by permission of The Future Foundation

Even shopping malls might include themed areas reflecting, for example, Disney World. As Brown puts it 'pretence of service... salesperson's adherence to script. rote responses, fake sincerity... not unpleasant (experience) but unreal, illusory'.

There is a degree of fragmentation in that consumption is frenetic. We have multiple roles, as discussed in the previous chapter and this means our group membership is not only varied but also constantly changing. We have disconnected lifestyles and are happy to switch brands as suggested or implied by different groups and their memberships. Furthermore, consumers are no longer passive receivers of marketing. They interact with it and, via group interaction, make their own meaning of advertisements and brands.

As Table 7.3 illustrates, some argue that our postmodern society is characterized by social dissolution, extreme individualization of taste and consumption patterns and a fragmentation of collective meanings (Firat and Shultz, 1997).

THINKBOX

FUTURE FOUNDATION RESEARCH

Have It All Society

'Have it all society' is about the way in which more and more people attempt to run several modes of existence simultaneously and demand products and services that can respond to their multiple identities. Time has become a more precious commodity as affluence has increased and opportunities broadened, and in many ways time management has become the most important driver of social change and innovation.

Many women return to work and their career after their first baby and within a year of the baby's birth – a function of enhanced access to careers and the pressure to sustain lifestyle expectation through income maintenance. Millions stretch the elastic of each day to try to cram more activities and meet more responsibilities – trying to maximize the efficiency of their time. Although life-stage is still important in shaping lifestyles, we now inhabit a society in which desires for sociability, economic gain, family involvement, leisure and self-improvement are less delineated by particular stages of life or gender. They are now constant and universal demands that must somehow be reconciled in the course of day-to-day living. While we clearly tend to lead richer and more fulfilling lives than those of our forebears, the other side of the coin is the pressure of expectation. We want it all and we expect our brands to have it all ready for us, even before we think of just what 'it' might be. Companies that understand the challenges and resolve the contradictions of the 'have-it-all' society will be very successful indeed. Those that do not will struggle, especially with the more affluent consumers who feel under most pressure of time.

This summary of the Future Foundation report of the same name links well with our coverage in Chapter 5 of demographics and Chapter 6 of psychographics, but also with Chapter 1 where we questioned the consumer society. What do you think of the findings summarized?

Reproduced by permission of The Future Foundation http://www.futurefoundation.net/

Marketers are using this by blurring message types and using metaphors. Consider the advertisement below for Brasher shoes; it borrows from the style of message more usually found in the personal advertisement columns, via what are called Extended Symbolic Messages (Brennan and Bahn, 2006):

Source: The Brasher Boot Company

Condition	Illustration
Openness/tolerance	Acceptance of difference (different styles, ways of being and living) without prejudice or evaluations of superiority or inferiority
Hyperreality	Constitution of social reality through hype or simulation that is powerfully signified and represented
Perpetual present	Cultural propensity to experience everything (including the past and the future) in the present, 'here and now'
Paradoxical juxtapositions	Cultural propensity to juxtapose anything with anything else, including oppositional, contradictory and essentially unrelated elements.
Fragmentation	Omnipresence of disjointed and disconnected moments and experiences in life and sense of self – and the growing acceptance of the dynamism which leads to fragmentation in markets
Lack of commitment	Growing cultural unwillingness to commit to any single idea, project or grand design
Decentring of the subject	Removal of the human being from the central importance she or he held in modern culture – and the increasing acceptance of the potentials of their objectification
Reversal of consumption and production	Cultural acknowledgement that value is created not in production (as posited by modern thought) but in consumption – and the subsequent growth of attention and importance given to consumption
Emphasis on form/style	Growing influence of form and style (as opposed to content) in determining meaning and life
Acceptance of disorder/chaos	Cultural acknowledgement that, rather than order, chaos and disequilibria are the common states of existence – and the subsequent acceptance and appreciation of this condition

Source: AF Firat and CJ Shultz, From Segmentation to Fragmentation, *European Journal of Marketing*, Vol 31, Nos 3–4 (1997), p. 186. Republished with permission, Emerald Group Publishing Ltd.

Table 7.3: Postmodern conditions

THINKBOX

Could the 'pastiche' and mixed up images that seem part of postmodernism lead marketers to employ more of the sort of participative and ambiguous messages that we discussed under gestalt psychology in Chapters 2 and 3?

The following could be two examples and if so, how do you react to the approach that encourages you to spot from which films the images are taken in A and which bands are symbolized by the images in B?

Source: Stella Artois

Source: Virgin

We recommend Stephen Brown's website: www.sfxbrown.com

VIRTUAL GROUPS

With the growth of the World Wide Web interface, the potential has been unleashed for the widespread creation of online virtual groups (communities) on a commercial basis. As Loader (1998) has observed:

> The global communication networks which make up cyberspace are claimed to be altering almost every facet of our lifestyles, including patterns of work and leisure, entertainment, consumption, education, political activity, family experience and community structures. (p 3)

Cyberspace has become a new kind of social terrain, crowded with 'virtual communities', in which people come together for sexual flirtation, business, idle gossip, spiritual exploration, psychological support, political action, intellectual discourse on all kinds of subjects – the whole range of human interests and needs. (Anderson, 1999).

More and more people are joining a variety of virtual groups; groups that may never meet in the physical world but are nevertheless influential social groups that can affect behaviour including consumption behaviour. Indeed, referring back to the previous chapter, the concept of the virtual self becomes pertinent. Here, non-real self personas can be created via such virtual group contexts as Second Life (Chapter 6).

Fundamentally, new technologies permit people to make direct connections with others by the elimination of the middleman, a process known as **disintermediation**.

Further, the like-minded come together irrespective of time and space issues to form groups and a variety of networks, a process known as 'aggregation'.

Some virtual group behaviour does lead to physical group behaviour. Clearly some who interact online may decide to meet in person, but an intriguing development is **flashmobbing**. Here, virtual groups agree to meet in the physical world for what some might regard as acts of pointless lunacy! On Thursday 28 November 2005 what was thought to be the biggest flashmobbing event to date, 3 500 people who had agreed (via an internet virtual group) to meet arrived at Paddington station concourse. Suddenly, to the amazement of the regular commuters, at 1918 precisely they all switched on their MP3 players to the same tune and stated to dance (McCormack, 2006). To the onlookers this would have been in silence and no doubt was a sight of surreal proportions. This again fits with the strange world of the postmodern consumer.

Some examples of flashmobbing have had a social cause; the opening of Heathrow Terminal 5 was plagued by technical ineptness but was also the scene of a demonstration against airport expansion. The flashmobbers turned up at the terminal and at the appointed time peeled off their top layer of clothing to reveal a uniform

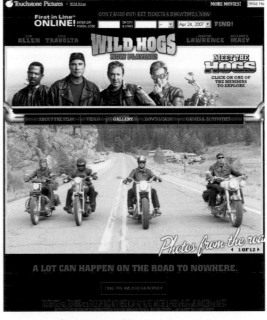

Source: www.wildhogs.movies.go.com

red T shirt with anti airport expansion slogans. They then proceeded to lie on the floor, together forming the shape of 'stop now'!

Howard Rheingold (1993) has observed that:

> The future of the Net is connected to the future of community, democracy, education, life – some of the human institutions people hold most dear, whether or not they know or care about the future of computer technology. (p 6).

Research by Robert Kozinets (1999) points towards Internet user experience as a key determinant – at least so far – of participation within a virtual community. People use networked computers for social relating and whether termed 'virtual communities' (Rheingold, 1993), 'brand communities' (Muniz, 1997), 'communities of interest' (Armstrong and Hagel, 1996), or **internet cultures** (Jones, 1995), research reveals that online groups are often market-oriented in their interests. Kozinets (1998) refers to 'virtual communities of consumption'.

There are specific sub-groups of virtual communities that explicitly centre on consumption-related interests.

Source: www.hog.com

They can be defined as 'affiliative groups whose online interactions are based upon shared enthusiasm for, and knowledge of, a specific consumption activity or related group of activities' (Kozinets, 1998) and in this way is the online version of the **brand community**.

Indeed, there are instances where the tribe is not only a rallying point for shared values but where these are expressed specifically through a brand. In Chapter 10 we discuss the case of the exceptional loyalty that some consumers have to Harley Davidson motorbikes. We also show that there are organized 'brandfests' at which Harley Owners Group (HoG) members can share common passions (see Chapter 11). This leads to the notion of brand community, which is defined as a 'specialized, non-geographically bound community, based on a structured set of social relations among admirers of a brand' (Muniz and O'Guinn, 2001:412).

Marketers are increasingly interested in engaging the consumer in brand developments and relationships, as Solomon (2003) explores consumers as co-designers.

EXAMPLE 7.4

Muniz and O'Guinn (2001) studied the consumption habits, family and leisure activities, interests, use of computer-mediated communications and what was perceived as important by some families and users of Saab cars and Macintosh computers in a small neighbourhood in the USA. Their findings revealed that members of the brand communities shared a strong sense of consciousness (e.g. 'we-ness') which transcended geographical boundaries (e.g. members used the Internet to communicate with other Saab and Mac users). Similarly, members developed a strong sense of oppositional brand loyalty (e.g. deriving important aspects of community experience from opposition to users of competing brands like BMW and IBM). Members shared brand stories and felt a sense of moral responsibility towards others.

Kozinets's research outlines four distinct virtual community 'types'. The first of the four types are the tourists who lack strong social ties to the group, and maintain only a superficial or passing interest in the consumption activity. Next are the minglers, who maintain strong social ties, but who are only perfunctorily interested in the central consumption activity. Devotees are opposite to this: they maintain a strong interest in and enthusiasm for the consumption activity, but have few social attachments to the group. Finally, insiders are those who have strong personal ties to the consumption activity.

McWilliam (2000) argues that online communities thrive because they offer the participants a number of benefits. First, the online community acts as a platform or a forum for exchanging common interests. For example, there can be discussion groups, regular forums on some topical issues, a research database which members can browse and use, a job exchange forum and a daily newsletter to keep members informed. Second, consumers get a sense of 'place', with codes of behaviour (e.g. shared rules and values) by using the online communities. Third, online communities promote dialogues and relationships among members through the use of discussion groups and other mechanisms. Fourth, online communities encourage active participation by everyone (not by just a few) as thousands of consumers can read the messages and post their responses on a bulletin board or a newsgroup.

EXAMPLE 7.5

The Case of My Nutella: The Community

Using a case study of 'My Nutella: The Community' promoted by the firm Ferrero in Italy, Cova and Pace (2006) analysed the power that a virtual brand community exerts over a brand of a mass-marketed convenience product. Findings suggested that the virtual community that gathers around a brand shows a new form of sociality and customer empowerment as it is not based on interaction between friends and peers, but more on personal self-exhibition in front of other consumers through the marks and rituals linked to the brand.

Source: Nutella

In a research project funded by the European Social Fund and the Direct Marketing Association (Evans, Wedande *et al.*, 2001) significant benefits emerged for those marketers who provide virtual communities on their commercial sites. In this study companies did, so were likely to be perceived more positively by at least a quarter of the users. Indeed, when asked directly, more than half of all respondents say they think it is a good idea for companies to provide virtual communities on their web sites. A third of respondents would also like to use a virtual community to communicate with the company itself.

Providing such facilities on a web site may also strengthen the relationship that consumers have with an organization. The concept of relational interaction between companies and consumers is discussed in Chapter 11.

From the same study (Evans, Wedande *et al.*, 2001), a third of respondents claimed to have purchased something via a virtual community site and 50% used the sites to find more information about products and services.

So, we propose several benefits of online communities that marketers can exploit:

- For the majority of virtual community participants, interacting within a virtual community is an effective way of connecting to a diverse group of people.
- Individuals can choose their level of interaction, gather and give information and advice and express their opinions – all while maintaining an important, perceived, level of control over the interaction.
- It helps them find information.
- They enjoy the interaction with other people and feel that they 'get something out of participating'.
- It's an opportunity to discuss topics that they are interested in.
- The majority of enthusiasts like to receive advice from other people. A smaller proportion like to give advice. This may be a good indicator for companies to use bulletin boards for posting product/service advice.

The *relational* potential of such communities is clear and because the locus of control is nearer the consumer, there is great scope for the online relational community (Figure 7.8). Consumers can take more of the initiative and be proactive in their interactions with other consumers and with companies.

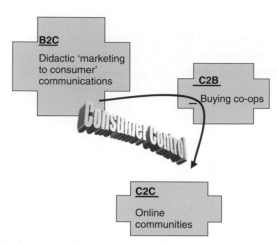

Figure 7.8: Consumer control over marketer–consumer interaction can increase via online communities

The following web site provides regular papers on a great variety of online communities:
http://www.onlinecommunityreport.com/

Brand Hijacking

Given the opportunities provided by the recent developments in technology and the ability of consumers to express themselves and their relationships with brands as and when they wish to do so, there is a concern about who owns the brand as online communities can assert on considerable claims on brand ownership with many viewing the brands as a shared cultural property rather the property of a business entity (Cova and Pace, 2006; Holt and Douglas, 2002). Indeed a brand can be hijacked, which means the brand is taken away from marketers by a brand community to enhance the brand's evolution (Wipperfürth, 2005). There are two ways in which brand hijacking occurs, the first being a serendipitous hijack in which brand fanatics seize control of a brand's ideology, use and persona. Secondly a co-created hijack can occur in which brand owners co-create a brand's ideology, use and persona, and pave the road for adoption by the mainstream consumers (Cova and Pace, 2006). In order to illustrate the re-balancing of power in company-consumer relations, Cova and Pace (2006) mention the case of Star Wars enthusiasts who feel so loyal and passionate about the brand that they make and exchange their own Star Wars movies, using digital camcorders and laptop computers. The response from the official owner of Star Wars is to act as an enabler on behalf of fans by distributing online 'reference', Star Wars sounds and visual effects that fans can insert into their DIY fan films.

THINKBOX

What virtual groups/communities do you belong to? Have you ever tried to hijack a brand? Do you know of someone who is involved in co-creation of brand? What is your relationship with them and do they influence your buying behaviour in any way? Explore some company web sites and the virtual communities they provide. How effective are these in developing greater relational interaction with their consumers?

Some online communities have evolved into social networking web sites. Facebook and Myspace are examples of these and allow people to post information about themselves and their interests and interact online with others. Many will become 'friends' even if they never meet physically. Again we explored aspects of this in the previous chapter but it is worth extending that analysis within the context of social group behaviour. In 2008 at Cardiff University, approximately 85% of the 26 000 students engaged with Facebook (Facebook, Cardiff University, 2008). There are concerns that people, especially young people, are posting too much about themselves on social networking sites. This is not only a treasure trove for identity thieves but also for marketers who can poach valuable information on, for example, brand interests and intentions to buy (together with personal details of the consumer).

We return to these issues in Chapter 11 and commend the case study given there by Sam Gould, titled 'Unitown Students' Union: Social Network Plunder'.

Marketers are encroaching onto consumer social networking space: Mars was the first to actually sell products on Facebook, for example (Jay, 2008a). Via Facebook consumers can buy Maltesers, for instance, and redeem a scanable mobile voucher at the checkout. Mars also has launched a radio show on Myspace which engages consumers in programme content and even delivery (Jay 2008b), but also clearly engages them with the brand as well.

CASE STUDY 7.1

The Grand Prize winner was a campaign that judges said "marked the shape of advertising in the future". They commended the winner for producing work that was "excellent, outstanding and beguiling, with witty and clever personalization".

It's a sad, yet true fact that as people get older they receive birthday cards. Guinness decided that a timely birthday message not only puts its drinkers in a good mood, but it's also a reminder of how best to celebrate another candle on the cake.

The brand wanted to encourage 360,000 members of its relationship marketing programme to celebrate their birthdays with friends and a few pints of the black stuff.

It chose the medium of email, as it thought this would appeal best to the younger, less traditional and more internet-savvy members of its database and achieve greater cut through than a paper-based or electronic birthday card.

Tullo Marshall Warren created a short movie showing a pub landlord wishing happy birthday to the recipient, with their name and age spoken by the publican. He then pulls a pint and tries to pass it through the screen.

Existing data was used to tailor the message to Guinness adorers or adopters. An email communication also had the added appeal of viral potential, giving members the ability to invite family members and friends to their birthday celebrations to enjoy a pint or two.

Of those who received the email, 60 per cent opened it and 95 per cent interacted fully. Every month 30,000 people used the email to invite their friends for a birthday pint.

One judge said: "it's the usual high quality you expect from Guinness, with an unusual personalised twist". Another remarked that it "was strong and innovative, with a good use of medium. It was a complex piece, yet simple in its execution and used technology and personalisation in a clever way".

FAMILY INFLUENCES ON CONSUMER BEHAVIOUR

The traditional form of the family in industrial societies is the *nuclear* or two-generation family, which consists usually of a mother, father and their children. Extended family comprises mother and father, numerous mature siblings who have spouses and who all live in one large joint-family arrangement (Childers and Rao, 1992). Extended families exist in collectivist cultures such as India, Pakistan, Thailand, Japan and China, whereas nuclear families prevail mostly in individualistic cultures such as the UK. A child in an individualistic culture is socialized to become a distinct, autonomous individual with emphasis on self and being different from others whereas a child in a collectivist culture is socialized to become an inherently integrated person with others who attach great deal of value to conformity to others in the group (Rose, 1999). However, in individualistic societies we see a trend toward different and often smaller families.

© Getty Images. Reproduced with permission

The extended family provides a very different type of environment for interaction among members in comparison with the nuclear family as there are multiple sources of influences based on observation and interaction of others, and family members may be considered as of greater importance than

	1950 (thousands)	2005 (thousands)
Marriages	408 000	247 805
Divorces	Around 30 000	141 750

Social Trends 2008

Table 7.4: Household composition in UK

outsiders. Hence, the probability that one gets influenced by a family member is higher in an extended family than in a nuclear family. This is quite significant given that family acts an important reference group.

There are now, for example, many more single households, single-parent households and childless couples than ever before, and Table 7.4 also reports on the rise in the divorce rate in UK which has an effect on the 'singles' market.

People in the Household	1971 (%s)	2007 (%s)
One	6	12
Couple: no children	19	25
Couple: dependent children	52	36
Lone parent	4	12

N.B. Some categories are not shown, therefore the figures do not total 100%

Consumer Behaviour by Family Type

The General Household Survey, published annually by the Office for National Statistics in UK, provides a wealth of data on household behaviour, including product ownership, consumption of social services and so on. Table 7.5 provides a glimpse into the Aladdin's cave of household data.

www. Have a look at the following web site, which provides more on the General Household Survey:
http://www.statistics.gov.uk/ssd/surveys/general household survey.asp

	Lone Parent %	Other families %
Ownership of satellite TV:	27	43
Access to Internet at home:	39	73

Source: General Household Survey, 2004.

Table 7.5: Household consumption

Intergenerational Influence

We learn our norms, attitudes and values from our families as part of our socialization and the effect of the family on our socialization is known as intergenerational influence (Childers and Rao, 1992). It is stated by Childers and Rao (1992) that a number of our behaviours including brand preferences, brand loyalties, information search, media usage and dependency and price sensitivity can be influenced by intra-family communications. In their study of US and Thai subjects, Childers and Rao (1992) found that intergenerational influence in Thailand was stronger for both luxuries and necessities whereas in the USA the influence was stronger for necessities than for luxuries. They concluded that the influence of family members was stronger in extended families (Thailand) than in nuclear families (USA). In a classic study, Young and Wilmott (1975) clearly demonstrated the influence of extended kin (e.g. grandparents, uncles) on the overall family's behaviour and decisions.

While some like Childers and Rao (1992) have compared the effect of different family types on consumer behaviours, it is still useful to explore the nuclear form of the family because it provides a good initial framework in the Western societies such as the UK.

The Family Life Cycle

The concept of a family life cycle shows how the family unit's interests and buying behaviour changes over time due to the progression from the single bachelor stage, to newly married, married with children, married with children who no longer live in the parental home ('empty nest'), and finally to the solitary survivor stage (Figure 7.9).

As per Murphy and Staples (1979) and others who have looked into family consumption habits, some of the traditional family life cycle stages are described in the following:

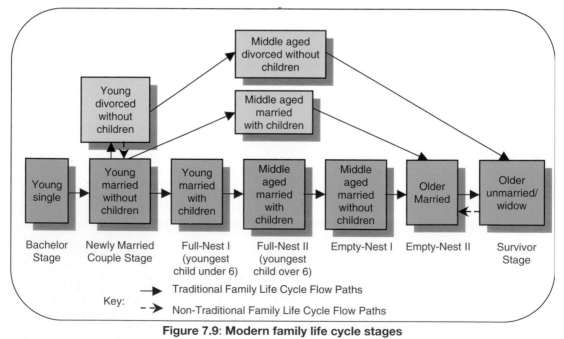

Figure 7.9: Modern family life cycle stages

Source: Murphy P E and Staples W A (1979) A modernized family life cycle, Journal of Consumer Research, Vol 6 (June), pp. 12–21

- Young Single (Bachelor) Stage

This stage usually starts at the age of 18 when a person starts living on their own as a household. The stage is characterized by below average income, high discretionary spending with a focus on personal growth and enriching personal experiences and tendency to buy products as an expression of individuality and newly achieved status.

- Young Married without Children Stage

This stage is normally described as the honeymoon stage and it tends to last for about two years or until the first child is born. At this stage, the focus is normally on the creation of a new family and meeting new obligations such as listening and negotiating with the partner in terms of allocating family resources. As both partners are able to work, the financial situation can be very good with a growing desire to establish some form of financial security.

- Young Married with Children (Full Nest I)

This stage starts at the arrival of first child which leads to some drastic changes to the lifestyle and financial situation. Parents start to feel loss of freedom but the focus remains on caring for home and the children. Parents tend to spend more on clothing, housing, childcare, food and healthcare and some pressures due to pester power start to emerge at this stage.

- Middle Aged Married with Children (Full Nest II)

This is a typical family life cycle stage which revolves around children and their educational activities. The family is often under pressure in terms of financial resources and often both partners need to work to provide for the family. Parents tend to spend more on housing, furnishing, computing and related household services. Parents are likely to change their brand preferences, giving in to the demands of children who have become better consumers on their own.

- Middle Aged Married without Children (Empty Nest I)

Children leave home as they grow older and the family is again in good financial situation with a tendency to spend more on vehicles and clothing.

- Older Stages (Empty Nest II and Survivor)

The family head may be about 65 and there are few time and financial commitments. Individuals may have made savings in the past and may enjoy good health with a tendency to focus on healthcare and travel related services. This stage is normally described as the grey market, which is good for targeting travel/leisure/healthcare/financial planning related products and services.

It is worth noting that as the family moves through various stages of the life cycle, needs and wants grow and subsequently the spending increases and remains high until falling sharply at the Empty Nest II or Survivor Stage. Figure 7.10 describes the average family in the UK and some of the consumption patterns.

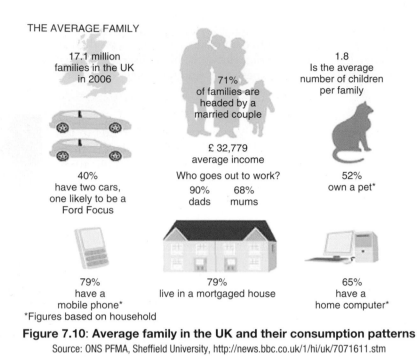

THE AVERAGE FAMILY

17.1 million
families in the UK
in 2006

71%
of families are
headed by a
married couple

1.8
Is the average
number of children
per family

40%
have two cars,
one likely to be a
Ford Focus

£ 32,779
average income
Who goes out to work?
90%   68%
dads   mums

52%
own a pet*

79%
have a
mobile phone*
*Figures based on household

79%
live in a mortgaged house

65%
have a
home computer*

Figure 7.10: Average family in the UK and their consumption patterns
Source: ONS PFMA, Sheffield University, http://news.bbc.co.uk/1/hi/uk/7071611.stm

Marketing is certainly cognisant of the family life cycle and uses the concept for segmenting markets. Here is an example of targeting according to FLC:

© ATOC Ltd. Reproduced with permission

Trends Affecting Family Life Cycle Stages

During the past couple of decades, there have been significant changes in terms of demographic characteristics, life style and family patterns and some of the noteworthy trends are as follows:

- Childless Couples: Many couples now decide not to have children at all and this may be due to more career-oriented married women and delayed marriages.
- Unmarried Couples: There is a growing acceptance of heterosexual and homosexual couples living together without formal marital arrangement and more babies are now born outside marriage than ever before. As per a recent BBC news report, two in five babies are born outside wedlock in the UK, which compares to one in 10 children born outside marriage 20 years ago.
- Single Parents: The divorce rate tends to be quite high (about 50% in the UK), which leads to an increase in single-parent households.
- Lonely Nation: According to a recent survey by the independent Family Policy Studies Centre (FPSC) reported by the BBC, fewer people in the UK are now getting married than at any time in the past 40 years. Also, more than 6.5 million people in Britain (about 28% of households) now live on their own, three times as many as 40 years ago.
- Back to the Extended Family!: In some cases, a family may have a structure that resembles the extended families often found in collectivist cultures. This is fuelled by a growing trend whereby young single-adult children return home to avoid the expenses of living alone while establishing their careers. Moreover, a divorced daughter or a son and grandchildren may return home to join parents/grandparents. Other examples include elderly parents who decide to move in with children to avoid healthcare costs. Some of the newlyweds may prefer to live with their in-laws. As per a recent BBC news report, half of working parents in the UK now rely on their parents or other relatives to look after their children and grandparents are playing a much more active role in their families' lives than in the past. Finally, due to the rising ethnic diversity, many of the ethnic minorities with extended family structure now co-exist with mainstream population.

THINKBOX

It is clear that each of these stages has its own implications for consumers' income and expenditure patterns. Family needs and the ability to satisfy them can be uniquely associated with each life cycle phase.

How would a family's needs change over time, for furniture, clothes, food, cars, financial services and holidays?

EXAMPLE 7.6

A recent promotional campaign by Barclays Bank depicted the life stages through which their customers go, by picturing a young single man, then a couple with a family and an older couple whose children had left home, and suggesting that the bank has financial service products to suit not just each stage 'now' but each individual as they progress through these stages of the life cycle.

The concepts here have been extended and applied within practical market analysis programmes such as SAGACITY (Research Services Ltd, 1981) given in Table 7.6. SAGACITY combines an abbreviated

1	Dependent			1.1	White collar
				1.2	Blue collar
2	Pre-family			2.1	White collar
				2.2	Blue collar
3	Family	3.1	Better off	3.11	White collar
				3.12	Blue collar
		3.2	Worse off	3.21	White collar
				3.22	Blue collar
4	Empty nest	4.1	Better off	4.11	White collar
				4.12	Blue collar
		4.2	Worse off	4.21	White collar
				4.22	Blue collar

Source: Research Services Ltd (1981).

Table 7.6: Twelve SAGACITY categories

family life cycle with income and occupation. The result is a series of 12 categories based on life stage, whether both partners are working or not, and on 'blue collar' or 'white collar' occupations.

Roles and Decision Making in the Family

As some of the traditional functions of the family have declined, others have taken on increased significance. Consumption planning has become a central function of the modern family in industrial societies and the different purchasing roles of various family members have become more important. A variety of role players, both within and external to the family, affect purchase decision-making. Thus Kotler (1972) distinguishes five buying roles, which must be taken into account in analyses of family buying behaviour (Figure 7.11). These are the initiator (the person from whom the idea of buying a certain product first comes), the influencer, (who consciously or unconsciously affects the purchase in some way, perhaps as an opinion leader), the decider (who makes any of the decisions or sub-decisions that determine the precise nature of the purchase), the purchaser (who actually carries out the final purchase), and the user (who makes practical use of the item bought). Almost all family decisions are affected by more than one of these consumer roles. For example, the selection of a venue for a family trip,

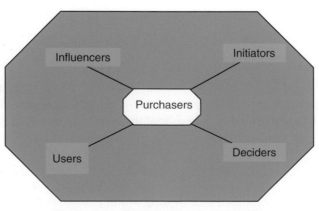

Figure 7.11: Buying roles in the family

although paid for and purchased by the parents, may be initiated and strongly influenced by children (see the pester power section, later in this chapter).

Husband–Wife Decision Making

A considerable amount of empirical consumer research has concerned the role behaviour of family decision units and within this research, the theme of husband–wife interaction in the decision-making process has predominated.

Komarovsky (1961) hypothesized that the amount of communication between husbands and wives varies directly with the egalitarianism and sharing of tasks displayed in the family. If one of the joint tasks is shopping, then the very scale and complexity of the operation demands considerable discussion between partners.

Summarizing the empirical evidence on husband–wife interaction, which might help confirm or refute this hypothesis, Komarovsky concluded that:

1. There is a tendency for wives to have more influence in decision making in the lower socio-economic groups (and this suggests that the symmetrical type of family is to be found more in the middle classes).
2. There appears to be a curvilinear relationship between the family's social class and the extent of joint involvement in its decision processes: both low- and high-income groups show low joint involvement whereas middle-income families tend to be high in joint decision making.
3. Joint involvement is greater among younger couples than among older ones. The possibility that either husbands or wives may predominate in decisions relating to particular products is confirmed by a well-known investigation of husband–wife relationships carried out by Kenkel (1961). The products mentioned by the couples were classified into five separate categories as shown in Table 7.7.

Davis and Rigaux (1974) analysed the influence exerted by husbands and wives at differing stages in the process of consumption planning and decision-making. Their investigation was designed to determine whether there are differences in partners' roles at different stages of the decision-making process and how husbands and wives perceive their roles at each stage of the process.

Husbands and wives in 73 households in Belgium were asked to provide information on their decision making relative to 25 products and services. Each respondent was required to specify the person who had been dominant in making the overall decision with regard to each of the 25 areas (Table 7.8).

According to Davis and Rigaux (1974), decisions can be classified in one of four ways for the families as a whole: husband-dominant, wife-dominant, syncratic and autonomic decisions. The last two categories require further explanation. When more than half the families made a joint decision with

1.	Wife personal	e.g. clothes, jewellery
2.	Wife household	e.g. washing machine, cooking utensils
3.	Husband	e.g. books, clothes, watch
4.	Joint family	e.g. furniture, TV, car
5.	Children e.g. toys, clothes.	

Table 7.7: Kenkel's division of labour

respect to an item, the decision was classified as syncratic; when fewer than half the families made the decision jointly, it was classed as autonomic.

THINKBOX

Think about your own family and the way in which decisions are made or were made when you were a child. How are decisions made now in your household? Identify the person who decides, the type of decision made and link these to the nature and type of product purchased (see Table 7.8 for some guidance).

Husband-dominant	Life insurance, other insurance
Wife-dominant	Cleaning products, kitchenware, child clothing, wife clothing, food, other furnishings
Autonomic	Cosmetics, non-prescription drugs, appliances, housing upkeep, husband clothing, alcoholic beverages, garden tools, saving objectives, forms of saving, car
Syncratic	Children's toys, living-room furniture, outside entertainment, vacation, school, housing, TV

Table 7.8: Davis and Rigaux's family decision-making roles

Having demonstrated that purchase decision can be classified in this way, Davis and Rigaux turned to the question of the nature of husband–wife interactions at three stages in the decision-making process. The selected stages are:

1. Problem recognition.
2. Search for information.
3. Final decision.

Figure 7.12 shows that marital roles appear to vary from phase to phase in the decision process but it has to be added that the differences are by no means large, and may not be statistically significant.

Resource Allocation and Factors Affecting Joint Family Decision Making

The household decision-making process and who ends up deciding can be a function of the sex role orientation of the family, which reflects the cultural norms and values of the society. For instance, in some societies men are expected to provide for the household and hence they may play a more dominant role in household decision making. However, perception of the role of women in society has changed over the years and many trends (e.g. advent of career women leading to more women contributing towards the resource of their families and/or taking the responsibility of running a household) have resulted in challenges to earlier beliefs about the role structures and the purchase influence of typical family members. Studies investigating resource allocation cover the flow and management of resources from the point at

	Phase 1	Phase 2	Phase 3
Husband dominant	2	3	2
Joint	17	15	8
Wife dominant	6	7	5
Totals	25	25	25

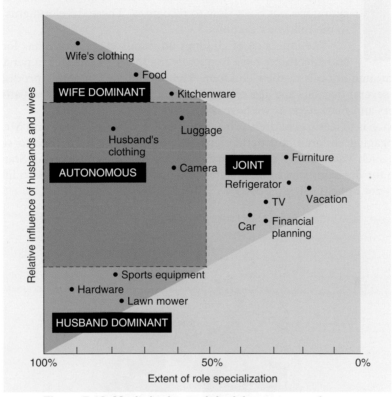

Figure 7.12: Marital roles and decision process phases

Source: HL Davis and BP Rigaux, Perceptions of Marital Roles in Decision Processes, Journal of Consumer Research, Vol 1 No 1 (1974)

which they enter the household to the point at which they are expended and as per the comparative resource theory whoever brings more economic and educational resources into the household is the one in control (Commuri and Gentry, 2005). Hence, while traditionally the wife would allow her husband to be in control of the household decisions, as she contributes more significantly to the household income, her overall influence in household decision making is likely to go up.

However, the focus on husband and wife roles tends to neglect the growing influence of children in consumption decisions and we now turn our attention to this.

Children and Pester Power

Children are becoming more brand literate and are more influential in the market place, whether it be via pester power or the levels of opinion leadership over other children that some will exert. In recent years

many organizations have focused on the children's consumer marketplace, because expenditure within and on behalf of this group of consumers is increasing rapidly and satisfying young consumers sets a course for predictable sales growth. As children get older so does their independence (from parents) and their disposition as consumers varies depending on their development (Piaget and Elkin, 1969). Since the early 1980s research has investigated factors affecting consumption choices made by children and for children (Moschis and Moore, 1979; Belch, 1985). Their degree of influence over other children and over parents is also a major factor in contemporary society and one which marketing has not been slow to recognize. These developments form the backdrop to the following sections.

The influence of children on family expenditure has long been recognized and advertisers have frequently made use of this fact to persuade parents to buy certain products through appeals to their children. The market for children's products has itself grown rapidly in the last several decades and the teenage market in particular is a very attractive segment for many manufacturers and marketers, as we have seen.

A related approach is to feature children as if adults. Recent Vauxhall Zafira and Meriva advertisements have done this, engaging children and perhaps pester power, but parents like to see children as little adults. Indeed one such Vauxhall TV commercial was reported to the Adverting Standards Authority as being irresponsible for depicting children acting as 'little dads' and using a jack to lift the front of a car. The complaint was not upheld (Singh, 2008a).

Source:© United Biscuits. Reproduced with permission

What some marketers do is to target their advertising at a slightly older age group so that the 'trickle down' theory operates – younger kids see the product being used by their elders and want to follow their lead. By the time it has trickled down to them the older ones have been enticed to the next craze.

When children are of primary school age it is often school friends who become more important product influencers than parents. Observation and word of mouth are then very important in developing children's preferences.

Many marketers have really taken this on board and have started to get into schools with various sponsorship and 'educational' ventures. Schools need the help to ease financial hardship associated with their budgets but some teachers might be uncomfortable with this way of getting to the children's market.

Any viewing of TV at 'children's' times will confirm saturation of commercials aimed at children. Younger children may merely watch these as entertainment but as they grow, the brand and image become important and salient in children's minds as a result of associative learning processes and vicarious learning (see Chapter 3).

Children's TV viewing (which of course includes advertisement viewing) is significant. In one study (Annenberg Public Policy Centre, 1999) it was estimated that children spend 60% more time per year in watching television than they spend in school.

In terms of the extent to which children can influence family consumer decision making, their age is an important factor. As children grow older, their request frequency goes down but parents may yield to their requests more often and this may be because parents often think that older children have gained some experience and consumer skills to act as better consumers in the marketplace. In particular, teenagers' ability to influence family decisions goes up when they have greater financial resources and when they know the product very well. Similarly, when teenagers are highly involved with a purchase or when they are the prime users of products (e.g. clothes, toys, snacks, breakfast cereal and school supplies), then their influence on family decision making is also likely to be very high (see for instance, Beatty and Talpade, 1994; Palan and Wilkes, 1997).

As well as child related-consumption, we are also concerned here with the role of children in determining more adult purchases, for example, which car the parents will buy and where to go on holiday and so on. The family is a decision-making unit, which means that there are different roles for each member. There will be deciders, influencers, buyers, users, gatekeepers (holders of information) and different members can play each of these roles at different times – including children. Indeed Lindstrom (2004) suggests that 8- to 14-year-olds are the most powerful gatekeepers of consumption information in many families. Children are increasingly influencing choice of housing, durables, clothes, TV, video, cars and holidays as well as in the more conventional areas such as sweets. Tinson and Nancarrow (2005) found that children thought of themselves as influencing 73% of family trips to the cinema, 63% of family holidays and 37% of family car purchases.

As per Horgan (2005), the average weekly income among 7–14 year olds has almost doubled since the mid 1990s, almost £9.00 now leading to a total disposable income of around £3.4 bn per year. Most of this is spent on food and drink (47%), clothing and reading/stationery (32% each) and home entertainment (24%).

Although the term 'pester power' is now common place, the less journalistic term is purchase request behaviour and McDermott *et al.* (2006) found that food advertising appears to encourage pestering by children with the result that some parents buy less healthy food products.

John (1999) reviewed 25 years of consumer socialization research dealing with what is known about children's development as consumers and the way they respond to marketing stimuli in different age groups. It was found that children pass through various stages of cognitive development whereby during the initial years (aged 4–5) they tend to focus on surface aspects of product and brand information, learn to identify TV ads and distinguish them from other forms of programming and tend to see the ads as a form of entertainment (e.g. the ad is funny). By the age of 7–8, they start to understand the intent of advertising (e.g. ads are trying to make you buy something). At the age of 8 years, children can also recognize whether the advertising is telling the truth and whether there is a bias in the message leading to a general lack of trust and less liking of advertising in general. In later years (ages 9–10) they are able to focus on deeper aspects of stimuli and become even more sceptical of advertising. When children are 11 and 12, they may start to behave very much like grown-ups (e.g. may have good knowledge about products/brand features). However, at this age, they still lack specific knowledge of what tactics and advertising appeals are used by an advertisement.

In this context, one can argue that young children (aged eight and less) can be at risk for being easily misled or deceived by the advertising message as they do not have enough cognitive defence mechanisms to interpret and comprehend the truth behind a commercial message (John, 1999; see also Zhang and Sood, 2002). Clearly there are ethical issues here. Children have not fully matured, by definition, yet marketers heavily target children, often in very subtle ways with a view to nurture brand preferences among children.

Although there is evidence to suggest that brands are not as stable as they used to be – we switch more regularly in many product-markets – once a brand has become a clear preference it may well remain within the repertoire of acceptable brands for a considerable period. Think of the effort that the banks make to target just one age 'year' – 18 year olds. As these go off to university their business is courted by most of the banks with offers such as discounts off CDs, free stationery, low bank charges and so on.

In Chapter 5 we reviewed other aspects of children's consumption behaviour and one question that was raised was possible links between media exposure, children's buying behaviour and their happiness. Perhaps it is worth posing this, here: UK children have been described as unhappy and parents have been described as being out of touch with their children. In the former case, the UNICEF found that of 21 nations in the developed world, British children are the unhappiest (Bradshaw, 2007). Perhaps children who are watching too much television and spend hours on the internet are 'greedy and unhappy' (NCC, 2007)? For the latter, further research suggests that parents are out of touch with their children (Glover, 2007), with two-thirds of parents not knowing their children have tried drugs and many not aware they are having sex.

THINKBOX

There are anecdotal stories of 10 year olds mugging and even killing for the 'right' brand of trainers in some urban areas of USA. How important for UK 10 year olds are 'brands'?

Most UK marketing trade bodies outlaw practices which exploit minors. How effective do you think these regulations are?

Many parents have succumbed to youth culture and look to their children for what is 'hip' to buy. In a survey for the BBC *Money Programme* (1997) it was found that 72% of parents admitted to £20 of their weekly spending being influenced by their children, 22% of parents thought up to £50 of weekly spending to be a result of pester power and even 4% thought that up to £100 of their weekly spending was based on this! This would amount to £5 billion per year if averaged across the UK. Lindstrom (2004) estimates that 'tweens' (8 to 14 year olds) influence and even control $1.18 trillion pa. It has even been suggested that up to 80% of brand choices (even those aimed at parents) are 'controlled' by teens (Millward-Brown, 2002).

EXAMPLE 7.7

The targeting of children to encourage pester power is not new, as Figure 7.13 shows; a 1950s advertisement for Bovril was aimed at both parents and children and the McDonald's bus will encourage children to want to eat more fast food (Figure 7.14).

Figure 7.13: Old and new examples of encouraging pester power
A similar approach was adopted by Rowntrees: 'Don't forget the fruit gums, Mum!'
Reproduced by permission of Robert Opie

Figure 7.14: Reminding children and parents of the 'fun' to be had as well as the food at McDonald's
Photograph: Martin Evans

THINKBOX

Next time you are in a supermarket, watch what happens as parents with young children go around the store.

Do the children pick up any items? Do they sometimes ask nicely for them, sometimes scream if they don't get them and sometimes surreptitiously put them in the basket – perhaps especially at the supermarket checkout?

Parent Power

Turning pester power on its head, there are marketers who recognize that some parents want their children to project a certain image (Brown, 2004). This is not the same as the children themselves saying what

Source: D&G Junior

they want. Lego has promoted its kindergarten brick, Duplo, with a £5 million campaign through direct mail, plus advertisements in magazines sent to mothers of pre-school children. The D&G advertisement appeared in up-market womens' magazines, clearly targeted at parents, to encourage brand purchase for their very young children.

However, a different perspective on pestering has been suggested by Benady (2008) who refers to positive pester power. Here, children's exposure to corporate social responsibility issues such as the environment and healthy eating could lead to pestering for the purchases of environmentally friendly and more healthy products.

Much of our development is shaped in childhood and the process through which we move from childhood to and through adulthood is socialization. This involves reciprocal interaction with others, including parents and friends. So not only do parents influence children but the reverse can apply as well, hence the potentially powerful application of this as positive pestering.

THINKBOX

Advertisements for very expensive designer childrenswear often appear in magazines aimed at 30–50-year-old ABC1 women, thereby not directly targeting children but their parents instead. Such a strategy exploits adults wanting to 'live through their children' and express their own self-concept vicariously through their children.

What are the implications of this for consumers (children and parents), marketers and society as a whole?

Schaninger and Lee (2002) A New Full Nest Classification Approach, Psychology and Marketing, Vol 19 No 1 pp 25–58, which explores family life cycle issues, especially the full nest stage, appears on the web site that accompanies this book:
www.wileyeurope.com/college/evans

The important analysis of marketing to children by Juliet Schor, Born to Buy (2004) could turn you into an activist!

THINKBOX

FUTURE FOUNDATION RESEARCH
The Networked Family

It is well understood by now that the concept of family is not as tightly drawn as it once was. Some have described this as a move from 'simple' to 'complex' family structures.

There is no evidence that these changes – the notionally cumulative impact of divorce, step-parenting, re-marriage, co-habitation – have weakened kinship links. Though it has a politically controversial dimension, the majority of parents stay close to all their children, many of which stay in the family home long after the traditional moment of departure has passed. Families are also much more democratized than they used to be – more decisions are shared on the basis of more internal discussion than ever before. The other obvious point is that women/partners/mothers are increasingly able to match the income potential of men/partners/fathers. Technology has largely been a driver of this trend, 'democratizing' information within the knowledge economy so that traditional authority paradigms, particularly among parents and children, are being dramatically altered (witness the numbers of children teaching and helping parents with daily decisions through their superior use of the internet). Yet whilst children are finding themselves more included in family decisions and dialogue, the paradox remains that protective/paranoid parenting may restrict their freedom in other ways.

What are your reactions to this summary of the Future Foundation's research on the family?

Reproduced by permission of The Future Foundation http://www.futurefoundation.net/

SUMMARY

■ Groups are specifically defined in behavioural science to refer to collections of individuals brought together to achieve a particular purpose. Primary groups are characterized by face-to face interaction and evolve norms, which influence the behaviour of their members. Reference groups are social artefacts, which the individual uses for purposes of comparison, aspiration and to obtain values and perspectives. Group membership usually imposes a degree of conformity on the person.

■ Consumers are vitally influenced by their group memberships and by their reference groups. Brand choice, conformity and independence depend to an extent on group affiliations, and reference group influences vary from product to product and brand to brand. Socially distant reference groups also have relevance for marketing but some segments of the population must be expected to regard them as negative reference points.

■ Reference group influence can be manifested in the form of information influence, utilitarian influence or value expressive influence and the extent to which these are effective depends upon the product type. There are some characteristic features of living in postmodern society including fragmentation, lack of commitment, hyperreality, and emphasis on form and style. While some argue that we now live in a society of isolated individuals, others argue for a reverse movement in which we join with others on the basis of sharing common passions, feelings and interest. Such a group of consumers is called a 'tribe' and there are many manifestations of tribal behaviour including the teenage groupings. Related to the idea of tribe is the notion of brand communities and online communities whereby consumers participate as groups.

■ The family is the context within which many consumer decisions are made and there is thus wide scope for the attitudes and behaviour of one family member to influence the purchase behaviour of another. The effect of the family in our socialization process is known as 'intergenerational influence' and some of our brand choices and brand preferences may be guided by such an influence. Consumer needs and the ability to satisfy them vary from stage to stage of the family life cycle. Shopping behaviour for some products varies significantly with life cycle stage. The roles of husbands and wives appear to vary from phase to phase of the decision-making process; specific products and decision areas can be classified as husband-dominant, wife-dominant, autonomic or syncratic. Children can influence family expenditure in the form of pester power but there are some ethical concerns regarding the targeting of children by marketers. This is particularly so in the context of young children who lack cognitive defence mechanisms to understand and comprehend the advertising intent and the use of persuasion, deception and bias in commercial messages.

www. Read the article Belch and Willis (2002), Family Decision at the Turn of the Century, Journal of Consumer Behaviour, Vol 2 No 2. This can also be accessed via the web site at www.wileyeurope.com/college/evans

QUESTIONS

1. How do advertisers try to use 'group influence'? Think about this through relevant theories of group behaviour and influence. Give specific examples, for illustration.

2. Give examples of marketing activity that reflect French and Raven's typology of social power.

3. What are virtual groups? Why do consumers participate in virtual groups and what are the implications for marketers?

4. Explore postmodern consumer behaviour and its implications for marketers.

5. Explain different stages of traditional family life cycle. Also, discuss variations in family life cycle due to changing lifestyle patterns.

6. Explore decision making in the family. Use examples to illustrate differences in different families and in different product-markets.

7. What ethical issues are there for marketers if they recognize the importance of pester (and parent) power?

FURTHER READING

Firat A F and Venkatesh A (1993) Postmodernity: The Age of Marketing, *International Journal of Research in Marketing*, Vol **10** pp 227–249

Moore E S, Wilkie W L and Lutz R J (2002) Passing the Torch: Intergenerational Influences as a Source of Brand Equity, *Journal of Marketing*, Vol **66**, No 2, pp 17–38. This is a very useful paper which convincingly explores the nature of intergenerational influences and identifies intergenerational influences for various products and brands.

Tajfel H (1981) *Human Groups and Social Categories: Studies in Social Psychology*, Cambridge: Cambridge University Press. This is a classic book on human groups and the social categories.

CHAPTER 8
CULTURE AND SUBCULTURE

CHAPTER OBJECTIVES

Having engaged with the material in this chapter you should be able to:

■ Explain what is meant by culture, cultural meaning and the role of shared consumption rituals.
■ Examine the nature of differing consumer values across cultures and their implications for national and international marketing and standardization versus customization.
■ Explore the nature and implications of 'country of origin' for marketers and consumers.
■ Explain what are subcultures, ethnic subcultures, ethnicity and ethnic identity and the implications of these for targeting.
■ Explain acculturation and the way it applies to the understanding of consumer behaviour of ethnic minority consumers.

INTRODUCTION

It might be a cliché to say that the world is getting smaller in terms of travel, communication, trade and population movements, but because more marketers are targeting more markets, this reinforces the importance of recognizing whatever diversity there is in these markets. There are plenty of examples of companies' international marketing strategies failing where this was not the case. Later in the chapter you will find some examples of brand names, which have not 'converted' well to international markets and other examples of a lack of understanding of how to interact with people in different societies. So, as markets and marketing become more international and in some cases global, it is increasingly important to recognize cultural differences and to respect different consumers' values, traditions and ways of life.

We need to bear in mind that societies differ radically, such that apparently homely materialities can assume startlingly different meanings as one passes from one social context to another. It is also the case that within a particular society, such as a country, there are often different subcultures reflecting a growing cosmopolitan mix within populations. Subcultures often differ in their place in, and understanding of, patterns of class, status, ethnicity and the like. With greater opportunities for travel, communication and immigration/emigration, many societies see original indigenous populations being enriched by the experiences and knowledge of those from different cultures. The resulting 'minorities' can be of significant and growing proportion and will retain their own values and lifestyles but within their new environments. Marketers need to respect them and to understand the consumption behaviour of these ethnic segments.

This chapter is structured around these issues. We start by exploring culture: its meaning and implications for consumers and marketers and then narrow the focus to examine the characteristics of subcultural behaviour.

CULTURE

There are many definitions and descriptions of culture in literature, many going as far back as the beginning of the twentieth century. Few provide as helpful a 'classification' as Johnson (1962). To him, culture comprises:

- *Cognitive elements and beliefs:* These are what a society 'knows' (and transmits from generation to generation) about the physical and social worlds and the way in which society works and its religious beliefs.
- *Values and norms:* These inform how the majority in the society are expected to behave. Nonnormative behaviour is how the individual responds and reacts to these more generalized societal norms.
- *Sign, signals and symbols:* These include language and the variety of conventions in a society for conveying meaning. In terms of language, it is sometimes said, jokingly, that the US and UK cultures are separated by a common language.

It is worth pointing out that culture is learned (not something that you are born with), collective (something that you share with others) and dynamic; it changes as new ideas come along and as the environment changes, for example as a result of climate change or technological change which in turn can effect changes in lifestyles. Marketing can also impact upon cultural change. In the UK, before McDonald's fast food restaurants opened, market research revealed a liking for waiter/waitress service and a dislike of brightly lit venues. But as the US style format appeared in UK, the British soon changed their lifestyles to fit and so one aspect of their culture was changed.

Indeed 'McDonaldization' is a term used to reflect the spread of American culture across other societies. The advent of the microwave and 'instant' meals provided impetus in many Western societies for the harried lifestyles of fragmented households and there is a 'chicken and egg' debate about which came first.

The process of learning your own culture is termed as 'enculturation' and that of learning a new/different culture is known as 'acculturation'.

Culture and Meaning

Culture can also be defined as the meaning system that members of any specific group use to inform their lives. This meaning system provides us with a sense of identity (who we are) and rationale for our actions (how we should behave and what we should be doing in different contexts). It also helps us to make sense of what other people and even objects stand for and how and in what sense we should deal with them. Consumer products are a part of this system of meaning, which is often culturally specific and shared, learned and transmitted through generations. The food we eat, the clothes we wear, the type of transport we use every day and the possessions we love all serve as a media for the expression of our cultural meaning.

McCracken (1986) argues that culture is the lens through which people see their world. It is also a blueprint of human activity. As a lens, culture determines how we see our world and as a blueprint, it determines how the world is fashioned by our efforts. However, culture cannot exist without perception, without the attribution of meaning (Chapman 1992). There can be no outsider accounts, no extracultural observers; we are all in cultures of our own, and a recognition of this is a step to understanding it (Jamal, 1997).

EXAMPLE 8.1

This point can be illustrated through an example. Imagine you are in India and you see two adolescent Hindu boys walking together holding their hands. You may instantly get the impression that the two boys are homosexuals. However, to the boys and to everyone around them in the Indian culture, the same act signifies friendship and solidarity with each other (Spradley and McCurdy, 1977). Similar examples of differences in classification and meaning systems can be found in family and kinship patterns around the world.

McCracken (1986) uses the term cultural category to represent the basic distinctions that a culture utilizes to divide up its world of everyday experiences. Examples of cultural categories include time (e.g. leisure vs. work time), space (e.g. personal vs. public) and person (e.g. gender). Such categorizations and distinctions help us understand and comprehend our world of everyday experiences. These categorizations are often culturally specific and could be subject to change. For instance, we in the West have a strong sense of private space, which requires some distance between us as individuals and others. However, such a distinction may not be that significant in some other cultures where conformity to a group is more important than valuing one's own individual self. The notion that culture is concerned with meaning implies that we should be mostly concerned with the study of people in groups, since meaning is a shared phenomenon and plays an important role in group life.

One aim of studying culture is then to find a way of understanding and describing the 'lenses' and 'blueprints' to which McCracken refers. We are also encouraged to investigate various cultural categories and cultural meanings that are important to each culture. In order to get a better understanding of cultural categories and meanings, marketers as well as consumer researchers need to think about adopting some *qualitative* and interpretive methods of investigation. One such interpretive approach is an ethnographic account of people and their meanings where time is spent observing and participating in consumption experiences of consumers in natural settings (Arnould and Wallendorf, 1994). Sufficient time should be spent (e.g. couple of months) meeting a sample of consumers on a regular basis and researchers should communicate with them through their language, from the 'native's point of view' (Geertz, 1973). You may find some other methods such as focus groups and long interviews (McCracken, 1988) to be quite effective as well.

Meaning Transfer Model

According to the meaning-transfer model (Figure 8.1) suggested by McCracken (1986), the meaning originally resides in the *culturally constituted world,* which is the world of everyday experiences in which

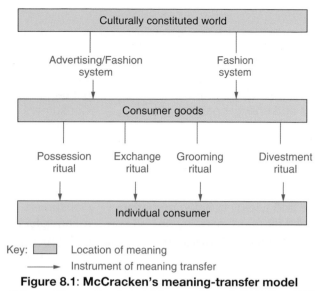

Figure 8.1: McCracken's meaning-transfer model
G McCracken, Culture and Consumption, Journal of Consumer Research, Vol 13 (June 1986), pp. 71–84.

consumers live and make sense of marketing stimuli. The meaning is then disengaged and transferred to consumer goods via macro mechanisms such as advertising and fashion systems. The meaning is finally transferred to individual consumers through a range of *symbolic actions* such as gift exchange rituals, possession rituals, grooming rituals and divestment rituals. Since rituals play an important part in consumers' lives and the way consumers make sense of the world around them, we will discuss them in the next section in further detail.

The underlying assumptions of the meaning transfer model appear to be that: cultural meaning is attached to consumer goods; cultural meaning can be communicated by goods; and consumers turn to consumer goods as a source of cultural meaning. This implies that consumers do not simply consume products for their material benefits but consume the symbolic meaning of those goods as portrayed in their images (Elliott, 1997). Consumption of products and brands thus becomes the very arena in which 'culture is fought over and licked into shape' (Douglas and Isherwood, 1980:57).

As per McCracken (1986), advertising facilitates meaning transfer by bringing the consumer good (e.g. a product or a brand) and a representation of the culturally constituted world together within the frame of a particular advertisement in such a way that the consumer perceives a symbolic equivalence between them. Consequently, the consumer starts making attributions to the brand or the product, certain properties that they know exist in the culturally constituted world. The 'known properties of the culturally constituted world thus come to reside in the unknown properties of the consumer good and the transfer of meaning from world to good is accomplished' (p.74). Once the meaning becomes resident in consumer goods, it moves from the consumer good into the life of the consumer through a second set of instruments of meaning transfer known as rituals, which represent a number of repetitive and apparently simple behaviours that we engage in our daily lives. For example, most of us go to work/study on a fairly regular basis. We also have to eat our food (sometimes alone and sometimes with the family) and go shopping (sometimes more than once a week). As per McCracken (1986), however, four types of rituals are important, each representing a different stage in a more general process by which meaning is moved from consumer good to individual consumer: exchange, possession, grooming, and divestment rituals (see Table 8.1).

For example, you may choose, purchase and present a product to another person as a gift and in doing so actually end up transferring meaningful properties from the product to that person through exchange ritual. This is because you may choose a gift (e.g. a beautiful dress) because it possesses certain meaningful

Name of ritual	Examples	Purpose of ritual
Exchange rituals	Gift giving at Christmas, Mother's Day, Father's Day, Valentine's Day, birthdays, weddings, etc.	Consumers to insinuate certain symbolic properties into the lives of gift recipients
Possession rituals	Time and energy spent on cleaning, discussing, reflecting, showing off, photographing cherished belongings such as a new car or a new house	Consumers extract the meaningful properties invested in consumer good out and transfer them to their own lives; allows consumers to claim ownership of newly acquired product and associated meanings
Grooming rituals	Time and energy spent in preparing oneself for public scrutiny on occasions such as going out	Consumers manage to exalt meaningful properties that exist in clothing, hairstyles, looks, etc., into their own lives
Divestment rituals	Cleaning and redecorating a newly bought house; disposing of a product (e.g. selling or giving away as charity)	Consumers can erase the meaning associated with previous owners; prior to disposal, consumers aspire to remove special meaning associated with an item that they have owned themselves

Table 8.1: Rituals as instruments of meaning transfer

properties (e.g. young, attractive) that you wish to see transferred to the recipient (e.g. by wearing the dress, the person finds herself to be young and attractive). Hence, as a gift giver, you end up acting as the agent of meaning transfer to the extent that you selectively distribute your gift with specific properties to the recipient who may or may not have chosen them otherwise. Citing Furby (1978), McCracken (1986) argues that many of the parental gifts to their children are motivated by a similarly notion, because such gifts contain symbolic properties that the parents would have their children absorb.

Moreover, possession rituals can also act as instruments of meaning transfer. For instance, we often spend quite a bit of our time in cleaning, discussing, comparing, reflecting, showing off and even personalizing our possessions. Through the use of such possession rituals, we manage to extract the meaningful properties that have been invested in the consumer good and transfer them to our own lives. In doing so, we take possession of the meaning of a consumer good and declare possessions to be our own. Other examples of instruments of meaning transfer include grooming rituals whereby consumers spend time and energy in grooming themselves for an occasion (e.g. going out on Friday night) or groom an object (e.g. personalizing an automobile).

The glamorous, exalted, meaningful properties that exist in consumer goods such as clothes, hairstyles and looks are transferred into the lives of consumers through grooming rituals and hence consumers acquire new powers of confidence, aggression, defense and feelings of achievement. Finally, divestment rituals act as instruments of meaning transfer in two ways. Firstly, when you buy a product previously owned by someone else (e.g. a house), you may engage in divestment rituals (e.g. cleaning, painting, redecorating) to erase the meaning associated with the previous owner freeing up the house from previous properties with a view to add meanings of your own. Secondly, when you dispose of a product (e.g. sell in a car-boot sale or give away in a charity), you may engage in divestment rituals making sure that some of the meaning attached with the object is removed prior to disposal.

Shared Consumption Rituals

In order to reflect many of our everyday as well as extraordinary experiences, Rook (1985:252) defined a ritual as: a type of expressive, symbolic activity constructed of multiple behaviours that occur in a fixed, episodic sequence, and that tend to be repeated over time.

Important features of a shared consumption ritual could include scripted behaviour, the use of artefacts, a serious and intense atmosphere, an audience, evocative and stylized staging, a community of believing participants and the symbolic meanings of actions (Gainer, 1995). Rituals involve a variety of social and psychological processes, which perform many individual and societal functions (Werner et al. 1988).

A significant underlying feature of a ritual is that it can be *public* or *shared* with others in some ways (Gainer, 1995). Although they look simple, shared consumption rituals link us to our physical, temporal, social and cultural environments. For instance, when we observe rituals associated with many of our communal events (e.g. communal feasts, weddings), we find that these events and their rituals convey a sense of collective identity, which mainly exists in the context of these events. An important function of these events is 'to instill and to celebrate a sense of group cohesiveness' (Werner et al., 1988:205). Such events draw us into groups, whereby our participation can be both a privilege and an obligation. Wallendorf and Arnould's (1991) study of Thanksgiving in the USA identified several behavioural patterns, including following prescribed rules of food preparation, fasting or eating very little prior to the meal, consuming abundant amounts of food at the meal, and enacting togetherness through storytelling and viewing photographs.

However, we need to bear in mind that a consumer's distinctive personal identity can also be conveyed through rituals associated with communal events such as birthdays, puberty rites and other rites of passage, including death. In these ceremonies, an individual's identity is highlighted through others including family members, friends and kin who also participate. Thus, the purpose of the shared consumption rituals can be to establish the self to one's self and to others.

Therefore, by studying ritualistic consumer behaviours, marketers can gain some really interesting insights into the way consumers view themselves and others around them. For instance, Gainer (1995) investigated how different features of a ritual characterized an art attendance (e.g. live performing arts) and reported three major findings. First, consumers undertook art attendance in order to pursue some interpersonal goals. For instance, while some had the desire to attend with others to socialize with them, others also wanted to express 'an image of themselves as sensitive and intellectual individuals' (p. 255). Second, consumers undertook art

attendance in order to build bridges to socially distant acquaintances. For instance, by attending the art performances, consumers had the opportunity to build and strengthen close ties and develop a sense of attachment with other people (such as work acquaintances and neighbours). Third, consumers undertook art attendance in order to manage individual and community identities. For instance, art attendance gave participants an opportunity 'to make the transition from one small world of connected individuals to another' (Gainer, 1995:257).

Using Goffman's (1959) notion of public behaviour as a performance and Turner's (1969, 1984) notion of social drama, Gainer (1995) conceptualized rituals of art performance as a social performance whereby symbolic meanings involving both the actors and the observers were communicated and confirmed. This allowed Gainer to go beyond the apparent meaning of the staged performance to individual consumers and to examine the art attendance as the provision of a venue whereby consumers established and maintained their membership in a small social world by communicating and sharing their values with others. Gainer went further and viewed art attendance as rituals of reproduction (Cheal, 1989) in which 'individuals in a dislocated and impersonalized post-industrial world participate in order to establish and maintain the bonds of a particular small world' (Gainer, 1995:254). That is, art attendance, in Gainer's view, served the function of constructing the relationships of a future social life in a specific small world. Other studies such as those by Errington (1987, 1990) reinforce the view that in shared consumption rituals, the self is established symbolically, not only through material objects, but also in terms of social connections to others (Gainer, 1995). The social connections are becoming quite explicit nowadays as an increasing number of people are joined together by strong emotional bonds such as the sharing of same tastes, habits, intellectual pursuits or participating in events like animal rights protests or anti-capitalism campaigns (Maffesoli, 1996).

VALUES

In Chapter 1, we explored consumer values in the context of what motivates consumers to buy as they do; and in Chapter 6, consumer lifestyles were shown to reflect (at least in part) the values that consumers hold. As we have seen (Chapter 1), Western values are characterized by 'separatedness' in the sense of people being relatively independent and individualistic. The individualistic Harley Davidson strapline reflects this, as does the other example in Figure 8.2. Non-Western cultures are more 'connected' (interdependent and collective) than Western ones.

Individualistic cultures (e.g. UK) tend to hold an independent view of the self, which emphasizes separateness, internal attributes and uniqueness of individuals. However, collectivist cultures (e.g. Japan) tend to hold an interdependent view of the self that stresses connectedness, social context and relationships. Both cultures have different time orientations. For instance, within an individualistic culture, time is viewed as a past/present continuum whereby it can be experienced and used in a linear way. Here time is also regarded as a tangible commodity, which can be spent, saved, wasted and lost.

In other words, time is prioritized in such a way that the relative importance of promptness of schedules is greater than the relative importance of social relationships. On the other hand, within a collectivist culture, time is treated as less tangible and more as a way of building relationships with others. Time is non-linear here (e.g. time is structured according to the seasons of the year, which come back every year) and relates to social processes and to conceptualization of the ordering of social life.

Connectedness–separatedness, or collectivism–individualism, is one continuum developed by Hofstede (1980) who also identified other values-related cultural constructs such as:

• Power distance: for example, the relatively informal culture of many Western societies compared with a more structured set of interpersonal relationships in some Asian societies.

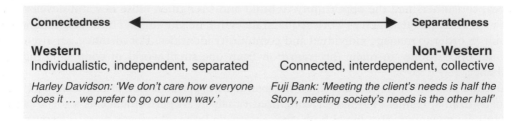

Figure 8.2: Social values continuum

- Uncertainty avoidance: the extent to which ambiguity is overcome by belief structures and societal institutions, for example organized religion and how significant an element of that society is.
- Long-term orientation: also termed 'Confucian dynamism' reflects the importance a society attaches to perseverance and values associated with preparing for and shaping the future, as opposed to a short-term, living-for-today orientation. In theory at least, the former should be more conducive to relationship marketing than the alternative short-term, profit-seeking cultures.
- Masculinity vs. femininity: this concerns the degree of assertiveness, doing and acquiring in societies such as the USA compared with more nurturing and thinking cultures such as some Asian societies. It also relates to sex roles in society. In some societies the role of women is to be the child bearer and housewife. Singer Sewing Machines, for example, decided that in order to be successful in some Middle Eastern countries some years ago, they could not target women, so they appealed to men, with the message that the sewing machine would make their wives more efficient.

THINKBOX

It is interesting to reflect on Hofstede's framework in the light of research conducted to evaluate its applicability. For example, research conducted by Pressey and Selasse (2003) reports aspects of culture as being less important in buyer–seller relationships than perhaps expected. The study used face-to-face interviews with senior import and export managers and a postal questionnaire distributed in 11 countries.

Do you think Hofstede's cultural dimensions can influence buyer–seller relationships in a business-to-business context? If yes, how and in what sense can culture have an impact? What is the best method to find out the impact of culture on buyer–seller relationships?

CULTURAL DIFFERENCES AND SIMILARITIES

On the one hand there is the proposition that due to the recent developments in technology and consumer tastes, a global market for global brands has emerged. Levitt (1983) argued that technology was a significantly powerful force that drove the world towards a converging commonality as consumers across the world wanted all of the brands that they had heard about, seen or experienced via the new technologies (e.g. the Internet, cable TV). The main argument was that the world's needs and desires were becoming 'homogenized' and that the entire world could be treated as one large marketplace. Organizations could create competitive advantage by benefiting from huge economies of scale in production, distribution, marketing and management, and translating these benefits into reduced world prices. Where consumers are seen to act in a relatively homogenous way in the consumption context, marketers have attempted to globalize the marketing mix as much as possible by standardizing products, promotion campaigns, brands, prices and distribution channels for all markets. The economic and competitive pay-offs for global marketing strategies are certainly great. Brand name, product characteristics, packaging and labeling are among the easiest marketing mix variables to standardize; media allocation, marketing communications, retail outlets and price may be more difficult. In the end, the degree of similarity among the various environmental and market conditions determines the feasibility of globalization for global marketers, or standardization for international marketers.

	UK		Rep. of Ireland		France		Italy	
	'81	'90	'81	'90	'81	'90	'81	'90
Confidence in:								
Companies	48	46	49	51	42	60	33	62
Press	29	13	44	36	31	37	31	40
More important:								
Freedom	69	63	46	45	54	48	43	42
Equality	23	31	38	52	32	42	45	44
Happy	38	38	39	43	19	25	10	16
Proud to be	55	52	66	76	33	32	41	41

Adapted by the authors from Heald (1982, 1993).

Table 8.2: Different perspectives in different countries, 1981 and 1990

Many, however, argue that there are important language and cultural differences (e.g. traditions, norms, customs, habits, attitudes and perceptions differ across cultural groups) across the globe. For instance, consumers in the Middle East and some parts of Asia use clean hands while eating whereas the Europeans tend to emphasize the use of knife and fork and other table manners. Still in other places (e.g. China), consumers tend to use chopsticks whereas in places such as India communal eating is common with the use of a common plate for eating by everyone. Moreover, cultural differences are also evident by looking at food choices: beef is avoided by Hindus whereas Muslims avoid eating pork; French would eat horse whereas such an idea would disgust some in the UK where horses, dogs and cats are treated as pets.

Given cultural differences, it is not surprising that many suggest using a customized approach. In international marketing, customization refers to products and marketing activities being modified according to cultural, regional and national differences. Table 8.2 reflects some attitudinal differences between nations according to an international Gallup survey (Heald, 1982, 1993). The survey revealed different attitudes in different countries to such issues as:

• confidence in companies and the press in each country;
• pride in being a national of each country; and
• whether freedom or equality were seen to be more important to the inhabitants.

The relevance of this is that marketers need to understand the frame of reference (Chapter 2) of the people in the countries they intend to target. The style of communications messages must acknowledge that people can hold different views. Even in the retail environment, some believe that recognizing local perceptions is important: 'labels in different fonts, staff dressed completely differently, even a different sort of fascia can have an effect' (Godliman, 2007). But doubts have been expressed over some American retailers' recognition of local markets (Gorman, 2007). The old joke about US and UK separated by a common language reflects only the tip of the problem: 'the management back in the States often doesn't acknowledge the degree of difference between there and the UK. They assume the rest of the world is like us until you tell us they're not.' (Stewart-Allen, 2007). This is a statement by the American founder of International Marketing Partners. This position appears to differ from some European companies' international marketing strategies: 'Zara is very careful when it goes into new markets and perfectly attunes itself to the local market' (Saunders, 2007).

This leads us to a popular marketing phrase: 'think global, act local' and it serves to reinforce the importance of not ignoring local culture. For example, a recent HSBC TV commercial includes an example from Thailand where feet should not be exposed.

This was included in Winick's 1961 study of cultural taboos. Nonetheless, it should be remembered that there are degrees of both customization and globalization. Neither strategy is implemented in its pure form. The debate will doubtless continue over which products can be fully globalised. For some products – such as soft drinks – a global marketing strategy, including advertising, seems to work well; while for other products – such as beer – strategies must accommodate local, regional, religious and national differences.

When a new product is developed, most companies will attempt to make it a global product with a common name and position. The pressure for standardization is particularly strong in Europe, where there is now considerable media overlap and fewer distinct distribution systems. However, a more difficult issue is whether or not to create a global brand when regional brands are in place.

Source: HSBC

When a brand is already established in a country, for example, it commands high awareness levels and will often have developed a set of associations that can be very valuable. Changing the name and/or position in order to simply conform to a standardized global brand may be extremely costly. The effort to change the Datsun name to the global brand Nissan in the United States in the early 1980s probably cost more than $1 billion. Five years after the name change, the Datsun name was still as strong as the Nissan name.

A new name also kills any associations that the old name might have developed. Heinz does not put its name on the products it acquires outside the United States because it wants to retain their associations.

EXAMPLE 8.2

Many international marketing blunders occur because of a failure on the part of marketers to understand the language and cultural differences in values, traditions, customs and norms. Even when the markets are apparently similar (e.g. the USA and the UK), there can be cultural differences that can influence the way the message is received and interpreted by consumers. For example, Caillat and Mueller (1996) compared cultural variables reflected in beer advertising messages developed in the USA and the UK. Findings revealed that different cultural values were represented differently in the two countries. While the US advertisements perpetuated values such as achievement, independence, modernity and newness, the UK ads perpetuated values such as tradition and history. Similarly, while the UK sample used *humour appeals* almost exclusively (89.5%), the US sample relied on *emotional* and *sex appeals* (78.9%). The two samples also differed in the way alcohol consumption was depicted through the advertising. UK advertisements more often presented characters drinking beer on ordinary occasions. However, the US ads tended to show characters drinking beer during special occasions or even tended to avoid representing the product being consumed at all. This suggested a difference in cultural attitudes towards drinking; the UK being more liberal and the USA being more conservative. Their research concluded that a standardized approach for the two countries was not appropriate because of differences in cross-cultural values.

In France, McDonald's has softened its American face, as Gravier, the McDonald's Vice President, France states, it is now 'less flashy...a cosy place with nice warm colours with free wireless where you might like to stay for an hour' (Gravier, 2008). The food also includes local cheeses and other French friendly products and the burger has even been localized: 'it's not a gourmet burger, but it's a big slice of beef with an old fashioned mustard sauce' (Gravier, 2008).

www.   **Have a look at the following web site, which provides more examples of such branding strategies:**
www.heinz.com

THINKBOX

If an existing name has weak associations, of course, it has little to lose by changing. In the late 1980s in the US market, Mars successfully changed the name of its Kal Kan dog food to 'Pedigree' and its Kal Kan cat food to 'Whiskas' to create worldwide names. In contrast to Kal Kan, which was mainly associated with cans, the name 'Pedigree' was associated with a quality, expensive pet that would only be served the best food, and the name 'Whiskas' was feline-sounding and likeable. Some brands are positioned quite differently in different countries. Clearly, it would be foolish to force a common position on such brands in order to achieve a standardized global brand.

You can probably think of a number of other brand names that have changed in recent years to reflect greater standardization across countries (Marathon chocolate bars became Snickers, Oil of Ulay cosmetics became Oil of Olay, Jif became Cif, etc.).

Did these name changes work for you and how do you think the name changes worked in different countries?

Table 8.3 shows the paradox of often needing to be relatively standardized across cultures because of high costs of new product development and at the same time the need to respond to more local differences in taste.

THINKBOX

For each of the following, consider the arguments for and against a standardized marketing approach across countries:
Cars
Beer
Fast food
Lingerie
Credit cards

	Japan	Poland	USA	Holland
Appearance	****	**	****	***
Interior	*****	****	*	****
Handling	***	****	*	***
Comfort	*****	****	***	**

Car clinics in different countries, product testing a new car (the more *'s the more that country, on average, likes the relevant dimension of the car being evaluated)
Implications for world cars – satisfy *some* well or *everyone* poorly?

Table 8.3: Standardization vs. customization

Earlier in the chapter we referred to Johnson's classification of the essential elements of culture. These included *signs, signals* and *symbols*. Examples of these are shown in Table 8.4.

Society	Symbol	Meaning
Iran	Blue	Funeral/mourning
Japan	White	Funeral/mourning
Latin America	Purple	Death

Table 8.4: Signs and symbols

EXAMPLE 8.3

- 'Come alive, you are in the Pepsi generation' – means 'Come alive out of the grave' (in Germany) and 'Pepsi brings your ancestors back from the grave' (in China).
  - Chevy Nova – in Spain means 'Doesn't go'.
  - Esso – phonetically the name means 'stalled car' in Japan.
  - Kellogg's Bran Buds – 'burned farmer' in Sweden.
  - A Chinese brand, 'Pansy', did not do well in the USA (it was a brand of men's underwear).
  - 'Fanny fish' and 'Krapp toilet paper' might be greeted with a different reaction outside their countries and so might 'Bonka coffee' outside Spain – actually there were three variations of Bonka!

This is your opportunity! You probably know of some examples of global marketing that ignore local culture, including language.
- Mitsubishi came under attack for naming one of their car models 'Pejero', which has been interpreted as 'wanker' in Spain.
- An old brand of throat lozenge (Zube) in the UK was promoted using the strap line ' suck a Zube'. But when it was promoted in the Arab Emirates, a poster depicting a horse modified the line to 'Feeling horse, go suck a Zube'. Unfortunately the company had not checked that Zube was one of many words in Arabic for penis.

Over to you: your favourite humorous and downright unacceptable blunders. . .

EXAMPLE 8.4

MarketingWeek

Climate Change Hits US Retail

US retailers are battling tough times in the UK, with clothes chain Gap poised to axe stores, and bookseller Borders likely to pull out of Britain to concentrate on its home business.

US grocery giant Wal-Mart was tipped to trail a blaze with its purchase of Asda in 1999, but has so far failed to ignite, while Toys 'R' Us is said to have fallen off the radar for many British consumers.

Setting up shop in rip-off Britain has caught out many US retailers. In the US, land is plentiful and rents are cheap. By contrast, square footage rates for prime sites in Britain can be notoriously high and stores have to maintain a consistently high footfall in order to pay their way.

Neil Saunders, consulting director at research company Verdict, says US retailers often wrongly price their UK merchandise. Clothes retailer Abercrombie & Fitch made headlines earlier this year when its first UK Store in London priced items at the same numeric amount as in the US, and it barred UK customers from comparing prices on its US website. The effect is a doubling of price.

Saunders says: ''There's a perception that you can change the dollar sign for a pound sign and get away with it.''

He says this does not work, especially in the clothing market, which has become extremely price sensitive. Spanish retailers, such as Zara, Mango and Sweden's Hennes & Mauritz (H&M) have moved into Britain, turning the high street into a battleground for retailers. Customers are increasingly expecting fast fashion at low prices as the norm.

Clothing store Brooks Brothers has been an established name in the US since 1818 and claims to be the country's oldest clothing retailer. In the past year it has opened two stores in London in a ''cookie cutter'' model of its format at home. It is known as a high street staple in the US, but plans to become a premium retailer in the UK, despite offering little different from its stores in the US.

Historical Viewpoint

Saunders warns it is hard to ask someone to pay a premium price without having the heritage of the brand to back it up. ''Brooks Brothers has a history in the US. The company has a very strong brand with a long heritage. In the UK, many haven't heard of it,'' he says.

Earlier this year, Borders reported its overseas operations had posted losses of more than £250,000. The group's international division represents 16% of sales, 70% of which comes from the 72 Borders and Books Etc stores in the UK and Ireland. Despite the disappointing performance, the whole UK bookselling market has been subjected to a malaise in the face of competition from online retailers and supermarkets.

Toys 'R' Us, the toy retailer, has also failed to set the market alight. Last year, its US division reported comparable store sales had increased just 0.6%, while the international division only managed to increase sales by 2.6% across its 678 overseas stores. The out-of-town retailer had ambitions, in the 1990s, to roll out a network of high street stores across Britain, but had to backtrack after the stores failed to make an impact.

Both of these so-called "category killers", who planned to destroy the competition with massive stores, are suffering the effects of the ultimate threat to physical stores – the internet. But, to ensure success abroad, adapting to the local market is imperative, according to Mike Godliman, director and retail consultant at Pragma Consulting. "Labels in a different font, staff dressed differently, even a different sort of fascia can have an effect," he says.

One US retailer to do well is TK Maxx (the discount retailer selling premium lines) because it is unique, knows its proposition in the UK and has adapted itself accordingly. It is also understood that office supplies giant Staples has not suffered in a similar way to its fellow Americans.

Gap's 1987 UK launch was expected to herald a wider US invasion. It quickly grew to become a cornerstone of the British high street. It now has 171 UK stores, but has struggled in recent years at home and abroad. In May, it reported its first quarter profits fell 26%. Where the company was once something of a novelty, critics say it has failed to respond to competition from European retailers.

In the past 18 months, Gap has completely overhauled its strategy abroad. Its European spokeswoman, Anita Borzyszkowska, says the company had historically operated a global strategy and collections and distribution were carried out centrally from the US. The company is reported to be reviewing its UK store portfolio to make possible cuts, but Borzyszkowska insists the company is continually looking at its portfolio.

The company now has a design and distribution team based in London working on a fairly autonomous basis. This autumn/winter, Gap's European stores will have all adult clothes designed in Europe. "We realised that customers in different markets have different needs," Borzyszkowska says.

European retailers are more comfortable localising their offer to different markets and making use of local management, according to Saunders. "Zara is very careful when it goes into new markets and perfectly attunes itself to the local market," he says. "There's a tendency with US companies to import the format into the UK without tweaking it. There's this view that because we speak the same language and are similar in other ways, we're all the same; but of course we're not."

State of Independence

Allyson Stewart-Allen, founder of International Marketing Partners, agrees. She is an American who has worked in Europe for more than 20 years and advises US and EU companies. She says: "The management back in the States often doesn't acknowledge the degree of difference between there and the UK. They assume the rest of the world is like us until you tell us you're not." Another retailing expert says: "Americans can struggle to adapt. Europeans tend to be more global in outlook."

Whole Foods Market, the supermarket group selling organic and natural foods, has just hit our shores to mixed reviews. From a vast store in Kensington, the retailer will be hoping to lure custom away from the likes of Marks & Spencer and Waitrose, which are leading the march in the race to be "green".

The shop has been panned by some for its layout and location. One expert questions whether the company has done its homework. The vast emporium has been criticised as a step too far from a British supermarket format. And the lack of parking at its central London location makes it unsuitable for a family to carry out a weekly shop. Both are factors that show little understanding of the UK market, one retail expert says.

After Gap entered the UK market, many experts predicted an explosion of US retailers setting up shop. There was speculation in the early 1990s that other category-killers, such as Home Depot, would enter the DIY market. However, the explosion never happened.

In Early 2008, Gap is launching its first Banana Republic store in the UK. As the clothes being stocked will be exactly the same as those found in its US stores, it remains to be seen whether the company has really learnt any lessons from its older cousin.

Marketing Week, 5th July 2007, p. 24–25. Reproduced with permission of Centaur Media Ltd.

USE OF HUMOUR

Since consumers are bombarded with so many commercial messages (we call this 'clutter'), many marketers use humour as a way of getting attention. Use of humour can be particularly effective when it comes to products that we buy on a fairly regular and repeated basis and so do not allocate much of our mental energies to evaluating information before making a purchase. As many of us enjoy watching humorous advertisements, it is possible that we may develop a liking for the advertisement and/or for the advertised brand. Research on comparing television advertising in the USA and the UK reveal that advertisers in the UK rely more on humorous advertisements than their counterparts in the USA (Weinberger and Spotts, 1989).

Humour involves the generation of some pleasurable feelings that can be triggered by the experiencing of some forbidden feelings, violating some uniform social standards or the social context in which it occurs (Spotts *et al.*, 1997).While humour is very effective in drawing consumers' attention and improving the likeability of the message, it may not always be effective in increasing the probability that the message will be properly understood and comprehended by consumers.

When it comes to conveying humour in different countries, marketers need to be careful in choosing the themes, situations and settings. In a cross-national study of TV ads in Germany, Thailand, South Korea and the United States, Alden *et al.* (1993) found that a substantial number of humorous advertisements in the four countries appeared to rely on expected/unexpected or possible/impossible contrasts. The study also found that the number of humorous advertisements portraying group-oriented situations (e.g. use of three or more characters) in Korea and Thailand was much higher than the number of similar humorous advertisements found in Germany and USA. This reflects Hofstede's collectivist–individualist dimension as Korea and Thailand are collectivist cultures whereas Germany and the USA are more individualistic cultures. Similarly, the number of humorous advertisements portraying characters of unequal status was much higher in Korea and Thailand than in Germany and the USA. This reflects Hofstede's power distance dimension, as both Thailand and Korea are low on this dimension in comparison with Germany and the USA.

SPANNING CULTURES

Consider the internet. Clearly this can have global reach and indeed everything which the marketer puts on an internet site is accessible from anywhere in the world unless access controls are put in place. Because internet sites can be accessed from anywhere, the law in many countries considers things done on the internet as being within their jurisdiction no matter where the computer hardware is sited. Many countries therefore apply their own laws, not the laws of the country where the computer hardware is or from where the internet communications originate.

Clearly marketers must consider the legality of what they wish to do under the laws of every country, not just their own.

EXAMPLE 8.5

1. Virgin Atlantic Airways maintained a web site, which included details of its trans-Atlantic airfares. The web site described a return airfare of under $500, but when a prospective passenger asked for one of these tickets he was told that this special price was no longer available and the alternative was a ticket costing a little over $500. Under US law the airline was obliged to keep the information up-to-date, and as it had inadvertently failed to do so it ended up paying the US Department of Transport $14 000.

2. The Italian company Tattilo Editrice SpA made erotic pictures available over the internet. The milder pictures were made available to all visitors to the web site, whether or not they had a subscription. More explicit pictures were available to those who wished to subscribe to a special service. Tattilo is an Italian company, based in Italy and both services were made available from computer equipment located in Italy. The domain name (that is the internet address) of the Web site was playmen. Playboy Enterprises Inc – the publisher of *Playboy* magazine – had failed to obtain protection for its Playboy trade mark in Italy in a previous case brought against Tattilo. However, Playboy brought proceedings against Tattilo in the New York courts claiming that Tattilo had infringed Playboy's US registration of the Playboy trade mark by – among other things – its use of the playmen site address because the service was available to US citizens. The court agreed and ordered Tattilo to either refuse subscriptions from US customers or shut down its internet site, even though that site was in Italy. Tattilo was also ordered to pay to Playboy the gross profits it had earned from subscriptions to the service by US customers and all gross profits earned from the sale of goods and services advertised on the playmen site. Interestingly, the court stated that 'Cyberspace is not a safe haven.' Evans *et al.* (2004).

Country of Origin Effects

We normally hear comments that certain products from certain countries are better than others in one way or another. For example, we may hear comments such as 'Japanese cars are more reliable' or 'Belgian chocolates are the best.' These comments represent well developed stereotypical beliefs that consumers have about products that originate from other countries (Hong and Wyer, 1989). Consumers often use the country of origin as an information cue to make inferences about products and their attributes such as quality and reliability. They can treat country of origin as an important  product attribute during product evaluation when more specific information relevant to the product is not readily available (Han and Terpstra, 1988). In this sense, country of origin serves an informational function by providing cues to the consumers regarding product attributes when consumers are unfamiliar with a product (Han and Terpstra, 1988).

Country of origin works as an *image variable*, which influences consumers' perceptions of a brand or a product to the extent that the evaluation of other salient and important attributes is affected (Janda and Rao, 1997). Furthermore, consumers can utilize country of origin as heuristics (these are quick rules of thumb, Chaiken, 1980) as a basis for evaluating products without considering other attribute information.

However, country of origin cues can also relate directly to a consumer's sense of affiliation with a nation or country and can reinforce a sense of national identity (Bruning, 1997). For instance, a less nationalistic and ethnocentric consumer is more likely to prefer a foreign product to domestic substitutes than a more nationalistic and ethnocentric consumer. Ethnocentric consumers have a tendency to feel proud of and attached to products originating from their own culture and a tendency to reject culturally dissimilar products.

SUBCULTURES

Subcultures refer to groups within a society which possess distinctive characteristics. Widely quoted examples include cultural groupings on the basis of geographical region, religion and ethnicity. However, the term subculture can also be used to refer to 'a distinctive subgroup of society that self selects on the basis of a shared commitment to a particular product class, brand, or consumption activity' (Schouten and McAlexander, 1995:43). We can therefore use the term 'subculture' to refer to, for example, the teenage subculture or that of the postmodern consumer and even that of 'tribes' or 'communities' (Chapter 7).

It is important for marketers to study subcultures because consumer behaviour often varies from one to another and some subcultures are based almost entirely on *cultural artifacts*, which are obtained in the marketing system. For example, a three-year ethnographic study of Harley-Davidson motorcycle owners classified them as a 'subculture of consumption' because they appeared to be a distinctive subgroup within the society with a shared commitment to the brand and a visible hierarchical social structure. This subculture also shared a unique set of beliefs and values and used unique jargons and rituals to express their identity (Schouten and McAlexander, 1995). The nearby Think Box will help you understand some of the emerging sub-groupings in our society, such as online communities.

We discussed tribal and postmodern behaviour in Chapter 7 and Generation X and Y in Chapter 5. Here we focus on some of the ethnic minority groups in the UK but first we will look at what is meant by ethnicity and ethnic identity.

THINKBOX

Many of the leading brands host online brand communities through bulletin boards, forums and chat rooms. McWilliam (2000) says that brands which are built around the idea of hosting and building online communities are community brands. An example is the Geocities web site, which is home to millions of community members 'living' in different 'neighbourhoods'. Would you say that the online community is an example of a subculture? Can you think of reasons why consumers join such communities? What are the implications in building strong relationships with consumers and what happens if a consumer in real life feels dissatisfied with a brand and spreads a negative word of mouth via online communities? How can marketers respond to such challenges?

Ethnic Subcultures

THINKBOX

Multiculturalism

British society is in a constant state of demographic and cultural churn – partly the benevolent inheritance of our colonial past and the modern movement of economic migrants into the UK. Around 7.5% of people living in Britain were born abroad. Travel and migration of all kinds are a daily incentive to try new things see different points of view, be aware that a national destiny is shared by a dynamic interaction of origins, faiths and traditions. While some political forces, with varying agendas, resist both multiculturalism and integration, the rest of Britain simply has to live with highly unstable but not necessarily disorienting concepts of 'Britishness'. We like chicken tikka and sushi. Our neighbours are Muslims and Australians. Our sitcoms poke light fun at Asian families who poke fun at indigenous Brits. Our beer and our waiters are Czech. We holiday in Majorca. We do not make jokes about ethnic accents. Our Europe is enlarged. We accommodate new-multiplied-by-old folk memories + practical experiences of the Windrush, Irish emigration, the disapora of the Balkans' poor, talented Brazilian footballers and fabulously wealthy Russian club-owners, Chinese cockle-pickers and Somalian asylum-seekers...multiculturalism is a paraphrase for diversity of all kinds. Gender or sexual inclination, for example, do not dictate either one's own life pattern or the reactions of others to it in the way that they used to. We are free to be different people in different phases. We can morph in and out of options for personal definition. The marketing community cannot assume that 'Britishness' is a stable concept, inhabited by a rounded and immutable national character. Commerically directed appeals to patriotism might well define Britain in a way that makes no sense to millions. Marketing has to be a continuous exercise in studied inclusiveness, one that does not leave aside or inadvertenly exclude any group stakeholding in UK plc.

Courtesy of the Future Foundation, (2008)

There have been immigrant groups in the UK throughout its existence, although these have varied in size and provenance; among the recent arrivals are, for example, South Asians (Indians, Pakistanis and Bangladeshis), Chinese, Black-Caribbean, Irish, Poles, Central European Jews, Cypriots and Turks. Ethnic subcultures as a whole represent the fastest growing segment of the total population and are particularly prominent in certain metropolitan areas (e.g. in half of the London boroughs, by 2011, ethnic 'minorities' will form the 'majority') with significant share in the school age population.

As per the 2001 Census, there were 4.6 million (or 7.9%) people belonging to non-White ethnic groups (see Table 8.5 and Figure 8.3).

We find that *cultural diversity* in the UK is already affecting and shaping many institutions (e.g. the educational institutions have to cope with a multicultural student body and staff) and culinary habits (e.g. the assimilation of a variety of ethnic foods into British cuisine – Jamal, 1996; 2003). You may note that cultural diversity brings many marketing opportunities as marketers can target new segments with suitable products but it also presents some challenges. In order to be successful, marketers need to look at differences in subcultures that drive differences in consumption patterns, responses to advertising and direct marketing efforts, media usage, brand choices and decision-making styles.

	Total population Numbers	Total population Percentages	Non-White population (percentage)
White	54 153 898	92.1	
Mixed	677 117	1.2	14.6
Indian	1 053 411	1.8	22.7
Pakistani	747 285	1.3	16.1
Bangladeshi	283 063	0.5	6.1
Other Asian	247 664	0.4	5.3
All Asian or Asian British	2 331 423	4.0	50.3
Black Carribean	565 876	1.0	12.2
Black African	485 277	0.8	10.5
Black Other	97 585	0.2	2.1
All Black or Black British	1 148 738	2.0	24.8
Chinese	247 403	0.4	5.3
Other Ethnic Groups	230 615	0.4	5.3
All minority ethnic population	4 635 295	100	100
All population	58 789 194	100	

National Statistics Online: http://www.statistics.gov.uk

Table 8.5: UK population by ethnic groups, April 2001

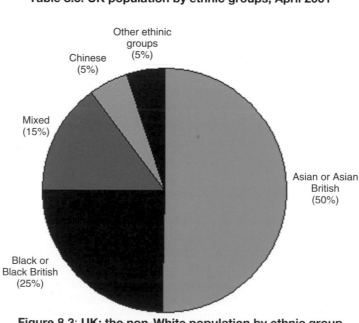

Figure 8.3: **UK: the non-White population by ethnic group**
National Statistics Online: http://www.statistics.gov.uk

Ethnicity and Ethnic Identity

Within the British context we normally use the term 'ethnic' to describe groups of relatively recent immigrants who are perceived to be sufficiently different from the mainstream Anglo-Saxon group.

However, the term could be used to describe any social group (mainstream or minority), irrespective of their cultural and social background. Therefore, a study of an ethnic group does not necessarily mean a study of an ethnic minority group. The term ethnicity implies many dimensions including 'a sense of common customs, language, religion, values, morality, and etiquette' (Webster, 1994:321).

In other words, ethnicity can be viewed as a characteristic of racial group membership on the basis of some commonly shared features. You can also describe ethnicity in terms of biological make-up of consumers and the extent to which genetic factors play their role in conveying aspects of ethnicity including consumption behaviour.

It is important to note that ethnicity exists 'in a context of oppo sitions and relativities' (Tonkin *et al.*, 1989:17). In other words, the basis of ethnicity is self-identification of the members mediated by the perceptions of the others. There are two sets of principles that operate within ethnicity: the inclusionary–exclusionary principle and the difference–identity principle. By excluding, one establishes difference. By including, one establishes identity. Both are, therefore, closely related (Venkatesh, 1995:33; emboldening added).

Hence what we are allows us to understand what we are not. That is why an increasing number of consumer researchers draw our attention to the fact that *intercultural contact* and the way we adapt and respond to other cultural groups can be a defining feature of a society. Ethnicity can be best understood by exploring the ways in which consumers interact with one another and with other important players in the society, such as marketers and businesses (Penaloza and Gilly, 1999).

We can also get a better understanding of ethnicity by 'looking at situations in which groups or group members present themselves to, and interact with, other groups and the outside society' (Costa and Bamossy, 1995:9). In a study involving two ethnic subcultures – English Canadians and French Canadians in Montreal – Laroche *et al.* (2003) reported that English Canadians demonstrated more positive perceptions towards the UK and its products than did the French Canadians. Similarly, French Canadians demonstrated more positive perceptions towards France and its products than did the English Canadians. This shows that consumers' subcultures and their perceptions of cultural similarity with other countries can influence their attitudes towards them (Laroche *et al.*, 2003).

You may note that the terms 'ethnicity' and 'ethnic identity' are often used interchangeably. This is because ethnicity can also be defined as a process of self-identification whereby individuals define themselves and others into specific groups using ethnic labels (Rossiter and Chan, 1998). At the individual level, the process of self-identification or ethnic identity is part of one's self-concept which is based on knowledge of membership in a social group(s) together with emotional significance and value that is attached to that membership (Tajfel, 1981). This discussion links up with our discussion of self in Chapter 6. You can say that a person's ethnic identity involves their sense of belonging to a group, as well as the feelings and thoughts that go with being part of that group. In this sense, ethnic identity could be viewed as a complex psychological process that involves perceptions, cognition, affect and knowledge structures about how a person thinks and feels about themselves and others in the society (Cuellar *et al.*, 1997; Tajfel, 1981).

The processes of thinking and feeling could play an important role in the lives of ethnic minority consumers. For instance, in an ethnographic study of British-Pakistanis in Bradford, Jamal and Chapman (2000) reported the coexistence of both positive and negative perceptions among the participants towards their own group as well as towards the mainstream society. These perceptions were important because they guided their thoughts and actions in terms of developing a sense of who they were, and who they were not. The perceptions also informed their consumer decision-making processes regarding which products to buy, where to buy and on what basis to buy. The nearby Think Box will help you comprehend the notion of situational, multiple but often coexisting identities.

THINKBOX

Bouchet (1995) argues that ethnicity is like a bricolage whereby one builds self-identity on the basis of heterogeneous elements taken from a diversity of *cultural representations* and practices. Oswald (1999) provided empirical evidence to support the coexistence of consumers' mixed emotions and their implications for ethnicity and ethnic identity, arguing that 'in consumer culture, ethnicity can be bought, sold and worn like a loose garment' (p 304). Stayman and Deshpande (1989) made a related argument by suggesting that ethnicity is not just about one's identification with a particular ethnic group but also about how strongly one identifies with that group in a particular situation. According to them, 'ethnicity is not just who one is, but how one feels in and about a particular situation' (p 361). They argued that social situation and one's perception of that situation influenced their felt ethnic identity. They concluded that persons in multicultural societies were likely to have a set of ethnic and other identities that might be differentially salient. In other words, they are expected to have multiple selves whereby they act differently in different situations and with different individuals (see also Markus and Kunda, 1986; Markus and Nurius, 1986).

On the basis of this, Donthu and Cherian (1994) cited the example of some Hispanics in the USA who behaved very much like the mainstream population all year round except while celebrating Cindo de Mayo or while visiting a Hispanic restaurant with family and friends. Similarly, Jamal (2003) argued that consumers not only feel a stable sense of identity but also a fluid sense of identity whereby they can play with different images of themselves. The discussion implies that one can experience or feel multiple and coexisting identities that can inform one's buying behaviours in different contexts and locations (Jamal and Chapman, 2000).

As a consumer, have you ever felt a sense of multiple identities in different situations?

As a marketer, what role can you play in facilitating the coexistence of a variety of modes of consumption and a sense of being?

Figures published by the National Statistics Online support our view that many of the non-White people in the UK describe themselves as British even though there are strong indications that they maintain their own cultural identifies while at home (Figure 8.4).

Ethnicity and Acculturation

Initially social researchers expected immigrants (mostly in North America, particularly in the USA) to abandon their own *cultural heritage* and conform to what was dominant in America at the time of their arrival there. It was assumed that over a period of time, immigrants would blend into a national whole (like a melting pot) and abandon their distinctive cultural features. However, a quick glance at many Western societies suggests that ethnic subcultures do not abandon their cultural features. Rather they

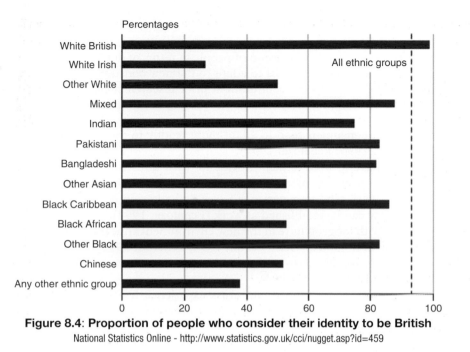

Figure 8.4: **Proportion of people who consider their identity to be British**
National Statistics Online - http://www.statistics.gov.uk/cci/nugget.asp?id=459

recreate their own small cultural worlds in their own ways (like a salad bowl where ingredients can coexist with one another). Therefore, consumer researchers now use the term acculturation to describe changes in consumer behaviours of ethnic subcultures.

Acculturation refers to the 'phenomena which result when groups of individuals having different cultures come into continuous first hand contact, with subsequent changes in the original culture patterns of either or both groups' (Redfield *et al.*, 1936, cited in Berry, 1980:9). Another way of looking at acculturation is to say that it is 'the general process of movement and adaptation to the cultural environment in one country by persons from another country' (Penaloza, 1994:33). An implicit assumption here is that the immigrant consumers can maintain some aspects of their original cultural values and traditions in addition to moving towards the culture of the host society.

In terms of acculturation, Berry (1980) raised two important questions. First, to what extent does an individual or a group have a sense of identification with their culture of origin; in other words, does an individual or a group feel it important to retain identification with the culture of origin? Second, to what extent does the individual or group want to have positive relations with the dominant society? On the basis of this, Berry (1980) identified four possible varieties of acculturation.

The first one is called assimilation, which refers to the situation where an immigrant consumer or group relinquishes their cultural identity over time and moves into the larger society. The second one is called integration, which refers to a situation when an immigrant consumer or group not only maintains their original cultural integrity but also makes a move to become an integral part of a larger societal framework. The third one is named as rejection, which refers to a situation where an immigrant consumer or group rejects the mainstream society while maintaining identity with the culture of origin. And the fourth is called deculturation, where an immigrant consumer or group rejects movement into the mainstream society as well as any identification with the culture of origin.

In an ethnographic study of Mexican immigrants in the USA, Penaloza (1994) identified a model of acculturation which appears to be applicable to most immigrant consumers in the Western context. Hence, in the following section, we discuss the key components of this model while keeping in mind the vast amount of research conducted on ethnic minority consumer behaviour.

Individual Differences

Immigrant consumers tend to be a diverse group of people in terms of demographic and other differences and hence they tend to have differential skills to adapt to the new consumer environment in the country of destination. For instance, in terms of acculturation, prior research suggests that the following factors can be very important in determining the pace and direction of acculturation:

- **Age**: younger immigrant consumers tend to adapt more readily to the new consumer culture than do older ones (Gentry *et al.*, 1995; Penaloza, 1994).
- **Gender**: Females may have to work to help provide for their households; this can lead to role tension for men and women accustomed to men being the sole provider for the household (Penaloza, 1994).
- **Work status**: those in work tend to experience fewer difficulties in adopting to new culture as more contacts with host society can be established at work (Penaloza, 1994).
- **Length of stay**: Those with longer tenure in the new environment appear to have less difficulty adapting than those who recently immigrated (Gentry *et al.*, 1995; Penaloza 1994).
- **Social class**: those with middle-class backgrounds appear to have an advantage over those with working-class backgrounds (Penaloza, 1994).
- **Urban/rural background**: those from urban areas experience fewer difficulties than do their rural counterparts as they normally inhabit a consumption environment similar to the one in the new culture (Jamal, 1997; Penaloza, 1994).
- **Sense of ethnic identity**: those with a strong sense of ethnic identification are more likely to recreate their own culture than those who care less about their ethnic origin (Cuellar *et al.*, 1997; Gentry *et al.*, 1995).
- **Degree of similarity between cultures/nations**: those immigrating from a collective culture may find it difficult when it comes to adjusting to the demands of an individualistic culture and society (Berry, 1997; Gentry *et al.*, 1995; Triandis, 1997).
- **Attitudes of local society**: this together with the state policies can have an impact on acculturation strategies adopted by immigrant consumers (Bourhis *et al.*, 1997).
- **Exposure to the host and ethnic media** can also impact acculturation strategies adopted by immigrants (Lee and Tse, 1994).

Acculturation Agents

We discussed the role of family and other reference groups in Chapter 7. For immigrant consumers, there are two sets of institutions that can act as important sources of group and personal influences. The first one includes family, friends and media, and commercial, educational and religious institutions back home. The second one includes family, friends and media, and commercial, educational and religious institutions in the culture of destination (Penaloza, 1994). Both sets of institutions are very important in terms of socializing and consumption behaviour and the extent to which immigrant consumers interact and rely on each set of institutions can significantly inform their modes of living and consumption patterns. Some recent research argues that there could be triple acculturation agents, the third one being the subculture with which one may associate (Wamwara-Mbuga *et al.*, 2008).

Acculturation Processes

Penaloza (1994) reported movement, translation and adaptation to be important acculturation processes. For instance, the acculturation process is often initiated when immigrant consumers move to new cultural environment and there are both push and pull factors (e.g. differences in pay, living conditions, availability of jobs and education for children, etc., in both countries and anticipated earnings and consumption patterns in the new country) which motivate such a movement of people. Moreover, once in the new culture, immigrant consumers go through the process of adaptation to the new cultural environment and in doing so rely on their translation skills in comprehending the complexities of the new culture.

Through the process of learning, the immigrant consumers adapt and adjust to the mainstream cultural environment in the way that they exhibit consumption patterns associated with the mainstream culture, their original culture or a hybrid combination of the two cultures. For example, Jamal and Chapman (2000) found that consumption patterns of British-Pakistanis in Bradford, UK, were a reflection of their Pakistani culture, UK culture and a combination of both. As stated earlier, the extent to which an ethnic minority consumer feels associated with their culture of origin can be an important predictor of some of their consumer behaviour. For instance, Deshpande *et al.* (1986) found that Hispanic-Americans who identified strongly with their culture of origin tended to use Spanish language media heavily, held a positive attitude towards advertising, were brand-loyal and were likely to buy brands advertised to their ethnic group as compared to those who identified weakly with their culture of origin.

One should also expect intergenerational differences when it comes to understanding consumer behaviours of ethnic minority consumers. For instance, Jamal (1997, 1998) reported strong generational differences in shopping orientations of British-Pakistanis who were born and raised in the UK in comparison with those who belonged to the first generation.

Acculturation Outcomes

Assimilation appears to be one possible outcome in the sense that most immigrant consumers assimilate many of the products and services associated with mainstream consumer culture (Jamal, 1997; Penaloza, 1994). However, in addition to assimilating mainstream products and services, many of the immigrant consumers also maintain various aspects of their original culture as reflected in their food, media, clothing, travel, financial and music choices. This obviously creates demand for ethnic products that are typically catered for by ethnic minority owned businesses (Iyer and Shapiro, 1999; Jamal, 2005; Ram, 1994). Moreover, while some immigrant consumers tend to dislike and resist adapting to certain aspects of mainstream consumer culture (e.g. materialism), others tend to segregate in certain rural areas with a view to drawing support from their own communities and recreating a new form of culture that does not resemble either the original or the culture of the host society. For instance, in an ethnographic work involving poor migrant women living in a Turkish squatter, Ustuner and Holt (2007) reported three modes of acculturation: the immigrant consumers reconstituted their village culture in the city, shutting out the dominant ideology; or they collectively pursued the dominant ideology as a myth through ritualized consumption; or they gave up on both pursuits, resulting in a shattered identity project.

It is also interesting to note that immigrant consumers sometime 'over-acculturate' (Wallendorf and Reilly 1983) or develop 'hyperidentification' (Mehta and Belk 1991). For instance, Mehta and Belk (1991) found that Indian immigrants to a number of countries were more traditionally Indian than those left behind in India in various product categories such as music, photographs, furniture, traditional dress, jewellery and religious objects. Moreover, Jamal (1996) cites the examples of British consumers who tend to over-acculturate when it comes to consumption of ethnic foods.

EXAMPLE 8.6

Ethnic identification can be expressed via shopping behaviours. This can be reflected through the choice of specific stores or preference for particular brands. For example, Herche and Balasubramaian (1994) looked into how ethnic minority consumers from different ethnic backgrounds varied in their shopping orientations. Their study involved 6000 respondents belonging to six ethnic minority consumer groups (i.e. Black, Hispanic, Chinese, Japanese, Italian and Korean) in the USA. They found that Black consumers had the highest level of ethnic identification as compared to other ethnic minority groups with respect to their buying attitudes and preferred to buy from Black-owned businesses.

EXAMPLE 8.7

Similarly, the behaviour of ethnic minority consumers can differ from that of their mainstream counterparts. For example, Chudry and Pallister (2002) reported some significant differences in British-Pakistani and native consumers' attitudes towards direct mail. The British-Pakistani group felt positive about the idea of direct mail but took personal involvement in direct mail much less seriously. The group did not want to reveal personal information and desired the direct mail to be accurately targeted and to be engaging. The group also depended much more heavily on advice from family and workmates than its counterpart. Similarly Jamal (1996, 1998) studied the food consumption experiences of British-Pakistani and mainstream consumers in Bradford, UK. His study found that there were significant differences between the food consumption experiences of both groups.

Also, Shim and Gehrt (1996) reported findings in relation to the shopping approaches of Hispanic, White and Native adolescents in the USA. They found that the Hispanic adolescents depicted a greater tendency to the *social/hedonistic shopping orientation* than did the White and Native American adolescents. The White adolescents, on the other hand, manifested a greater tendency toward the *utilitarian approach to shopping* than did Hispanic and Native American adolescents. Hispanic adolescents also manifested a greater tendency towards novelty/fashion consciousness, recreational and brand-loyal orientations as compared to their White and Native American counterparts. Hispanic adolescents were the most likely to interact with parents while making purchase choices. They were also the most likely to enjoy printed media, to be receptive to television advertising, and to believe that school is a good source of consumer education.

Impact of Acculturation

An important feature of acculturation is that it recognizes the fact that the process of cultural change is a reciprocal one because we are talking about contact and interactions among different cultural groups (one being the immigrant group and the other being 'every other' group in the society). Hence, changes can and do happen among any of the groups including the mainstream consumers. To illustrate, consider the case of the popularity of ethnic foods (e.g. Indian, Chinese, Thai and Mexican) both inside and outside the home in the UK where ethnic foods are now a regular part of the weekly shopping of many consumers (Key Note, 2007). The total expenditure on ethnic eating, including restaurants and takeaways, is well over £1 billion per annum and there are thousands of ethnic restaurants across the country suggesting a significant change in the dietary habits of the nation. According to Jamal (1996), such changes happened partly due to frequent cultural encounters between the cultural categories of mainstream population and those of ethnic subcultures and ethnic minority businesses such as restaurants and corner shops. For example, Figure 8.5 illustrates the reciprocal nature of cultural change. The Chinese have a well-established history of migration to the UK and as a consequence of frequent interaction between the

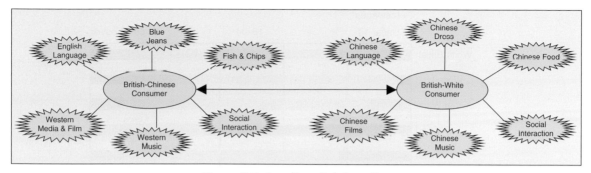

Figure 8.5: Acculturation in action

UK and the Chinese cultural categories there could be changes in preferences for language, dress, food, media, music and friends among both the Chinese immigrants living in the UK and the British-White consumers.

However the impact of acculturation is not limited to a given society or a nation rather the forces of change are acting at a global level. Hence, we find groups of consumers across the globe (e.g. teenagers) adopting and acculturating to different cultural dimensions. The 20th century has witnessed an ever-increasing interdependence and integration throughout the world, giving rise to a florescence of social changes at local, regional, and international levels (Costa and Bamossy, 1995; Penaloza and Gilly, 1999). Global forces of capitalism, global transport, communications, marketing and advertising, and transnational cosmopolitanism have thus interacted to bring forward cultural change and contributed toward the emergence of a homogeneous global consumer culture (Cleveland and Laroche, 2007). Main drivers of acculturation to global consumer culture include cosmopolitanism, exposure to global media and to marketing activities of global firms, increasing preference for the use of English language, social interactions including travel and interactions with foreigners and an openness and desire to adopt different cultural values (Cleveland and Laroche, 2007).

THINKBOX

Think about your family and household consumption. Can you recall your experiences of eating out in an ethnic restaurant? Do you mind or love eating ethnic food like Sushi or a curry? Do you occasionally wear any ethnic dresses? Watch any ethnic films? Listen to any ethnic music? Speak any ethnic language? How about your friends? Do they all belong to the same culture as that of yours? What do you notice about their food, dress, music, lifestyle choices? To what extent are they similar to or different from yours?

The Need for Understanding Ethnic Subcultures in the UK

There are a number of reasons for developing a better understanding of consumer behaviour of ethnic minority consumers in the UK. First, irrespective of the country of origin, the ethnic minority community (as a whole) has been the fastest-growing segment of the total population in the UK (Clegg, 1996; Suzman, 1996) with about 30% of London's population expected to come from the ethnic minorities in 15 years' time (Timmins, 1995). 'Ethnic minorities will make up the majority in half of London's boroughs. The country's ethnic population as a whole is growing by 2.5% annually and is set to double

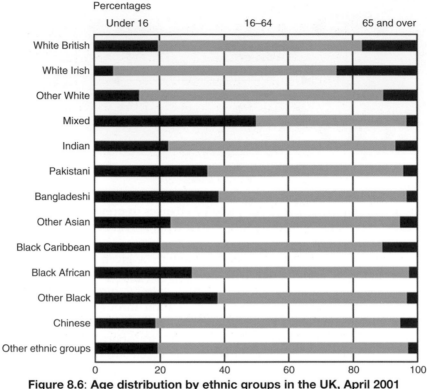

Figure 8.6: **Age distribution by ethnic groups in the UK, April 2001**
National Statistics Online: http://www.statistics.gov.uk/cci/nugget.asp?id=456

over the next 50 years' (Sclater, 2002). For many marketers, the growing number of ethnic minority consumers could soon mean some important market niches to target. However, to target them effectively, marketers need to have a good understanding of the way ethnic minority consumers live and construct their lives in the UK.

www.
Have a look at the following web site:
www.raceforopportunity.org.uk
This provides information on the 'Race for Opportunity' survey conducted in 2002. The survey found that banks and building societies filled six of the top ten private sector organizations in terms of enlightened approaches to ethnic minorities.

Second, marketers are always interested in instilling brand loyalties in their target customers particularly when they are relatively young; children are likely to develop strong brand loyalties over time. As reflected in Figure 8.6, ethnic minority groups tend to have younger age structure than the White British and current media reports suggest that they already enjoy a significant share in the school-age population of many urban areas of the UK (e.g. London, Birmingham, Bradford).

Moreover, media reports also suggest that some of the cleverest children in the UK's schools today are likely to be of ethnic minority origin as they are increasingly outperforming their mainstream counterparts. The view is well supported by figures released by the National Statistics Office Online (Figure 8.7) according to which, in 2004, Chinese pupils were the most likely to achieve five or more GCSE grades A*-C in England, with 79% of Chinese girls and 70% of Chinese boys respectively. Indian pupils had the next highest achievement levels: 72% of Indian girls and 62% of Indian boys achieved these levels.

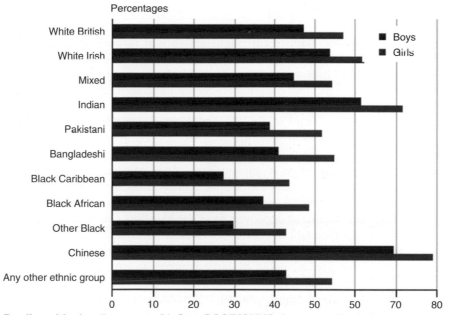

Figure 8.7: Pupils achieving 5 or more A*-C at GCSE/GNVQ: by sex and ethnic group, 2004, England

National Statistics Online: http://www.statistics.gov.uk/cci/nugget.asp?id=461

Figure 8.8: Ethnic minority advertising

© Media Reach Advertising. Reproduced with permission

Third, marketers are also interested in targeting customers that are relatively affluent. In the case of the ethnic minority consumers, positive attitudes towards hard work and family life have led to the creation of many millionaires owning high street brands like Joe Bloggs Clothing, Horne Brothers, Ciro Citterio fashion shops, Colorama, Time computers and Binatone telephones. Furthermore, many of the ethnic minority consumers are self-employed, leading to a stable stream of income.

Fourth, marketers of health products (such as GPs, the NHS and pharmaceutical companies) are strongly interested in exploring the consumption patterns of ethnic minority consumer groups because of their different health patterns as compared to mainstream consumers. For instance, ethnic minority consumer groups from the Indian subcontinent are more likely to have diabetes and coronary heart disease than mainstream consumers.

Targeting Ethnic Subcultures

There is a debate about whether mainstream marketers should target ethnic segments differently or go for 'inclusive marketing'. The latter is exemplified by an advertising campaign by the British Navy (Figure 8.9), featuring people of different racial origins. The idea is not to exclude but rather to attract as many as possible from different ethnic segments. As we have seen, ethnic segments have their own cultures, languages, religions and distinct requirements. It is not always appropriate for them to be targeted with more general products and services by merely changing advertisements for them. Different coloured skin, for example, has different moisture content, and the formulation of cosmetics should be different (as they are in the Revlon range in USA), not merely suggesting how people of different colours can select from existing ranges to arrive at appropriate colour combinations. Revlon and Marks and Spencer do now produce special cosmetics products for ethnic consumers (Sclater, 2002).

There are examples of differentiating product ranges, such as the organic baby food range from Boots the Chemist, which includes halal-approved food for Muslims (according to Islamic law for food preparation) and BT has a multilingual call centre in Leicester (Sclater 2002).

There could be two main effects of not targeting ethnic minority consumers properly. First, the ethnic minority consumers may feel alienated by large companies and their marketing and advertising campaigns, leading to a sense of exclusion from mainstream society (Suzman, 1996). Second, marketers of mainstream brands can miss out on opportunities to take advantage of the £10 billion ethnic minorities spend every year, because of misplaced marketing and advertising drives (Suzman, 1996). However, there are some small businesses that have been very active in identifying and serving the needs of ethnic minority consumers. One can look at their marketing practices because they have been quite successful in establishing a variety of commercial enterprises such as corner shops, grocery stores, cash and carrys, restaurants, takeaways, ethnic supermarkets, food wholesaling, electronics and textiles. Some of these businesses particularly target specific ethnic minority consumer groups; others target both the ethnic minority consumers as well as the mainstream population in the UK. However, what makes them significantly different from mainstream marketers is that they do understand the needs and requirements of ethnic minority consumers.

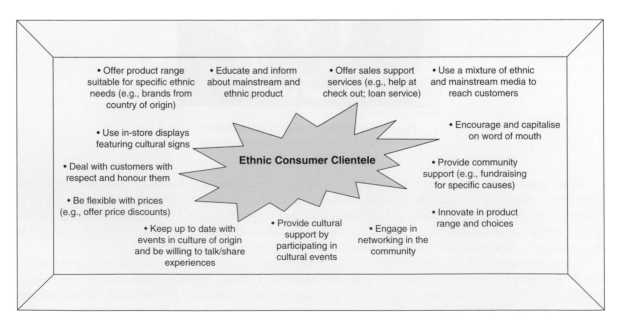

Figure 8.9: Marketing strategies for targeting ethnic minority consumers

For instance, in a recent study of ethnic minority enterprises such as grocery stores, corner shops, mini-supermarkets and restaurants, Jamal (2005) reported that the enterprises successfully adapted their marketing mixes to suit the needs of their co-ethnic consumers. This meant they provided a full range of ethnic as well as non-ethnic products for the needs of their consumers and followed a differential pricing strategy, offering special discounts to opinion leaders and formers in the community. They also promoted themselves not only via traditional media (newspapers, radio) but also via the extensive use of word of mouth advertising and by participating in community events. Others (e.g. Penaloza and Gilly, 1999) have also identified some effective strategies employed by ethnic marketers. Figure 8.10 illustrates the marketing strategies that could be used by marketers in their attempts to market products and services to ethnic clientele.

There are now market research agencies that offer specialized services to research ethnic segments, so the argument of a decade or so ago that they are difficult to research is not as strong as it once was. Indeed the 2001 Census included additional questions about ethnicity and these led to the more accurate identification of the locations and characteristics of ethnic communities in UK (the Census being available for commercial purposes). Also, with the developing **ethnic minority media** it is equally possible to reach ethnic minority segments with marketing messages. There are newspapers, magazines and now, of course, an expanding range of dedicated radio and TV channels (via cable and satellite) which together with the internet not only communicate with ethnic segments in their own language (see Figures 8.9 and 8.11) and using the same frame of reference, but do this interactively. This has changed rapidly, there are now many ethnic media TV channels, commercial radio stations, magazines and web portals. But Sclater (2002) suggests, many ethnic segments don't read, listen or watch the mainstream media, yet many marketers appear slow to run campaigns via the more specialized targeted media now available. Research by Emslie *et al.* (2007) reinforce these issues and add that the lack of market research among ethnic segments is another reason why marketers have not responded as fully as they might. There are some ethnic omnibus surveys but relatively less market research than among the rest of the population.

Figure 8.10: Lynx advertisement

Yes, there are notable exceptions, such as the West Bromwich Building Society's research which led to a mortgage product especially for Muslims (Gray, 2004). It is perhaps disappointing that despite clear progress, all of these issues were also cited over 30 years ago (Piper, 1977).

However, many marketers are reluctant to target ethnic communities. Indeed a research project was proposed (by one of the authors), believing that direct mail campaigns would benefit from understanding ethnic communities' reaction to the medium. Although a number of direct marketing agencies agreed, they stated that they were wary of how the research might be portrayed in 'the media'. The feeling was that it would be taken to be racist.

THINKBOX

Figure 8.11: Communicating with a multiracial society
© Commission for Racial Equality (CRE). Reproduced by permission

If ethnic segments differ in their needs and values, they should be treated differently. But if they are, is that discrimination? Also, is the targeting of ethnic segments in any way racist? The relatively recent increase in migration from Eastern European countries also charges the ethnic and sub cultrual mix in the UK. Explore this issue.

Crossing Cultures

An interesting variation on the analysis so far concerns the behaviour and opinions of those who move from one culture to another – for example, foreign students going to study in another country. For instance, Davies and Fitchett (2003) found some emotional, symbolic and pragmatic issues related to crossing of cultures. *Emotional factors* included loneliness and being unable to feel part of a group.

Symbolic issues included difficulty in understanding and interpreting social rules in the new society, especially in social situations and overcoming communication problems. *Pragmatic issues* included, for example, getting used to public transport, getting used to new food and eating habits, and sorting out personal financial arrangements. Overall a significant majority of their sample reported experiencing 'culture shock'. Less than 2% said that their experiences in the UK matched exactly with expectations held prior to arrival, so marketers need to be aware of the disorientation of culture-crossers. This will especially apply where there are large concentrations of foreign visitors, such as university towns with significant numbers of foreign students.

THINKBOX

If you are from another culture, or know people who are, how is crossing culture 'culture shock' manifested? Could your University town or indeed University itself do more to help overcome this phenomenon?

 Have a look at the following article, which is accessible from the accompanying web site at www.wileyeurope.com/college/evans:
Keillor, D'Amico and Horton (2001) Global Consumer Tendencies, Psychology and Marketing, Vol 18 No 1pp 1–19
This paper provides some evidence to suggest the emergence of a global consumer.

CASE STUDY 8.1

TNS CASE STUDY: The Apache Motorcycle Advertising Campaign in India

Poonam V. Kumar TNS – Asia Pacific & Middle East & Prasad Narasimhan TVS Motor Company India
NB: refer to the Apache case in Chapter 1 for the first instalment.

Liberation – Life, Here I come!

With increasing competition, the dialogue between the consumer and marketer grows in sophistication and the balance of power shifts to the consumer. Marketing then has to shift from push to pull. From selling and product-focused marketing, the market moves to a need for brands that connect with consumer emotion. The Indian two-wheeler market was waiting for brands like Apache that understood this and met more than just the need for great mileage and reliability.

NeedScope, through the use of a needs based model and an archetypal framework, uncovered the needs landscape, identified the market essentials and the discriminating needs. The underlying motivations were validated and quantified in terms of the commercial opportunity offered. Brands were mapped and measured on the same frame of reference and market gaps identified. TNS, a leading global marketing research agency, partnered the client in bringing the segments to life, development of concepts and guidance to the advertising and design team.

On the basis of this customer research, described more fully earlier in Chapter 1, an opportunity for marketing a motorbike was identified – that of fulfilling a desire for freedom – the need for Liberation.

The Taste of Success

Apache has been voted as the bike of the year by almost all stakeholder groups. The brand struck a deep chord with the Auto experts, the auto media and most importantly with the consumers.

A Final Word

This case is not just about bold decision making and creating the right concept. The execution and implementation remained true to the archetypal positioning and delivered the perfect tonality. Advertising created was completely different from anything TVS had done before and was a complete break from the corporate image. To ensure that the planners remained true to the archetype and did not give in to the temptation of resorting to a comfortable direction that had worked before, a principle of NOTness was used to develop the advertising and marketing communication.

Apache is...

- _Not_ doing stuff by himself, but with a group – to be different from Potency and to avoid the temptation of showing an all-man, rugged terrain bike that conquers elements and space.
- _Not_ with a girlfriend – to keep away from the hackneyed boy-girl story that all youth brands tell. Instead, the bike was about having NO commitments.
- _Not_ aspirationally upwardly mobile, or about success at work – again a temptation of all new launches to ride the optimism of the 'Shining India' mood. The bike was not about status or success – instead the optimism was captured by a carefree attitude that enables living of life without worrying about tomorrow.
- _Not_ about family and the responsibilities that come with family – to avoid temptation to capture not just the youth, but family people as well.
- _Not_ overtly premium – although modernity and premiumness were conveyed through features and styling rather than by exclusivity. The bike SPOKE the archetype.

And finally, there was realization that to target Liberation, the planners and brand managers had to feel and live the archetype. They had to break out of their Brahmin engineering, rooted in the rationality mindset. The team therefore had fun spending several Friday afternoons observing young people and testing the waters at the several pubs and cafes of Bangalore.

Questions

1. Is 'cool' a relevant concept for this product?
2. Does Apache have the ingredients to be 'cool' and is the concept of consumer tribe relevant?
3. Is 'cool' a global phenomenon?

This case study is based on a paper given at ESOMAR Annual Congress, Berlin, September 2007 by Poonam Kumar, Motivational Research, APAC Region, TNS Asia, India & Prasad Narsimhan TVS Motor Company, India (ESOMAR Copyright).

A full version of this case study appears on the accompanying web site for this book: www.wileyeurope.com/college/evans

SUMMARY

■ Culture could be defined in numerous ways but it can refer to what a society knows about its physical and social world including its religious beliefs, what it considers to be appropriate forms of conduct, and the language and other forms of conveying meanings that it uses for communication. Culture is dynamic and continuously in the process of changing and is transmitted from one generation to another. It can also refer to the overall meaning system that a group of people uses to inform their lives and to make sense of the world around them. Brands and services are part of this system of meaning, which acts as a lens through which people see their world and make sense of it. We realize the power of our own culture when we encounter a different one. Cultural categories are the distinctions that a culture uses to divide up its world of everyday experiences. There are many examples of such distinctions, including time and space.

■ Meaning originally resides in the culturally constituted world and can be transferred to consumer brands and goods via advertising and fashion systems. Meaning is transferred at an individual level through a range of ritualistic behaviours. Rituals are repetitive behaviours, which help us link up with our environment including brands and services. While some rituals are private and personal, others are shared, conveying a sense of collective identity and belonging to a group.

■ Different cultures have different values, with Western cultures often emphasizing individualism with focus on the individual self and Eastern cultures emphasizing collectivism with focus on conformity to the group. However, some argue that due to the recent developments in technology, global trade and migration, consumers are becoming homogenized and hence a standardized approach to target them is effective. Others argue that there exist very strong cultural differences (e.g. differences in norms, values, beliefs, attitudes and languages) and therefore one should adopt a customized approach. Companies often use a middle-of-the-road approach combining some elements from both approaches.

■ Since consumers are exposed to large numbers of marketing stimuli, use of humour can be very effective in getting their attention. However, it is important to bear in mind that cross-cultural differences exist in the way humour is interpreted and that extra care is needed in choosing the themes, situations and settings while using humour. Some consumers have a stereotypical belief about products that originate from other countries and thus the country of origin can act as an important information cue (or a heuristic) during the product evaluation stage of consumer decision-making. Some consumers have ethnocentric tendencies as they tend to favour products made or processed in their own cultures and countries.

■ Subcultures refer to smaller groups within a society which possess certain distinctive features (e.g. teenage subculture or ethnic minority subculture). Many of the Western societies can be described as culturally diverse where ethnic minority subcultures are growing in size and have increased purchasing power accompanied by heightened political and cultural awareness and ethnic pride. Ethnicity can be viewed as a characteristic of racial group membership on the basis of some commonly shared features. It can also be described in terms of the biological make-up of individuals and the extent to which genetic factors play their role in conveying aspects of ethnicity including consumption behaviour. However, for many, ethnicity is also a process of self-identification whereby individuals define themselves and others into specific groups using ethnic labels. Ethnicity exists in the context of oppositions and relativities and the process of self-identification is mediated by the perceptions of others. Acculturation is the approach utilized by many to understand the consumer behaviour of ethnic minority consumers. The extent to which ethnic minority consumers feel attached to their original culture can influence their decision-making and shopping behaviours. Marketers can respond to consumer differences with differentiation and segmentation strategies and adapt their marketing mix according to the cultural aspirations, needs and wants of the target group.

QUESTIONS

1. **What is meant by 'culture'? What do you think of the idea that culture is the meaning system that members of any specific group use to inform their lives?**

2. **Using examples of your own, discuss the meaning transfer model suggested by McCracken (1986).**

3. **What issues are involved in adopting a standardized vs. customized approach to targeting consumers around the globe? Which are most important? Use examples to illustrate.**

4. **What are the effects of country of origin and the use of humour in consumer behaviour?**

5. **What is 'acculturation'? How does it help to understand consumer behaviour of ethnic minority consumers?**

6. Critically discuss and evaluate the key components of the acculturation model identified by Penaloza (1994).

7. Why do marketers need to study ethnic minority consumer behaviour? Identify and explain different strategies that marketers can adopt while targeting ethnic minority consumers.

FURTHER READING

Arnould E J and Thompson C J (2005) Consumer Culture Theory (CCT): Twenty Years of Research, *Journal of Consumer Research*, Vol **31** No 4 pp 868–883. This paper provide a very good overview of the past 20 years of consumer research dealing with socio-cultural, experiential, symbolic and ideological aspects of consumption.

Cova B and Cova V (2001) Tribal Aspects of Postmodern Consumption Research: the Case of French Inline Roller Skaters, *Journal of Consumer Behaviour*, Vol **1**, No 1, pp 67–76.

Gladwell M (1997) The Coolhunt, The New Yorker, March 17.

Knobil, M (2002) What Makes a Brand Cool? Market Leader, *Journal of the Marketing Society*, issue 18.

Maffesoli M (1996) *The Time of the Tribes: The Decline of Individualism in Mass Society*, trans. D Smith, Sage, London.

Mick D G (1986) Consumer Research and Semiotics: Exploring the Morphology of Signs, Symbols, and Significance, *Journal of Consumer Research*, Vol **13**, No 2, pp 196–213. This is a classic paper which comprehensively outlines the emergence and principal perspectives of semiotics (the study of meanings and symbols) and then discusses its applications and implications for consumer research.

Nancarrow C and Nancarrow P (2007) Hunting for Cool Tribes, in *Consumer Tribes*, Cova B, Kozinets R V and Shankar A (Eds), Sage, London.

Robbins D (1991) *The Work of Pierre Bourdieu*, Open University Press, Milton Keynes.

Smith S (2003) How to Bottle Cool, Sunday Times Style, 10 August, pp 24–25.

Thornton S (1995) *Club Cultures: Music, Media and Subcultural Capital*, Polity, Cambridge.

Wallendorf M and Reilly M (1983) Ethnic Migration, Assimilation, and Consumption, *Journal of Consumer Research*, Vol **10**, December, pp 292–302. This is a classic article in consumer research dealing with issues of ethnicity and assimilation.

Here, at end of Part 2, we present an article by Mckechnie and Tynan (2006) in *Journal of Consumer Behaviour* that extends our coverage of rituals in a cultural sense and contextualizes these in the social meanings of Christmas in UK.

Q 1 Discuss the application of McCracken and Holt within this research.

Q 2 How do the findings relate to your own meaning of Christmas?

PART 2   JOURNAL ARTICLE

SOCIAL MEANINGS IN CHRISTMAS CONSUMPTION: AN EXPLORATORY STUDY OF UK CELEBRANTS' CONSUMPTION RITUALS

Sally McKechnie* and Caroline Tynan
Nottingham University Business School, UK
Reproduced from Journal of Consumer Behaviour 5: 130–144 (2006)

Although much has been written about the celebration of Christmas from a variety of perspectives, limited attention has been paid in the consumer behaviour literature to understanding the behaviours of consumers surrounding this event. Apart from insights gained from prior work on consumption rituals and meanings of festivities, our knowledge of meaning creation through Christmas consumption is partial, and written mainly from a North American perspective. Since consumer behaviour is shaped by cultural and social contexts, understanding the relationship between consumption objects and the social meanings that consumers ascribe to them is a research imperative. This paper explores the ways in which the British Christmas is consumed as a shared consumption experience, by bringing together two different approaches taken by consumer researchers and sociologists to analysing social consumption patterns. These are drawn from structuralist and post-structuralist thinking. The findings of an exploratory qualitative study are used to demonstrate how an enhanced understanding of consumption meanings associated with this particular cultural context can lead to new insights into how consumers create social meanings through special, as well as ordinary, behaviours.

Introduction

Christmas is one of the few rituals which is annually celebrated around the world, even in countries which do not have a Christian tradition. Typically, Christmas involves family gatherings and gift giving. In the UK it

*Correspondence to: Sally McKechnie, Nottingham University Business School, Jubilee Campus Wollaton Road, Nottingham NG8 1BB, UK.
E-mail: sally.mckechnie@nottingham.ac.uk

is observed along with the following day, Boxing Day, as a public holiday and part of a 'twinpeaked festival' (Miller, 1995, p. 6) comprising the Christmas and New Year celebrations.

This paper aims to gain a better understanding of meaning creation through consumption, by examining the ways in which consumers create social meanings through the consumption rituals of the Christmas celebration. Although there has been some work on consumption rituals (Rook, 1985; McCracken, 1986; Gainer, 1995) and on the meanings of the celebrations generally (Caplow *et al.*, 1982) as well as specific studies of Hallowe'en (Belk, 1990; Levinson *et al.*, 1992), Thanksgiving (Wallendorf and Arnould, 1991) and Christmas (Belk, 1987, 1989a; Hirschman and LaBarbera, 1989), these have largely been from a North American perspective. While the origin of Christmas myths and rituals in the cultural context of the UK are well researched within the fields of anthropology and sociology (see Pimlott, 1962; Hubert, 1999; Law, 2003), there has been little consumer behaviour research into British Christmas consumption, apart from recent studies by Miller (1995) who compared Christmas across a range of cultural contexts,[1] and Gurau and Tinson (2003) who examined attitudes towards Christmas commercial campaigns.

Christmas is built upon a variety of consumption practices and, as a central component of the retail calendar, is a worthy focus of study. It represents the major holiday shopping season (Ruth *et al.*, 1999) which has resulted in rising levels of festive spending and commensurate consumer debt (BBC News, 2003). Furthermore, there is an ongoing need for explanations of consumer behaviour from an experiential perspective that focuses on the symbolic, hedonic and aesthetic nature of consumption (Holbrook and Hirschman, 1982, p. 132). According to Belk and Bryce (1993, p. 277) 'Christmas is, for the predominantly Christian western world, the distilled essence of contemporary consumption' and provides an opportunity to compare the bridges and rifts between ideology and praxis (Wallendorf and Arnould, 1991).

The findings of an exploratory study are used to demonstrate how an enhanced understanding of consumption meanings associated with this particular cultural context can lead to new insights into how consumers create social meanings through Christmas consumption behaviours. However, before discussing the results of the study, the paper first reviews the literature on Christmas consumption, and considers two different approaches to analysing patterns of social consumption. A conceptualisation is then presented which brings these two approaches together to capture the nature of special and ordinary behaviours imbued with social meaning. This is followed by an explanation of the research methodology. The key findings of the empirical analysis are then discussed, and conclusions are drawn.

Literature review

The rituals of the American Christmas have been likened to a 'conspicuous cluster of symbolic and practical acts' by Caplow (1992, p. 383). They were first examined in terms of their impact on the family unit and culture at large by Barnett (1954) and

---

[1] These contexts were the USA, Japan, Britain, Sweden and Trinidad.

then by Caplow *et al.* (1982). However, it took another thirty years before the impact of such rituals on consumer behaviour began to be examined. First, Rook (1985) considered Christmas to be a clearly defined ritual, which was widely observed in Western culture and associated with gift-giving rituals and ritual symbols such as coloured lights, mistletoe, wreaths, Santa Claus and food and drink. He raised concerns over ritual scripts[2] and role uncertainty due to the decline in church attendance and rise of single-person households and multiple marriage families. Next, Hirschman and La Barbera (1989) reviewed the limited prior research on Christmas and identified the following common themes: gift giving, sociability and family togetherness, commercialism and materialism, hedonism and sensuality, and religious tradition and spirituality. Then, from their own empirical work, they described the multidimensional meaning of Christmas using bipolar descriptors, highlighting the importance of sacred/secular and positive/negative affective dimensions.

Around the same time, Belk (1989a) conducted the first of two historical analyses of the development of Christmas meaning and symbolism reflected in, as well as influenced by, various popular media. He concluded that Christmas was considered to be a largely secularised celebration of commercialisation, materialism and hedonism. He also noted the opposition of sacred and profane values, and in a separate study highlighted the importance of the performance of sustaining rituals as a means of maintaining sacredness through consumption (Belk *et al.*, 1989). A second historical analysis compared the Christmas shopping experience portrayed in two films (Belk and Bryce, 1993).

Arguably, the basic ritual foundations of the Christmas celebration in the UK may not necessarily be that different from the USA. Indeed, the burgeoning literature on the rituals of Christmas gift shopping (see Fischer and Arnold, 1990; Otnes *et al.*, 1993; Laroche *et al.*, 2000) and gift giving (see Mortelmans and Damen, 2001; O'Cass and Clarke, 2002) bear testimony to this fact. However, the focus of the present study is not to compare consumption rituals between US and UK consumers (as undertaken by Miller, 1995), but rather to gain a better understanding of consumption meanings, by specifically examining the ways in which UK consumers create social meanings through a range of Christmas consumption rituals.

A key assumption of this paper is that two different approaches, namely structuralist and poststructuralist, taken by consumer researchers and sociologists to analysing social consumption patterns, can aid our understanding of meaning creation through Christmas consumption rituals. These approaches will now be considered in turn.

Meaning transfer model

The first approach to analysing social consumption patterns is a structuralist model developed by McCracken (1986, 1988) which is firmly embedded in the stream of 'object signification' research. This theoretical model of the movement of cultural meaning through marketing and consumption was chosen for analysing Christmas consumption, because it examines the relationship between culture and consumption in the Western world

---

[2]An unwritten script which guides the ritual role player and identifies appropriate behaviour and artefacts.

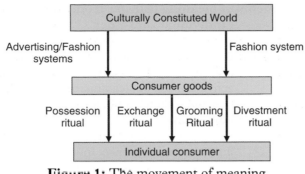

Figure 1: The movement of meaning
Source: McCracken (1986, p. 72).

and embraces the notion of the creation of meaning involving individuals, objects and associated rituals – all key components of this event. Consumer meanings move in a one-way trajectory between three locations: the culturally constituted world; consumer goods; and the individual consumer (see Figure 1). By resurrecting trickle-down theory, McCracken demonstrates how advertising and fashion systems[3] serve as instruments of meaning transfer from the world to goods, while four types of consumption rituals (possession; grooming; exchange; and divestment) transfer cultural meanings from goods to individuals.

These rituals, which are described in Table 1 below, represent ways in which goods are used by consumers to position and define themselves within a socio-cultural context.

Structuralist thinkers such as McCracken subscribe to the view that there is a one-to-one relationship between consumption objects and their social meanings and uses. While such a position on the locations of symbolic meaning and their use by consumers is supported by researchers such as Appadurai (1986) as well

as Lunt and Livingstone (1992), McCracken's model has been subject to criticism. The first stage of meaning transfer, which he conceptualised as a one-way trajectory, is criticised on the grounds that a two-way process exists, whereby consumers derive meaning from the culturally constituted world via advertising and fashion systems, as well as create cultural meaning by their actions. For example O'Donohoe and Tynan (1997) found that consumers play an active role in linking product and consumption meanings, with the implication that advertisers should tap into this pool of consumer understandings and ideas in order to seek to establish meanings that can be associated credibly with their product offerings in the marketplace. As for the second stage of meaning transfer, Arnould *et al.* (2004) argue that rituals are not the only forms of symbolic action which transfer meaning from goods to consumers, and that ordinary (as opposed to special) behaviours contribute as well.

Further shortcomings of McCracken's model have been identified. For Joy (1989), the model focuses on how meaning structures are formed at an individual level, but

---

[3]In a recent adaptation of this model by Arnould *et al.* (2004) the instruments of meaning transfer have been updated to include the participation of the 'art system' which operates in tandem with 'fashion systems', and the substitution of 'integrated marketing communications' (IMC) for 'advertising'.

Table 1: Instruments of meaning transfer from consumer goods to individual consumer

Possession rituals	Taking a purchased good to the place of consumption and claiming its possession as one's own; involves activities such as cleaning, discussing, comparing, reflecting, showing off, and photographing personal possessions.
Exchange rituals	Gift giving and receiving as a means of exercising interpersonal influence; involves choice of gift that possesses certain symbolic properties that the giver wishes to see transferred onto the receiver.
Grooming rituals	Situations where cultural meanings have to be drawn out repeatedly due to perishable nature of some of the special properties of goods; involves grooming the consumer as well as grooming the good.
Divestment rituals	Used by consumers to relinquish meaning associated by previous owner for second-hand goods, or to erase any personal meaning attached to a good being disposed of.

Source: Adapted from McCracken (1986, pp. 78–80).

fails to address how this gives rise to conflict at group level. Also, it considers the role of the socio-cultural context in defining and shaping consumer behaviour, yet ignores the socio-economic or political context. By comparison, Belk (1989b) noted the model's failure to take into account the shift in a consumer culture away from utilitarianism towards hedonism and novelty-seeking behaviour, as well as to consider non-consumption rituals; while Sherry (1989) considered the model's development from a mainly Euro- American perspective to be a weakness.

Notwithstanding these criticisms, this model offers a logical approach to the analysis of Christmas consumption, since the four rituals in the second stage of meaning transfer comprise a range of special behaviours which are reflected in the Christmas celebration. However, since the model helps to gain a better understanding of meaning creation only at an individual rather than a group level, an alternative poststructuralist approach to analysing social consumption patterns was considered.

Typology of consumption practices

Poststructuralist thinking makes allowances for the possibility of variation in the manner in which consumers understand and use consumption objects (Holt, 1997). Rather than adopting an object-based perspective, which seeks a one-to-one relationship between consumption objects and their social meanings and uses, an intersubjective perspective is taken which examines patterns of consumption practices instead. This work also embraces the notion of hedonism unlike McCracken's (1986) model (Belk, 1989b).

Holt's (1995) typology of consumption practices was chosen to analyse Christmas consumption, because

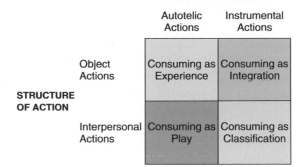

Figure 2: Metaphors for consuming.
Source: Holt (1995, p. 3)

it captures a range of ordinary consumption behaviours and provides an opportunity to examine ordinary modes of meaning transfer (using the metaphors of consuming as experience, integration, play and classification). Unlike McCracken's approach, this conceptualisation of consuming is based on empirical work and takes into account the structure of the action in terms of whether consumers directly engage with the consumption object (i.e. object actions) or interact with other people (i.e. interpersonal actions), and the purpose of the action in terms of whether it is an end in itself (i.e. autotelic actions) or a means to an end (i.e. instrumental actions) (see Figure 2).

These four ordinary modes of meaning transfer can be classified in two ways: those which are hedonic meaning transfer activities (experiencing and playing) and those which are utilitarian ones (integrating and classifying); and those which help individuals to establish social identity (playing and classifying) as opposed to those which help to establish individual identity (experiencing and integrating). Furthermore, in Holt's study of how spectators consume professional baseball, he established 10 separate types of behaviour, which

were found to best explain and describe the most important and distinctive features of these modes of meaning transfer (see Table 2).

Since Holt's framework analyses consumption practices according to the structure and purpose of actions, as well as the nature of the meaning transfer activities, it offers another approach to analysing Christmas consumption. Specifically, it serves as a means of enhancing our understanding of the creation of social meanings as opposed to individual ones, by highlighting those ordinary behaviours which help consumers to establish social identity (i.e. playing and classifying) and are therefore imbued with social meaning.

Conceptualisation

Bringing the two approaches of McCracken and Holt together, the following conceptualisation encompasses the range of special and ordinary behaviours associated with Christmas consumption and distinguishes between those which create social as opposed to individual meanings (see Figure 3, where Consumer A is portrayed as interacting with fellow Consumer B and so forth). The purpose of this conceptualisation is

Table 2: Modes of meaning transfer via ordinary behaviours

Meanings	Modes	Behaviours	Definitions
Social/ Hedonic	Playing using consumption objects as resources to interact with fellow consumers	Communing	Sharing consumption experiences with others.
		Socialising	Using personal (past or present) consumption experiences to entertain others.
Social/ Utilitarian	Classifying looking at ways consumer classify themselves with regard to 'relevant others'	Via objects	Using shared meanings of consumption objects to classify oneself or others.
		Via actions	Using the manner in which one experiences a consumption object or event to classify oneself or others; mentoring novice consumers.
Individual/ Hedonic	Experiencing consumers' subjective reactions to consumption objects	Accounting	Typifying actions and objects, assigning them specific meanings and values, then contextualising the account to enrich it.
		Evaluating	Making comparisons to norms, history, and conventions.
		Appreciating	Applying aesthetic and emotional frameworks to actions and to objects.
Individual/ Utilitarian	Integrating using methods to enhance the perception that a valued consumption object is a constitutive element of one's identity	Assimilating	Using methods to become a competent participant.

(continued)

Table 2: (*continued*)
Modes of meaning transfer via ordinary behaviours

Meanings	Modes	Behaviours	Definitions
		Producing	Using methods to enhance perception of being that they are significantly involved in production of the object or action.
		Personalising	Adding extra-institutional elements to consumption to assert the individuality of one's relationship to the object or action.

Source: Adapted from Holt (1995, pp. 1–16) by Arnould *et al.* (2004, p. 143).

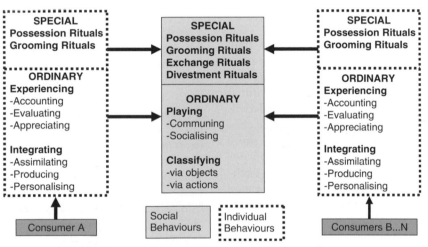

Figure 3: Christmas consumption practices.
Source: Adapted from McCracken (1986, pp. 78–80) and Holt (1995, p. 4)

not to have it subjected to empirical testing, but to use it to interpret and better understand the findings of the exploratory study. Since the focus of the present paper is on gaining insights into how consumers create social meanings through their Christmas consumption behaviours, the only part of the conceptualisation which will be examined empirically will be the special and ordinary social behaviours used to interact with fellow consumers.

Methodology

Given that this work is of an exploratory nature, qualitative methods were adopted as being appropriate for exploring people's 'lived experience' and for focusing on 'naturally occurring ordinary events in natural settings' (Miles and Huberman, 1994, p. 10). The limited time frame for data collection, severe time constraints on participants, and therefore the need to minimise participant recall loss (Cleveland *et al.*, 2003), necessitated the adoption of a multi-method approach.

To gain a meaningful understanding of phenomena 'which emerge out of sharing and discussing issues, exchanging opinions, revising perceptions and highlighting differences' (Carson *et al.*, 2001, p. 115) focus groups were chosen. Emerging themes were then explored through depth interviews.

Sample

The study is based on a relatively small judgement sample of female participants, who were selected using the snowballing technique from an initial pool of volunteers who responded to posters. Female participants were chosen to enable the study to be more focused, and participants were purposively selected to increase the likelihood of gaining insights into a range of Christmas experiences by including those with and without children; aged either under 39 or 40 years or older; and with or without full-time jobs. (See Appendix A for vignettes of participants of both stages of the study (after Huffman *et al.*, 2000)).

Data collection

Two exploratory focus groups were conducted with 10 and 7 female participants, respectively three to four weeks before Christmas. These approximately 75 min group discussions were conducted in an informal environment. Participants were informed initially that the purpose of the study was to gain an understanding about their feelings, experiences and perceptions relating to Christmas. Chronological flow (Miles and Huberman, 1994) was maintained through the adoption of a processual approach, addressing consumption in three phases: the anticipation of and preparation for Christmas; the experience of Christmas; and the post-festivity clearing up and reflection on the whole process. Depth interviews were then conducted with six of the original participants four to six weeks after Christmas. They lasted between 65 and 135 min, and typically began with the participants being asked to reflect on their expectations of Christmas and then chronologically considering their actual experience.

Data analysis

The style of questioning was informal for both stages and involved asking semi-structured questions around themes and processes, beginning with open-ended questions and gradually focusing on actual experiences rather than allowing the discussion to remain at an experience-distant, abstract level as advised by Thompson and Haytko (1997). Each interview was audio-recorded and then transcribed verbatim. The text was analysed independently by the authors following the generalised sequence of steps (data reduction and transformation, data display and conclusion drawing/verification) as described in Miles and Huberman (1994, p. 10).They individually developed a holistic understanding of each transcript and, as the fieldwork progressed, also noted the patterns and themes, which were similar across scripts. This approach allowed for earlier readings of the text to inform later readings, and more pertinently in this research, to allow for later readings of the transcripts from the depth interviews to explore patterns not noted on the initial analysis of the focus group data (Thompson and Haytko, 1997). At this stage, similarities and differences across their separate analyses were compared and the data integrated.

Findings and discussion

Special behaviours

Most of the participants felt that Christmas was becoming too commercialised, which is nothing new as the debate on whether or not Christmas is losing its traditional meaning can be traced back to 1890, when Christmas was likened to a 'festival of store-keepers' (O'Neil, 1981) and supports earlier research by Hirschman and La Barbera (1989), Belk (1989a) and Belk and Bryce (1993). While only some of the participants were aware of the common theme used by major advertisers in their Christmas campaigns of encouraging consumers to participate in 'the magical experience of Christmas', most were of the opinion that, for adults at least, Christmas was less of a reality-suspending event and more of an occasion demanding a lot of hard work instead.

> I always think when you go out in the community . . . you never get a feeling of excitement or that people are actually bothered . . . I've noticed like if you go into a shop and buy something and say like 'Merry Christmas' . . . they are like surprised or taken aback.
>
> (Stella[4] – over 40, 3 children, working part-time)

Participants confirmed that the annual nature of the Christmas celebration meant that cultural meaning in the home had to be re-established through various rituals. To reflect the importance and public nature of the holiday, there was evidence of the household possession ritual of cleaning and redecorating. Indeed, the household cleaning routine went into overdrive before, during and after Christmas, giving rise to tension and conflict at both an individual and a group level. Some participants were driven to anger by the seasonal clutter of cards, wrappings and gifts. Although everyone was aware of the Twelfth Night tradition for taking down decorations, most of them were relieved to take theirs down around New Year's Day. Other participants complained about over-enthusiastic guests taking over their customary cleaning and tidying chores. Conflict at group level was neither explicitly addressed in the conceptualisation in Figure 3, nor in McCracken's (1986) model (Joy, 1989).

> Christmas is not Christmas unless you can smell paint somewhere in this house, and it's true . . . he's always decorating, my husband is, a couple weeks before. Yep, just to get it like all spick and span.
>
> (Pam – over 40, 1 grown-up son, working full-time)

After the ritual pre-Christmas cleaning, decorations were brought out of storage for grooming rituals to begin. The excitement of unpacking Christmas decorations was evident,[5] in anticipation of the Christmas to come, yet at the same time nostalgically evoking memories of Christmases past.

> We always know when we put the tree up that Christmas is coming, and something me and my mum always do

---

[4]Pseudonyms are used for people and places to ensure the anonymity of participants.
[5]Although in a work context there were reservations about whether or not Christmas decorations should be put up for fear of offending non-Christian colleagues or customers.

(is) we always put the tree up and decorate it. Dad has to go up into the loft and get all the boxes down, and then we decorate with a glass of sherry.

(Charlotte – under 40, no children, working full-time)

With the exception of Pam, who aspired to a minimalist lifestyle, it was apparent that the participants' homes were being extensively and increasingly expensively groomed for Christmas. There was mention of purchases of multiple Christmas trees, new sets of exterior and interior Christmas lighting, candelabras, wreaths and dedicated Christmas tableware, largely driven by the advertising and fashion systems (see Figure 1) promoting elegantly colour-coded decor through glossy magazines, television 'makeover' programmes and retail displays. However, Penny rejected the notion of 'tasteful decorations', favouring a riot of gaudy colours to create her notion of a 'winter wonderland'.

We really doll the house with lights and tinsel and everything tacky ... really it's what you make it. You get excited. I don't know what it'd be like when we've got children.
(Penny – under 40, no children, not working)

The Christmas tree, the universally adopted symbol of Christmas, exists in various forms from the huge real forest tree to a minimalist twig or fibre optic one bought from a DIY warehouse. For most participants there was the dilemma of choosing between a traditional real tree or an artificial one. It was evident that the former was perceived to be of a higher status and aspired to, whereas the latter was deemed to be more practical in terms of long term cost and ease of transportation. Tree decoration was considered to be a public statement by the head female in the household. Judy's home had in fact six trees, partly explained by the fact that her children were forbidden to help decorate the main tree, but were given little trees for their bedrooms to decorate as they liked. While some participants did allow their children to help, Stella would rearrange the decorations once they went to bed. For Pam, an empty nester, her tree was used for individual as well as social meaning.

I'm very particular when it comes to my tree ... I don't know why. I'm almost territorial.
(Stella – over 40, 3 children, working part-time)

... and I've got the most beautiful sparkly twig tree that I bought from B&Q and I stand that on the hearth and it looks absolutely beautiful and minimalist, and anyone who walked into the house said how beautiful the tree was and that was my Christmas tree.

(Pam – over 40, 1 grown-up son, working full-time)

External decorations such as wreaths and outdoor lighting were also clearly catching on as a public sign of celebration. Charlotte's father reluctantly put lights up for the first time to please her mother, who had purchased them earlier in the year. Pam, however, strongly disliked this type of grooming, remarking on it just looking 'so cheap and dirty' and being most prevalent in the poorest neighbourhoods. She would only make an exception, if it were done for charity. Finally, the absence of Christmas grooming rituals for the home was interpreted as making no effort and thus overtly insulting Christmas guests.

These findings provide some support for the criticism mentioned earlier that a two-way process exists at the first stage of meaning transfer in

McCracken's (1986) model, as participants such as Penny and Pam were able to articulate examples of meaning creation through their actions or actions of others, rather than deriving meaning from the cultural values and symbols (see Figure 1). Counterintuitively, there was very little evidence in the data of personal grooming rituals (see Table 1) apart from mentions of grooming the children for the annual family Christmas Day video recording, and going with work colleagues to a health spa for some 'pampering' instead of the usual Christmas night out.

While Christmas is a major occasion for gift shopping (see Fischer and Arnold, 1990; Otnes *et al.*, 1993; Laroche *et al.*, 2000) and gift giving (Mortelmans and Damen, 2001; O'Cass and Clarke, 2002), the associated exchange rituals are complex and difficult to both decode and to renegotiate. Buying Christmas presents is a social obligation for close family members, although consumers do have some choice in how wide their recipient group should be. When joining a new family on marriage or when extended families expand, gift giving norms for the participants often needed to be re-evaluated and a consensus established.

> One of the things that really sticks with me about my first year of marriage ... um ... Arthur's sisters were already married and they'd got families and he said buy for the kids and I got a little gift for his sisters. And one of them actually said 'We don't buy for each other' ... She hadn't refused my gift but said 'What have you done this for?' She didn't say it in a very nice way. She said 'We only buy for the children' ... I wish she'd told me before! (Marion – over 40, 3 grown-up children, working full-time)

Buying a gift of the appropriate perceived value is paramount, with over- or underspending causing loss of face (Wooten, 2000).

> I think the money side of it with presents was bang on. It was quite nice, the gifts we were receiving were roughly the same as we were giving out, like cost wise ... you don't want to look like a cheapskate or like you've been mad.
> (Penny – under 40, no children, not working)

While some paid for gifts from personal savings via the use of 'The Diddlum'[6], others spread the cost through the use of credit cards, or buying gifts throughout the year. Surprisingly, Christmas shopping for some 'early evangelists' (Gurau and Tinson, 2003) began as early as Boxing Day the previous year, so that the participants could avail themselves of sales bargains. This required them not only to store the purchases for twelve months, but also to remember where they had stored them, a challenge not always met.

Choosing presents for children was facilitated by getting them to write a wish list (O'Cass and Clarke, 2002) and then employing different strategies (Otnes *et al.*, 1993) to bring any unrealistically high expectations to a more manageable level. Parents tended to seek good quality, practical gifts rather than Christmas novelty items or 'one day wonders'. Despite the marketers' efforts to encourage consumers to buy more gifts, value for money and quality were uppermost in these participants' minds rather than

---

[6]'The Diddlum' is an intergenerational wartime informal Christmas weekly savings system, which was still operating in several households and workplaces as a way of meeting the additional expense of Christmas.

volume. However, purchases of inexpensive humorous presents for adults who 'don't need anything' was also mentioned.

I'd rather buy one quality thing that I think they (children) really want or appreciate; you know what I mean, rather than loads of things.
(Stella – over 40, 3 children, working part-time)

Unwrapping gifts and sharing the pleasure of opening sacks, stockings, boxes and pillowcases of presents clearly had its own sense of time and place for each family. For those with children, the final stage of the gift exchange would involve playing with the children's new acquisitions. This was seen as part of the intergenerational, 'once in a year' opportunity to participate in a shared activity.

... if they've had any games (as Christmas presents) we play a game. My youngest daughter had 'Rumble in the Jungle' this year so we had to set all that up ... It's an actual board game ... ... she got some videos so she wanted to watch a video as well. I like to sit and watch the videos with her, at least one.
(Stella – over 40, 3 children, working part-time)

The other important exchange ritual mentioned was the sending and receiving of Christmas greeting cards. Some participants felt that this widespread and expensive practice was getting out of hand, especially for people they saw every day or have not seen for many years, but they would have felt extremely sad to receive only a few. Others were cynical about charity cards in terms of how much money went to charity. Finally, the difficulty of competing with 'Round Robin'

newsletters from families with 'perfect' lives caused some anxiety.

Well I'm not into this Round Robin which I hate when I get one ... I can't be bothered to read them mostly, while at the same time I'm interested in people I haven't seen for 20 years. I am interested in what they are doing but ... they have perfect lives and I can't write like that ... My son failed his A levels you know and my daughter split up from her boyfriend ... it's hard to put in these things, isn't it? ... Without sounding tragic or 'over the top' or cheesy!
(Selma (focus group) – over 40, 3 grown-up children, not working)

Complex divestment rituals were in evidence. For one participant's mother, the purchase of second-hand goods as Christmas gifts proved to be problematic, when she was given a second-hand jumper from the church bazaar by her mother-in-law. Otherwise, most participants would have items such as real trees and holly wreaths re-planted or composted and Christmas cards recycled, as their particular meaning drew to a close at the end of the holiday. Stella would also keep some cards as mementoes for her family tree (Belk *et al.*, 1989) or to make gift tags for the following year.

Ordinary behaviours

While playing is discussed earlier in the context of special behaviours associated with exchange rituals, it is classified by Holt (1995) as an ordinary mode of hedonic meaning transfer which helps consumers to establish social identity (see Figure 2 and Table 2). Sharing Christmas as a communal experience was clearly in evidence for most participants, who went to nativity plays, pantomimes, concerts, ballets, the cinema, employees' Christmas nights out, and shopping. Several mentioned making their annual visit to church to take part in some enjoyable carol singing. All participants engaged in a range of social activities such as going to pubs, restaurants and nightclubs, or visiting relatives. Not every participant wanted to be with her extended family over the holiday period. Out of boredom, Pam had recently broken the family tradition of 'house swap' Christmas visiting (where the same members visited each other's homes day after day) so that she could regain some 'quality time' with her immediate family. In short, these social activities were no different from the rest of the year, but occurred more frequently over a shorter space of time, leading to burnout. Judy clearly had the most hectic Christmas social diary, which she admitted caused her to 'hibernate' in January. These findings confirm the themes of sociability and hedonism identified in earlier research (Hirschman and LaBarbera, 1989; Belk, 1989a).

It just happens, we always go to the same pub in Bestford (on Christmas Eve) but no ... we don't plan who we're going to meet there, we don't know that the people are going to be there. We saw a lot of people we knew, had a good chat with them and caught up.

(Charlotte – under 40, no children, working full-time)

By comparison, the ordinary mode of utilitarian meaning transfer which helps consumers to establish social identity is classifying through objects or actions (see Figure 2 and Table 2). In order to create the perfect Christmas to impress her guests via objects, Judy had been engaged in extensively buying Christmas-related purchases,

only to admit, on subsequent reflection, that she might have got 'a bit carried away'.

When you are setting the table you have got to have the perfect napkins and you go out and buy the candles for around the house ... and you've got to have the lights and everything has got to be just right and you've got to have fresh flowers ... .

(Judy – under 40, 3 children, not working)

As for classification via actions, the self classification of novice and expert hostess became apparent. Penny, aspiring to be 'the hostess with the mostest', had never celebrated Christmas Day in her own home before and was having a large family gathering, which was somewhat hampered by her inexperience at food shopping and cooking, as well as a degree of role uncertainty (Rook, 1985) with regards to how best to interact with her recently widowed father-in-law's fiancée. There was evidence of Marion, by comparison, who was quite adept at organising such gatherings and had considerable expertise in cooking, as well as arranging extravagant Christmas floral displays.

It would be the first year that I would actually hold Christmas at my house. Er ... a bit traumatic, a bit hectic getting everything in. My expectations, having a nice, sort of time, my family at my own house and just hoping everything went smoothly.

(Penny – under 40, no children, not working)

Conclusion

To date our knowledge of meaning creation through Christmas consumption has been partial and mainly written from a North American perspective. Therefore, research into consumption meanings within another cultural context leads to an enhanced understanding of how consumers create meanings through the consumption rituals associated with the celebration of this holiday, and is also of interest to marketing practitioners.

The focus of this research has been to examine how British consumers create social meaning through their consumption of the festival of Christmas. This paper contributes to theory building about meaning creation by bringing together two approaches to examining social consumption patterns in order to investigate the behaviours imbued with social meaning. Building on the work of McCracken (1986) and Holt (1995), a conceptualisation was developed to capture the range of special and ordinary behaviours at both individual and group level, and subsequently used to interpret the findings of the exploratory study.

Our study has tried to capture a range of Christmas consumption experiences, which has resulted in a rich dataset, but the participants were restricted to females only. A full investigation at the level of the family/household may prove more fruitful. Since there was little evidence of religious observance amongst the participants, it may be worth comparing the behaviours of practising Christians, non practising Christians and those of other faiths. Secondly, the difficulty of getting participants to commit time for the research even with a substantial financial incentive, suggests that alternative methods of data collection such as observation and archival material might also be considered.

The study provided an opportunity to compare ideology and praxis (after Wallendorf and Arnould, 1991). The participants' stories revealed examples of how products and consumption activities took on and communicated meaning about themselves and their relationships with others, through the four types of special consumption rituals: possession; grooming; exchange; and divestment. There were examples of meaning conflict, such as Marion's discomfort from differing inter-family exchange rituals on marriage, or the anxiety caused by 'Round Robin' newsletters. The importance of family togetherness and sociability (Hirschman and LaBarbera, 1989) was confirmed through evidence of hedonic communing and socialising behaviours. However, there was some evidence of meaning negotiation within extended families with regard to where adult children should celebrate Christmas; the nature of the present-opening ritual; and the renegotiation of children's wish lists. Examples were found of classifying behaviours to establish social identity. However, Holt's (1995) study was set in a different research context and therefore his conceptualisation does not embrace the ordinary caring and nurturing behaviours of parents, which are what turn Christmas into a reality suspending event for both the younger and older generation. Practitioners should note that in spite of high expenditure and responsiveness to new festival fashions, these purchases merely provide a backdrop to the focal family-centred celebration as identified by Caplow *et al.* (1982) and thus are vulnerable to changes in consumption meanings.

To conclude, social meanings are rich and complex in nature. The conceptualisation which has been presented makes a preliminary attempt at developing a deeper understanding of how consumers create social meanings through the consumption rituals of Christmas, but it could also be examined in other settings such as the increasingly commercialised festivals in the UK retail calendar of Easter, Halloween and Bonfire Night.

Acknowledgements

The authors acknowledge the helpful comments of the editors and three anonymous reviewers on earlier drafts of this paper.

Biographical notes

Sally McKechnie is a Lecturer in Marketing. Her research interests are in the areas of customer behaviour and marketing communications. She has published in journals such as the Journal of Marketing Management, International Journal of Advertising, Journal of Marketing Communications, Journal of Customer Behaviour, International Journal of Bank Marketing, and International Small Business Journal.

Caroline Tynan is a Professor of Marketing and Head of the Marketing Division at Nottingham University Business School, Chair of the Academy of Marketing and visiting Professor of Marketing at The University of Ljubljana in Slovenia. Her research interests include relationship marketing, particularly within business- to-consumer and cross-cultural contexts, consumption rituals and services marketing. She has published in a number of journals including the Journal of Business Research, The European Journal of Marketing, The Journal of Marketing Management and The Journal of Strategic Marketing.

References

For full references to this text please see the website.

Appendix 1. Participant descriptions

Name	Profile	Life themes and values	Life projects	Current Christmas-related concerns
Charlotte	24 years; single; lives with parents and older brother; works full-time as a secretary at a university	Enjoying life and being with family; wants to get married and have a family of her own; not career-minded	Spending quality time with family; maintaining family traditions especially for Christmas; socialising	Buying multiple gifts for family, boyfriend and friends (starts process at Boxing Day sales)
Judy	39 years; married with 3 young children; has not worked for 10 years, but is a qualified primary school teacher	Being the perfect spouse to a successful businessman; a good mother and hostess	Promoting family togetherness; spending time with children; shopping for useful or educational gifts	Giving up control of Christmas celebration away from home; being caught up with the trappings of Christmas
Marion	54 years; married with 3 grown up children, works full time as a hospital warden	Being a good mother, especially to daughter with learning difficulties; helping others less fortunate	Hosting family gatherings and creating an enjoyable big family Christmas (with in-laws as well)	Replacing refrigerator and cooker which broke down just as 11 guests arrived to stay for Christmas week
Pam	48 years, married with one grown-up son; works full time as clerk at a hospital	Being a good mother to her only son; values scarce resources like time and money	Minimalist de'cor (strong aversion to untidiness and clutter); minimal socialising with extended family; retail therapy	Expects to give a lot through the Christmas season; seeking out good quality sales bargains
Penny	26 years, married, no children, not working but is qualified as a nurse	Purchasing in moderation and with 'value for money' in mind; inconspicuous consumption; having a family of her own	Hosting family reunions (a sister in Antipodes); being a good friend	Hosting Christmas celebration for first time; being seen as 'hostess with the mostest' for guests
Stella	40 years, married with three children, working and studying part-time	Being a good mother; being optimistic and making the best with what she has	Making a better family life for her children than the one she experienced	Paying for Christmas as money is tight and wants to treat her children

PART 3

INTEGRATED APPROACHES TO
CONSUMER BEHAVIOUR

CHAPTER 9   New Product Buying

CHAPTER 10   Repeat, Loyal and Relational Buying

CHAPTER 11   Data-Based Consumer Behaviour

CHAPTER 12   Consumer Misbehaviour

CHAPTER 13   Organizational Buying Behaviour

ARTICLE: P A Norberg and D R Horne (2007) Privacy Attitudes and
Privacy–Related Behavior, *Psychology & Marketing*, Vol 24(10):
829–847.

The final Part of the book extends the coverage of some of the distinct concepts that we introduced in the other Parts, within integrating approaches to explaining consumer behaviour.

We start (Chapter 9) with an exploration of how consumers react to new products and services. We show that there are different market segments that adopt new products in different ways over time. There are further important implications here, in the recognition that some can be used to 'spread the word' to others. The use of multi-step flows of communication by markets is a reflection of this as they often use celebrities or journalists to endorse a product as a way of encouraging its adoption. We extend our analysis of opinion formers, opinion leaders and market mavens and include ideas on stimulating opinion leadership and associated new developments such as Buzz marketing, conversational marketing and Retro marketing. Our coverage in this edition includes product placement, the TAM model and the KAI approach. We also provide new evidence on the dubious ethics associated with some marketing that targets opinion formers and opinion leaders, especially in medical markets.

This analysis is furthered in Chapter 10 with coverage of repeat buying and the extent to which marketers can encourage and exploit loyal and even relational buying. Models of repeat and loyal buying are presented along with marketers' attempts to capture loyalty through, for example, loyalty schemes. Whether the same sort of relationship can exist between companies and consumers as between people is analysed and evaluated. What is certain, though, is that marketers want to develop relationships with their best consumers. We present examples of how this has been done but we also show the difficulties of achieving relational consumption. This edition extends coverage of the NBD/LSD model, DIRICHLET Model, loyalty theory, relational and experiential buying. We are also privileged to be able to present cutting edge developments from TNS, in their TRI*M model.

Chapter 11 takes this even further. The relatively recent use of consumers' personal details has led to more personalized targeting by marketers. Sources of data include consumers' transactional data and geodemographics. In addition, consumers can be 'tracked' via new radio frequency identification (RFID) tags in the products they buy and via global positioning satellites (GPS), which can monitor the location of their mobile phones. There are new ways of analysing consumer data and sophisticated data mining software is presented here. As well as clear benefits to marketers, for example in being able to target individual consumers with offers for products and services in which they are known to have an interest, the extent of personal details available to marketers (and others?) is questioned. This leads some consumers to be concerned about 'big brother' privacy issues, not least in the aftermath of data losses by both government and private companies. We explore how marketers use transactional data and a vast range of other personalized data sources that, combined, form biographics. This worries us a little because biographics can be great for the what, when and how of buying but not necessarily for the 'why'. These are issues that we examine and significantly update and extend in the new edition.

If there are any concerns over marketers' behaviour, Chapter 12 delves into the darker aspects of consumer (mis)behaviour. Consumers can indulge in shoplifting, they might not always own up to being given too much change at the checkout, they can illegally download music and buy bootleg copies of films. This chapter examines a large range of such behaviour along with some of the reasons why consumers misbehave. Marketers might also consider anticonsumption as misbehaviour on the part of consumers. But there can be philosophical reasons why some are concerned about the proliferation of planet-damaging products and people-damaging marketing techniques. As a result some consumers consume little and others will react negatively toward marketing techniques and even act as consumer terrorists. We have updated and extended our coverage of misbehaviour in terms of theory, practical examples and implications for marketers and consumers.

Our new chapter on organizational buying behaviour provides further integration of much of the previous coverage in the text. There is application of both social and individual influences within this different buying context. We differentiate between the characteristics of consumer markets and business markets, analyse buying situations, the concept of the buying centre, the organizational buying decision-making process and discuss the major influences on business buying decisions. We provide analyses from both theory and practice perspectives, again with examples and case studies to illustrate application in the real world.

This Part is concluded with a research paper into the nature and influences on market mavernism.

We also remind you that the accompanying web site houses many other articles, along with links to relevant web sites, which provide further coverage and examples of the issues, theories and concepts that we explore in the text.

As in the previous Parts, we include clippings from *Marketing Week*, cases from the DMA and TNS and reports from the Future Foundation and are most appreciative of the permissions granted for these inclusions.

CHAPTER 9
NEW PRODUCT BUYING

CHAPTER OBJECTIVES

After engaging with the material presented in this chapter and its associated exercises and reading, you should be able to:

- Explain new product buying behaviour by drawing from the conceptual framework provided by diffusion-adoption of innovations theory.
- Exemplify how multi-step flows of communication can operate.
- Explore the implications for understanding consumer behaviour, of opinion-forming and opinion leadership, together with the characteristics of different adopter categories.
- Examine related, but alternative, ways of explaining innovative-adaptive behaviour among consumers.

INTRODUCTION

Introducing new products is important for marketers because it allows them to compete effectively in a highly competitive marketplace. That is why all marketing texts deal with new product development and **product life cycle** (PLC) strategies. The key proposition behind the product life cycle concept is that marketers should adapt their marketing as products go through various stages (e.g. 'introduction', 'growth', 'maturity' and 'decline') of their life. This is predicated on the facts that: markets usually become increasingly competitive over the life cycle; and that customers change over time – the more innovative will be the earlier adopters and the less innovative will be later adopters. The latter is the starting point for this chapter. There are also issues of how consumers perceive new products and the factors that can lead to acceptance or rejection of these. In addition, the nature of flows of communication concerning new products is relevant, especially when both the marketer and the consumer use opinion formers or opinion leaders to disseminate and receive information respectively. These topics hold many implications for marketing generally, for introducing new products and services and for explaining new and repeat purchasing behaviour.

This chapter explores these areas, starting with some foundation theory (**diffusion-adoption of innovations**) and follows this through to current research into 'innovative' and 'adaptive' behaviour by consumers. There are strong links with other topics covered elsewhere in the book, notably 'person-ality' in Chapter 6, 'sequential models' of consumer response to marketing (Chapters 2, 3 and 4) and 'involvement' (Chapter 4). The issues are then furthered by coverage in Chapter 10 of loyal, switching and relational behaviour.

FOUNDATION THEORY

Diffusion-Adoption of Innovations

The processes of spreading innovations through a society and how individuals 'adopt' these, is the domain of diffusion-adoption of innovations theory. Diffusion refers to how the innovation is communicated and distributed through society over time – it is a macro concept concerned with aggregated adoption behaviour. We will describe each component in turn:

Innovation and its Types

An **innovation** is anything (e.g. idea, concept, product or service) perceived as being new in the marketplace. Robertson (1967) categorized innovations in terms of the amount of disruption and behavioural change they cause in existing consumption patterns (Figure 9.1).

Discontinuous innovations ←	Dynamically continuous innovations	Continuous innovations ⇒
High level of disruption and behavioural change		Low level of disruption and behavioural change
Internal combustion engine in the first car	The first hatchback car	Car fitted with satellite navigation and pollen filter
Personal computer	Portable laptop PC	Faster 'chips' and larger memory

Figure 9.1: **Degrees of disruption: more of a continuum than categories**

Discontinuous Innovations

Radically new products which have maximum disruptive effect are termed 'discontinuous innovations'. In their day, the internal combustion engine and television came into this category. 'Disruption' is not necessarily a problem to be overcome: the internal combustion engine provided revolutionary, convenient transportation for work and leisure, and the TV dramatically changed entertainment and informational and educational media, which in turn changed lifestyles. As time moves on, of course, a new version of one of these products, today, creates less disruption and would be called a 'continuous innovation'.

Dynamically Continuous Innovations

This is the 'in-between' type of innovation, creating some change in how consumers behave but not perceived to be dramatically important changes by those individuals. Electric lawnmowers, for instance, do the same job as manual versions but faster and with less effort and therefore do a known job differently. This is called a 'dynamically continuous innovation': the result is evolutionary, not revolutionary.

Continuous Innovations

These are variations on familiar products: 'new improved' shampoos, 'mark 2' models of cars, for which the radiator grill has been slightly redesigned and perhaps fuel economy improved, and second editions of successful textbooks. These are minimally disruptive of established consumption patterns; they allow life to go on much as before but provide the benefits of the most recent developments in technology and thought. These are continuous innovations and most of the new product launches each year tend to fit into this category.

Genuinely discontinuous innovations are few and far between. When such an item is introduced it is the first brand in a wholly new product class, right at the beginning of the product life cycle (Howard and Moore, 1982).

Alternative Types of Innovation

An alternative to the continuum approach (Figure 9.1) has been suggested by Hoyer and McInnes (2001). They suggest that innovations can also be 'functional innovations', 'aesthetic or hedonistic innovations' and 'symbolic innovations'. The first of these, *functional innovations*, have functional performance benefits over existing products. Examples are often technology-driven, such as the combined shampoo/conditioner or ever more powerful laptop computers. Successful aesthetic or hedonistic innovations appeal to consumers' more sensory, creative, pleasure-seeking or creative needs (such as Maslow's levels 5, 6 and 7). Symbolic innovations are related to new associations with, for example, social groups or tribes (see Chapter 7). Symbolic innovations can be invested with other symbolic meanings as well because 'a complete ensemble of consumption objects may be able to repeat the diverse and possibly incongruous aspects of the total self' (Belk, 1988). As a result, our possessions, including the brands we buy, extend our self-image (see Chapter 6) to others and to ourselves. So some new products and services will be especially relevant to consumers' self-concept.

Criteria for Acceptance of Innovations

People are often suspicious of radical innovations and Rogers (1959, 1983) proposed several criteria useful for determining the likely success of new products. Some of these dimensions are more directly involved with facilitating trial, while others both facilitate trial and encourage brand loyalty. We discuss each in turn.

Compatibility

'Compatibility' refers to the degree to which a product is consistent with consumers' current values, cognitions and behaviours. Other things being equal, a product that does not require an important change in consumer values, beliefs, purchase or user behaviours is more likely to be tried by consumers. For example, a shampoo and conditioner in one bottle requires little change on the part of consumers to try the product, and both 'features' are congruent with consumers' behaviours.

Relative advantage

'Relative advantage' refers to the degree to which an item has a sustainable, competitive, differential advantage over other product classes, product forms and brands. There is no question that relative advantage is a most important product characteristic not only for obtaining trial, but also for continued purchase and the development of brand loyalty. The main question raised by this characteristic is: 'Which attribute makes this product better than competitive products'? The shampoo/conditioner, providing it does the job as well as separate products, requires less effort and time.

Relative advantage is a very important element of successful product strategies. However, such an advantage can seldom be sustained through technology or modifications of product attributes alone. One of the most important sources of sustainable relative advantage is product symbolism (as discussed in Chapters 1 and 2 and in the article at the end of Part 1).

Trialability

'Trialability' refers to the degree to which a product can be tried on a limited basis or divided into small quantities for an inexpensive trial. Other things being equal, a product that facilitates a non-purchase trial or limited-purchase trial is more likely to influence the consumer to try the product. Test-driving a car, trying on a sweater, tasting bite-sized pieces of a new snack bar, trying the free sample-sized bottle of a new shampoo 'banded' onto a magazine are ways that consumers can try products on a limited basis with reduced risk.

Observability

'Observability' refers to the degree to which a product or its effects can be sensed by other consumers. New products that are public and frequently discussed or seen are more likely to be adopted rapidly. For example, many clothing styles become popular after consumers see celebrities wearing them, and new cars are also highly observable. There is tremendous importance here, as is discussed shortly, in using opinion formers and opinion leaders to communicate the new product.

Speed

'Speed' refers to how fast the benefits of the product are experienced by the consumer. Because many consumers are orientated towards immediate rather than delayed gratification, products that can deliver benefits sooner rather than later have a higher probability of at least being tried. For example, diets that promise results within the first week are more likely to attract consumers than are those that promise results in six months (but 'hype' can be exposed by the 'observability' characteristic, in this instance).

Simplicity

'Simplicity' refers to the degree to which a product is easy for a consumer to understand and use. Other things being equal, a product that does not require complicated assembly and extensive training for the consumer to use it, has a higher chance of trial. For example, many computer products are promoted as being 'user-friendly' to encourage purchase. The trial or adoption of a new cooking sauce might be delayed if it involved complicated preparation and cooking, especially when many consumers tend to expect 'convenience' in such products.

Perceived Risk

If the perceived (physical, financial or social) risk of the new product is low, it is more likely to be adopted. Products with a high level of perceived risk, such as dangerous or expensive sports, will generally have a lower adoption rate, as can internet banking if security of personal data or finance is perceived to be at risk.

Product Symbolism

Product symbolism refers to what the product or brand means to the consumer and what the consumer experiences in purchasing and using it. Consumer researchers recognize that some products possess symbolic features, and that consumption of them may depend more on their social and psychological meaning than on their functional utility (see Chapter 1). For example, the jeans market is dominated by major brands but there are functional and even design similarities among these. It seems clear that jeans branding and imagery have meanings and symbolize different values for consumers.

Indeed, Hoyer and MacInnis (2001) include 'symbolic innovations' in their framework for categorizing innovations, as mentioned above. To them, symbolic innovations are those that convey some sort of associative meaning such as belonging to a peer or reference group (see Chapter 7). It might not always be a new product in the conventional sense, but rather new symbolic meaning, such as when a long-established drink brand which had an 'old-fashioned' image is repackaged and relaunched and aimed at a young, trendy market.

Aesthetic or Hedonistic Innovations

Aesthetic or hedonistic innovations are also cited by Hoyer and MacInnis (2001) in their categorization of innovations and we can consider them as being important in determining likely acceptance of new products. They appeal to our sensory or pleasure-seeking needs, and include such things as new clothing styles, new forms of dance, new food flavours and textures, so for those who really want to try new things and are motivated by new experiences (see 'Adopter Categories', below) these will be further dimensions that can facilitate trial and adoption.

Innovation Overload

We can add a more general factor: innovation overload (Schiffman and Kanuk, 2000) which is where consumers are faced with a bewildering array of new products across many categories and the increase in the number of, and speed of change within, categories leaves the time-hungry consumer unable to make informed decisions or even any decisions. This can help explain resistance to a new product but is not so much to do with that new product per se, but rather with a general marketing and consumption environment that might be seen to be too active.

The Communication of Innovation

This element of the diffusion process is concerned with direct and deliberate personal forms or less formal, indirect ones that perhaps allow some of the natural opinion leadership flows of information to take their usual course. This can be of crucial importance – often a local opinion leader will be more persuasive than a paid-for expensive advertising campaign. But how to 'influence the influencers' is the inevitable question here. Because different adopter categories have varying characteristics in terms of the sources of information – and even type of message – to which they will respond, different communications approaches will be required: sometimes direct and personal approaches such as personal selling, sometimes less personal such as advertising, and sometimes of the 'article' type – for example as produced through press releases. These aspects are discussed in more detail later in this chapter.

The Social System

Innovations are targeted at specific segments (the 'social system' in terms of the constructs of innovation theory). Again based on adopter category characteristics, some consumers will be more influential within their particular social system (segment) than others, and a later section discusses in some detail the role of opinion formers and opinion leaders and the implications of targeting these in order to speed up the diffusion process.

Time

Some adopters go through the sequence of pre- and post-purchase stages in ways that lead to adoption more quickly than others do, so the time element is an important variable in determining the innovativeness of adopters and in turn who to target and on what basis.

Another aspect of time relates to how quickly the 'new behaviour' required becomes accepted and therefore how quickly discontinuous innovations become dynamically continuous and then continuous innovations.

Adoption

The **adoption** process is really the other side of the same coin: indeed the same dimensions of 'innovation', 'time', 'social system' and 'communication' operate here. Adoption is not merely purchase (that can happen during 'trial') but rather it is more regular or committed purchase behaviour. The adoption process is often shown to be reflected in a series of stages through which consumers progress:

$$\text{Awareness} \Rightarrow \text{Interest} \Rightarrow \text{Evaluation} \Rightarrow \text{Trial} \Rightarrow \text{Adoption}$$

There are variations on the theme here and such sequences are also known as 'hierarchy of effects models' (see Chapters 2–4). The one above makes no allowances for skipping stages and feedback is not catered for. Another early model was proposed by Lavidge and Steiner (1961), as mentioned in Chapter 2 and this includes the following stages:

$$\text{Awareness} \Rightarrow \text{Knowledge} \Rightarrow \text{Liking} \Rightarrow \text{Preference} \Rightarrow \text{Conviction} \Rightarrow \text{Purchase}$$

This was possibly the first adoption model to be based on an 'information–attitude–behaviour' theory of the communications effect (see Chapter 3).

Another problem-solving model lists four stages:

$$\text{Knowledge} \Rightarrow \text{Persuasion} \Rightarrow \text{Discussion} \Rightarrow \text{Confirmation (Rogers and Shoemaker, 1971)}$$

These hierarchy of effects models have been criticized by Ehrenberg (1975) in the context of well-established and regularly advertised brands. In such circumstances, Ehrenberg proposes that consumer behaviour is more to do with habit. Even in his 'Awareness, Trial, Reinforcement' (ATR) model (Figure 9.2) the focus is on reinforcement which can lead to repeat purchase. This would be based on the operant conditioning approach discussed in Chapter 3.

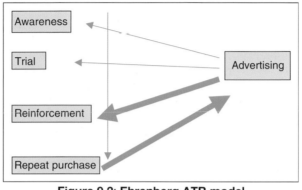

Figure 9.2: Ehrenberg ATR model
The heavy lines denote the major effects.

Whichever model is favoured, an important implication is that the more innovative consumers go through the sequence at a speedier rate than those who are less innovative. As we say, the same elements as for diffusion are appropriate here: the progression through these stages 'over *time*' due to individuals' *innovativeness*, which in turn can be related to their position in *society* and how they influence others and/or are influenced by others and the *communications* sources they seek and are influenced by.

Most prefer to wait and see what happens to the first adopters before they themselves make a purchase. The consumers who do buy at this stage are usually highly involved in the product field. They are heavy users of whatever preceded the innovation (e.g. radio and films in the case of television). In Chapter 6, we discussed rather inconclusive attempts to link consumer personalities with the products and services they buy. One problem with that approach was that consumers do not always recognize the totality of their personalities and, even if they do, some will want to disguise certain traits and project other traits in different social contexts. However, research is much more affirmative over one particular trait: an apparent 'need for newness' or **innovativeness**. Some want to be the first to try novel ideas and thereby to communicate them to others, whereas more cautious consumers buy later, if at all. The more innovative often display a strong personal interest in the product field, which links with 'involvement' as covered in Chapter 4.

A major focus of consumer research has been to identify the characteristics of the more innovative consumers and their differences from other consumers. A review of this research found that the more innovative tend to be more highly educated and younger, and to have greater social mobility, more favourable attitudes towards risk (more venturesome), greater social participation, and higher opinion leadership than other consumers (Gatignon and Robertson, 1985).

It should be noted that the five adopter categories and the percentages in Table 9.1 are somewhat arbitrary. Their validity has not been fully supported in consumer research, particularly not for low-involvement products (Gatignon and Robertson, 1985). It is a useful framework, however, in indicating the relative incidence of the different adopter segments.

Segment	Proportion of eventual total adopters
Innovators	The first 2.5% of the total number of eventual adopters of a new product
Early adopters	The next 13.5% to adopt
Early majority	The next 34% to adopt
Late majority	The next 34% to adopt
Laggards	The last 16% to adopt

Table 9.1: Adopter categories

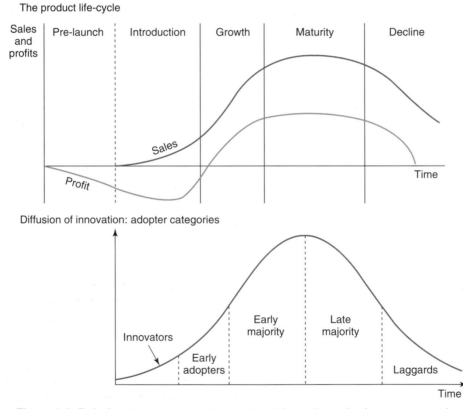

Figure 9.3: **Relationship between the product life cycle and adopter categories**

The idea that different types of consumers become adopters of products in different stages of the product's life cycle does have important implications for marketing strategy (Figure 9.3). Promotion and other elements of marketing strategy should change across time to appeal to different types of consumers. Remember our reference to the product life cycle at the beginning of this chapter. We believe that identifying different adopting segments over time provides more marketing value than the PLC in its more narrow sense and indeed we consider it to be an important base for segmenting markets.

Adopter Categories

The characteristics of adopter categories were well summarized by McCarthy (1977) over 30 years ago:

Innovators are eager to try new ideas. They do not need much persuasion. They are fairly well off and are willing to take risks. They tend to be younger and to have higher status and education. Their reading goes beyond 'local' and mass media communications. They have the closest contact with scientific and specialist sources of information and in general rely on impersonal sources. They seek social relationships outside their local peer circle. They are extrovert in a jet-set sense. They have a broad range of interests and are socially mobile.

Early adopters tend to have the greatest contact with salespeople and local people and are often leaders in local clubs and organizations. They exhibit the greatest opinion leadership and are highly 'localite'. They have a high status and are fairly well off. They are highly respected in local society and are often asked for their opinions and advice.

Early majority have contact with mass media and salespeople, but also with early adopters. They do not exhibit so much opinion leadership and they deliberate over adoption decisions.

Late majority tend to be sceptical and need much pressure from peers before they adopt. They are below average in terms of income, status and education, etc. They adopt when they perceive little risk, perhaps when they see others like themselves using an innovative product.

Laggards are bound in tradition and often use other laggards as sources of information. The past is their frame of reference. Some are semi-isolates who do not use the mass media or salespeople as information sources. They tend to be older and from lower socio-economic groups and are less wealthy. They might become adopters when innovators are adopting the next innovation.

Some consumers may appear to be almost laggardly *non-adopters* but instead do not adopt because they are actively against the usage of a product; for instance anti- or non-smokers, vegetarians, or people that do not possess a car for pro-environmental reasons. These could, in some cases, be innovators in the sense of adopting an (e.g.) anti-materialistic stance.

It becomes clear, on considering this description of the various adopters, how there can be segmentation over time, because each category is quite different from the others in terms of innovativeness, demographic profile and sources of information used. It is worth pointing out that the earliest innovator is not incredibly young, wealthy and well-educated, but is more so than others in the market concerned. In other words, if we are concerned with the over-50s market, innovators are usually nearer 50 than 90 and more affluent than most within the over-50s market, and so on.

What is also evident, however, is that there is a reasonably logical 'cascading' sequence from innovators through to early majority consumers. The 'big divide' could be between early and late majority. For the latter, the 'newness' appeal is precisely why these people are not already adopters. So it means the appeals should change to being less based on newness, even turning this around to state a degree of longevity in the market, 'tried and tested' and so on. It might also mean prices falling a little, to appeal to the late majority. If so, then the whole character of the brand is being changed – perhaps too much for the earlier adopters?

For Moore (1991) the big divide (or 'chasm') is between the early adopters and early majority in the market for hi-tech products: 'the difficulty . . . in accepting a new product if it is presented in the same way as it was to the (preceding) group' (p17).

Another approach, suggested by Gladwell (2002) is that the main influencers of others are: the connectors (these convey messages to many others – they know lots of people), the mavens (see later, but these share information across product categories and act as gatekeepers – they know about lots of innovations) and then there are the salespeople (who are not salespeople (!) but consumers with the charisma to persuade others).

THINKBOX

Tec Shoes is a specialist manufacturer of high-quality athletic footwear. The company has been manufacturing scientifically designed specialist shoes for top runners, racket-sports players and other athletes for several years.

Now the company feels that most people interested in sport could benefit from wearing this footwear because of the increased care and protection of the feet they can provide, because of the contribution that the medical profession as well as experienced footwear and fashion designers make to the creation of the products.

Tec Shoes has been concerned only with top sportspeople on a personal basis and is unsure about how to reach a wider target market. One company executive suggests that different promotional approaches be used to reach different adopter categories over the products' life cycle.

What promotional mixes (advertising, publicity, sales promotion, direct marketing, personal selling) should be used to reach each of these market segments which adopt in different ways 'over time'? How should the 'message' change for each segment?

Adoption in Technological Markets

The Technology Acceptance Model (TAM) extends traditional adoption theory via linkages with attitude models. In Chapter 4 we explored various attitude models and Davis (1989) proposed the amalgam of cognitive, affective and behavioural dimensions when investigating acceptance of computer based information systems (see Figure 9.4).

In addition, perceived ease of use (for example, its complexity) and perceived usefulness (similar to relative advantage) are proposed as being contributors to adoption. This is a simple model and was extended again by Venkatesh and Davies (2000) with the inclusion of the subjective norm construct (how we perceive significant others' feelings about how we should or shouldn't act).

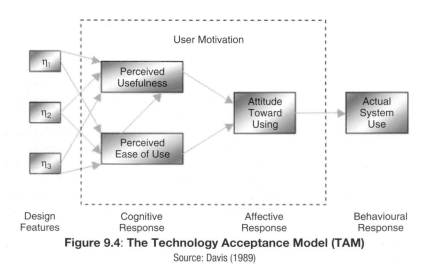

Figure 9.4: **The Technology Acceptance Model (TAM)**
Source: Davis (1989)

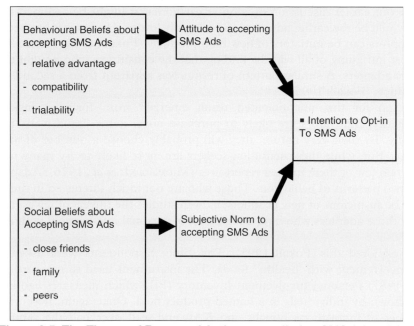

Figure 9.5: The Theory of Reasoned Action as applied to SMS Advertising
Source: Muk (2007)

Again relating back to Chapter 4, but in this case to the Theory of Reasoned Action, Muk and Babin (2006) and Muk (2007) investigated the adoption of mobile SMS advertising via a model that combined components of both traditional adoption theory and the Reasoned Action attitude model (see Figure 9.5).

ADAPTERS VS INNOVATORS

Cognitive style is concerned with how individuals make decisions and solve problems. The **Kirton Adaption Innovation Inventory** (KAI [1994]) scales can identify individuals' positions along one particular continuum of cognitive styles: an adapter–innovator continuum. It was developed in the 1970s in a management context. The scales used relate to the ease or otherwise of how the respondent finds it to project themselves consistently over time as (for example: patient, thorough, having ideas and so on). The more innovative (remember this is a continuum not a rigid categorization) thinks in risky or unexpected ways, is not particularly respectful of the past, questions rules and can be a change agent. On the other hand, the adaptor is more methodical and reliable and is more concerned about group cohesion. In the original management context, innovators included marketing and R&D managers and fashion buyers, whereas the adaptors included bank managers and civil servants.

In the consumption context the identification of the 'initiator' (earlier adopter of products) is strategically important for four reasons (Goldsmith and Flynn, 1992). First, they represent the immediate source of cash flow to the company eager to start retrieving the expenses of new product development; the fact that initiators are usually heavy users of the product class in question means that they play a disproportionate role in recouping developmental costs. Second, they may provide market leadership and help set up barriers to new competition that prevent other firms making a fast entry into the market. Third, they provide important feedback to the company on further new product development (see later in this chapter for the implications of democratizing innovation). Fourth, they communicate the innovation to the less active sections of the market, the bulk of the market who will eventually provide the high levels of sales and profits.

Following from our earlier discussion of adopter categories, it might be assumed that innovators (in the KAI context) would be the earlier adopters and adaptors less so. However it has been found that both innovators and adaptors can be initiators of new food products (Foxall, 1995) indeed 40% of the sample were adapters. Most intriguing of all was the finding that the consumers who bought the largest number of new brands were adapters. A similar pattern of results was apparent from a second study, this time of 'healthy' food products (Foxall, 1995).

A possible reason for this unanticipated result emerged from further consideration of adaption–innovation theory. Innovators are likely to purchase novel items impulsively, independently and perhaps haphazardly. By their very nature, they will probably choose a number of innovative products just to try them out. But, while these sensation-seekers are more likely to try many new products, they are also likely to retain few of them in their repertoires (Mittelstaedt *et al.*, 1976). Adapters, however, will presumably show two patterns of behaviour. Those who are not much interested in the product field will, as we might think, be suspicious of new products; in both studies the buyers of fewest brands or products were adapters. Yet those adapters who have a high level of personal involvement with a product field will act quite differently.

A third study explored this (Foxall, 1995). This time, respondents were asked to indicate their level of personal involvement with 'healthy' foods. The instrument used to measure this construct was the Zaichkowsky (1987) Personal Involvement Inventory (PII) which measures ego-involvement or the personal interest shown by individuals in a named product field. Once again, no correlation was found between the number of innovations bought and KAI, and well over half the sample were adapters. More importantly, the results confirmed the hypothesis: the highest level of purchase was shown by more-involved adapters.

Let us pause a moment to consider the implications of these findings. It appears that the post-launch market for new foods is not a homogeneous collection of innovators whose personalities predispose them to be venturesome, risk-taking, flexible and self-assured *early adopters*, as our earlier framework within this chapter suggested. Rather, the market consists of three psychographic segments, each with its own personality profile: less-involved adapters (who buy least), innovators (who buy an intermediate number regardless of their level of involvement), and more-involved adapters (who buy most). Moreover, each of these segments has its own distinctive style of decision-making. Each segment is likely to become aware of new brands/products in a different fashion, to search and evaluate information in its own way, to choose uniquely and to have a distinctive post-decisional reaction. The launch marketing strategy for a new product needs to accommodate all three.

Two further investigations have taken the use of personal computers as their focal interest: the use of a range of software is usually thought to be highly involving; personal computers are well past the introduction stage of their product life cycle; the research involved consumption rather than purchasing, and it allowed situational variables to be examined (Foxall, 1995).

Whereas in the case of new foods adapters buy most; for software applications innovators were found the most likely to adopt most applications. Involvement is a crucial factor in each case and overall the conventional wisdom is sometimes correct, but unsophisticated, and our conclusion is that marketing strategies must thus be multifaceted. In particular the general involvement level engendered by the product is very important. The market for new 'healthy' foods contains innovators, more-involved adapters, and a significant group of less-involved adapters. That for new software applications contains more-involved adapters, more-involved innovators, plus groups of less-active, less-involved adapters and innovators. Because new product marketing relies on the diffusion sequence over time, none of these can be ignored, even at the launch stage. What consumers absorb about an innovation at that stage may colour their impressions for a long time to come.

Marketing strategies should, therefore, be sensitive to the coexistence of adapters and innovators in both the initial and established markets for new products. A marketing strategy directed towards, say, the adapters is likely to alienate the innovators. Perhaps the failure of marketing campaigns which aimed principally at innovators, and ignored the fact that initial adopters and use-initiators may be adapters, have contributed to the high failure rates of new consumer products. But the crucial question now is the likely implications of adaptive–innovative cognitive styles for future marketing campaigns.

The conventional wisdom provides easy prescriptions for managerial action: just focus on the more innovative, but the research indicates that there are three problems with that. First, each launch segment has a unique decision-making style. Second, each active segment, therefore, requires its own launch marketing mix, reflecting the decision style and involvement level of its members. Third, post-launch markets – the markets for imitators – are also segmented by decision style and require multifaceted marketing.

An important extension of this research is the linkage with stages in the decision process. Foxall and Bhate (1993) propose that for the problem recognition stage the less involved adaptor is less likely than the innovator to seek problems and ignore radical or discontinuous innovations. More involved adaptors, however, show the highest level of awareness of new products.

As for search and evaluation, adaptors show their cautious but thorough characteristics by being deliberate though these stages. Innovators are more likely to be more wide ranging in searching for and evaluating alternatives (not just in the same product category) and can be less meticulous.

At the decision stage adaptors will be much more cautious than innovators who can display greater impulsiveness. Indeed innovators can be rather blasé about discontinuous innovations, where adaptors perceive discontinuities in less disruptive newness. Highly involved adaptors, however, can decide positively on a wider range of innovations than those adaptors who are less involved with the product category or even than innovators.

When it comes to the post purchase stage, adaptors reflect more thoroughly and justify decisions based on their more extensive earlier deliberations, compared with innovators. The latter can switch brands more easily and quickly compared with adaptors.

THINKBOX

Have a go at completing the following table:

Decision Styles of Market Segments

Stage in the Adoption Decision Process	Less Involved Adapters	Innovators	More Involved Adapters
Problem recognition Search	Passive, reactive	Superficial but extensively based within and across product class boundaries	

Decision Styles of Market Segments

Stage in the Adoption Decision Process	Less Involved Adapters	Innovators	More Involved Adapters
Evaluation			Careful, confined to considerations raised by relevant product category but executed confidently and (for adapter) briskly within frame of reference
Decision	Conservative selection within known range of products, continuous innovations preferred		
Post purchase evaluation		Less loyal, constantly seeking novel experience through purchase and consumption	

See website for the full version.

TWO- AND MULTI-STEP FLOWS OF COMMUNICATIONS

As will have been deduced from the initial framework, a major factor in speeding up the diffusion process is the use of 'recommendations' by those who are seen to have **source credibility**, which can involve perceived expertise and trustworthiness. **Source attractiveness** is where the consumer perceives the source of a message to be similar to themselves and this has been found to increase the persuasiveness of the source (Woodside and Davenport, 1974).

Consumers receive information about new products from a variety of sources including from those who are thought to possess special knowledge and expertise. These intervening participants are often regarded as credible because they are perceived to be trustworthy and because they are believed to have expertise in a particular product area. This is Lazarsfeld's (1944) proposition, and led to his 'two-step' flow of communications model (Figure 9.6).

Katz and Lazarsfeld (1955) presented these initial ideas following research into the voting and purchase behaviour of Americans. They identified individuals who not only received information but also processed and re-presented the information to others and in doing so were able to influence their decision-making. Therefore, information received directly from personal influence channels is regarded as generally more persuasive than information received through mass media. Those people who influence others are usually referred to as **opinion leaders**, and are often product class- or domain-specific. Those who are opinion leaders across categories are known as **market mavens** (see later section).

Some people have status conferred upon them by their peer group (Raven and French, 1959; and see Chapter 7). Through recognition of their expertise, prowess or particular knowledge or skills, these opinion leaders are able to guide and lead the thoughts of others in particular product areas. Opinion leaders often rely on word-of-mouth communications to influence others and often do so, as Kingdom (1970) says, passively, by being observed. Bristow *et al.* (2005) reaffirm the importance of opinion leaders who do not just communicate by word of mouth (WOM) but by being observed. They refer to such opinion leaders as **opinion shapers**. In this way, the key point is that they are change agents however they communicate with others. Featherstone (1991) describes symbol specialists, style leaders, taste makers and leading edge consumers, but it all amounts to the same general paradigm of influence.

However, the model can be enhanced. Some influencers have a status of expertise bestowed upon them by the nature of their employment or training (e.g. journalists). These are referred to as opinion formers: people who are actively and deliberately involved in the process of shaping and forming the thoughts of others with regard to specific products and services. Very often they will use the mass media to communicate their reprocessed information (journalists) while all can be regarded as active influencers, or talkers (Kingdom, 1970).

Opinion Formers and Opinion Leaders

To illustrate the difference between the two types of influencer, an accountant who has particular taxation skills may be an opinion former to their clients. Communications might be expected to be more formal and direct. To their peers they may be an important advisory/influential person and thus be an opinion leader. Communications in these circumstances may be more informal and indirect (word-of-mouth).

Sender $------\blacktriangleright$ Opinion leader $------\blacktriangleright$ Receiver

Figure 9.6: Two-step model of communication

Just as the role of the influencer can be considered to be relatively complex, so can the role of the receivers or opinion followers. Some actively seek information from the social networks within which they participate (two-step) while others prefer to rely on mass media communications (one-step) for information and guidance (Robinson, 1957).

The **two-step model of communication** has a number of strengths and weaknesses. Opinion formers and leaders are assumed to pass on positive information, but communication planners need to be sure that they will not reprocess and transmit the information in a negative manner and so reverse the intentions of the source of the message. Furthermore, not only can opinion leaders be difficult to identify but also it can be difficult to measure the degree of impact they have in influencing opinion followers. Opinion formers, on the other hand, are more easily identified but potentially less effective than opinion leaders.

Real Opinion Formers

Broadcast entertainment programmes are sometimes used to convey messages. An example of this is the Russian radio 'soap' *House Seven, Entrance 4* which is part funded by the EU Know-How Fund with the aim of giving advice on living in a market economy (Bailey, 1997). The then British Prime Minister, Tony Blair, even appeared on this programme as an opinion former conveying a message about the importance of education.

> # THINKBOX
>
> Next time you listen to a 'news' programme, count the number of times phrases like: 'X is likely to announce Y today' occur. In such cases, news is not being reported, but press releases are. Should we therefore have two categories of 'news': *actual* news and *future* news? We even hear music being announced as a 'future hit'. Such reports by credible news or music presenters are examples of opinion-forming.
>
> 'Free features Ltd provides an online database of copy that can be downloaded by any editor free of charge provided they include information from a commercial sponsor' (Katbamna, 2005).
>
> Could it be that 'news is something someone, somewhere doesn't want printed, the rest is just public relations' (Humphries, 1995) and that, with or without regulation among the ranks of 'invisible persuaders', influence over the media is as 'powerful as it remains utterly unnoticed' (Michie, 1998:316)?
>
> What do you think?

In Chapter 3 we introduced celebrity endorsers in the context of associationist learning theory: a brand can be associated with the characteristics and personality of a celebrity. We return to celebrity endorsement here because celebrities can be used as opinion formers. Indeed, Till *et al.* (2008) show how celebrity endorsers are the conditioned stimuli in associative learning, but the 'pairing' of brand and celebrity needs to be appropriate. If it is, brand attitudes can be strong and lasting.

So, generally there should be a degree of congruity between the celebrity used and the brand itself (Kamins, 1990; Misra and Beatty, 1990) but congruence can be on different levels: some logical link, such as a sports person endorsing sporting equipment; or merely emotional, where a comedian endorses a relatively frivolous or 'wacky' brand.

Since consumers perceive some celebrities as highly trustworthy, believable, persuasive and likeable, marketers often rely on them to endorse their products. In the UK, for example, the image of Sainsbury's supermarkets has been greatly enhanced by its use of a TV chef (Jamie Oliver) in its advertising messages, and Oliver spearheaded a campaign to improve school dinners in 2005. His expertise as a chef invested him with opinion-forming powers.

In 1979 when Sony introduced the Walkman, the company gave samples of the product to film stars and models, who were thus used as opinion formers to show that there was a fashion benefit as well as functionality. As the company's public relations manager states, 'The most powerful way of telling someone that something is a good product is if someone who is credible tells you that it is' (Goodman, 1997).

EXAMPLE 9.1

A problem with this approach is that the celebrity might do something to dilute or even degrade the association. For example, Adidas pulled out of a campaign using the athlete Dwain Chambers when he was found guilty of using banned drugs. Indeed Amos *et al* (2008) found negative news about a celebrity can be very harmful in an advertising campaign. Even if they are good boys and girls, it can cost the marketers large sums. For example, in 2003 David Beckham was reported to be earning, from such endorsements: £2 million from Vodafone, £1 million from Marks & Spencer, £1 million from Rage Software, £1 million from Police brand sunglasses, £1 million from Brylcreem and £5 million from Adidas (among others) (Hopkins, 2003). This is not to say that he isn't an effective opinion former, but how cost-effective?

However, the use of celebrities to endorse brands is not new. Figure 9.7 shows the use of Shirley Temple, a child actress of the 1930s, being portrayed on a cereal pack. Note that her film company also gets a mention. We couldn't resist the other historical example of an opinion former which depicts a nurse, possessing a degree of expert knowledge recommending a product.

THINKBOX

Are you influenced to think of a brand differently if promoted using a well-known celebrity (be honest)?

A related issue is the number of different product types a celebrity is endorsing at a given time. For instance, Tripp *et al.* (1994) investigated the effects of a number of products endorsed by a celebrity on consumer attitudes and purchase intentions. Their findings revealed a negative link between multiple products endorsed by a celebrity and consumer attitudes towards the advertisement.

Figure 9.7: Shirley Temple and Evansol Antiseptic
Shirley Temple – Reproduced by permission of Robert Opie
Evansol – Image courtesy of The Advertising Archives

Figure 9.8: Some recent opinion-forming celebrity endorsers
Images courtesy of the Advertising Archives

Perhaps it is an example of the cynical and marketing-savvy environment in which we all now live that consumers know that companies might want to make some sort of relevant association between the product and the endorser but that the endorser may or may not even use the product, never mind like it. Silvera and Austad (2004) concluded from their experimental research into the effectiveness of celebrity endorsement, that marketers could pay more attention than they do to 'making strong and believable explanations for why endorsers truly do like the products they endorse'. This is based on their findings that consumers can be persuaded more if they believe the endorser likes what they are endorsing. Some rather more recent opinion-forming celebrity endorsers are shown in Figure 9.8.

Another issue concerns how well celebrities 'travel' in global marketing campaigns. Research is less well developed in this area and Chao *et al.*'s (2005) exploratory study advocates further research. The use of celebrities can be further explained with reference to types of social power: social power, referent power, information power, legitimate power, expert power, reward power and coercive power (Raven and French, 1959; and see Chapter 7).

Small businesses have scarce resources and cannot really afford to compete with the large advertising budgets of some of their powerful competitors. So, rather than booking expensive television advertising campaigns to target the final consumer, it is often recommended that they consider targeting business correspondents of the local newspapers and magazines as opinion formers, so that they might achieve some editorial coverage of their new ranges or other aspects of their business.

These correspondents are read as if they possess a degree of knowledge and credibility regarding the subject matter and act as opinion formers, sometimes in a far more persuasive way than a paid-for advertising campaign. On a larger scale, this is why, for example, the top fashion designers are keen to 'show' at the major fashion shows in order to get editorial coverage in the leading fashion and women's magazines and national newspapers. The 'saleability' of their collections is often only secondary to achieving 'exposure' via the opinion-forming fashion journalists. In this way there is a multi-step flow of communications: designers to opinion-forming journalists to buyers in chain stores and their designers, then to opinion-leading consumers and on to the following 'majority' in the market place.

Similar methods are employed in the motor market (Evans and Fill, 2000) where public relations (PR) people possess databases of motoring correspondents and categorize these in terms of their opinion-forming credentials with the consumer – or at least in terms of circulation figures for their newspapers and magazines.

Some PR managers said they targeted a few carefully selected motoring journalists, with some going more for blanket coverage of the motoring press and others recognizing the different levels of likely persuasion possible from regional and national newspapers and the motoring magazines. Some even recognize more of a pecking order among named journalists, such as one who has a list of 1700 motoring journalists but selects 600 of the 'top' journalists for some events and just six for other events.

Selected journalists might be taken, via first-class travel, to (for example) South Africa (in the case of one car launch) where they road-tested the new car, enjoyed the sunshine, food and hospitality (and even partners were paid for, though only at second-class rates!) and were given a 'press release'. Now, this is not merely a list of technical specifications but will usually be full of favourable adjectives, many of which can reappear in road reports in the press. Most car manufacturers employ in-house PR specialists, many having previously been motoring journalists themselves.

The consumer will read these road reports as if from some totally objective and independent source. An editor of one such magazine has admitted that there is pressure on editors by the advertisers. If less glowing reports are published, he says, there have been occasions when the advertiser has informed the editor that they will advertise elsewhere for a while.

This goes even further. A PR consultant confessed that they regularly check the daily press and estimate that two-thirds to three-quarters of the news/editorial (that is, ignoring all advertising content) originates from some PR source or another. This type of publicity isn't advertising, it comes from an (objective) business journalist, so again the cognitive defences on the part of the readership are not raised.

The findings confirmed that, in the case of motor industry PR personnel, nearly all of their campaigns targeted journalists, that this approach was important to their strategy and that it was very effective. This confirms the general multi-step flow proposition. The main methods of so targeting journalists is via press releases and 'events' such as launches.

In a major study by Lewis *et al.* (2008) it was found that 60% of press articles and 34% of stories broadcasted were sourced from PR or wire services. This study confirmed the one by Evans and Fill (2000) in that journalists are more pressed for time today and ready-prepared material helps them – but does it help the consumer if objectivity is less clear?

The use of opinion polls has also been called into question recently in a related context (Nancarrow *et al.*, 2004). Pressure groups increasingly want to convince legislators of their cause and sometimes use biased question wording in their opinion polls, encourage supporters of the cause to 'pile in' as respondents or distort the statistical data so the results are more favourable to the cause than they really are. This can be a sort of reverse opinion-forming, where (supposed) public opinion is used in attempts to influence politicians, but the claimed objectivity of x% wanting 'whatever' is used to form the opinions of others.

Simulated Opinion Formers

The BBC's *The Archers* has been used as an opinion former to convey messages about farming practice and indeed one of its original aims when launched was to educate farmers about new methods after the Second World War. The characters are fictional but possess a degree of perceived credibility in the farming sphere.

Other UK 'soaps' frequently portray issues that have been either influenced by, or worked through in conjunction with, a sponsor of some kind. For example, a storyline concerned with euthanasia was prompted by a press release from the Morphine Information Service, demonstrating the multi-step flow model. The show's producer has stated, 'We cannot get away from the fact that people will have an interest in putting a message across in (our) stories' (Mellis, 1997). Other 'soap' stories have originated from the UK government (adult literacy) and the National Schizophrenia Fellowship (a storyline concerning schizophrenia). These are strong examples of how opinion formers, albeit 'simulated' opinion formers (the characters exist only in fiction), can be powerful formers of opinion.

Indeed as Turner (2008) reports, the government is being urged by a Treasury backed report to use such vehicles more often to convey social marketing campaigns such as being cautious with money and credit.

EXAMPLE 9.2

An example is a totally mythical character, Roy of the Rovers. The comic of this name was bought by a sportswear company and whereas there was little advertising in the publication the sporting hero, Roy, was always wearing that company's brand of sportswear.

Many films and television programmes are subject to 'product placement', where brands are shown or mentioned in the film. Viewers do not put up their cognitive defence to the same extent as they might if the same products appeared in commercials. The suppliers pay for the privilege, of course. A classic example concerns the James Bond series. Many products are mentioned or shown, often just once, and part of the idea is that James Bond is some sort of aspirational reference point for some of the audience, an opinion former in effect, and if he wears a Seiko watch, shaves with a Philishave, drinks Bollinger champagne and drives an Aston Martin, BMW or even a Citroen 2CV, then followers should do so as well! This is a classic example of a simulated opinion former.

EXAMPLE 9.3

MarketingWeek

TV soaps should educate consumers on debt issues

The Government should use popular soap operas such as Coronation Street and East- Enders to educate consumers about financial services, according to a new Treasury-backed report.

The Thoresen Review of Generic Financial Advice, written by Otto Thoresen, the chief executive financial services group of Aegon UK, also suggests the financial services industry could save £57m in marketing costs each year by supporting a government-backed cash education scheme.

The final report published this week sets out a number of recommendations for the government and industry backed generic financial advice scheme, Money Guidance. It follows an interim report, published last year, which said an ad budget of up to £30m could be set aside to support the proposed free advice scheme (*MW* November 1, 2007).

The Government has pledged £12m for a large-scale trial of the service, which will be led by the Financial Services Authority (FSA). Thoresen suggests television could play a "big part" in the engagement strategy and recommends positioning the service within a storyline of "one of the popular soap operas" or creating a Money Guidance-themed "lifestyle" series. He urges the Government to use initiatives to form part of the trial.

The report further details how the industry-backed service could save it money. It says that the industry spends around £1.5bn a year on advertising and promotion, with a further £4bn in commissions to intermediaries.

Thoresen says that the industry's advertising and marketing campaigns will be more effective if targeted at an audience that understands basic financial facts.

He adds: "Any attempt to put a value on this would be purely speculative, but if the figures quoted could be reduced by just 1%, this would generate savings across the industry of £57m a year".

Marketing Week, 6th March 2008, p.5. Reproduced by permission of Centaur Media Plc.

'Real' Opinion Leaders

As for using real opinion leaders, an early experiment conducted by Mancuso (1969) demonstrates the potential influence they can exert. A pop record was produced, but not distributed widely. In some university towns, sociometric research was conducted. This entailed asking each student, in isolation from the rest of the group, with which other members of the class they would most like a conversation about buying music (sociometric research, see 7.3). Those students  mentioned by many others were identified as possessing a degree of credibility in terms of music and records. They were then thought to be higher in opinion leadership than others. A copy of the record was mailed to these opinion leaders, as a token of appreciation.

As a 'control group', a copy of the record was mailed to other students in other universities. In this case, however, student names were selected at random from class lists. Some may have been opinion leaders, but this would have been a coincidence and it is assumed that fewer of them would be opinion leaders than those selected in the other universities through sociometric research. Distribution for the record was set up in the university towns that were used as both experimental and control groups. For those towns in which 'real' opinion leaders were selected, the record moved into the charts, but in the control towns, where few opinion leaders were targeted, the record was not a 'hit'.

This research demonstrates the potential power of targeting opinion leaders. It also indicates the complexity that is often encountered when attempting to identify real opinion leaders, by name and address.

As mentioned earlier, Bristow *et al.* (2005) use the term 'opinion shapers' because, to them, this extends word of mouth (WOM) influence to non-verbal communication such as that which vicarious learning (Chapter 3) would explain. They also report an interesting study which found that opinion shapers in the financial services market (consumers) were twice as likely to say that they sought out finance TV programmes as the rest of the respondents. Financial services marketers should clearly either 'buy into' such programme's advertising 'spots' or even sponsor the programme (or perhaps try to influence the content?). The same research found that opinion shapers in the 16- to 34-year-old group were more than 1.3 times the average likely to watch US entertainment and fashion programmes. So again there are useful clues for the marketers wishing to reach opinion leaders/shapers in the consumer market.

In Chapter 7 we explored family influence and it is interesting to note that the government in the UK targets parents, as opinion leaders to children, with a view to reducing drinking among children. The Youth Alcohol Action Plan (Singh, 2008b) also offers advice to parents on when to introduce their children to drinking alcohol in the home. Similarly, a social marketing advertising campaign has depicted how young children follow the lead set by parents by copying their smoking behaviour, albeit at an early age by mimicking smoking using crayons (Weissberg, 2008). These campaigns are supposed to show parents the opinion leading influence they exert over their children in these potentially health damaging areas.

EXAMPLE 9.4

Another example is the marketing of the Tamagotchi (virtual pet) in the late 1990s. In Japan, teenagers were recruited to 'spread the word' to their friends about the new product and even to form queues outside stores to simulate strong demand (Murphy, 1997).

In pharmaceutical markets, for example, the approach was described by a medic, Michael Rawlins (1984) in the *Lancet* – in somewhat critical terms. He described how medics in UK are targeted by the pharmaceutical industry and are classified as either 'conservatives' or 'risk takers'. The more innovative are identified by sales representatives who discuss doctors' prescribing habits with local pharmacists. This information can be used to target the more innovative when a new drug is being launched. To their peers these are opinion leaders and are invited to various 'events', seminars, lunches and so on. The effect is for a substantial proportion of them to start prescribing the new drug. Their behaviour is observed by the less innovative and is emulated, thus demonstrating the two-step flow of communication. Rawlins is critical of the industry for the approach but also lays a charge of potential corruption at the door of some medics. They expect such rewards in return for sometimes needless prescribing habits.

To take this further, some years ago the drug Flosint was launched. It treated rheumatoid arthritis and the launch was based on selected medics (opinion leaders among peers in their field) being taken to Switzerland for a weekend 'conference' with plenty of food and drink and an all-expenses paid trip on the *Orient Express*. Many went back to prescribe Flosint and they were copied by the followers. The approach can clearly be effective in speeding up the diffusion rate. The final twist to this particular case history was that, within a few months of its launch, Flosint was associated with several deaths and it was banned.

THINKBOX

'Young influentials' is a term used to describe opinion leading tweens and teens (Carey, 2004). It is suggested that not only does the opinion leading concept apply in these younger markets, but it can be especially persuasive here. They are at school and want to be different from children younger than them and also to be different from people older than they are. Such differentiation can be sought from other tweens and teens who are seen to be especially well connected (they participate in many school and non-school activities), communicate via mobile phones and social networking sites more than many do, have more friends than others, are respected by their followers and, as with the classic opinion leader, are asked for views by other kids. They themselves seek information and could even verge on being seen to possess the 'expert' status according to French and Raven (1959). Young influentials have been found to be involved in more household decisions as well (Carey, 2004).

Could their influence help to explain the near epidemic spread of some new products, especially fashion and music?

Is there a link here with the concept of the memetic (Chapter 1)?

The Lewis (2008) report, cited above, also concluded that health was the area most influenced by PR. It is, perhaps, mildly reassuring that in some quarters the next generation of medics is savvy to the PR techniques and are blocking pharmaceutical reps from educational and clinical locations of Universities (Marcus, 2007). Several universities ban medics from accepting gifts, including the proverbial free lunch. The problem is likely to be obvious to students when guest lecturers are sometimes found to be company reps espousing, albeit subtly, their companies' drugs. Indeed in the US, third-year medical students were recipients of a gift or lunch by a drug company each week (Marcus, 2007).

The strict rules on gifts and hospitality within pharmaceutical marketing are somewhat weak: 'in the Munich European Conference for cardiologists the big companies hold quizzes . . . doctors sit on stools at a table, fingers on buzzers, or crowd round the posters filling in questionnaires about the company drugs . . . is everyone a winner . . . many doctors wander around the stands with bags crammed with booty' (Guardian, 2004).

It has even been reported that some medical test results on drugs have been affected by the drug company that sponsored the academic research with some research articles being ghostwritten by the company and therefore bringing into question the validity of the research paper, even though it appears in a reputable medical journal (Healy, 2004). Such use of medical articles would come into the category of opinion forming because the reputation of the journal itself is of that status. If named authors are perceived by peer medics as specialists then the author would be an opinion leader.

If pharmaceutical companies manage to restrict the amount of data from the trials of a drug to be released to the academic researchers who had agreed to analyse and write up the trials for publication in peer-reviewed refereed medical journals, then the supposedly credible and objective reporting of findings can be questioned on both grounds. The Parliamentary Select Committee inquiry (Healy, 2005) into pharmaceutical marketing heard that if medics were not especially influenced by freebies, travel and lunches, what really influenced them was the medical evidence about new drugs from randomized control trials as published in opinion-forming peer-reviewed journals such as *The Lancet* and the *British Medical Journal*. It has been alleged that drug companies sometimes manage to influence how these articles are written, for example, by not releasing the full trial data, so the results might be distorted. This was an implied allegation in the case for P&G's *Actonel* brand (Baty, 2005).

The drug Vioxx was withdrawn in 2008 and it is alleged that the drug company concerned, Merck, only released selected data from the drug trials (on deaths from using the drug) to the US Food and Drug Administration (Boseley, 2008). In addition, papers released during the litigation process here, suggested that 'papers published in journals on the results of Vioxx trials were ghostwritten by employees or contracted medical writers and that leading doctors were later invited to be named as authors. Financial links were sometimes but not always declared' (Boseley, 2008).

Professor Murray of the Institute of Psychiatry is reported as stating 'academics, particular academic pharmacologists, have somehow begun to believe that it is acceptable to present company data as if they were a hired gun' (2004). Indeed the Chief Executive of MIND (Brook, 2004) resigned from the industry's regulatory committee (*British Medicines and Healthcare Products Regulatory Agency*) partly because he saw a tension between safeguarding the public and the power of the pharmaceutical industry in maintaining the status quo. Professor Andrew Herxheimer also expressed concern over this tension (2005) and Sismodo (2007) found ghost management of pharmaceutical information to be extensive and calls for tighter regulation and greater questioning of sources of medical information.

Political lobbying is also based on the general principle here. PR companies maintain computerized databases of all Members of Parliament, their political and non-political interests. When the small print of proposed legislation is scrutinized by these companies on behalf of their clients and something is discovered that might affect the client, the PR agents set to work on opinion-leading politicians. Often it will not be members of the Cabinet who are targeted but those known to have an interest in and credibility over the issue. These Members of Parliament will be dined and receive a presentation in favour of the PR consultant's client. If they go back to Parliament and set up 'working committees', they will probably be more influential because they are seen to have greater (opinion leading) credibility than other Members of Parliament in the issue concerned.

THINKBOX

Does the use of opinion leaders in medical and political areas raise concerns over the ethics of such approaches? Why, or why not?

An interesting twist to opinion leadership is the phenomenon of democratising innovation, which we introduced in Chapter 7. Here, companies are increasingly turning to those consumers who are highly involved with their products category and engage with social networking and company sponsored online communities, for ideas for new products. This is a sort of reversed opinion leadership because it is trickle-up from consumer, rather than trickle-down from the company.

 www. **Have a look at this web site, which provides more on pressure groups in politics:** http://www.historylearningsite.co.uk/pressure_groups.htm

We feel that the addition of the opinion former transforms the original two-step flow model into a multi-step flow model. Here the sender will target opinion formers directly and deliberately and may or may not target opinion leaders (perhaps depending on the complexity involved with identification). Opinion leaders may receive information from the sender and/or from opinion formers, as suggested in Figure 9.9.

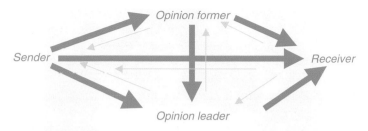

Figure 9.9: **Multi-step flows of communication and the integration of opinion-forming and opinion-leading**
M Evans and C Fill Extending the Communication Process, *International Journal of Advertising*, Vol 19 No 3
(2000), pp 377–396.
Reproduced by permission of the World Advertising Research Center

www. Take a look at the article by Nancarrow, Nancarrow and Page (2002) An Analysis of the Concept of *Cool* and its Marketing Implications, Journal of Consumer Behaviour, Vol 1 No 4 pp 311–322 on the web site at `www.wileyeurope.com/college/evans`.

This paper explores cultural capital and cultural intermediaries within the context of investigating style leaders' consumption.

Identifying opinion leaders can be time consuming, as with the application of sociometrics in Mancuso's research above. Other techniques have been used as well, such as 'self report'. For example, Corey (1971) suggested that individuals can be asked:

'When it comes to . . . Which of the following statements comes closest to describing you:

Friends and relatives usually come to me for advice and information (to identify leaders)

I usually go to friends and relatives for advice and information (to identify non-leaders).

We introduced Gladwell's notion of 'connectors' earlier. He asked respondents how many people with one of the family names listed (100) did they know. Those who said they knew several whose family name is the same (e.g. Evans, Jamal, Foxall) might be more 'connected' than those knowing few with the same family name. This is useful but could be misleading – in Wales everyone might know 150 Evanses and there could be a similar preponderance in the Pakistani community with Jamal. The method does not necessarily indicate the level of engagement with all of these 'contacts'.

Simulating Opinion Leaders

As was seen earlier, those in the early adopter category are more likely to be higher in opinion leadership, and they possess certain demographic characteristics. This means that with some further research into specific markets, it is usually possible to identify the *sort* of people who are opinion leaders. These characteristics can then be depicted in promotional campaigns. Levi's employ different advertising campaigns for the 15- to 19-year-olds in the style press in order to 'reach the key opinion leaders in that age group' (Edmonson, 1993).

In the study of the motor market (Evans and Fill, 2000) reported above, relatively few motor PR campaigns target opinion-leading consumers, instead using the opinion forming power of celebrities.

Figure 9.10: **George the Bear**
Source: Hofmeister
Image courtesy of the Advertising Archives

Some years ago the brewing industry wanted to change the image of lager as being a feminine drink. The approach was to advertise more macho images of men drinking lager and to associate, through sponsorship, lager with energetic and aggressive sports. All of this probably contributed to the 'lager lout' image but certainly demonstrated effective campaigns. The simulated opinion leadership approach was prohibited in that anything vaguely communicating a lager lout stereotype could not be used. One company took the simulation even further and introduced George the bear who was only a stone's throw away from being a lager lout himself (figure 9.10). Even this approach was banned, serving to reinforce its potential effectiveness.

Stimulating Opinion Leadership

This is concerned with encouraging people to talk about an issue. An early example of this was when British Gas introduced a seminal advertising campaign selling company shares. This was in an era when share ownership among the general public was low and at an early stage of development. The campaign featured the 'tell Sid' strap line and depicted ordinary people being interested enough in the new concept that they thought that spreading the word was important.

Contemporarily, consumers are increasingly turning to social networks and blogs for advice, from peers, about products and services (Hampton, 2008). Those with a degree of perceived expertise or opinion leadership could be 'stimulated' into such engagement. In recent times, marketers have been harnessing the power of word of mouth – or rather word of 'mouse', via blogs and social networks. By 'seeding' discussions, in ways favourable to the brand, markets have come under attack when they do not make it clear that they are not 'ordinary' consumers, but representing the brand (Jay, 2008c).

Other examples of what is rapidly becoming known as **buzz marketing** include 'planting' company representatives in a social setting, where they talk loudly about a product or service category, so that they are obviously going to be heard by others in the bar, or wherever they are. Once it appears that others are concentrating on this conversation, the 'plants' stand up and announce the company and hand out leaflets. This version has been termed **conversational advertising** (Flack, 2007). It fits with the idea of stimulating opinion leadership by encouraging discussion and forwarding to others.

The much publicized relaunch of the Wispa bar has been credited to a virtual whispering campaign by consumers nostalgic for the old Wispa bar. Whether it really was true that Facebook members

Figure 9.11: Simulated opinion leaders
He's not real but James Bond can lead opinion.
Reproduced by permission of Omega SA

were so vociferous about this that Cadbury reintroduced the product will only be known to the company, but the story demonstrates the potential power of stimulating opinion leaders across virtual social network media (Parry, 2008). Although not a focus of the current discussion, this is also an example of the contemporary phenomena of **Retro Marketing,** whereby nostalgia can inform product design, fashion design, product re-launches and advertising campaigns. There are 70s nights, traditional 'bangers and mash' on the menus of upmarket restaurants and the revival of old style music players.

The overall implication is to communicate with the opinion leaders first (by formal marketing activities) and then through a two-step or even multi-step flow of communication and influence, the 'followers' are persuaded.

Market Mavens

Feick and Price (1987) identify an extension of the gatekeeper role (see Chapter 7). Market mavens not only hold useful information for others about products but also they are so interested in buying and consumption generally that they can provide information about prices and availability at different stores as well as details of the products themselves. They may not, however, have purchased these products themselves – they are almost 'consumerist hobbyists' (Clark and Goldsmith, 2005). Transferred to the Internet they are termed **infomediaries** and act in a similar 'agony aunt' role for other consumers. Indeed they have been found to be motivated by a desire to share information, to help others and by the joy of disseminating information about products (Walsh *et al.*, 2004).

Such sharing and dissemination can be orchestrated by marketers via viral or network marketing campaigns in which the targeted consumer is encouraged to send the message (chain letter-like) on to many of their friends. Thomas (2004) extends network, pyramid and viral marketing into 'buzz marketing'. He defines this as where marketers' initial efforts are 'amplified by third parties'. The Internet facilitates this via chat rooms and online communities and he shows how even irate consumers can be

Figure 9.12: **Retro Marketing**
Source: Monsoon and Martin Evans

used positively if their problems can be sorted out, because they are often more involved and are likely to share experiences. So again we have the importance of involvement in the influence process.

An adaptation of the market maven concept has been adopted by the 118 118 telephone advice service. From May 2008 this extended beyond directory enquires to a more general information service: as if 118 118 is a market maven. The company also linked this with the popular conception that London taxi divers have opinions on lots of things and so a launch campaign installed telephones in some London taxis allowing passengers to contact 118 118 (free) to ask anything! (O'Flaherty, 2008)

Diffusion Patterns

In some markets – for example, fashion – it is typical for marketing to use multi-step flows of communication; in this instance from designers to fashion shows, to fashion editors and journalists, to retail buyers to consumer fashion opinion leaders to fashion followers, in early and late 'majority' categories. Again in this instance, fashion opinion leaders are characterized as young, gregarious and high in status (Katz and Lazarsfeld, 1955). However, fashion opinion leaders can be found at both the top and bottom of the socio-economic scale (Midgeley and Wills, 1979). If they are so spread for a single fashion then there can be difficulties in maintaining consistent marketing communications. Other researchers have come up with theories of 'trickle down' (from designers to the general public), 'trickle across' (spreading within social strata) and even 'trickle up' (especially punk fashions in 1970s). Evans (1988) explored what was considered to be a confusing set of 'trickle theories in the fashion contexts and suggested that self-concept theory (see Chapter 6) could be a useful addition.

SUMMARY

■ The manner in which a new innovation is communicated and distributed in a society is called 'diffusion' and there can be many types of innovations such as discontinuous, dynamically continuous and continuous innovations. Important characteristics of innovations include compatibility, relative advantage, triability, observability, speed, simplicity, perceived risk, product symbolism, hedonism and innovation overload. This chapter has shown that some consumers progress through unawareness to repurchase sequences more quickly than others. It is also clear that there are several different categories of adopters and that this helps greatly in understanding how consumers behave toward new products.

■ The concept of two- or multi-step flows of communication (from more innovative opinion leaders to the followers) is especially helpful in speeding up the diffusion rates for new products and services. There are also, however, some ethical concerns over some uses of this knowledge. It is probably not generally realized how much of the editorial and news content of our media is derived from publicity sources. Such sources target opinion formers, especially, based on their pivotal and powerful role in multi-step flows of communications.

■ Conventional wisdom, which assumes a uniform process of consumer decision-making, should, it appears, be modified to include considerations not only of level of involvement but also of consumers' differing cognitive styles as measured by such methods as the KAI inventory.

QUESTIONS

1. **Which discontinuous innovations, dynamically continuous innovations and continuous innovations have you personally experienced?**

2. **How much have you influenced others and how much have you been influenced by others in a buying context? Did any of the roles of market maven, opinion leader, or opinion former apply?**

3. **What ethical issues are involved with the targeting journalists or politicians via the model of multi-step flows of communication?**

4. **Explore the issues involved with Kirton's Adapter-Innovator paradigm in the context of innovative buying.**

5. **What is the Technology Acceptance Model and how can it explain consumer behavior with respect to new products?**

6. **Discuss the concepts of real, simulated and stimulated opinion leadership in a consumer market of your choice.**

FURTHER READING

Foxall G R (2003) Consumer Decision Making: Process, Level and Styles, in Baker M (ed.), *The Marketing Book*, Butterworth Heinemann. This chapter is an excellent summary of the extension of innovation theory to take account of different consumer decision styles. The work draws from Kirton's original 'adaptive-innovative' theory and reports more recent research. Integrated with this is involvement theory and there are cautionary words about over-emphasizing consumers' cognitive processes in their consumption behaviour.

Moore G (1995) *Crossing the Chasm*, Harper Business, New York. This important work extends the traditional concept of the normal curve of adopter categories by adding a significant gap or 'chasm' between the early adopters and early majority of adopters of technological products.

Gladwell M (2002) The Tipping Point: How little things can make a big difference, Abacus

CHAPTER 10
REPEAT, LOYAL AND RELATIONAL BUYING

CHAPTER OBJECTIVES

After engaging with the material presented in this chapter and its associated exercises and reading, you should be able to:

- Extend the concepts of adoption processes and repeat purchase into prediction models of new product buying.
- Explain the nature, characteristics and measurement of switching, defection and repeat purchasing.
- Critically examine what 'loyalty' means in theory and practice and how it should be measured and encouraged.
- Analyse and evaluate the nature and benefits of relational interaction between consumers and organizations.

INTRODUCTION

From a marketer's point of view, customer loyalty is an important concept because greater loyalty can lead to a number of benefits such as reduction in marketing costs, increased opportunities for brand extensions and an improved market share. Loyal customers are a good source for spreading positive word of mouth and the most positive are advocates. They also offer greater resistance to competitive offerings. More and more companies now realize the significance of retaining their existing customers and increasingly develop marketing programmes (e.g. relational marketing activities) to improve **retention** rates. They are aiming to improve customer loyalty and encourage customer–firm dialogue and relationships as a way of creating competitive advantage. From consumers' perspective, greater levels of loyalty may mean they have a great deal of passion and **commitment** to the brand, reduction in search costs, **perceived risk** and enhancement of self-concept.

Beyond loyalty there is the possibility of relational buying where consumers engage with brands on such emotional levels that the interaction between consumer and brands/companies involves reciprocated affective relationships. Some consumers experience consumption in holistic ways if all their senses are involved along with their emotions, as a result of the symbolic nature of their consumption.

In this chapter we cover **repeat purchasing behaviour,** loyalty and **relational buying** behaviours from both the consumer and marketer perspective.

REPEAT PURCHASING BEHAVIOUR

One of the earlier approaches to customer loyalty includes looking at the repeat buying of low-priced, frequently-bought products, which appears to be a well-defined act and tends to be easy to measure using **consumer panel** data. Here, repeat purchasing behaviour is what matters, irrespective of any **affective** dimensions of what goes on in consumers' minds.

THINKBOX

In a number of product categories (e.g. groceries) consumers often buy the same products or brands on a repeated basis either on the same purchase occasion or as several distinct purchases in a given time period.

Consider your own grocery shopping. To what extent do you repeat buy the same brands?

Does this make you loyal to those brands?

Repeat purchasing behaviour can be explained using the operant conditioning learning model (see Chapter 3). If the purchasing of the same product or service is reasonably rewarding it can become repetitive. There is a stimulus–response sequence here and, together with methods of quantifying sequential purchases, it is possible to use **probability theory** to predict which brand will be purchased next, after whatever sequence of brands was previously bought. Models using this 'probability' approach based on purchase sequence are termed **stochastic models**. These models make predictions about repeat purchasing using consumer panel data. Consumer panels involve households that agree to report on their buying behaviour or media habits over a period of time. Panel households are often asked to go through their shopping baskets when they return home and 'scan' all their purchases (Figure 10.1). The point that the same households report over a period of time is significant: it means individual household buying patterns can be monitored, including levels of repeat buying.

Landmark approaches to repeat buying using consumer panels date back to the 1950s and 1960s and include works by Brown (1952–1953) and Parfitt and Collins (1968). The *Chicago Tribune* ran a consumer panel and Brown studied the behaviour of 100 of the panel members. He found marked consistencies in the patterns in which brands of various products were bought, and on this basis, proposed four 'patterns' of loyalty:

- *Undivided loyalty*: within a product category, the consumer buys just one of the brands;
- *Divided loyalty*: the consumer buys from a repertoire of alternative brands in a product category on different buying occasions;

- *Unstable loyalty*: which is really brand switching because the consumer switches from 'undivided' loyalty to one brand to a similarly regular pattern for another brand;
- *No loyalty*: the consumer doesn't even buy from a repertoire of brands, but appears to buy haphazardly from all the brands available.

Figure 10.1: Consumers scan their purchases
Photo: Martin Evans

The Parfitt–Collins model also utilized panel data, in their case to calculate the penetration of the market and the repeat purchasing rate in order to estimate eventual brand share. It is thus a predictive model. Figure 10.2 shows how panel households bought different brands (T, R, and S) in the same product category, from the time (week 1) that new brand (T) was launched. In week 1, two households purchased this brand for the first time, so this is the cumulative number of new buyers for week 1. In the second week, household numbers 3 and 4 buy T for the first time, bringing the cumulative number of new buyers to four in week 2 and so on. When expressed as a percentage of those buying in the product category, this provides the market penetration rate.

In Figure 10.3 the cumulative number of buyers for the first few weeks was projected forward as an estimate of what the eventual penetration percentage would be. In this case, it was estimated that 34% of those buying in the product category would have tried T once. Figure 10.3 shows only seven households from a panel that might have comprised several thousand. From the entire panel an average period for repurchase is calculated. Some buyers in this category will buy every week, some every two weeks, and others less frequently. The average repurchasing period in this case was estimated to be a fortnight. The first repeat purchase period is not weeks 2 and 3 for every household, but the two-week period immediately following the time of first purchase by each household: weeks 3 and 4 for households 3 and 4, weeks 4 and 5 for households 5, 6 and 7, and weeks 2 and 3 for the first two households.

In each repeat purchase period, the percentage of all purchases in the product category that were of brand T, is calculated. This is the repeat purchase rate. As can be seen from the first repeat purchase period: of ten purchases, six were of T, and of ten purchases in the second repeat purchase period, five were of T and so on. This figure is projected forward after calculating it for just a few weeks, to give an estimate of the eventual stable level of repeat purchase. In this case the prediction is for a 25% repeat purchase rate (Figure 10.3). Thus, 34% of the market will (it is estimated) eventually have bought T once, and 25% of these will go on to buy it on a repeat purchase basis (which in this instance means every fortnight).

If T is consumed at average levels for the product category (i.e. that is, once every fortnight), the prediction for its eventual brand share will be 25% of 34% of the market (which is 8.5%). If T is consumed more than other brands, obviously more will be sold and it will have a higher market share. A buying level index can be calculated, again from the panel data, for the level of usage of T. If it is purchased more than every fortnight, on average, a corresponding 'weight' of something more than 1 will increase

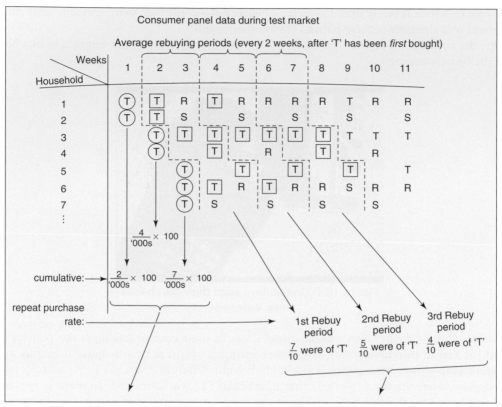

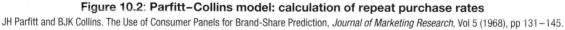

Figure 10.2: **Parfitt–Collins model: calculation of repeat purchase rates**

JH Parfitt and BJK Collins. The Use of Consumer Panels for Brand-Share Prediction, *Journal of Marketing Research*, Vol 5 (1968), pp 131–145.

the estimated 8.5% to an appropriate level. Likewise, if T is bought only (say) half as frequently as other brands, then a buying level index of 0.5 will weight the 8.5% down to the appropriate level (4.25%).

Households 2 and 7, for example, have purchased different brands but we might predict that they are more likely to buy S next time. This is only an estimate in the Parfitt–Collins model, which does not take the reinforcement construct into account. But if we also knew that these households were pleased with their recent purchases of S, the likelihood of repurchase could be strengthened.

The approach, however, proved to be robust as a conceptual underpinning, which informed later models. However, there are more variables at work than those monitored by time and frequency of purchase. As we saw in Chapter 3 (operant conditioning), if a purchase is rewarding there is a greater chance of repeat purchasing.

There is also a 'habit' factor in repurchase. Many consumers will continue to buy the same brand merely because of inertia, unless and until they are activated to reconsider their purchasing. Sometimes the advertising of a new brand or temporary unavailability of the existing brand can trigger a re-evaluation, which may or may not lead to brand switching.

NBD/LSD Model of Consumer Buying Behaviour

Following from the logic of the above approaches, Ehrenberg and various collaborating researchers have extensively explored the prediction of repeat brand purchase and it is worth referring to Ehrenberg (1988). The major theory to emerge from this work is what is known as the *negative binomial distribution* (NBD)

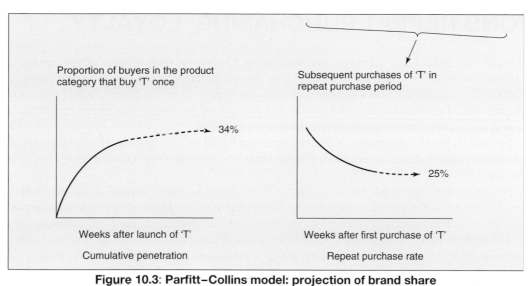

Figure 10.3: Parfitt–Collins model: projection of brand share

JH Parfitt and BJK Collins. The Use of Consumer Panels for Brand-Share Prediction, *Journal of Marketing Research*, Vol 5 (1968), pp 131–145.

theory. The mathematics of the theory is beyond the scope of this book but briefly, the proposition is that the number of purchases that a consumer makes within a certain time period is reflected in a negative binomial distribution. But further, that when a brand has a relatively low penetration of its market, the distribution of buying occasions across consumers is reflected in a *logarithmic series distribution*. Hence the nomenclature of NBD/LSD. It helps estimate the number of consumers who might lapse in their buying in one time period which follows another period in which they had bought. NBD/LSD can also help predict the likely number of consumers who buy, relatively, in two time periods of differing lengths. It only requires the average frequency of purchase of the product concerned within a specific time period and the percentage of the total number of consumers buying the same product in the same time period. The model provided evidence that when there are no particular sales trends, those who lapse in one time period do not necessarily leave that market but are merely infrequent buyers. Different propensities to purchase are, over time, pretty much random, for each consumer. There can be problems with the model's predictability when looking at very short time periods of buying, for those consumers are really heavy buyers and when the product concerned is especially frequently or especially infrequently purchased. Ehrenberg developed a computer programme (Program NBD) to analyse penetration, purchase frequency and time period data in order to predict repurchase rates.

Dirichlet Model

Ehrenberg, together with Goodhardt and Chatfield (Goodhardt, Ehrenberg and Chatfield, 1984) refined and extended the above stochastic model into what is now known as the **Dirichlet Model**. This has proved to be extremely successful and some even suggest that there are no published occasions of it failing (Sharp and Driesener, 2000). It enables comparisons across brands whereas the earlier model focused on the single brand context. The model assumes each consumer to have relatively stable purchase propensities to buy any particular brand; there being different propensities for buying different brands and indeed different consumers' propensities vary greatly in terms of their brand repertoires and frequencies. The model applies to those markets that do not exhibit any particular trends (i.e. they are stationary markets) and where brands are close substitutes. The latter condition is a reality in many markets, despite 'marketing' activity.

BEYOND REPEAT PURCHASING: LOYALTY

Whereas stochastic models are relatively mechanistic and based on probabilities of recurring behaviour, **deterministic models** are based more on cognitive processes. Here, it is presumed that repeat purchase 'loyalty' involves commitment and a stronger affective motivator. Even if a cheaper alternative is available, the consumer would continue to buy the first brand because of greater commitment and/or **trust**. More variables will be involved here to explain regular buying patterns.

One approach is to consider stages of decision-making based on a progression from when organizations acquire consumers through to the processes involved in how consumers are retained (and therefore become regular buyers).

The 'awareness through to adoption' (Chapter 9) sequence is one of several such 'sequential models' (Chapters 2, 3 and 4) of consumer response to marketing activity. Here we present another sequential model but one which is especially relevant to the theme of this chapter. Figure 10.4 depicts the progression that consumers make from being attracted to a brand/company through to not only being regular buyers/patrons of it, but also to feeling they are in a relationship with that brand/company. This also shows that, as with the product life cycle (and indeed some human relationships) there can be 'decline' stages and perhaps a degree of recovery of the relationship as well. We summarize these stages but focus more on the later ones which move us onto *affectively* positive repeat purchasing, which is predicated on attitudinal loyalty and relational buying.

It is worth referring back to Chapter 2 in which we discussed 'exposure' and 'attention' because the nature of consumer behaviour and corresponding marketing techniques in these respects provide the basis for acquisition of new customers. It is important to select appropriate media with which to communicate with potential customers, based on their media habits. Chapter 2 provided coverage of media selection and a number of ways of gaining attention, which are also relevant in the first stage of the acquisition-retention continuum: attraction.

Attraction

Here, consumers and organizations see each other as potential 'partners' in terms of buying and selling.

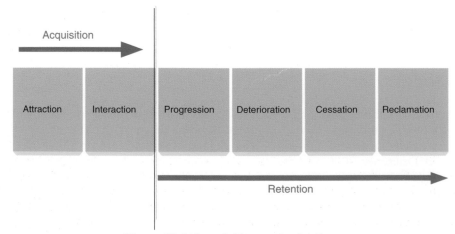

Figure 10.4: Acquisition and retention
M Evans, L O'Malley and M Patterson, *Exploring Direct and Customer Relationship Marketing*, Thomson Learning, London, 2004.

Organizations might see the consumer as being a likely prospect because, for example, they match the profile of existing good customers. The main criterion for the organization relates more to the financial value that the consumer might contribute to profitability than anything particularly attitudinal or emotional on the part of the organization or consumer. (See the next chapter for more on the new 'metrics' which are underpinning interaction between organization and consumer.)

EXAMPLE 10.1

Winos R Us is an online wine company and might want to acquire new customers. The company can profile its existing customers because, being online, it will have details of their purchase transactions as well as their personal details such as name and address. *Winos R Us* can deploy some of the metrics discussed in Chapter 11 and can identifying its 'best' customers: those who buy regularly from them, frequently and who have high monetary values of their orders. These 'best' customers' addresses can then be profiled. Chapter 11 again shows the mechanics of this: postcodes can be profiled into different categories (geodemographics). *Winos R Us* can then buy a list of names and addresses of others who are in the same 'geodemographic' categories as their best customers. In this way *Winos R Us* is able to attract new customers on what we term the Identikit method of acquisition.

Consumers are perhaps attracted to a particular organization's advertising, which seems to promise the benefits they seek to derive. In turn consumers are probably more concerned with getting the value they seek than in a desire to have a relationship per se with the organization. There will be some consumers, however, who undoubtedly develop strong bonds with the brands they buy.

EXAMPLE 10.2

'Pre-consumers', that is school-aged children who might be interested in joining the British Army when old enough, were encouraged to join a 'club'. This involved receiving a magazine several times a year and receiving emails about events, exhibitions and competitions to engage their interest even before they were old enough to join the Army. There was also a web site with which the teenagers could engage. Many of those *attracted* (before they could 'buy' into the service) were indeed converted into enlisters (DMA Award, 2001). In 2001 the programme had attracted 50 000 members and by 2006 there were 250 000 members (Hoffbrand, 2006).

Interaction

Following the initial attraction, organization-prospect dealings can become interactive. For example, we are seeing an increase in the marketing use of interactive digital outdoor media such as interactive posters, such as those shown here and as can be seen, consumers can interact with the medium itself. In some, it is possible to download content to mobile phones via Bluetooth or infrared.

© Russell Signs. Reproduced with permission.

Consumers can interactively sample Sony's Singstar (below) but the rest of the high street can (probably unfortunately) sample that consumer's rock star aspirations.

Source: Sony Computer Entertainment Europe.

Such interactive and digital technology is even being included at the design stage of certain projects: Heathrow's Terminal 5 has been cited as perhaps the first public building to have been so included (Croft, 2008a).

EXAMPLE 10.3

1. Kitten owners *interacted* with Pedigree Masterfoods before they were customers. The company advertised free Whiskas kitten care packs and the result was that 30% of kitten-owning consumers were recruited. (DMA Award, 2001).

2. Cat food manufacturer Felix produced a Felix Kitten taster pack, aimed at recruiting and educating new kitten owners. Those who signed up also received a kitten newsletter with tips. In year one, 65 429 consumers participated, with 92% being new to the Felix database. Monthly Felix Kitten sales rose by 56% in the first six months and achieved incremental sales of £624 000.

3. The BBC TV licensing is constantly aware that many students do not buy licenses in their student accommodation (which they need to, even if the TV at 'home' is licensed). In an effective acquisition campaign, students were not merely reminded (via flyers at universities and mailings to home addresses) but were encouraged to interact by posting 'silly' humour on 'It's not funny' website. The silliest student humour won a comedy gig at their university.

This winner of the DMA Awards Strategy: Customer Acquisition Gold Award was marked out as a 'strong performer year-on-year with a novel twist'. One judge added that it 'encouraged kids to think about the consequences and also targeted parents'.

In order to motivate students to buy a TV licence at the start of the academic year, BBC TV Licensing appointed Proximity London to encourage sales and customer loyalty.

Research suggested that young people were wary of patronizing marketing approaches so the campaign aimed to use word-of-mouth and digital opportunities.

The central idea was that being caught without a licence isn't funny. An 'anti-humour' website encouraged students to submit a video of their own unfunny jokes, which could also be sent on as viral marketing. The site was promoted at university student unions and through brand ambassadors who referenced it on their social networking profiles. Mailings were sent to students' family homes before termtime, a poster and leaflet were left in halls of residence rooms and activity took place on the day they moved to university and at freshers' fairs.

The website had 82 000 unique visitors and the campaign had a ROI of 12:1. It maintained the 24% sales growth of the previous year and achieved a sales increase year-on-year of 5%.

© Direct Marketing Association. Reproduced with permission.

A different take on interaction with prospects before they buy, is via current customers. The 'member-get-member' approach is where existing customers are encouraged to 'recruit' friends or others as new customers. The recruiting existing customers usually receive some minor reward in the form of a gift or discount and sometimes the recruited are also offered discounts on first purchases.

EXAMPLE 10.4

This winning campaign of the 2007 DMA Awards Strategy: Customer Loyalty Award had, according to the judges work 'that has clearly been lovingly created'. It had a quirky theme, a stand out creative and very strong results.

The Glenmorangie Company's Aardbeg distillery opened in 1997 after being mothballed in the 1980s. The company initially used in-pack leaflets to build a CRM programme for the Aardbeg single malt whisky and introduced a website, aardbeg.com. This continuing customer loyalty campaign aims to increase sales using mail and online channels. More recently, it has used online word-of-mouth recommendations to encourage visits to the distillery and, as of 2006, move the brand into the luxury sector.

The loyalty programme is called the Aardbeg Committee and aims to inspire devotion and commitment. It has a worldwide membership, so digital and direct mail are the preferred channels of choice for campaigns. Its quarterly newsletter, *Momentous Minutes*, also plays an important role and mailings are often collected by the whisky's fans. Digital executions are also very successful. In 2006, a viral and email campaign launching the £2100 Aardbeg 1965 led to all of the bottles being sold in days. The programme has 37 000 members across 120 countries and since 1997, production has reached a million litres.

© Direct Marketing Association. Reproduced with permission.

Progression

Potential customers now become customers. Because the relationship between the consumer and the organization reflects a degree of collaboration providing benefits for both sides, the relationship 'progresses' to variously enduring degrees. Efforts to strengthen relationships with satisfied customers include inviting their participation in consumer clubs and providing exclusive services for high-value customers.

EXAMPLE 10.5

1. *The Times* newspaper has populated its database with the interests of its readers. Indeed readers can update these by choosing from different categories such as sport, politics and gardening. Each Friday they receive an email tailored to these interests indicating what stories will appear in the paper over the weekend (Murphy, 2006). This is clearly a technique that does not expect consumers to blindly continue buying but recognizes their interests and reminds them how the product is still relevant. The personalization aids with the progression of the relationship.
2. Progression can also be reflected in cross-selling campaigns. For example, Islay whisky brand, Aardbeg, introduced a variant named Arigh Nam Beist (in Gaelic this means 'shelter of the beast'). Members of its relationship marketing programme were mailed a book of spoof stories tailored to the scariness of Halloween, when they were timed to arrive. The new version was positioned to be appropriate to calm the nerves; 49% of the stock was sold via these mailings (DMA, 2007c).
3. Sainsbury's rewarded top customers with a highly personalized birthday card, including a voucher to be exchanged for a gift relevant to their purchasing behaviour. Up to 400 000 cards were sent each month. Since personalized cards replaced generic ones in May 2004, redemption were increased from 28% to 40%, with incremental revenue up 110% each.

© Direct Marketing Association. Reproduced with permission.

Deterioration

All things must pass. Relationships rarely move directly from a state of progression to dissolution, but deteriorate gradually. Deterioration is where commitment and loyalty fade perhaps because the consumer becomes attracted to an even more enticing organizational offering elsewhere, or because their own circumstances change (a new stage of their family life cycle (Chapter 7)) or maybe because the organization repositions itself, perhaps after a merger or takeover.

EXAMPLE 10.6

Personalization is particularly important to Amazon.co.uk. Consumers are able to edit the personalized recommendations they receive (Figure 10.5) by rating their purchases to build a picture of what they like. A 'wish list' service allows customers to tell their friends and family what they would like for Christmas and birthdays, while the site's 1-Click ordering system means consumers can buy products with one click of the mouse without having to fill in order forms. Updates are sent to consumers during the steps of the ordering process. As a result there is not merely a purchase–sale transaction, but *progression* is facilitated by the personalized offers based on interests gleaned from transactional records.

Figure 10.5: Progression personalization
Source: www.amazon.co.uk

EXAMPLE 10.7

Older female consumers were found to be feeling somewhat alienated by the style of Lever Brothers' advertising of the Persil washing powder brand, which targeted young women. Many of these older consumers were therefore becoming less enthusiastic about the brand. But they had not entirely defected.

The company targeted 'modern grandmas' with a mailing which asked for their laundry tips, based on their wider and fuller experience of life. Eight thousand tips were sent in. In this way they were encouraged to feel 'wanted' and this helped stave off *deterioration* of their interaction with Persil (DMA Award, 2001).

Cessation

It is probably inevitable that many relationships between consumers and organizations will end. The organization, for example, might eliminate the product/service concerned or the consumer's new circumstances might mean the product simply isn't relevant any more (e.g. in the case of Mothercare and the woman whose children have grown up).

Reclamation

However, organizations should not always totally forget these consumers. Telecoms companies, for example, are realizing the benefits of reclaiming profitable customers. They must analyse the reasons behind relationship cessation in order to assess the possibility of reclaiming the consumer and estimate the costs of doing so.

EXAMPLE 10.8

1. The rather quaint tradition in the UK of having one's milk delivered in the morning has come under pressure as more consumers include milk in their supermarket shopping trips and because more have already left home for work before the milk is delivered. Associated Co. Creameries recognized this trend and tried to stop the decline. The company left empty milk bottles on the doorsteps of lapsed customers with a note proclaiming the benefits of having milk delivered (Figure 10.6). The *reclamation* programme produced a 26% increase in milk delivery customers on those milk rounds that employed the technique at a cost of just 49p per customer (DMA Award, 2001).

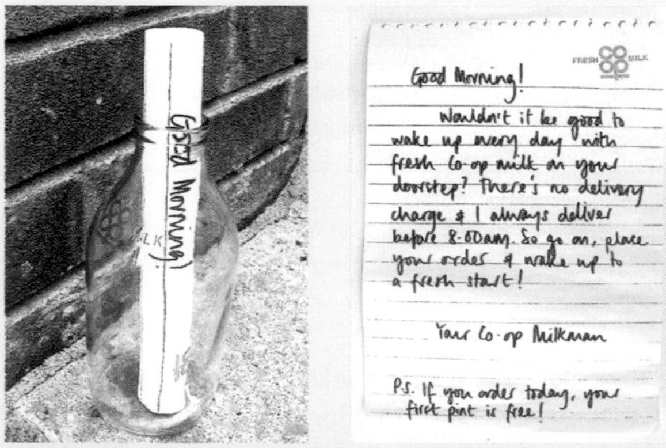

Figure 10.6: Reclaiming doorstep milk delivery consumers
Photos: Martin Evans

Loyalty programmes are another device used to retain customers. These are proving increasingly popular with both consumers and organizations and therefore are deserving of greater attention within a conceptual framework of *loyalty*, to which we now turn.

EXAMPLE 10.9

Tesco wanted to find out why previously loyal customers had stopped shopping at its supermarkets. It sent them a message on a till receipt, from their local checkout, telling them Tesco missed them and that life was not the same without them. An attached money-off coupon was used to tempt them back. Judges remarked that 'despite the amount of data that Tesco holds, this campaign was not over-elaborate'.

© Direct Marketing Association. Reproduced with permission.

LOYALTY

Reichheld (1988) argued that consumers' repeat purchase patterns may not reveal their true loyalty behaviour as they may be trapped by inertia or they may be indifferent to brands or there may be high exit barriers imposed by the brand. Also, a consumer who is actually a loyal one may not buy on a repeated basis because of a reduced need for a given product or brand.

Dick and Basu (1994) also propose a framework that conceptualizes loyalty as combining both behavioural and attitudinal approaches to the understanding of loyalty. They conceptualized loyalty as the relationship between the relative attitude shown by a person towards a brand/product/store and their patronage behaviour. Relative attitudes take into consideration the notion that we all compare brands relevant to a given consumption context in which our perceptions and attitudes towards brands coexist in our minds. Therefore, our attitude towards a given entity is always in relation to some other entity. A person's relative attitude is said to be at its highest when the person associates the target brand with a strong attitude and clearly differentiates this from other brands with which the consumer has weaker attitudes. Similarly, a person may have a weak attitude but if that attitude is strongly differentiated from competitors, then it also leads to a high relative attitude and may contribute towards loyalty. On the contrary, a person may have a positive attitude but they do not perceive the target brand to be much different from the competition. In this case, the person is likely to show a multi-brand loyalty because all alternatives are perceived as equally good. So the key points here are the extent to which a person perceives a focal brand to be different from other brands in the marketplace and the strength of attitude. As long as the consumer perceives significant differences among competing brands, their relative attitude towards a focal brand is likely to be high and this may contribute towards loyalty.

The conceptualization which linked relative attitudes with repeat patronage led to four categories of loyalty, each of which has managerial implications (Table 10.1). The four categories of loyalty provide a far richer conceptualization of loyalty than previously existed. The first one is loyalty, which exists when consumers have high relative attitude and high repeat patronage behaviour. Very often, marketers aim to create this form of loyalty whereby consumers like their brand much more than any other brand and buy the brand on a regular basis. The second one is latent loyalty, which exists when consumers have high relative attitude but low repeat patronage. The low repeat patronage may be due to some normative or situational influences such as unavailability and marketers need to tackle them through marketing communication or distribution efforts. The third one is spurious loyalty, which exists when consumers have low relative attitude but high repeat patronage. This reflects typical repeat buying of low-value, low-involvement and frequently purchased items. This behaviour may be driven by habit or inertia or by some situational cues (e.g. familiarity with a shelf position or a convenient location of a store). The fourth one is no loyalty, which exists when consumers have a low relative attitude and a low repeat patronage.

Loyalty and Satisfaction

It would be logical to expect loyalty to depend, to at least some extent, on 'satisfaction'. As a result, measures of consumer satisfaction have been widely used as proxy measures for loyalty. However, research from the Ogilvy Loyalty Centre suggests that 85% of automotive industry users report being satisfied but only 40% repurchase, while for FMCG goods, 66% of people who identified a favourite brand admitted to having bought another brand most recently (McKenzie, 1995). As a result, satisfaction measures have proved to be ineffective measures of loyalty (Reichheld, 1988). But are marketers really wrong in assuming that satisfied customers will automatically be loyal?

As we might expect, the picture is more complicated. In extensive research in a number of different product markets, Jones (1996) reported that the degree of claimed satisfaction is critical to levels of repeat purchase (Figure 10.7). In other words, those who claimed to be completely satisfied were more loyal than those who stated that they were merely satisfied. Figure 10.7 presents the satisfaction scale whereby consumers are asked to rank their satisfaction levels using a five-point scale from very satisfied (5) to very dissatisfied (1). The difference between repeat purchase behaviour for someone who scores '4' on a five-point satisfaction survey and those who score '5' is sixfold. That is, mere satisfaction (e.g. '4') is manifested in repeat purchasing far less than when it is extremely high satisfaction (e.g. a score of '5'). It is not enough, therefore to satisfy customers, but to 'delight' them.

Jones and Sasser (1995) in fact propose another version of a loyalty grid, which groups consumers into four distinct groups on the basis of their satisfaction and loyalty levels (Figure 10.8).

- Group 1 Loyalists These are completely satisfied consumers who claim to have high levels of satisfaction and loyalty. They stay with firms and remain supportive of the firm's activities. Some of these can even

		Repeat patronage	
		High	**Low**
Relative attitude	**High**	Loyalty	Latent loyalty
	Low	Spurious loyalty	No loyalty

Source: AS Dick and K Basu Customer Loyalty: Toward an Integrated Framework, *Journal of the Academy of Marketing Science*, Vol 22 No 2 (1994), pp 99–113. Reproduced by permission of Sage Publications Inc.

Table 10.1: Loyalty segments

Figure 10.7: The need to 'delight' consumers
Source: TO Jones, Why Loyal Customers Defect, Keynote Presentation, IDM Symposium, 6 June 1996.
© T. Jones. Reproduced by permission

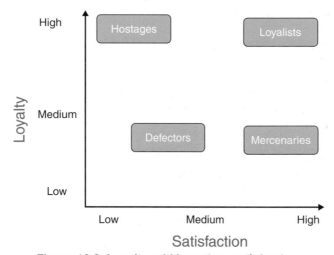

Figure 10.8: Loyalty grid based on satisfaction
Source: TO Jones and WE Sasser, Why Loyal Customers Defect, Harvard Business Review (1995), pp 88–99.
Reproduced by permission of Harvard Business School Publishing

turn into advocates (those who are so satisfied and delighted that they share their experiences with others by engaging in positive word of mouth).

• Group 2 Defectors They have low to medium levels of satisfaction and loyalty. These include those who claim to be completely dissatisfied, quite dissatisfied and even neutral when asked about their satisfaction levels. They normally switch brands due to unsatisfactory experiences. Some of them can even become **consumer terrorists**. These have such a bad experience that they can't wait to tell others about their bad and frustrating experiences. They will be positioned at the left of the horizontal axis and anywhere along the vertical. When bad word of mouth spreads, it can get worse each time a story is told and the actual facts can become distorted. They can spread ill will concerning the organization or even play games such as swapping loyalty cards to be awkward or to see what happens to their 'targeted' offers (see Chapter 12).

- Group 3 Mercenaries These show high levels of satisfaction but low to medium levels of loyalty. They normally do not stay with the firm long enough to become profitable customers for the firm.
- Group 4 Hostages They show low to medium levels of satisfaction but high levels of loyalty. These consumers are stuck with the companies (due to lack of choice or the monopolistic position of firms, such as those in the telecommunications and airline industries).

The following case study affords not only interesting insights into the practical applicatioin of the above loyalty models, but also important extensions of them. We are very grateful to Professor Clive Nancarrow, Gemma Camp and TNS for allowing us to share this with you.

CASE STUDY 10.1

TNS CASE STUDY: A Marketing Research Model by TNS to Measure Loyalty

Gemma Camp (TNS) and Clive Nancarrow (Bristol Business School, UWE)

The cost of losing customers

It costs five to six times as much to recruit a new customer as to retain one. That is why customer retention is so important to marketers and why good measures of customer retention are needed to help organizations establish how they are doing in terms of fostering loyalty.

To start with you need to know how many loyal customers you have and how many might be vulnerable to competitors' offerings. In addition, understanding what drives loyalty is clearly vital. What are the competitive attributes of your product or service that encourage loyalty and which attributes do not. This certainly should feed into your marketing plan.

There are behavioural and attitudinal measures of commitment or loyalty to an organization.

Behavioural measures of loyalty include how recently a customer bought or used your product or service, how often they use it as well as how much they spend in total on your brand and whether or not they buy across the range and are trading up to your more expensive offerings. In competitive terms, and appreciating some customers use more than one brand, it is useful to know how their share of expenditure breaks down across your brand and its competitors.

Attitudinal measures that indicate loyalty include whether or not a product is seen to deliver satisfactorily, the likelihood of purchasing in the future, the likelihood of recommending the product to someone else and the degree to which the product is seen to have a competitive advantage over competitors.

Behavioural measures	Attitudinal measures
Recency, Frequency, Monetary Value (RFM)	Perceived overall performance
Buy across range/trade-up	Declared intent to consider/purchase
Share of budget/wallet on your product	Disposition to recommend
Recommended brand/product to others	Perceived competitive advantage

TNS, a global marketing research agency, combines four attitudinal measures to provide an Index of retention. The TRI*M Index is a single number measure that characterizes the intensity of retention of specific customer groups.

This measure is a weighted aggregate of the four proven key indicators of retention:

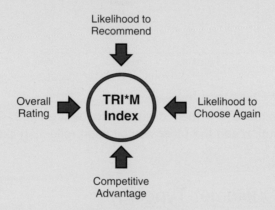

1. Overall Rating: An overall measure of the company's performance, products and services. The first step in creating a climate of retention.
2. Advocacy: Likelihood to recommend your company to a friend or colleague – key indicator of satisfaction and one of the most powerful ways that your customers can help your bottom line.
3. Repurchase: Likelihood to continue as a customer, or to buy other products and services from the same supplier. A critical component of retention and a claim that the customer will 'put his money where his mouth is'.
4. Competitive Advantage: Perceived advantage of dealing with your company rather than another. Does your company offer something different from other suppliers? This is a key factor in moving from satisfaction to retention but is often a difficult measure to drive up. As such, it is all the more important as a hard measure of retention.

TNS has developed a weighting scheme for the four questions when calculating the Index. The weights attached to each question reflect the relative importance of each question in producing the most accurate Index of loyalty. The Index has been proven to link to actual customer churn, cross-sales and share of wallet over time.

Once the index is calculated, one can monitor the level of likely customer retention over time and establish whether your campaigns to retain customers are working:

The TRI*M Index measures Customer Retention over time

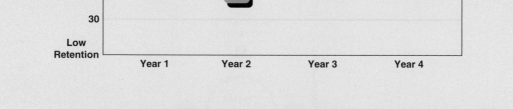

The four questions are then divided into two groups – one combination reflecting customer satisfaction and the other combination reflecting likely customer loyalty for that customer.

TRI*M Customer Typology
It is not enough to simply satisfy customers...

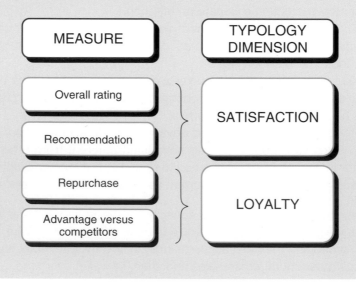

Using these two derived measures (satisfaction and loyalty) TNS segment customer experiences into four types based on earlier work by Jones and Sasser (1995). The distinction between satisfaction and loyalty addresses the age old paradigm – why do satisfied customers sometimes defect?

TRI*M Customer Typology

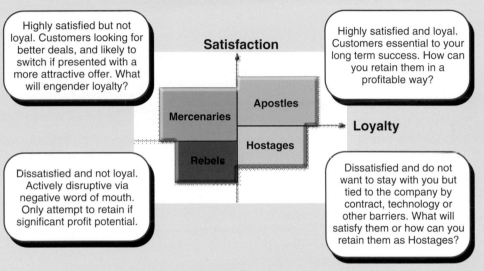

Source: Jones / Sasser, Why satisfied customers defect, Harvard Business Review, 1995

TNS is then able to analyse the customer experience profile by two balances:

- The balance of Apostles (true advocates) to Rebels who will be spreading negative feedback. Clearly it is desirable to have a greater number of Apostles than Rebels. Here TNS can calculate the likely word-of-mouth resulting from these experiences, to discover whether the overall balance is positive or negative.
- The balance of Hostages to Mercenaries. This provides an understanding of what is driving market share. In the case of Hostages, this is likely to be contracts, lack of alternatives or other barriers to switching; this can be dangerous if the barriers are removed. If there is a high proportion of Mercenaries, the company's offering does not result in loyalty and may even encourage shopping around (such an offering is often price-driven). This position is likely to be expensive to maintain.

It is now possible to compare one's own customer profile in terms of the size of the four customer experience segments with the profiles for competitors.

An understanding of topline customer retention is clearly not enough. A company will need specific, actionable information to identify which changes to their business will bring about overall improvements in retention and customer value.

TNS has a tool to understand the diagnostic elements of customer relationships – the TRI*M Grid. This is a map detailing the relative importance of and a company's performance on a set of service related attributes. They use three steps to achieve this:

a. Draw a full picture of the customer relationship.
b. Measure how much each element of the relationship matters.
c. Measure how well a company performs on each element.

QUESTIONS

1. Why is retention important?
2. What could you use as measures of retention?
3. Why is the Jones/Sasser inspired TNS TRI*M typology useful?
4. Once the brand is established, how might you determine if purchasers would remain loyal to the brand. What would be the things you would seek to measure as indicators of loyalty?

Reproduced by permission of TNS

THINKBOX

Reichheld's Net Promoter Score (NPS) is based on the question 'how likely is it that you recommend Company X to a friend or colleague?' on an eleven point scale. Those scoring nine to eleven are promoters. Those scoring zero to six are detractors. The NPS is the percentage of promoters minus the percentage of detractors.

The NPS approach has also been subjected to four criticisms:

1. Respondents, who say they would recommend, do not necessarily do so: a usual problem with surveys in that claims are not always manifested in behaviour.
2. There might be 75% promoters and just 25% detractors, giving an NPS of 50. Or, there might be 50% promoters and 0% detractors, giving the same NPS. Both categories would show detractors but lots of zeros might reflect a significant number of consumer terrorists who are probably more concerning than a significant number giving six scores.
3. Scores can vary wildly month-by-month, depending on media exposure of company issues or recent extreme experiences of consumers.
4. NPS has often not replaced traditional satisfaction research: many companies merely add NPS questions to the satisfaction survey.
Is Reichheld's NPS useful?

Customer Switching Behaviour

Many consumers routinely defect from brands and companies and this may happen for a variety of reasons. Sometimes we are simply not happy with our experiences with a brand, whereas on other occasions we get a better deal or better alternative elsewhere. Keaveney (1995) identified more than 800 critical behaviours of service firms that led customers to switch their service providers. On the basis of this, Keaveney grouped reasons for customer defection into the following eight categories:

1. Core service failure. Consumers defect due to mistakes (e.g. billing errors) or other technical problems with the service itself.
2. Service encounter failure. Consumers defect because in their interactions with employees they found employees to be uncaring, impolite, unresponsive and lacking sufficient knowledge.
3. Employee responses to service failures. Consumers defect because service providers were unable to handle the situation properly (e.g. reluctant response, failure to respond or negative response).
4. Pricing. Consumers defect because the existing service provider charges a high price, has high service charges or has increased the price recently.
5. Inconvenience. Consumers defect due to inconvenient location, working hours or waiting time to get an appointment.
6. Attracted by a competitor. Consumers defect because a competitor makes a better offer.
7. Ethical issues. Consumers defect because of perceived illegal, immoral, unsafe or other unhealthy behaviours of the firms.
8. Involuntary switching. Caused by factors that are beyond consumers' control (e.g. customer moving house).

Also, DeSouza (1992) cited following reasons for customer defections:

1. Defection in order to purchase a superior product from a competitor.
2. Defection due to market related factors – defecting to a different market. For example, a transport company which has moved out of road haulage therefore no longer needs to buy trailers.
3. Defection due to technology related reasons – a consumer who has converted from using one technology to another. Customers who abandoned high street banks in favour of banks that provide dedicated telephone or Internet banking would fall into this category.
4. Defection due to organizational related factors – switching as a result of ethical or political pressures. For example, many customers who switched to the Co-Operative Bank did so because they preferred to support the ethical position held by that bank.

Reichheld (1996) argues that the longer a customer stays with a firm, the better it is for the firm because the customer is likely to buy more and become less sensitive to price. Furthermore, in certain industries, if companies can manage to reduce their customer defections from, say 15% to 10%, they can double their profits (Reichheld, 1996).

EXAMPLE 10.10

Revisit Example 4.1 concerning Professor Jones (the same Jones as cited in this chapter) and his BMW ash tray. He became an 'advocate' for Lexus after being *satisfied* with BMW for over a decade, but clearly not *delighted*.

Do you or does anyone you know have any similar experiences – in any product/service context?

What are the implications for consumers and for marketers?

Customer Loyalty and Loyalty Programmes

A loyalty programme (Figure 10.9) normally aims to build customer loyalty (or just repeat purchase?) by rewarding consumers for their cumulative purchasing over time. In most cases, the aims of loyalty programmes are:

* to retain customers by providing them value and satisfaction
* to increase spending by existing customers
* to cross-sell other products of which existing customers might not be aware.

There are many examples of loyalty programmes but a very famous one is that of Tesco Clubcard, which was introduced in 1995 to retain existing customers and to increase spending by them. The card is swiped at the point of sale, earning points for each pound spent, and the transaction details are then fed into a centralized database overnight. Consumers receive vouchers on a quarterly basis. In this case, consumers get rewarded after a time period (a quarter). However, there are other loyalty schemes, which reward your behaviour immediately (e.g. an instant scratch card). Similarly, you can have direct rewards (product related) and indirect rewards (non-product related). Yi and Jeon (2003) found that, under high-involvement conditions, direct rewards were perceived to be more valuable than indirect rewards. Under low-involvement conditions, immediate rewards were perceived to be more valuable than delayed rewards.

The Nectar scheme is an example of one that operates across partner companies. These started with the four named on the card in Figure 10.9. but despite Debenhams dropping out in 2008 (they say, due to the difficult retail environment (Alaroon, 2008; Hoffbrand, 2008a)), it continues to expand, including (at the time of writing): AA, Abebooks, Adidi, Advanced MP3 Players, Alienware, All Posters, Allsaints, Amazon, American Express, Ancestry, Angel Fancy Dress, AOL Broadband, Appliance Deals, Appliances Direct, Appliances online, A Quarter of, Arena Flowers, Argos, Audible, Austin Reed, Autoglass, Avon. The eagle-eyed reader will note that these are just the 'As'. Check the Nectar website for the full alphabetical list. There are 160 online brands (Anon, 2007).

Today many organizations are being forced into running a loyalty programme, simply because their competitors are offering them. However, loyalty programmes represent a considerable investment, and

Figure 10.9: Nectar loyalty scheme
It has been suggested that the Nectar scheme is a template for the UK State ID scheme (Ambler, 2002).
Loyalty Management UK Ltd. Reproduced by permission.

takes at least two to three years to achieve any return on investment. Often there can be 'loyalty' to the programme rather than the organization and as soon as a more attractive offer – or scheme – comes along, the consumer might defect (or at least keep multiple loyalty cards). So some are 'deal loyal' rather than 'real loyal'. The former might act like cats and go where the offer is juiciest (from a repertoire of sources/brands) the latter more like dogs with less wavering loyalty.

EXAMPLE 10.11

The phone company O2 calculates the optimum tariff for each customer and every quarter notifies whether a change would benefit the customer. You might think this is a way of reducing a company's revenue. But instead the reduction in defection to other brands was 24%. Each 1% drop in defection increased revenue by £5m. In addition, satisfaction scores were 6–10 percentage points higher (IDM, 2003).

THINKBOX

Consider this: a consumer is on a diet – or at least his wife thinks he is. He uses his loyalty card at the supermarket for most of the groceries but pays cash for the chocolate biscuits because he doesn't want his wife to be sent offers for similar goodies, because such offers might be a 'give-away' to his wife about his lack of self control (Sasse, 2005).

A study investigating supermarket loyalty schemes (Evans *et al.*, 1997) based on qualitative group discussions found that irrespective of demographic profile through the groups there was a high degree of similarity in the main issues raised. These themes were as follows:

1. The schemes were widely used.

2. The schemes were seen to be potentially money saving, but even among some of the adopters this potential was not always seen to be fully realized and was not enough to prevent switching behaviour between schemes.

3. There were very clear concerns over revealing personal details. Many (especially, but not exclusively) women participants did not like divulging personal details such as marital status, age, household numbers, telephone numbers, bank accounts, type of dwelling or home contents. This was seen to be intrusive. They were unhappy about the fact that their personal details and their purchases could be linked together on databases for various ulterior purposes. (We explore the use [and abuse] of consumers' personal details and transactional data in Chapter 11.)

Having said this, research by TNS (Hummerston, 2008) found that at least one loyalty card is held by 85% of UK households and research by GI Insight reports that in 2008 there were twice as many loyalty schemes in UK compared with 10 years ago (Hummerston, 2008).

THINKBOX

You personally may have at least one loyalty card, which might encourage you to frequent that store more often but does it engender a feeling of greater emotional attachment with the store?

Is it the convenient location of the store or the fact that you can get what you want there?

So, do you have any *affective* feelings of loyalty to the organization?

What, for you, *is* 'loyalty'?

www. Have a look at the following web site:

http://www.nectar.com/NectarHome.nectar

This is the web site for the major loyalty scheme, Nectar, which is a partnership between many well known companies.

BEYOND LOYALTY: RELATIONAL CONSUMPTION

Can loyal consumers go even further with their interaction with organizations and develop 'relationships' with them? This is an area of particular interest in recent years and many organizations have appointed 'relationship marketing managers' and claim to have developed relationship marketing programmes. So what is relational consumption (at least normatively)?

Based on the Evans *et al.* (2004) definition of *relationship marketing*; relational consumption involves the identification, specification, initiation, maintenance and (where appropriate) dissolution of long-term relationships between consumers and brands/organizations through mutual exchange, fulfilment of promises and adherence to relationship norms in order to satisfy the objectives and enhance the experience of the parties concerned.

For customers, true relational interaction can be very satisfying:

• They feel an affinity with the organization beyond mere repeat purchase and this can add to the 'experiential' nature of much current consumer behaviour (see section below). They can feel 'known'

to the organization, not just as an anonymous consumer but akin to the personal interaction between restaurateur and regular consumer.
- They often receive special treatment and extra pampering by the organization.
- They are likely to receive timely and relevant communications of offers that would be of interest to them at that moment.

Combining organizational and consumer motivations, it becomes clear that the successful implementation of *relational marketing* would also make marketing more efficient because (wasteful) expenditure on advertising and promotion could be reduced.

The template that is most generally (but not necessarily appropriately) employed to explore relationships, is that of marriage. In the early 1980s Theodore Levitt made a striking comparison between business relationships and contemporary marriage. According to Levitt (1983): 'the sale merely consummates the courtship. Then the marriage begins. How good the marriage is depends on how well the relationship is managed by the seller.'

In talking about commercial relationships as marriages, we assume that the parties in the relationship are on an equal footing, and there are certain values that we implicitly rely on. For example, we assume that relationships involve partners who should be committed and loyal. The long-term nature of the relationship is emphasized compared with the one-night stand, and there is an underlying suggestion that such relationships should be monogamous. But as with many 'theories' in (especially) economics and other disciplines, over-qualification (of 'we assume') can lead to unreality.

From a relationship perspective, Fournier (1998) views customer loyalty as a committed and affect-laden partnership between consumers and their brands which grows and evolves over time. Fournier

Figure 10.10: Interdependence with Tesco
© Tesco Stores Ltd. Reproduced by permission

(1998) identified many attributes of brand-relationship quality including the following, many of which have appeared in different guises elsewhere in the book:

- Love/passion – this describes the emotional attachment of consumers with brands – consumers often have a passion to possess a brand and will feel anxiety if the brand is not available (Chapter 1).
- Self-concept connection – brands provide a mechanism for connecting to the self and to the notions of who one is (Chapter 6).
- Interdependence – brands play a central role in consumers' day-to-day lives and routine (Chapters 1 and 5). Consider Figure 10.10, where Tesco is not just concerned with 'selling groceries' but with engagement within consumers' daily lives.
- Commitment – as consumers pass through different stages of their life cycles, they stick with the brands (both in good times and bad times; see Chapters 9 and 10).
- Intimacy – consumers feel a sense of extensive familiarity with brands and very good understanding of their attributes (this chapter).
- Partner quality – consumers perceive brands to have qualities that they normally associate with their partners (e.g. dependability, credibility, trustworthiness and reliability). Brands are perceived as active, contributing members of the dyadic relationship (this chapter).
- Nostalgic attachment – brands allow consumers to imagine their past. They can bring back vivid memories of the past as brands remind consumers of their past consumption contexts and situations (Belk, 1988). (We discussed this aspect in Chapter 5 where we explored generational cohorts.)

www. **Have a look at the following web site:**
http://www.tesco.com/
This is the web site for Tesco but have a look at the range of products and services the company provides. Many people need venture little further for their purchases across most product/service categories: books, CDs, DVDs, electricals, DIY, flowers, gardening, music downloads, credit cards, loans, mortgages, savings, insurance, telecoms (broadband, dial-up Internet), advice on diets and healthy eating, holidays, flights, games, delivered wine, legal advice, gas and electricity – oh, and food.
Does this represent an all-pervasive relational interaction?

www. **Take a look at the article by Woodside (2004), which is accessible from the accompanying web site at** www.wileyeurope.com/college/evans. **We referred to the same article in Chapters 1 and 3 because it integrates concepts from those chapters with Fournier's relational typology.**

Key Relational Constructs

There are a number of concepts commonly employed to explain and describe successful relationships.

Trust

Trust is considered to be the basis for exchange and the glue that holds a relationship together. Conversely, in the absence of trust, exchange becomes increasingly difficult. Scott (2002) highlights that it is useful to:

Think of trust as a natural resource, like water. It oils the machinery of human interaction in everything from marriage and friendship to business and international relations. There are reserves of trust, in a perpetual state of replenishment or depletion. And in this parched and suddenly sweltering spring, it is not just water supplies that are looking ominously low.

Unless there is a minimum level of trust between parties, it is unlikely that a relationship will be initiated at all. Similarly, if trust breaks down the relationship is likely to be dissolved. Furthermore, it remains difficult to identify exactly why trust intensifies or decreases. In practice, trust may be a function of the reputation and perceived expertise of the organization and its employees. Organizational reputation is communicated to customers through corporate and brand image, through advertising, through product and service quality and through the behaviour of its employees.

Trust is particularly important for services, which by their nature are highly intangible (for example, banks and insurance companies) because there is a need for a minimum level of consumer trust before service delivery is initiated (Liljander and Strandvick, 1995). As a result, organizations must carefully consider the implications of the promises they make. Equally, visible elements of the organization's activities (e.g. personalized communications) signal to customers the quality of other, less visible, organizational activities. Thus, engendering trust also involves paying attention to the details that matter to customers.

Commitment

In addition to trust, commitment is also considered to be central to successful relationship marketing (Morgan and Hunt, 1994). An initial level of commitment is required to initiate the relationship and, as the relationship deepens, so too does the existence and evidence of commitment. Moreover, without commitment, no relationship is believed to exist. Referring to consumer markets, De Wulf *et al.* (2001) define commitment as 'a consumer's desire to continue a relationship... accompanied by this consumer's willingness to make efforts at maintaining it' (De Wulf *et al.*, 2001). Furthermore, commitment involves behavioural, attitudinal, affective and calculative components (Geyskens *et al.*, 1996).

- Behavioural commitment refers to the actual behaviour of parties in the relationship, the efforts they make and the choices they take. The earlier discussion of repeat purchase rates is an example of consumers' behavioural commitment and the level of organizational investment in helping and interacting with individual consumers is a reflection of their behavioural commitment.
- Attitudinal commitment refers to 'an implicit or explicit pledge of relational continuity' between relational partners (Oliver, 1999).
- Affective commitment relates to positive feelings towards the organization. As a result of these feelings, the consumer is not tempted to seek alternatives or to engage in any cost-benefit analytical schemes. Affectively committed customers voice strong intentions to remain in the relationship and are willing to invest in that relationship (Samuelsen and Sandvik, 1997).
- Calculative commitment, in contrast, is partly instrumental. In this case, calculative commitment may be the outcome of a perceived lack of alternatives or estimation that the switching costs might outweigh likely benefits. Customers who remain in a relationship as a result of calculative commitment will only do so as long as their cost-benefit analysis provides no incentive to leave. However, such customers are only loyal while it is instrumentally rewarding for them to be loyal (Samuelson and Sandvik, 1997).

Figure 10.11: Relational constructs
Reproduced by permission of Kia Motors (UK) Ltd.

Perhaps marketers, whether tongue in cheek or pure coincidence, appear to be incorporating relational constructs in their advertising (Figure 10.11).

EXAMPLE 10.12

MarketingWeek

T-Mobile focuses on value and 'relationships' in ads

T-Mobile is positioning itself as the best-value network and highlighting its focus on relationships with its new ad campaign and strapline, "Life's for Sharing". The £17m campaign breaks tomorrow (Thursday) during the Euro 2008 semi-final.

The strapline replaces "Simply Closer". T-Mobile head of brand and communications Karen Phipson says: "The Simply Closer strapline was a step in the right direction towards our goal of being a relationship focused brand. 'Life's for Sharing' really cements our focus in this area."

The campaign, which has been created by Saatchi & Saatchi London, shows "people from different walks of life" searching for minutes in unusual places, such as a medium at a séance looking for minutes in the afterlife and an archaeologist discarding Roman artifacts as he hunts for minutes.

A national press, online, and outdoor campaign will also be launched. The media, which was planned and booked by MediaCom, includes the IMAX and will also feature people looking for minutes in obscure locations.

The mobile operator will also challenge Britain to "find more minutes for £30" and it will offer new and existing customers £30 price plans and will match or beat the amount of free minutes offered by four other operators.

Marketing Week, 26th June 2008, p.6. Reproduced by permission of Centaur Media Plc.

Mutual Goals

Mutual goals are important because they explain the motivation for relationship development. However, the goals of relational partners do not have to be the same. Rather, both parties must simply have the possibility to achieve their goals through the relationship. For example, an organization wishes to engender loyalty among its customers because it has been proven that it is more profitable to service existing customers than to constantly attract new ones. (Reichheld and Sasser, 1990). Similarly, customers may wish to reduce the time and effort (search costs) of shopping around and this is possible by remaining loyal to a good supplier. Customers may also accrue the extra benefits of shopping in a familiar environment and having the product or service customized to their requirements at no extra cost (Sheth and Parvatiyar, 2000).

Satisfaction

Customers are not motivated to engage in relationships unless they are satisfied with the offer made by the organization (Tzokas and Saren, 1997). However, buyers evaluate satisfaction on other criteria also. For example, economic satisfaction refers to an 'evaluation of the economic outcomes that flow from the relationship' and social satisfaction to the 'psychological aspects of [the] relationship' (Geyskens et al., 2000). Thus, satisfaction is a multidimensional construct (as we discussed in chapter 4) that must include the quality of the core product or service as well as the economic and social aspects of the relationship. Linked to this is the comparison level of alternatives, which simply acknowledges that satisfaction is always relative. That is, customers are happy to remain in any given relationship so long as they believe there are no better alternatives out there. To a large extent, this concept explains why individuals remain in relationships in which they express unhappiness.

Cooperation

Cooperation is another variable that recognizes the interdependent and interactive nature of relationships. Relational partners must be willing and able to work together to improve relational outcomes. Cooperation is essential for achieving mutual goals and is a necessary prerequisite for any adaptations to products, services, systems or processes to occur.

It is interesting to note that research in the B2B sector suggests that relational partnerships with suppliers or client companies can sour over time and that it can be the very relational constructs that, over time, deteriorate (Anderson and Jap, 2005; Grayson and Amber, 1999).

Clearly there are links with the affective interaction that consumers have with certain brands. This has been going on for decades, as marketers have created emotional associations with their brands, but relationship marketers have picked it up again in their context of 'brand relationships' (Smit et al., 2006) and 'consumer–brand relationships' (Veloutsou, 2007).

EXAMPLE 10.13

1. To help cement relationships with its (top) customers, Sainsbury's sends up to 400 000 birthday cards every month to its loyalty card users (DMA, 2004).
2. Nectar card holders receive a map of their local area showing where they can find Nectar consortia retailers (Kimberley, 2006)

THINKBOX

It is interesting that one of the architects of customer relationship programmes, Clive Humby – of DunnHumby, the company that manages the loyalty schemes for a number of organizations including Tesco – has actually questioned the appropriateness of 'relationships' in the business context. In the keynote speech at the IDM's annual lecture, Humby (2004) said that it would be more appropriate to use the 'R' word to mean 'relevance' rather than relationship.

What do you think?

Relational marketing has been described as being composed of interaction, relationships and networks (Gummesson, 1994). Although this is relational 'marketing' not 'consumption', it is worth a brief analysis of some relevant issues here. First, 'interaction'. We have seen how consumers are increasingly interacting with marketers in a two-way sense: in Chapters 2 and 3 we explored participation by consumers (e.g. Gestalt psychology) with marketing activity and earlier in this chapter we discussed interaction as a stage in the acquisition-retention continuum, which itself could be regarded as part of a broader continuum, from acquisition to retention to loyalty to relationship. The relationships construct has been explored in the paragraphs above, but it is worth examining the network construct.

In a relationship 'marketing' context this relates to connections and partnerships up and down the supply chain, with collaborative partners as in, for example, the Nectar scheme (even if some are competitors). But networks also apply to the C2C contexts. We have again explored some of this, for example in Chapter 7 in the context of virtual social groups, but also in Chapter 9 with the influence of opinion formers and opinion leaders over followers.

Consumers are engaging in relational consumption with each other, even if much of the time this is a virtual engagement. Online Blogs and social networking sites bulge with product reviews by consumers, both positive and negative.

GIZMODO

Gizmodo, the gadget guide. So much in love with shiny new toys, it's unnatural.

view by category

TIPS@GIZMODO.COM

Yamaha YSP-900 Delivers 5.1 Sound From a Single Speaker

T-man says:

Yamaha YSP-900 Delivers 5.1 Sound From a Single Speaker

No it doesn't.

02/16/07 10:21 AM

BlindsidesDork says:

Only issue with these virtual surround sounds but…what are the room requirements for this to effectively work?

02/16/07 10:22 AM

kevjohn says:

I'll believe it when I see it. Err, hear it.

adholmes says:

I don't get these products. It looks like it works if you believe the lovely marketing drawings, but the same thing happens with all types of speakers. The sound from your TV bounces off the walls too. Doesn't mean it "sounds" like its coming from behind you.

02/16/07 10:07 AM

europria says:

It will work in a perfect world. Oddly shaped rooms, our sound absorbent materials will render it useless. More, speaker size matters.

02/16/07 10:19 AM

Source: www.gizmodo.com

An interesting trend is what we have introduced previously (Chapter 9) as 'democratizing innovation'. Here consumers are contributors to new product development in a more direct way than in previous eras. Hoffbrand (2006), for example, has shown how the relationship network includes consumers' product ideas as posted on social networking sites. Häagen Dazs encourages consumers to post their ideas for the next new ice cream recipe. Other consumers vote for their favourite of these and the company may launch that recipe. Von Hippell (2005) is a leading exponent of this approach under his terminology of democratizing innovation. Roberts and Baker (2005) also explore the phenomenon using the term co-creation and report on the new relationship between producer and consumer which in our terms, here, is a different manifestation of the 'network' construct of relationship marketing.

THINKBOX

Is relational consumer behaviour stronger (or even only possible) where there is some personal contact with a real person in the organization?

Doss it matter that we have contact with different staff at each contact (e.g. checkout or call centre)?

Egan (2003) concludes that 'the attempt to force fit relational strategies in markets where interpersonal interaction is low, promotes the use of technology . . . as a supposed substitute for personal closeness. . . . There is nothing inherently wrong in this approach except when companies start to believe there is more to their relationship than is in fact the case' (p 153).

How can relational interaction work under such conditions?

Guanxi

It is worth pausing to consider a different relational paradigm; that from within Chinese culture, called *Guanxi*.

This is similarly concerned with connections but at the face-to-face level. The relationships are not based on written agreements as might be the case in Western society, with, for example opt-in/permission marketing, but rather on personal trust. The connections require reciprocal obligation (Brunner and Koh, 1988). Wong and Leung (2001:5) succinctly provide the underpinning for *Guanxi*: 'The traditional Confucian concept of the group taking precedence over the individual . . . the five relationships, emperor–subject, father–son, husband–wife, brother–brother and friend–friend, perpetuate its influence in modern China.' They show how gifts and hospitality can be used at what we would refer to as the attraction and interaction stages of acquisition. But emotional relationships (*ganqing*) evolve with further bonding so that the outsider actually becomes an insider and this is when and how business deals work effectively.

Experiential Consumption

We introduced the concept of experiential consumption in Chapter 1 where we posited an extension beyond the buying of benefits to the buying of experiences. In terms of consumer behaviour theory, this is informed by several of the concepts we have also introduced, such as gestalt psychology (Chapter 3) because there is a synergy of the four Ps of marketing (product, price, place and promotion) with how the product engages with a range of the consumer's senses (Chapter 2). From this we learn that our perceptual processes and senses are important. We have now explored the relational approach in the current chapter, as this advocates reciprocal interactive involvement between company/brand/product and consumer.

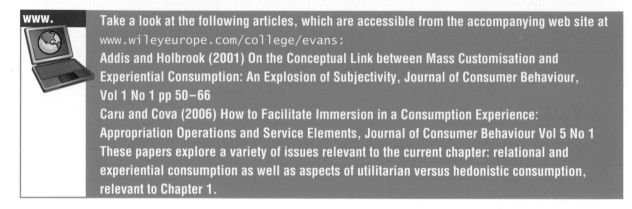

www. Take a look at the following articles, which are accessible from the accompanying web site at www.wileyeurope.com/college/evans:

Addis and Holbrook (2001) On the Conceptual Link between Mass Customisation and Experiential Consumption: An Explosion of Subjectivity, Journal of Consumer Behaviour, Vol 1 No 1 pp 50–66

Caru and Cova (2006) How to Facilitate Immersion in a Consumption Experience: Appropriation Operations and Service Elements, Journal of Consumer Behaviour Vol 5 No 1

These papers explore a variety of issues relevant to the current chapter: relational and experiential consumption as well as aspects of utilitarian versus hedonistic consumption, relevant to Chapter 1.

Marketers refer to **experiential marketing** and we consider this from the consumer's perspective as experiential consumption. This can be sense consumption, which targets several of the consumer's senses.

EXAMPLE 10.14

An example of using consumers' senses in an experiential marketing campaign is afforded by the Coca-Cola Magic Ride campaign. Here, consumers watched a three-dimensional show during which they *heard* the (digitized) sound of fizzing cola, *smelt* the aroma of the cola, *felt* cold air bubbles and then *tasted* the product itself.

Feel consumption exploits consumers' emotions.

EXAMPLE 10.15

When the VW Beetle was re-launched, the early campaigns emotionally portrayed feelings of nostalgia for the 1960s version. If you remember what we have said about possessions defining consumers and especially the nostalgic role that possession can play (Belk, 1988) you will see the logic of this approach. It is useful at this point to revisit our coverage of Retro Marketing in chapter 9.

Then there is think consumption, which is a form of experiential marketing that 'appeals to the intellect with the objective of creating cognitive, problem solving experiences that engage consumers creatively' (Schmitt, 1999). We refer you back to our coverage of the FCB grid in Chapter 4 because this involves 'think' and 'feel' products.

Relate consumption encompasses all and incorporates the brand within the consumer's core existence, and in this way is closest to the relational marketing paradigm discussed here.

Such approaches can have a clear edge over other, non-participatory, campaigns in encouraging trial of the product. Some researchers even suggest that experiential marketing will not only be a major plank for gaining competitive advantage but also for increasing brand loyalty (Barrett, 2003).

EXAMPLE 10.16

It was back in 1983 that Harley Davidson introduced their relationship marketing strategy, via the owners club (Harley Owners Group – HOG). The brand has long been an icon in the motorcycle world and this has been reinforced by the strong associations of its appearance in such films as *Easy Rider* and *Terminator II*. Harley's relationship strategy was kick-started by the informal meetings held by Harley fans. They nicknamed the bikes 'HOGS' in any case, so it wasn't a huge jump to set up the 'HOG' relationship club. The relationship with the brand and other owners is a good example of what we discussed in Chapter 6 concerning the extended self-concept, but also of both individualism and tribal behaviour.

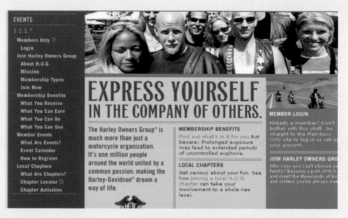

Source: www.hog.com

To add a more social slant to the image of bikers, Harley Davidson associated the company with the Muscular Dystrophy Foundation and hold events to promote the charity. Now Harley owners hold rallies and rides for quite a range of charities. The strength of emotion toward the brand is reflected in the feeling that it is driveway jewellery. Indeed, via the Owners Group, this is supported by the range of bike merchandising including accessories, jackets and caps. It all adds to a way of life that HOG members have bought into and there are few relationship strategies that are so 'affectively' based. There are tangible retention devices as well: customers can up-grade to a bigger model one year after purchase with trade-in at full value.

Now, potential owners of second and even third bikes are targeted for relational treatment.

The channels of relational interaction are also extensive:

multi-lingual customer care will be provided through a newly centralized call centre, allowing the delivery of dedicated bespoke service to HOG's 70 000 strong user base. Customers can use telephone, fax, e-mail, or mail to find out about forthcoming rides, event tours and merchandise with a view to offering a web and SMS service in future. (Rubach, 2003a)

Consider the emotional, symbolic and experiential consumption aspects of the potential relational consumption that are afforded HOGs.

THINKBOX

Experiential consumption, according to Caru and Cova (2007) includes the following attributes:

'Consumers are not only consumers, consumers act within situations, consumers seek meaning, consumption involves more than mere purchasing' (p 5).

They report Arnold *et al*. (2002) as describing experiential consumption stages as:

'The pre-consumption experience, which involves searching for, planning, day-dreaming about, and foreseeing the experience.

The purchasing experience, which involves choosing the item, payment, packaging and the encounter with the service and the environment.

The core consumption experience, which involves sensation, satisfaction, dissatisfaction, irritation and transformation.

The remembered consumption experience and the nostalgia experience in which photographs are used to relive a past experience based on narrative and arguments with friends about the past, is something that tends toward the classification of memories' (Caru and Cova, 2007:7).

Or is it just buying and using? What do you think, why and give some examples of your position?

This brings us a long way from the starting point of this chapter, which focused on behavioural repeat purchasing. It shows how marketers and consumers can benefit from reciprocal engagement beyond the mere sale–purchase exchange.

SUMMARY

■ Customer loyalty is important as it provides benefits to both consumers and to firms. One of the earlier approaches to loyalty included measuring repeat purchasing behaviour using panel data and researchers predicted consumer behaviour using stochastic models. A deterministic, cognitive-based approach to explaining loyalty is also suggested and the concept of retention strategy might be a relevant one to integrate in this respect. Repeat purchasing may not always lead to loyalty and the much-hyped loyalty scheme is sometimes in danger of being little more than short-term sales promotion or even an oxymoron.

■ Loyalty as opposed to repeat purchasing includes attitudinal constructs in addition to the behaviour of just buying repeatedly. Customer satisfaction is an important antecedent to customer loyalty but one should note the effects of those who are merely satisfied and those who are completely satisfied or delighted with a firm's offering. Those who are delighted can become advocates and can recommend the brand to others whereas merely satisfied and dissatisfied customers are likely to switch brands.

■ Relational consumption is an important concept and many have advocated its principles of reciprocal affective interaction. Indeed brands are not lifeless entities: the amalgam of consumers' purchases can even define them – they can be perceived as being a live and active central part of consumers' lives. Consumers often show a great deal of involvement, passion, love and commitment towards them. It is important to consider the relationship that develops, grows and evolves over time between a consumer and the brands they buy.

QUESTIONS

1. **What is repeat buying? How is this different from the loyalty models proposed by Dick and Basu (1994) and Jones and Sasser (1995)? Use examples to illustrate.**

2. **What must organizations do to overcome criticisms that their loyalty programmes are nothing more than sophisticated sales promotions?**

3. **For the following contexts, which key relational constructs are likely to be most important for a consumer: financial services company, supermarket, mail order firm, expensive restaurant?**

4. **What parallels are there between the elements of 'relationship' you have with people close to you and any relationship you have with brands or companies?**

5. **How much do you engage in experiential consumption? Can this approach lead to relational buying? Why, or why not?**

6. **Analyse and evaluate the TRI*M model in terms of explaining and measuring consumer loyalty and retention.**

7. **Provide examples of how a marketer might use the acquisition-retention continuum.**

FURTHER READING

Caru A and Cova B (2007) *Consuming Experience*, Routledge.

Ehrenberg A S C (1988) *Repeat Buying*, 2nd edn, Charles Griffin, London. This is a seminal monograph which reports extremely extensive empirical research into consumer repeat purchasing behaviour.

Humby C, Hunt T and Phillips T (2007) *Scoring Points: How Tesco Continues to Win Customer Loyalty*, Kogan Page. This text takes repeat purchasing into the twenty-first century with an in-depth discussion of how Tesco's loyalty scheme operates. It is a rich source of insights into the use of customer data for marketing purposes.

CHAPTER 11
DATA-BASED CONSUMER BEHAVIOUR

CHAPTER OBJECTIVES

After engaging with the material presented in this chapter and its associated exercises and reading, you should be able to:

■ Explain the trend toward behavioural-based knowledge of consumer behaviour via transactional data and the emergence of biographics.

■ Evaluate the role and relevance of a variety of consumer surveillance approaches available to marketers to track consumers' behaviour.

■ Analyse and evaluate the role and nature of geodemographics and *contemporary* lifestyle research in understanding and profiling consumer behaviour.

■ Elucidate how consumers react to individualized consumer–organization interaction.

INTRODUCTION

The two previous chapters discussed how a greater understanding of new and repeat buying can move toward loyal and even relational buying behaviour. This chapter continues this theme by analysing how consumer behavioural information and further sources of individualized profile data can be used not only to explain and predict consumers' behaviour but also to facilitate individualized consumer–organization interaction.

First, we explore personalized behavioural data and its contribution to understanding how consumers behave. These data include consumers' **transactional data** such as are gathered via loyalty cards or on-line purchases. There is also the use of pre-purchase data such as that from monitoring Internet searches via, for example, Google. There is also an increasing range of other sources of **behavioural data**, including: **radio frequency identification 'tags' (RFID)**, Internet **cookies, global positioning systems (GPS)** based on satellite tracking.

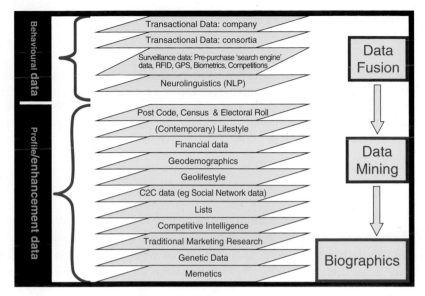

Figure 11.1: Sources of data

We then turn to personalized (or near personalized) **profiling** databases, such as **geodemographics** and contemporary lifestyle research, which claim to provide further explanations of consumer behaviour. There is continuous debate over the use of **genetic data** by, for example, insurance companies to increase ability to predict probabilities of risk based on the health profile of consumers, perhaps tacked back through their generations.

Some of this might sound a bit sinister, but these are personalized behavioural data sources used by some current and probably by many future marketers, to understand and target consumers.

Figure 11.1 provides a summary of some of these sources of data that marketers are now increasingly turning to, to help them 'know' their customers.

The trend toward trying to understand consumers as individuals means that marketers are increasingly targeting them as such (or at least within smaller and smaller segments). This goes further, as our discussion of relational consumption in Chapter 10 proposed, because it has the potential for individualized consumer–organizational interaction.

The chapter then concludes with an exploration of wider social implications of the 'data-based consumer' and indeed how consumers themselves are reacting to being targeted more precisely.

UNDERSTANDING CONSUMER BEHAVIOUR FROM PERSONALIZED BEHAVIOURAL DATA

Transactional Data: Company

When companies are able to track individual buying behaviour, via loyalty schemes (Chapter 10) or from mail order purchases or on-line transactions, they collect transactional data.

These data are used to help explore consumer behaviour in two main ways: to identify and predict what will be bought; and to identify the 'better' consumers.

Identifying and Predicting What Will be Bought by Whom and What to Sell

By linking items purchased with specific named consumers, their patterns of consumption can be tracked in order to target them, as individuals or small segments. Transactional data is 'refreshed daily and weekly, thereby providing a dynamic insight, not only into how and what consumers are buying but describing individual behaviour across different channels . . . payment methods and their typical conversion performance, all in near real time' (Morris, 2006).

EXAMPLE 11.1

An inspection of a retail loyalty scheme database revealed, for a certain 'Mrs Brown', her address and a variety of behavioural information including: she shops once per week, usually on a Friday, has a baby (because she buys nappies), spends £90 per week on average and usually buys two bottles of gin every week (Mitchell, 1996). By knowing what individual consumers buy, the retailer might be able to target them with relevant offers while the consumer saves money at the same time.

Even credit and debit card data is used. It is typical for the 'small print' of the terms of use of these to state that personal data, including transactional data, will be used within the 'group' (do we all know the constituent members of our credit card group?). 'Use' often includes assessing financial risk and developing relationships with customers. Transactional and any other data that credit card companies hold can, not surprisingly in today's environment, be accessed for the detection of crime and other legal reasons.

THINKBOX

Credit card companies often state that they will share personalized data with companies outside of the 'group', with our permission or sometimes not, if that company provides a service to the credit card company itself- or to the consumer:

'Never before have consumers carried around in their wallet their own database of all the brands they have bought or all the promotions they have responded to' (Shaw, 2004).

Think about this: every time you Chip & PIN or give someone the details of your plastic friend, you might never be entirely sure who else gets to know about you.

So, transactional data provides scope for analysing who buys what, when and through what form of payment, but also, purchase patterns can be revealed for different geographic locations, store branches, seasons of the year and all of this for each customer.

THINKBOX

Loyalty card data can identify, for a Mrs Spender, that she bought a pair of shiny tight-fit trousers, size 10, colour red at £39.99 and a plunge-neck skinny-fit sequined top, size

10 at £49.99 and a pair of pink men's boxer shorts size M at £12.99. She paid by credit card number 1234 5678 9101 1213, at 16.03 on 14 February this year, at the Cardiff branch of Cheeky Fashions.

If you also have data showing she is a regular shopper, of both women's and menswear, and brought some friends along to a fashion evening in December, of what use would these data be to Cheeky fashions?

Inferences about consumer interests and likely future buying behaviour can be made from transactional data over a period of time. Such inferences can lead the organization to target individual consumers at what are hoped to be appropriate times with relevant offers. If consumers do indeed see this as timely and relevant and there are repeated and reciprocated personalized interactions, a relationship between consumer and organization/brand might develop.

EXAMPLE 11.2

Tesco was aware that their petrol stations were not as profitable as they could be, because margins are low on fuel, but they saw potential of more sales from non-fuel items. Transactional data across petrol stations were analysed by number of visits, spend per visit and so was cross-spend between supermarket and petrol station. New lines were added to selected petrol stations according to the segmentation that emerged (DunnHumby, 2007).

Data mining software is often used to trawl through the mountains of transactional data that many marketers now have, in order to understand, monitor and predict consumer behaviour. The Venn diagram below is an illustration of SmartFocus's 'Viper' data mining package and how it can extract those customers on its database who have bought product item 'B' via the 'E' channel and paid by credit card. The less exciting looking space underneath would be completed with the actual names and addresses of those customers.

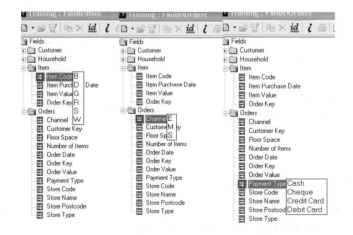

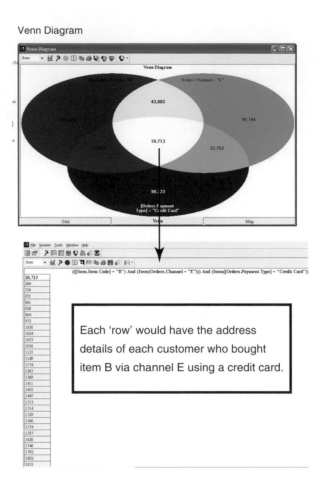

Venn Diagram

Identifying the 'Better' Consumers

Personalized consumer researchers can identify the **recency, frequency and monetary value (RFM)** of customer orders. Recency – just knowing they have purchased from us in the past is important but not sufficient; we are probably less interested in those who bought from us 10 years ago and not since. Frequency – a one-off purchase may also make a customer less attractive (depending, of course, on the product market in which we operate). So knowing how often they buy from us is an important measure. Monetary value – small orders are usually less attractive than larger ones, so this is yet another measure of significance. Indeed marketers are increasingly concentrating on their 'better' customers – those who have the highest monetary value (and frequency) of purchase and are segmenting on the basis of 'volume' because in this way they are more cost-effective, because they concentrate on those who bring greater returns.

THINKBOX

Next time you are in a supermarket queue at a checkout, have a look at the items in the trolley in front of you (surreptitiously and without causing offence, of course!). In the meantime, consider Figure 11.2.

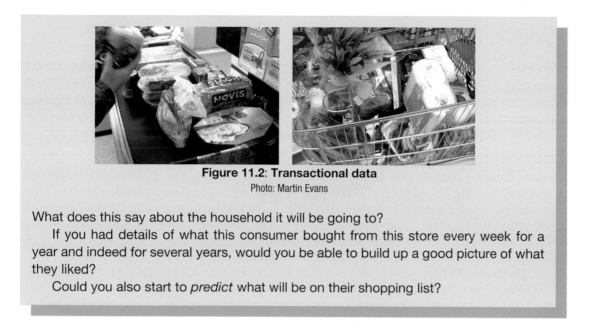

Figure 11.2: Transactional data
Photo: Martin Evans

What does this say about the household it will be going to?

If you had details of what this consumer bought from this store every week for a year and indeed for several years, would you be able to build up a good picture of what they liked?

Could you also start to *predict* what will be on their shopping list?

Vilfredo Pareto's theory of income distribution has been transferred and borrowed by marketers to support the proposition that 80% of sales come from just 20% of customers – in many markets the ratio can be even more polarized (95:5 is not uncommon). For RFM analysis transactional data must be tracked by the database – actual purchase history is needed. Figure 11.3 shows a screenshot from the RFM tool within the Viper data-mining software product. Actually names and addresses (withheld here, but IDs shown) of those customers who have ordered more than 20 times with an average order value of over £200 and whose most recent order was in 2008 (the most recent for that dataset) are extracted very quickly from the customer database.

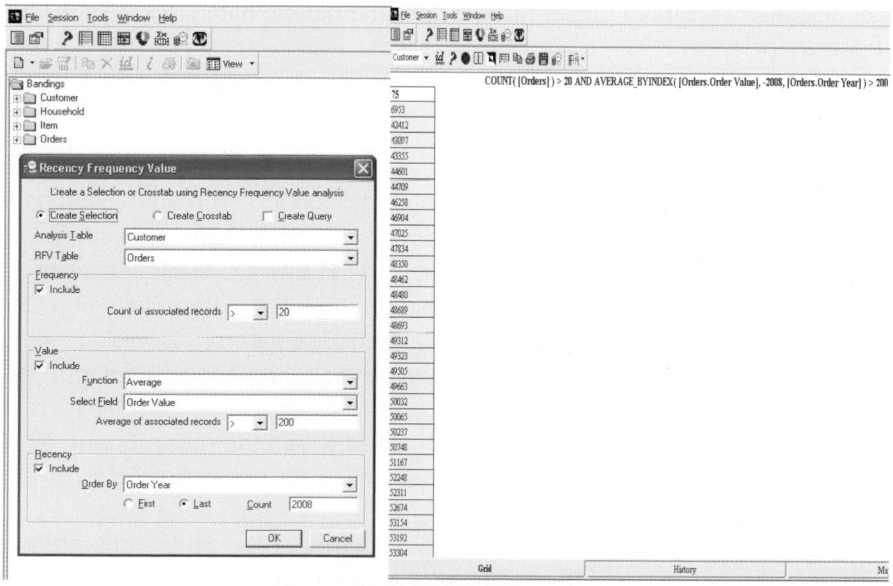

Figure 11.3: VIPER data-mining
VIPER can identify RFM categories

EXAMPLE 11.3

The short break company, Center Parcs employed such metrics when analysing customer behaviour by activity, spend, type of booking and party profiles. They segmented their database using tree names: Redwoods are frequent visitors but not big spenders, Cedars have high spend value but are less frequent visitors, Birch's spend and visits are low, Saplings have booked but not visited as yet and Oaks are the most loyal (Benjamin, 2008).

However, those consumers who do *not* contribute as much to profit as the company might wish and have a low RFM might be excluded. This might lead to some disaffection among the less attractive segments when they realize that others are being presented with the 'better' offers. It has been suggested, even from within the industry, that alienated customers might even see this as something 'Orwellian in nature' (Wright, 1999). Tesco for example has described the student loyalty card (which was discontinued) 'impossible to profit from using loyalty marketing techniques' (Humby *et al.*, 2007).

Indeed, Larrington-Wright (2008) has been critical of the Egg bank for closing the credit card accounts of over 160 000 of its customers. He stated that 'it is doing it because these customers aren't making it any money'. It was clear that many of the customers were not bad debtors (as the company had claimed in the context of the credit crunch of 2007-8) because they paid their balances in full each month and many had already repaid their mortgages. It was probably the very fact they were not paying interest on their credit that the bank saw them as in a low RFM segment.

Transactional Data: Consortia

Not only can many companies collect and analyse transactional data from their own customers, but increasingly there are data consortia in which collaboration between the company members allows a sort of Gestalt of customer behaviour: 'the sum really is greater than the sum of the parts...data co-operatives...mail order companies, catalogers and charities are ahead of the game...multi source data on a pool of customers creates a bigger picture than standalone databases' (Anon, 2006).

THINKBOX

If you have a Nectar card, are you aware of all of the organizations in the consortia?

They include BP, Barclaycard, Sainsbury's, First Quench (Thresher, Victoria Wine, Wine Rack, Bottoms Up, Drinks Cabin, Haddows, Huttons), Adams, Ford, Vodafone, EDF Energy, London Energy, Seeboard Energy, SWEB Energy, Hertz, Brewsters, TNS Market Research surveys, Blockbusters, Nuffield Health Fitness and Wellbeing Centers, Alton Towers, Argos, Winemark, AllSports, Magnet, Beefeaters, eBookers, Carphone Warehouse, Racecourses and 160 online brands (Anon, 2007) check the nectar website for changes.

The 'small print' states that data will only be used within the group & where needed to operate the system. You may want a relationship with some but how do you feel about 'all'?

Transactis hosts a data consortia of mail order companies whose customer transactional data is pooled to provide profiles of the 'best' mail order consumers across sectors – even by RFM score (Anon 2004).

Personalised 'Surveillance' Data

Pre-Purchase Search Engine Data

Transactional data provides, by definition, an historical perspective on a customer's buying patterns. Consider Google: many consumers search for information on products they are *about* to buy, via search engines. By tracking this behaviour online, marketers are perhaps able to identify those consumers who are about to buy specific products or services and can target them at this most salient point, with their own offer. 'Facebook and MySpace are other examples: individuals building profiles about themselves – personal databases – on a mass scale, to reveal information about their attitudes, preferences, circumstances, lifestyles and interests. No traditional market research or transaction-based database could ever match these personal databases once they reach maturity' (Mitchell, 2008).

THINKBOX

How do you feel about ALL your Google searches being tracked by marketers, to be targeted at what they would claim to be appropriate times and with relevant offers?

It is also clear that there are concerns abut marketers' tracking of social network sites: (Facebook) 'pays for itself by allowing marketers to access demographic and behavioural information' (Mann 2008).

EXAMPLE 11.4

MarketingWeek

Google gives Tesco Clubcard information technology lesson

It could be one of the competitive battles of the early 21st century. The battleground: Phoenix, Arizona (of all places). The contestants: upstart newcomer Tesco with its new Fresh & Easy format versus leviathan incumbent Wal-Mart, with a new concept called Marketside. Why is it so significant? Because Tesco's model of many small local stores linked by a super-efficient and flexible replenishment network could have found Wal-Mart's Achilles heel.

Wal-Mart rose to be the biggest company in the world on the back of its formula of big box out-of-town stores. Its influence is huge. For example, it has over 50 000 Chinese suppliers, making it China's seventh largest trading partner – bigger than most nations. Yet Tesco believes it can pretty much match Wal-Mart on price while offering shoppers much greater convenience, freshness and quality. So it's game on.

One weapon Tesco has yet to deploy, however, is Clubcard. Perhaps it's just a matter of time, but there might also be competitive/contractual issues relating to Tesco subsidiary DunnHumby's work for Kroger. It may also have something to do with the nature of Clubcard itself.

With Clubcard, Tesco has earned global admiration as a pioneer and innovator, demonstrating the power of a business driven operationally by customer data. It gives us a glimpse into the future. Clubcard data is now embedded into virtually everything Tesco does: ranging, pricing, promotions, space allocations and store designs, store locations, marketing communications, the lot.

Using this data, Tesco can do things other retailers can only dream of: countless small experiments – tweaking this, trying that – so that it keeps improving details of its operations, most of which remain invisible to its competitors but which nevertheless add up to a formidable competitive advantage.

Yet as far as marketing as a whole is concerned, Clubcard is just a magnificent dead-end because the combination of things that make it so powerful do not apply to most businesses. Imagine a similar loyalty scheme for an electricity supplier, holiday company, clothes shop, bank or petrol station. None of these businesses has customers constantly returning once or twice a week, 52 weeks of the year. None of them has customers buying 40 or 50 different items each time from within a range of tens of thousands of stock keeping units. So none of them has Tesco's infinite potential to tweak offerings.

Reliable picture

Few of them share Tesco's sweet spot "share of customer requirement" either. The petrol station or clothes shop's share of the individual's total category spend may be so small that any data they collect will fail to give them a reliable picture of the customer's overall spending patterns. On the other hand, the electricity supplier or bank may have 100% of the customer's business, which means they lack the one thing that makes Clubcard so successful – the ability to expand their share of customer spend.

Tesco has the best of both worlds: a big enough share of category spend to get a good profile of customer attributes and behaviours, but with plenty of room for growth. (Even if you have 75% of a customer's category spend, if you can increase this by just 1% over 10 million customers you are talking mega bucks.) And that's not counting the ability to use the same data to ease entry into new markets.

I could go on – the size of the customer base, the fact that the food you buy says an awful lot about your values and lifestyle (much more than your electricity). However, Clubcard is a freak, rather like a giraffe standing tall among all other jungle beasts. For most businesses (aside from a few international retailers with similar characteristics), trying to copy its "secrets of success" isn't feasible.

Does this mean the dream of the data driven company is a mirage after all? No, it simply means Tesco is not the one showing us the way forward. The real opportunities lie elsewhere. Take Google as one example. With Google, individuals volunteer information about what they are interested in buying, and when they are interested in buying it. This provides data that Clubcard can never capture: before-the-event information about what somebody is planning to buy rather than after-the-event information about what they have bought. In marketing terms, that's nirvana – and Google is just the start.

Facebook and MySpace are other examples: individuals building profiles about themselves – personal databases – on a mass scale, to reveal information about their attitudes, preferences, circumstances, lifestyles and interests. No traditional market research or transaction-based database could ever match these personal databases once they reach maturity.

Now factor in the many other ways individuals could volunteer information if they were so minded and if the appropriate mechanisms, infrastructure, incentives and safeguards were in place – communication preferences (opt ins and opt outs), factual updates ("I have moved home"), questions and queries, orders and specifications, complaints and suggestions, peer reviews and peer advice, expressions of interest, future plans and intentions, doubts and fears, and so on.

Elicited, processed and combined in the right way, these sorts of volunteered information will reach levels of richness, scale, granularity, immediacy and flexibility that make Clubcard look like a beached whale.

Transactional data

Our current model of customer relationship management (CRM) – gathering transaction data about customers, storing it in a huge centralised database inside a single corporate silo, and then trying to infer patterns and make predictions on the basis of this data – is reaching its sell-by date. But that doesn't mean "the death of CRM". Big companies still need CRM systems for legal and operational reasons. But the cutting edge of marketing and competitive advantage – spotting emerging opportunities for innovation, responding quickly to changing market trends, eliminating waste from the marketing process by knowing who to talk to, about what, when – is rapidly moving to a completely different arena.

With volunteered information the underlying infrastructure is incredibly decentralised; the individual rather than the corporation is the key data generator; success comes from the ability to respond rapidly to real signals of demand rather than from building models, making predictions and running "campaigns".

Over the pond in the US, Tesco is poised to prove the superiority of fast, flexible and local. But back here, its information model is an echo of Wal-Mart – big, cumbersome, centralised and hugely expensive. By all means, admire Tesco for what it has achieved with Clubcard, but try adopting the same approach at your peril.

Tesco Clubcard: Will not be used in its Fresh & Easy stores Stateside because its old-style data collection methods is an echo of Wal-Mart
Marketing Week, 24 January 2008, pp 26–27. Reproduced by permission of Centaur Media Plc.

RFID Tags

To date, the tracking of transactional data in the 'bricks and mortar' shopping environment has been via bar-coded items linked with some mechanism for identifying the individual consumer (e.g. loyalty cards). In the future, bar codes might be replaced by radio frequency identification tags (RFID) which are extremely small (grain of sand) radio transmitters embedded within products or their packaging. They emit radio signals which can be collected by hand-held or static scanners. Their main current use is to track goods as they move through supply chains and help in the stock control and ordering processes. However, they are being used in experiments by various retailers, such as Marks & Spencer, House of Fraser and Tesco, to track items in-store. Not only can this lead to more accurate shelf-stacking, but also to in-store personalized targeting. Here, consumers will soon be able to push their **smart trolleys** around supermarkets. Smart trolleys will be able to access consumers' transactional profiles once their loyalty cards are swiped (on *entry* to the store) in order to target relevant offers in real time and indeed in the right location within the store.

Another application is in tackling theft. As items are taken off the shelves, they can be tracked through (and out of) the store and matched with what was actually paid for. Some tags will even incorporate a miniature camera that can help identify thieves (BBC, 2003).

You might have an RFID under your skin! The members of some European bars and clubs have RFIDs implanted in their arms. They don't need to show ID and don't need to carry cash or cards: the money is recorded on the RFID and balances change as their 'arm' is scanned for each purchase (Usborne, 2007). RFID cards might also appear in loyalty cards, allowing the customer to be identified as they enter the store and for their transactional data to be accessed in real time. From this, relevant offers can be sent to them while still in the store via their mobile phones. Is this something you would welcome?

EXAMPLE 11.5

Biometrics

The film *Minority Report* demonstrated real-time recognition of customers as they entered a store or even just walked around a shopping mall. Recognition was via automatic retina identification (biometrics) and on this basis customer transactional and profile records were accessed and relevant promotions and offers delivered at the same time. This might have been futuristic at the time of the film's release (in 2002) but the technology is certainly available and perhaps RFID will even replace this. A London department store and a casino have already introduced biometric recognition (facial recognition software) so that their 'special' customers can be recognized as soon as they enter and then quickly greeted personally by a manager (Steiner, 2002), RFID could be an alternative way of identifying customers – as long as they didn't swap clothes! Invasion of privacy is a possible implication of this new trend, as suggested by London (2003) and Shabi (2003), but what invasion of privacy is to some is not to others.

GPS and Cookies

The future use of such tags might be much broader, however, and could include tracking products where they are after purchase (or theft) and even through to disposal. Global positioning systems (GPS) via satellites, can track these tags. GPS can also track the location of mobile phones to within several metres without the owner knowing. This can lead to personalized targeting (in real time) by marketers who are geographically in close proximity to the individual consumers; for example, as a consumer approaches a particular store.

The RAC identifies the location of a vehicle breakdown via the GPS tracking of the customer's mobile phone.

There is also the covert surveillance of web traffic, via technology such as cookies: the 'surfing' behaviour of those visiting web sites can provide valuable information about how prospects and customers behave on the Internet.

Behavioural data: Competitions

Competitions have long been used not only as a form of sales promotion but also to gather personalized data. It is obvious that those entering a competition could be existing customers but equally they might never have had any contact with the organization concerned. As a result, the competition is a good way to gather data from prospects as well as to upgrade existing data on customers, depending on the sorts of questions asked. These questions can sometimes be the main purpose of the competition, even if, to the entrant, the competition itself is more clearly *their* intent. Entering a competition is behavioural, but it is more usually used to profile possible prospects for customer acquisition campaigns.

EXAMPLE 11.6

Mobile telephony is also a major new medium. The film company Twentieth Century Fox has a 'home entertainment' unit and for the launch of the DVD version of the film *Minority Report*, they used a sound clip from the film. Receivers of this telephone message were surprised to hear a man drawing breath and then saying, 'Where's my *Minority Report*?' and then screaming: 'Do I even have one?' The voice was that of Tom Cruise, the star of the film. The message ended: 'Don't miss out on your *Minority Report*. Buy it now on DVD and video.' This led to complaints to the Advertising Standards Authority (ASA) based on the phone message being offensive and that it could have caused distress and indeed that it did not make clear it was an advertisement. Some people who received the message had to pay to call their answer phone to retrieve the message if they had not been able to answer their phone when it was initially sent. Twentieth Century Fox Home Entertainment justified this by saying that it was only sent to those who had registered their details on the company's web site (30 000 of them) and had actually asked for communications concerning films and DVDs. So the company considered it appropriate to communicate with those who had 'opted-in' for relational interaction. The company also thought that most people who had expressed this sort of interest would be familiar with Tom Cruise's voice. However, the ASA upheld the complaints on the basis that when consumers are out of the film context and going about their daily routine they would not necessarily be thinking of receiving a message from Tom Cruise and the nature of the message could indeed be seen to be somewhat menacing and could therefore cause offence (Rosser, 2003).

THINKBOX

Does the prospect of being tracked every minute of the day, through the items we carry or wear, represent an invasion of personal privacy?
  Why, or why not?

Behavioural Data NLP

In Chapter 5 we explored the use of neurolinguistic programming in the context of the gendered brain. Without repeating the underlying principles, it is worth including the approach here, as another source of personalized behavioural data: the way the brain behaves when, for example, processing marketing information.

UNDERSTANDING CONSUMER BEHAVIOUR VIA PERSONALIZED PROFILE DATA

Post Codes, Census, Electoral Roll, Contemporary Lifestyle and Geodemographics

We need to start with the national census, here. Originally the census was devised to help government and social planners determine infrastructural, community and social requirements for the next few years. But more recently it has also been used by companies to understand consumers. The first commercial use of the census was a marketing watershed and from 1981, in the UK, the national census has been available for marketing purposes.

The use of the national census in the UK led to the development of geodemographic systems and was a major catalyst in providing alternatives to anonymized market research samples. Although names and addresses cannot be revealed from the census, a link via the postal code system with the electoral roll means that it is possible to identify individual households and their characteristics. In November 2001 a member of the public won his case against Wakefield Council after that council had not been able to confirm that his electoral roll data (name and address) would not be supplied to third parties (such as marketers) without his consent (Acland, 2001). This had been a worry of the Information Commissioner who had been concerned that the electoral roll is compiled for voting purposes and should not be used for another purpose (one of the principles of the data protection legislation). The result has been the inclusion of opt-out options for electoral roll submissions and this should help to alleviate privacy concerns. But this means that only a smaller and, by definition, an incomplete electoral roll can be used. Even within months of the electoral roll opt-out being introduced, over 10 million people had opted out (Larkins, 2003) and by 2004 this had risen to over 29% of the population (indeed over 70% in some individual local authority areas) (May, 2005). So there are problems for marketers in the database's lack of geographical coverage.

The reduced completeness of the roll could lead to an increase in poor (junk) targeting (Rubach, 2003b). Another source of geodemographic data comes from (contemporary) lifestyle data.

Lifestyle Profiles

We explored traditional (anonymized) lifestyle research in Chapter 6. Here, however, we review an alternative approach to lifestyle research which has developed since about the late 1980s.

Contemporary lifestyle research, as we term this, asks respondents to tick those responses that apply in terms of products and services in which they claim an interest or actual purchase. Table 11.1 demonstrates some typical questions, some of which will be sponsored by specific companies.

Table 11.1 reflects just a portion of typical current lifestyle surveys. Many more questions are included covering claimed buying behaviour across many different product and service categories. Some questions will be sponsored by specific companies; for example, a car insurance company might sponsor a question asking for the month in which the car insurance is renewed. Because these surveys are not anonymized (the data will be filed in a database by name and address of respondent) it is likely that in the month prior to that respondent's renewal date, they are very likely to receive direct mailings soliciting defection to the sponsoring company.

The difference between the more traditional form of lifestyle segmentation discussed in Chapter 6 and the current approach is that the former builds psychographic profiles from segments from relatively small (anonymized) data sets and expands these to generalize patterns within the larger population. The latter, however, has the ability to list specific names and addresses of those who claim to be interested in specific products, brands and services.

 www. www.prospectlocator.com is Experian's online 'list' site. It shows how consumers can be selected (by name and address and even telephone number), according to a variety of characteristics including geodemographics and specific factors from lifestyle lists.

Please indicate your marital status:
single
married
divorced/separated
widowed
What is your name and address?........
What is your partner's full name?........
Holidays:
How much are you likely to spend per person on your next main holiday?
up to £500 ☐   £501–£999 ☐   £1000–1499 ☐   £1500–£2000 ☐ £2000+ ☐
In which country are you likely to take your next main holiday?........
In which month are you likely to take your main holiday?........

Table 11.1: Contemporary lifestyle research

Financials

The fusion with financial data is partly based on the origins of some of the geodemographic companies. Experian for example used to be CCN, the credit referencing arm of Great Universal Stores (CCN stood for Consumer Credit Nottingham). The value of being able to score consumers according to their use, or abuse of credit is obvious to marketers. Consumers with a poor credit history might be avoided as customers, unless the context is financial services, in which case those who do not, for example pay their credit card balances each month, are the ones that make money for the financial services company! We return to this particular issue when discussing the de-selection of customers later in this chapter and this is relevant to the credit crunch from 2007.

Geodemographics

There are several geodemographic products but two leading ones are **Acorn** and **Mosaic** from the companies Consolidated Analysis Centres Incorporated (CACI) and Experian respectively. They overlay analyses of census data with a variety of data sources including financial data such as county court judgements (CCJs) for bad debt, electoral roll and Royal Mail (post code and address) data. The result is a profile of neighbourhoods, often at full postcode level of around 15 households. The basic rationale behind geodemographics is that 'birds of a feather flock together', making neighbourhoods relatively homogenous. An easy criticism in riposte, however, is that 'I am not like my neighbour'.

Geodemographic systems are not restricted to the UK, and a number of similar systems have been operating around the world for many years. In other European countries similar systems exist and several geodemographic companies now operate throughout many European countries and even, recently (in the case of Mosaic) into China.

It is straightforward to profile the area around a postcode in terms of geodemographic categories (Gonzalez-Benito and Gonzalez-Benito, 2005). This could be the catchment area of an existing retail outlet, bank, pub and so on, or it could be the profiling of a 'drive time' area of one of several possible locations to site a new branch of a multiple retailer. It is likely that the retailer (in this case) would know the geodemographic profile of existing best customers and from the geodemographic profile of the new area would be able to purchase (from Experian or CACI, for example) the names and addresses of those who match this profile, for potential for direct mail or telemarketing contact.

EXAMPLE 11.7

Figure 11.4 depicts the sort of neighbourhood profiling offered by geodemographic systems (MOSAIC in this case). The 11 groups here are further subdivided into 61 'types'. To illustrate the depth of consumer behaviour 'knowledge' that can be gleaned from just one of these types, Table 11.2 provides a summary.

There is now a full geodemographic analysis of the Target Group Index (TGI), which is an annual report in 34 volumes of buyer profiles in most product markets, based on samples of over 20 000. From this, each geodemographic category's interest in the product concerned can be determined. In fact the TGI sample design is now based on geodemographic categories and so sample design is an application of geodemographics. In addition, the National Readership Survey is similarly analysed by geodemographics and this can provide readership profiles for media selection purposes. The TGI is fused with BARB TV panel data in order to estimate media habits, lifestyle, product purchase and geodemographic profiles of the population, hence the depth of analysis in Table 11.2.

Group A: Symbols of success

Group B: Happy families

Group C: Suburban comfort

Group D: Ties of community

Group E: Urban intelligence

Group F: Welfare borderline

Group G: Municipal dependency

Group H: Blue collar enterprise

Group I: Twilight subsistence

Group J: Grey perspective

Group K: Rural isolation

Figure 11.4: Geodemographic groups

© Experian Ltd. Reproduced by permission

Consumer values *Conservative values* appreciates personal contact rather than impersonal transaction channels. Here people will naturally turn to professional advisors when key decisions need to be made. They like to discuss with shopkeepers or their sales assistants the relative merits of different brands and products, assuming that they will get unbiased advice. They use financial advisors. By contrast they are not very IT-literate and are not people to purchase over the Internet. However, having time at their disposal, many residents take very seriously the opportunities for searching out information on different products and will be well informed on new consumer issues such as the use of chemicals and ingredients in foods, and genetically modified crops. Preferences in food and fashion are conservative, and the opening of a local branch of Marks & Spencer would be seen as a major benefit.

Nevertheless residents are willing to support local shopkeepers and local suppliers, particularly if they can establish a personal relationship with them. Range, freshness and quality of service are more important than price and conformity with latest fashion trends. These people are likely to support their local church and give generously to charities. Perhaps on account of its age, this type has remained loyal to the Conservative Party notwithstanding its recent electoral vicissitudes.

Consumption patterns *Conservative values* represents a good market for the financial services industry and for long-haul travel. Much money is also spent on gardening products, on personal services such as laundry, dry-cleaning and hairdressing, and on quality food brands. By contrast, relatively little is spent on home improvement, on home furnishing or on clothing. People in these areas seldom smoke and prefer visits to country restaurants to evenings at the local pub.

Culture and consumer psychology *Conservative values* represents a very mainstream type in terms of tastes, values and lifestyle. These people are as practical and pragmatic in their consumption decisions and choices, as they probably are in all aspects of daily life. Unlikely to hold strong views on major issues, they are nevertheless 'switched on' to world and local events, through reading the better-quality papers and watching national and regional TV news programmes. They are likely to be careful with money even to the point of thriftiness but have developed money management skills over the years and are likely to be quite financially astute. They keep a close eye on the stock market and other investments, to stretch their savings and maintain financial security. There may also be some interest here in the possibility of raising cash from the equity in their homes.

Conservative with a small 'c', their attitude towards and engagement with consumption is confined to routine provisioning. These consumers are not likely to be tempted into trying new products which they have seen advertised, and will tend to stick with familiar brands. Even though they are careful with the pennies, they are not bargain hunters and, indeed, shopping holds no particular interest for them. Probably the type of people who maintain values dating from a time when things were bought to last, they will tend not to see the point of buying new clothes or household furnishings when those they have are still perfectly adequate. The same goes for new gadgets and appliances. These consumers are not likely to try any new-fangled equipment and may simply have no need for them in their traditional homes and lifestyles. In consumer behaviour terms, these are the 'laggards' when it comes to new products and brands. Appearances are not important, either, although their interest in their neat and pleasant gardens suggests their homes are neat and pleasant inside, albeit in a dated kind of way.

Moderate TV viewing is likely to revolve around informative programmes such as *Antiques Roadshow* and *Gardeners' World*, with a little *University Challenge* to keep the grey cells ticking over and *Songs of Praise* for spiritual edification. Grandchildren feature highly among this type, and it may be that the *conservative values* consumers are likely to splash out a little more where they are concerned.

They do enjoy a comfortable and cosy lifestyle, however, and will indulge themselves to some extent with frequent holidays and short breaks – possibly coach tours or even cruises–which they may well take with a group of like-minded friends. For the rest of the time, however, they lead orderly lives, moving into old age in a comfortable and familiar daily routine.

Table 11.2: Mosaic type 16: conservative values

Figure 11.5 demonstrates how geodemographics can profile a catchment area (for example) for the potential citing of a retail outlet. The Mosaic (in this case) category overlays of the local map show where different segments live. If, for example, the retailer is mainly targeting the 'stylish single' segment, the map shows the area of greatest concentration of this segment. Indeed names and addresses of those in this segment can be purchased in order to target these potential customers personally. This particular map shows a five-minute off-peak drive time from Cardiff Business School (CF10 3 EU). Table 11.3 then shows how market potential can be estimated from a geodemographic profile of a (potential) catchment area.

Most geodemographic systems are also now heavily fused with financial data so it is not surprising, therefore, that such consumer data is of interest to government departments. CACI, for example, have an entire department dealing exclusively with government contracts for Acorn and related products. The Inland Revenue would have particular interests in the financial details of households to check financial details and trends against tax returns from those they want to investigate further.

It is interesting to note that for the 2001 census, the British Government, for the first time 'officially added commercial business to the list of users' of the census (Exon, 1998). New questions potentially relevant to the marketer and market researcher were added, including a clever question revealing the sexuality of partners (Exon, 1999; Brindle, 1999). The question wording asked for names of partners in the household and presumably marketers will assume same or different sex partners to indicate sexuality – the gay market being an important one for many marketers to target (see 'Sexuality' in Chapter 5).

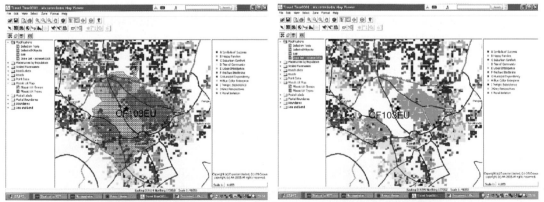

Figure 11.5: Five-minute off-peak drive time from CF103EU

The following shows how the area around a car dealership can be analysed by geodemographics.

Geodemographic group	% of area	×	Model X index	=	Area sales potential
			Table Catchment area analysis		
1	1.4	×	61	=	0.85
2	–	×	108	=	–
3	9.7	×	84	=	8.15
4	7.9	×	39	=	2.92
5	–	×	41	=	–
6	11.4	×	53	=	6.04
7	–	×	34	=	–
8	13.9	×	124	=	17.80
9	29.4	×	230	=	66.93
10	22.5	×	217	=	48.82
11	3.1	×	84	=	2.60
Total					154.11

If Model X would be bought by 5% of the national population and the catchment area is 10 000, a sales potential of 10 000 × 5% = 500 would be expected. But the index here is 154.11, so for this catchment area the sales potential is 500 × 1.5411 = 770.

Table 11.3: Market potential

However extensive the census becomes, the major limitation of census data relates to the difficulties associated with updating information, particularly because in the UK the census is only carried out every ten years and the 2011 census might be the last of its kind in the UK. It is likely that a range of data sources from different government departments and elsewhere will form the basis of the census after that date.

Another issue concerns the generic nature of geodemographics. These have traditionally been off-the-shelf systems from which marketers can profile their existing customers according to postcode or select a sample of certain geodemographic clusters for research purposes. But all this is fine as long as the underpinning clustering of the specific data included is relevant to the marketer's purposes. If *different* census questions are analysed and overlaid with *different* financial and other details, to form more tailored clusters relevant to specific marketer's needs, then the customized geodemographic system might be even more useful in uncovering consumer behaviour.

Also, as sophisticated as geodemographics might be, it *profiles* consumers; it does not in itself explain why they behave as they do and neither does it provide individualized information on what they buy: remember it is based on aggregated data for neighbourhoods.

www.

Take a look at the following article, which can be accessed via the accompanying book web site at www.wileyeurope.com/college/evans:

Duchessi, Schaninger and Nowak (2004) Creating Cluster-Specific Purchase Profiles from Point of Sale Scanner Data and Geodemographic Clusters: Improving Category Management at a Major US Grocery Chain, Journal of Consumer Behaviour, Vol 4 No 2, pp 97–117

Geo-lifestyle

The clustering of lifestyle data and then inferring similar profiles for others in similar postcodes is **geo-lifestyle** profiling. This is the major approach adopted by Claritas with their PRIZM system.

EXAMPLE 11.8

MarketingWeek

Direct Route to Primary Target

There is an equation which explains how direct marketing works: budget ÷ population = targeting. Since you cannot afford to appeal to everybody in the country, you have to find ways to narrow the field.

Over the decades, the DM industry has developed increasingly accurate ways to target and direct marketers have an array of alternatives to consider. From geodemographic classifications of the entire population to near realtime hot leads from current purchasers, there is a system to suit almost any pocket.

However, many in DM agencies are disparaging about what is on offer. "Demographic classification systems are solutions looking for problems – they are the lazy weapon of choice in the data planner's tool kit," says Neil Johnson, data planning director at Claydon Heeley.

Jed Mooney, managing director of Datahold, believes the reasons for dissatisfaction with prospect data lie in improved access. "Analytical tools are becoming more accessible via software on the marketer's desktop. So the way direct marketers are selecting data is becoming more intelligent," he says.

DLG communications director Richard Webster adds that geodemographic systems are not targeted enough for direct marketers looking to employ direct mail. "The weaknesses of geodemographics are particularly evident in urban and cosmopolitan areas, which are typically where the young, affluent targets for marketers live," he says. "Very different groups are living close together, which mixes up the assumptions made 25 years ago."

Against this he sets individual level data, directly derived from the consumer, which allows for the personalised offers and targeting the DM industry advocates. For some advertisers, the single most valuable variable they are looking for is that an individual is currently looking to make a purchase. Hot lead data of this sort is not cheap, nor plentiful, but it is powerful.

"Consumers have freedom of information, movement and economy. So it is harder to make a judgement based on where they are living or limited demographics. We live in a more flexible society than ever and want to be treated as individuals," he says.

This is the most powerful argument for the new generation of individualised data sets, but geodemographics are not going away any time soon, either as a core marketing tool or as influences over each and every one of us.

Webber can justifiably be called the godfather of geodemographics, having developed the first-ever classification system, Acorn, and its major rival, Mosaic. He has just completed work on the UK's first ethnological classification, Origins.

"The power of geography is more true than it has ever been, but it is very easy to misunderstand," says Webber, now managing director of Origins Information.

Neighbourhood Knowledge

A major criticism of geodemographic clustering is that diversity in each segment is considerable. But Webber points out: "People in one type of neighbourhood are no more diverse than people of the same age or set of qualifications. Knowing occupation is less predictive than knowing neighbourhood."

Difference is the core of what marketers are looking for – any indicator that their specific target audience can be identified from among the mass. They also want some prediction that their campaigns will influence behaviour in the right way. Knowing that a geographically-defined cluster is more likely to respond is a powerful way of getting this uplift.

Hybrid Solution

A hybrid solution that seeks to bridge geodemographics and individual-level systems is Personicx from Acxiom. Based on directly-derived data from 60% of the UK population, it uses 3,000 variables to generate clusters that are highly predictive of buying behaviour.

"Personicx is behaviourally optimised," says Ian Stewart, head of product sales at Acxiom. "It maximises understanding at an individual level, rather than the segment level in geodemographics."

Stewart adds: "Many clients have built predictive models for cross- and up-selling to existing customers. But when it comes to prospecting, they have no way to access and action those same models."

Paradoxically, the way those models can be overlaid into Personicx is via the geodemographic system Acorn. Acxiom has those codes associated against its own clusters, so if a client is using them to identify its most valuable customers, it can pick out the same people in the prospect pool.

Choice is one of the hot words used by marketers. When it comes to the tools available to themselves, they are now spoiled for choice, and the reality is that, unless you are mass market, you need to segment. The only way to work out which system is best is to test it.

Marketing Week 25 October 2007, p 37. Reproduced by permission of Centaur Media Plc.

C2C Social Network Data

As discussed under pre-purchase surveillance, marketers are monitoring social networking sites such as Facebook in order to identify prospective customers on the basis of what they reveal on these sites.

CASE STUDY 11.1

Unitown Students' Union: Social Network Plunder

Following the arrival of several new nightclub rivals, Unitown University's Students' Union, has seen a sharp decline in attendance and drink sales for its events. In order to maintain its strong position in the market, Unitown University's Students' Union investigated how it could use the social networking website, Facebook, as a means of promoting various events such as the many gigs it organizes for students at its nightclub.

The Union knows that online relationship marketing with the student community can be highly effective with many students. Indeed it has learned that over 80% of students at many universities use Facebook. Furthermore, many 16–25s spend more time online than they do watching TV.

Social networking is, however, much more than 'social': it is an evolving business relationship phenomenon. In its investigation the Union found that student night promoters Rough Hill integrates its website with Facebook, so when visitors view and 'tag' themselves in photos of an event on the website, these are automatically added to their Facebook profile, thus encouraging consumer participation and engagement as part of the relationship process. When a Rough Hill event ticket is purchased, friends of the student are informed via their Facebook profiles. Rough Hill captures complete demographic and other profile data of those who interact with them and this is a large number because over 80% of visitors are also Facebook members.

This enables individualized targeting to particular students. They can be sent reminders of events, birthday cards or VIP access on their birthday. They can be emailed about the next event, with eTickets or photo galleries and even about jobs.

Unitown Students' Union has even found that the Facebook community 'groups' can provide a quick, informal and effective way that students can communicate about music played by a DJ for example. Online discussion boards proved to be more effective, much speedier and less confrontational than a formal complaints or feedback process. In return for group membership to a particular club night, club promoters often rewarded members with VIP and guest list entry as part of their relationship marketing process. Furthermore, many promoters would add their customers as friends on Facebook to enable them to more easily invite them to events and communicate their messages.

Fresher's Week is a major opportunity to collect personal preference and other details from students. Student event promoters employ attractive and provocatively dressed 'guys & gals' to give away ice creams or other free incentives when freshers complete forms to enable them to receive promotional information and offers. Their details, of course, go on a database, but the individualized targeting can lead to a positive relationship. When the freshers arrive at their first event, they are greeted by the same promotional staff who collected their details. This continuance of the personal relationship from Fresher's Week helps new students feel more comfortable about visiting a large and new event when they are themselves new at a large and sometimes overwhelming University.

What are your experiences of this? Were you aware of the sophistication behind the targeting of new students? Were you aware of 'marketers' lurking in the background of your Facebook interactions? Is this good relational buying or an intrusion into students' private lives? Which methods do you think Unitown University's Students' Union should use to interact with its students?

NB Check out the following:
Fatsoma, which is a complete online marketing solution for event promotion. [WWW]<URL: http://www.fatsoma.com/promotions/> [Accessed 11 March 2008]

Rough Hill – Premium Events for Yound People. [WWW] <URL: http://www.roughhill.co.uk/> [Accessed 11 March 2008]
Sam Gould, Total Students Ltd.

Lists

Based on much of the above analysis of sources of personalized customer data, there are thousands of lists available for purchase. Such lists provide names and addresses, together with other personal details, such as demographics and geodemographics and sometimes with transactional data (as with Transactis, as mentioned previously). Experian and CACI, for example, sell lists of people in each of their geodemographics groups and types. List brokers compile and sell other lists. For marketers in the gardening market, for example, there are lists of consumers who subscribe to gardening magazines, who enter gardening competitions, who buy plants and garden equipment via mail order or the Internet and so on. Experian even offers an online list service through which a marketer can select, themselves, any number of prospects based on lifestyle data, MOSAIC, financials, geographic location, claimed purchase patterns and other characteristics.

Competitive Intelligence

AC Nielsen with MMS run a consumer panel (see Chapter 9) in which consumers store the direct mail they receive. The panel provides marketers with a profile of the sort of consumers who receive direct mail in different product markets and the nature of that direct mail. This means that although marketers know what THEY have sent, they can now see what is being sent by competing firms to which market segments.

Marketing Research

This text is not about market research but we have already introduced motivation research methods in Chapter 1. It is pertinent to remind us that traditional market research, especially qualitative research, can provide great insight into the 'why' of consumer behaviour. It is pertinent because the current chapter has focused on the relatively new era of data-informed marketing. In short, we have 'data' that can help us 'know' what consumers buy, when, through which channel, by which methods of payment, and so on, but does 'data', as in this chapter, really provide sufficient insight into the 'whys' or 'why nots'?

THINKBOX

'Data' can become a surrogate for consumer insight. For example Mitchell (2001) recently quoted a director of one of the largest retailers in the UK:

We've given up trying to understand our customers...helping us cut a lot of complexity from our business. The academic's instinct is to gather a large amount of information, formulate a theory, and apply it to a situation...(this) creates waste in the form of the wrong information at the wrong time, leading to the wrong decisions...or...fruitless attempts to predict or alter customer behavior.

The favoured approach by this company, 'sense and respond' (Haeckel, 2001), is to react quickly on the basis of customer contact via call centres, Internet, interactive digital TV and infomediaries. This is understandable in the current context of pressure to achieve short-term profit in order to provide shareholder value. However, it can lead to a subordination of the key component of the marketing concept itself – namely, customer satisfaction – to over-emphasis on tracking transactional data. Another example concerns a major data consortium, Jigsaw, which is run by Cadbury, Kimberley Clark and Unilever. This consortium has announced the scrapping of attitudinal data in favour of transactional data (Walker, 2001).

Might this even lead to companies 'dictating' what we put in our shopping baskets because they know what we have bought previously and think they understand us so well? (Richardson, 2000)

In other words, marketers have so much data on individual consumers – their personal details, profile and purchase patterns – that there is less of a need for the kind of market research which tries to answer the 'why' questions of consumer purchase or non-purchase behavior.

What do you think about this?

Genetic Profile Data

Further issues arise in the realm of genetic data and assessing insurance risk (Specter, 1999). Clearly, for financial services companies, it would be useful to be able to assess risks on the basis that gene patterns can indicate individuals' future potential susceptibility to illness or disease (Borna and Avila, 1999). In the UK some patient data is available in the NHSnet database that can be accessed by healthcare professionals (Introna and Powloudi, 1999). In a survey of 3 000 UK households, three-quarters were against genetic tests for insurance underwriting, 85% against insurance companies rejecting applicants on this basis and 78% against insurance companies charging higher premiums on the basis of genetic tests. Indeed, 68% of the sample thought that this use of genetic data should be prohibited by law (Borna and Avila, 1999). Introna and Powloudi (1999) report that medics have expressed concern over this trend. The logical extension of the scenario is that those who don't need insuring will be insured and the rest will be excluded. This is an example of the corollary of the RFM type of metrics introduced above: it can result in those consumers who are less valuable or more costly to a service being excluded.

At the time of writing there is a moratorium on the use of genetic data in the UK for insurance purposes. The 'concordat' on this (HM Government, 2005) states: 'insurers should not treat customers who have an adverse predictive genetic test result less favourably than others without justification'. But the Genetics and Insurance Committee (GAIC) is considering applications to approve the use of tests for 'single gene disorders that are inherited . . . (and where there is) a high probability that those with the gene will develop the disorder' (HM Government, 2005). What 'without justification' really means and indeed whether there is a lack of clarity over the entire concordat and moratorium, will, hopefully be resolved soon, but although a review was announced for 2008, the current situation can hold until 2011.

Memetics

We discussed memetics in Chapter 1 and again it is worth revisiting this. A meme acts as a sort of 'horizontal' communicator of how to behave - from person to person, similar to vicarious learning as we discussed in Chapter 4. The difference, however, is that memes work more like a viral contagion. The suggestion, for example, by Marsden that marketers might produce computer programs to simulate and instigate consumer behaviour based on memetic communication is perhaps fanciful. But it is likely that much of the contents of this chapter would have been seen that way 50 years ago. On the other hand, are we on the eve of the kind of 'hidden persuasion' that brought the industry under the ethical spotlight of the late 1950s (Packard, 1957)? It is interesting to revisit Packard at this point, who wrote: 'Eventually – say by A.D. 2000 – perhaps all this depth manipulation of the psychological variety will seem amusingly old-fashioned. By then perhaps the biophysicists will take over "biocontrol", which is depth persuasion carried to its ultimate' (Packard, 1957:195).

BIOGRAPHICS AND INDIVIDUALISM

Biographics

The fusion of transactional and profile data leads to a significant trend in consumer behaviour research, namely **biographics**. Consumers are being analysed in ever more sophisticated and detailed ways and this is leading to the identification and targeting of smaller but better defined (at least in theory) segments. But although this gives the impression that we have moved to one-to-one marketing, this is not the norm and perhaps is more rhetoric than reality. There might be personalized targeting, in the sense that the individual is addressed by name, and there might be some data-driven offer that matches the data-mining outcome for the segment to which the individual is allocated, but this is not the same as understanding customers on a truly individual basis as we would in a human relationship context.

WWW.

Take a look at the following web sites:

www.dunnhumby.com, **the company that deals with the loyalty scheme data for several organizations, including Tesco.**

www.talkingnumbers.com, **which is the web site of a company that specializes in data-driven solutions – there are case studies and other useful information here.**

Individualism

In Chapter 6 we reported how the Henley Centre (1978) predicted the trend toward individualism and the more fragmented cellular household.

One reason for such fragmentation of markets is consumers' desire to be treated more as individuals (see Chapter 6). Evidence of the trend toward individualism was uncovered during the 1970s and led, among other things, to the Regan and Thatcher election campaigns from the late 1970s and into the 1980s based on 'self-reliance' (BBC, 2002). 'Standing on one's own feet' and 'freeing the individual from the state' were the sorts of mantras of those elections and were manifestations of research at the time that revealed individualism (McNulty, 2002).

THINKBOX

Individualism is manifested in greater pluralism within society, evident in the high street where pluralism in clothing styles is observable.

Is the logical extension of this that if more consumers want to express individuality then it provides marketers with opportunities to treat them individually and not only offer more self-expressive products but also to target them as individuals?

CONSUMER REACTION TO INDIVIDUALIZED CONSUMER–ORGANIZATION INTERACTION

As society continues to be time-poor due to long working hours (see Figure 11.6) many consumers seek time-saving purchasing methods, such as via direct mail, telephony and the Internet, which are the manifestations of the new personalized and data-informed consumer–organization interaction.

However, Evans *et al.* (2001) found that the situation is complex. At the same time as participating in direct reciprocal interaction, consumers also express various concerns. They are, for example, simultaneously, street-wise and cynical. Various dimensions of privacy were revealed, as we summarize below.

Figure 11.6: Time-hungry cash-rich commuters
Harried commuters interact with companies via phone, mail and Internet
Source: Digital Vision. Reproduced with permission

Physical/Interaction Privacy

Although direct personalized targeting is clearly a convenience to the time-constrained contemporary consumer, it can also be its own worst enemy because the consumer can be bombarded by unwanted or untimely (junk) information (Evans *et al.*, 2001).

'Physical/interaction privacy' relates to the physical intrusion of marketing communications (for example, direct mail, telesales, emails) into the daily lives of consumers. In 1994 '7% of UK consumers received more than six items of direct marketing in the post each week. [By 2004] over 34% of consumers fall into that category' (Mitchell, 2004).

The 'hottest' prospects are, somewhat obviously, targeted most heavily, such as those with the highest spending power. Ungoed-Thomas and Nuki (1998) reported their uncovering of a 'Midas' list of those between 25 and 45, earning more than £50 000 pa, who own lots of electronic products and engage in relatively expensive leisure activities. They 'are being sent 250 mailshots a year, five times the national average'. If these people enjoy receiving information about even more things they can spend their money on, then there probably isn't a problem, as long as they can sustain such expenditure levels. However, many will feel this is just too much – as one consumer reported: 'every day it comes through the door . . . it's relentless . . . I don't read it on principle because Britain is turning into a huge buying experience and I hate it' (Rule, 1998).

Outbound unsolicited telephone calls also cause concern and annoyance to many and there is a continual rise in the number of consumers who sign-up to the Telephone Preference Service (TPS). This makes it legally binding for companies to screen their databases against the TPS list and if they don't and still call an 'opted-out' consumer, the company could be fined. At the time of writing about two-thirds of UK phone numbers were so registered, reflecting a concern over physical (phone) privacy.

We all know that most email is actually unwanted 'spam', another example of the invasion of physical privacy. It has been reported that over 97% of all emails sent in December 2007 were in this category (Softscan, 2008).

Information Privacy

Evans *et al.* (2001) also reveal a 'privacy paradox' in that some consumers are somewhat cynical about 'relational' interaction and concerned about divulging personal information but are participants nevertheless. There might be a desire on the part of organizations to develop relationships with customers but customers do not always want to reciprocate. It is likely that the cynicism is predicated upon a lack of trust resulting from business scams, unfulfilled promises and marketing hype.

'Information privacy' refers to the extent to which individuals can *control* who holds their data, and what is done with those data (Westin, 1967). In the USA, many consumers already believe that they have lost all control over how information about them is used, with some even suggesting that if they could, they would add privacy to their constitutional rights to life, liberty and the pursuit of happiness (Schroeder, 1992). Indeed there has been a plethora of books written on this issue in the USA in recent years (Rothfeder, 1992; Chesbro 1999; Rosen, 2001; Larson, 1994; Charrett, 1999).

EXAMPLE 11.9

In the UK the Information Commissioner's office ran a hard-hitting advertising campaign aimed at marketers who deal with personalized consumer databases (Figure 11.7).

Figure 11.7: **Information Commissioner's advertisement to database marketers**

© Information Commissioner's Office. Reproduced by permission

The marketers themselves might delight in having access to this sort of data on the consumers they want to target, but how might they feel about their own data being available like this?

We have already, in both this chapter and in Chapter 7, raised concerns over the security of social networking sites such as Facebook. Shaw (2007) for instance has cautioned that criminals seeking personal data can extract what they need for identity fraud from such sites.

Marketers are already monitoring these sites to compile lists for targeting, based on the interests and lifestyle of those posting such detailed and copious data about themselves. The problem is that social networks are usually the vehicle for engagement in virtual social environments and those involved do not necessary know or want others with a more commercial objective to highjack their data. It is equally possible of course that some social networkers use totally different personas from their real ones, as we discussed in Chapter 7 under postmodernism, and therefore their data would be suspect.

There have been many high profile examples of the infringement of information privacy over recent years. Data losses by both government and private companies have hit the national headlines:

'Computer discs holding sensitive personal data on 25 million people and 7.25 million families have gone missing, Chancellor Alistair Darling has admitted to MPs.

He said the details included names, addresses, dates of birth, Child Benefit numbers, National Insurance numbers and bank or building society account details.' (BBC News web site, www.bbc.co.uk/news, 20 November 2007)

'Hackers stole the bank details of millions of British and American shoppers in what is thought to be the world's biggest credit card heist, it has been revealed.

The crooks stole 45.7 million credit and debit card numbers from the US and British-based computer systems of the American retailer that owns bargain chain TK Maxx.

The data was accessed on TJX's systems in Watford, Herts, and Massachusetts over a 16-month period and covers transactions dating as far back as December 2002.' (BBC News web site, www.bbc.co.uk/news, 30 March 2007)

'The HSBC banking group has admitted losing a computer disc with the details of 370,000 customers. The disc was lost four weeks ago after being sent by courier from the bank's life insurance offices in Southampton.

The customers' details included their names, dates of birth, and their levels of insurance cover.' (BBC News web site, www.bbc.co.uk/news, 7 April 2008)

Further information privacy concerns have been raised over the lax behaviour of banks, many of whom have been found to just dump customer details with the normal household rubbish on the streets (Ford *et al.*, 2006) where ID fraudsters can easily pick out data needed for their dastardly deeds.

Many might think that these events were mere slips and that companies would be keen to ensure they did not happen again, but research shows that many companies do not think such breaches of information privacy would affect their reputations (Hoffbrand, 2008b, 2008c).

Accuracy

A further concern over the marketing use of personal data is whether it is used accurately. Consumers move house, some die and others add their names to the opt-out Preference Services. If marketers do not screen their databases against 'gone away' files, 'bereavement registers' and, for example, the TPS, the there will be privacy invasion on terms of poor accuracy of targeting. Unfortunately, many of these errors (or cynical omissions) continue. Indeed, 40% of consumer records on leading UK company databases have been described as unusable (for these sorts of reasons) (Hummerston, 2007). Similar research focusing on just the charity sector is equally damning, 'only 12% of mailings were screened against the Gone Away Suppression File (GAS) and only 9% were screened against the Bereavement Register (TBR)' (Kimberley, 2008).

As a result of these privacy conflicts between consumers and organizations, Westin envisages a rise in what he calls 'consensual databases' **(permission marketing)**, where consumers consent to information surrender in return for some type of reward such as coupons, samples or money (Westin, 1992). Giving consumers more control over their data is worth exploring as a possible solution to information privacy problems and (Croft, 2008b) has shown how consumers can be more in control. However, as Mitchell states:

> Permission isn't enough . . . is ticking a box once, permission to spam me for the rest of my life . . . there's only one way out: to put consumers in the driving seat, empowering them to specify what sort of messages they are looking for by time, place and category. (Mitchell, 2002)

In reality there may be no easy solution.

THINKBOX

How do you feel about reciprocal personalized interaction with companies?
Do you have concerns in terms of physical and information privacy and accuracy?
Why or why not?

For a fuller discussion of the wider social implications of personalized data-informed marketing, see Evans (2005).

SUMMARY

- Transactional data provide the means to assess consumer behaviour in terms of what they buy, when, how and where. This is personalized when linked with loyalty schemes or online cookies. There is a range of other data sources, such as RFIDs, NLPs, cookies and genetics, all of which have specific implications for explaining consumer behaviour.

■ A major catalyst in consumer-profiling research was the marketing use in 1981 of the census which led to the first geodemographic product in the UK. These are now widespread around the world and census data is overlaid with data from a variety of other sources such as financial and lifestyle data.

■ The combination of data profiles with transactional data provides the new biographics which marketers often claim can help generate the sort of relational interaction discussed in the previous chapter. However, there are concerns that 'data' drives too much and becomes the surrogate for real consumer insight, which might be derived from a more psychologically and socially informed consumer behaviour paradigm.

■ New metrics can be applied to this data to identify the best – and worst – consumers in order to focus on the former and (often) to exclude the latter. New media facilitate personalized interaction between consumer and organization and allow individualism to be manifested.

■ However, there are wider social concerns over the use and potential misuse of personal data and consumers and marketers need to come to a mutually amicable arrangement over how such data is used.

QUESTIONS

1. What are the implications for consumers and marketers of the trend toward biographics?

2. What is meant by 'geodemographics'? How might the approach explain consumer behaviour?

3. As a consumer, are you comfortable knowing that marketers have lots of your personal details? Why or why not?

4. What consumer data is a car dealership likely to hold? What external sources might it fruitfully buy in? How could this data explain consumer behaviour?

5. The coverage in this chapter of the *Minority Report* film reports:
   a. How consumers can be biometrically recognized, individually, as they enter a shopping mall; and
   b. How consumers can be targeted as individuals via mobile phones.
   c. What are the issues for both marketers and consumers that these two developments present?

6. What is meant by physical privacy, information privacy and accuracy?

7. What are the implications of consumers' use of social networking sites for marketing?

FURTHER READING

Evans M, O'Malley L and Patterson M (2004) *Exploring Direct and Customer Relationship Marketing*, Thomson Learning, p 544. This is an extensive exploration of what some refer to as 'the new marketing' based around the use of very personalized consumer data for segmenting and targeting purposes.

Lace S (ed.) (2005) *The Glass Consumer: Life in a Surveillance Society,* Policy Press/National Consumer Council. This is a collection of readings which critically examines the use of personal consumer data in public and private sectors. The readings are not only concerned with marketing applications, but also with wider issues of technology and society, social policy as well as consumption.

CHAPTER 12
CONSUMER MISBEHAVIOUR

CHAPTER OBJECTIVES

After engaging with the material presented in this chapter, its associated exercises and reading, you should be able to:

■ Appreciate that we can all misbehave as consumers.
■ Explore a range of misbehaviours and their consequences for the company, the consumers and society.
■ Differentiate between illegal and abnormal consumer behaviour.
■ Be aware of some of the reasons for consumer misbehaviour.
■ Appreciate how consumer misbehaviour can be related to each aspect of marketing activity and indeed toward capitalism, multi-nationals and the materialistic society.

INTRODUCTION

This chapter recognizes that consumers themselves are not always angels. They might indulge in consumption behaviours that might harm themselves or others in some ways. According to Fullerton and Punj (2004), consumer misbehaviour refers to 'behavioural acts by consumers which violate the generally accepted norms of conduct in consumption situations and thus disrupt the consumption order'. This could be extended to include consumption and related behaviours which also disrupt other consumers, the environment and society at large (even though they may be generally accepted forms of behaviours). While a simple example would be queue-jumping at checkouts, a more delicate example would be the case of purchasing products that can harm our environment.

Several writers adopt sequential frameworks to buying behaviour. Holbrook (1987) for example explores acquisition of things, consumption and then disposal of them. Muncy and Vitell (1992) apply these stages to ethical considerations and define consumer ethics as 'the moral principles and standards that guide the behaviour of individuals or groups as they obtain, use and dispose of goods and services' (Muncy and Vitell, 1992:298).

The American term 'jaywalker' (someone who dangerously crosses streets; for example, when not indicated to do so by the pedestrian crossing lights) has been adapted to refer to consumers who misbehave. Lovelock (1994) uses the phrase **jaycustomer** to refer to consumers who:

- Do not pay for goods or do not pay the full price.
- Break the rules of consumer–organization interaction, by, for example, queue-jumping at theme parks or in supermarkets.
- Are overly angry with company personnel.
- Vandalize company property or equipment.
- Fail to pay for goods or services not because of criminal intent but just due to lack of concern or interest.

Another example of misbehaviour is 'de-shopping' which has been defined as 'deliberate return of goods for reasons other than actual faults in the product, in its pure form premeditated to and during the consumption experience' (Schmidt *et al.*, 1999:2). It is interesting to note that not only is there evidence that de-shopping is fairly widespread but also that there appears to be a lack of awareness on the part of many consumers that de-shopping is illegal (King and Dennis, 2006).

As discussed in Chapter 10, there are also **consumer terrorists**: those who are dissatisfied with a particular company or brand and spread ill will about it and who generally try to undermine its credibility and even its activities (Jones and Sasser, 1995). An otherwise well-behaved person might misbehave while on board a plane with a group of friends. A minority of football fans act as a hooligans before, during and after matches. Both of these are examples of consumption misbehaviours. More obvious instances would be shoplifting, illegal drug-use, under-age drinking and binge-drinking. Some consumers dispose of plastic shopping bags in ways that litter our streets and pollute the environment (they may take up to 500 years to decompose when buried in a landfill site). We use cars even though we know that cars seriously pollute our environment and contribute towards global warming.

Sometimes consumer misbehaviour is encouraged by marketers, such as eating disorders induced by the sort of unrealistic body images portrayed in advertising, as discussed in Chapter 6. Could it be that the entire marketing industry is guilty of encouraging shallow materialism?

We focus here on misbehaviours that violate the generally accepted norms of conduct and that are of concern or threat to others and to the environment.

THINKBOX

It is likely that many who are now good citizens engaged in petty shoplifting or vandalism as teenagers. Does this mean that you think such youth misbehaviour to be harmless? Why, or why not?

CONSUMER MISBEHAVIOUR TYPOLOGIES

Consumers can misbehave in many ways. Table 12.1 summarizes some of the more obvious forms of misbehaviour. It classifies misbehaviour into four categories depending on whether the behaviour is abnormal or illegal and whether the misbehaviour occurs during the acquisition stage of consumption or is related to the use of the products and services (Hoyer and McInnes, 2001).

	Misbehaviour in acquiring products	Product misuse
Abnormal consumer behaviour	Excessive buying	Addictive
	To compensate for psychological problems Sometimes over-stretching financial resources leading to bad debt or bankruptcy cases	Buying drugs Alcohol Gambling Binge-eating/drinking Smoking
Illegal consumer behaviour	Theft, shoplifting, black markets, bootlegging, counterfeiting brands	Under-age drinking Under-age smoking Under-age sex-related products and services misuse Drug use and abuse

Source: Adapted by the authors from WD Hoyer and DJ MacInnes, *Consumer Behavior*, 2nd edn, Houghton Mifflin, Boston, 2001. Copyright ©2001 by Houghton Mifflin Company. Adapted with permission

Table 12.1: Consumer misbehaviour typologies

Misbehaviour in Acquiring Products

Abnormal Behaviour

One type of abnormal behaviour is known as 'compulsive consumption behaviour' and is defined by O'Guinn and Faber (1989) as a 'response to an uncontrollable drive or desire to obtain, use, or experience a feeling, substance, or activity that leads an individual to repetitively engage in a behaviour that will ultimately cause harm to the individual and/or to others' (p 148). For instance, some people have a tendency to buy more products than are appropriate for satisfying their needs. It will be interesting to see whether the sort of austerity-themed propaganda of the 1940s (see below) might return as a reaction to world food crises and shortages.

Some consumers also buy products that they cannot afford but they still have an urge and desire to keep on buying. Hence the satisfaction comes from the act of buying and not from owning the product or using the product. Indeed as we explored in Chapter 1, there can be dissatisfaction from buying when the promises associated with acquisition are not met, quite apart from the credit related problems of repeatedly over-extending one's budget in search for happiness. The effects can lead to a sort of macro consumer misbehaviour when the economy is threatened by uncontrolled credit expansion: some consumers can be as much to blame as can profligate financial services companies.

THINKBOX

Are we as consumers over-consuming?

- We change a mobile every 18 months on average.
- Last Christmas 6 million PCs were left on standby in offices.
- 1.5 million PCs are thrown away each year yet 99% work perfectly.

Has consumerism become more powerful than any religion & reached everywhere in the world?
Smith (2007)

Examples of compulsive consumption include: drug abuse, excessive eating, alcoholism, excessive sexuality and gambling. By definition, compulsive behaviour is repetitive in nature and carries negative consequences for the individual even though there can be some short-term rewards. Once a consumer fully develops this behaviour and becomes used to it, they face great difficulty in controlling it even though they are fully aware of the negative consequences. For instance, Faber *et al.* (1995) reported that compulsive buyers are significantly more likely than non-compulsive buyers to be diagnosed as having an eating disorder.

According to O'Guinn and Faber (1989), physiological, genetic, psychological, social and cultural factors contribute towards the development of compulsive behaviour. Compulsive buyers have low levels of self-esteem and a high ability to fantasize, which allows them to escape reality (O'Guinn and Faber, 1989). Some consumers may have 'obsessive personalities' which contribute to this behaviour. Anecdotally, one teenager spends around 10% of her gross weekly wage on nail varnish alone. The effects on finances and social relationships can be devastating if such buying cannot be sustained. Moreover, in a study involving undergraduate students, Hassay and Smith (1996) found that compulsive buyers were more likely to return products, to exhibit greater concerns for store return policies, and to report higher return volumes than non-compulsive buyers.

A survey of young adults (aged 20 to 32) in the USA revealed that family structure is related to compulsive buying and to materialism (Rindfleisch *et al.*, 1997). Those whose parents were divorced or separated showed much higher levels of compulsive buying and materialistic values than those whose parents were not divorced. Moreover, family resources (e.g. household income, parental support, role modeling and guidance) and family stressors (e.g. lack of stability, parental conflict, loss of friends and relatives, and changes of adult caregivers) appeared partially to mediate the relationship between family structure and compulsive buying.

Illegal Behaviour

There are many instances in which consumers seek products through illegal means (e.g. shoplifting or illegal use of products). Some goods are especially prone to being stolen in-store. Razor blades and DVDs have been among the first to be RFID-tagged (see Chapter 11) and there is also the possible use of subliminal audio messages in store ('I must not steal') in an attempt to reduce pilferage.

EXAMPLE 12.1

MarketingWeek

Call for action over music copyright theft

The International Federation of the Phonographic Industry has called for "urgent action" on co-operation between internet service providers and governments to stop music copyright theft.

The trade body made the comments as it reported the latest download sales for 2007. The Digital Music Report 2008 shows that sales of single track downloads increased by 53% to 1.7 billion in 2007 but sales have slowed compared to 2006, when sales grew by 89%.

It adds that record companies "continued their transition" into digital businesses in 2007 but that the spread of unlicensed music on ISP networks is "choking revenues to record companies and investment in artists despite the healthy increase in digital sales".

It calls for co-operation with ISPs, using filtering and disconnecting people that infringe copyrights, to clampdown on piracy. IFPI points to proposed legislation in France to make ISPs responsible for file sharing as "groundbreaking" and a "three strikes and you're out" policy for users that repeatedly infringe copyrights.

Marketing Week, 25 January 2008. Reproduced by permission of Centaur Media Plc.

Product Misuse

Abnormal Product Use

Addictions, here, are examples of what can happen when compulsive behaviour gets out of hand after purchase. Drink, gambling and drugs can lead to dependency which in turn can lead to other social and personal disasters such as financial ruin, job loss and family break-up.

Binge-drinking has been a social evil for several years. The damage that 40 or more units of alcohol in one night can do to the individual, those around them, the police and health services is clearly not a worry for those concerned, at the time of bingeing, but there are consequences nonetheless. It is not only the young who are accused of binge drinking. In 2008 a government campaign was aimed at the over 50s with the objective of encouraging sensible drinking (Singh, 2008b): the strapline being 'think you might be drinking too much?'. Singh reports Alcohol Concern's research shows that there has been a 75% increase since 1990s in women over 65 who exceed alcohol recommended limits. Indeed, another government campaign targeted women who are drinking heavily, with warnings about liver failure and breast cancer (Singh, 2008b).

Illegal Product Use

There are several activities which are regulated by law. These include smoking, driving and sexual intercourse. Teenagers, however, are 'finding themselves': they are developing their own identity, which means becoming more distant from parents and even rebelling against them and 'the establishment'. Hence there is always a clash between 'teenage kicks' and the law. In terms of illegal drug use, this can lead to crime, to violent gangs vying for catchment areas for 'dealing', and personal misery, ill-health and even death. As with crime in general, there can be a deliberation over the costs of being caught and the benefits of success (Becker, 1968; Wilson and Hernstein, 1985). It is disturbing to read reports of British teenagers being the 'worst behaved in Europe' (Roberts, 2006) and that the current concerns over knife crime in the UK (Ford, 2008) prompted the Chief Constable of South Wales to declare 'tribal loyalty has replaced family loyalty and gang culture based on violence and drugs is a way of life' (Wilding, 2008). This is in part predicated on consumer misbehaviour with respect to the use of drugs and acquisition of weapons. It also reminds us of our coverage in Chapter 7 of tribal behaviour and in the same chapter of family influences on consumer behaviour.

 www. Take a look at the article that follows this chapter, Fitchett and Smith (2002) Consumer Behaviour in an Unregulated Market. This can also be found on the accompanying web site at www.wileyeurope.com/college/evans.

THINKBOX

Under-age smoking, drinking and sex are illegal and the consumption of many products related to these activities (by the under-aged) represents consumer misbehaviour.
   Do you agree?
   What issues does this raise?

IDEALISTIC RATIONALE FOR MISBEHAVIOUR

The postmodern era sees consumption as integral to societal behaviour and norms. This contrasts with earlier times (e.g. 1960s and 1970s) when materialism and capitalism were rebelled against (Gabriel and Lang, 1995). It was also possible to use legitimate consumption behaviour as a manifestation of misbehaviour. For example, the punk era of the late 1970s saw teenagers dressing in bin bags with safety pins through their ears as symbols of rebellion against the 'prescribed' fashions of expensive fashion designers and marketers. The current version of this is the battle between massive multinational corporate power and anti-corporation activism on the part of some sections of consumers (Klein, 2001).

We have already shown, in Chapter 7, how flashmobbing was used to organize a mass demonstration in 2008 at Heathrow Terminal 5 against airport expansion in principle.

A footbridge near the Students Union in Cardiff sported catchy graffiti, presumably intended as a protest against the invasion of Tesco and the possible concomitant demise of the corner shop.

Prosser (2007) describes several methods used by consumers to avenge what they see as unethical company behaviour, some of which are, perhaps, themselves unethical: or does the end justify the means? He reported 'web rage' and illustrated this with the web site 'ntl-hell.co.uk' which, before its closure, was full of anti NTL vitriol. We have already discussed the power of the negative word of 'mouse'. He also describes 'direct action' and provides an example of the then environment minister who encouraged consumers to leave unwanted packaging at the checkout with the aim of encouraging companies to reduce the amount of wasteful packaging that we (still) see in the 21st century. 'Waste their time and cash' is another of Prosser's categories of consumer

Photo: Martin

rebellion and can also be described as consumer misbehaviour because it involves, for example, constant and repetitive complaining, sometimes over relatively trivial matters. His 'turn the tables' category is exemplified by the web site 'moneysavingexpert.com', which advises consumers on how to use the 'small print' in company literature to their advantage, where there are loop holes that benefit the consumer. His final category is the 'consumer boycott'. Here, he cites the Co-operative bank's research that found that over half of consumers avoided dealing with one or more company in 2006 because of poor company reputation.

Consumer Boycotts

A consumer boycott is defined as 'an attempt by one or more parties to achieve certain objectives by urging individual consumers to refrain from making selected purchases in the marketplace' (Friedman, 1985:97). Boycotting behaviour is considered by many as a collective action and a form of pro-social behaviour similar to voting in which consumer actions are intended to benefit many rather than a single person (John and Klein, 2003; Klein *et al.*, 2004).

Sometimes consumers boycott a company's products because they feel the company operates in unethical ways. Examples are Nestlé and the controversy surrounding its selling of powdered milk to poor African communities, or L'Oréal and its use of animals to test its cosmetics. Other prominent examples include consumers' boycott of Shell because of its plan to sink the Brent Spar oil platform at sea and that of Nike over alleged sweatshop conditions at Asian suppliers (Klein *et al.*, 2004). Such consumer behaviour could be construed as *mis*behaviour by the companies concerned, but sections of society could see this to be highly ethical behaviour which sometimes manages to reverse what they see as *company* misbehaviour. It can be seen from Table 12.2 that there are some wide ranging motives for participation in boycotts.

The notion of 'de-coupling' attitudes towards production from attitudes towards consumption is explored by Salzer-Morling and Strannegard (2008). They recognize the paradox of, on the one hand, concerns over some production practices (e.g. child and other exploitative labour practices) yet, on the other hand, the same brands that are perceived this way are often still bought by the same consumers who might at the same time protest about them.

Motive	Explanation
Perceived egregiousness	When consumers believe that a company has engaged in an egregious or outrageous action, they are very likely to boycott.
Make a difference	When consumers believe that by participation they can make a difference (e.g. make the company reverse its decision), they are likely to boycott.
Self-enhancement	Regardless of boycott outcome, some consumers are likely to boycott when they perceive themselves as moral persons or when the social and personal self-esteem associated with supporting a cause is high.
Counterarguments	Consumers are less likely to boycott when they have some valid counterarguments (e.g. boycotting may lead to unintended harm; actions are too small to get noticed; other consumers are taking active part, so I don't need to, etc.).
Constrained consumption	Those whose consumption is most constrained by boycotting are less likely to boycott (e.g. heavy users of a brand may not wish to participate as they might perceive their action to be too costly for them).

Table 12.2: Consumer motivations to participation in boycott as per Klein *et al.* (2004)

The proposition here is that brands can be so powerful that consumers de-couple the 'functional' (production processes, etc.) from the more aesthetic and 'expressive' aspects that brands communicate and deal with each separately and differently. Many organizations outsource their production to concentrate on image development and communication. So in the same way that the 'functional' is separated from the 'expressive' by companies, consumers might be mirroring this.

Some argue that business and marketing activities have a macro effect in shaping attitudes and values which lead to consumer misbehaviour (Fullerton and Punj, 2002). In other words, most of the misbehaviour is an 'unintended consequence of the marketing activities of firms, which seek to promote a philosophy of consumption so that consumers will buy more' (p 240). This reflects the **cultural authority perspective** in which marketers are viewed as cultural engineers with strong abilities and techniques (e.g. use of persuasive communications, segmentation and targeting techniques) to shape consumer desires, feelings and actions and to promote a consumer culture in which consumers implicitly grant authority to the marketers to organize their tastes (Holt, 2002). We explored some of these dimensions in Chapter 1 where we raised questions about marketing's exploitation of human drives. These motivate us to aspire to more and more, without necessarily satisfying us, regardless of how much we buy and own.

In such a context, some consumers fight back by allocating products with oppositional meanings, by using them in more idiosyncratic ways (which may be viewed as misbehaviour by others) and by seeking out social spaces in which to produce their own culture and identities (Firat and Venkatesh, 1995; Holt, 2002). Holt (2002) argues that conflict between consumers and marketers arises 'when firms attend to their internal interests rather than seek to meet consumer wants and needs' (p 70). Consumers can feel rebellious when there is huge perceived 'social distance' between a large, multinational organization and the consumer. Anti-commercial consumer rebellion has been defined by Austin *et al.* (2006) as 'open and avowed resistance to institutionalised marketing practices' (p 62). They conceptualize this as being composed of:

1) **Artifice**. Consumers often perceive marketing practices to be inherently deceptive (e.g. distorted product claims).

2) **Avoidance**. Company actions can damage the plant and steamroller over cultural values. Some consumers 'avoid' companies that receive bad press (but some seem to de-couple this from actual consumption behaviour, as discussed above by Salzer-Morling and Strannegard (2008)).

3) **Cynicism**. Despite pseudo philanthropic actions by 'big business' many consumers see through these ploys in a cynical perception of companies' and marketers' real intentions.

4) **Manipulation**. Packard's (1957) hidden persuaders reappear here in the guise portrayed by Austin *et al.* (2006). Consumers, they suggest, see company self-interests and unethical interaction with markets as manipulative of consumers from birth.

This is congruent with Holt's (2002) analysis that consumers can hold negative attitudes towards large organizations because there can be a big gap between the GDP figure for many underdeveloped countries and the profits of big multinational corporations. It might be due to the multinational imposing its own values and/or practices on other countries. In some cases it might be because there is not the personal contact between organization and consumer that might have existed in previous eras.

For example, the 'corner shop' catchment area and its inhabitants were well known by the shopkeeper on a personal basis but the more impersonal retail chains can't achieve this even through their attempts of loyalty scheme surrogacy (as discussed in the two previous chapters). As a result, social distance is even greater and might lead to the view that some forms of misbehaviour are almost legitimate (Houston and Gassenheimer, 1987).

So far our attention has been focused on anti company and anti commercalization as well as specific boycotts. However, as the recent cartoon controversy in the Danish media has revealed, boycotts can be at the societal level and may be triggered by some geopolitical, religious or even historical tensions between countries or nations or even regions (Ettenson *et al.*, 2006). Six months after the publication of a series of caricatures of the prophet Muhammad (PBUH) in a Danish paper, Arla Foods a Danish dairy giant lost annual sales worth US $430 million due to backlash by Muslims across the Middle East. Moreover, Ettenson *et al.* (2006) argue that not all consumer protests are boycotts, rather they are a type of protest which encourages consumers to buy some brands in support of a certain cause (e.g. buy dolphin-friendly tuna). This leads to our next topic which is consumer animosity towards other countries or nations.

---

www. **Have a look at the following web sites:**
`http://www.corporatewatch.org/`
`http://www.adbusters.org`
These are good examples of anti-corporate online communities for consumers to exchange views and negative experiences of company and marketing activity.

THINKBOX

Sometimes there can be a rejection of the consumption and materialistic world. Some consumers 'make do' from cheap supplies or charity shops. Could either of these phenomena be considered 'consumer misbehaviour'?

Consumer Animosity and Ethnocentrism

In Chapter 8, we discussed country of origin effects and stated that ethnocentric tendencies of certain consumers make them avoid foreign made products. However, there could be past or present hostilities

iMac For Men   iMac For woman

Figure 12.1: Spoof ads and buy nothing campaign posters by Adbusters.org

Source: www.adbusters.org

between nations and hence consumers may have animosity against a specific country or nation which can influence their willingness to buy products made in that country. Klein *et al.* (1998) defined consumer animosity as 'remnants of antipathy related to previous or ongoing military, political or economic events' (p 90). In an empirical study, Klein *et al.* (1998) reported that Chinese consumers' animosity towards Japan was negatively related to their willingness to buy products made in Japan but interestingly this effect was independent of their judgements about the quality of Japanese products. In other words, though the Chinese consumers thought highly of the product quality, they were still unwilling to buy Japanese products due to their animosity towards Japan. Moreover, Klein and Ettenson (1999) found that US consumers' animosity towards Japan had similar effects. In particular those who held higher levels of animosity towards Asians and ethnocentrism were more likely to be patriotic and members of unions. Subsequent studies involving other nations have largely supported the negative effects of animosity on willingness to buy (Riefler and Diamantopoulos, 2007).

CONSUMER MISBEHAVIOUR WITH RESPECT TO MARKETING ACTIVITIES

Whatever the motive, consumer misbehaviour influences not only consumers themselves but also other consumers, marketers and the environment in which we all live. Consumers can display misbehaviour in the way that they interact with, and react to, specific marketing activities.

EXAMPLE 12.2

Table 12.3 summarizes consumer misbehaviours with respect to a number of marketing activities including the ones in which we as consumers, either consciously or unconsciously, cause trouble to the environment and to others.

Marketing activity	Consumer misbehaviour
Products and services	Anti-social product use and misuse, such as in Figure 12.1
	Abuse of services, such as 'bad behaviour' when travelling on planes or when on holiday
	Use of environmentally damaging products such as cars, airline travel, fur garments, TV and sound systems with remote control
	Disposal of products in an environmentally damaging manner
	Knowingly investing in companies which exploit child labour and use other socially undesirable practices
	Purchase of pornographic products which exploit and damage women in particular and sometimes children
	Damaging brand reputation of companies perceived to be politically or socially irresponsible
	Buying products to indulge in sports which damage the environment, such as non-degradable fishing lines which can kill birds, guns to shoot wildlife
	Consumption of foods we know will damage our health

Table 12.3: *(continued)*

Marketing activity	Consumer misbehaviour
Price	Avoidance of paying, not owning up to being undercharged or given too much change, or falsely claiming the reverse Knowingly taking advantage of loans and credit when financial position won't sustain these Credit card fraud
Distribution	Vandalism of shops and shopping malls Illegal or unethical distribution of counterfeit goods Use of unauthorized distribution to sell bootleg products Physically damaging in-store displays and carpets
Promotion	Adding graffiti to posters Distorting (via word of mouth or online communities) advertising messages to damage the reputation of a brand out of spite Relationship marketing Deliberately distorting purchase details in loyalty and marketing database schemes by, for example, swapping loyalty cards Identity theft, abuse of personal details of other consumers
Relationship marketing and marketing databases	Misusing or stealing consumers' personal information and credit card details from marketing databases for fraudulent use
Market research	Poll rigging Deliberately mis-responding
Marketers' employees and other consumers	Being abusive to front-line marketing staff such as call centre operatives, complaints departments, store-till operators and service staff Double standards adopted by the same individual in their capacity as a marketer and consumer

Table 12.3: Consumer misbehaviour and marketing activities

THINKBOX

Whereas some consumers' behaviour is clearly unethical, such as when they break the law or seriously affect other people, there are grey areas depending on our personal stance.

From Figure 12.2 and Table 12.3, which do you think are *not* examples of consumer misbehaviour? Why do you think so?

As a cinema commercial, this certainly made an impact: the model walking up the cat-walk reaches the end, turns and at the same time flings the fur coat over her shoulder. But imagine the power of this on the big screen, when that action involved the blood from the animal from which the coat was 'skinned' being thrown over the catwalk audience and back along the catwalk.

© People for the Ethical Treatment of Animals (PETA). Reproduced by permission

Souce: LYNX

Figure 12.2: Fur misbehavior Why kill–for vanity?

Fullerton and Punj (2002) report a range of consumer misbehaviour directed against marketers' merchandise, their physical and electronic premises, financial assets and even employees. They report seven important motives for such misbehaviour.

1. When consumers are unable to fulfill their consumption goals through legitimate means, they are likely to engage in misbehaviours such as theft and fraud.
2. Some consumers find the act of misbehaving to be a thrilling experience in which they defy basic legal and moral strictures and hence they misbehave.
3. An absence of moral constraint can lead to misbehaviour. In other words, the acts of misbehaviours may not be perceived as bad or undesirable.
4. In certain groups (e.g. teenagers), misbehaviour may be perceived as a way of promoting a group's identity by positioning itself differently from others in the society. Here, an act of misbehaviour reinforces one's sense of belonging to the group.
5. Strong negative attitudes towards large institutions and particular ownership of businesses can trigger misbehaviour.
6. Certain situational factors (e.g. crowding, unsettling amount of heat and noise) can trigger powerful impulses to misbehave.
7. Some consumers engage in rational weighting of the risks and rewards associated with misconduct, which can trigger misbehaviour.

Consumer Misbehaviour with Respect to Products and Services

Shoplifting costs billions of pounds to retailers every year and consumers not only steal products but also engage in insurance fraud, hotel thefts and phone service fraud, which also costs millions of pounds every year. Indeed the fastest growing crime in the UK is identity theft where some consumers steal personal information from other consumers and will not mind looking into your rubbish bins, steal your handbag, open your mail box or meet you at your door step pretending to be representative of a legitimate organization.

www.

Visit the following website for information on Identity Theft in the UK, what the UK government is doing to prevent it and what consumers need to know if they become a victim:

http://www.identity-theft.org.uk/protect-yourself.asp

While you may think that it may be only professionals or some teenagers who would engage in illegal behaviours such as shoplifting, the reality is that consumers from all walks of life are involved. The Think Box will help you imagine the extent of this growing problem which is facilitated by the growth of self-service retail service culture (Phillips *et al.*, 2005; Tonglet 2002). According to a recent BBC New 24 report, more than 3.5 million people in the UK admitted shoplifting during the past five years, each taking an average of £105 worth of goods (BBC News 24, 2005). The shoplifters can shoplift literally anything that can be sold quickly including razor blades, air fresheners, batteries, CDs, DVDs, electronic gaming, music equipment and alcohol.

THINKBOX

Shoplifting and Celebrities!

Hollywood actress Winona Ryder was convicted on 6 November 2002 of stealing up to $5500 in Beverly Hills' Saks Fifth Avenue. She was accused of stealing 20 items, which included socks, hair accessories and a white Gucci dress worth $1595. Ryder, when approached, told the guards that a film director told her to shoplift to prepare for a forthcoming role. She was given 480 hours of community service, ordered to seek counselling, to pay more than $10000 in fines and three years probation.

How do you feel about shoplifting behaviour? Is this a characteristic feature of a particular group of consumers (e.g. teenagers or celebrities), gender group (e.g. female)? Do those involved in shoplifting share their experiences with others?

Sources used:

http://news.bbc.co.uk/1/hi/entertainment/showbiz/2406069.stm

http://www.dailymail.co.uk

Table 12.3 lists several examples of misbehaviour with respect to product purchasing. Is it misbehaviour to buy products which damage our planet and the life it supports? Consider, for example, the cases of the buying of fur, snakeskin and cars. Figure 12.2 summarizes the problems with buying fur garments. From mid-2000, fur is back in fashion and as a result more than 30000 baby seals were shot, speared and clubbed to death in Canada in March 2005. Over a thousand hunters were employed to strip the pups of their fur. They are helpless, 'can't swim or get away' (Beeston, 2005) and some are 'still alive after they had been skinned' (Aldworth, 2005).

'It (snakeskin) is an almost entirely unregulated trade where species are pushed to the brink' (Mesure, 2007). Celebrities are important users of snakeskin and as we have seen in Chapter 9, celebrities can act as powerful 'endorsers'. Warwick (2007) who is a reptile biologist with the Animal Protection Agency also claims that 'snakes caught in the wild are nailed to a tree and skinned alive taking days to die'. Is it consumer MISbehaviour to support such trade through purchase behaviour?

Figure 12.3: A consumer's struggle against car usage
Why worship the car?
© IEESDS. Photograph: Thierry David. http://www.decroissance.org

Figure 12.3 shows Car Buster's co-founder who set off across the countryside of southern France on foot in July 2004, with a donkey at his side, to highlight the need for an alternative to consumerism (in this case car travel) and economic growth, and to promote conviviality along the way. But to what extent are consumers willing to buy cars that wouldn't pollute the environment or even consider alternatives to having a car in the first place?

THINKBOX

Clothing Brands and Child Labour

© Getty Images. Photographer: Peter MacDiarmid. Reproduced with permission

In recent years, consumer groups have been putting a lot of effort in highlighting the terrible working conditions in which factory workers in less developed countries such as Bangladesh and India have to work to produce leading designer labels and fashion brands. A recent BBC Panorama programme reported widespread use of subcontracting in the manufacture of embroidered goods for Primark, including the employment of homeworkers under extremely bad conditions and possible instances of child labour.

To what extent does this illustrate consumer misbehaviour in terms of buying brands and ignoring the conditions under which these are produced?

Visit for more information:
http://www.labourbehindthelabel.org/
http://news.bbc.co.uk/1/hi/programmes/panorama/7471041.stm

Similarly, consider the case of holidays. Are we as consumers willing to forego our beloved foreign holidays because planes damage the Earth's environmental balance? Indeed, do we misbehave too much on holidays anyway? Club 18–30's recent campaigns are an interesting example of marketing's encouragement of misbehaviour on holiday.

This links with our coverage of Freudian motivation in Chapter 1 where we explored the superego diminishing effect of alcohol and different societal constraints when on holiday. Should youth market segments indulge so much in sex, alcohol and drugs while on holidays? These can damage their country's reputation, physically damage the holiday destination's infrastructure, and violence and rape can sometimes be consequences of certain sorts of holiday purchase.

THINKBOX

Is there a degree of hypocrisy regarding recycling products and waste? Many of us claim to recycle bottles or paper, but consider the following research findings:

89% thought their household is environmentally conscious
and
81.8% recycled more rubbish in the past 12 months
but
only 6.3% chose a more eco friendly car
and
11.4% used rail or sea for foreign travel
Haygarth (2007)

Consumer Misbehaviour with Respect to Price

Overcrowded, shortened and cancelled trains in the Bristol area in 2007 led to a consumer rebellion over 'paying'. It was claimed that a couple of thousand commuters used fake tickets with the brand 'Worst Great Western' (mocking the actual train company 'First Great Western') and refused to pay fares in this direct action protest (Prosser, 2007).

If a consumer has a standard rail ticket, yet occupies a seat in a first-class compartment, this is misuse of a service but it also is an example of use without paying, which, in many guises, is misbehaviour over price. There are a great many reasons why consumers misbehave over price. One of the earliest is the gap between their consumption/ownership aspirations and the financial means to realize these (Merton, 1968; Brokaw, 1993).

Perhaps one of the most obvious examples here is shoplifting. But as Fullerton and Punj (2004) also state, it can include returning goods such as clothing or DIY tools after one use only in order to get a refund. They also cite the switching of price tags in an attempt to get an item for much less than should be paid for it. Daspin (2000) also cites driving away from a petrol station without paying and this is again theft, as is leaving a restaurant without paying.

Another example of misbehaviour which in effect means that proper prices have not been paid includes failing to own up to a cashier's error and leaving with more change than is due. Steenhaut and Van Kenhove (2005) found that this depends on the level of the consumer's commitment to the retailer; if there is high commitment and large amounts of change involved, the consumer is more likely to 'own up'. But if the consumer has low commitment and large excess of change, they are less likely to own up. Steenhaut and Van Kenhove (2005) say this can be explained by opportunism on the consumer's part.

If a consumer submits a fraudulent insurance claim hoping to be reimbursed for items not stolen or destroyed, then this is a further example of misbehaviour, which in effect means that proper prices have not been paid.

Are consumers, who acquire tickets for a concert by the latest and trendiest rock band and then sell to other consumers at several times their face-value price, abusing price? Black markets do not represent normality even if they have become commonplace.

The downloading of music has largely been illegal and the artist does not get paid when it occurs. Increasingly though, provision is made for royalty payments, as iPods, Internet-enabled mobile phones and MP3 players (and indeed music web sites) become more common and the industry recognizes that rather than see downloading as a threat it can turn it into an opportunity.

THINKBOX

Is there any parallel between consumer misbehaviour with respect to music piracy (the unauthorized downloading of music or buying of pirated music) and the buying of counterfeit brands?

For this, read: Chiou, Huang and Lee (2005); and Gentry, Putrevu and Shultz (2006)

The latter is accessed via the accompanying web (www.wileyeurope.com/college/evans). It explores the implications of increasingly 'convincing' counterfeits and suggests, among other things, that consumers might buy a counterfeit brand as part of the 'trial' stage of the adoption process (Chapter 9) and if it is rewarding enough may go on to buy the 'real thing'.

www.
Take a look at the article on consumer misbehaviour by Tonglet (2002) Consumer Misbehaviour: An Exploratory Study of Shoplifting, Journal of Consumer Behaviour, Vol 1 No 4 pp 336–354, which can be accessed via the accompanying web site at www.wileyeurope.com/college/evans.

Consumer Misbehaviour with Respect to Distribution

The examples listed in Table 12.3 under this heading include the vandalism of shops and shopping centres. 'Bootlegging' is where illegal copies of, for example, DVDs or videos are made and sold, so it can be a distribution misbehaviour as well as a pricing one, as discussed above. Counterfeiting of brands is also distribution misbehaviour as well as pricing misbehaviour. Some people go to inordinate lengths to produce, sell and consume fake brands. Before the Iron Curtain came down, Levi's jeans labels were smuggled into the Soviet Union and sewn into 'ordinary' jeans. Consumers were more than happy to buy these: the jeans were cheaper than the real thing but conveyed the same image. However, Levi's branding, advertising and merchandising was 'ripped off' in the process.

Consumer Misbehaviour with Respect to Promotion

Consumers can be incredibly powerful. Consider the following:

> Whether directed against customers, employers or entire organizations, satirical messages created by activist organizations and even disapproving comments posted by customers can be quite damaging. Consumers weigh negative word of mouth far more heavily than they do positive comments about a product or service. According to a study by the White House Office of Consumer Affairs, 90% of *unhappy* customers will not do business with a company. Each of them is likely to share their grievance with at least nine other people and 13% of these disgruntled customers will go on to tell more than thirty people of their negative experience (Solomon, 2003).

In terms of consumers defacing marketing messages, the addition of graffiti to posters is fairly common. This might reflect random attacks of mindless vandalism, if the posters are conveniently located and relatively easy to write on (compared with brick, for example). Or there could be some deeper reason for the graffiti, such as a political or another activist slogan, targeting the specific brand or company concerned (Figure 12.4). Examples of consumers defacing posters can be seen around the country. Following the earlier mention of some consumers' perception that Nestlé operates unethically, a poster for Nescafé was defaced with the graffiti: 'Nescafé kills babies.'

Figure 12.4: Activist poster graffiti
© JP Dafault/eyevine. Reproduced by permission

Consumer Misbehaviour with Respect to Relationship Marketing and Marketing Databases

The previous chapter discussed aspects of consumer misbehaviour with respect to relationship marketing and marketing databases. It is a possibility, for example, that marketing databases could be used to target burglaries. That is, the destination of goods could be gleaned from customer databases in order to determine premises to burgle.

Some consumers engage in other illegal activities relating to personal data and its electronic storage. For example, the increase in credit card fraud and identity theft has been fuelled by the availability of personal details stored electronically by marketers.

In Chapter 10 we mentioned the consumer who hid his chocolate biscuit consumption from his wife. He did this by paying cash, for these items only, and putting the rest of the grocery purchases on his wife's loyalty card. He felt that without doing this she might be targeted with chocolate offers as a result of the company's analysis of the transactional records. Is this consumer misbehaviour? Or is it an example of marital misbehaviour?

Consumer Misbehaviour with Respect to Market Research

Some pressure groups are becoming adept at using opinion polls to influence policy decisions. They can orchestrate the 'piling in' (Nancarrow *et al.*, 2004) by other like-minded consumers to, for example, online polls. You may consider the following questions:

- Is it respondent misbehaviour to give answers which you think the interviewer wants to hear?
- Is it respondent misbehaviour to give any old answer just to get the interview over?
- Is it respondent misbehaviour to give answers which are generally known to be public opinion even if you yourself feel differently about the issue?
- Is it respondent misbehaviour to give a deliberately 'outlying' response out of bloody-mindedness?

Consumer Misbehaviour with Respect to Marketers' Employees and Other Consumers

Fullerton and Punj (2002) summarize several examples of this form of misbehaviour, including verbal abuse by consumers of marketing staff and in some cases the physical abuse of them. Harris and Reynolds (2004) extend this to include vindictive revenge and sexual predation of front-line marketing staff. They also reinforce the view that misbehaving consumers do not represent the minority but indeed the majority of consumers. In another study, Harris and Reynolds (2003) provide clear evidence of the damaging effects on marketing front-line staff of the abusive and aggressive consumer: 'More than 93% of employees interviewed indicated that dysfunctional customer behaviour negatively affected their emotional state.' They also found that few companies had policies to deal with the problem. There is even a web site – http://customerssuck.com – which is set up by some front-line employees as a forum for employees to share their grievances about awkward consumers.

THINKBOX

Might the 'exclusion' of some consumers on the grounds of not contributing much to sales or profit (as discussed in the previous chapter) be extended to exclusion based on misbehaviour?

Could it be that a manifestation of 'the customer is always right' perspective is that a degree of misbehaviour is tolerated? There might be a pragmatic view that a certain level of abuse is tolerated even if the same abuse might not be in a different social setting. Does this encourage even more abuse by consumers?

BEHAVIOUR BALANCES

We have norms and expectations which might determine the extent to which behaviour is perceived as misbehaviour (Fullerton and Punj, 2002). In a marketing context, consumers have expectations of how firms and their employees should behave whereas marketers also expect their consumers to behave in certain ways. Furthermore, consumers have certain expectations regarding the behaviour of *other* consumers in a particular situation. Figure 12.5 suggests that the wider societal perspective of consonant behaviour requires that the three components of the 'exchange triangle' interact smoothly.

Any dissonance between them can violate impersonal trust. Impersonal trust is where people who do not normally interact have faith in each other. Where there is either no misbehaviour or that which

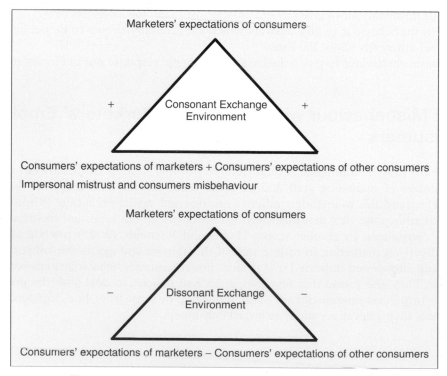

Figure 12.5: Impersonal trust and consumer behaviour

does exist has relatively minimal impact on the other parties, there is a consonant exchange environment. But where there is significant misbehaviour and/or it impinges upon the lives of the other parties more dramatically, there is a dissonant exchange environment and misbehaviour has a wider and negative effect on society.

THINKBOX

What were your motives for any consumer misbehaviour in which you might have indulged?

Should marketers do anything to address consumer misbehaviour?

Why, or why not?

If 'yes', what sort of measures would be effective?

THINKBOX

FUTURE FOUNDATION RESEARCH
Ethical Consumption

'Ethical Consumption' refers to the growing importance of concerns beyond mere price and quality that stimulate consumers' product choices. It covers a range of philosophical concerns in peoples' minds at the point of purchase and the conversion of these into measurable market behaviour. Examples might include not buying a product because you believe it to have been produced in a socially or environmentally reprehensible way or because it might say something about you to others, or perhaps actively choosing a product because it gives money to charitable causes or is locally produced. Rising incomes and higher levels of educational attainment, combined with real competition in many markets, have given modern consumers the space to incorporate this kind of thinking into their purchasing decisions – and companies the responsibility to deal with them and retain customer loyalty. The potent and media-savvy voice of lobbies and campaigns (relating to anything from GMOs to animal welfare to human rights to global warming) are constantly prodding us to use our buying power in what they would define as politically constructive ways – turning ethical consumption into a lively debate in the UK, with customers receiving plenty of advice and encouragement to participate. Companies have fast started to respond to this trend.

There is hardly a company these days operating in the branded consumer goods sector that does not offer some kind of morally upright identity and image to its customers. It is as if there is a constant battle in the corporate mindset to anticipate and to meet any shifts or intensification of the ethical instincts of consumers. For as long as economic conditions remain broadly favourable, we should expect this phenomenon to expand. Consumers want sophisticated debate about life from the companies selling in the British marketplace.

Do you? Why or why not?

Reproduced by permission of The Future Foundation http://www.futurefoundation.net/

SUMMARY

■ Consumer misbehaviour has serious consequences for all: those who indulge in such behaviours as well as others including members of the society, marketers and even the environment. Consumer misbehaviour occurs when someone violates the socially accepted norms of conduct in a consumption situation. However, it can also be extended to include other behaviours that have some negative consequences for consumers or society or the environment. Consumer misbehaviour can be categorized as abnormal and illegal behaviour.
Compulsive buying behaviour is one form of abnormal behaviour and it can make a person repeatedly engage in the behaviour in such a way that it would eventually cause some harm to the person.

■ There are many motives for consumer misbehaviour including the temptation to fulfill some unfulfilled aspirations, the desire to seek thrill and adventure, lack of moral constraint, some perceived coherence and affiliation with a group, strong and negative attitudes against capitalism and firms working within it, situational factors like crowding or being in a group of people and some rationalistic assessment of risks and rewards.

■ We live in a society which is dominated by a consumerist culture. Sometimes, though, marketing activities may be perceived as too controlling, too intrusive and being too powerful in shaping our desires, feelings, attitudes and consumption habits. Some consumers do not like the idea of not being in control of their lives and rebel against corporate and marketing culture. There are many instances in which consumers misbehave towards the marketing activities involving product, price, distribution, marketing communication, marketing research and even employees of the firm.

QUESTIONS

1. What is consumer misbehaviour? Why do consumers engage in such behaviour?

2. Does marketing encourage consumption so far as to make it damaging to the individual and to society?

3. Have you ever engaged in any of the 'misbehaviour' activities discussed in this chapter? To what extent do you consider this to be misbehaviour? Why, or why not? What are the implications of your stance for marketing, for consumers and for society?

4. Is marketing at fault for, for example, making shoplifting easy, for encouraging binge-drinking, for encouraging aspirations to unrealistic self-images?

5. Are we all too willing to buy things which damage the planet (e.g. cars, fur, etc.)? What shall we do as consumers and as marketers to stop such misbehaviour, or don't you see it as misbehaviour?

6. Critically discuss consumer motivations to participate in consumer boycotts.

7. What is consumer animosity and ethnocentrism?

FURTHER READING

Klein N (2001) *No Logo*, Flamingo, London. A wonderfully irreverent – but not irrelevant – exposition on anti-capitalism. This one will make you think as much as Packard's *Hidden Persuaders* (Chapter 1).

Gabriel Y and Lang T (1995) *The Unmanageable Consumer*, Sage, London. As well as exploring consumers' behaviour in terms of 'chooser', 'communicator', 'hedonist' and so on, Gabriel and Yang also delve into the darker side of consumer behaviour: 'consumer as rebel', 'consumer as activist'.

CHAPTER 13
ORGANIZATIONAL BUYING BEHAVIOUR

CHAPTER OBJECTIVES

After engaging with the material presented in this chapter, its associated exercises and reading, you should be able to:

- Appreciate the nature and various types of business products and markets.
- Differentiate between the characteristics of consumer markets and business markets.
- Appreciate business buying situations and the concept of buying centre.
- Explore various stages of the organizational buying decision-making process.
- Be aware of major influences on business buying decisions.

INTRODUCTION

We have left this chapter to the end because it builds on much of the rest of the book. There are links with Chapter 1 on motivation, with Chapters 2 to 4 where a sequential model of buying was explored and with Chapter 7 where group and family buying was discussed. The previous chapters of Part 3 are also relevant to the coverage here: we draw from Chapter 9 and the concept of opinion formers, from Chapter 10 on relationship marketing and from Chapter 11 where personalized data was shown to be important for understanding and targeting individual buyers, and even from Chapter 12's coverage of misbehaviour.

The chapter recognizes that there are some fundamental differences between consumer markets and business markets and hence the context in which buying decisions are made is very different when it comes to organizational buying behaviour. In Chapter 7 we discussed the role of reference groups and family in decision making and there may be some parallels that you can draw between household decision making and organizational buying as both reflect some degree of joint decision making. Indeed, the term **Decision Making Unit** is often applied to both, to reflect the amalgam of buying roles and influences within these respective groups. Therefore, the chapter first looks at various types of business markets and then highlights the differences and similarities between the consumer and organizational contexts. This sets the scene for our exploration of organizational buying behaviour.

Organizational buying is 'a decision making process carried out by individuals, in interaction with other people, in the context of a formal organization' (Webster and Wind, 1972:157). Hence, organizational buying is very much influenced by budget, cost and profit considerations as well as group dynamics since there can be more than one person involved in decision making.

You will sometimes see different terminology used for the broad context of this chapter's focus. 'Industrial buying behaviour' generally refers to buying by manufacturers, for example the gear boxes purchased by a car manufacturer from a component supplier. The term 'procurement' is sometimes used to describe the process of sourcing products and services for an organization: this could relate to fire engines for a local authority or submarines for the navy. You will also come across the phrase 'B2B' (Business to Business) which relates to companies' buying and selling processes between each other. Our context is a little wider and we use the more universal terminology of 'organizational buying'. This encompasses the buying behaviour of organizations as diverse as hospitals or universities (e.g. for computer equipment or travel for professionals attending conferences), airlines (e.g. for aircraft seats) and advertising agencies (e.g. buying TV commercial slots for their clients). Not all organizational buying will, therefore, be by 'businesses' that operate on commercial or profit related lines. Some will be not-for profit organizations such as charities and many public sector organizations.

It is worth mentioning at this stage that some products are clearly identified as organizational (e.g. a jet engine to be used in an airplane or a digger to be used by a construction company), whereas other products (e.g. a van) intended for use by an organization can also be purchased by consumers (Gross et al., 1993). Table 13.1 presents a product classification that is relevant to organizational markets.

Another distinction worth making is that most of this book has used the term 'consumer' to refer to the end-user or buyer. Organizational buyers are not usually described as consumers, but as *customers*. That is, when a restaurant buys a catering pack of 'sausage and mash' from its supplying food manufacturer, it is a customer, but when Gordon orders his sausage and mash in that restaurant he is the consumer. This introduces another aspect of much organizational buying: it is for the development, construction or delivery of products or services aimed at others, e.g. consumers. The health care and education sectors have huge buying budgets but not for their own purpose, but rather for the delivery of appropriate services to the population. There can be a sort of trickle-down effect from organizational customer to organizational customer and eventually to the final consumer. For example, a company might make rivets and one of its customers might be a shipyard. The shipyard's customers might include a Cruise company and when Gordon goes on his holiday cruise, he is the final consumer.

THINKBOX

It is interesting to think about different types of organizational products and the way in which these could be marketed to their customers. Identify channels of distribution for each product type presented in Table 13.1. Also, think about the amount of expenditure involved in buying such products and the extent to which an organization would engage in extensive decision making when purchasing such products and services.

Product type	Examples	Important features
Capital equipment and investments	Land, buildings, machinery, boilers, compressors, etc.	These tend to require significant financial expenditure
Accessory equipment	Personal computers, furniture, hand-held drills, forklift trucks, etc.	These can be standardized and are relatively lower in cost
Component parts	Batteries, tyres, headlights, timing motors, automotive windshields, etc.	Some parts are standardized to conform to industry specifications while others are custom made as per the requirement of the buyer
Process materials	Chemicals and additives, sheet metals, textiles, cement, electronic circuit wiring, etc.	They tend to lose their identity when used in a final product
Maintenance, repair and operating supplies	Office supplies, cleaning agents, tools, paints, light bulbs, petrol for company cars, etc.	These do not become part of the final product but are used to facilitate operation of the company
Raw materials	A variety of livestock, poultry and fish by-products are used to produce tallow, which is then used for making soaps, cosmetics and paints	These are the products of fishing, lumbar, hunting, aqua-cultural, agricultural (e.g. farming, livestock) and extractive (e.g. gas, mining, petroleum) industries
Services	Repair contracts for computers and other machinery, software development and maintenance, health care facilities and cleaning services, etc.	Some of these are technical (e.g. repairing of machines) and others are non-technical (e.g. cleaning services)

Table 13.1: Organizational products classification
Adapted from Gross *et al.*, (1993)

CHARACTERISTICS OF ORGANIZATIONAL MARKETS AND ORGANIZATIONAL BUYING

Geographic Concentration

Organizational markets tend to be more geographically concentrated than consumer markets in the sense that manufacturers of certain products or services or indeed the whole industry may locate in certain regions of the country to take advantage of availability of some raw material and/or skilled work force. For instance, back in 1950s, Bradford and Sheffield in the Yorkshire region of the UK were world renowned for textile and steal industries respectively. South Wales was a centre of the coal mining industry (for obvious reasons) and this led to the development of a very extensive railway network up and down the South Wales valleys to take to the mined coal to the major ports of Newport, Cardiff and Swansea for exporting. Other suppliers to the industry were again often located near to its centre. Clearly, our history shows that things change.

THINKBOX

Do some research to identify centres (regions or towns) that used to be 'known' for certain products or services.

For example:

Town/City/Region	Famous for:
Stoke-on-Trent	Ceramics industry
Nottingham	Fine lace
Leicester	Shoe factories
Cornwall	Tin mines
Bradford/Sheffield	Textiles and engineering
Tyneside	Shipbuilding, coal and steel

What other towns/regions had concentrations of industries and how have they changed for the 21st century and why?

Size and Number of Buyers

An organizational 'buyer' is usually not just one person, although micro businesses of just one person making handicrafts would be an exception. They will still need to buy-in the (for example) sewing materials and this, after a certain level of sales, will also have implications for VAT taxation and pricing, which makes another distinction from the consumer market where consumers can not reclaim VAT!

Compared with consumer markets, business markets tend to have limited number of buyers as each buyer (so this means organization) may buy in bulk quantities. For example, depending on the production capacity and the requirements dictated by the market, a washing machine manufacturer such as Bosch may buy thousands of spin speed motors, drums, sensors, LCD panels, door hinges, water pipes, etc. at one given time, which means such purchases have to be taken very seriously by both supplying and buying firms. Obviously, for some suppliers it might be that they only supply one large manufacturer and hence they could be quite vulnerable if there is a drop in the sales of the manufacturer. One of your writers remembers a business woman of the year award in Newcastle upon Tyne. Over 90% of the winning company's output of womenswear was to Marks and Spencer. This was at a time when that company had a policy of sourcing from within the UK. A question from the floor, at the award ceremony, was to the effect of 'are all your eggs in one basket?' The reply was that the company was very happy with a mutually beneficial relationship with Marks and Spencer. It is not known what happened subsequently, but it does alert suppliers to the potential risk of being beholden to one large buyer. It is a dangerous extreme of the 80:20 concept: almost all of one's profit coming from one customer.

Given that industrial buyers are limited in number, each one can be targeted via personal selling and other direct marketing efforts, as shown by the following two cases.

EXAMPLE 13.1

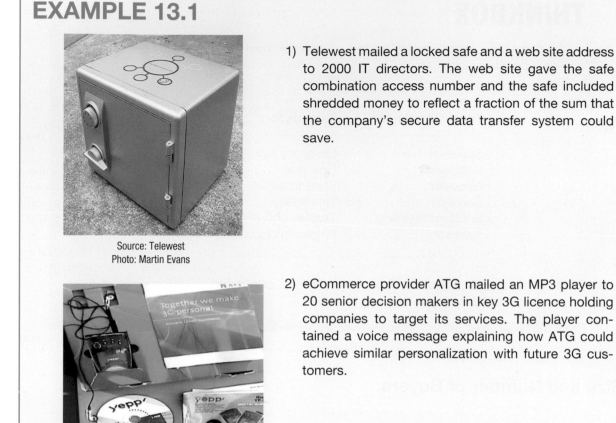

1) Telewest mailed a locked safe and a web site address to 2000 IT directors. The web site gave the safe combination access number and the safe included shredded money to reflect a fraction of the sum that the company's secure data transfer system could save.

Source: Telewest
Photo: Martin Evans

2) eCommerce provider ATG mailed an MP3 player to 20 senior decision makers in key 3G licence holding companies to target its services. The player contained a voice message explaining how ATG could achieve similar personalization with future 3G customers.

Source: ATG
Photo: Martin Evans

These approaches show that organizational buyers are being appealed to with 'task' orientated messages, but the way of conveying them can be more emotional, entertaining, interactive and fun. In one, only 20 individuals were targeted.

Nature of Demand

Within organizational markets, the demand for products and services is often linked with the demand for consumer products and services. This is called **derived demand**. For instance, when you buy a Nokia mobile phone, you are not only supporting Nokia but also hundreds of suppliers and business marketers who supply materials and components to Nokia phone manufacturer. Hence, any slow down in consumer demand for Nokia phones is likely to have an impact on the sale of Nokia phones but also many of its suppliers. Similarly, if the sales volume of major clothing retail store suffers on a longer term basis, the company may decide to get rid of some of its suppliers and put some extra demands on the remaining ones in order to cope with the low consumer demand for its clothing range. This indeed happened at Marks and Spencer back in 2001 when the company experienced a sharp decline in sales and consequently the retailer ditched some of its British suppliers in favour of cheaper overseas manufacturers in order to help improve profit margin. As mentioned above, it is not known if the 'business woman of the year', as described, suffered from this particular fall-out. The rise in petrol and food prices and the problems associated with the credit crunch from 2007 impacted consumer confidence and profit warnings were issued by many in the retail sector. This is a good example of how demand for consumer products can influence demand for organizational products.

Another implication of derived demand is the effect on **elasticities of demand**. Consider a change in price (to a TV manufacture) of a 'widget' component. The price for this (to the manufacturer) might have increased even by as much as 100%, but if this were a small element of the overall cost to the manufacturer for making the TV, then the price of the finished TV to the consumer may not rise at all, so consumer demand remains unaffected. In such a case, demand for the widget would be inelastic. Inelastic demand is where the percentage change in demand is less than the percentage change in price. This means that it is not unusual for demand for products in the organizational market to be inelastic.

Sometimes business marketers also have to stimulate demand at consumer level by advertising in mass media. For example, Intel advertises directly to consumers with a view to increasing its brand profile and enhancing confidence in their processors, which are actually sold to computer manufacturers. So although their product is just a component, they target consumers with the aim of encouraging them to seek 'Intel Inside' computers. In this way, there could be relatively inelastic demand for Intel based computers than for computers using central processing chips supplied by other manufacturers. Indeed, component suppliers who market in this way, move their products out of 'commodity' status and into desired brand status.

Marketing Mix

Organizational markets also differ from consumer markets in terms of marketing mix and Table 13.2 illustrates these differences very well.

THE DECISION-MAKING PROCESS

Rationality

Since there may be more than one person involved, the decision-making process tends to be more complex in terms of number of people involved, time taken to make decisions, the procedures and criteria applied while making decisions. For instance, decision makers and influencers can work at different functional levels and hence it is a time-consuming job to deal with all of them if you are one of the suppliers. Moreover, the decision-making process is more formal and professional than with consumers. This is because decision makers work in an organizational context and have to  comply with the rules and procedures established by their organization. Also, many organizations invest heavily in regular staff training making sure that those directly involved in the buying function have the right type of knowledge and expertise to deal with a range of suppliers.

Although organizational buying is largely dictated by organizational goals and objectives and hence is predicated on the rational, logical and efficient, it is too simplistic to assume that the more 'emotional' is not relevant, as we explore shortly.

However, the emphasis is often more on quality, price, accuracy of delivery schedule and after-sales service and support. Price is not necessarily the over-riding criterion: rational thinking can be quite evident when a buyer considers this to be of less importance than supplier attributes, such as the ability to provide products to the required specifications and to meet delivery deadlines.

	Business to business markets	Business to consumer markets
Product	This could be technical in nature and hence may require additional support in the form of support services (e.g. demonstration, installation and after sale care by qualified personnel). Equally the product might be simple nuts and bolts.	Can be less technical in nature and require less support compared to business products. But equally, a consumer might be buying a complex solar heating system for their house, which would require support and servicing.
Price	Suppliers may have to negotiate prices and offer special discounts particularly if large volumes are involved; may have to engage in competitive bidding against other suppliers; may work on list prices for standard items. Price changes can be manifested in inelastic demand if a large increase in price of the small component concerned, has negligible effect on the final price of the finished item.	Sellers often use list prices and some generic sales promotions (no face to face contact required to negotiate prices in most cases) although this does happen in some markets, e.g. when buying a vehicle from a car dealer. In times of recession, consumers often turn to 'value' brands which are cheaper and many believe the quality to still be acceptable. The organizational buyer might need to put rigid product specifications above price.
Promotion	Strong case for using direct marketing with emphasis on face to face contact in the form of personal selling; other tools used in support.	Emphasis on using advertising, sales promotions, public relations; direct marketing is also increasingly popular.
Distribution	Normally direct channels to market and hence the channel tends to be short with fewer intermediaries involved.	Use of intermediaries quite common; disintermediation is also getting popular particularly given the tremendous growth of internet and other direct channels.
Customer relations	Buyer–seller relations tend to be dynamic, complex and often personal.	Customers may feel emotionally involved with the brand but frequency of contact with the supplier is relatively limited, despite claims by marketers of 'relational interaction'.
Decision-making process	More and diverse groups of people working at different functional departments may be involved; hence the decision-making process tends to complex within a DMU.	The consumer can make most of their decisions on their own; in the case of household decision making, joint decision making is possible, so there is an equivalent of the DMU.

Table 13.2: Marketing Mix Differences between Business to Business and Consumer Marketing

Risk

Moreover, buyers' perception of the degree of risk involved can be very high, which means more time is spent in deliberation and evaluating alternatives, making sure that the risk of product/service failure is minimized. For example, imagine a car manufacturer placing an order for an important component that is used in the assembly of the car but the supplier not being able to deliver on time, due to some production fault at their factory. This may have serious implications for the car manufacturer because stopping the production line even for one single shift can cause huge financial problems. In other cases, the supplier may end up in delivering a substitute component that is not up to the standard and complaints being generated by the final consumer of the car. This happens quite often in many business markets and hence the product recalls by the manufacturers or retailers involved leading to expensive advertisements placed in national press. The Trading Standards Central website in the UK provides up-to-date information regarding product recalls by many leading brands and Example 13.2 presents some product recalls appearing in UK national press in recent months.

EXAMPLE 13.2

Recent Product Recalls in the UK

Date: 24th June 2008

IKEA RECALLS BARNSLIG BABY SLEEPING BAG
BARNSLIG BABY SLEEPING BAG article numbers: 30133409, 40133404, 70130079, 90130078

If you have bought a BARNSLIG baby sleeping bag IKEA kindly ask that you return it to your local IKEA store where you will receive a full refund.

IKEA has received two customer reports where the zip bottom stop has detached from the zipper which also makes it possible for the zip slider to detach. Both parts could produce a choking hazard to small children. No injuries have been reported.

Date: 21st May 2008

Product Recall: Tefal Smart clean Fryer
Tefal have identified a potential component failure within the Smartclean Fryer, ref FR400915 and FR400916 which may lead to overheating and risk of damage to the surrounding area. If the name of your product matches the one in the picture, then check the rating plate (situated on the base of the fryer) for the reference, FR400915 or FR400916 and the date code. If the last two digits of the date code are 06 or 07 your product is affected.

FREEPHONE: 0800 983 0983 Lines open Monday–Friday 8:30am–5:30pm and Saturday–Sunday 10am–4pm

The cause of the failure was poor quality of the zipper. IKEA have stopped the sales and production of BARNSLIG sleeping bags and we are now reviewing our routines to ensure the future quality of BARNSLIG sleeping bags.

We apologize for any inconvenience this may cause. For more information visit www.IKEA.co.uk or call Customer Services on 0845 358 3364.
IKEA

If you have purchased this product, we would advise you to stop using it immediately and contact our helpline (above) for details of how to return the affected product and obtain a free replacement. PLEASE NOTE ONLY THE PRODUCT PICTURED IS AT RISK, ALL OTHER FRYERS PRODUCED BY TEFAL ARE UNAFFECTED
We would like to thank you for your co-operation and apologize for any inconvenience.

Tefal www.tefal.co.uk

Source: http://www.tradingstandards.gov.uk/cgi-bin/newsitem.cgi?file=safe1005.txt&area=safe

The concept of risk originated from the Buygrid Model, which we discuss in the next section, because this was predicated on perceived risk. This was described as being a combination of importance of the purchase, how complex it was, the speed needed to make a decision and the level of uncertainty associated with the purchase. An extension of this is the risk continuum as developed by Johnston and Lewin (1996) and further explored by, for example, Thompson *et al.* (1998). The continuum includes the propositions that as the risk attached to an organizational purchase increases, the buying centre becomes larger, more people will be involved, previously proven suppliers will be preferred, search will be wide and varied, relationships and networks will become more important but there will also be an increase in conflict between the parties (Johnston and Lewin, 1996).

Thompson *et al.* (1998) used this framework and found that although some of these propositions held, 'large high risk purchase decisions, buying centres, laden with the conflicting agendas of the various parties, are being replaced by process-driven buying teams. In leading companies value is no longer seen to be created by not making mistakes but by suppliers working with customers to create customer value and wealth for both businesses'. This is a precursor to our coverage of the relational approach to organizational buying behaviour with which we conclude the chapter.

It is also akin to the relatively recent emergence of category management, where suppliers and buyers work together to grow a product category rather than the supplier being exclusively interested in selling-in their specific brand to the supermarket, for example.

BUYING CLASSES AND PHASES

Not all organizational purchases are the same and hence the amount of time spent in deciding what to buy, from where to buy and on what conditions to buy, can be different depending on the nature and type of buying. Purchases can be classified into three categories depending on the newness of the buying 'class': new task buying, modified re-buying and straight re-buying.

New Task Buying

In new task buying, the organization buys a product or a service for the first time and hence there can be a lack of experience in terms of handling suppliers or using a particular product/service. Therefore, in such buying, the organization might need a significant amount of information about the new product/service and its suppliers. Moreover, there is no history of prior purchase and evaluation, hence, there is a greater amount of risk involved and the organization often ends up operating under extensive problem solving mode. This means that the organizational buyers engage in extensive information search and evaluation before a final decision can be made. New task buying poses some specific challenges to those who wish to supply to the organization as they need to understand the buying organization's buying criteria and motives, understand their problems and align with their ways of working. If you are already supplying to the buying organization, then it is obviously to your advantage as you may already know quite a lot about what is bought by whom and why.

Modified Re-buying

A company may have bought an item before and based on usage experiences, the company might feel that some benefits could be derived by looking into the possible alternatives again. This could be triggered by a bad performance of an existing product/service or an existing supplier and hence the need to re-evaluate the alternatives. Since the buyers have been through the decision-making process before, they may operate in limited problem solving mode and might have some well-defined criteria while in re-buying situations. Since existing suppliers are familiar with buying firms' expectations and motives, they are in a better position to respond to the changing needs of the buying firm. However, a new supplier with stronger profile and resources can secure business by offering better quality and an enhanced buyer-seller interface.

Straight Re-buying

This reflects repeat purchases and corresponds very well to the idea of routine grocery shopping for the household. For instance, an organization might be running out of routine supplies such as paper, ink cartridges, pens and other stationary items as indicated by existing stock levels and hence might wish to replace them by placing a repeat order. The need is mostly recurring in nature and buyers are likely to have all the information that they need to place an order. Hence, they are very likely to operate under routine problem-solving mode with limited need for new information both about the product/service and the suppliers. Given the advent of new technologies, most repeat orders can be handled very well with a technological interface between the buyers and suppliers, for example via Electronic Data Interchange (EDI) systems. This means that once the stock levels go below a certain level, a straight re-order can be placed automatically with the same supplier for a pre-established quantity, without the need for humans! This does not mean that companies do not re-evaluate their suppliers but rather that it is done at different time intervals. For instance, after a certain period of time (say a year), a company might wish to re-evaluate all suppliers including the ones that supply on a routine basis. There have been some comical examples of EDI not working quite as intended: a consumer who was constantly woken and annoyed by what turned out to be telephone calls made by a Coca Cola machine to its supplier! In one case an elderly woman was rung up through the night by a public lavatory in a park in Leicester because it had developed a fault!

These classes of buying have been integrated within the famous and long lasting 'Buygrid' model (Figure 13.1), developed by Robinson *et al.* (1967). This model divides the purchase process into eight stages starting from recognizing the problem to evaluating its performance. The eight buy phases are in line with the three-buy class framework.

The Buyphases refer to the sort of sequential model that we covered in Chapters 2 to 4 in the consumer context. These phases or stages are explained in the following section.

Stage 1: Anticipation or recognition of problem

This stage triggers the purchasing process within the buying organization. The recognition of the problem can range from the need for raw materials, replacement of worn out machines to buying new products or a need to invest in a new technology as a result of changing consumer demand patterns. Understanding the organization's needs, on the part of the supplier, can initiate early involvement in the buying process. (Hutt and Speh, 1981).

Buyphases	Buyclasses		
	New task	Modified re-buy	Straight re-buy
1. Anticipation or recognition of a problem (need) and a general solution			
2. Determination of characteristics and quantity of needed item			
3. Description of characteristics and quantity of needed item			
4. Search for and qualification of potential sources			
5. Acquisition and analysis of proposals			
6. Evaluation of proposals and selection of supplier(s)			
7. Selection of an order routine			
8. Performance feedback and evaluation			

Figure 13.1: The Buygrids framework for an industrial buying situation
Source: Robinson *et al.* (1967)

Stage 2: Determination of characteristics and quantity of needed item

Here, the features of the items needed to solve the problem are determined. The problem can be defined as a routine task, a modified task or as a completely new buying task facing the organization. This will have an impact on the extent to which the organization considers the remaining stages of the buying process. In either case, the buying centre needs to assess the problem and determine the possible options to solve those problems.

Stage 3: Description of the characteristics and quantity of the needed item

This sets out the description and required quantity of a particular product. This is the key stage where the knowledge about the desired characteristics and the quantity demanded can place the marketer at a competitive advantage (Hutt and Speh, 1981). In the case of a modified re-buy or new task situation, the buying centre specifies what the product must be and how it must perform to meet the organizational needs. This is important for the suppliers as they can respond by offering products and services that can match what the buying organization is looking for.

Stage 4: Search for and qualification of potential sources

Once the buying centre establishes what is required to meet or solve the problem, it can then start the process of searching for and evaluating the potential suppliers and their product offerings. There might already be an approved list of potential suppliers or a new and fill search might have to be initiated. The stage involves a formal analysis and evaluation of current and potential suppliers using some well defined criteria including the product specifications established in the earlier stage.

Stage 5: Acquisition and analysis of proposals

The buying organization can request quotations or proposals in order to meet its requirements. Obviously the key task is to find a supplier who can provide best value to the buying firm and can help meet organizational goals and objectives. A closer look at the strengths and abilities of the potential suppliers including size, capacity, service commitment and technical competency can be very helpful at this stage.

For complex products more time and effort is spent on this stage for getting the information and various price quotations.

Stage 6: Evaluation of proposals and selection of suppliers

At this stage, a formal contract may be offered to a particular supplier which may be an outcome of lengthy negotiations about product features, pricing, delivery schedules and contract terms and conditions. The buying firm often seeks to protect itself from the downsides of single sourcing and inflexible pricing and hence might wish to use a range of suppliers in order to reduce uncertainty and risk involved. Sometimes a supplier is unique as it may be the only one in the area and hence the buying firm may wish to develop a long-term relationship with the supplying firm. The overall buying philosophy of the buying firm is also very important at this stage because some companies have a policy of developing long-term relations with most of their suppliers. Some firms wish to support local businesses with a view to strengthening their social responsibility credentials and hence the focus could be to choose local suppliers even though they might be expensive to manage. Large multinational companies have the resources and capability to source globally and hence a supplier can be chosen globally.

Stage 7: Selection of order routine

This is where purchase orders are drawn up and follow-up activities determined including liaison with suppliers but also with the internal department that initiated the process.

Stage 8: Performance feedback and evaluation

At this stage, the final purchase outcome is evaluated by looking at how best the product and the supplier met the criteria with a view to making adjustments to the product specification or taking a corrective action against those suppliers who failed to deliver as per the agreement.

THE BUYING CENTRE: ROLES AND COMPLEXITY

As introduced at the beginning of this chapter, we discussed reference group and family influences in Chapter 7, and as in household decision making, there are different people involved, playing differential roles in organizational buying and decision making (Webster and Wind, 1972). Depending on the size of the company, one person can perform all of these roles if it is a small firm but often more than one person is involved. There can be any number of users, influencers, deciders, gatekeepers, policy makers and technologists (Turnbull and Leek, 2003).

For instance, users are individuals who actually use a product or service within the organization. They may or may not be directly involved in the actual decision-making, but they can play an important role in determining what is bought by initiating the purchase process via need recognition and product specification. For instance, imagine the lecturers who work for your college or university. They may be using a computer in their office and can make a request to buy a new one with some specific product specification in mind, but the request might be denied because others make that decision. Similarly, gatekeepers (e.g. a purchasing officer in a procurement department) control the flow of information or material directed towards different members of the buying centre. For many sales people, they may be the first point of call even if they wish to contact other members of the buying centre, or Decision Making Unit (DMU).

Influencers influence organizational buying process either directly or indirectly by providing relevant information and/or criteria to be used for evaluating alternatives. The role can be performed by someone from within the organization (e.g. a quality control engineer) or an external party such as a technical consultant. Due to their knowledge and expertise, these resemble opinion formers and opinion leaders in a consumer behaviour context.

Deciders or formal decision makers are those who actually choose and decide among alternatives. The role can be played by the head of a purchasing department, a purchase committee or even the CEO of a company who wants to decide given the strategic importance of purchase. Buyers are individuals who have the formal responsibility and authority for contracting with suppliers. These are the people who are actually employed by the company to design, control and deliver all procurement policies.

The size and structure of the buying centre and the level of involvement by its members often depend on product type, product complexity and importance of purchase in a given situation. 'Buying centre size refers to the number of people actively involved in a purchase situation across the various stages of the decision process' (Lewin and Donthu, 2005:1383). When buying low value and routine items such as office stationery, there may be less people involved in making a decision. However, when it comes to making huge investments on a highly complex and important machinery, you should expect more people involved in decision making. In such a situation, buying centre participants may place a lot of emphasis on using formal rules and procedures during the decision making process and this is known as buying centre formalization (Lewin and Donthu, 2005). The buying centre participants may belong to different functional departments within the organization and/or hold key positions at senior levels. The number of departments represented in the buying centre is known as lateral involvement whereas the level of management involved in or influencing the decision-making process is known as vertical involvement (Lewin and Donthu, 2005).

Given the lateral and vertical involvement, business marketers face the challenge of identifying specific members of the buying centre with a view to approaching and influencing key participants involved in organizational buying process. In particular, due to complex organizational structures, it is often very difficult to isolate those involved in the buying centre, to determine the relative influence of each one of them and to identify the criteria that each one applies while evaluating alternatives. This is why you may find business marketers advertising in national press or even on TV as they wish to influence the opinions of members of the buying centre which are otherwise very difficult to reach. In this context, Ronchetto *et al.* (1989) suggested following strategies to identify power or relevant members of the buying centre:

- Isolate the personal stakeholder Sometimes an individual may have a personal stake and hence they may have a more powerful role to play in the decision making. For example, a production manager may wish to have a stronger say in which production equipment to buy as installation of new equipment might affect the efficiency of the production department.
- Follow the information flow Within the organizational context, the crucial information is often directed towards those who play a key role in decision making and hence following the flow of information makes it easier for the supplying firm to identify an important member of the buying centre.
- Identify the expert This can be very helpful because those with relevant expertise and knowledge can act as opinion leaders and opinion formers.
- Trace the connection to the top It is very likely that those who play a dominant role in the buying centre also have stronger links with the top management.
- Understand purchasing's role In certain buying situations such as straight re-buy, personnel with official responsibility to procure play a crucial role and hence identifying their role within the overall buying centre could be very crucial.

Some of these may act as opinion formers or opinion leaders as we explored in Chapter 9. An example is in medical markets, where nurses have been targeted via advertisements in the *Nursing Times*, as influencers over the adoption of drugs and treatments – they, after all, have the closest and most sustained contact with patients and can have a real influence over the medics who have the authority to make purchases.

MAJOR INFLUENCES ON ORGANIZATIONAL BUYING BEHAVIOUR

Webster and Wind (1972) identified four sets of variables that influenced organizational buying behaviour: environmental, organizational, interpersonal/social and individual (Figure 13.2).

Environmental Factors

Unlike consumer decision making, organizational buying is influenced by a range of environmental factors such as economic trends in the marketplace, supply conditions, technological changes, political stability and environment, and social-cultural issues. As indicated earlier, demand for business products/services fluctuates as per changes in demand for consumer products and hence a change in economic conditions (e.g. rate of economic growth, disposable income, interest rates and unemployment levels) can have a significant impact on what to buy, how much to buy and at what price to buy. The Think Box on the following page will help you imagine the extent of the problem when there are fluctuations in the economic conditions of a country.

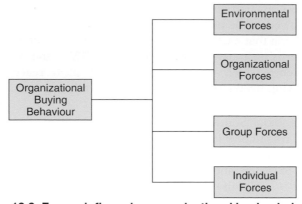

Figure 13.2: Forces influencing organizational buying behaviour
Source: Hutt and Speh, 1981, p 70

THINKBOX

In the current economical downturn, house prices have falten and the demand for new houses has slowed considerably. This had an impact on the economy which showed signs of slowing down and of a low consumer confidence in the face of redundancies, rising fuel and food prices. The credit crunch and the fall of sub-prime lending meant that UK banks were finding it increasingly difficult to borrow money in order to lend it on to their customers. This was expected to have a detrimental effect on many in the construction industry, which according to the Department for Business, Enterprise and Regulatory Reform (BERR) consisted of over 250 000 firms employing 2.1 million people in a variety of roles. Imagine the range and type of businesses affected by exploring who is involved in the construction industry. You may think of the obvious suppliers of construction materials and products but there are building services manufacturers, providers and installers, contractors, sub-contractors, professionals, advisors, construction clients and organizations that are relevant to the design, build, operation and refurbishment of buildings.

Sometimes supply of a specific raw material is restricted due to some unavoidable circumstances (e.g. a strike at the supplier's production facility), which might trigger unexpected order placement at an alternative supplier. Technological advancements and the rate of technological change can also have an impact because businesses have to reconsider their product/service portfolio on a continuous basis and hence what is a very popular product today may become outdated in the future. Moreover, business buyers tend to use latest technologies to make their procurement efforts more efficient. Similarly, business buyers have to operate under certain legal constraints (e.g. environmental protection legislation), which influence the nature and type of products that can be purchased by them. Similarly, some business purchases are of such a strategic importance to a given country that often lobbying has to be done at the most senior level to secure jobs.

Organizational Factors

Unlike consumer buying, organizational buyer behaviour is influenced by factors related to the buying organization such as its objectives and goals, purchasing policies, resources, the size and composition of the buying centre and organization structure. For example, in some organizations, the buying centre may be centralized, which means only a few participants hold meaningful influence over the purchase decision process irrespective of the number of participants in the buying centre (Lewin and Donthu, 2005). Moreover, the extent to which a buying firm is modern or bureaucratic, innovative or traditional, open or close ended, dynamic or static can influence its purchase decisions because the overall orientation and business philosophy can determine attitude towards buying and dealing with other firms. For instance, certain firms have a business philosophy of creating and maintaining long-term relationships with their suppliers and the hence the emphasis is not on price only but on value creation that can be mutually beneficial to both parties. Organizational culture (e.g. promoting excellence or emphasizing value) can affect the mindset of different participants involved in the buying centre. Moreover, some companies have a centralized buying department and buyers acting in such a context may focus more on negotiating lower prices and standardizing the products so that these could be used across the organization. However, in other firms, the buying function is very much decentralized with local purchase offices scattered throughout the organization at different locations. Buyers working in such a context may pay more attention to the needs of local units and their managers. Also, the resources (e.g. level of expertise and information available and nature and type of technology to be used) available at the buying centre might vary in different organizations, which can influence the organizational buying behaviour.

Interpersonal/Social Factors

Since the buying centre consists of human participants, they are very much likely to be influenced by social factors like the extent to which they get along with one another and whether they have the right type of skills to work in a group environment where decisions may be made either by consensus or via persuading others. Though organizational buying occurs in the context of a formal organization and its goals and objectives, the needs of individual participants are still important determinants of business decisions (Figure 13.3). This is because participants of the buying centre have attitudes, values and belief systems which interact with those of the organization and hence various personality types and individual preferences can influence organizational buying. The act of buying can become part of organizational politics in which some members use their position, authority and status to increase their influence in the organization. Buying centre participants may disagree on their expectations about specific suppliers or products or may apply different criteria in evaluating suppliers and hence conflicts might generate. There are many conflict resolution strategies that are applied by participants of the buying centre including persuasion and bargaining, politicking and use of power (Johnston and Lewin, 1996).

Individual Factors

Members of a buying centre are not only team members but individuals in their own right. They will have different personalities, have their own way of perceiving the world and learning about the organization and its buying processes (links with Chapters 1 to 4 and Chapter 6) can be from different cultures (Chapter 8) and have different cognitive styles (Chapter 9). The amalgam of members' characteristics can lead to unique team approaches by each buying centre team. Suppliers need to explore 'the person', not just 'the process'.

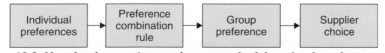

Figure 13.3: How buying centres make group decisions in choosing suppliers
Source: Wilson (1996, 1998)

Less Rational

The sections above reflect the generally more rational, structured and formalized approach to buying by organizations as compared with that of consumers. However, as the last point made clear, organizational buyers are people, too!

The organizational buyer might skip some of the 'stages' or formalized/rational processes because they see a compromise between satisfying these requirements and maximizing personal time. This might sometimes verge on 'misbehaviour' especially if corners are cut too much, but often buyers will think 'this supplier worked OK for us before, it might not be the most rational choice, but no real damage will be done'.

Deals can be done that involve 'back-handers' and 'slush funds' because that is how an organizational buyer might choose a supplier. In some countries this might not be unethical or illegal but elsewhere it will be seen as misbehaviour and a step away from the 'rational man' model of buying. We have already, in Chapter 9, explored the ethics of 'incentives' used to persuade buyers or influencers in medical and motor markets.

Economic man would be swayed by price/quality/delivery/service issues, but individuals within the buying centre will balance their own personal goals with those of the organization and the compromise may not be entirely 'rational'. There might be misplaced loyalty to a supplier perhaps because of a personal friendship which, if not there, might lead to the replacing of that supplier.

Overall the balance between the 'rational' and 'non-rational' will not be fixed. It will change as both individual and organization evolve and change. It is possible that when the range of suppliers' offers are relatively homogeneous, there could be more scope for the buyer being influenced by personal and non-rational motives. Where suppliers' offers are very different then 'the rational' might be more in evidence.

CASE STUDY 13.1

Source: Photo Martin Evans

As a Travel Agency, there might be many rational reasons for recommending a specific car hire company to consumers, but this case shows that organizational buyers are also appealed to on other grounds: the 'incentive' of a £1000 prize for the agency an the emotional, fun game. This involved applying 'yes' stickers (provided by the supplying company, Holiday Autos) to any part of the body of any agency member and photographing this with the camera, which was also sent to the agency. The camera was then to be mailed back and the 'winning' photos (in terms of humour, taste and daring) uploaded to a web site for all entrants to view and, no doubt, have a giggle. The Winning Travel Agency won the £1000 prize and the name 'Holiday Autos' was, probably, likely to be on that agencies' list of recommended hire car companies for its clients.

Buyer-Seller Relationships

Within business markets, buyer-seller relationships are often intense as both parties tend to be interdependent on each other. Indeed, relational buying in the consumer context, as we discussed in Chapter 10, originated, in part, from the notion of relationship marketing that evolved within organizational markets. The **Industrial Marketing and Purchasing Group** (**IMP**) is a consortium of researchers in the UK and Europe, that has developed the **interaction model** of buyer-seller relationships, which are seen to be complex and dynamic (Ford *et al.*, 2003).

Each transaction between organizations is not isolated; it is dependent on past experiences of both companies and their expectation of future business (Ford, 2004). Does this sound a little familiar? It would be useful to revisit our coverage of relationship marketing in chapter 11 where we introduced the constructs of interaction, relationships and networks.

A single relationship cannot be understood in isolation, it is a part of the complex networks of relationships (Ford, 2004). Buyer-seller partnership is defined as a type of strategic alliance between two organizations where they tend to enter into high involvement relationships if there is perceived mutual benefit. The IMP group also introduced more constructs that we explored in Chapter 11: relationships are characterized by long-term interaction where factors such as trust, commitment, social bonds, communication and even friendship ties are important ingredients (Forsström, 2005).

There can also be **reciprocal trading**, that is, two-way trading between organizations. Organization A might make the widgets that organization B needs to make computers. An agreement can be that organization B becomes the supplier to A of its office computers.

There could be high switching costs involved in terms of searching and evaluating new suppliers and in investing in supplier training, etc., and hence many organizational buyers exhibit strong loyalty to their existing suppliers. This has implications for new suppliers as they have to break into the mind set of new clients and communicate extensively in order to negotiate prices, delivery schedules, finance terms and may offer customized product features. Sometimes, buyers can have strong buying power which may lead to the notion of reverse marketing in which a buyer aggressively persuades a supplier to supply products that closely match their requirements (Gross *et al.*, 1993). Many retailers, for example, dictate specifications to their suppliers. Powerful players in distribution channels, such as Tesco and Marks and Spencer require their suppliers to produce to product specifications and to price points.

Relational selling strategy is defined as a strategic approach adopted by an organization with a view to developing long-term and mutually beneficial relationships with some of its customers (Guenzi *et al.*, 2007). Not all customers are the same and hence a business marketer may wish to identify those with whom long-term relationships could provide strategic advantage and value. Such customers are called key account customers and indeed there are many benefits in identifying and managing key accounts properly (Crosby *et al.*, 1990; Dwyer *et al.*, 1987).

Interestingly a key account can be identified and targeted by either the selling firm or the buying firm as in both cases working interdependently leads to value creation such as lowering of transaction cost or joint product development. Sales people play a very important role in identifying key accounts as they normally act as the eyes and ears of their respective organization and have considerable knowledge and expertise about their clients. Key account sales people need very strong social and communication skills and an ability to relate to important personnel in the buying firm at different levels of the management. Given the importance of relational selling in business-to-business contexts, Wilson (1993) argued that in addition to prospecting, appointment setting, letter writing, travelling, training and administration, many sales people are also responsible for a number of other tasks that underpin successful implementation of relational strategy within their organization:

1. **Customer Partner**: Sales people work with customers to create strategic advantage for both the buying and the selling firm and create a win-win situation.

2. **Buyer Behaviour Expert**: Sales people need to know and understand the buying criteria used by the buying firm, identify the key participants of the buying centre and issues relevant to the decision-making process.
3. **Buyer-Seller Team Coordinator**: Sales people need to manage the buyer-seller relationships using back-up specialists from both buyer and seller organizations to solve their customers' problems.
4. **Customer Service Provider**: Sales people coordinate the after-the-sale efforts including the provision of technical advice, financing, deliveries and after-sales service.
5. **Information Gatherer**: Sales people glean and pass back the information to their own organization about market trends and the needs and requirements of their customers.
6. **Sales Forecaster**: Sales people provide information upon which senior management can base strategic planning and quota setting.
7. **Market Analyser and Planner**: Sales people monitor changes on a continuous basis and devise strategies to adjust to them.
8. **Market Cost Analyser**: Sales people focus on profitable sales rather than sales volume.
9. **Technologist**: Sales people adopt new technologies to improve their performance.

As in the consumer market, there is an element of database marketing (see our coverage in Chapter 11) that is now impacting B2B marketing, at least to provide data on potentially relevant organizational buyers. For example, Flack (2008) describes how exhibition and other 'events' organizers incorporate barcodes or RFID tags in the badges of delegates. As a badging company director states: 'most of us have had our badge scanned by an exhibitor or handed over a business card only to find that no contact is made after the show. If exhibitors do nothing with the data they gather, then obviously the exercise is a waste of time' (Clayton, 2008). Such technology can track the movements of a delegate around an exhibition and even know when important buyers approach your stand.

EXAMPLE 13.3

…against unsafe translations

If you don't take proper precautions when choosing a language partner, you might find yourself with a nasty STD (Substandard Translation Disaster) on your hands.

There is more to making a website work in foreign markets than simply translating the words. At Mother Tongue, our aim when we adapt web copy for overseas use is to create something which reflects not just the content of the original, but also its freshness and emotional appeal.

So don't just jump into bed with any old company. Practice safe translation and benefit from the skill, sensitivity and experience of our market-based foreign-language copywriters.

Mother Tongue Writers
020 7371 0686
writers@mothertongue.com
www.mothertongue.com

Source: Mother Tongue

1. One of your writers received a condom through the university post. This was not a spoof or a student trying to convey some sort of message. It was a legitimate business mailing properly addressed using his professional salutation and using the university postal address correctly. Because he had attended a trade fair on internet marketing, his name was on the delegate list and an internet marketing company used the list to target prospects for their copywriting service which promises 'safe translations' in global markets.
2. Organizational relational buying is monitored and acted on via 'data'. For example, a major computer retailer has a B2B arm and so deals with organizational customers such as companies, local and central government departments.

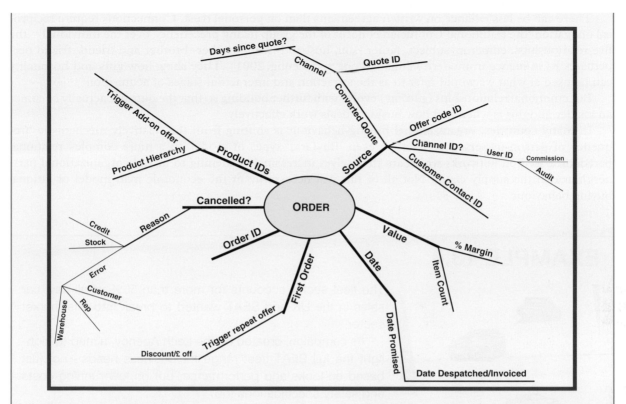

As the 'time line' below suggests, each order is tracked and monitored from initial contact through to attempts to reclaim lapsed customers:

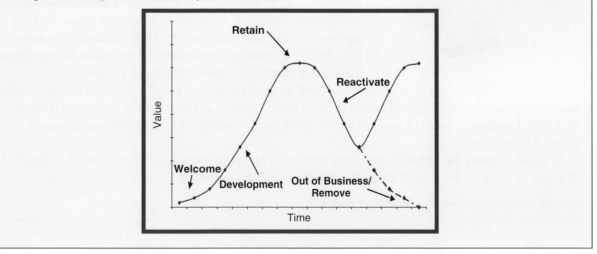

In the Chinese context, relationships (*Guanxi*) are even more important for understanding organizational buying, but less based on 'data' and more on personal interaction cultivated over what can be a long period of time.

There can be less reliance on written agreements than on personal trust. Connections require reciprocal obligation 'the traditional Confucian concept of the group taking precedence over the individual. . .the five relationships, emperor–subject, father–son, husband–wife, brother–brother and friend–friend perpetuates its influence in modern China' (Wong and Leung, 2001). They show how gifts and hospitality can be used at what we would refer to as the attraction and interaction stages of acquisition.

But emotional relationships (*ganqing*) evolve with further bonding so that the outsider actually becomes an insider and this is when and how business deals work effectively.

In many countries, organizational buying behaviour is shifting from the relatively mechanistic 'frequency of person-to-person contact' or even 'BuyGrid' types of model, to a more complex relational paradigm based on networks which are themselves increasingly widening to include organizational partners through the supply chain. Not all of this will necessarily fit the economic man model of rational buying behaviour.

EXAMPLE 13.4

The fleet sector accounts for more than 50% of all new car sales in the UK and SEAT wanted to break into this market sector.

Its campaign, created by the Leith Agency, aimed to highlight the full SEAT fleet range for business needs – not just based on looks and performance, but on low-running costs and safety specifications too.

Creative used and made fun of the irritating things people have to deal with at work, positioning the choice of a SEAT company car as the factor that makes it all worthwhile. An A3 flipchart, ridiculing elements of business speak and management techniques, was sent to 3 000 account managers in the UK and an adopted A1 version of the same flipchart was mailed to a smaller number of business people.

As well as launching the SEAT brand to this particular market sector, the campaign was used to build and develop a dedicated fleet database. It resulted in a 44% increase in sales of new cars since work began, equating to an additional sales value of about £1.3 million.

Judges praised the concept, saying it "delivered fantastic insight as offices are full of jargon". The use of humour, they said, showed understanding and empathy.

SUMMARY

■ In this chapter, we have explained some of the differences between consumer markets and business markets and argued that the context in which organizational buying decisions are made is very different when it comes to organizational buying behaviour. There are different types of organizational products each requiring different strategies when it comes to targeting and approaching organizational buyers. Moreover, business markets differ from consumer markets in many ways and hence the marketing mix needs to be adapted for the business markets keeping in mind the characteristics of organizational markets and organizational buying.

■ Organizational buying decisions are often made by more than one individual and the criteria used in making choices tends to be rational and driven by organizational factors and objectives. Not all buying situations are the same and it is often the new task buying situation that requires an extensive information search about the product and supplier, more time spent in evaluating the alternatives and the application of strict rules and procedures dictated by organizational philosophy and policies.

■ The buy phases relevant to organizational buying are anticipation or recognition of a need, establishment of characteristics and quantity of needed item, description of the characteristics and quantity of the needed item, search for and qualification of potential sources, acquisition and analysis of proposals, evaluation of proposals and selection of suppliers, selection of order routine and performance feedback and evaluation. You may recall that consumer decision making also involves many stages and there may be some parallels that can be drawn between the two.

■ In this chapter, we also discussed the concept of the buying centre which is very much similar to our discussion of reference group and family influences in Chapter 7. Organizational buying involves multiple participants from different levels of management playing differential roles in organizational buying and decision making. It is obviously a tedious job to identify and isolate each participant of the buying centre and establish ways of communicating with them.

■ Unlike consumer decision making, organizational buying is influenced by a number of factors related to the environment, to the organization itself and interpersonal/social factor. Even individual factors play their role which may make the whole organizational decision making less rational and objective in nature.

■ In organizational markets, both buyers and sellers tend to be interdependent on each other and hence the need to identify and manage key accounts can have strategic relevance and impact on the performance of the organization. Obviously not all customers are key accounts and hence the importance and significance of sales people who can play a very crucial role in identifying and managing key accounts.

QUESTIONS

1. **Compare and contrast the similarities and differences between business markets and consumer markets.**

2. **Imagine you work for an organization selling computer parts to a computer manufacturer. In what sense will the marketing mix for your company be different from the one designed for a company selling fast moving consumer goods such as a cereal?**

3. **What is organizational buying? Compare and contrast organizational buying process with consumer decision making process.**

4. **Explain the concept of buying centre. Which factors can influence the size and structure of buying centre and the level of involvement by its members? What are the implications for targeting buying centre members?**

5. **'Consumer behaviour is irrational, organizational buying is rational'. Discuss.**

6. **Discuss the major influences on organizational buying behaviour.**

7. **Analyse and evaluate the IMP Group's approach to organizational buying.**

FURTHER READING

Gilliland D I and Johnston W J (1997) Toward a Model of Business-to-Business Marketing Communications Effects, *Industrial Marketing Management*, Vol **26**, pp 15–29.

This is a seminal paper as it argues to consider the differences between business-to-business marketing and consumer marketing while proposing a model of business-to-business marketing communications effects. The paper is worth reading if you are interested in knowing how marketing communications work in a business-to-business marketing context.

Millman T and Wilson K (1995) From key account selling to key account management, *Journal of Marketing Practice: Applied Marketing Science*; Vol **1**, No 1, pp 9–21

Another seminal paper worth reading as it proposed a key account management relational model which takes into account the level of involvement with a customer and the nature of relationship that a firm might expect to have with its potential or existing customers.

Wotruba T R (1996) The Transformation of Industrial Selling: Causes and Consequences, *Industrial Marketing Management*, Vol **25**, pp 327–338.

In this classic paper, the author explains some of the changes and trends impacting industrial selling and the effects of those changes on industrial selling.

The academic article at the end of Part 3 is concerned with one of the most significant developments in marketing and in the understanding of consumers: namely, the shift to collecting and analysing personalized consumer data. Norberg and Horne (2007) in *Psychology and Marketing* raise the vexed question of the inconsistency between what consumers say about privacy and their continual engagement with what they also often see as privacy invasive marketing.

Q 1 Discuss why and how the attitude-attribution framework proposed here could explain the mismatch between consumers' negative attitudes toward what they might see as privacy intrusion and their more positive engagement with privacy damaging disclosures of personal information.

Q 2 How should the framework be operationalized via a research programme?

PART 3 JOURNAL ARTICLE

PRIVACY ATTITUDES AND PRIVACY-RELATED BEHAVIOR

Patricia A. Norberg* Daniel R. Horne**

Reproduced from Psychology & Marketing, Vol. 24(10): 829–847
(October 2007)

A significant body of research has arisen over the last few decades describing the causes of observed incongruity between attitudes and behaviors. Recent work in the area of privacy has demonstrated this type of situation, in which people with negative attitudes toward the provision of personal information will disclose this very same information for no apparent benefit. However, little theoretical work has been developed to explain why this paradoxical anomaly exists. This paper suggests that attribution plays a crucial role and should be taken into account with regard to both the assessment of behavioural outcomes and the examination of attitude formation. The purpose of the current work, thus, is to consider the contribution of the two theoretical areas, attitude formation and attribution, in explaining the correspondence between privacy-related attitudes and behaviors. This represents a critical first step in understanding the antecedents of privacy-related behaviors and in further developing the understanding of attitude models in general. As such, the paper suggests a framework and a set of propositions to guide future research and theoretical development.

Introduction

There is a significant body of research that has developed over the last few decades describing the causes of observed incongruity between attitudes and behaviors (Ajzen, 2001; Bagozzi, 1993; Fazio, Powell, & Williams, 1989; Fazio, 1989; Fazio, 1986; Smith, Haugtvedt, & Petty, 1994; Ryan, & Bonfield, 1975).

*Quinnipiac University
**Providence College

When an attitude-behavior incongruity becomes apparent in an area that is the subject of considerable individual and media attention, with concomitant calls for governmental intervention, the nature and cause of the incongruity must be understood in order to fully recognize the commercial and social implications of any public policy changes. Certainly, the matter of collection and use of personal information in marketing fits this description, where recent empirical work in the area of privacy has demonstrated that people with negative attitudes toward the provision of personal information will disclose this very same personal information for *de minimus* benefit (Norberg, Horne, & Horne, 2007).

From an organizational perspective, the collection and analysis of personal information has several benefits including, at the most basic, more effective offerings and more efficient communications (Franzak, Pitta, & Fritsche, 2001; Pitta, Franzak, & Laric, 2003), thus enhancing profitability prospects. From the consumer perspective, benefits such as the increased availability of products and services that more closely meet needs and communications that more readily address specific concerns, could be quite attractive if actually proffered. However, consumers also face the negative impact of loss of privacy when they offer up their personal details (White, 2004). To complicate matters, this loss is felt in varying degrees across individuals (Graeff & Harmon, 2002) and, furthermore, differs across categories of information (Phelps, Nowak, & Ferrell, 2000).

Although some insights into privacy issues have been gained from past research, it is still an area in need of further theoretical development to help explain the findings to date and the observed marketplace behaviors in which attitude-behavior incongruity is exhibited. One can look to attitude theory to explore this issue of low correspondence, but attitude research alone is likely to leave a gap in understanding. For instance, when attitudes are strong but not activated, are biased, or are nonexistent, there is a need to understand the factors that might contribute to attitude activation or bias, or the drivers of behavior when prior attitudes do not exist.

This paper discusses how attitude formation and strength contribute to the understanding of privacy attitude-behavior consistency, while also considering how attributional processes lead to an (mis)alignment of privacy attitudes and privacy behaviors. The paper focuses on one specific type of privacy-related behavior, *active* personal information disclosure, or the disclosure situations in which consumers overtly provide some personal data in commercial exchange. The paper does not directly discuss covert data collection that occurs via passive methods (scanner data, video surveillance, or credit card transaction data), nor does it include other privacy-related behaviors, such as keeping one's home phone number unlisted, installing spam blockers, deleting cookies, and so on. However, these other consumer data collection and usage (privacy) areas also can be understood better using the framework and propositions developed in this paper, and the paper briefly discusses the implications for these other privacy-related activities in the closing sections.

To provide a backdrop for the topic of interest in this paper, some of the relevant research on personal information disclosure in the context of consumer privacy is presented. Then, reviews of attitude and attribution constructs believed to be most relevant to the phenomenon of interest are presented. The sections emphasize attitude strength and formation with regard to privacy and the attribution process and biases that affect privacy attitude-behavior consistency. Although an extensive review of both theory areas is beyond the scope of this paper, it is hoped that the work will spark the interest of researchers who might contribute to the ideas put forth herein. Next, each theoretical area is applied to the issue at hand in the privacy attitude-behavior framework section, followed by a set of propositions offered to address the unique concerns about personal information disclosure outcomes. The framework and propositions form a first step in exploring the underlying theoretical underpinnings of the privacy attitude-behavior paradox, while helping to guide future research. The paper closes with a discussion of how attitude and attribution theories foster better understanding of consumer disclosure and how this new understanding can contribute to developing public policy initiatives that yield outcomes better suited to satisfying multiple constituents – consumers, marketing practitioners, and policy makers.

Privacy

While consumers continue to express concerns about loss of privacy, and while electronic and print media pay increased attention to the matter, academic researchers have been attempting to disentangle this multifaceted concept. Early efforts focused on attitudes toward incursions into a felt sphere of privacy, with some studies describing the levels of these attitudes across broad populations (e.g., Harris/Equifax, 1993; 1995; 1996) and others examining differences across demographic characteristics (Graeff & Harmon, 2002; Wang & Petrison, 1993). Recent research has also focused on technology, often the Internet, and its impact on felt privacy deprivation (Hoffman & Novak, 1996; Miyazaki & Fernandez, 2000; Mascarenhas, Kesavan, & Bernacchi, 2003). Still other researchers delved deeper into the origins and characteristics of the concept of privacy itself by exploring it from a legal/rights basis (cf. Schoeman, 1984; Murphy, 1996).

Consumer researchers have been more concerned with what defines the sphere of privacy that surrounds individuals and how interactions with the external environment affect consumers (Nowak & Phelps, 1995). For example, White (2004) argues that the disclosing of some types of personal information is of concern, because in a social context the information could be embarrassing. Other types of information, according to White (2004), are the subjects of concern because consumers do not want the information used without consent, indicating a desire for control over use. It is interesting to note the latter could result in consequences that are relatively benign (e.g., receiving unwanted direct mail offerings) or that are extremely negative (e.g., the denial of employment because of a previous medical condition).

Research efforts that combine both privacy-related attitudes and actual behavior are less frequently reported. An early attempt to investigate both attitudes and behavior found that people who utilized services of direct marketers had significantly different attitudes about how the direct mail methods used represented a threat to their personal privacy (Horne & Horne,

1997). Sayre and Horne (2000) found that negative privacy attitudes did not impact consumers' willingness to provide personal information to a grocer when enrolling in a loyalty program. In a study that examined information disclosure in an online purchase environment, Spiekermann, Grossklags, and Berendt (2001) demonstrated that even consumers who stated concern about privacy became highly communicative about personal information once engaged in a shopping task. Finally, a recent empirical investigation utilizing a market research environment provided evidence that privacy-related attitudes and personal information disclosure behaviors differ considerably (Norberg, Horne, & Horne, 2007). Here, consumers explicitly stated that they would not supply specific pieces of personal information that they subsequently did provide for no real benefit.

The studies noted earlier suggest that the degree to which one can rely solely on attitude research in the construction of personal information disclosure policies and practitioner directives is uncertain. Answering the question of why a significantly large incongruity between attitudes/willingness to disclose personal information and actual disclosure behavior in the marketplace exists should be started with a more theoretical approach to ongoing research in this area. The following sections on attitude and attribution are offered as a springboard for greater theoretical development and testing.

Attitude

Under the Fazio (1986) formulation, attitudes are associative networks made up of nodes encompassing all of the beliefs and emotions that relate to an attitude object. On a general level, attitudes range from nonattitudes through weakly held attitudes to those that are strongly held. Strongly held attitudes are expected to be more predictive of behavior (Fazio, 1989; Fazio, Powell, & Williams, 1989; Holland, Verplanken, & Van Knippenberg, 2002) and more stable over time (Holland, Verplanken, & Van Knippenberg, 2002), and emotion surrounding an encounter with an attitude object is less likely to influence behavior if attitudes are well developed (Smith, Haugtvedt, & Petty, 1994). Strongly held attitudes are more likely to be spontaneously or automatically retrieved prior to a related behavior than ones that are weakly held (Fazio, 1989). Accordingly, spontaneous retrieval of strong attitudes reduces an individual's inclination to rely on environmental factors when making behavioral decisions (Holland, Verplanken, & Van Knippenberg, 2002), a process that occurs when attitudes cannot be accessed, are construed on the spot, or do not exist. In other words, individuals with weak attitudes are less able to retrieve these from memory and are therefore more reliant on available cues in the exchange environment (Holland, Verplanken, & Van Knippenberg, 2002). In these instances, individuals utilize accessible environmental information to guide decisions at the time a behavior is required.

The structure of an attitude (the associative network) influences strength of the attitude in behavioral situations. The effects of source reliance (secondary information access versus experience), valence of information, and the conditions under which the information is perceived as relevant are important in attitude formation, and thus strength, considerations (Fazio, 1986). The following discussion treats each independently, although all three effects actually operate simultaneously in the attitude formation process in a complex environment like that of privacy.

The processing of information accessed via secondary means or via firsthand experience affects the degree to which an attitude might influence one's behavior. As developed through vicarious learning, the structure of privacy attitudes, for example, can be formed by relying on information received through media and other external sources that emphasize privacy issues. However, Fazio and Zana (1978) examined cognitive properties of attitudes and found that those formed based on actual experience are better predictors of behavior than attitudes that are formed based upon secondary information (see also Aarts, Verplanken, & Van Knippenberg, 1998; Fazio, 1986; Thøgersen, 2002). Therefore, consumers who *recognize* that their privacy has been compromised by a sharing of their information would have stronger privacy attitudes than those individuals whose attitudes were formed based on media coverage of general privacy violations.

In addition to the information sources that shape attitudes, the valence of information affects attitude development. Ajzen (2001) reiterates that positive and negative information encountered is processed differently, in that negative information impacts attitude formation more than other (neutral or positive) information. With regard to development of attitudes about privacy, individuals therefore may attend more to information that emphasizes risk, such as information that is available to the consumer from news coverage or other sources (Kuran & Sunstein, 1999). For example, media coverage of privacy breaches[1] (negative information) is likely to contribute to privacy attitude formation, whereas communications regarding the receipt of benefits derived from exchanges of personal information (positive information) may not contribute to privacy attitude formation. Thus, strong negative attitudes may be held by those who have not experienced and recognized a violation of their privacy because the attitudes result from an overweighting of negative information and underweighting of positive information from secondary sources.

Finally, the relevance of the attitude to a specific behavioral situation affects the attitude's strength relative to that behavioral situation. For attitude to be predictive of behavior, one must consider the consumer's ability to generalize from one situation to another, and thus specificity of an attitude is likely to impact the degree to which it is accessed in a behavioral situation (see Bassili, 1996). With respect to privacy attitudes, the general nature of concern if formed by relying on secondary sources of information, or the specific nature if formed due to a particular privacy violation that was recognized, may not tie directly to the various marketing exchanges encountered. For example, the extent to which a consumer, who receives unwanted telephone calls about special deals from a video rental chain after providing their phone number, refrains in the future from providing their phone number or other information when signing up for loyalty cards,

---

[1] Privacy breach, as used here, is defined as situations by which personal information was used in an unauthorized way, a way other than that for which the data was originally collected, or a way other than that which the consumer has been informed.

renting cars when on vacation, and so on, is unknown.

Also to be considered is the general nature of the marketing environment whereby people gain experience with information exchanges. Consumers are experienced with exchange in an information-rich environment in the United States. Why then are their attitudes not updated with repeated exposures to a marketplace requiring more and more personal information? The answer may be addressed by considering how consumers make attributions about the outcomes of exchange. A discussion of attributional processes, thus, is warranted to build a more comprehensive framework for understanding what drives disclosure behavior, why attitudes are not updated based on marketplace exchanges, and under what conditions attributions would prompt attitude update about privacy in such a way as to bring attitudes in line with behavior.

Attribution Theory

Attribution is the process by which a person judges the causes of an outcome and the impact of these judgments on future behavior (Weiner, 1985; 2000). According to Weiner's (1985, 2000) attributional theory of motivation,[2] individuals have initial affective responses to outcomes that influence future behavior. He suggests that attributions exert influence after an outcome is experienced but before the next choice and that more attributional search occurs after failures (negative outcomes). The causal dimensions that affect one's "rationale" as to why a specific outcome

was experienced include locus (an outcome is caused by either the self or another), control (an outcome can or cannot be controlled by the self), and stability (the factors leading to the outcome are situational or recurrent). A follow-up emotional response is tied to each dimension, and the combination of cognitive evaluation of causal properties and affective consequence influences follow-up behavior when similar situations are encountered. For example, if a consumer experienced a negative outcome perceived to be because of his/her own action, but for which he/she perceived a lack of ability to perform well (locus), then that consumer may feel frustrated and upset if feelings about his/her skill level and thus chances of success (control) could not be improved. The consumer would refrain from future behavior because the same poor performance would be expected in similar situations (stability). Thus, negative affect combined with the locus, control, and stability attributions would prompt an individual to discontinue the kind of performance that led to the initial failure.

Other researchers have examined additional factors affecting attributional activity that are also important in explaining the current phenomenon (cf. Crittenden, 1983; Johnson, & Drobny, 1985; Griffin, Babin, & Attaway, 1996; Pierro, Mannetti, Kruglanski, & Sleeth-Keppler, 2004; Robins, Mendelsohn, Connell, & Kwan, 2004; Wang, 2004). Of the studies in motivation, framing, learning, attribution, attitude, and combinations therein, this review contains those that contribute strongly to the understanding of attribution bias, which is quite relevant to the topic at hand.

---

[2]Although significant literature exists before Weiner (e.g., Heider 1958, Jones & Davis 1965, Kelley 1967), his introduction of a more comprehensive, and importantly dynamic, model serves well as a foundation for examining the phenomenon of interest here.

First, Fazio, Shook, and Eiser (2004) examined learning and attribution asymmetries and showed that, where value is uncertain, engaging in goal-based behavior is likely to take place if gains are perceived as significant/large relative to any perceived loss (approach tendencies increase). Fazio, Shook, and Eiser (2004) also demonstrated that people tend to experience more positive than negative events, even though they also believe there are more negative situations that are encountered in general. This reflects that individuals perceive themselves as good judges of the environment, although they might not be making accurate assessments. Applying this to personal information exchange with marketers, a consumer may believe that he/she is successfully engaging in an exchange when he/she provides personal health details to an online pharmacy for some health care tips. Whether or not value of the tips is truly equal to the cost of giving up personal information, however, cannot be completely assessed at the time of the exchange. Possible future unwanted outcomes, such as solicitations from drug companies or denial of health claim benefits, have not yet been encountered and are not considered by the person who judged the information sharing as a successful exchange.

Thomas and Mathieu (1994) argue that individuals use feedback information following performance to conduct self-evaluations, and a greater discrepancy between a person's performance and their intended goal will spark self-evaluation (Bandura, 1989). If an outcome is ascribed to a stable, enduring cause, then that same outcome will be anticipated in the future, as noted earlier. Continuing the previous example, if the consumer believes he/she is a good judge of the environment and believes he/she knows when to engage in a behavior (exchanges personal health details for some healthcare tips), he/she will continue the same suboptimal behavior stemming from the undiagnosed poor judgment based on a lack of understanding about subsequent unauthorized use of the health information provided. Thus, repeated failure may occur unless feedback is provided that leads to attributional reevaluation (Fazio, Shook, & Eiser, 2004). In other words, for the consumer to recognize that performance did not *in reality* lead to the achievement of an intended goal or outcome, feedback must be received (Thomas & Mathieu, 1994). If a noted authority made the consumer aware that other companies had access to and subsequently used the personal health data that was provided to the online pharmacy, then he/she would become aware of the negative effects of information disclosure. At that point, the consumer would likely reevaluate the exchange value and potentially classify it as a failure.

Second, Pierro, Mannetti, Kruglanski, and Sleeth-Keppler (2004) showed that positive cues are perceived as more relevant than negative cues during exchange and are more likely to be attended to. The authors also demonstrated that early presentation of relevant information has a stronger influence on behavior than information presented later. Combined, these two findings suggest that consumers may be prompted to focus on the positive and overlook (future) negative outcomes of disclosure because (1) the marketing frame is positive and (2) the positive outcome of receiving an immediate benefit precedes negative future outcomes related to secondary use of personal information. The marketplace is the arena in which consumers expect exchange benefits, and this positive nature of the marketplace marks the frame of reference on which consumers rely during exchanges and the positive cues available can prompt disclosure behavior in absence of concern.

Third, information ambiguity can bias attributions. Chaiken and Maheswaran (1994) found that although high importance, ambiguous messages induce individuals to increase cognitive processing, which in turn leads to greater attitude-behavior consistency, heuristic processing can bias systematic processing when ability to process is constrained (Chaiken & Maheswaran, 1994). Similarly, Van Dijk and Zeelenberg's (2003) findings that there is a tendency to discount ambiguous information, which lowers the likelihood that decisions will be based on such information, might be related to heuristic processing that is used to deal with processing constraints. Thus, correspondence bias, the incongruity between attitude and behavior, in constrained situations is heightened (Chaiken & Maheswaran, 1994). Because marketing exchanges are often characterized by time constraints, greater reliance on heuristic cues in the environment is likely.

Finally, with regard to attribution bias and ambiguity, Johnson and Drobny (1985) examined the effects of proximity on attribution, with proximity having both temporal and causal (number of intervening events between cause and result) components. They demonstrated that when outcomes are not temporally or causally distant from the actions that lead to the outcomes, individuals tend to rate the outcomes as more foreseeable, and the individuals who engage in the behavioral actions perceive more control over the outcomes. These findings suggest that greater temporal and causal distance leads to more ambiguity in discerning control and foreseeability of outcomes. Thus, if a consumer provides information during an exchange and privacy violations occur in the future, the consumer might not be able to make the causal connection. This argument is similar to the discussion presented by Ang, Gorn, and Weinberg (1996) on time-dependent attributes.

Attitude-Attribution Framework

Attitudes develop and may be reinforced by media distributions of a negative nature highlighting commercial violations of consumer privacy (e.g., Cavoukian & Hamilton, 2002; Knapp, 2004). Such attitudes might contradict observed marketplace behaviors because individuals are more likely to focus on the immediate benefits of the disclosure, and therefore an actual exchange will not be likened to those that consumers often hear about in the news and through other secondary sources.

Alternatively, consumers who directly experience and explicitly recognize that the negative outcomes are a result of their own disclosure behavior will hold attitudes that are closely aligned with their observed behaviors. The more the consumer experiences these negative causal relationships, the stronger and more predictive the attitude will be. However, individuals are not likely to experience multiple incursions, or make the causal connections even if they do, because of temporal and causal distancing coupled with the absence of feedback mechanisms that prompt a gap between behavior and successful outcomes.

When consumers interact directly with the marketplace, they may provide their personal details in the process of searching for goods and services that will satisfy a particular need state (goal-based behavior controlled by self). Privacy attitudes might not be invoked during marketplace transactions where the attitude is actually relevant, however, because the current attitude schemas may not include the variety of actual marketplace situations. This leads one to continually utilize marketplace cues to guide behavior, mitigating attitude update.

Recall that an overweighting of negative information can contribute to negative attitudes toward privacy, yet positive information from the environment can influence behavior. When framing effects create an environment that is perceived as positive, consumers are likely to rely on heuristic processes (positive contextual cues) while engaging in goalbased behavior of achieving marketplace benefits. This goal-based behavior in the context of the positive marketplace frame prompts the consumer to (mis)judge the attributional dimensions of locus and control. Consumers that engage in goal-based behavior believe that the outcomes of that behavior are due to their own actions. Environmental cues likely trigger performance of the act, which might subsequently be repeated because of an evaluation of the outcome as positive when immediate exchange benefit for information provided is received.

Thus, attributional biases mitigate the ability for individuals to revise their attitudes (cf. Chaiken & Maheswaran, 1994). When a marketer requests personal information from a consumer, the marketer emphasizes the benefit of providing the personal information during that exchange. When consumers sign up for loyalty cards, the discounts on items or points collected toward future rewards are emphasized as the reason for the exchange. When one registers online on a Web site, it is often for information access, Web site personalization, and so on. These types of benefits are likely very attractive to consumers who purchase many items frequently and can enjoy the benefits of loyalty programs or visit websites specifically to access available/customized information or offers. In these cases, then, the consumer may focus on a gain without much thought about any losses associated with providing the information, especially when the benefit is instantaneous and specific (Johnson & Drobny, 1985). Based on Pierro *et al.*'s (2004) findings with regard to attribution, it is possible that the positive frame presented by the marketer requesting information might *not* be overridden by subsequent thoughts about negative effects that might occur because (1) positive information is perceived as more relevant or alternatively the cost of negative information is unknown or minimized, or (2) the first information presented has greater influence over later information. Should consumers give any consideration to potential losses at all, the uncertainty surrounding the likelihood and severity of potential losses in the consumers' minds are likely to be discounted. As mentioned earlier, because consumers might feel they are good judges of outcomes, they will likely carry out goal-based activity to achieve benefits associated with providing information (approach behavior). The learning that takes place is based on the receipt of immediate benefit, which acts as direct feedback on goal achievement (Fazio, Shook, & Eiser, 2004; Thomas & Mathieu, 1994) because it directly compares to the benefit expected to be received.

Exacerbating the problem of favoring environmental cues are constraints to the decision process. As Chaiken and Maheswaran (1994) demonstrated, heuristic processing can bias systematic processing when incoming information is ambiguous, and this bias will be heightened when incoming information is constrained. When a marketer requests information, the consumer's ability to process the request is often constrained by time. In such a case, based on Chaiken and Maheswaran's (1994) arguments, an individual is more likely to attribute a requestor of information's true intention from the environmental cues that are easily processed using heuristics.

However, these constraints are not present when the negative outcomes (privacy breaches) are incurred, and so one would conclude that a more thoughtful investigation of why the breach occurred would take place. One also must remember, however, that the temporal and causal distances between the negative outcome(s) and the initial exchange will bias the attribution (Johnson and Drobny, 1985). Thus, as time passes, there are multiple explanations that might be considered in the absence of heuristic cues that were present during the actual exchange. It is therefore quite possible that consumers do realize when they experience a negative outcome (e.g., identity theft, unwanted telephone calls or e-mails, credit declines); they just do not necessarily link these to their own personal information provision behaviors. Given the marketing frame used when collecting information and the temporal/causal distance between negative outcomes and the initial disclosure, the likelihood of connecting these outcomes to the disclosure behavior is low. The attributions that drive behavior are often biased and thus the correspondence between privacy attitudes reflecting a low willingness to disclose personal information and actual personal information disclosure behavior is likely to be low.

Propositions

Based on this review, behavior is proposed to be a function of both attitudes and the attributions made about expected outcomes of that behavior. Correspondence between attitudes and behavior is in part dependent on unbiased attributional activity that results in attitude update (Chaiken & Maheswaran, 1994; Crittenden, 1983). It is proposed that the spontaneous attributions made by consumers during disclosure situations, and the subsequent misattributions made when negative outcomes are experienced, explain why people hold, sometimes strongly, attitudes that reflect an unwillingness to provide personal information even though they exhibit behavior in which they readily and willingly disclose personal information. Given misattribution, attitudes about privacy concern are stored without reference to specific marketing contexts, because they are not likely to be updated based on marketplace behaviors. Instead, the attitudes are held at a general level whereas behavior is activated in the presence of specific positive marketing cues in the environment. Only when attitudes are updated via accurate attributions regarding the overall value of outcomes resulting from disclosure will they be in line, and influence, disclosure behavior.

With personal information disclosure, outcomes are multiple and occur over time (immediate benefit, followed by an annoying telephone solicitation some time in the future, for example), and feedback from the marketplace that aides the consumer to link future and negative outcomes to one's own disclosure behavior is required for consumers to engage in a reevaluation and attitude update. Without such a mechanism, it is quite possible that not all outcomes are tied back to the original disclosure because of the (1) asymmetry of gain/loss perceptions, (2) the relevance of the cues, and (3) the order of presentation and timing of the outcomes. The linking of multiple outcomes to the actual behavior of disclosing information and the ability to generalize that linking are proposed to influence the degree to which attitudes about privacy correspond to observed behaviors.

These arguments are stated in the following propositions:

P1: Privacy attitude-behavior congruency is a function of attitude strength and formation, which is influenced by attributional activity.

P2: The strength of an attitude's influence on behavior is a function of:

P2a: the specificity of the attitude (e.g., privacy attitudes are more general than the marketplace exchanges that characterize actual disclosure situations).

P2b: the unbiased recognition of actual marketplace exchange outcomes.

P3: The degree to which biased attributions reduce the correspondence between attitudes and behaviors is a function of:

P3a: the number of outcomes resulting from an action,

P3b: the valence of these outcomes,

P3c: the timing of each outcome,

P3d: the sequence of these outcomes,

P3e: feedback on behavior and achievement of the outcomes.

P4: Feedback provided that emphasizes or makes apparent the negative effects linked to disclosure behavior will prompt update to attitudes, increasing the correspondence between attitude and behavior.

Discussion and Future Research

The focus of this paper is to propose a theoretical framework and set of propositions to guide future investigation of why privacy-related attitudes and behaviors appear to be inconsistent. When one examines how attitudes are formed/updated given the behavioral environment that likely drives attributions in this context, one begins to develop an understanding of why people say they will behave in one way but then actually behave in another. This creates an opportunity to more precisely inform the development of public policy. Thus, it is important to think about both attitude development and attributional processes that take place during personal information exchanges. Although this conceptual framework suggests a number of empirical examinations that would further this understanding, it is not intended to be exhaustive, nor could it be given the rapidly changing environment.

What happens under repeated exposure, even with the temporal distance of staged outcomes? Do the negative outcomes become linked to the prior behavior over time? If so, when and how? Is it possible that the negative outcomes will link to one's own behavior if the repeated exposures are stable, and the consumer can generalize across disclosure situations? Finally, how many repeated bad outcomes after a series of good or neutral outcomes does it take for reevaluation to occur? These are the questions that relate directly to the propositions offered above and provide fertile ground for future examination in both the privacy area and multiple-outcome exchanges in general.

Further examination also is warranted on the dimensions that influence attribution. Specifically, the control dimension appears particularly interesting and ties to past research in privacy. Given the ability of the marketplace to provide feedback to consumers regarding the overall value of outcomes incurred from disclosure behavior, attitude updating will lead to greater correspondence with behavior. However, this assumes that individuals will feel a sense of control in that he or she can choose whether or not to provide data. When consumers perceive that they are forced to provide information in exchange for marketplace benefits or perceive lack of control over the information environment (Goodwin, 1991), even if the environment is stable and consistent, they will still exhibit behaviors that are potentially inconsistent with attitude, due to a situational attribution made about lack of control.

Consider one situation not discussed in the framework and propositions – when the consumer does indeed connect their disclosing of personal information to some of the negative outcomes that are incurred in the future. Examples of this condition include a consumer's understanding that providing a telephone number, address or e-mail to a marketer may lead to unwanted marketing calls, direct mail, and SPAM. In these instances, attributions might be unbiased and can lead to accurate and accessible attitudes. The consumer who perceives that they can control the situation will make an attribution that the marketer will not detect whether or not the information provided is accurate. Disclosure to the marketer in this instance will be modified by omitting or misrepresenting pertinent personal details in order to achieve the attainment of marketplace benefits while minimizing negative outcomes of disclosing. Given the importance placed on (accurate) information by a consumer-driven economy, future research should consider this and other alternative marketplace conditions and the impact on attributions, attitudes, and behaviors.

Implications

With the push for policy and legislative remedies[3] and the diffused set of conditions that describe the area of personal privacy and commercial information usage, it becomes necessary to fully understand the underlying relationship between attitudes and behavior and the drivers of that relationship. Although privacy attitudes typically reflect concern in varying degrees based on individual differences, the types of information requested, and the relationship between the individual and the party requesting information (Milne & Boza, 1999), disclosure behavior does not appear to be fully driven by these concerns. Although attitudes are something that policy makers want to rely on as indicators for

---

[3]In 2004, 31 U.S. states were considering proposed legislation dealing with various aspect of personal privacy. In New York State alone, there were 33 different bills at a variety of stages of deliberation (National Conference of State Legislatures, 2004).

solutions to appropriately address the core needs of affected consumers, it is proposed that they also examine additional processes that may influence attitude-behavior linkages or precede attitude development. Specifically, it is suggested to consider both the contribution of attitude theory in understanding disclosure behavior and that of attribution theory. Although attributions can lead to attitude update, one must note that inaccurate or lack of attribution can preclude the development of strong, reliable attitudes that are indicative of behavior, and thus an understanding of the attributional process in personal information exchanges should prompt policy developers to focus more on what must happen to aid consumers in making attributions that are accurate and more closely aligned with behavior.

Although it is often difficult to make the jump from theoretical work to application, in the realm of privacy this leap is quite necessary. Current public policy is in a state of flux as new technologies emerge which allow the faster and cheaper acquisition, storage, analysis and distribution of consumer data, whereas legal and ethical systems have difficulty keeping up. In the United States, executive regulation and legislative answers are currently being sought at both the federal and state level and yet, without a firm grasp of why people express certain attitudes, it is quite likely that proposed solutions will yield less overall utility. Recent antispam legislation (the Can-Spam Law of 2003) has come under attack because it addressed concerns and needs at the time of the legislation's enactment that have been far outstripped by subsequent technological advances and entrepreneurial creativity. The motive for the current work is to develop an understanding of how attributions made during personal

information exchanges influence the extent to which privacy attitudes professed so vehemently actually impact consumer disclosure behavior in the marketplace. The hope is that with this increased understanding comes efforts, both by businesses and governmental bodies, that will solve real problems both today and into the future.

Certainly, if future empirical research supports the propositions presented herein, a number of implications may be drawn. The current *behavioral* evidence suggesting that consumers are relatively unconcerned could have one of two bases. In the first, consumers may consciously view the provision of personal information as fair in exchange for the benefits they receive. In the second, information asymmetries create a situation in which the consumer has little knowledge or understanding of the impact of collection, analysis, and distribution of personal information. It is argued here that the latter case is more prevalent, and helps account for the concept that direct experience will create stronger attitudes that are more closely attuned with actual behavior only when the consumer ties all outcomes to that behavior.

Should the attribution-attitude-behavior propositions be refined, tested, and supported, or revisited and then tested/supported as other researchers contribute to development of the framework, results can be utilized in the future to assess the effects of educational or other initiatives that policy makers institute. As initiatives are carried out, subsequent testing might be used to determine if such initiatives are changing attitudinal structures in ways that truly contribute to attitude-behavior alignment, as opposed to just measuring one's overall attitude, which might not really reflect on true behavior. In addition, an improved knowledge of privacy related behaviors such as personal information disclosure could yield a better understanding of consumers' interactions with businesses in the marketplace as information needs continue to increase. Measurement at this more granular level will lead to better analysis and development of policies/business practices that truly impact consumer decision making in this realm in a positive way.

References

For full references to this text please see the website.

GLOSSARY

Absolute sensory thresholds. Physiological limits to sensory perception.

Acculturation. This refers to the phenomena which result when a particular ethnic or cultural group come into continuous first-hand contact with another group and the subsequent changes that occur in the original culture patterns of either or both groups.

Acculturation agents. This refer to institutions or mechanisms such as family, friends, media and commercial, educational and religious institutions that can facilitate the cultural changes occurring among an ethnic or immigrant group.

Acorn. A classification of residential neighbourhoods – the first geodemographic system in UK, introduced by Consolidated Analysis Centres Incorporated. This, as with other geodemographic systems, is based on analysis of census data at postcode level. All UK households are profiled according to a clustering of similarities. Acorn profiles are now supplemented by a range of other data sources but the census is the key source. Links with the electoral roll allow individual addresses to be identified.

Action. Consumer behaviour as a result of information processing, which may take the form of trying the product, adopting it, consuming it, searching for information about it, and so on.

Actual self-image congruence. A subjective experience generated due to a psychological comparison involving an interaction between product-user image and a person's actual self.

Adoption. Regular or committed purchase behaviour. A one-off purchase is not sufficient for adoption. The adoption process is often shown to be reflected in a series of stages through which consumers progress: awareness $\Rightarrow$ interest $\Rightarrow$ evaluation $\Rightarrow$ trial $\Rightarrow$ adoption.

Advertisement Avoidance. The deliberate avoidance of specific advertising message or indeed deliberate avoidance of advertising in general.

Advertising wearout. The effect of an advertisement's repetition such that each additional exposure to it has a less than proportionate influence on consumers.

Advocacy. Consumers recommending a brand/store/company.

Affective motives. Motives whose achievement results in satisfying emotional states.

Aided recall method. A technique of advertising research that involves asking respondents to reproduce or 'play back' sufficient of the ad to show that they have seen it.

AIO Analysis. Traditional lifestyle analysis, referring to activities, interests and opinions.

Alderfer ERG Model. Alderfer's model is similar to Maslow's and includes existence, relatedness and growth motivation levels.

Approach. Behaviour directed towards a goal or object. This may include physical movement or thinking or feeling about an entity.

Aspirational group is a group to which a person aspires to belong.

Assimilation refers to the phenomena that result when an immigrant consumer or group relinquishes their cultural identity over time and adapts the cultural values and traditions of the larger mainstream society.

Assimilation effect. Selectively perceived message about an issue seen as more favourable than perhaps it really is, if the message is within their latitude of acceptance.

Associationist learning. *See* **Classical conditioning.**

Associative reference group. Those people who more realistically represent our current equals or near equals. Examples include our friends, neighbours and co-workers

Attention. The stage in the persuasion process at which the consumer merely notices the message.

Attribution theory. Consumers seek explanations for the causes of outcomes.

Attitude. A consumer's evaluative response to an object or person; their feelings or affective reaction towards it.

Attributes. Any elements or features of a product or service judged salient by a consumer to their purchase behaviour.

Autonomic decisions refer to those decisions that are spontaneous and are involuntary in nature.

Avoidance. Behaviour that involves moving away from an object or goal; this may be physical or mental.

Baby boomers. The generation born following the Second World War; usually regarded as those born between 1945 and 1965.

Bandwagon effect. The tendency of respondents in attitude research to give the answers they imagine the interviewer wants them to give.

Behavioural data. Data which provide personalized facts about how consumers behave. The main source is transactional data, but Internet **cookies** can track consumers' paths through the Internet, global positioning satellites (**GPS**) can locate where a consumer's mobile phone is geographically, and radio frequency identification 'tags' (**RFID**)), if not 'switched off ' at the checkout, can track consumers' purchases into use and even disposal.

Bernays. Edward Bernays was the nephew of Sigmund Freud and is accredited with being the first to link the subconscious with buying behaviour.

Biogenic drives. Needs that are biological in origin, e.g. for food, water, sex.

Biographics. The combination of behavioural data and profile data. Analogous to the 'biography' in literature, biographics can provide a 'buying biography' of individual consumers.

Body image. How consumers perceive their bodies and how they would like their bodies to be. Can be influenced (not always positively or healthily) by idealized images as shown in marketing messages. Sometimes leads to physical alteration of one's body via cosmetic surgery, piercing and tattooing.

BOGOF. Buy one and get one free.

BRAD. British Rate and Data – provides prices of advertising media.

Brand attributes refer to brand-related features such as price, quality and durability.

Brand community is a grouping of individuals which is specialized, non-geographically bound and has a structured set of social relations among participants. Buying centre – this is based on the idea that organizational buying decisions can be made by multiple participants working at different levels of management. Buying centre formalization – buying centre participants placing a lot of emphasis on using formal rules and procedures during the organizational decision making process.

Brand hijacking. The brand is taken away from marketers by a brand community to enhance the brand's evolution, either by a serendipitous hijack in which brand fanatics seize control of a brand's ideology, use and persona, or a co-created hijack can occur when brand owners co-create the brand's ideology, use and persona, and pave the road for adoption by the mainstream consumers.

Buying centre size. Number of participants in the buying centre.

Buying roles refer to different roles that a consumer can play in the buying process.

Buyphases. These are the stages involved in organizational buying.

Buzz Marketing. The 'planting' of company reps in a social setting to talk loudly about the company in a positive way, but initially not revealing that they are company reps.

Calibration. What consumers think they know and what they actually know can be different and this is the level of correspondence between objective and subjective knowledge.

Cellular household. The notion that many households, especially in Western cultures, are more fragmented than used to be the case. Household members have their own 'cells': children have their TVs and computers in their bedrooms and there is less communal activity than in more integrated households.

Central route to persuasion. Attitude change that is the result of the consumer's deliberative involvement with information.

Chronological age. Number of years that a person has lived since birth.

Classical conditioning. The process in which an initially neutral stimulus, through constant pairing with an unconditioned stimulus that elicits a given, unconditioned, response, acquires the capacity to elicit a similar response itself even in the absence (for a time) of the unconditioned stimulus. The hitherto neutral stimulus is now known as the conditioned stimulus and the similar response is the conditioned response.

Classification system is the systematic grouping of objects, thoughts and ideas into categories on the basis of structural relationships between them.

Clutter. Bombardment of consumer with information to the extent that they cannot distinguish one message from another.

Coercive power encourages conformity by explicitly or implicitly threatening some form of intimidation.

Cognitive age. The consumer's self-perceived age, the age they feel. It is related to the consumer's self-concept.

Cognitive elements and beliefs. Elements of culture that reflect what a society 'knows' (and transmits from generation to generation) about the physical and social worlds and the way in which society works including religious beliefs.

Cognitive consistency. The theory that consumers attempt to maintain a degree of balance between the cognitive and affective elements of their attitudes. Attitude change results from the homeostatic modification of one or other element.

Cognitive dissonance. A person who holds two or more contradictory cognitions (beliefs, attitudes, intentions, etc.) is said to experience cognitive dissonance, an emotional state that motivates them to drop or modify one of the cognitions in order to reduce the dissonance.

Cognitive motives. Motives whose fulfilment engenders a sense of meaning in the individual.

Collectivist cultures tend to hold an interdependent view of the self that stresses connectedness, social context and relationships with others.

Commitment. A component of reciprocal relationship consumption which means that both parties are so comfortable with the relationship that they don't feel the need to look for alternative partners.

Compulsive buying. Buying products or brands one had not planned to purchase.

Conformity to group is one's tendency to follow the norms, traditions, rules and regulations prescribed by the group.

Connectors. A method of identifying opinion leaders. Gladwell asked respondents how many people with one of 100 family names listed they knew.

Consequences. The outcomes of behaviour that determine the rate at which that and similar behaviours are subsequently performed: usually conceptualized as rewards (reinforcers) and punishments (punishers).

Conspicuousness refers to something which is obvious, easy to notice or attracts attention by being unusual.

Consumer acculturation refers to the overall process of movement and adaptation to the cultural environment in one country by persons from another country.

Consumer Animosity and Ethnocentrism. Consumers avoid some foreign made products because of past or present hostilities between nations or because of animosity toward a specific country or nation for any reason at all.

Consumer boycott. Rejection of a brand or company and the encouragement of others to so not deal.

Consumer Brand knowledge. The personal meaning about a brand including brand features, brand attributes, benefits provided by the brand, brand imagery, thoughts and feelings associated with the brand and attitudes and experiences relevant to the brand.

Consumer misbehaviour is consumption behaviour that can have adverse effects on themselves or others in some way. Such misbehaviour infringes accepted societal norms.

Consumer panels. A form of marketing research in which the same respondents report over a period of time. The resulting longitudinal data can be especially useful in identifying trend over time. Typical consumer panels report on media habits or the consumption of fast-moving consumer goods such as groceries.

Consumer susceptibility to interpersonal influences (CSIN). Consumers vary in their susceptibility to interpersonal influences and some consumers can be more susceptible to social or interpersonal influences than others and vice versa. This susceptibility is likely to be enhanced when a consumer is highly worried about the inferences other people make or may make about their behaviour.

Consumer terrorists. Consumers who have such a bad experience that they tell others about their bad and frustrating experiences. They might also be subversive and swap loyalty cards in order to damage the integrity of consumer databases.

Contemporary lifestyle. Based on personalized surveys which ask respondents to 'tick' those responses that apply in terms of products and services in which they claim an interest or actual purchase. The data is attributed to the respondent's name and address and is used to compile lists for contact via mail, telephony or email.

Contrast effect. A message which is within a consumer's latitude of rejection can be interpreted as even more unfavourable than perhaps it really is.

Conversational advertising. Where apparently ordinary conversations between members of the public are actually planned brand communications messages delivered by field promoters role playing ordinary people having (loud) conversations.

Cookies. Web messages which can identify visitors to web sites. Repeated visits can lead to customized web pages being developed for the consumer.

Country of origin refers to the place or country where the brand or product is manufactured or assembled.

Country of origin effect refers to the stereotypical beliefs that consumers have about products or brands originating from specific countries.

Crossing culture. The behaviour and opinions of those who move from one culture to another – for example, foreign students going to study in another country.

Cultural authority perspective. A view which considers marketers to be cultural engineers and in control of, as well as having the ability and technique (for example, persuasive communications), shaping consumers' desires, ideals and what they buy and consume.

Cultural category represents the basic distinctions that a culture utilizes to divide up its world of everyday experiences.

Cultural dimensions. The notion implying that culture is multifaceted and has many aspects or dimensions.

Cultural rituals refer to repetitive and expressive behaviours that are shared by a group of people.

Culture refers to socially learned behavioural patterns, arts, beliefs, institutions, and all other products of human work and thought. The term also refers to the meaning system that people use to inform their lives, providing them with a sense of identity and rationale for their actions. Culture helps people to make sense of what other people and even objects stand for, and how and in what sense one should deal with them. Customers – a term used for organizational buyers.

Customer satisfaction. The difference between pre-purchase expectations and post-purchase evaluations, leading to a positive or negative effect felt by the consumer toward the product, store or brand at the post-purchase stage of the buying cycle.

Customization refers to products and marketing activities being modified according to cultural, regional and national differences.

Data consortia. Alliances between companies that share data at varying levels, from generalised campaign effectiveness results to personalised transactional data.

Decider is the person who makes any of the decisions or sub-decisions which determine the precise nature of the purchase.

Decision-making style. A mental orientation characterising a consumer's approach to making shopping choices.

Decision-Making Unit. A term that is often applied to both consumer buying and organizational buying to reflect the amalgam of buying roles and influences within these respective groups.

De-coupling. Attitudes toward production separated from attitudes toward consumption, so although a consumer might object to a company's production methods (eg use of child labour in developing countries) they are still able to consume that brand.

Deculturation refers to the phenomena that result when an immigrant consumer or group rejects movement into the mainstream society as well as any identification with their own culture of origin.

Demand Mapping. Banks of attitudinal statements are presented to respondents in order to uncover their outlook on life and central values and aligning a brand's emotional and functional components with these.

Democratizing innovation. Consumers become an integral part of the new product development process, sometimes as if they were part of the company team itself.

Demographics. Consumer characteristics which are objective: age, gender, marital status and occupation.

Derived demand. The idea that the demand for a product/service can be linked with the demand for another product/service.

De-shopping. Predetermined purchase and use of a product but which is then returned even though it is not defective.

Deterministic models. Models of repeat purchase and loyalty, based on cognitive processes. Repeat purchase 'loyalty' here involves commitment and affective dimensions, not just behavioural repeat purchasing.

Diffusion. How an innovation is communicated and distributed through society over time.

Diffusion-adoption of innovations. The conceptual framework for how new products and ideas are spread through society and how they are received, accepted and adopted.

Direct Marketing is the interaction between customer and marketer which is, to varying degrees, personalized, such as via telephony, mail, internet and so on.

Disconfirmation paradigm. A means of understanding the causes of consumer satisfaction in terms of pre-purchase expectations and their subsequent confirmation or disconfirmation.

Disintermediation is the process of taking away any middleman or intermediary.

Dissociative reference group. Those people that we would not like to be like. Examples include famous celebrities having a very bad public image.

Diversity refers to variety. The term is often used to mean the existence of a variety of ethnic groups in a marketplace or a society.

DIRICHLET Model. Applies especially in stationary markets and assumes each consumer to have relatively stable purchase propensities to buy any particular brand; there being different propensities for buying different brands and indeed different consumers' propensities vary greatly in terms of their brand repertoires and frequencies.

DRTV is direct response television advertising. Some form of response mechanism is included in the advertisement itself, such as a telephone number or web site address.

Ego. *See* **Freudian motivation.**

Elaboration likelihood model. The theory that advertising messages provoke different likelihoods of the consumer becoming involved and therefore of highly elaborating the message by taking the central route to persuasion or failing to become involved and thus taking the peripheral route.

Elasticities of demand. Refer to the extent to which demand for consumer product/service responds to changes in the price charged for the product/service.

Emphasis on form/style refers to the condition of Western society in which there is a growing influence of form and style (as opposed to content) in determining meaning and life.

Enduring involvement. Sustained interest in a particular product category.

Equity theory. Evaluation of what you consider as fair or right based on a comparison of outcomes (e.g. value, utility and pleasure gained out of the transaction) relative to inputs (e.g. cost and effort involved) in a market exchange situation.

Ethnic identity refers to a set of behavioural or personal characteristics by which an individual is recognizable as a member of a group. This reflects a person's knowledge of membership in a social group(s) together with emotional significance and value that is attached to that membership.

Ethnic media refers to the media that communicate in a particular ethnic language and is normally targeted at a particular ethnic group.

Ethnic segment refers to a grouping of ethnic consumers that may potentially be targeted by marketers.

Ethnicity can be viewed as a characteristic of racial group membership on the basis of some commonly shared features such as common customs, language, religion and values.

Ethnocentric consumer refers to a consumer who believes in the superiority of their own ethnic group or culture or country over others.

Evoked set. Brands within a particular category that consumers bring to mind, some of which they consider purchasing (the 'consideration set').

Experiential marketing. Where markets encourage consumers to use multiple senses to experience a brand, at any or all the pre and post purchase stages of the buying process.

Expert power is where there really is a good degree of generally known expert knowledge on the part of the referent.

Exposure. Consumers' contact with marketing activity is selective, so the marketer needs to ensure that the marketing message is placed where the consumer is more likely to have contact and similarly that marketing offerings are distributed through relevant channels.

Exposure effect. Reflects tendency among consumers to join a reference group based on the frequency of interaction and being exposed to others.

Extended family normally consists of a patriarchal or matriarchal figure and some mature siblings who have spouses and children and who all live in one joint family system.

Extended Symbolic Message. Where messages borrow from the style of message more usually found in the personal advertisement columns.

External motivation. Motivation generated by the possibility of acquiring extrapersonal things such as products.

Family buying behaviour. The buying behaviour of a family as a unit.

FCB grid. A framework reflecting consumers' involvement and their salient knowledge, meanings and beliefs about the product. Some products are considered primarily in terms of rational factors, such as the functional benefits of using the product ('think' products) in the grid model. In contrast, 'feel' products are considered by consumers primarily in terms of non-verbal images and emotional factors. The grid was originally used by the Foote, Cone and Belding (FCB) Advertising Agency.

Feel products. Products that the consumer considers primarily in terms of emotional factors such as their putative psychological and social benefits.

Felt ethnic identity refers to one's sense of belonging to a group and the feelings and thoughts that go with being part of that group in a particular situation.

Flashmobbing. Virtual groups agree to meet in the physical world for what some might regard as acts of pointless lunacy.

FMCG. Fast-moving consumer goods, such as groceries.

Focal attention. Deeper cognitive engagement with a persuasive message.

Focal vision. What we see centrally in our vision.

Forgetting. Inability to retrieve previously stored information. This could be caused by many factors including the probability that the information was never encoded into long-term memory in the first place (encoding failure) or that, for some reason, we are unable to retrieve the information from long-term memory (retrieval failure).

Formal group is an officially organized group of people having a proper structure and procedures to be followed.

Fragmentation refers to the condition of Western society in which disjointed and disconnected moments and experiences in life and a sense of self are omnipresent and there is a growing acceptance of the dynamism which leads to fragmentation in markets.

Fragmentation of collective meanings refers to the demise of collective meanings.

Frame of reference. The framework into which consumers perceive a particular product or brand as fitting or belonging.

Frankfurt School. A group of social thinkers in Germany who saw social symbolism of products often outweighing their more practical use values.

Frequency. The number of times a message is placed or shown during a given period of time.

Freudian motivation. The motivating states realized in the individual as the result of conflict among the id and superego as they are regulated by the ego. The id is the unconscious and instinctive source of selfish motivation, immediate gratification. The idea that comes closest to that of the superego is that of the conscience, a socially learned device that regulates one's motives; in Freudian motivation it tends to inhibit the antisocial influences that have their origin in the id. The ego is the seat of reason, the self, which attempts to create a balance between id and superego so that the individual can function effectively.

Generation X. The generational cohort following the **baby boomers** and born approximately between 1966 and 1976. The name 'Generation X' was coined by Douglas Coupland in 1991.

Generation Y. The generational cohort following **Generation X** and born between 1977 and 1994. Sometimes also called the Millennial Generation or the 'N-Gen' after 'the net' and the 'information revolution' which were such significant technological events of the time.

Generational cohort. Division of age groups based on a 20-year span to allow individuals to develop.

Genetic data. Data on an individual's evolutionary development, for example, their family medical history.

Geodemographics. The amalgam of a variety of sources of data using the Census as the motherload, providing profiles of neighbourhoods around postcodes.

Geo-lifestyle. The clustering of data from contemporary lifestyle research, with the results transferred to the population as a whole by inference of similar clustering in similar postcodes.

Ghost writing. Writing of a piece by someone other than the named author.

GPS. Global positioning system. When signals are beamed (e.g. from mobile phones) to a number of satellites, the triangulation of that signal can position the source of the signal.

Group cohesiveness refers to a condition of cohering in which group members show their attraction to and attachment with a group.

Group conformity refers to the notion of acting or behaving in correspondence with socially accepted standards, conventions, rules or laws prescribed by the group.

Habitual buying. The apparently unthinking behaviour of consumers in repeatedly selecting a particular product, store or brand.

Habituation. We attend less to messages that are repeated too often – we become too accustomed to them.

Hemispheral lateralization. Different sides of the brain deal with different functions such as processing different pieces of information.

Heuristics refer to quick rules of thumb that consumers utilize while making decisions or while evaluating and processing information.

Hierarchy (or sequence) of communication effects. The cumulative sequential effects of advertising or other persuasive messages in generating consumers' exposure to the message, their giving their attention to it, followed by perception, cognitive learning, attitude formation and change, intentionality and action. It may also include post-purchase behaviours such as cognitive dissonance reduction.

Homeostasis. A process that promotes balance and harmony of working. Initially employed to denote autonomous physiological processes that reduce irregularities in blood pressure or body temperature, the term is also used somewhat metaphorically to refer to social and psychological processes that generate equilibrium.

Husband-dominant decisions are those decisions in which the husband is the decision-maker and/or exerts a major influence in the joint decision-making process.

Husband–wife decision-making refers to the notion that both spouses can engage in joint decision making.

Hyperreality. An especially postmodern phenomenon which translates 'hype' into consumer desires to experience simulation more than reality: e.g. man-made theme parks rather than nature-made natural environments.

Id. See Freudian motivation.

Ideal self-image congruence. A subjective experience generated due to a psychological comparison involving an interaction between product-user image and a person's ideal self.

Ideal social self-image congruence. A subjective experience generated due to a psychological comparison involving an interaction between product-user image and a person's ideal social self.

Inbetweenies. 11–12 year olds – not quite teens but older than younger children.

Impulse buying. Act of purchasing driven by unplanned and sudden decision making.

Independence from group is a person's tendency to break away from the group or show some defiance of the group by not explicitly following the norms, traditions, rules and regulations prescribed by the group.

Individualism is the tendency to hold an independent view of the self, which emphasizes separateness, internal attributes and uniqueness of individuals.

Individualistic cultures tend to hold an independent view of the self, which emphasizes separateness, internal attributes and uniqueness of individuals.

Industrial buying behaviour. Generally refers to buying by manufacturers.

Industrial Marketing and Purchasing Group (IMP). This group was originally formed in the mid 1970s by a group of researchers representing five European countries and universities investigating industrial marketing and purchasing. The group is now an informal, international network of scholars and researchers who continue to approach industrial marketing and buying from an interactive perspective.

Inept set. Known brands that consumers reject as purchase possibilities because of poor experience with them or negative information towards them.

Inert set. Brands consumers know but to which they are indifferent.

Influencer refers to the person who consciously or unconsciously affects the purchase in some way, perhaps as an opinion leader.

Infomediaries. Provide a sort of brokerage service to consumers by collecting information about their buying patterns and requirements and providing information about different potential suppliers.

Informal group is a grouping of people on the basis of common interests and geographical proximity with no formalities or rigid structure.

Information influence occurs when an individual enhances their knowledge of the environment and their ability to cope with some aspect of this environment (e.g. purchasing a brand) by seeking specific information from their reference group (e.g. family, experts).

Information power operates when a consumer perceives someone as possessing knowledge about the issue.

Initial attention. First scanning of information to determine its relevance.

Initiator refers to the person from whom the idea of buying a certain product first comes.

Inner-directed. Riesman used social character to explain personality type. Inner-directeds have a strong personal (inner) sense of what sort of behaviour is correct.

Innovation. A product, service or idea which is perceived as new by a significant proportion of consumers in a market.

Innovativeness. A personality trait which reflects the individual's interest in trying and using new products.

Insight. The capacity of the untrained person or animal to structure information in order to produce effective behaviour.

Instrumental learning. *See* **Operant conditioning**.

Instrumental values. Things that are desired only because they lead to wanted consequences.

Integration refers to the phenomena that result when an immigrant consumer or group not only maintains their original cultural integrity but also makes a move to become an integral part of a larger societal framework.

Interaction model of buyer-seller relationships. The model assumes that organizations in the contemporary marketplace are interlinked and interdependent and hence the notion of business exchange cannot be understood as disjointed or stand alone events but rather as complex relationships between buying and selling organizations where what is exchanged is created in the interaction itself.

Intergenerational influence is the effect of the family in the socialization of a person.

Intergenerational value transmission. The cultural passing on of desires, usually from parents to their children but conceivably from children to grandparents (or within any other combination of generations).

Internal motivation. Intrapersonally generated motivation.

Internet cultures are cultures that exist in the context of the Internet.

Interpretive approach refers to a variety of non-traditional perspectives on the study of consumer behaviour. Generally speaking, an interpretive approach to consumer research aims to understand the meaning of consumer behaviour by focusing on the context and by utilizing qualitative data and qualitative analysis, and by frequently using an emergent research design and procedures.

Intrinsic information cues. Those that are specific to a particular product and include the physical attributes such as shape, design, style and ingredients of a product.

Involvement. Extent of personal interest and engagement the consumer has with a product, brand or buying situation.

Jaycustomer. Lovelock's transfer of the jaywalker concept to those consumers who are over-awkward or malicious toward companies, brands and/or marketers.

Joint decision-making refers to two or more consumers making decisions jointly. Within the household context, it could be husband and wife engaging in joint decision making.

Jungian motivation. Carl Jung proposed an alternative theory of the subconscious. Experiences that are equally unconscious but which derive from our previous ancestral existence(s) lead to motives that are hidden in the unconscious reflect a more spiritual collectivism from the past. He also proposed a series of 'archetypes', or image-types that we all possess, albeit at the unconscious level.

Key account. A customer having some strategic relevance for the buying firm

Kinesics. The use of body and movement as well as eye positioning to indicate feelings.

Kirton Adaption Innovation Inventory. Developed by Kirton to measure individuals' self-perceived cognitive styles. The main application in consumer research is to identify innovators who try different ways of solving problems and adaptors who do things in ways which are more familiar to them.

Knowledge. What we know and what we have stored in our memory as a function of learning. Knowledge can be of two types: objective knowledge which is the actual information about a stimulus stored in the memory and subjective knowledge which reflects our own perceptions of what or how much we know about the stimulus.

Lack of commitment refers to the condition of Western society in which individuals are increasingly unwilling to commit to any single idea, project or grand design.

Lateral involvement. Number of departments represented in a buying centre.

Law of effect. Behaviours which have pleasant consequences are repeated; those that have unpleasant outcomes are not.

Law of closure. Making 'whole' something that initially appears to be ambiguous or incomplete.

Learning (cognitive). The storing of a message in **memory** and the processing of message information by memory.

Legitimate power is where a consumer thinks that the position of the referent confers authority in the context concerned, for example, police officers in the law enforcement context.

Lifestyle. A mode of living that reflects consumers' opinions, values, attitudes and activities.

Lifestyle segments. Groups of consumers identified by marketers as per their modes of living which reflect their opinions, values, attitudes and activities.

Likert scaling. The presentation of a series of attitude statements to respondents and asking for their degree of agreement with each statement.

Lists. Lists of prospects (names and addresses and perhaps phone numbers) collected from, for example, subscribers to specialist magazines or competition entrants. There are also lists available from providers of geodemographic and contemporary lifestyle data.

Long interview refers to an in-depth face-to-face interview lasting for around an hour and a half during which the interviewer tries to understand what things mean to the person who is being interviewed.

Long-term memory. Organization and storage of new pieces of information, often tied up with other bits of information that already exist. Long-term memory can be categorized into semantic memory which refers to the organizing and storing of factual information (independent of context) and episodic memory which refers to the organizing and storing of information specific to a particular context (e.g. as to where and when an event happened).

Long-term orientation reflects the importance a society attaches to perseverance and values associated with preparing for and shaping the future, as opposed to a short-term, living-for-today orientation.

Looking-glass self. Consumers' perceptions of who they are based on their interpersonal interactions in the society and how others perceive them.

Loyalty. The tendency to repurchase a particular brand, variously conceived as a behavioural phenomenon (simply the rate at which the consumer chooses Brand A over other brands) and/or as an attitudinal phenomenon (the amount of positive affect the consumer has towards the brand, which may manifest itself behaviourally when an opportunity to purchase presents itself).

Mainstream marketers refer to marketers of mainstream brands and products.

Marital roles in decision-making refer to the role played by husband and wife in the decision-making process.

Market mavens. Consumers who transmit information about new products and services to others. They may or may not be early adopters themselves but act more as active gatekeepers of information about a range of new products.

Market-orientated. An extrovert attitude on the part of the firm which (logically, if not always chronologically) begins by establishing what consumers want and are willing to pay for before commencing production and distribution.

Marketing concept. The business philosophy that sees the consumer as the final arbiter of commercial success which leads the firm to orientate all of its functions and efforts towards the profitable satisfaction of consumer wants.

McDonaldization. The spread of American culture across other societies.

Meaning-transfer model. The meaning originally resides in the culturally constituted world, which is the world of everyday experiences in which consumers live and make sense of marketing stimuli. The meaning is then disengaged and transferred to consumer goods via macro mechanisms such as advertising and fashion systems. The meaning is finally transferred to individual consumers through a range of symbolic actions such as gift exchange rituals, possession rituals, grooming rituals and divestment rituals.

Means–end chains. The sequence in which consumers' perceptions of product attributes and outcomes reveal their basic values.

Memetics. The theory that humans' imitative behaviour can be explained in terms of ideas (memes) that 'jump from brain to brain' as people observe others' behaviour. Just as the gene is the replicator in natural selection, so memes are cultural replicators that communicate socially acceptable practices.

Memory. The storing of information and its processing by association with other mental information such as attitudes, motivations and ideas.

Misbehaviour. Behaviour by consumers that crosses the line of what is usually accepted as appropriate in the purchase process and in buying, consumption and disposal situations.

Modified Re-buying. A buying situation in which an organization decides to buy a product/service again but with different criteria.

Moore's Chasm. The particularly large gulf between the early adopters and early majority in high tech markets.

Mosaic. The brand name of Experian's geodemographic system, developed by Richard Webber after he moved from CACI where he had pioneered **Acorn**, the first geodemographic system in UK.

Motivation. The energizing state that arises from internal needs and drives and orients the individual's behaviour towards achieving an appropriate goal. A complete state of motivation requires both the inner drive and the external means of satisfying it to be present. Positive motivation is that which leads to **approach** behaviour; negative motivation that which leads to **avoidance**.

Motives. *See* **Motivation**.

Multiple identities refer to the notion that a person can experience many identities at a given time.

Multisensory brands. Brands that appeal to two or more senses rather than a single modality.

NBD/LSD Model. The Negative Binomial Distribution/Logarithmic series distribution model estimates the number of consumers who might lapse in their buying in one time period which follows another period in which they had bought. The model requires the average frequency of purchase of the product concerned within a specific time period and the percentage of the total number of consumers buying the same product in the same time period.

Needs and wants. A need can be understood as an internal state of an organism that it will strive to fulfil *or* as whatever will serve to overcome that inner state of deprivation. Needs in the first sense are often treated as drives that arise biologically (e.g. towards food or sex) or as resulting from social pressures (e.g. for status). Hence they are often referred to as biogenic or socio- (or psycho-) genic. In either case, they denote what the organism requires in order to function as a biological or social entity. Wants, which are whatever the individual desires and demands, are generally thought to arise entirely from acquired social and psychological considerations. Hence, we may be born with a need for food but develop a taste or want for chocolate chip cookies as a result of social experience.

Negative reference group is a group or individual whose behaviour, beliefs or values the individual deliberately avoids adopting as their own.

Net Promoter Score. The net difference between detractors and promoters as measured by questioning whether the consumer would recommend a company/brand.

Neurolinguistic programming. How individuals think, process information and experience their world.

New Task Buying. A buying situation in which an organisation buys a product or a service for the first time.

Noise. Distraction from an advertising message as a result of clutter.

Non-membership groups. A notion that consumers may not formally belong to a particular reference group but still aspire to belong to the group.

Normative influence. see utilitarian influence

NRS. The National Readership Survey provides data on readership patterns and profiles for national and local print media.

Nuclear family normally consists of two spouses and a small number of children living together and representing one family unit.

Online communities refer to communities that exist in the virtual environment, like the Internet.

Operant conditioning. An operant is a behavioural response that *operates* on the environment to produce positive or aversive consequences ('rewards' and 'punishments') that control the rate of future emission of the response. Operant conditioning is the process in which an operant response is controlled by its being followed by a reinforcer or punisher. Any feature of the environment that is present when this conditioning occurs may come to control the response, even when the reinforcer or punisher is not presented. Operant conditioning is said to be complete when this (discriminative) stimulus alone controls the rate of the response.

Opinion formers. Individuals who actively and deliberately shape and form the thoughts of others, from a (usually impersonal) position of some perceived level of expertise, for example, motoring journalists or TV personalities.

Opinion leaders. Individuals who are seen, usually at a more local peer group level, to be knowledgeable about a specific product category and from whom others are willing to take advice.

Opinion shapers. See opinion leaders.

Oppositional brand loyalty refers to loyalty towards a specific brand, based on a perceived opposition and dislike of competing brands.

Organizational buying. 'A decision making process carried out by individuals, in interaction with other people, in the context of a formal organization' (Webster and Wind, 1972:157.)

Outer-directed. Riesman used social character to explain personality type. Other-directeds' values, attitudes and behaviour are largely acquired from others.

Paralanguage. The conscious and deliberate choice of words in conveying information.

Parent power. Some parents want their children to project a certain image and the appeal reflects parents' (sometimes) desire to live through their children.

Passive learning. The effects of information on consumers' mental structures which take place even though they are not involved with the message.

Peer. Immediate associates such as friends or colleagues.

Perceived risk. This is where consumers see some less desirable consequences of a purchase or product and can often, but not always, be greater when the purchase is expensive and the product more complex.

Perceptual defence. The avoidance of messages which are incongruent with one's current world view.

Perceptual vigilance. Where consumers seek messages that are of interest to them.

Perceptual maps. The mental dimensions on which consumers construe brands in order to categorize and compare them.

Peripheral route to persuasion. Attitude change that results from the individual's limited level of involvement with the message.

Perceptual vigilance. Being open to what one is interested in to the extent of seeking information about it.

Peripheral vision. Messages not in our central path of vision, the core of one's eye and here, left peripheral messages being dealt with in the right brain and right peripheral message elements dealt with in the left hemisphere.

Permission marketing. The equivalent of an 'opt-in', where consumers agree to specific elements of a relationship with an organization.

Persistent attention. Continued scanning of information once its relevance has been established.

Personality. The amalgam of an individual's physical, psychological and social characteristics as reflected in their natural and acquired behaviour, opinions and ideals.

Personality big five. Extraversion, openness, agreeableness, conscientiousness and emotional stability.

Personality traits. Specific characteristics which individuals possess and display in responding to the social and physical environment. Examples are aggression, honesty, anxiety, independence and innovativeness.

Personality types. Classifications of individuals into groups, such as extrovert or introvert.

Pester power refers to the influences exerted by children on the decision-making of parents.

Planned impulse buying – act of purchasing driven by unplanned and sudden decision making based on prior intentions to buy.

Pleasure principle. The human tendency to seek satisfaction without necessarily considering the consequences for others. In Freudian theory these drives are unconscious.

Pluralism refers to the notion that many different distinct ethnic, religious and cultural groups coexist and are tolerated within a society and considered to be desirable and socially beneficial.

Possible selves. The notion that consumers can have more than one self.

Positive pester power. Children's exposure to (e.g.) social issues could lead to pestering of their parents for the purchases of environmentally friendly and more healthy products.

Postmodern. The late 20th century and early 21st century have seen a dramatic expansion of communications and the trend away from standardization of mass production. There is also pluralism in society and as a result there is a fragmentation of society and many different ways for consumers to behave.

Postmodern consumer is a consumer showing or revealing the cultural tendencies associated with postmodernity.

Postmodern consumer behaviour is consumer behaviour showing or revealing the cultural tendencies associated with postmodernity.

Postmodern society refers to the Western society with all the features and characteristics associated with postmodernity.

Post-purchase. The stage in the buying process in which the consumer evaluates what they have bought and reaches a level of satisfaction or dissatisfaction with it.

Power distance is the extent to which less powerful members of a society or country accept the fact that power is not distributed equally in the society.

Primacy effect. Where the most recent and similarly presented stimulus determines how the newly presented stimulus is perceived.

Primary group is normally the immediate group to which one belongs, such as family and friends.

Privately consumed luxuries are those products that are not visible to others when consumed, are exclusive and conspicuous in nature and are not commonly owned.

Privately consumed necessities are products that are not observed when being consumed and are also commonly owned by others.

Probability theory. The statistics of calculating the likelihood of an event occurring.

Procurement. A term that is sometimes used to describe the process of sourcing products and services for an organization.

Product attributes refer to features such as price, quality and durability.

Product life cycle. Products and services are seen to ape the biological time clock and have stages of development, maturity and decline.

Product-orientated. A tendency of firms to look inwardly towards what they are capable of producing rather than outwardly towards what consumers want to buy.

Profiling. Data about the characteristics of consumers can help categorize them into different segments for targeting.

Projective tests. Methods of revealing consumers' underlying motivations and understandings by requiring them to project themselves into situations of purchase and consumption in which they role-play or describe the behaviour of others, explaining what is going on in the situation and why.

Proquinquity. Include the physical closeness to the group of its members or potential members.

Proxemics. How people use physical space to convey information.

Psychogenic drives. Needs that are socially inculcated, e.g. for prestige.

Psychographics. The identification, analysis and use of consumer personality, lifestyle and self-concept characteristics to understand consumer behaviour.

Publicly consumed luxuries are those products that are visible to others when consumed, are exclusive and conspicuous in nature and are not commonly owned.

Publicly consumed necessities are products that are observed when being consumed and are also commonly owned by others.

Purchase request behaviour. Another term sometimes used for pester power.

Purchaser is the person who actually carries out the final purchase.

Pure impulse buying. Act of purchasing driven by unplanned and sudden decision making based on novelty or escapism.

Reach. The percentage of target audience that would be exposed at least once to an advertised message in a medium.

Reactance. Consumer's motive responsible for their desire to maintain freedom.

Reality principle. The pleasure principle is constrained by how the individual sees societal norms and behaviour.

Reasoning. The process in which consumers deduce conclusions from information.

Reciprocal trading. Two-way trading between organizations.

Recognition method. A technique of advertising research that involves showing an advertisement to consumers and asking whether they have seen it before.

Reference group refers to any individual or a group of individuals that can significantly influence one's behaviour.

Referent power operates when a consumer identifies with or admires a group or person.

Reinforcement. A behavioural consequence that increases the frequency with which the behaviour is subsequently enacted.

Relational buying. Reciprocally favourable emotional engagement between company and consumer in the buying context.

Relational selling strategy. A strategic approach adopted by an organization with a view to developing long-term and mutually beneficial relationships with some of its customers (Guenzi *et al.*, 2007).

Reminder impulse buying. Act of purchasing driven by unplanned and sudden decision making based on memory recall (examples are stocks are low or recall of a purchase intention).

Repeat purchasing. Degrees of purchase recurrence.

Retention. Retaining customers over a period of time. It is often cheaper to develop strategies to keep customers than to acquire new customers.

Retro Marketing. Consumer nostalgia for an earlier era can inform product design, fashion design, product re-launches and advertising campaigns.

Reward power operates when responding favourably to the referent results in positive reinforcement by the group.

RFID. Radio frequency identification (tags) which emit a radio signal which can be decoded by relevant radio receivers. Used mostly to track items through the supply chain.

RFM. Recency, frequency and monetary value of individual consumers' buying patterns with a specific company.

Ritual refers to a kind of expressive, symbolic activity constructed of multiple behaviours that occur in a fixed, episodic sequence, which is repeated over time.

Schema discrepancy. The capacity of a message to evoke surprise by being unusual or discrepant.

Scripted behaviour. Refers to behaviour that occurs repeatedly and is pre-programmed, predetermined with some degree of predictability attached.

Secondary group is made up of more than one primary group such as a students' union.

Selective attention. Consumers can notice certain messages but even if exposed to others they can screen them out and avoid attending to them.

Selective exposure. Consumers, consciously or subconsciously, avoid some media but not others.

Selective perception. Consumers can extract from a message certain elements which fit their own frame of reference, even if they tend to distort the intention of the message.

Selective retention. Consumers retain elements of a message which might not reflect the intention of that message, but which are congruent with the consumer's frame of reference.

Self-actualization. The state of having fulfilled all of one's potential capacities. In Maslow's hierarchy of needs system, this is the final stage of development, achievable only after the individual has fulfilled all their biogenic and sociogenic needs.

Self-concept refers to the totality of thoughts and feelings that a person has of himself or herself as an object.

Self-expression refers to an individual expressing personality, feelings and ideas (within the marketing context, this is said to happen via brand consumption).

Self-image. How we see ourselves.

Self-image congruence. A subjective experience generated due to a psychological comparison involving an interaction between product-user image and a person's self-concept.

Semantic differential. A method of attitude assessment that requires respondents to place an object on a seven- or nine-point scale bounded by antonyms.

Semiotics. The study of how meaning is derived. An object might be a brand and it's advertising message is a sign. How a receiver of the message gives meaning to it and the brand is the process of semiotics.

Senses. Usually taken to include the modalities of vision, hearing, smell, taste and touch, but sometimes including also balance.

Sensory memory. Very short representation of information while being processed via our senses. The sensory memory forms automatically without any attention or interpretation.

Sexual Identity. How a person sees themselves along a continuum from masculinity to femininity, regardless of biological gender.

Short-term memory. Conscious and active processing of incoming information but limited in capacity and is short lived meaning information is stored for short durations, even as little as 30 seconds.

Situational involvement. Interest in a product category that is sustained only by the current situation and which dissipates when the situation changes.

Smart Trolleys. In-store customer trolleys that are equipped with technology such as view screens which can show targeted messages.

Social class. The stratification of society.

Social grade. Marketing's surrogate for social class in the UK, based on occupation of the chief income earner in a household.

Social judgement theory. A highly involved consumer might not accept many other opinions on the issue (they have a narrow 'latitude of acceptance') and instead might reject many others (a wider latitude of rejection).

Social network data. The use by marketers of personal profile and other data posted by individuals on social networking sites such as Facebook.

Social power is the ability or official capacity to exercise control and authority by a group of individuals acting together.

Social pressure is a type of pressure exerted on an individual by members of their social group.

Social self-image congruence. A subjective experience generated due to a psychological comparison involving an interaction between product-user image and a person's social self.

Socialization is the process by which a person, beginning at infancy, acquires the habits, beliefs and accumulated knowledge of society through education and training for adult status.

Sociogram is a sociometric chart plotting the structure of interpersonal relations in a group situation.

Sociometry is the quantitative study of interpersonal relationships in populations, especially the study and measurement of preferences.

Source attractiveness. This is where the consumer perceives the source of a message to be similar to themselves. This has been found to increase the persuasiveness of the source.

Source credibility. This is when the source of a message is perceived as having relevant expertise and to be trustworthy.

Standardization refers to products and marketing activities being modified according to cultural, regional and national differences.

Stochastic models. These models make predictions, usually based on probabilities, about repeat purchasing using longitudinal data.

Store Atmospherics. In-store techniques that target consumers' senses, such as the use of colour, lighting, aromas.

Straight Re-buying. A buying situation in which an organization routinely re-purchases previously bought items without any modifications to the product/service specification.

Subcultures refer to groups within a society, which possess distinctive characteristics. The term can also be used to refer to a distinctive subgroup of society that self selects on the basis of a shared commitment to a particular product class, brand, or consumption activity.

Subliminal messages. Persuasive influences that affect behaviour at the unconscious level without the individual who is subject to them registering that they have impinged upon them.

Suggestion impulse buying- act of purchasing driven by unplanned and sudden decision making without any prior knowledge of the product.

Superego. *See* **Freudian motivation**.

Symbolic interactionism. There is meaning that consumers attach to many things, often at a symbolic level. The meaning of any product or consumption situation is dependent upon how the consumer interprets the symbols.

Syncratic decisions refer to those decisions that are taken out of mutual consent with a second party.

Target Group Index (TGI). One of the most significant sources of consumer data, based on survey research conducted by the British Market Research Bureau (BMRB). The survey was launched in 1969 in the UK but is now run in over 60 countries. In the UK the fieldwork is conducted throughout the year, from an annual sample size of around 24 000 adults and data released quarterly. The data presents profiles of consumers in many product-markets and includes demographic and lifestyle data.

Technology Acceptance Model. Davis' extension of attitude modelling to include perceived ease of use, perceived usefulness and further refined to include a subjective norm.

Terminal values. Things desired as ends in themselves.

Theory of the triple appeal. The view that in order to be successful in persuading an audience, a message must appeal simultaneously to the **id, ego** and **superego**. A message that appeals only to the id will provoke a counter-appeal from the superego which will render the message unpersuasive. It is necessary therefore that the message assuage the superego as well as making a guarded appeal to the id. An appeal only to the superego will tend to invite conformity to it which will not arouse any of the want-generating mechanisms controlled by the id; such a message is unlikely to be persuasive unless the advertiser is promoting a very socially acceptable behaviour, such as altruism. An appeal to the ego (reason) alone is likely to be ineffective because it engenders neither an id-related desire nor the mental conflict whose resolution is likely to be achieved by buying the product advertised.

Think products. Products that the consumer considers primarily by reasoning about them, e.g. in terms of their functional benefits.

Third-person tests. Methods of revealing consumers' motivations and understandings by involving the idea of a typical consumer of a particular product or brand about whom the respondent is asked such questions as 'What is she like? 'Why does she buy this?' In this way, the respondent may more readily provide access to her own feelings and motives than if she is asked 'head-on' what she thinks.

Traditional lifestyle. Anonymized market research which presents a series of attitude (**Likert**) statements reflecting the respondent's activities, interests and opinions. Generalized clusters of similar responses lead to the identification of the 'sorts' of consumers who fit the profile of each lifestyle segment but names and addresses are not available, in contrast to contemporary lifestyle research.

Traits. Some unique and distinguishing qualities or characteristics that consumers possess as individuals.

Transactional data. Data from individual purchase transactions with a company. Over time, what a consumer buys from a company can provide useful information to predict future purchasing behaviour. It can also identify the RFM scores of each consumer.

Tribe is a grouping of heterogeneous consumers, with different demographic features, who are capable of collective action and act as advocates for their causes.

TRI*M Model. TNS's proprietary model which weights overall rating of a company/service/brand, likelihood of recommendation and likelihood of re-buying and perceived advantage of dealing with the company rather than another.

Trust. The mutual favourable confidence between company and consumer. Each sees the other as being reliable and not likely to damage the other.

Two-sided arguments (two-sided appeals). Advertisements that provide counter as well as positive arguments about the pros and cons of buying a brand.

Two-step model of communications. Where information is communicated from an initial source to some form of intermediary and from there onward to a final receiver.

Unawareness set. Brands within a product or service category of which consumers do not know.

Uncertainty avoidance is the extent to which people in a country or society feel threatened by uncertainty and ambiguity and try to avoid them.

Undesired self. Marketing and other consumers can influence an individual's perception of self and some consumers will try to avoid appearing in particular ways as a result.

User is the person who makes practical use of the item bought.

Utilitarian influence occurs when a person complies or conforms to the aspirations and expectations of reference group because they perceive that their behaviour is visible or known to the group members and that the group can mediate some rewards or punishment.

Value expressive influence occurs when an individual uses a reference group to express their image and self-concept.

Values are enduring beliefs that a particular action or mode of conduct is personally or socially acceptable and desirable. Values include abstract social entities such as justice and mercy, as well as socially and marketing-contrived desires like fresh breath confidence and being a 'good' parent.

Vertical involvement. Levels of management involved in buying centre.

Vicarious learning. Learning as a result of observing the behaviour of others, especially when they are overtly rewarded or punished for their actions.

Viper. A data-mining package from SmartFocus, Bristol.

Virtual communities refer to communities that exist in the virtual environment, like the Internet.

Virtual groups refer to groups that exist in the virtual environment, like the Internet.

Virtual self image. The projection of a real or alternative self via online channels such as social networking sites.

Voluntary exposure. Wanting to see messages – for example opting-in to receive direct mail, mobile phone or email messages.

Wants. *See* **Needs and wants**.

Wearout. Similar to habituation, where the consumer has seen the message so many times that its effect is 'wearing out'.

Wife-dominant decisions are those decisions in which wife is the decision maker and/or exerts a major influence in the joint decision-making process.

Word of mouth (WOM). Communication with others over, for example, positive or negative experiences with brands or companies. Often, today, we can use 'WOM' to refer to 'word of mouse' because so much of this sort of communication is via computer/internet channels.

Word-of-mouth advertising. Consumers pass on information about brands, stores and companies to others, orally, or by others observing their behaviour.

Zapping. Channel-surfing or -hopping to avoid advertisements.

Zipping. Fast-forwarding through advertisements.

REFERENCES

Aaker J (1997) Dimensions of Brand Personality, Journal of Marketing Research, Vol 35, August, pp 347–356

Aaker J (1999) The Malleable Self: The Role of Self Expression in Persuasion, Journal of Marketing Research, Vol 36, February, pp 45–57

Aaker J and **Fournier** S (1995) A Brand as a Character, a Partner, and a Person: Three Perspectives on the Question of Brand Personality, Advances in Consumer Research, Vol 22 pp 391–395

Acland H (2001) Ruling Puts DM Industry Firmly on Back Foot, Marketing Direct, December

Adam Smith Institute (1998) The Millennial Generation, London

Addis M and **Holbrook** M B (2001) On the Conceptual Link between Mass Customisation and Experiential Consumption: An Explosion of Subjectivity, Journal of Consumer Behaviour, Vol 1 No 1 pp 50–66

Addison T (2005) More Science: More sense or nonsense? Admap, May, pp 24–26

Advertising Research Foundation (1964) Are There Consumer Types?

Ahmad R (2002) The Older or Aging Consumer in UK, International Journal of Market Research, Vol 44 No 3 pp 337–361

Ajzen I (1988) Attitudes, Personality and Behaviour, Milton Keynes, Open University Press

Ajzen I and **Fishbein** M (1970) The PredIction of Behaviour from Attitudinal and Normative Variables, Journal of Experimental Social Psychology, Vol 6, pp 466–487

Ajzen I and **Madden** T J (1986) Prediction of Goal-Directed Behaviour: Attitudes, Intentions and Perceived Behavioural Control, Journal of Experimental Social Psychology, Vol 22 No 5 pp 453–474

Alarcon C (2008) The Carphone Warehouse joins Nectar Scheme, Marketing Week, 14 February, p 9

Alba J W and **Hutchinson** J W (1987) Dimensions of Consumer Expertise, Journal of Consumer Research, Vol 13, No 4, pp 411–435

Alden D A, **Hoyer** W D and **Lee Chol** (1993) Identifying Global and Culture-Specific Dimensions of Humour, Journal of Marketing, Vol 57 No 2 pp 64–73

Alden D A, **Mukherjee** A and **Hoyer** W D (2000) The Effects of Incongruity, Surprise and Positive Moderators on Perceived Humor in Television Advertising, Journal of Advertising, Vol 29 No 2 pp 1–14

Alderfer C P (1972) Existence, Relatedness, and Growth, The Free Press, New York

Aldworth R (2005) in Beeston R (2005) Killing in the Name of Fashion, The Times, 31 March p 3

Allen D E and **Olson** J (1995) Conceptualising and Creating Brand Personality: A Narrative Theory, Advances in Consumer Research, Vol 22, pp 391–395

Ambler T (2002) Why Big Brother Believes Loyalty is Good for You, Marketing, 17 October, p 10

Amos C, **Holmes** G and **Strutton** D (2008) Exploring the Relationship between Celebrity Endorser Effects and Advertising Effectiveness, International Journal of Advertising, Vol 27, No 2, 209–234

Anderson E and **Jap** S D (2005) The Dark Side of Close Relationships, MIT Sloan Management Review, Spring, pp 75–82

Anderson J R (1976) Language, Memory and Thought, Erlbaum, Mahwah, NJ

Anderson J R (1983) The Architecture Of Cognition, Harvard University Press, Cambridge, MA

Anderson W T (1999) Communities in a World of Open Systems, Futures, Vol 31 pp 457–463

Andruss P L (2001) FedEx Kicks up Brand through Humor, Soccer and Line of Naked Men, Marketing News, 30 July, Vol 35 No 16 pp 4–5

Annenberg Public Policy Centre (1999) reported in **Lindstrom** M (2004) Child's Play, The Marketers, CIM, Maidenhead, July/August, pp 23–24

Anon (2006) Sizeable Issue, Precision Marketing, December, p 25

Anon (2007) Nectar boosts portal with 60 new retailers, Precision Marketing, 30 November, p 5

Argyle M (1969) Social Interaction, Methuen, p 220

Armstrong A and **Hagel** J (1996) The Real Value of On-Line Communities, Harvard Business Review, May/June, pp 134–141

Arnold M J and **Reynolds** K E (2003) Hedonic Shopping Motivations, Journal of Retailing, Vol 79, No 2, pp 1–20

Arnold E, **Price** L and **Zinkhan** G (2002) Consumers, McGraw-Hill

Arnould E J and **Thompson** C J (2005) Consumer Culture Theory (CCT): Twenty Years of Research, Journal of Consumer Research, Vol 31, No 4, pp 868–883

Arnould E J and **Wallendorf** M (1994) Market-Oriented Ethnography: Interpretation Building and Marketing Strategy Formulation, Journal of Marketing Research, Vol 31, No 4, pp 484–504

Arrowsmith (2007) reported by Benady (2007) Is It Still as Simple as ABC? Marketing Week, 2 August, pp 31–32

Asch S (1955) Opinions and Social Pressure, Scientific American, November

Atkinson J W (1958) Motives in Fantasy, Action, and Society, Van Nostrand, Princeton, NJ

Atkinson R L *et al.* (eds) (1999) Introduction to Psychology, 12th edn, Wadsworth

Austin C G, **Plouffe** C R and **Peters** C (2006) Anti-Commercial Consumer Rebellion: Conceptualisation and measurement, Vol 14, No 1, pp 62–78

Babin B J, **Darden** W R and **Griffin** M (1994) Work and/or Fun: measuring hedonic and utilitarian shopping value, Journal of Consumer Research, Vol 20, No 4, pp 644–656

Baier K (1969) What is Value?: An Analysis of the Concept, in **Baier** K and **Resher** E (eds), Values and the Future, Free Press, New York

Bailey J (1997) Tune in to the Power of the Viewing Public, PR Week, 17 October

Baines P (2006) Recapturing our Lost Youth, Management Focus, Cranfield, November , p 21

Barak B (1987) Cognitive Age: A New Multidimensional approach to measuring age identity, International Journal of Ageing and Human Development, Vol 25, pp 109–128

Barak B and **Schiffman** L G (1981) Cognitive Age: A Nonchronological Age Variable, Advances in Consumer Research, Vol 8 pp 602–606

Barnes R (2001) High Impact Mail, Marketing Direct, November, pp 51–53

Barrett L (2003) Getting Touch-Feely with UK Consumers, Marketing Week, 26 July p 22

Bashford S (2000) Generation X Uncovered, Marketing Direct, October, pp 17–19

Baty P (2005) Data Row Sparks Research Debate, Times Higher, 25 November, p 8

Baudrillard J (1999) The Consumer Society: Myths and Structures, Sage, London

Bauman Z (1992) A Sociological Theory of Postmodernity, in **Beilharz** P, **Robinson** G and **Rund- ell** J (eds), Between Totalitarianism and Postmodernity, MIT Press, Cambridge, MA, pp 149–162

Bayley G and **Nancarrow** C (1998) Impulse Purchasing: A Qualitative Exploration of the Phenomenon, Qualitative Market Research, Vol 1 No 2 pp 99–114

BBC (1997) Money Programme, 16 October

BBC (2002a) Century of the Self, November

BBC (2002b) Happiness Machine, Century of the Self, BBC 2, 29 April

BBC (2003) Beyond the Bar Code, In Business Series, Radio 4, 2 October

BBC News 24 (2005) What do people shoplift? http://news.bbc.co.uk/1/hi/magazine/4477596.stm (Accessed 28 November 2005)

Bearden W O and **Etzel** M J (1982) Reference Group Influence on Product and Brand Purchase Decisions, Journal of Consumer Research, Vol 9 pp 183–194

Bearden W O, **Netemeyer** R G and **Teel** J E (1989) Measurement Of Consumer Susceptibility To Interpersonal Information, Journal of Consumer Research, Vol 15, No 4, pp 473–481

Beatty S E and **Talpade** S (1994) Adolescent influence in family decision making: a replication with extension, Journal of Consumer Research, Vol 21 No 2, pp 332–341

Becker G S (1968) Crime and Punishment, Journal of Political Economy, Vol 762 pp 169–217

Beeston R (2005) Killing in the Name of Fashion, The Times, 31 March p 3

Belch G (1985) Parental and teenage Influences in Family Decision Making, Journal of Business Research, Vol 13, No 2, pp 163–176

Belk R (1985) Materialism: Trait aspects of living in a material world, Journal of Consumer Research, December, Vol 12, No 3, pp 265–280

Belk R W (1988) Possessions and the Extended Self, Journal of Consumer Research, Vol 15 pp 139–168

Belk R W, **Ger** G and **Askegaard** S (2003) The Fire of Desire: A Multisited Inquiry into Consumer Passion, Journal of Consumer Research, Vol 30 No 3 p 326

Bellenger D and **Korgaonkar** P (1980) Profiling the Recreational Shopper, Journal of Retailing, Vol 56, No 3, pp 77–92

Benady D (2008) The Positive Power of Pestering, Marketing Week, 18 January

Benjamin K (2007) It's DM – but not as we know it, Marketing Direct, February, pp 32–34

Benjamin K (2008) Center Parcs Gets Personal, Marketing Direct, April, p 35

Berger D (1986) Theory into practice: The FCB Grid, European Research, January, pp 35–46

Bernstein D (1975) Creative Advertising, Longman, Harlow, p 128

Berry W J (1980) Acculturation as Varieties of Adaptation, in **Padilla** A M (ed.), Acculturation: Theory, Models and Some New Findings, Westview Press, Boulder, Colorado, pp 9–46

Berry J W (1997) Immigration, Acculturation, and Adaptation, Applied Psychology: An International Review, Vol 46, Issue 1 (January), pp 5–34

Beverland M, **Lim** E, **Morrison** M and **Terziovski** M (2006) In Store Music and Consumer Brand Relationships: Relational transformation following experiences of (mis) fit, Journal of Business Research, Vol 59, pp 982–989

Blackmore S (1999) The Meme Machine, Oxford University Press

Block, R (1992) Sales Talk, BBC Radio 4, January

BMRB (2008) Target Group Index

Bodey K and **Grace** D (2007) Contrasting "complainers" with "non-complainers" on attitude toward complaining, propensity to complain, and key personality characteristics: a nomological look, Psychology & Marketing, Vol 24, No 7, pp 579–594

Bond C (1997) Frightened and Fifty, Marketing, 22 May, pp 27–28

Borna S and **Avila** S (1999) Genetic Information: Consumers' Right to Privacy Versus Insurance Companies' Right to Know: A Public Opinion Survey, Journal of Business Ethics, Vol 19 pp 355–362

Boseley S (2008) Drug Firm Accused of Death Rate Failures, Guardian, 16 April, p 10

Bowie D (1972) All the Young Dudes (for Mott the Hoople), Columbia Records

Bouchet D (1995) Marketing and the Redefinition of Ethnicity, in **Costa** J A and **Bamossy** G J (eds), Marketing in a Multicultural World, Sage, London, pp 68–104

Bourhis R Y, **Moise** L C, **Perreault** S, and **Senecal** S (1997) Towards an Interactive Acculturation Model: A Social Psychological Approach, International Journal of Psychology, Vol 32, No 6, pp 369–386.

Bourne F S (1956) Group Influence in Marketing and Public Relations, Foundation for Research on Human Behaviour, p 8

Bradshaw J (2007) Report Card 7, Child Poverty in Perspective: An Overview of Child Well-being in Rich Countries, UNICEF

Brennan I and **Bahn** K (2006) Literal versus Extended Symbolic Messages and Advertising effectives, Psychology and Marketing, Vol 23, No 4, pp 273–295

Brindle D (1999) Census Check on Partners, Guardian, 5 March, p 12

Bristow L, **Tinson** J and **Nancarrow** C (2005) How to Target Movers and Shakers, Admap, May, pp 40–42

British Market Research Bureau (1988) The Target Group Index

Brokaw T (1993) The Lost Generation, The Brokaw Report, Livingston, Burelle's Information Services, New Jersey

Brook R (2005) Evidence to the Parliamentary Select Committee (2005) Influence of the Pharmaceutical Industry, 14 October

Brown S (2003) Postmodern Marketing: Everything must Go! in **Baker** M (ed.) The Marketing Book, Butterworth Heinemann

Brown C (2004) Top Brands Wake up to the Rise of 'Parent Power', Precision Marketing, 1 January, p 11

Brown G H (1952–1953) Brand Loyalty – Fact or Fiction, Advertising Age, 23 June 1952 – January 1953 (series)

Broyles S J (2006) Subliminal Advertising and the Perpetual Popularity of Playing to People's Paranoia, Journal of Consumer Affairs, Vol 40 No 3 pp 392–406

Bruning E R (1997) Country of Origin, National Loyalty and Product Choice: The Case of International Air Travel, International Marketing Review, Vol 14 No 1 pp 59–74

Brunner J A and **Koh** A C (1988) Negotiations in the People's Republic of China, Journal of Global Marketing, Vol 2 No 1 pp 33–55

Brunso K, **Scholdere** J and **Grunert** K (2004) Closing the Gap between Values and behaviour: a means – end theory of Lifestyle, Journal of Business Research, Vol 57, pp 665–670

Buttle F and **Burton** J (2002) Does Service Failure Influence Customer Loyalty?, Journal of Consumer Behaviour, Vol 1 No 3 pp 217–227

Caillat Z and **Mueller** B (1996) Observations: The Influence of Culture on American and British Advertising: An Exploratory Comparison of Beer Advertising, Journal of Advertising Research, May/June, pp 79–85

Cairns W (2006) Bringing up baby with brands, Marketing Week, Vol 6, June, pp 30–31

Calder B J and **Ross** M (1973) Attitudes and Behaviour, General Learning Press, Morristown, NJ

Carling E (1999) Grappling with the Grey Market, Marketing Direct

Carey R (2004) The Anxiety of Influence, Research, October, 40–43

Caru A and **Cova** B (2006) How to Facilitate Immersion in a Consumption Experience: Appropriation Operations and Service Elements, Journal of Consumer Behaviour, Vol 5 No 1

Caru A and **Cova** B (2007) Consuming Experience, Routledge

Celsi R L and **Olson** J C (1988) The Role of Involvement in Attention and Comprehension Processes, Journal of Consumer Research, Vol 15 No 2 pp 210–224

Chaiken S (1980) Heuristics Versus Systematic Information Processing and the Use of Source Versus Message Cues in Persuasion, Journal of Personality and Social Psychology, Vol 39, November, pp 752–766

Chandon P, **Wansink** B and **Laurent** G (2000) A Benefit Congruency Framework of Sales Promotion Effectiveness, Journal of Marketing, Vol 64. No 4, pp 65–81

Chao P, **Wuhrer** G and **Werani** T (2005) Celebrity and Foreign Brand Names as Moderators of Country of Origin Effects, International Journal of Advertising, Vol 24 pp 2173–2192

Chapman M (1992) Social Anthropology and International Business: Some Suggestions, paper presented at the AIB Conference, Brussels, 20–22 November

Charret S (1999) Identity, Privacy and Personal Freedom: Big Brother V New Resistance, Paladin Press, Boulder, Colorado

Chaudhuri A (2002) A Study of Emotion and Reason in Products and Services, Journal of Consumer Behaviour, Vol 1 No 3 pp 267–279

Cheal D (1988) The Gift Economy, Routledge, London

Cheal D (1989) The Postmodern Origin of Ritual, Journal of Theory of Social Behavior, Vol 18 No 3 pp 269–290

Chesbro M (1999) Privacy for Sale: How Big Brother and Others are Selling Your Private Secrets for Profit, Paladin Press, Boulder, Colorado

Childers T and **Houston** M (1984) Conditions for a picture superiority effect on consumer memory, Journal of Consumer Research, Vol 11, p 652

Childers T L and **Rao** A R (1992) The Influence of Familial and Peer-Based Reference Groups on Consumer Decisions, Journal of Consumer Research, Vol 19 No 2 pp 198–211

Childwise (2006) The Monitor Trends Report, Norwich

Chiou J S, **Huang** C Y and **Lee** H H (2005) The Antecedents of Music Piracy Attitudes and Intentions, Journal of Business Ethics, Vol 57 pp 161–174

Chudry F and **Pallister** J (2002) The Importance of Ethnicity as a Segmentation Criterion: The Case of the Pakistani Consumers' Attitudes towards Direct Mail Compared with the Indigenous Population, Journal of Consumer Behaviour, Vol 2 No 2 pp 125–137

Churchill G A and **Suprenant** C (1982) An Investigation into the Determinants of Customer Satisfaction, Journal of Marketing Research, Vol 19, November, pp 491–504

CIM (2000) Consumer Research: Advertising and Gender, Chartered Institute of Marketing, Maidenhead

Clark R A and **Goldsmith** R E (2005) Market Mavens: Psychological Influences, Psychology and Marketing, Vol 22, No 4, pp 289–312

Clayton K (2008) cited in Flack J A (2008) Getting the Measure of Data, Marketing Week, 12 June

Clegg A (1996) Marketing Week: Cover Story: Colour Blind, 21 June

Clegg A (2008) An Open Door Policy, Marketing Week, 3 January, pp 11–18

Cleveland M and **Laroche** M (2007) Acculturaton to the Global Consumer Culture: Scale development and research paradigm, Journal of Business Research, Vol 60, No 3, pp 249–259

Cleveland M, **Barry** J B, **Laroche** M, **Ward** P and **Bergeron** J (2003) Information Search Patterns for Gift Purchases: A Cross National Examination of Gender Differences, Journal of Consumer Behaviour, Vol 3 No 1 pp 20–47

Cohan J A (2001) Towards a New Paradigm in the Ethics of Women's Advertising, Journal of Business Ethics, Vol 33 No 4 pp 323–337

Cohen A, **Stotland** E and **Wolfe** D (1955) An Experimental Investigation of Need for Cognition, Journal of Abnormal and Social Psychology, Vol 51 pp 291–294

Cohen J B (1967) An Interpersonal Orientation to the Study of Consumer Behaviour, Journal of Marketing Research, Vol 6 pp 270–278

Collins A (2004) reported in Taylor Nelson Sofres, Are You a Member of Your Kid's Generation? (http://www.tns-global/corporate/doc/0/2vmqq3513e0419caj02jk5176f/247) accessed 23 March 2004

Commuri S and **Gentry** J W (2005) Resource Allocation in Households with Women as Chief Wage Earners, Journal of Consumer Research, Vol 32 No 2, pp 185–195

Consumer Insight (2005) http://www.insightmc.com/insightmc_groups3.htm, last accessed 6 June 2005

Cooper P (2003) in Sclater I, Challenging Perceptions, Marketing Business, February, pp 16–17

Cooper P and **Tower** R (1992) Inside the Consumer Mind, Journal of the Market Research Society, Vol 34 No 4 pp 299–311

Cooper S, **McLoughlin** D and **Keating** A (2005) Individual and Neo-Tribal Consumption: Tales from the Simpsons of Springfield, Journal of Consumer Behaviour, Vol 4 No 5

Corey L G (1971) People Who Claim to be Opinion Leaders: Identifying their Characteristics by Self Report, Journal of Marketing, October, pp 48–53

Costa J A and **Bamossy** G J (1995) Perspectives on Ethnicity, Nationalism, and Cultural Identity, in **Costa** J A and **Bamossy** G J (eds) Marketing in a Multicultural World, Sage, London, pp 26–67

Coupland D (1991) Generation X: Tales for an Accelerated Culture, Abacus

Cova B (1997) Community and Consumption: towards a Definition of the Linking Value of Product or Services, European Journal of Marketing, Vol 31, No 3/4

Cova B and **Cova** V (2001) Tribal Aspects of Postmodern Consumption Research: The Case of French In-Line Roller Skaters, Journal of Consumer Behaviour, Vol 1, No 1, pp 67–76

Cova B and **Cova** V (2002) Tribal Marketing: The Tribalisation of Society and its Impact on the Conduct of Marketing, European Journal of Marketing, Vol 36, No 5/6, pp 595–618

Cova B and **Pace** S (2006) Brand Community of Convenience Products: New Forms of Customer Empowerment – the Case of 'My Nutella The Community', European Journal of Marketing, Vol 40 No 9/10 pp 1087–1102.

Cova B, **Kozinets** R and **Shankar** A (2007) Consumer Tribes, Butterworth Heinemann

Crawford G and **Melewar** T C (2003) The Importance of Impulse Purchasing Behaviour in the International Airport Environment, Journal of Consumer Behaviour, Vol 3, No 1, p 85

Croft M (2008a) Consumers in Control, Marketing Week, 10 April, pp 29–30

Croft M (2008b) Poster Sites Make Digital Switch, Marketing Week, 10 April, pp 33–34

Crosby LA, **Evans** KR and **Cowles** D (1990) Relationship Quality in Services Selling: an interpersonal influence perspective, Journal of Marketing, Vol 54 (July), pp 68–81

Cubitt E (2004) Battle Erupts to Exploit Joy of Sex, Precision Marketing, 23 April, p 12

Cubitt E (2008) A Clearer Picture, Data Strategy, March, pp 23–24

Cuellar I, **Nyberg** B and **Maldonado** R E (1997) Ethnic Identity and Acculturation in a Young Adult Mexican-Origin Population, Journal of Community Psychology, Vol 25, No 6, pp 535–549

Cummins B (1994) Time Pundits, Marketing Week, 8 April, pp 29–31

Dabholkar P A, **Thorpe** D I and **Rentz** J O (1996) A Measure of Service Quality for Retail Stores: Scale Development and Validation, Journal of the Academy of Marketing Science, Vol 24 pp 3–16

Darley W K and **Smith** R E (1995) Gender Differences in Information Processing Strategies: An Empirical Test of the Selectivity Model in Advertising Response, Journal of Advertising, Vol 24, No 1, pp 41–56

Daspin E (2000) The Cheater Principle, Wall Street Journal, August, pp 1–16

Datamonitor (2003) Report on the Grey Market, reported by Sclater I, Challenging Perceptions, Marketing Business, February, pp 16–17

Davidson A (2003) From Why to Z, Research, February, pp 31–33

Davies F D (1989) Perceived Usefulness, Perceived Ease of Use and User Acceptance of Information Technology, MIS Quarterly, Vol 13, No 3, pp 319–339

Davies A and **Fitchett** J A (2003) Crossing Culture: A Multi-Method Enquiry into Consumer Behaviour and the Experience of Cultural Transition, Journal of Consumer Behaviour, Vol 3, No 4, pp 315–330

Davis F D (1989) Perceived Usefulness, Perceived Ease of Use, and User Acceptance of Information Technology, MIS Quarterly, Vol 13, No 3, 319–339

Davis H L and **Rigaux** B P (1974) Perceptions of Marital Roles in Decision Processes, Journal of Consumer Research, Vol 1, No 1

Davis S, **Inman** J and **McAlister** L (1992) Promotion has a Negative Effect on Brand Evaluations – or Does It? Additional disconfirming evidence, Journal of Marketing Research, Vol 29, pp 143–148

Dawkins R (1989) The Selfish Gene, Oxford University Press, Oxford

Dawn Lerman D (2006) Consumer Politeness and Complaining Behaviour, The Journal of Services Marketing, Vol 20, No 2, p 92

De Wulf K, **Odenkerken-Schroder** G and **Iacobucci** D (2001) Investments in Consumer Relationships: A Cross Country and Cross Industry Exploration, Journal of Marketing, Vol 65, pp 33–50

Delozier W and **Tillman** R (1972) Self Image Concepts – Can they be used to Design Marketing Programs, Southern Journal of Business, Vol 7, No 4, pp 9–15

Deshpande R, **Hoyer** W D and **Donthu** N (1986) The Intensity of Ethnic Affiliation: A Study of the Sociology of Hispanic Consumption, Journal of Consumer Research, Vol 13, September, pp 214–220

DeSouza G (1992) Designing a Customer Retention Plan, Journal of Business Strategy, March/April, pp 24–28

Dick A S and **Basu** K (1994) Customer Loyalty: Toward an Integrated Framework, Journal of the Academy of Marketing Science, Vol 22 No 2 pp 99–113

Dishman P (1997) A Survey of Nudity in Advertising and Offensiveness Responses with Regard to Gender. Gender and Consumer Behaviour, 2, pp 164–170

Dittmar H (2007) A new look at 'compulsive buying': Self-discrepancies and materialistic values as predictors of compulsive buying tendency. Journal of Social and Clinical Psychology

Dittmar H (2000) Impulse Buying in Ordinary and Compulsive Consumers, in **Weber** E, **Baron** J and **Loomes** G (eds.) Conflict and Tradeoffs in Decision Making, Cambridge University Press, Cambridge

DMA (2001) Camouflage Case, Book of the Night, Direct Marketing Association, London

DMA (2004) Annual Award Case: Consumer Direct Mail (High Volume), Silver Award

DMA (2005a) Annual Award Case: FMCG Markets, Bronze Award.

DMA (2005b) Annual Award Case: Retail Markets, Bronze Award.

DMA (2007a) Annual Award Case: Customer Acquisition, Gold Award

DMA (2007b) Annual Award Case: Consumer Direct Mail (Low Volume) Silver Award.

DMA (2007c) Annual Award Case: Consumer Direct Mail (Low Volume) Gold Award

Dodd C, **Linaker** A and **Grigg** N P (2005) He's Gotta Have It: Shopping Dependency and the Homosexual Male Clothing Consumer, Journal of Consumer Behaviour, Vol 4 No 5

Donthu N and **Cherian** J (1994) Impact of Strength of Ethnic Identification on Hispanic Shopping Behaviour, Journal of Retailing, Vol 70 No 4, pp 383–393

Dorlich I (1969) Congruence Relationships between Self Images and Product Brands, Journal of Marketing Research, Vol 6, pp 80–84

Dornoff and **Tatham** (1972) Congruence between personal image and store image, Journal of the Market Research Society, January

Douglas M and **Isherwood** B (1980) The World of Goods: Towards an Anthropology of Consumption, New York

Duchessi P, **Schaninger** C M and **Nowak** T (2004) Creating Cluster-Specific Purchase Profiles from Point of Sale Scanner Data and Geodemographic Clusters: Improving Category Management at a Major US Grocery Chain, Journal of Consumer Behaviour, Vol 4 No 2 pp 97–117

DunnHumby (2007) Creating Customer Focused Product Ranges for Supermarket Petrol Stations, Data Strategy Awards, Data Strategy, December, p 25

Du Plessis (2005) Advertisers' new insight into the brain, Admap, May, pp 20–23

Durgee J F (1991) Interpreting Dichter's Interpretations, in **Hartwig-Larsen** H, **Mick** D G and **Alsted** C (eds), The Handbook of Consumer Motivation, Handelshøjskolens Forlag, Copenhagen, pp 52–74

Durvasula S, **Lysonski** S and **Andrews** JC (1993) Cross-cultural Generalizability of a Scale for Profiling Consumers' Decision-making Styles, Journal of Consumer Affairs, Vol 27, No 1, pp 55–65

Dwyer FR, **Schurr** PH and **Oh** S (1987) Developing Buyer – Seller Relationships. Journal of Marketing, Vol 51 (April), pp 11–27

Dylan (1965) Subterranean Homesick Blues, Warner Brothers Music

East R (1997) Consumer Behaviour: Advances and Applications in Marketing, Prentice Hall

Edmonson R (1993) reported in Levi Zips into Youth Market with Hip Ads, Marketing, 17 June

Egan J (2003) Back to the Future: Divergence in Relationship Marketing Research, Marketing Theory, Vol 3, No 1, pp 145–157

Ehrenberg A S C (1988) Repeat Buying: Theory and Applications, 2nd edn, Charles Griffin, London

Ekman P and **Freisen** V (2003) Unmasking the Face, A Guide to Recognising Emotions from Facial Expressions, Major Books

Ellen P S and **Bone**, P F (1998) Does It Matter if It Smells? Olfactory Stimuli as Advertising Executional Cues, Journal of Advertising, Vol 27 No 4 pp 29–40

Elliott R (1997) Existential Consumption and Irrational Desire, European Journal of Marketing, Vol 31, No 3/4, pp 285–296

Elliott R and **Elliott** C (2005) Idealised Images of the Male Body in Advertising: A Reader-Response Exploration, Journal of Marketing Communications, Vol 11, No 1, pp 3–20

Emslie L, **Bent** R and **Seaman** C (2007) Missed Opportunities? Reaching the ethnic consumer market, International Journal of Consumer Studies, Vol 31, No 2, pp 168–173

Engel J F, **Blackwell** R D and **Miniard** P W (1986) Consumer Behaviour, 5th edn, Dryden Press, Chicago; 8th edn, 1995

Errington F (1987) Reflexivity Deflected: The Festival of Nations as an American Cultural Performance, American Ethnologist, Vol 14, pp 654–667

Errington F (1990) The Rock Creek Rodeo: Excess and Constraint in Men's Lives, American Ethnologist, Vol 1, 7 pp 628–645

Escalas J E and **Bettman** J R (2005) Self-construal, Reference Groups and Brand Meaning, Journal of Consumer Research, Vol 32, No 3, pp 378–389

Ettenson R, **Smith** N C, **Klein** J and **John** A (2006) Rethinking Consumer Boycotts, MIT Sloan Management Review, Summer, pp 6–7

Evans F B (1959) Psychological and Objective Factors in the Prediction of Brand Choice, Journal of Business, p 39

Evans M (1989) Consumer Behaviour Toward Fashion, European Journal of Marketing, Vol 23 No 7 pp 7–16

Evans M (2005) The Data Informed Marketing Model and its Social Responsibility, in **Lace** S (ed.) The Glass Consumer: Life in a Surveillance Society, Policy Press/National Consumer Council

Evans M and **Blythe** J (1994) Fashion: A Paradigm of Consumer Behaviour, Journal of Consumer Studies and Home Economics, Vol 18 No 3, September, pp 229–237

Evans M and **Fill** C (2000) Extending the Communication Process, International Journal of Advertising, Vol 19 No 3 pp 377–396

Evans M, **Nairn** A and **Maltby** A (1999) Gender Differences for Financial Services Direct Mail, Journal of Financial Services Marketing, Vol 4 No 2 pp 139–162

Evans M, **Nairn** A and **Maltby** A (2000) The Hidden Sex Life of the Male and Female Shot, International Journal of Advertising, Vol 19 No 1, February, pp 43–65

Evans M, **O'Malley** L and **Patterson** M (2001) Bridging the Direct Marketing-Direct Consumer Gap: Some Solutions from Qualitative Research, Qualitative Market Research: An International Journal, Vol 4 No 1 pp 17–24

Evans M, **O'Malley** L and **Patterson** M (2004) Exploring Direct and Customer Relationship Marketing, Thomson Learning, London

Evans M, **Patterson** M, **O'Malley** L and **Mitchell** S (1997) Consumer Reactions to Database-Based Supermarket Loyalty Programmes, Journal of Database Marketing, Vol 4 No 4 pp 307–320

Evans M and **Rowland** G (1996) Semiotic Contexts: on Reading Bar Codes, Research, February, pp 12–13

Evans M, **Wedande** G, **Ralston** L and **van t'Hul** S (2001) Consumer Interaction in the Virtual Era: Some Solutions from Qualitative Research, Qualitative Market Research: An International Journal, Vol 4 No 3 pp 150–159

Eysenck H Y *et al.* (1975) An Encyclopaedia of Psychology, Fontana

Exon M (1998) The Moral Marketing Maze, Precision Marketing, 28 September, p 12

Experian (2004) MOSAIC Multimedia CD ROM Guide, Nottingham

Faber, R J, **Christenson**, G A, **De Zwaan**, M and **Mitchell**, J. (1995) Two Forms of Compulsive Consumption: Comorbidity of Compulsive Buying and Binge Eating, Journal of Consumer Research, Vol 22, No 3, p 296

Facebook (2008) http://en-gb.facebook.com/ accessed 16.8.08

Featherstone M (1991) Consumer Culture and Postmodernism, Sage, London

Feick L F and **Price** L L (1987) The Market Maven: A Diffuser of Marketplace Information, Journal of Marketing, Vol 51, pp 83–97

Felder D, **Henley** D and **Frey** G (1976) Hotel California, Fingers Music/Cass County Music/Red Cloud Music

Festinger L (1957) A Theory of Cognitive Dissonance, Stanford University Press, California

Festinger L (1964) Behavioural Support for Opinion Change, Public Opinion Quarterly, Vol 28 pp 404–417

Fifield P (2002) New Age Marketing, Marketing Business, December/January, pp 34–37

Firat A F, **Dholakia** N and **Venkatesh** A (1995) Marketing in a Postmodern World, European Journal of Marketing, Vol 29 No 1 pp 40–56

Firat A F and **Schultz** II C J (1997) From Segmentation to Fragmentation: Markets and Marketing Strategy in the Postmodern Era, European Journal of Marketing, Vol 31, No 3–4 pp 183–207

Firat A F and **Venkatesh** A (1993), Postmodernity: The Age of Marketing, International Journal of Research in Marketing, Vol 10 pp 227–249

Firat A F and **Venkatesh** A (1995) Liberatory Postmodernism and the Re-enchantment of Consumption, Journal of Consumer Research, Vol 22, December, pp 239–267

Fischer E and **Arnold** S J (1990) More than a Labor of Love: Gender Roles and Christmas Gift Shopping, Journal of Consumer Research, Vol 17 No 3 pp 333–345

Fishbein M (1973) The Search for Attitudinal-Behaviour Consistency, in **Kassarjian** H H and **Robertson** T S (1973) Perspectives in Consumer Behaviour, Scott Foresman, pp 210–220

Fishbein M and **Ajzen** I (1975) Belief, Attitude, Intention and Behavior: An Introduction to Theory and Research, Addison–Wesley, Reading, MA

Fitchett J A and **Smith** A (2002) Consumer Behaviour in an Unregulated Market: The Satisfactions and Dissatisfactions of Illicit Drug Consumption, Journal of Consumer Behaviour, pp 355–368

Flack J (2007) Military Operations Break Cover, Marketing Week, 24 May, pp 45–46

Flack J A (2008) Getting the Measure of Data, Marketing Week, 12 June

Flynn M (2005) How to Use the Senses for a Better Brand Experience, Admap, May, pp 31–33

Ford D (2004) Guest Editorial, The IMP group and International Marketing, International Marketing Review, Vol 21, No 2, pp 139–141

Ford R (2008) Top Police Officer Barbara Wilding: Gang life replacing family life, The Times, 2 July

Ford D, **Håkansson** H, **Gadde** L E and **Snehota** I (2003) Managing Business Relationships, Wiley, Chichester

Ford R, **Miles** A and **Rumbelow** H (2006) Banks are Dumping Account Details on the Street, Times, 28 October, p 1

Forsström B (2005) Value Co-Creation in Industrial Buyer-Seller Partnerships – Creating and Exploiting Interdependencies An Empirical Case Study, ABO Akademi University Press

Forster S (1997) Direct Marketing in the Travel and Tourism Sector, IDM lecture, UWE, Bristol, May

Fournier S (1995) The Brand as Relationship Partner: An Alternative View of Brand Personality, Advances in Consumer Research, Vol 22, pp 391–395

Fournier S (1998) Consumers and Their Brands: Developing Relationship Theory in Consumer Research, Journal of Consumer Research, Vol 24, pp 343–373

Foxall G R (1995) Cognitive Styles of Consumer Initiators, Technovation, Vol 15, pp 269–288

Foxall G R (2003) Consumer Decision Making: Process, Level and Styles, in **Baker** M (ed.), The Marketing Book, Butterworth Heinemann

Foxall G and **Bhate** S (1993) Cognitive Style and Personal Involvement as Explicators of Innovative Purchasing of Healthy Food Brands, European Journal of Marketing, Vol 27, No 2, 5–16

Foxall G R, **Goldsmith** R E and **Brown** S (1998) Consumer Psychology for Marketing, 2nd edn, International Thomson Business Press, London and New York

Friedman M (1985) Consumer Boycotts in the United States, 1970–1980: Contemporary Events in Historical Perspective, Journal of Consumer Affairs, Vol 19, No 1, pp 96–117

French J R P and **Raven** B (1959) The Bases of Social Power, in **Cartwright** D (ed.), Studies in Social Power, MI Institute for Social Research, pp 150–167

Fulberg P (2003) Using Sonic Branding in the Retail Environment: An Easy and Effective Way to Create Consumer Brand Loyalty While Enhancing the In-Store Experience, Journal of Consumer Behaviour, Vol 3 No 2, December, pp 193–198

Fullerton R A (2008): Mr MASS Motivations Himself: Explaining Dr Ernest Dichter, Journal of Consumer Behaviour, Vol 6, No 6, pp 369–382

Fullerton R A and **Pung** J G (2002) Repercussions of Promoting an Ideology of Consumption: Consumer Misbehaviour, Journal of Business Research, Vol 57, pp 1239–1249

Future Foundation (2000) Responding to the Future, London

Future Foundation (2007) cited in Anon (2007) UK Consumers give in to their indulgent impulses, Precision Marketing, 15 June, p 13

Future Foundation (2008) Collective Individualism, London

Gabriel Y and **Lang** T (1995) The Unmanageable Consumer, Sage, London

Gainer B (1995) Ritual and Relationships: Interpersonal Influences on Shared Consumption; Journal of Business Research, Vol 32 No 3, March, pp 253–261

Gardner A (2008) The 30 second seduction: How Advertisers Lure Women Through Flattery, Flirtation and Manipulation, Seal Press

Gatignon H and **Robertson** T S (1985) A Propositional Inventory for New Diffusion Research, Journal of Consumer Research, March, pp 849–867

Geertz C (1973) The Interpretation of Cultures, Basic Books

General Household Survey (2004) Social Survey Division of the Office of National Statistics, London

Gensch D and **Javagali** R (1987) The Influence of Involvement on Disaggregate Choice Models, Journal of Consumer Research, Vol 15, pp 210–224

Gentry W J, **Sunkyu** J and **Patriya** T (1995) Consumer Acculturation Processes and Cultural Conflict: How Generalizeable Is a North American Model for Marketing Globally?, Journal of Business Research, Vol 32, pp 129–139

Gentry H J W, **Putrevu** S and **Shultz** C J (2006) The Effects of Counterfeiting on Consumer Search, Journal of Consumer Behaviour, Vol 5, No 6

Geyskens I and **Steenkamp** J-B (2000) Economic and Social Satisfaction: Measurement and Relevance to Marketing Channel Relationships, Journal of Retailing, Vol 76, No 1, p 13

Gillespie M (2003) In Search of Lost Youth, Research February, pp 28–29

Gimba G J (1998) Color in Marketing: Shades of Meaning, Marketing News, 16, Vol 38, No 6, March, p 6

Gladwell M (2002) The Tipping Point: How little things can make a big difference, Abacus, London

Glover J (2007) Worlds Apart: Polls Find Parents Out of Touch, Guardian, 24 February, p 1

Goddin S (1999) Permission Marketing, Simon & Schuster, New York

Godliman M (2007) cited in Gorman M (2007) Climate Change hits US Retail, Marketing Week, 5 July 24–25

Goffman E (1959) The Presentation of Self in Everyday Life, Doubleday, New York

Gofton K (2001) Firms Fail to Relate to Customers, Marketing Direct, January, p 10

Goldsmith R E and **Flynn** L R (1992) Identifying Innovators in Consumer Product Markets, European Journal of Marketing, Vol 26, No 12, pp 42–55

Gonzalez-Benito O and **Gonzalez-Benito** B J (2005) The Role of Geodemographics in Retail Location Strategy, International Journal of Market Research, Vol 47, No 3, pp 295–316

Goode P (2008) reported in Turner C (2008) Ad Industry Eyes Phone Advances, Marketing Week Social Media and Search, April, pp 5–8

Goodhardt G, **Ehrenberg** A and **Chatfield** C (1984) The Dirichlet: A Comprehensive Model of Buying Behaviour, Journal of the Royal Statistical Society, Vol 147, pp 621–655

Goodman S (1997) as reported by Murphy D in Money Where your Mouth Is, P R Week, 9 October, pp 35–36

Gorman M (2007) Climate Change hits US Retail, Marketing Week, 5 July 24–25

Gorn G J (1982) The Effects of Music in Advertising on Choice Behavior: A Classical Conditioning Approach, Journal of Marketing, Vol 46, pp 94–101

Goulding C and **Shankar** A (2002) Age is Just a Number: Rave Culture and the Cognitively Young Thirty Something, European Journal of Marketing, Vol 38, No 5/6, pp 641–658

Graeff T R (1996a) Using Promotional Messages to Manage the Effects of Brand and Self-Image on Brand Evaluations, Journal of Consumer Marketing, Vol 13

Graeff T (1996b) Image Congruence Effects on Product Evaluations: The Role of Self Monitoring and Public/Private Consumption, Psychology and Marketing, Vol 13, No 5, pp 481–499

Graeff T (1997) Consumption Situations and the Effects of Brand Image on Consumers' Brand Evaluations, Psychology and Marketing, Vol 14, No 1, pp 49–70

Grass R and **Wallace** W (1974) Advertising Communication: Print Vs TV, Journal of Advertising Research, Vol 14, pp 19–23

Gravier E (2008) cited in Shanaham A. (2008) Why did France fall in love with McDonald's? Guardian, 24 July 2008, p. 3

Gray R (2004) Ethnic Insight, Marketing, 4 March

Grayson K and **Amber** T (1999) The Dark Side of Long Term Relationships in Marketing Services, Journal of Marketing Research, February, pp 132–141

Green H (1995) Welcome to Your Over-Friendly Supermarket, Independent on Sunday, 20 August, pp 10–11

Gross A C, **Banting** P, **Meredith** L and **Ford** I D (1993) Business Marketing, Houghton Mifflin

Grove S J, **Carlson** L and **Dorsch** M J (2002) Addressing Services' Intangibility through Integrated Marketing Communication: An Exploratory Study, Journal of Services Marketing, Vol 16, No 5, pp 393–411

Grubb E L and **Grathwohl** L H (1967) Consumer Self-Concept, Symbolism and Market Behaviour: A Theoretical Approach, Journal of Marketing, Vol 31, No 4, pp 22–27

Grubb E and **Hupp** G (1968) Perception of Self, Generalised Stereotypes and Brand Selection, Journal of Marketing Research, Vol February

Grubb E and **Stern** B (1971) Self Concept and Significant Others, Journal of Marketing Research, Vol August

Guardian (2004) Gifts to Doctors, 4 October

Guenzi P, **Pardo** C and **Georges** L (2007) Relational sSelling Strategy and Key Account Managers' Relational Behaviors: An exploratory study, Industrial Marketing Management, Vol 36, pp 121–133

Gummesson E (1994) Making Relationship Marketing Operational, The International Journal of Service Industry Management, Vol 5, No 5, pp 5–20

Gunter B (1998) Understanding the Older Consumer, Routledge

Gutman J (1982) A Means-End Chain Model Based on Consumer Categorisation Processes, Journal of Marketing, Vol 46, Spring, pp 60–72

Habershon J (2004) in Need to Know, Research, MRS, June, p 10

Haeckel (2001) reported in Mitchell A, Playing Cat and Mouse Games with Marketing, Precision Marketing, 16 March, p 14

Hafstrom JL, **Chae** JS and **Chung** YS (1992) Consumer Decision Making Styles: comparison between United States and Korean young consumers, Journal of Consumer Affairs, Vol 26, No 1, pp 146–158

Haire M (1950) Projective Techniques in Marketing Research, Journal of Marketing, Vol 14, pp 649–656

Haley R I (1968) Benefit Segmentation: A Decision Oriented Research Tool, Journal of Marketing, July, pp 30–35

Hallberg G (1995) All Consumers Are Not Created Equal, John Wiley & Sons

Hampton F (2008) Recommendation Generation, Marketing Week, 24 April, pp 34–35

Han C (1989) Country Image or Summary Construct?, Journal of Marketing Research, Vol 26, No 2, pp 222–229

Han C and **Terpstra** V (1988) Country-of-Origin Effects for Uni-National and Bi-National Products, Journal of International Business Studies, Vol 19, No 2, pp 235–255

Hansen T (2005) Perspectives on Consumer Decision Making: An Integrated Approach, Journal of Consumer Behaviour, Vol 4, No 6

Harrell G (1986) Consumer Behaviour, Harcourt Brace Jovanovich

Harris L and **Reynolds** K (2003) The Consequences of Dysfunctional Customer Behaviour, Journal of Service Research, Vol 6, No 2, pp 144–161

Harris L and **Reynolds** K (2004) Jaycustomer Behaviour: An Exploration of Types and Motives in the Hospitality Industry, Journal of Services Marketing, Vol 18, No 5, pp 339–357

Harris Research (1998) European Values Research Report, London

Harrison-Walker J L (2001) The Measurement of Word-of-mouth Communication and an Investigation of Service Quality and Customer Commitment as Potential Antecedents, Journal of Service Research, Vol 4, No 1, pp 60–75

Hassay D N and **Smith** M C (1996) Compulsive Buying: An Examination of the Consumption Motive, Psychology & Marketing, Vol 13, No 18, pp 741–752

Hawkins D, **Mothersbaugh** D and **Best** R (2007) Consumer Behaviour, Building Marketing Strategy, McGraw Hill, London

Haygarth (2007) Consumer Attitudes to the Environment, cited in Baxter T (2007) Lacking in Green Conviction, Marketing Week, 13 September, pp 28–29

Heald G (1982) A Comparison between American, European and Japanese Values, World Association for Public Opinion Research Annual Meeting, Maryland, USA, 21 May

Heald G (1993) Changing Values 1981–1990, Market Research Society Annual Conference, Birmingham

Healy D (2004) Select Committee on the Influence of the Pharmaceutical Industry, Westminster, October

Healy (2005) Evidence to the Parliamentary Select Committee, Influence of the Pharmaceutical Industry, 14 October

Heider F (1958) The Psychology of Interpersonal Relations, John Wiley & Sons, New York

Heilman C M, **Nakamoto** K and **Rao** A G (2002) Pleasant Surprises: Consumer Responses to Unexpected In-Store Coupons, Journal of Marketing Research, Vol 39, No 2, pp 242–252

Hemsley S (2007) Let the Music Play, Marketing Week, 19 April, pp 33–34

Henley Centre for Forecasting (1978) Planning Consumer Markets, London

Henley Centre for Forecasting (1992) Presentation to Market Research Society, 5 March, Bristol

Henry P C (2005) Social Class, Market Situation, and Consumers' Metaphors of (Dis)Empowerment, Journal of Consumer Research, Vol 31, No 4, pp 766–778

Herche J and **Balasubramanian** S (1994) Ethnicity and Shopping Behaviour, Journal of Shopping Centre Research, Vol 1 No 1, Fall, pp 65–80

Herxheimer A (2005) Evidence to the Parliamentary Select Committee, Influence of the Pharmaceutical Industry, 14 October

Hibberd B (2008) reported in Marie Claire (2008) Miss Bimbo Website Fury, 25 March

Hirschman A (1970) Exit, Voice, and Loyalty: Responses to Declines in Firms, Organizations, and States, Harvard University Press, Cambridge, MA

HM Government (2005) Concordat and Moratorium of Genetics and Insurance, Department of Health, London

Hoffbrand J (2006) Army Unleashes Youth Blitz, Precision Marketing, 3 November, p 1

Hoffbrand J (2007) Blurring the Line between Consumers and Producers, Precision Marketing, 5 May, p 12

Hoffbrand J (2008a) Debenhams Exits Nectar in Review of Loyalty Strategy, Precision Marketing, 8 February

Hoffbrand J (2008b) Data Breach to Spark Mass Boycott of Errant Brands, Precision Marketing, 10 August, p 2

Hoffbrand J (2008c) How Safe is Consumer Personal Data in your Hands, Precision Marketing, 2 May, p 11

Hofstede G (1980) Culture's Consequences, Sage, Thousand Oaks, CA

Hogg M K and **Bannister** E N (2001) Dislikes, Distastes and the Undesired Self: Conceptualising and Exploring the Role of the Undesired End State in Consumer Experience, Journal of Marketing Management, Vol 17, No 1–2, pp 73–104

Holbrook M B (1987) What is Consumer Research, Journal of Consumer Research, Vol 14, No 1, pp 28–32

Holbrook M B and **Schindler** R M (2003) Nostalgic Binding: Exploring the Role of Nostalgia in the Consumption Experience, Journal of Consumer Behaviour, Vol 3, No 2, pp 107–128

Holt D B and **Douglas** B (2002) Why Do Brands Cause Trouble? A Dialectical Theory of Consumer Culture and Branding, Journal of Consumer Research, Vol 29, No 1, pp 70–91

Holt-Hansen K (1971) Perceptual and Motor Skills, Vol 33, No 3, pp 101–103

Hong S T and **Wyer** R S Jr (1989) Effects of Country-of-Origin and Product Attribute Information on Product Evaluation: An Information-Processing Perspective, Journal of Consumer Research, Vol 16, No 2, pp 175–187

Hopkins N (2003) Advertisers Reject Thrills and Spills of the Race to Promote Programmes for Third World, Time Business, 19 April, p 55

Horgan S (2006) The Kids are All right, Marketing Week, 19 October, pp 30–31

Horney K (1950) Neurosis and Human Growth, Norton, New York

Houston F S and **Gassenhemer** J B (1987) Marketing and Exchange, Journal of Marketing, Vol 51, pp 3–18

Hovland C I, **Janis** I L and **Kelley** H H (1953) Communication and Persuasion, Yale, New Haven, CT

Hovland C I and **Weiss** W (1951) The Influence of Source Credibility on Communication Effectiveness, Public Opinion Quarterly, Vol 15

Howard J A and **Moore** W L (1982) Changes in Consumer Behavior over the Product Life Cycle, in **Tushman** M L and **Moore** W L (eds) Readings in the Management of Innovation, Pitman, Boston, MA, pp 122–130

Hoyer W D and **MacInnes** D J (2001) Consumer Behavior, 2nd edn, Houghton Mifflin, Boston

Humby C (2004) R is for Relevance, Annual IDM Lecture, London

Humby C, **Hunt** T and **Phillips** T (2003) Scoring Points: How Tesco Is Winning Customer Loyalty, Kogan Page

Humby C, **Hunt** T and **Phillips** T (2007) Scoring Points, Kogan Page, p 84

Hummerston G (2007) Client Customer Data 'Shambles', Precision Marketing, 23 March, p 1

Hummerston G (2008) Consumers Stay Loyal to Loyalty Cards, Precision Marketing, 8 February, p 12

Humphries J (1995) Institute of Management Conference

Hutt M and **Speh** T (1981) Industrial Marketing Management, CBS College Publishing, Illinios

IDM (2003) O2: Business Performance Award Finalist Case Study, Institute of Direct Marketing

Institute for Family Policy (2008) The Evolution of the Family in Europe 2008, European Parliament, Brussels

Introna L and **Powloudi** A (1999) Privacy in the Information Age: Stakeholders, Interests and Values, Journal of Business Ethics, Vol 22, pp 27–38

IpsosMORI (2005) Baines P (2006) Recapturing our Lost Youth, Management Focus, Cranfield, 21 November

Iyer GR and **Shapiro** JM (1999) Ethnic Entrepreneurial and Marketing Systems: Implications for the Global Economy, Journal of International Marketing, Vol 7, No 4, pp 83–110

Jack L (2007) A Charper for Copycats? Marketing Week, Vol 18, October, pp 22–23

Jackson M and **Fulberg** P (2003) Sonic Branding, Palgrave, Basingstoke

Jaffe L and **Berger** P (1994) The Effect of Modern Female Sex Role Portrayals on Advertising Effectiveness, Journal of Advertising Research, Vol 34, No 4, pp 32–42

Jagger M and **Richards** J (1965) (I can't get no) Satisfaction, Chess Studios, Chicago

Jamal A (1996) Acculturation: The Symbolism of Ethnic Eating among Contemporary British Consumers, British Food Journal, Vol 98, No 10, pp 14–28

Jamal A (1997) Acculturation and Consumer Behaviour: A Study of Cross Cultural Differences, Inter-Ethnic Perceptions and Consumption Experiences in Bradford, unpublished PhD thesis, University of Bradford, United Kingdom

Jamal A (1998) Food Consumption among Ethnic Minorities: The Case of British-Pakistanis in Bradford, UK, British Food Journal, Vol 100, No 5, pp 221–228

Jamal A (2003) Marketing in a Multicultural World: The Interplay of Marketing, Ethnicity and Consumption, European Journal of Marketing, Vol 37, No 11/12, pp 1599–1620

Jamal A (2004) Retail Banking and Customer Behaviour: A Study of Self Concept, Satisfaction and Technology Usage, The International Review of Retail, Distribution and Consumer Research, Vol 14, No 3, pp 357–379

Jamal A (2005) Playing to Win: An Explorative Study of Marketing Strategies of Small Ethnic Retail Entrepreneurs in the UK, Journal of Retailing and Consumer Services, Vol 12, No 1, pp 1–13

Jamal A and **Chapman** M (2000) Acculturation and Inter-Ethnic Consumer Perceptions: Can You Feel What We Feel?, Journal of Marketing Management, Vol 16, pp 365–391

Jamal A and **Goode** M (2001) Consumers and Brands: A Study of the Impact of Self-Image Congruence on Brand Preference and Satisfaction, Marketing Intelligence and Planning, Vol 19, No 7, pp 482–492

Jamal A and **Naser** K (2002) Customer Satisfaction and Retail Banking: an assesment of some of the key antecedents of customer satisfaction in retail banking, International Journal of Bank Marketing, Vol 20, No 4, pp 146–160

Jamal A and **Al-Mari** M (2007) Exploring the Effects of Self-Image Congruence and Brand Preference on Satisfaction: The Role of Expertise, Journal of Marketing Management, Vol 23, No 7–8, pp 613–629

Jamal A and **Gboyega** A (2008/9) Customer Employee Relationships: The Role of Self Employee Congruence, European Journal of Marketing, Vol 41 (forthcoming)

Jamal A, **Davies** F, **Chudry** F and **Al-Mari** M (2006) Profiling Consumers: A Study of Qatari Consumers' Shopping Motivations, Journal of Retailing and Consumer Services, Vol 13, No 1, pp 67–80.

Janda S and **Rao** C P (1997) The Effect of Country-of-Origin Related Stereotypes and Personal Beliefs on Product Evaluation, Psychology and Marketing, Vol 14, No 7, pp 689–703

Janiszewski C (1989) Preconscious processing effects, Journal of Consumer Research, June, pp 76–87

Jansson C, **Marlow** N and **Bristow** M (2004) The Influence of Colour on Visual Search Times in Cluttered Environments, Journal of Marketing Communications, Vol 10, September, pp 183–193

Japan Consumer Marketing Research Institute Tokyo http://www.jmrlsi.co.jp/english/sizing/insights/2004/cons2.gif

Jay R (2008a) Facebook Launches Mars Products Shopping Service, Marketing Week, 13 February

Jay R (2008b) Mars Launches first Myspace radio Show, Marketing Week, 20 May

Jay R (2008c) Sowing the Seeds of Change, Marketing Week, 29 May, pp 18–19

John D R (1999) Consumer Socialization of Children: A Retrospective Look at Twenty Five Years of Research, Journal of Consumer Research, Vol 26, December, pp 183–213

John A and **Klein** J G (2003) The Boycott Puzzle: Consumer Motivations for Purchase Sacrifice, Management Science, Vol 49, No 9, pp 1196–1209

John O P and **Srivastava** S (1999) The Big Five Trait Taxonomy: History, Measurement, and Theoretical Perspectives, in **Pervin** L A and **John** O P (eds), Handbook of Personality: Theory and Research, 2nd edn, , New York, Guilford, pp 102–138

Johnson H M (1962) Sociology, Routledge & Kegan Paul, pp 86–95

Johnston W J and **Lewin** J E (1996) Organisational Buying Behaviour: toward an integrative framework, Journal of Business Research, Vol 35, pp 1–15

Jones S (1995) Understanding Community in the Information Age, in **Jones** S G, Cybersociety: Computer-Mediated Communication and Community, Sage, Thousand Oaks, CA, pp 10–35

Jones T O (1996) Why Loyal Customers Defect, Keynote Presentation, IDM Symposium, 6 June London

Jones T O and **Sasser** W E (1995) Why Loyal Customers Defect, Harvard Business Review, pp 88–99

Kacen J J (2000) Girrl Power and Boyyy Nature: The Past, Present and Paradisal Future of Consumer Gender Identity, Marketing Intelligence and Planning, Vol 18, No 6/7, pp 345–355

Kamins M A (1990) An Investigation into the 'Match-Up' Hypothesis in Celebrity Advertising: When Beauty May Only be Skin Deep, Journal of Advertising, Vol 19, No 1, pp 4–13

Kanner B (1989) Color Schemes, New York Magazine, 22–23 April

Kassarjian H H and **Robertson** T S (1973) Perspectives in Consumer Behaviour, Scott Foresman, p 292

Katbamna M (2005) This article is not an advertisement – or is it? Independent Media Weekly, 4 April, p 21

Katz E (1960) The Functional Approach to the Study of Attitudes, Public Opinion Quarterly, Vol 24, pp 163–204

Katz E and **Lazarsfeld** P F (1955) Personal Influence, Free Press, New York

Kauffman S E, **Silver** P and **Poulin** J (1997) Gender Differences in Attitudes toward Alcohol, Tobacco and Other Drugs, Social Work, Vol 42, No 3, pp 231–241

Kaufman-Scarborough C (2001) Accessible Advertising for Visually-Disabled Persons: The Case of Color-Deficient Consumers, Journal of Consumer Marketing, Vol 18, No 4/5, pp 303–318

Keaveney S M (1995) Customer Switching Behaviour in Service Industries: An Exploratory Study, Journal of Marketing, Vol 59, pp 71–82

Keillor B D, **D'Amico** M and **Horton** V (2001) Global Consumer Tendencies, Psychology and Marketing, Vol 18, No 1, pp 1–19

Keller K L (1987) Memory Factors in Advertising: The Effect of Advertising Retrieval Cues on Brand Evaluations, Journal of Consumer Research, Vol 14, No 3, pp 316–333

Keller K L (2003) Brand Synthesis: The Multidimensionality of Brand Knowledge, Journal of Consumer Research, Vol 29, No 4, pp 595–601

Kempner T (1976) A Dictionary of Management, Penguin

Kenkel W F (1961) Husband Wife Interaction in Decision-Making and Decision Choices, Journal of Social Psychology, Vol 54

Key W B (1973) Subliminal Seduction, Signet, Englewood Cliffs, NJ

Key Note (2007) Ethnic Foods, September, Hampton

Kilby N (2006) Villains at the School Gate, Marketing Week, 21 September, pp 26–27

Kimberley S (2006) Nectar gets personal in local map mailing, Precision Marketing, Vol 25, August, p 2

Kimberley S (2008) Charities Blasted for £11.5m Waste, Precision Marketing, 22 February, p 1

King T and **Dennis** C (2006) Unethical Consumers: De-shopping behaviour using qualitative analysis of theory of planned behaviour and accompanied (de) shopping, Qualitative Market Research: An International Journal, Vol 9, No 3, pp 282–296

Kingdom J W (1970) Opinion Leaders in the Electorate, Public Opinion Quarterly, Vol 34, pp 256–261

Kirton M J (1994) A Theory of Cognitive Style, in **Kirton** M J (ed.), Adaptors and Innovators: Styles of Creativity and Problem-Solving, 2nd edn, Routledge, London, pp 1–36

Kitchen P and **Spickett-Jones** G (2003) Information Processing: A Critical Literature Review and Future Research Directions, International Journal of Market Research, Vol 45, No 1, pp 73–98

Klein N (2001) No Logo, Flamingo, London

Klein J G and **Ettenson** R (1999) Consumer Animosity and Consumer Ethnocentrism: An analysis of unique antecedents, Journal of International Consumer Marketing, Vol 11, No 4, pp 5–24

Klein J G, **Ettenson** R E and **Morris** M D (1998) The Animosity Model of Foreign Product Purchase: An Empirical Test in the People's Republic of China, Journal of Marketing, Vol 62, pp 89–101

Klein J G, **Smith** N C and **John** A (2004) Why We Boycott: Consumer Motivations for Boycott Participation, Journal of Marketing, Vol 68, pp 92–109

Komarovsky M (1961) Class Differences in Family Decision-Making, in **Foote** N N (ed.), Household Decision-Making, New York University Press

Kosfeld M, **Heinrichs** M, **Zak** P J, **Fischbacher** U and **Fehr** E (2005) Oxytocin Increases Trust in Humans, Nature, Vol 435 No 7042, 1 June, pp 673–676

Kotler P (1972) Marketing Management, Prentice-Hall, p 113

Kozinets R (1998) On Netnography: Initial Reflections on Consumer Research Investigations of Cyber-culture, in **Alba** J and **Hutchinson** W (eds), Advances in Consumer Research, Vol 25 pp 366–371

Kozinets R (1999) E-Tribalized Marketing? The Strategic Implications of Virtual Communities of Consumption, European Management Journal, Vol 17 No 3 pp 252–264

Knox J (2002) Archetype, Attachment, Analysis: Jungian Psychology and the Emergent Mind, Routledge, Abingdon

Kressmann F, **Sirgy** M, **Herrmann** A, **Huber** F, **Huber** S and **Lee** D (2006) Direct and Indirect Effects of Self Image Congruence on Brand Loyalty, Journal of Business Research, Vol 59, pp 955–964

Kring A M and **Gordon** A H (1998) Sex Differences in Emotion: Expression, Experience, and Physiology, Journal of Personality and Social Psychology, Vol 74, March, pp 686–703

Krugman H E (1965) The Impact of Television Advertising: Learning without Involvement, Public Opinion Quarterly, Vol 29 pp 349–356

Laaksonen P (1994) Consumer Involvement: Concepts and Research, Routledge, London and New York

Lace S (ed.) (2005) The Glass Consumer: Life in a Surveillance Society, Policy Press/National Consumer Council

Larkins V (2003) 10 million Tick Electoral Roll Opt-Out Box, Marketing Business, February, p 6

Larrington-Wright S (2008) cited in Kimberley S, Experts Blast Callous, Stupid Egg, Precision Marketing, 8 February, p 1

Laroche M, **Papadopoulos** N, **Heslop** L and **Bergeron** J (2003) Effects of Subcultural Differences on Country and Product Evaluations, Journal of Consumer Behaviour, Vol 2 No 3 pp 232–247

Larson E (1994) The Naked Consumer: How Our Private Lives Become Public Commodities, Penguin, New York

Lasswell H D (1948) The Analysis of Political Behaviour, Routledge & Kegan Paul

Lavidge R J and **Steiner** G A (1961) A Model for Predictive Measurements of Advertising Effectiveness, Journal of Marketing, Vol 25 pp 59–62

Lawson J (2007) Super Rich Set Agenda, Marketing Week, 12 July, pp 30–31

Lawson R W (1988) The Family Life Cycle: A Demographic Analysis, Journal of Marketing Management, Vol 4 No 1 pp 13–32

Laybourne P and **Lewis** D (2005) Neuromarketing: The Future of Consumer Research?, Admap, May, pp 28–30

Lazarsfeld P *et al.* (1944) The People's Choice, Duell, Sloan & Pearce Inc., New York

Lee M and **Lou** Y-C (1996) Consumer Reliance on Intrinsic and Extrinsic Cues in Product Evaluations: A Conjoint Approach, Journal of Applied Business Research, Vol 12, Issue 1, pp 21–29

Lee W-N and **Tse** D K (1994) Changing media consumption in a new home: acculturation patterns among Hong Kong immigrants to Canada, Journal of Advertising, Vol 23, No1, March, pp 57–70

Legg D and **Baker** J (1996) Advertising Strategies for Service Firms, in **Lovelock** C H (ed.), Services Marketing, 3rd edn, Prentice Hall

Leighton N (2004) They're Reading Our Minds, Sunday Times, 25 January, p 9

Lerman D (2006) Consumer Politeness and Complaining Behavior, The Journal of Services Marketing, Vol 20, No 2, p 92

Levitt T (1983) The Marketing Imagination, Free Press, New York

Lewin J E and **Donthu** N (2005) The Influence of Purchase Situation on Buying Center Structure and Involvement: a select meta-analysis of organizational buying behavior research, Journal of Business Research, Vol 58, pp 1381–1390

Lewis J, **Williams** A, **Franklin** B, **Thomas** J and **Mosdell** N (2008) The Quality and Independence of British Journalism, Cardiff University, Rowntree Trust, Mediawise Report

Lewisohn M (1988) The Complete Beatles Recording Sessions, Hamlyn, EMI, London, p 109

Liljander V and **Strandvick** T (1995) The Nature of Customer Relationships in Services, Advances in Marketing and Management, Vol 4 pp 141–167

Lindstrom M (2004) Child's Play The Marketers, CIM, Maidenhead, July-August, pp 23–24

Lindstrom M (2005) Sensing an Opportunity, Sensory Appeal, The Marketers, CIM, Maidenhead, No 10, February, pp 6–11

Littlewood F (1999) Attention Seekers, Marketing, 13 May, p 31

Loader B (ed.) (1998) Cyberspace Divide: Equality, Agency and Policy in the Information Society, Routledge, London, pp 3–16

London S (2003) Radio ID Tags Spread Waves of Anger among Privacy Activists, Financial Times, 1 March, p 1

Louden D L and **Della Bitta** A J (1993) Consumer Behaviour, McGraw Hill, New York

Lovell C (1997) IDM Guest Lecture, University of the West of England, 30 January, Bristol

Lovelock C (1994) Product Plus, McGraw Hill, New York

Lysonski S and **Durvasula** S (1996) Consumer Decision Making Styles: a multi-country investigation, European Journal of Marketing, Vol 30, No 2, pp 10–21

Madden T J, **Hewett** K and **Roth** M S (2000) Managing Images in Different Cultures: A Cross-National Study of Color Meanings and Preferences, Journal of International Marketing, Vol 8, No 4, pp 90–107

Maffesoli M (1996) The Time of the Tribes: The Decline of Individualism in Mass Society, Sage, London

Magrath A J (1992) The Death of Advertising has been Greatly Exaggerated, Sales and Marketing Management, Vol 144, No 2, February, pp 23–24

Mancuso J R (1969) Why Not Create Opinion Leaders for New Product Introductions?, Journal of Marketing, Vol 33, pp 20–25

Mann S (2008) Legal Column, Data Strategy, April, p 20

Mano H and **Oliver** R L (1993) Assessing the Dimensionality and Structure of the Consumption Experience: Evaluation, Feeling and Satisfaction, Journal of Consumer Research, Vol 20, December, pp 451–466

Manyiwa S and **Crawford** I (2002) Determining Linkages between Consumer Choices in a Social Context and the Consumer's Values: A Means-End Approach, Journal of Consumer Behaviour, Vol 2, No 1, pp 54–70

Marcus J (2007) US Medical Students say 'no' to firms' free lunches, The Times Higher, 21-28 December, p 10

Market Research Society (1981) Working Party Report on Social Grade, MRS, London

Market Research Society (2004) Occupation Groupings: A Job Directory, 5th edn, Market Research Society, London

Marketing Week (2008) ASA Condemns Littlewoods Ads, 10 January, p 6

Markus H R and **Kunda** Z (1986) Stability and Malleability of the Self Concept, Journal of Personality and Social Psychology, Vol 51, No 4, pp 858–866

Markus H R and **Nurius** P (1986) Possible Selves, American Psychologist, Vol 41, No 9, pp 954–969

Marsden P S (1998) Memetics: A New Paradigm for Understanding Customer Behaviour and Influence, Marketing Intelligence and Planning, Vol 16, No 6

Marsden P S (1999) Help Advertising Evolve: Clone Consumer Thought-Patterns, Admap, March, pp 37–39

Marx K (1867/1967) Capital, Vol 1, International Publishers, New York

May M (2005) Electoral Roll Reveals Final Opt-Out, Marketing Direct, February, p 7

May R (2005) Consumer White Paper 2004: Changing Consumption Patterns, Japan Consumer Marketing Research Institute, Tokyo, http://www.jmrlsi.co.jp/english/sizing/insights/2004/cons2.gif

McAlexander J H, **Schouten** J W and **Keonig** H F (2002) Building Brand Community, Journal of Marketing, Vol 66, No 1, pp 38–55

McCarthy E J (1977) Basic Marketing Learning Aid, Irwin, Homewood, IL

McClelland D C (1961) The Achieving Society, Van Nostrand, Princeton, NJ

McCormack H (2006) Record Breaking Flashmobbers Come Dancing, Independent, 2 December, p 15

McCracken G (1986) Culture and Consumption: A Theoretical Account of the Structure and Movement of Cultural Meaning of Consumer Goods, Journal of Consumer Research, Vol 13, June, pp 71–84

McCracken G (1988) The Long Interview, Sage

McDougall J and **Chantrey** D (2004) The Making of Tomorrow's Consumer, Young Consumer, Vol 5, p 4

McDermott L, **O'Sullivan** T and **Hastings** G (2006) International Food Advertising, Pester Power and its effects, International Journal of Advertising, Vol 25, No 4, 513–540

McGuire W (1974) Psychological Motives and Communication Gratification, in **Blummer** J F and **Katz** E (eds) The Uses of Mass Communications: Current Perspectives on Gratification Research, Sage, Beverly Hills, pp 106–167

McGuire W (1976) Some Internal Psychological Factors Influencing Consumer Choice, Journal of Consumer Research, Vol 2, No 4, pp 302–319

McKenzie S (1995) Distinguishing Marks, Marketing Week, 17 November, pp 13–15

McNulty C (2002) interview on BBC, Century of the Self, November

McNulty C and **McNulty** R (1987) Applied Futures: Social Value Groups, Taylor Nelson

McWilliam G (2000) Building Stronger Brands through Online Communities, Sloan Management Review, Vol 4, 1 No 3, pp 43–54

Mehta R and **Belk** R W (1991) Artifacts, Identity, and Transition: Favorite Possessions of Indians and Indian Immigrants to the United States, Journal of Consumer Research, Vol 17, No 4, pp 398–412

Mellis R (1997) as quoted in Bailey J, Tune in to the Power of the Viewing Public, P R Week, 17 October, p 7

Merton R K (1968) Social Theory and Social Structure, Free Press New York

Mesure S (2007) Passion for Python Puts Stars at War with Animal Rights Groups, Independent on Sunday, 12 August, p 12

Meuter M L, **Ostrom** A L, **Roundtree** R I and **Bitner** M J (2000) Self-service Technologies: understanding customer satisfaction with technology-based service encounters, Journal of Marketing, Vol 64, No 3, pp 50–65

Meyers-Levy J and **Maheswaran** D (1991) Exploring Differences in Males' and Females' Processing Strategy, Journal of Consumer Research, Vol 18, June, pp 63–70

Michaelidou N and **Dibb** S (2006) Product Involvement: An Application in Clothing, Journal of Consumer Behaviour, Vol 5, 442–453

Michie D (1998) Invisible Persuaders, Bantam Press

Mick D G (1986) Consumer Research and Semiotics: Exploring the Morphology of Signs, Symbols, and Significance, Journal of Consumer Research, Vol 13, No 2, pp 196–213

Middleton T (1997) The Pink Pound, Direct Response, February, pp 49–53

Midgely D and **Wills** G (1979) Fashion Marketing Lateral Marketing Thoughts, Bradford: MCB Prem, p 131

Miller R L (1962) Dr Weber and the Consumer, Journal of Marketing, January, pp 57–62

Milliman R E (1982) Using Background Music to Affect the Behavior of Supermarket Shoppers, Journal of Marketing, Vol 46, Summer, pp 86–91

Millward-Brown (2002) Brand Child Study, reported in Lindstrom M (2004) Child's Play, The Marketers, CIM, Maidenhead, July-August, pp 23–24

MINTEL (2001) Gay Lifestyles, May

MINTEL, (2004) Men's Underwear, March

Mishan E J (1971) 21 Popular Economic Fallacies, Pelican, Harmondsworth

Misra S and **Beatty** S E (1990) Celebrity Foundations of the Endorsement Process, Journal of Consumer Research, Vol 16, No 1, pp 310–321

Mitchell A (1996) You and Yours, Interview transcribed from BBC Radio 4, January

Mitchell A (2001) Playing Cat and Mouse Games with Marketing, Precision Marketing, 16 March, p 14

Mitchell A (2002) Permission to Target in Not a Licence to Spam, Precision Marketing, 12 July, p 14

Mitchell A (2004) Innovation must be at the heart of opt-in revolution, Precision Marketing, 13 August, p 12

Mitchell A (2006) Demand Mapping and the Art of Customer Attitude Profiling, Marketing Week, 9 November, pp 24–25

Mitchell A (2008) Google Gives Tesco Clubcard Information Technology Lesson, Marketing Week, 24 January, pp 26–27

Mitchell V W and **Walsh** G (2004) Gender Differences in German Consumer Decision-Making Styles, Journal of Consumer Behaviour, Vol 3, No 4, pp 331–346

Mittal B (2002) Services Communications: From Mindless Tangibilization to Meaningful Messages, Journal of Services Marketing, Vol 16, No 5, pp 424–431

Mittelstaedt R A, **Grossbart** S L, **Curtis** W W and **DeVere** S P (1976) Optimal Stimulation Level and the Adoption Decision Process, Journal of Consumer Research, Vol 3, pp 84–94

Mizerski R W, **Golden** L L and **Kernan** J B (1979) The Attribution Process in Consumer Decision Making, Journal of Consumer Research, Vol 6, No 2, pp 123–141

Moir A and **Moir** B (1998) Why Men Don't Iron: The Real Science of Gender Studies, HarperCollins, London

Molesworth M and **Suortti** J P (2002) Buying Cars on Line: The Adoption of the Web for High Involvement, High Cost Purchases, Journal of Consumer Behaviour, Vol 2, No 2, pp 155–168

Moore E S, **Wilkie** W L and **Lutz** R J (2002), Passing the Torch: Intergenerational Influences as a Source of Brand Equity, Journal of Marketing, Vol 66, No 2, pp 17–38

Moore G (1991) Crossing the Chasm, Harper Business, New York

Moreno J L (1953) Who Shall Survive?, Beacon House

Morgan R M and **Hunt** S D (1994) The Commitment–Trust Theory of Relationship Marketing, Journal of Marketing, Vol 58, pp 20–38

Morris C (2006) Transactional Data Comes of Age, Precision Marketing, December, p 24

Mortimer K (2001) Services Advertising: The Agency Viewpoint, Journal of Services Marketing, Vol 15, No 2, pp 131–140

Moschis G P (2003) Marketing to Older Adults: An Updated Overview of Present Knowledge and Practice, Journal of Consumer Marketing, Vol 20, No 6, pp 516–525

Moschis G and **Moore** R (1979) Decision-Making among the Young: A Socialisation Perspective. Journal of Consumer Research, Vol 6, September, pp 101–112

Mourali M, **Laroche** M and **Pons** F (2005) Individualistic Orientation and Consumer Susceptibility to Interpersonal Influence, Journal of Services Marketing, Vol 19, No 3, pp 164–173

Muk A (2007) Cultural Influences on Adoption of SMS Advertising: A Study of American and Taiwanese Consumers, Journal of targeting, Measurement and Analysis for Marketing, Vol 16, No 1, pp 39–47

Muk A and **Babin** J (2006) US Consumers' Adoption–non Adoption of Mobile SMS Advertising, International Journal of Mobile Marketing, Vol 1, No 1, pp 21–29

Muncy J and **Vitell** S (1992) Consumer Ethics: an investigation of the ethical beliefs of the final consumer, Journal of Business Research, Vol 24, pp 297–311

Muniz A M (1997) Brand Community and the Negotiation of Brand Meaning, in **Brucks** M and **MacInnis** D J, Advances in Consumer Research, Vol 24, Association for Consumer Research, Provo, UT, pp 308–309

Muniz A M and **O'Guinn** T C Jr (2001) Brand Community, Journal of Consumer Research, Vol 27, No 4, pp 412–431

Murphy D (1997) Money Where your Mouth Is, P R Week, 9 October, pp 35–36

Murphy D (2006) The Times, Direct Response, 22–23 November

Murray I (1995) Bare Faced Cheek of a Naked Butt, Marketing Week, 17 November, Vol 94

Murray R (2004) cited in Broseley S (2004) Junket Time in Munich for the Medical Profession – and its all on the drug firms, Guardian, 5 October

Myers J G (1967) Determinants of Private Brand Attitude, Journal of Marketing Research, Vol 4

Nairn A (2006) What's Going on These Days, Presentation at a Marketing and Strategy Research Seminar, Cardiff Business School, 8 November

Nairn A, **Ormond** J and **Bottomley** P (2007) Watching, Warning and Wellbeing: Exploring the Links, NCC

Nancarrow C and **Nancarrow** P (2007) Hunting for Cool Tribes, in **Cova**, B, **Kozinets** R and **Shankar** A (eds) Consumer Tribes, Butterworth Heinemann, London

Nancarrow C, **Wright** L T and **Alakoc** B (1999) Top Gun Fighter Pilots Provide Clues to More Effective Database Marketing Segmentation: The Impact of Birth Order, Journal of Marketing Management, Vol 15, pp 449–462

Nancarrow, C, **Nancarrow** P and **Page** J (2002) An Analysis of the Concept of *Cool* and its Marketing Implications, Journal of Consumer Behaviour, Vol 1, No 4, pp 311–322

Nancarrow C, **Tinson** J and **Evans** M (2004) Polls as Marketing Weapons: Implications for the Market Research Industry, Journal of Marketing Management, Vol 20, No 5–6, pp 639–655

National Consumer Council (NCC) (2007) Watching, Wanting and Wellbeing: Exploring the Links, London

Netemeyer RG, **Boles** JS, **McKee** DO and **McMurrian** R (1997) An Investigation Into the Antecedents of Organizational Citizenship Behaviors in a Personal Selling Context, Journal of Marketing, Vol 61, No 3, pp 85–98

Nokes B (1994) The Good the Bad and the Sexist, Marketing Week, Vol 11, February, pp 50–51

North A C, **Hargreaves** D J and **McKendrick** J (1999) The Influence of In-Store Music on Wine Selections, Journal of Applied Psychology, Vol 84, pp 271–276

O'Brien S and **Ford** R (1988) Can We at Last Say Goodbye to Social Class?, Journal of the Market Research Society, Vol 30, pp, 289–332

O'Donahoe S and **Tynan** C (1998) Beyond Sophistication: Dimensions of Advertising Literacy, International Journal of Advertising, Vol 17, pp 467–482

Oakenfull G K and **Greenlee** T B (2005) Queer Eye for a Gay Guy: Using Market-Specific Symbols in Advertising to Attract Gay Consumers without Alienating the Mainstream, Psychology and Marketing, Vol 22, No 5, pp 421–440

O'Flaherty K (2008) The Number 118 118 Launches London Taxi Campaign, Marketing Week, 6 June

O'Guinn T C and **Faber** R J (1989) Compulsive Buying: A Phenomenological Exploration, Journal of Consumer Research, Vol 16, No 2, pp 147–158

Oliver R L (1980) Cognitive Model of the Antecedents and Consequences of Satisfaction Decisions, Journal of Marketing Research, Vol 17, November, pp 460–469

Oliver R L (1993) Cognitive, Affective, and Attribute Bases of the Satisfaction Response, Journal of Consumer Research, Vol 20, No 3, pp 418–430

Oliver R L (1997) Satisfaction: A Behavioural Perspective on the Consumer, McGraw-Hill, New York

Oliver R L (1999) Whence Consumer Loyalty, Journal of Marketing, Vol 63, pp 33–44

Onkvisit S and **Shaw** J (1987) Self-Concept and Image Congruence: Some Research and Managerial Implications, Journal of Consumer Marketing, Vol 4, No 1, pp 13–23

Opie R (1999) Remember When: A Nostalgic Trip Through the Consumer Era, p 116, Octopus Books, London

O'Reilly C A, **Chatman** J and **Caldwell** D F (1991) People and Organizational Culture: a profile comparison approach to assessing person-organization fit, Academy of Management Journal, Vol 34, No 3, pp 487–516

Orth U R, **McDaniel** M, **Shellhammer** T and **Lopetcharat** K (2004) Promoting Brand Benefits: The Role of Consumer Psychographics and Lifestyle, Journal of Consumer Marketing, Vol 21, No 2, pp 97–108

Oswald R L (1999) Culture Swapping: Consumption and the Ethnogenesis of Middle-Class Haitian Immigrants, Journal of Consumer Research, Vol 25, March, pp 303–318

Packard V (1957) The Hidden Persuaders, McKay, New York

Palan K M and **Wilkes** R E (1997) Adolescent-parent interaction in family decision making, Journal of Consumer Research, Vol 24 No 2, pp 159–170

Palda K S (1968) The Hypothesis of a Hierarchy of Effects: A Partial Solution, Journal of Marketing Research, May, pp 131–145

Parasuraman A, **Zeithaml** V and **Berry** L (1985) A Conceptual Model of Service Quality and its Implications for Future Research, Journal of Marketing, Vol 49, Fall, pp 41–50

Parfitt J H and **Collins** B J K (1968) The Use of Consumer Panels for Brand-Share Prediction, Journal of Marketing Research, Vol 5, pp 131–145

Park G W and **Lessig** V P (1977) Students and Housewives: Differences in Susceptibility to Reference Group Influence, Journal of Consumer Research, Vol 4, pp 102–110

Park W C, **Mothersbaugh** D L and **Feick** L (1994) Consumer Knowledge Assessment, Journal of Consumer Research, Vol 21, No 1, pp 71–73

Parliamentary Select Committee (2005) Influence of the Pharmaceutical Industry, 14 October

Parry C (2008) From Wispa to Bandwagon, Marketing Week, 29 May, 20–21

Parsons A (2004) Sensory Stimuli and E-Tailers, Journal of Consumer Behaviour, Vol 4, No 6

Patterson M (1998) Direct Marketing in Postmodernity: Neo-Tribes and Direct Communications, Marketing Intelligence and Planning, Vol 16, No 1, pp 68–74

Pavlov I P (1928) Lectures on Conditioned Reflexes: The Higher Nervous Activity of Animals, 1, trans. **Gantt** H, Lawrence & Wishart, London

Penaloza L (1994) Atravesando Fronteras/Border Crossings: A Critical Ethnographic Exploration of the Consumer Acculturation of Mexican Immigrants, Journal of Consumer Research, Vol 21, June, pp 289–294

Penaloza L and **Gilly** M C (1999) Marketer Acculturation: The Changer and the Changed, Journal of Marketing, Vol 63, July, pp 84–104

Peters J P and **Olson** J C (2005) Consumer Behaviour and Marketing Strategy, McGraw Hill, New York

Petty R E and **Cacioppo** J T (1983) Central and Peripheral Routes to Persuasion: Application to Advertising, in **Percy** L and **Woodside** A G, Advertising and Consumer Psychology, Lexington Books, Lexington

Petty R E, **Cacioppo** J T and **Schumann** D (1983) Central and Peripheral Routes to Advertising Effectiveness: The Moderating Role of Involvement, Journal of Consumer Research, Vol 10, No 2, pp 135–146

Phillips S, **Alexander** A and **Shaw** G (2005) Consumer Misbehavior: The Rise of Self-Service Grocery Retailing and Shoplifting in the United Kingdom c 1950–1970, Journal of Macromarketing, Vol 25, No 1, p 66

Piacentini M and **Mailer** G (2004) Symbolic Consumption in Teenagers' Clothing Choices, Journal of Consumer Behaviour, Vol 3, No 3, pp 231–264

Piaget J and D **Elkin** (1969) Studies in Cognitive Development, Essays in honour of Jean Piaget. Oxford University Press, Oxford

Pincus J (2004) The Consequences of Unmet Needs: The Evolving Role of Motivation in Consumer Research, Journal of Consumer Behaviour, Vol 3, No 4

Piper J (1977) Britain's Ethnic Markets, Marketing, January

Precision Marketing (2006) Volvo Blitz reaches out to Mothers, 3 November, p 3

Pressey A D and **Selassie** H G (2003) Are Cultural Differences Overrated? Examining the Influence of National Culture on International Buyer-Seller Relationships, Journal of Consumer Behaviour, Vol 2, No 4, pp 354–368

Prosser D (2007) Hell Hath No Fury Like a Modern Customer Scorned, Independent, 27 January, Save and Spend, pp 4–5

Pringle H and **Binet** L (2005) How Marketers Can Use Celebrities to Sell More Effectively, Journal of Consumer Behaviour, Vol 4, No 3, pp 201–214

Publicis (1992) presented by Block, R, Sales Talk, BBC Radio 4, January

Pulham A (2003) reported in Sclater I, Challenging Perceptions, Marketing Business, February, pp 16–17

Rainbow TV (1997) research reported in Middleton T, The Pink Pound, Direct Response, February, pp 49–53

Ram M (1994) Unravelling Social Networks in Ethnic Minority Firms, International Small Business Journal, Vol 12, No 3, pp 42–53

Raven J R P and **French** B (1959) The Bases of Social Power, in **Cartwright** D (ed.), Studies in Social Power, MI Institute for Social Research, pp 150–167

Rawlins M (1984) Doctors and Drug Makers, Lancet, Vol 4, August, pp 276–278

Redfield R, **Linton** R and **Herskovits** M J (1936) Memorandum on the Study of Acculturation, American Anthropologist, Vol 38, No 2, pp 149–152

Rees J (1995) Calvin Klein Makes 'Offensive' Ads Pay, Marketing Week, 8 September, Vol 23

Reichheld F F (1988) Loyalty and the Renaissance of Marketing, Marketing Management, Vol 2, No 4, pp 10–21

Reichheld F F (1996) Learning from Customer Defections, Harvard Business Review, Vol 74, No 2, March/April

Reichheld F F and **Sasser** W E (1990) Zero Defects: Quality Comes to Service, Harvard Business Review, September/October, pp 105–111

Reichert T, **Heckler** S and **Jackson** S (2001) The Effects of Sexual Social Marketing Appeals on Cognitive Processing and Persuasion, Journal of Advertising, Vol 30, pp 13–20

Reichert T and **Lambiase** J (2003) Sex in Advertising: Perspectives on the Erotic Appeal, Lawrence Erlbaum Associates, Mahwah, NJ

Research International (1996) Materialism or New Realism, Research International Ltd, London

Research Services Ltd (1981) SAGACITY: A tool for more Effective Market Analysis and Media Planning, London

Revolution Awards (2002) Haymarket, London

Reynolds T J and **Gutman** J (1988) Laddering Theory, Method, Analysis and Interpretation, Journal of Advertising Research, February/March, pp 11–31

Rheingold H (1993) The Virtual Community: Homesteading on the Electronic Frontier, Addison–Wesley, Reading, MA

Richardson L (2000) You Can Run But You Can't Hide, Revolution, September, pp 12–15

Richardson P S, **Dick** A S and **Jain** A K (1994) Extrinsic and Intrinsic Cue Effects on Perceptions of Store Brand Quality, Journal of Marketing, Vol 58, No 4, pp 28–37

Richins M L (1983) Negative Word-of-Mouth by Dissatisfied Customers: A Pilot Study, Journal of Marketing, Vol 47, Winter, pp 68–78

Richins M (1991) Social Comparison and the Idealised Image of Advertising, Journal of Consumer Research, Vol 18, pp 71–83

Riefler P and **Diamantopoulos** A (2007) Consumer Animosity: A Literature Review and a Reconsideration of its Measurement, International Marketing Review, Vol 24, No 1, pp 87–119

Ries A and **Trout** J (1986) Positioning: The Battle for Your Mind, McGraw Hill, New York

Riesman D (1950) The Lonely Crowd, Yale University Press, New Haven, Conn.

Rindfleisch A, **Burroughs** J E and **Denton** F (1997) Family Structure, Materialism, and Compulsive Consumption, Journal of Consumer Research, Vol 23 No 4 pp 312–325

Ritchie K (1995) Marketing to Generation X, Lexington Books, New York

Roberts L (2006) British Teenagers are 'Worst Behaved' in Europe, Daily Mail, 2 November

Roberts D and **Baker** S (2005) Can We Learn Together? Co-creating with consumers, International Journal of Market Research, Vol 47, No 4, pp 407–444

Robertson T S (1967) The Process of Innovation and the Diffusion of Innovation, Journal of Marketing, Vol 31 pp 14–19

Robertson T S (1971) Innovative Behaviour and Communication, Holt, Rhinehart & Winston

Robinson J P (1957) Inter-Personal Influence in Election Campaigns: Two-Step Flow Hypothesis, Public Relations Quarterly, Vol 40, pp 304–319

Robinson P J, **Faris** C W and **Wind** Y (1967) Industrial Buying and Creative Marketing, Allyn and Bacon, New York

Rogers E M (1959, 1983) Diffusion of Innovations, Free Press, New York

Rogers E M and **Shoemaker** F (1971) Communication of Innovation, Macmillan, p 103

Rokeach M (1968) Beliefs, Attitudes and Values, Jossey-Bass, San Francisco

Rokeach M (1973) The Nature of Human Values, Free Press, New York

Ronchetto J R Jr, **Hutt** M D and **Reingen** P H (1989) Embedded Influence Patterns In Organizational Buying System, Journal of Marketing, Vol 53, No 4, pp 51–62

Rook D W (1985) The Ritual Dimension of Consumer Behaviour, Journal of Consumer Research, Vol 12, December, pp 218–240

Rook D W (1987) The Buying Impulse, Journal of Consumer Research, Vol 14 No 2 pp 189–200

Rook D W and **Fisher** R J (1995) Trait and Normative Aspects of Impulsive Buying Behaviour, Journal of Consumer Research, Vol 22 No 3 pp 305–313

Rose G (1999) Consumer Socialisation, Parental Style and Development Timetables in US and Japan, Journal of Marketing, Vol 63 No 3 pp 105–119

Rosen J (2001) The Unwanted Gaze: The Destruction of Privacy in America, Vintage Books, New York

Rosenberg M (1979) Conceiving the Self, Basic Books, New York

Ross (1971) Self Concept and Brand Preference, Journal of Business, Vol 44, No 1, pp 38–50

Rosser M (2003) 20th Century to Persist with Voicemail Ads, Precision Marketing, 14 February, p 1

Rossiter J R and **Chan** A M (1998) Ethnicity in Business and Consumer Behaviour, Journal of Business Research, Vol 42, pp 127–134

Rossiter J R, **Percy** L and **Donovan** R J (1991) A Better Advertising Planning Grid, Journal of Advertising Research, October/November, pp 11–21

Rothfeder J (1992) Privacy for Sale: How Computerisation Has Made Everyone's Private Life an Open Secret, Simon & Schuster, New York

Rothschild M and **Houston** M (1977) the Consumer Involvement Matrix, in **Greenberg** B and **Bellenger** D (eds.) AMA Educators' Conference, Vol 41, pp 95–98

Rubach E (2002) Up Close and Too Personal, Precision Marketing, 1 February, p 12

Rubach E (2003a) Harley Gears up for Euro Loyalty Assault, Precision Marketing, January, p 1

Rubach E (2003b) Industry Hail Robertson Defeat, Precision Marketing, 23 May, p 1

Rudolph H J (1947) Attention and Interest Factors in Advertising, Funke Wagnalls, New York

Rule J (1998) reported in Ungoed-Thomas J and Nuki P, Mailshot Firms Blitz 'Midas' Consumers, Sunday Times, 17 May

Rust R T and **Oliver** R W (1994) The Death of Advertising, Journal of Advertising, Vol 23 No 4, December, pp 71–77

Salzer-Morling M and **Strannegard** L (2008) Ain't Misbehavin' – Consumption in a Moralized Landscape, Marketing Theory, Vol 7, No 4, pp 407–425

Samuelsen B and **Sandvik** K (1997) The Concept of Customer Loyalty, in 26th Annual EMAC Conference: Progress, Prospects and Perspectives, Warwick Business School, Coventry, England

Sasse A (2005) Effective Security and Privacy: Protecting People Not Just Data, International Symposium on Confidentiality, Privacy and Disclosure in the 21st century, University of Manchester, UK, 3 May

Saunders N (2007) cited in Gorman M (2007) Climate Change hits US Retail, Marketing Week, 5 July 24–25

Schaninger C M and **Lee** D H (2002) A New Full Nest Classification Approach, Psychology and Marketing, Vol 19 No 1 pp 25–58

Schewe C D and **Meredith** G (2004) Segmenting Global Markets by Generational Cohorts: Determining Motivations by Age, Journal of Consumer Behaviour, Vol 4 No 1 pp 51–63

Schiffman L G and **Kanuk** L Z (2000) Consumer Behaviour, 7th edn, Prentice Hall, NJ

Schmidt R, **Sturrock** F, **Ward** P and **Lea-Greenwood** G (1999) Deshopping: The Art of Illicit Consumption, International Journal of Retail and Distribution Management, Vol 27, No 8, pp 209–301

Schmitt B H (1999) Experiential Marketing: How to Get Customers to Sense, Feel, Think, Act and Relate to Your Company and Brands, Free Press, New York

Schor J K (2004) Born to Buy, Scribner

Schouten J W (1991) Selves in Transition: Symbolic Consumption in Personal Rites of Passage and Identity Reconstruction, Journal of Consumer Research, Vol 17, No 4, pp 412–425

Schouten J W and **McAlexander** J H (1995) Subcultures of Consumption: An Ethnography of the New Biker, Journal of Consumer Research, Vol 22 No 1 pp 43–62

Schramm W and **Roberts** D (eds) (1971) The Process and Effects of Mass Communication, University of Illinois Press, Urbana, IL

Schroeder D (1992) Life, Liberty and the Pursuit of Privacy, American Demographics, June, Vol 20

Schwartz S H and **Bilsky** W (1987) Toward a Universal Psychological Structure of Human Values, Journal of Personality and Social Psychology, Vol 53, pp 550–562

Sclater I (2002) Race Relations, Marketing Business, September, pp 31–33

Sclater I (2003) Challenging Perceptions, Marketing Business, February, pp 16–17

Scott J (2002) Once Bitten, Twice Shy: A World of Eroding Trust, New York Times, 21 April, p 5

Shabi R (2003) The Card Up Their Sleeve, Guardian Weekend Magazine, 19 July, pp 14–19

Sharp B and **Driesener** C (2000) The Dirichlet's Buyer Behaviour Assumptions Really Do mater, Australian and New Zealand Marketing Academy (ANZMAC) Conference, November, Griffith University, pp 1144–1148

Shaw J (2004) Chip and Pin, Campaign Supplement, 9 April, p 7

Shaw A (2007) The Secrets We Share with Strangers, Independent on Sunday, 12 August

Shaw D, **Grehan** E, **Shui** E, **Hasaan** L and **Thomson** J (2005) An Exploration of Values in Ethical Consumer Decision Making, Journal of Consumer Behaviour, Vol 4 No 3 pp 185–200

Shepherdson N (2000) Life's a Beach 101, American Demographics, May

Sherif M and **Hovland** C (1964) Social Judgement, Yale University Press

Sheth J N and **Parvatiyar** A (eds) (2000) Handbook of Relationship Marketing, Sage, Thousand Oaks, CA

Shibutani T (1955) Reference Groups as Perspectives, American Journal of Sociology, Vol 60

Shim S and **Gehrt** K C (1996) Hispanic and Native American Adolescents: An Exploratory Study of Their Approach to Shopping, Journal of Retailing, Vol 72 No 3 pp 307–324

Shiv B and **Huber** J (2000) The Impact of Anticipating Satisfaction on Consumer Choice, Journal of Consumer Research, Gainesville, Vol 27 No 2, September, pp 202–217

Shoffman M (2006) UK Falling Behind in Gay Market, Pinknews, 23 May

Shovlin C (2007) Cracking the Colour Code, Marketing Week, 11 October, pp 28–29

Silvera D H and **Austad** B (2004) Factors Predicting the Effectiveness of Celebrity Endorsement Advertisements, European Journal of Marketing, Vol 38 No 11/12 pp 1509–1526

Simcock P and **Sudbury** L (2006) The Invisible Majority? Older Models in UK TV Advertising, International Journal of Advertising, Vol 25, No 1, pp 87–106

Singh J (1988) Consumer Complaint Intentions and Behavior: Definitional and Taxonomical Issues, Journal of Marketing, Vol 52, No. 1, pp 93–107

Singh S (2008a) ASA Turns Down Request to Investigate Vauxhall Ad, Marketing Week, 6 March p 8

Singh S (2008b) Government Targets over 50s in Sensible Drinking Campaign, Marketing Week, 10 April

Sirgy J M (1982) Self-Concept in Consumer Behaviour: A Critical Review, Journal of Consumer Research, Vol 9, No 3, pp 287–300

Sirgy J M, **Grewal** D, **Mangleburg** F T, **Park** J-O, **Chon** K-S, **Claiborne** C B, **Johar** J S and **Berkman** H (1997) Assessing the Predictive Validity of Two Methods of Measuring Self-Image Congruence, Journal of the Academy of Marketing Science, Vol 25, No 3, pp 229–241

Sirgy M J, **Grewal** D and **Mangleburg** T F (2000) Retail Environment, Self-Congruity, and Retail Patronage: An Integrative Model and a Research Agenda, Journal of Business Research, Vol 49, No 2, pp 127–138

Sismodo S (2007) Ghost Management: How much of the medical literature is shaped behind the scenes by the pharmaceutical industry, PloS Medicine, September, pp 4–9

Skinner B F (1938) The Behaviour of Organisms, Appleton-Century-Crofts, New York

Small M (1999) Nosing out a Mate, Scientific American Presents, Vol 10 No 3 pp 52–55

SmartFocus (2004) Viper Print Out, Bristol

Smigel E O (1956) Public Attitudes toward Stealing as Related to the Size of the Organisation, American Sociology Review, Vol 21, pp 320–327

Smit E, **Bronner** F and **Tolboom** M (2006) Brand relationship quality and its value for personal contact, Journal of Business Research, Vol 60, pp 627–633

Smith D (2007) Stop Shopping . . . or the planet will go pop, Observer, 8 April, pp 8–9

Social Trends (2005) Office for National Statistics, London

Softscan (2008) Spam hits all time high, Precision Marketing, 11 January, p 5

Solomon M (2003) Conquering Consumerspace; Marketing Strategies for a Branded World, Amacom, New York

Solomon M (2004) Consumer Behaviour: Buying, Having and Being, Pearson, Upper Saddle River, New Jersey

Solomon M (2006) Consumer Behaviour: Buying, Having and Being, Pearson, London, p 162

Solomon M, **Bamossy** G and **Askegaard** S (2003) Consumer Behaviour, Prentice Hall

Speck P S and **Elliott** M T (1997) Predictors of Advertising Avoidance in Print and Broadcast Media, Journal of Advertising, Vol 26 pp 61–76

Specter M (1999) Cracking the Norse Code, Sunday Times Magazine, 21 March, pp 45–52

Spies K and **Hesse** F (1997) Store Atmosphere, Mood and Purchasing Behavior, International Journal of Research in Marketing, Vol 14 pp 1–17

Spotts H E, **Weinberger** M G and **Parsons** A L (1997) Assessing the Use and Impact of Humor on Advertising Effectiveness: A Contingency Approach, Journal of Advertising, Vol 26 No 3 pp 17–33

Spradley J P and **McCurdy** D W (1977) Conformity and Conflict: Readings in Cultural Anthropology, 3rd edn, Boston, Little Brown

Sproles G B and **Kendall** E L (1986) A Methodology for Profiling Consumers' Decision-Making Styles, Journal of Consumer Affairs, Vol 20 No 2 pp 267–280

Sprott W H (1958) Human Groups, Penguin Books, p 9

St Elmo Lewis E (circa 1900) cited in **Barry** T E and **Howard** D J, A Review and Critique of the Hierarchy of Effects in Advertising, International Journal of Advertising, Vol 9 pp 121–135

Stafford J E (1966) Effects of Group Influences on Consumer Brand Preferences, Journal of Marketing Research, Vol 3

Stayman D M and **Deshpande** R (1989) Situational Ethnicity and Consumer Behaviour, Journal of Consumer Research, Vol 16, December, pp 361–371

Steenhaut S and **Van Kenhove** P (2005) Relationship Commitment and Consumer Behaviour in a Retail Setting: The Case of Recovering Too Much Change at the Checkout, Journal of Business Ethics, Vol 56 pp 335–353

Steiner R (2002) Watch Out, Big Spenders, Big Brother is Watching You, Sunday Times Business, 11 August, p 1

Stephens N (1991) Cognitive Age: A Useful Concept for Advertising?, Journal of Advertising, Vol 20 No 4 pp 37–48

Stern B (1991) Literary Criticism and Consumer Research, Journal of Consumer Research, Vol 16 pp 322–333

Stern H (1962) The Significance of Impulse Buying Today, Journal of Marketing, Vol 26 pp 59–62

Sternthal B and **Craig** C S (1973) Humor in Advertising, Journal of Marketing, Vol 37 No 4 pp 12–18

Sternthal B and **Craig** C S (1974) Fear Appeals: Revisited and Revised, Journal of Consumer Research, Vol 1 No 3

Stewart-Allen A (2007) cited in **Gorman** M (2007) Climate Change hits US Retail, Marketing Week, 5 July 24–25

Stokes D (1997) cited in **Darby** I, Printing Gets all Creative, Marketing Direct, January, pp 52–56

Sulloway F (1995) Birth Order and Evolutionary Psychology: A Meta-analytic overview, Psychological Inquiry, Vol 6, No 1, pp 75–80

Suzman M (1996) Advertisers Miss Out on Ethnic Minority Market, Financial Times, November, Vol 19

Szmigin I and **Carrigan** M (2000) The Older Consumer as Innovator: Does Cognitive Age Hold the Key?, Journal of Marketing Management, Vol 16 No 5 pp 505–528

Szmigin I and **Carrigan** M (2001) Learning to Love the Older Consumer, Journal of Consumer Behaviour, Vol 1 No 1 pp 22–34

Tadajewski M (2006) Remembering Motivation Research: Toward an Alternative Genealogy of Interpretive Consumer Research, Marketing Theory, Vol 6, No 4, pp 429–466

Tajfel H (1981) Human Groups and Social Categories: Studies in Social Psychology, Cambridge University Press, Cambridge

Tauber E M (1972) Why Do People Shop?, Journal of Marketing, Vol 36 No 4 pp 46–49

Taylor Nelson Sofres (2004) Are You a Member of Your Kid's Generation? (http://www.tns-global/corporate/doc/0/2vmqq3513e0419caj02jk5176f/247) accessed 23 March 2004

Telegraph Group (1999) reported in **Carling** E (1999) Grappling with the Grey Market, Marketing Direct

Thaler R H and **Sunstein** C R (2008) Nudge: Improving Decisions about Health, Wealth and Happiness, Yale University Press

Thomas G (2004) Building the Buzz in the Hive Mind, Journal of Consumer Behaviour, Vol 4 No 1

Thompson C J, **Locander** W B and **Pollio** H R (1990) The Lived Meaning of Free Choice: An Existentialist-Phenomenological Description of Everyday Consumer Experiences of Contemporary Married Women, Journal of Consumer Research, Vol 17

Thompson K, **Mitchell** H and **Knox** S (1998) Organisational Buying in Changing Times, European Management Journal, Vol 16, No 6, pp 698–705

Till B, **Stanley** S and **Priluck** R (2008) Classical Conditioning and Celebrity Endorsers, Psychology and Marketing, Vol 25, No 2, pp 179–196

Timmins N (1995) London's Ethnic Balance Shifting, Independent, 12 December

Tinkham S and **Reid** L (1988) Sex Appeal in Advertising – Revisited, Proceedings of the AMA Conference, pp 118–123

Tinson J and **Nancarrow** C (2005) The Influence of Children on Purchases, International Journal of Market Research, Vol 47, No 1, pp 5–28

Todd S (2001) Self-Concept: A Tourism Application, Journal of Consumer Behaviour, Vol 1, No 2, pp 184–196

Tonglet M (2002) Consumer Misbehaviour: An Exploratory Study of Shoplifting, Journal of Consumer Behaviour, Vol 1, No 4. pp 336–354

Tonkin E, **Chapman** M and **McDonald** M (eds.) (1989) History and Ethnicity, Routledge, London

Tosdal H (1925) Principles of Personal Selling, Shaw, Chicago, p 61

Treguer J P (2002) 50 + Marketing, Palgrave

Triandis H C (1997) Where is Culture in the Acculturation Model?, Applied Psychology: An International Review, Vol. 46, Issue 1 (January), pp 55–58

Triplett T (1995) Carmakers Driven by Quest to Find Tomorrow's Color, Marketing News, Vol 29 No 18, 28 August, pp 38–39

Tripp C, **Jensen** T D and **Carlson** L (1994) The Effects of Multiple Product Endorsement by Celebrities, Journal of Consumer Research, Vol 20 No 4 pp 535–548

Tsiros M, **Mittal** V and **Ross** W T Jr (2004) The Role of Attributions in Customer Satisfaction: A Re-examination, Journal of Consumer Research, Vol 31, No 2, pp 476–483

Tuan Yit Fu (1980) The significance of the Artefact, Geographical Review, Vol 70 No 4 p 472

Tunney D (1999) Harnessing the Subconscious to Bolster Sales, Marketing, 13 May, p 20

Turnbull P and **Leek** S (2003) Business to Business Marketing: Organisatinal buying behaviour, relationships and networks, in **Baker** M (ed.) The Marketing Book, 5th edn, pp 142–170, Butterworth Heinemann

Turner C (2008) TV Soaps Should Educate Consumers on Debt Issues, Marketing Week, 3 August, p 5

Turner V (1969) The Ritual Process, Aldine, Chicago

Tzokas N and **Saren** M (1997) Building Relationship Platforms in Consumer Markets: A Chain Approach, Journal of Strategic Marketing, Vol 5 No 2 pp 105–120

Ulgado F M and **Lee** M (1993) Consumer Evaluation of Bi-National Products in the Global Market, Journal of International Marketing, Vol 1, No 3, pp 5–22

Ungoed-Thomas J and **Nuki** P (1998) Mailshot Firms Blitz 'Midas' Consumers, Sunday Times, 17 May

Usborne (2007) Smart Arms, Independent, 9 May, pp 10–11

Ustuner T and **Holt** D B (2007) Dominated Consumer Acculturation: The Social Construction of poor Migrant Women's Consumer Identity Projects in a Turkish Squatter, Journal of Consumer Research, Vol 34, No 1, p 41

VALS (2005) http://www.sric-bi.com/VALS/presurvey.shtml, last accessed 6 June 2005

van Raaij W F and **Schoonderbeek** W M (1993) Meaning Structure of Brand Names and Extensions, European Advances in Consumer Research, Vol 1, pp 479–484

Veblen T (1899) The Theory of the Leisure Class, in The Collected Works of Thorstein IN Veblen, Vol 1 Reprint (1944), Routledge, London

Veloutsou C (2007) Identifying the dimensions of the product-brand and consumer relationship, Journal of Marketing Management, Vol 23, No 1–2, pp 7–26

Venkatesan M (1966) Consumer Behaviour: Conformity and Independence, Journal of Marketing Research, Vol 3

Venkatesh A (1995) Ethnoconsumerism: A New Paradigm to Study Cultural and Cross-Cultural Consumer Behaviour, in **Costa** J A and **Bamossy** G J (eds.), Marketing in a Multicultural World, Sage, London, pp 26–67

Venkatesh V and **Davies** F D (2000) A Theoretical Extension of the Technology Acceptance Model: Four Longitudinal Field Studies, Management Science, Vol 46, No 2, pp 186–204

Venkatraman M (1988) Investigating differences in the roles of enduring and instrumentally involved consumers in the diffusion process, in **Houston** M (ed.) Advances in Consumer Research, Association of Consumer Research, Duluth, MN

Vinson D J S and **Lamont** L (1977) The Role of Personal Values in Marketing and Consumer Research, Journal of Marketing, Vol 41, April, pp 45–50

Von Hippel E (2005) Democratising Innovation, MTI Press

Voorhees C M, **David** M K and **Horowitz** M (2006) A Voice From the Silent Masses: An Exploratory and Comparative Analysis of Noncomplainers, Journal of the Academy of Marketing Science, Vol 34, No 4, pp 514–527

Wahb M A and **Bridwell** L G (1976) Maslow Reconsidered: A Review of Research on the Need Hierarchy Theory, Organisational Behaviour and Human Performance, Vol 15, pp 212–240

Wakefield K L and **Blodgett**, J G (1999) Customer Response to Intangible and Tangible Service Factors, Psychology and Marketing, Vol 16 No 1 pp 51–68

Walker C (2001) US Threat to Axe Data Treaty Puts Multinationals on Alert, Precision Marketing, 6 April, p 1

Wallendorf M and **Arnould** E J (1991) We Gather Together: Consumption Rituals of Thanksgiving Day, Journal of Consumer Research, Vol 18, June, pp 13–31

Wallendorf M and **Reilly** M (1983) Ethnic Migration, Assimilation, and Consumption, Journal of Consumer Research, Vol 10, December, pp 292–302

Walsh G, **Henning-Thurau** T, **Wayne-Mitchell** V and **Wiedmann** K-P (2001) Consumers' Decision-making Style as a Basis for Market Segmentation, Journal of Targeting, Measurement and Analysis for Marketing, Vol 10, No 2, pp 117–131

Walsh G, **Gwinner** K P and **Swanson** S R (2004) What Makes Mavens Tick? Exploring the Motives of Market Mavens' Initiation of Information Diffusion, Journal of Consumer Marketing, Vol 21 No 2 pp 109–122

Wamwara-Mbugua L W, **Cornwell** T B and **Boller** G (2008) Triple acculturation: The role of African Americans in the consumer acculturation of Kenyan immigrants, Journal of Business Research, Vol 61, No 2, p 83

Warwick C (2007) cited in **Mesure** S (2007) Passion for Python Puts Stars at War with Animal Rights Groups, Independent on Sunday, 12 August, p 12

Webster C (1994) Effects of Ethnic Identification on Marital Roles in the Purchase Decision Process, Journal of Consumer Research, Vol 21, September, pp 319–331

Webster F E, Jr and **Wind** Y (1972) A General Model for Understanding Organizational Buying Behavior, Journal of Marketing, 36 April, pp 12–19

Weinberger M G and **Gulas** C S (1992) The Impact of Humor in Advertising: A Review, Journal of Advertising, Vol 21 No 4, December, pp 35–60

Weinberger M G and **Spotts** H E (1989) Humor in US Versus UK TV Commercials: A Comparison, Journal of Advertising, Vol 18 No 2 pp 39–44

Weinberger M G, **Spotts** H, **Campbell** L and **Parsons** A L (1995) The Use and Effect of Humor in Different Advertising Media, Journal of Advertising Research, Vol 35 No 3, May/June, pp 44–56

Weiner B (2000) Attributional Thoughts about Consumer Behaviour, Journal of Consumer Research, Vol 27, No 3, pp 382–388

Weissberg T (2008) Anti-Smoking Campaign Targets Parents, Marketing Week, 2 June

Werner C M, **Haggard** L M, **Altman** I and **Oxley** D (1988) Temporal Qualities of Rituals and Celebrations: A Comparison of Christmas Street and Zuni Shalako, in **McGrath** J E (ed.), The Social Psychology of Time: New Perspectives, Sage, London, pp 203–254

Westbrook R A and **Black** W C (1985) A Motivation-Based Shopper Typology, Journal of Retailing, Vol 61 No 1 pp 78–103

Westfall R (1962) Psychological Factors in Predicting Brand Choice, Journal of Marketing, Vol 26

Westin A (1967) Privacy and Freedom, Athencum, New York

Westin A (1992) Consumer Privacy Protection: Ten Predictions, Mobius, February, pp 5–11

Wetzer I M, **Zeelenberg** M and **Pieters** R (2007) 'Never eat in that restaurant, I did!': Exploring why People Engage in Negative Word-of-mouth Communication, Psychology & Marketing, Vol 24, No 8, pp 661–668

White R (2005) Why Grey Matter Matters, Admap, May, pp 18–19

Wicker A (1969) Attitudes Versus Actions: The Relationship of Overt Responses to Attitude Objects, Journal of Social Issues, Vol 25 pp 24–32

Wilding B (2008) cited in **Ford** R (2008) Top Police Officer Barbara Wilding: Gang life replacing family life, The Times, 2 July, p 55

Williams R (2002) Memetics: A New Paradigm for Understanding Customer Behaviour, Marketing Intelligence and Planning, Vol 20, No 3, pp 162–167

Willmott M and **Nelson** W (2003) Complicated Lives: Sophisticated Consumers, Intricate Lifestyles, Simple Solutions, John Wiley & Sons, Chichester

Wilson K (1993) Managing the Industrial Sales Force of the 1990s, Journal of Marketing Management, Vol 9, pp 123–139

Wilson E J (1996) Theory Transitions in Organizational Buying Behaviour Research, Journal of Business and industrial Marketing, Vol 11, No 6, pp 7–19

Wilson D F (1998) Why Divide Organizational and Consumer Buyer Behaviour?', European Journal of Marketing, Vol 34, No 7, pp 780–796

Wilson J Q and **Hernstein** R J (1985) Crime and Human Nature, Simon & Schuster, New York

Winick C (1961) Anthropology's Contributions to Marketing, Journal of Marketing, Vol 25

Wipperfürth A (2005) Brand Hijack: Marketing Without Marketing, Portfolio, New York, NY

Wong Y H and **Leung** T K P (2001) Guanxi: Relationship Marketing in a Chinese Context, International Business Press, New York

Woodruffe-Burton H, **Eccles** S and **Elliott** R (2002) Towards a Theory of Shopping Behaviour, Journal of Consumer Behaviour, Vol 1 No 3 pp 256–266

Woodruffe-Burton H, **Eccles** S and **Elliott** R (eds) (2005) Special issue: Toward a Theory of Shopping, Journal of Consumer Behaviour, Vol 4 No 4

Woods R (2004) Exploring the Emotional Territory for Brands, Journal of Consumer Behaviour, Vol 3 No 4 pp 388–403

Woodside A and **Davenport** W (1974) The Effect of Salesman Similarity and Expertise on Consumer Purchasing Behaviour, Journal of Marketing Research, May, pp 198–202

Woodside A G (2004) Advancing Means-End Chains by Incorporating Heider's Balance Theory and Fournier's Consumer-Brand Relationship Typology, Psychology and Marketing, Vol 21 No 4 pp 279–294

Wright B (1999) reported in **Beenstock** S (1999) Supermarkets Entice the Ultra Customer, Marketing, 15 April, p 15

Yi Y and **Jeon** H (2003) Effects of Loyalty Programs on Value Perception, Program Loyalty, and Brand Loyalty, Academy of Marketing Science, Vol 31 No 3 pp 229–240

Youjae Y and **Hoseong** J (2003) Effects of Loyalty Programs on Value Perception, Program Loyalty, and Brand Loyalty, Academy of Marketing Science Journal, Greenvale, Vol 31 No 3, Summer, pp 229–241

Young M and **Wilmott** P (1975) Family and Kinship in East London, Routledge & Kegan Paul

Zaichkowsky J L (1985) Measuring the Involvement Construct, Journal of Consumer Research, Vol 12, No 3, pp 341–352

Zaichkowsky J L (1987) The Personal Involvement Inventory: Reduction, Revision and Application to Advertising, Discussion Paper number 87-08-08, Simon Fraser University, Faculty of Business Administration

Zavestoski S (2002) Anticonsumption Attitudes, Psychology and Marketing (Guest Editorial), Vol 19, No 2, pp 121–126

Zeithaml V A (1981) How Consumer Evaluation Processes Differ between Goods and Services in **Donnelly** J and **George** W (eds), Marketing of Services, American Marketing, Chicago, pp 186–190

Zelin A (2003) Good Housekeeping, Research, February, pp 24–25

Zhang S and **Sood** S (2002) Deep and Surface Cues: Brand Extension Evaluations by Children and Adults, Journal of Consumer Research, Vol 29, No 1, pp 129–142

Zimbardo P and **Ebbesen** E B (1970) Influencing Attitudes and Changing Behaviour, Addison–Wesley, p 20

Zimmerman A and **Dahlberg** J (2008) The Sexual Objectification of Women in Advertising, Journal of Advertising Research, pp 71–78

INDEX

Note: page numbers in *italics* refer to figures, tables, thinkboxes or example boxes.

A

ABC1 social grading, 183–8
abnormal consumer behaviour, 437–9
abnormal product use, *437*, 439–40
absolute sensory thresholds, 78
abusive consumers, 453
acculturation, 285, 304–9, 318
    agents, 306
    impact, 308–9
    outcomes, 307–8
    processes, 306–7
action stage, consumer response model, 45, 46,
    125–9
activities, interests and opinions (AIO) analysis,
    191, *193*
actual self-image congruence, 215
adapter–innovator continuum, 349
addiction, *437*, 439–40
adoption of products *see* diffusion-adoption theory
advertising
    conversational, 365
    ethnic minority, *311*, *313*
    reach, 49
    wearout, 98
advocacy, 47
aesthetic innovations, 341, 343
affective commitment, 395
affective component of attitudes, 106, *107*,
    112
affective motives, 15
after-sales service, 139
age factors in consumption, 154, 155, 188

see also young people
aggregation, virtual groups, 261
aggressive consumers, 453
AIDA (attention–interest–desire–action), 45
aided recall method, 103
AIO (activities, interests and opinions) analysis,
    191, *193*
airports, impulse buying in, *128*
alcohol misuse, *437*, 439–40, *450*
aloneness cult, *161*
anti-corporation activism, 440
anti-sabbaticalism, *161*
Applied Futures lifestyle typology, *193*
approach, 10
art attendance, 290
aspirational groups, 252
assimilation, 305
assimilation effect, 143
associationist learning, 92–7, *93*, 354
atmospherics, 64–5
attention gaining/holding, 45, 46, 51–63, 298
attitude
    privacy and, 484–6
    relative, 381
    see also attitudes to marketing activities
attitude–attribution framework, 488–90
attitude toward object model, 110–12
attitudes to marketing activities, 45, 46, 105–22
    affective component, 106, *107*, 112
    behavioural component, 107, 112, 115–20
    changing, 115–21
    cognitive component, 106, *107*, 112

attitudes to marketing activities, (*continued*)
    conative component, 107, 112
    functional models, 114–15
    involvement and, 141–50
    measuring, 108–12
    planned behaviour theory, 113, *114*
    reasoned action theory, 113, *113*
    reinforcement, 120
    structural models, 106–7
attitudinal commitment, 395
attraction, consumer–company relations, 374–5
attribution theory, 486–8
autonomic decisions, 273
avoidance, 10
avoidance groups, 252
Awareness, Trial, Reinforcement (ATR) model, 345, *345*
awkward customers, 453

B
baby boomers, 162–3, *166*
baby busters, 160–1
balance theory, 107–8
bandwagon effect, 109
behaviour
    organizational buying, 458–79
    privacy-related, 481–94
behavioural commitment, 395
behavioural component of attitudes, 107, 112
behavioural learning, 92–7
    see also operant conditioning
'better' consumers, identifying, 405
binge-drinking, 439–40
biogenic (physiological) drives, 7
biographics, 428, 433
biological age, *157*
biometric recognition, *414*
Blair, Tony, 353
body image, 212
body modifications, 213, *213*
bootlegging, 451–2
boycotts, 441–3
brand attributes, 104
brand communities, 261, *300*
brand hijacking, 264–5
brand identity creation, services, 85–6
brand imagery, 104
brand loyalty *see* loyalty
brand names

global standardization, 293, *294*
    stimulus generalization, 103
brand personality, 205–6
brand valency, 253
branded clothing symbols, 343
brand–relationship quality, 394
Buyer Behaviour Expert, 476
buyer–seller relationships, 474–8
buyer–seller team, 476
buyers, sizes and numbers, 461–2
BuyGrid Model, 466, 467, *468*, 478
buying case, 470–71
buying center, 470
buying classes and phases, 467–9
buying role, 272
buzz marketing, 365, 366

C
C2C social network data, 424
calculative commitment, 395
capitalism, 440
cartoon tests, 33, *33*
celebrities
    associationist learning, *95–6*
    credibility, 117
    motor market campaigns, 364
    as opinion formers, 34–6
cellular households, 162, 429
census data, 416–17, 421
central route to persuasion, 147
cessation, consumer–company relations, *374*, 380
children
    ethnic subcultures, 310
    family consumption and, 273, 275–9, 168–70
    see also teenagers
Christmas consumption study, 320–35
chronological age, 156
classical conditioning, 92–7, *93*
cliques, 250
closure, law of, 63, 70
clothing symbols, 343
clutter, 52
coercive power, 252, 356
cognitive age, 157, *157*, 163
cognitive component of attitudes, 106, *107*, 112
cognitive dissonance, 10, 23–4, 135–41
cognitive learning, 99–100
cognitive motives, 15

cognitive styles (information processing), 178–80, 349

cohesiveness, 250

collective meanings, 257

collectivist cultures, 29, 266, 290, 298

colour
cultural differences, 73–4, *74*, *295*
perceptions of, 73–6
to gain attention, 53

commitment, 394, 395–6
brand, 369
lack of, 281

communications, responses to, 45
children, 277–8
content and organization, 117–20
misbehaviour, 442
privacy conflicts, 430
see also new product buying; hierarchy of communication effects

compatibility of innovations, 341–2

competitions, 415

competitive intelligence, 426

complaining behaviour, 132
see also cognitive dissonance

compulsive buying, 24

compulsive consumption, 438, 440

conative component of attitudes, 107, 112

conditioned response, 58

conditioning
classical, 90–7
operant, 11, 97–8, 370
to gain attention, 58

conformers, *195*

conformity, 247–50, 286

Confucian dynamism, 291

congruence, self-image, 215–18

connectedness–separatedness continuum, 290

conscious mind (superego), *16*, 17

consensual databases, 432

conservative values, *420*

conspicuousness, 252

consumer boycotts, 441–3

consumer–brand relationship (Fournier typology), 394

consumer demographics *see* demographic variables

Consumer Insight's Social Value Groups, *195*

consumer loyalty *see* loyalty

consumer misbehaviour *see* misbehaviour

consumer motives *see* motivation

consumer panels, 370

consumer psychographics *see* psychographics

consumer psychology, *120*

consumer responses to marketing actions *see* communications, responses to

consumer satisfaction *see* satisfaction/dissatisfaction

consumer terrorists, 383, 436

consumer values *see* values

consumption patterns, 405, *420*

consumption, Christmas study of, 320–35

contemporary lifestyle, 191

continuity, law of, 72

continuous innovations, *340*, 341

contrast effect, 143

conversational advertising, 365

cookies, 404, 414–15

cooperation, relational partners, 397–9

counterfeit goods, *452*

country of origin, 129

country of origin effects, 299–300

credibility effect, attitudes, 116

cultural artifacts, 300

cultural authority perspective of marketers, 442

cultural capital, *6*

cultural categories, 286

cultural diversity, 301
see also ethnic subcultures

culture(s), 7, 284–318, *420*
acculturation, 304–9, 318
classification, 285, *295*
colour perceptions, 73–4, *74*, *295*
country of origin effects, 299–300
crossing, 298–300, *299*, 314–15
definitions, 285, 317
dynamic nature of, 285–6, 317
family structure, 266
global marketing, 291–8
humour, 298, 318
individual difference, 306
Internet and, 298–300
meaning and, 285–6, 317
neighbourhood profiling example, *418*
rituals, 287–8, 289–90, 317
values, 29–30, *30*, 290–1, *293–4*, 318
see also subcultures

customer loyalty *see* loyalty

Customer Partner, 475

Customer Service Provider, 476
customization, 292, *295*

D
data-based consumer behaviour, 404–33
  biographics, 428, 433
  individualism, 429, 433
  misbehaviour, 453
  personalized behavioural data, 404, 405–16,
    430–2
    'surveillance', 411
    transactional, 404, 405, 428, 432
  personalized profile data, 405, 416–28
    biographics, 428
    genetic, 427–8
    geodemographic, 416–17, 418–22
  social implications, 406–7, 431–2
    information privacy, 416, 430–2
    physical/interaction privacy, 431–2
data mining software, 407
data protection, 416, 431–2
decider, 272
decider role, 272
decision making
  autonomic, 274
  buying, 469–71
  husband-dominant, 274
  husband–wife, 273–4
  in families, 272–5, 279–81
  joint, 242, 274–5
  organizational buying behaviour, 463–6
  rationality, 463
  styles, 204–5, 350
  wife-dominant, 274
Decision Making Unit (DMU), 458, 470
deculturation, 305
defection, 383
demand, 462–3
demand mapping, 196–223
demographic variables, 154–89
  age, 156–70, 154
  gender, 154, 170–80
  sexual identity, 180–3, 422
  social grade, 154, 183–8, *183*
  see also ethnicity; families
derived demand, 462
deterioration, consumer–company relations, *374*,
  379–80
deterministic models, 374

difference–identity principle, 303
diffusion-adoption theory, 340–9
  adopter categories, 343, *346*, 347
  adoption, 344–6
  communication of innovations, 343
  innovation acceptance criteria, 341–3
  types of innovation, 340–1
  see also new product buying, communication
    flows
diffusion patterns, 366
direct marketing
  ethnic minority consumers, *308*
  id appeals, 22
Dirichlet model of consumer buying behaviour,
  373
disassociative groups, 252
disconfirmation paradigm, 130–1
disconnected, the, *195*
discontinuous innovations, 340, *340*
discrepancy in messages, 116
disintermediation, 261
disposal behaviour, 141
dissatisfaction *see* satisfaction/dissatisfaction
distribution, misbehaviour with, *446*, 451–2
diversity, 284
divorce assumption, *161*
down-nesting, *161*
drug consumption, 438, 440
dynamically continuous innovations, 341

E
early adopters, *346*, 347, 349, 364
early majority consumers, *346*, 347
effect, laws of, 97
ego, 16, *16*, 17–22
ego-defensive attitudes, 114, 115
elaboration likelihood model, 147–8
elasticities of demand, 463
electoral roll data, 416
enculturation, 285
enduring involvement, 142
environment
  influence on organizational buying behaviour,
    471–2
  misbehaviour and, 450
equity theory, 131–2
esteem-seekers, *195*
ethical issues
  advertising to women, 172, *173*

consumer boycotts, 441–3
marketing to children, 277–8
ethnic identity, 300, 302–4, *302*, *303–4*
ethnic minority consumers, 303
see also ethnic subcultures
ethnic minority media, 313
ethnic segments, 285
ethnic subcultures, 301, 318
acculturation, 304–9, 318
need for understanding, 309–11
targeting, 312–14
ethnicity, 300, 302–5, 318
ethnocentric consumers, 300, 443–5
ethnographic research, 286
evoked sets, 84
excessive buying, *437*
expectations, 130–1
experiential consumption, 399–402
expert power, 251, 356
exposure effect, 252
exposure to marketing activities, 45, 46, 47–51,
98
extended family, 266
extended self, 212–13
extrinsic cues, 104–5
eye cameras, 56, *57*

F
facial recognition software, *414*
fake brands, 452
families, 266–81
behaviour by family type, 267, *267*
buying roles in, 272–80
cellular, 162, 429
children, 273, 275–9
compulsive buying and, 438
decision making in, 272–5, 279–81
ethnic subcultures, *309*
extended, 266, 267
intergenerational influence, 268
life cycle, 268–71
networked, 280–1
nuclear, 266, 267
parent power, 279–80
pester power, 275–8, *276*, *279*
family branding strategy, 103
family buying behaviour, 158
FCB grid, 148, *148*, 149
fear, persuasion through, 117

feel consumption, 400
feel products, 148
FCB grid model, 149
felt ethnic identity, *304*
feminine cultures, 29
financial data, 418
Fishbein's multi-attribute model, 110–12, *113*
flashmobbing, 261
FMCG goods, 382
focal attention, 52
focal vision, 57
form and style, emphasis on, 281
formal groups, 242
Fournier's consumer–brand relationship
typology, 393–4
fragmentation, 50, 220
of collective meanings, 257
frames of reference
cultural differences, 292
selective perception, 82–3
within country differences, *71*
Frankfurt School, 9
free association tests, 32
frequency, 50
of purchasing (RFM), 408–10
Freudian theory of motivation, 15–22
functional innovations, 341

G
gambling, *437*, 438
ganqing, 478
gay consumer behaviour, 180–2, 422
gender issues, 154, 170–80, 188
cultural values, 291
Generation X, 160–1
Generation Y, 158–9
generational cohorts, 156–70
generational factors
family socialization, 266
value transmission, 30
genetic profile data, 405, 427–8
geodemographics, 405, 416–17, 418–22, 433
geography
of organizational buying behavior, 460
geo-lifestyle, 423
gestalt psychology
learning, 100–4
perception, 70–3
global marketing, 291–8, 443

golden section technique, 56, *56*
GPS (global positioning satellite) tracking, 404, 414–15
graffiti, 452, *452*
group cohesiveness, 250
group conformity, 254
groups *see* social groups
Guanxi, 399, 477

H

habitual buying, 98
habituation, 52
hedonistic innovations, 341, 343
Heider's balance theory, 107–8
heuristics, 300
hierarchy of communication effects, 45–7
    action, 45, 46, 125–9
    attention, 45, 46, 52–63
    attitudes, 45, 46, 105–22
    exposure, 45, 46, 47–51, 98
    involvement, 141–50
    learning, 45, 46, 90–104
    perception, 45, 46, 64–86
    post-purchase, 45, *46*, 125, 129–41
hierarchy of effects models, 45, 89, 344
    see also diffusion–adoption theory; hierarchy of communication effects
homeostasis, 7, *7*
hostages, Jones–Sasser grid, 384
humour, 61–2, 298, 318
husband-dominant decision making, 273
husband–wife decision making, 273–4
hyperidentification, 307
hyperreality, 162

I

id, 16–17, *16*
ideal self-image congruence, 215
illegal behaviour, 414, *438*, 439
illegal product use, 439
image variable, 300
impersonal trust, 454
impulse buying, 126–9
incentives, 474
inclusionary–exclusionary principle, 303
income, 188
independence, 201, 247–50
Indian motorcycle market case study, 35–42, 315–17

individual factors, buying and, 473–4
individualism, 15, 220, 221–3, 429, 433
individualistic cultures, 29, 290
    family structure, 266
    humour and, 298
industrial buying behaviour, 459
Industrial Marketing and Purchasing Group (IMP), 475
inept sets, 84
inert sets, 84
influencer role, 272
infomediaries, 366
informal groups, 242
Information Commissioner, 416, *430–1*
Information Gatherer role, 476
information influence, groups, 244
information power, 251, 356
information privacy, 430–2
information processing
    Scottish Executive case study, 150–1
    styles, 178–80, 349
initial attention, 51–2
initiator role, 272
inner-directedness, 15, 207–9, 218–23
innovation overload, 343
innovations
    adapter–innovator continuum, 349
    categorization, 340
    diffusion-adoption theory, 340–9
        adopter categories, 343, *346*, 347
        adoption, 344–6
        communication of innovations, 343
        criteria for acceptance, 341–3
        types of innovation, 340–1
    see also new product buying, communication flows
innovativeness, 209, 345
innovators, *346*, 347
    adapter–innovator continuum, 349
    lifestyle typologies, *195*
insight, in learning, 100
instrumental function of attitudes, 114
instrumental learning (operant conditioning), 11, 92, 97–8, 370
instrumental values, 28
insurance, genetic data, 427
integration, 305
interaction, consumer–company relations, *374*, 375–6

interaction privacy, 430
intergenerational differences, 307
intergenerational influence, 268, 281–2
intergenerational value transmission, 30, *30*
Internet
    cookies, 414–15
    crossing cultures, 298–300, *299*
    cultures, 261
    infomediaries, 366
    online virtual groups, 260–6, *300*
interpersonal factors, buying and, 473
interpretative methods of research, 286
interviews, long, 286
intrinsic cues, 104–5
involvement, 125, 141–50
    adapter–innovator continuum, 349
    measurement, 144
    hierarchy of effects and, 144–50

J
jaycustomers, 436
    see also misbehaviour
Jungian motivation, 22–3
junk information, 430
just noticeable difference (JND), 51–2

K
Keynote, 155
kinesics, 67
Kirton Adaption Innovation Inventory (KAI), 349
knowledge, 104–5
knowledge function of attitudes, 114, 115

L
lack of commitment, 281
laddering, means–end chain, 33–4
laggard consumers, *346*, 347
language differences, *295*
late majority consumers, *346*, 347
latent loyalty, 382
leadership, social groups, 250–1
    see also opinion leaders
learning, 45, 46, 90–104
    behavioural, 92–9
    cognitive, 99–100
    gestalt contributions, 100–3
    measurement of, 103
    stimulus discrimination, 103
    stimulus generalization, 103

vicarious, 11, 99
vs memory, 90
    see also operant conditioning
legitimate power, 251, 356
life cycle, family, 268–71
lifestyle, 191–6, 196–223
    contemporary, 191
    traditional, 191–6, 224
    profiling, 417, *417*
Likert scales, 109–10, 191, 218
lists, personalized fata, 426
longevity, *170*
long-term memory, 91–2
long-term orientated cultures, 291
loyalists, Jones-Sasser grid, 383, *383*
loyalty, 47, 369, 374–81, 390–2, 402–3
    case study, 384–8
    cohesiveness and, 250
    consumer–company relationship sequence, 374–81
    customer switching behaviour, 389
    Dick and Basu's model, 381
    Jones and Sasser grid, 383
    measuring repeat purchasing, 370–3
    programmes for building, 381, 390–2
    relative attitude, 381
    satisfaction and, 382–4, 402
    see also relational consumption
loyalty programmes, 381, 390–2
    data from *see* transactional data

M
marital roles, decision making, 272–3
Market Analyser and Planner, 476
Market Assessment, 155
Market Cost Analyser, 476
market mavens, 353, 365
market orientation, 3, *4*
market research, misbehaviour with, *446*, 453
marketing communication responses, 45
    children, 276–7
    hierarchy model *see* hierarchy of communication effects
    misbehaviour, 442
    privacy conflicts, 430–2
    see also diffusion-adoption theory
marketing databases, misbehaviour with, *446*, 453
    see also data-based consumer behaviour
marketing mix, 463, *464*

marketing research, 426–7
masculine cultures, 29
Maslow's hierarchy of needs, 11–15
materialism, 438–9
McDonaldization, 285
meaning systems, 285–6, 317
meaning transfer model, 286–8, 322–4, *324*, *326*
means–end chains, 33–4
medium reach, 49
me-ism, *161*
memetics, 23, 429
memory, 46, *90*
  vs learning, 90
  long-term, 104
  short-term, 104
  types, 90–2
men, 154, 170, 172–3, 178–80
  husband–wife decision making, 273–4
  role in non-Western cultures, 291
mercenaries, Jones–Sasser grid, 384
Millennial Generation, 158–9
MINTEL, 47, 155, 183
misbehaviour, 24, 435–57
  in acquiring products, 437–9
    theft, 414, 439, 450–1
  behaviour balances, 454–5
  consonant exchange environment, *454*
  consumer terrorists, 383
  customer animosity, 443–5
  ethnocentrism, 443–5
  definitions, 435–6
  idealistic rationale for, 440–5
  with respect to marketing, 445–54
    distribution, *446*, 451–2
    market research, *446*, 453
    marketers' employees, *446*
    marketing databases, *446*, 453
    motives for, 445
    price, *446*, 450–1
    products, *446*, 447–50
    promotion, *446*, 452
    relationship marketing, *446*, 453
    services, *446*, 447–50
  typologies, 437–40, *437*
  in use of products, *437*, 439–40, 447–50
misuse of products, *437*, 439–40, *446*, 447–50
mobile telephony, *415*
modified r-buying, 467
monetary value of purchases (RFM), 408–9, 490

Mosaic profiling, 418, *418*, *420–1*
motivation, 3–28
  cognitive dissonance, 23–4, 135
  external, 10–11
  Freudian theory of, 11, 15–22
  internal, 10–11
  involvement and, 149–50
  Jungian, 22–3
  McGuire's classification, 15
  Maslow's hierarchy of needs, 11–15
  memetics, 23
  negative, 10
  positive, 10, *11*
  research techniques, 31–3
  Rossiter–Percy Grid, 149–50
  and shopping, 24–8
movement, use of, 53–4
multicultural societies, *301*
multinational corporations, 442–3
multiple identities, 211
multisensory brands, 65
multi-step communication flows, 352–3, 356, 357, *363*, 365
music
  generational cohorts, *158*
  perceptions of, *64*
mutual goals, relational partners, 397

N
N-Gen (Generation Y), 158–9
national census data, 416–17, 421
national identity, 300
NBD/LSD model of consumer buying behaviour, 372–3
needs, 3–5, 34
  higher level *see* values
  Maslow's hierarchy of, 11–15
  see also motivation
negative binomial distribution (NBD) theory, 372–3
neighbourhood profiling, *418*
network marketing, 366
neurolinguistic programming (NLP), 68, 178, *178–80*
new product buying, 339–68
  adapter–innovator continuum, 349
  communication flows, 352–67
    diffusion patterns, 366
    market mavens, 365

multi-step, 352–3, 356, 357, *363*, 365
   opinion formers, 353–8, 362, *363*
   opinion leaders, 353, 359–65
   opinion shapers, 353, 360
   two-step model, 353, 361, 365
   word of mouth, 353, 360
  diffusion-adoption theory, 340–9
   adopter categories, 343, *346*, 347
   adoption, 344–6
   communication of innovations, 343
   criteria for acceptance, 341–3
   types of innovation, 340–1
new task buying, 467
nostalgia, legislated, *161*
novelty, use of, 60–1
nuclear household, 429

O

observability of innovations, 342
occupational classification, 183–8, *183*
Oliver, Jamie, 354
online polls, 453
online virtual groups, 260–6
  see also Internet
operant conditioning, 11, 92, 97–8, 370
opinion formers, 339, 353–8, 363
  cognitive dissonance and, 135
opinion leaders, 339, 353, 359–65
  cognitive dissonance and, 135
  diffusion patterns, 366
  simulated, 364, *365*
opinion polls, 362, 453
opinion shapers, 353, 360
opportunities to see (OTS), 50
oppositional meanings, 442
organizational buying behavior, 458–79
  characteristics, 460–3
  major influences on, 471–8
organizational factors
  buying behaviour and, 472
organizational markets, 460–3
outer-directed personality, 207–9, *208*
over-50s, 163–7, *165*
over-acculturation, 307

P

paralanguage, 67
parent power, 279–80
  see also families

Pareto principle, 409
Parfitt–Collins repeat buying model, 371–2, *372*
participation
  Generation X, 160–1
  to aid learning, 100–4
  to hold attention, 62–3
passive learning theory, 99, 142
Pavlov, I., 92–3
peer group, 156
perceived risk, 369
  of innovations, 343
perception of marketing activities, 45, 46, 64–86
  evoked sets, 84
  Gestalt processes, 70–3
  intangible services, 84–6
  just noticeable difference, 51–2
  perceptual organization conventions, 68–73
  selective, 82–3
  sensory marketing research, *66*, 67
  sensory systems, 64–7
  sensory thresholds, 78
  symbolism, 86
perceptual defence, 82
perceptual maps, 83
perceptual vigilance, 82
peripheral route to persuasion, 147
permission marketing, 432
persistent attention, 52
personal age, *157*
Personal Involvement Inventory (PII), 350
personality, 12, 190, 201–3, 224
  brand, 205–6
  impulse buying, 128
  inner-directed, 207–9, *208*
  innovation adopters, *346*
  outer-directed, 207–9, *208*
  psychoanalytic theory, 201
  self-concept, 209
  social character research, 207–9
  trait theory, 201, *201–3*
  type theory, 205
  see also self-concept
personality big five factors, 201, *202*
personalization, 63, *379*
personalized behavioural data, 404, 405–16, 430–1
personalized profile data, 405, 416–22
pester power, 273, 275–8
physical/interaction privacy, 431–2

physiological (biogenic) drives, 7
planned behaviour theory, 113, *114*
pleasure principle, 16
pluralism, 219, 221, *429*
political lobbying, 362
positioning of messages, 56–7
positive pester power, 280
possible selves, 212
postcodes, profiling by, 416–17, 418
poster graffiti, 452, *452*
postmodern society, 4, 220, 253–9, 281, 439
post-purchase stage, consumer response model,
   45, *46*, 125, 129–41
power, social, 251–2, 356
power–distance cultures, 29, 290, 298
press releases
   motor market, 356
   news programmes, *354*
price, misbehaviour with, *446*, 450–1
primary groups, 242
privacy, 481–94
   relational interactions, 416, 430–2
privacy-related behaviour, 481–94
private actions, 132
privately consumed luxuries, 244
privately consumed necessities, 244
probability theory, 370
product attribute, 252
product innovations *see* innovations
product life cycle, 339, *346*
   see also new product buying
product misuse, *437*, 439–40, 447–50
product orientation, 3
product perception, 83
product symbolism, 343
product valency, 253
progression, consumer–company relations, *374*,
   378, *378*
projective tests, 31–3
proquinquity, 252
proxemics, 67
psychoanalytic theory, 15–22, 201
psychodrama tests, 33
psychogenic (sociogenic) drives, 7
psychographics, 190–238
   lifestyle, 191–6
   personality, 190, 201–3
   self-concept, 190, 209–23
public relations campaigns, 357, 362, 364

publicly consumed luxuries, 244
publicly consumed necessities, 244
purchase request behaviour, 277
pyramid marketing, 366

R
radio frequency identification (RFID) tags, 404,
   414, 439
reach of promotional messages, 49
reactance, 248
reality principle, 17
reasoned action theory, 113, *113*, 348, *349*
reasoning, 99
recency, frequency and monetary value (RFM),
   408–10
reciprocal trading, 475
reclamation, consumer–company relations, *374*,
   380–1, *380*
recognition cue, 104
recognition method, 103
reference group, 156, 242–4, 280
   aspirational, 252
   information influence, 244
   membership, 252–3
   negative, 252
   non-membership, 252–3
   self-concept theory, 246–7
   symbolic interactionism, 213
   utilitarian influence, 244, 252
   value expressive influence, 244
referent power, 251, 356
reinforcement
   of attitudes, 121–2
   operant conditioning, 11, 97
relate consumption, 400
relational buying, 370
relational consumption, 392–402
   commitment, 394, 395–6
   cooperation, 397–9
   definition, 392–4
   experiential consumption, 399–402
   Fournier's typology, 393–4
   Guanxi 399
   Harley Davidson, *401*
   mutual goals, 397
   satisfaction, 397
   trust, 394–5
relational marketing, 393

relationship marketing, misbehaviour with, *446*, 453
  see also relational consumption
relative advantage, of innovations, 342
relative attitude, 381
relevant power, 251
repeat purchasing, 47
repeat purchasing behaviour, 370–3
  Brown's model, 370–1
  consumer–company relationship sequence, 374–81
  loyalty programmes, 390–2
  NBD/LSD model, 372–3
  Parfitt–Collins model, 371–2, *372*
  Dirichlet model, 373
  satisfaction and, 382–4
  switching, 389
  see also relational consumption
repetition effects
  attitude change, 120
  learning, 98–9
resource allocation, family decision making and, 274–5
responses to marketing activity, 45
  children, 276–7
  hierarchy model *see* hierarchy of communication effects
  misbehaviour, 442
  privacy conflicts, 430–2
  see also diffusion-adoption theory
retention, 369
Retro Marketing, 365, *366*
reward power, 252, 356
RFID tags, 414, 439
risk
  of innovation, 343
  organizational buying, 465–6
rituals, 287
  cultural, 287–8, 289–90, 317
  of reproduction, 290
Rokeach Value Survey (RVS), 28, *28*
role playing, 33
Rossiter–Percy Grid, 149–50

S
SAGACITY, 271, *272*
Sainsbury's, 354
Sales Forecaster, 476
satisfaction/dissatisfaction, 129–30

loyalty and, 382–4, 402–3
post-purchase dissonance, 132
relational partners, 397
schema discrepancy, 60
Scottish Executive case study, 150–1
scripted behaviour, 289
secondary groups, 242
selective attention, 104
selective exposure, 47, 104
selective perception, 82–3
selective retention, 104
self-actualization, 12
self-actualizers, *195*
self-concept, 190, 209–23
  actual self, 210, 211
  actual self-image congruence, 215
  baby boomers, 162–3, *166*
  dimensions of self, 210–11
  ethnic identity, 303
  extended self, 212–13
  ideal (looking-glass) self, 210, 211
  ideal self-image congruence, 215
  measuring, 218–23
  media image effects on, case study, 228–38
  multiple selves, 212
  possible selves, 212
  reference groups and, 213, 244, 246–7
  research mechanism, 217–18
  self-image congruence, 215–18
  social self-image congruence, 215
  symbolic interactionism, 213
  undesired self, 223
  virtual self-image, 213–14
self-concept theory, 367
self-explorer segment, *193*, *194*
self-expression, 193, 218–23
self-identity
  cultural rituals, 289
  ethnicity, 303
self-image congruence, 215–18
self-monitoring, 209
self-realization, 12
semantic differential scales, 109
  self-concept research mechanics, 217–18
semiotics, 86
semiotics triad, *86*
sense consumption, 400
sensory marketing research, *66*, *67*
sensory memory, 90–1, *91*

sensory systems, 64–7
sensory thresholds, 78
separatedness-connectedness continuum, 290
sequential models *see* hierarchy of effects models
services
    misbehaviour with, *446*, 447–50
    perceptions of, 84–6
sexual identity, 180
sexuality, 180–3, 422
shoplifting, 414, 439
shopping motives, 24–8
shopping orientation, *307–8*
short-term memory, 91
signs, cultural differences, *295*
similarity, law of, 69
simplicity of innovations, 342–3
situational involvement, 142
sizing of messages, 57
smart trolleys, 414
smell perception, *64*, 65
SMS advertising, 348
social age, *157*
social capital, *6*
social character research, 207–9
social class, 155, 183
social connections, 290–1
social distance, 442
social factors, buying and, 473
social grade, 154, 183–8
social groups, 241–53
    aspirational, 252
    cohesiveness, 250, 289
    conformity, 247–50, 254, 286
    disassociative, 252
    families *see* families
    independence, 247–50
    informal, 242
    leadership, 250–1
    negative reference, 252
    postmodern behaviour, 253–9, 281
    power, 251–2
    primary 242 *see also* families
    reference, 213, 242–4, 252
    secondary, 242
    symbolic interactionism, 213
    tribal behaviour, 253–9, 281
    virtual, 260–6
    see also subcultures

social judgement theory (Sherif), 143
social norms
    conformity, 247–50
    tribal group behaviour, *255*
social power, 251–2, 356
social pressure, 247
social self-image congruence, 215
social symbolism, 9
socialization, 280
socio-economic classification (SEC), 187–8
sociogenic (psychogenic) drives, 7
sociograms, 250, *250*
sociometry, 250
Sony Walkman, 354
sound
    attention, 55
    perception, *64*, 65, 79
source attractiveness, 352
source credibility, 352
spectacularism, *161*
speed of product benefits, 342
spurious loyalty, 382
standardization, 291, 293, *295*
stereotyping
    country of origin effects, 299
    gender, 170, 171, 173, 174, *174*, 188
stimulus discrimination, 103
stimulus generalization, 103
stimulus–response model, 92, 93, 370
stochastic models, 370
store atmospherics, 64–5
straight re-buying, 467–70
Strangelove reproduction, *161*
strivers, *195*
subconscious mind (ego), 16, *16*, 17–22
subcultures, 284–5, 200–17, 318
    ethnic, 301, 301–14, 318
    see also Generation X; Generation Y; tribal behaviour
subcultures, 284
subjective age, *157*
superego, *16*, 17
surprise, use of, 60
'surveillance' data, 411
switching behaviour, 389
symbolic consumption, 343
symbolic innovations, 341, 343
symbolic interactionism, 213
symbolic meanings, 9

symbolism, perceptual interpretation, 86
  see also symbolic consumption
symbols, cultural differences, *295*
syncratic decision making, 273

T

Target Group Index (TGI), 47, 48, 155, 191, *418*
taste perception, *64*
Taylor Nelson's lifestyle typology, *193–4*
Technologist role, 476
Technology Acceptance Model (TAM), 348
teenagers
  ethnic minority, *308*
  family consumption and, 277
  misbehaviour
    compulsive buying, 438
    illegal product use, 440
    rationales for, 442
    tribes, 241
  see also Generation Y
television ratings (TVRs), 50
television viewing, by children, 277
Temple, Shirley, 355
terminal values, 28
theft, 414, 439, 453
think consumption, 400
think–feel constructs, FCB model, 148
third party actions, 132
third-person tests, 31
thirds, law of, 56
time-poor consumers, 429, *429*
touch perception, *64*
tradition-directed personality, 207
traditional lifestyle, 191
traditionalists, *195*
trait theory, 201, *201–3*
transactional data, 404, 405, 428, 432
  company, 405
  consortia, 410
trialability of innovations, 342
tribal behaviour, 253–9, 281
tribes, 241
trickle theories, 367
triple appeal theory, 20
trust
  attitude change and, 116
  impersonal, 454, *454*
  relational partners, 394–5
  2 + 2 = 5-ism, *161*

two-sided appeals
  for attitude change, 120, *120*
  cognitive dissonance and, 137
two-step communication flows, 352–3, 365

U

unawareness sets, 84
uncertainty-avoidance cultures, 29, 291
unconscious mind (id), 16–17, *16*
undesired self, 223
utilitarian influence, 244, 252

V

valencies, reference group influence, 253
VALS (values and lifestyle) research, *193*, *194*
value expressive attitudes, 114, 115
value expressive influence, 244
values, 5, 28–31, 290–1, 318, 196–223
  conservative, *420–1*
  consumer, *420*
  cross-cultural, *293–4*
  of Generation X, 161, *161*
  lifestyle typologies, *194*
  means–end chain analysis, 33–4
  neighbourhood profiling, *418*
vandalism, 452
vicarious learning, 11, 99
Viper data-mining software, 407, 409
viral marketing, 366
virtual groups, 260–6
  see also Internet
virtual self-image, 213–14
visual perception, *64*
voice, post-purchase, 132
voluntary exposure, 51
voter's block, *161*

W

wants (desires), 3–5, 7, 34
  see also motivation
warranties, 139
wearout, 50
wife-dominant decision making, 273
women, 154, 170–80
  role in non-Western cultures, 291
  wife–husband decision making, 273–4
word association tests, 32
word-of-mouth, 47, 120, 129, 133–4
  consumer terrorists, 383

word-of-mouth, (*continued*)
   new products, 353, 360
   power of negative, 452
World Wide Web, 260
   see also Internet

Y

young people
   ethnic minority, *308*
   family consumption and, 278
   misbehaviour
      compulsive buying, 438

   holidays, *450*
   illegal product use, 440
   rationales for, 442
tribes, 241
see also Generation Y
yuppie wannabes, *161*

Z

Zaichkowsky Personal Involvement Inventory
   (PII), 350
zapping, 46
zipping, 46